Corporate Accounting

Volume I

Balavant M.P.

ATLANTIC

PUBLISHERS & DISTRIBUTORS (P) LTD

Published by
ATLANTIC
PUBLISHERS & DISTRIBUTORS (P) LTD
7/22, Ansari Road, Darya Ganj,
New Delhi-110002
Phones : +91-11-40775252, 23273880, 23275880, 23280451
Fax : +91-11-23285873
Web : www.atlanticbooks.com
E-mail : orders@atlanticbooks.com

Branch Office
5, Nallathambi Street, Wallajah Road,
Chennai-600002
Phones : +91-44-64611085, 32413319
E-mail : chennai@atlanticbooks.com

Printed in India at Nice Printing Press, A-33/3A, Site-IV, Industrial Area, Sahibabad, Ghaziabad, U.P.

PREFACE

A good number of standard textbooks on Accountancy are available in the market to cater to the needs of various academic and professional studies. But, there are no such books available to cater to the needs of the revised syllabus of Second Year B.Com. of Karnatak, Bangalore and Gulburga universities. This book will no doubt, serve the said purpose, as it is written strictly according to the revised syllabus. Though this book is primarily meant for the B.Com. Part-II Course of Karnatak, Bangalore and Gulburga universities, it will also be very useful for the B.Com., B.B.A., B.B.M., M.Com. and M.B.A. students of all Indian universities and Institutes and those pursuing C.A.I.I.B., C.A., I.C.W.A., A.C.S. or preparing other examinations of professional courses.

Although syllabus-based, book is a rare blend of the theoretical and practical aspects. After the theoretical discussion in a very lucid style, a 'ruling of account' concerned is presented so as to enable the students to follow the principles and their practical applications with ease. This volume provides exhaustive explanations, suitable examples and various graded illustrations along with working notes. As per the new question paper pattern, short questions, simple problems and practical exercises have been given, at the end of each chapter, for the benefit of the students.

Suggestions from all quarters for further improvement of this book will be appreciated and gratefully acknowledged.

Balavant M.P.

ACKNOWLEDGEMENTS

I take this opportunity to express my gratitude to Prof. A.G. Sunkad and Prof. K.R. Shegunasi, Dept. of English for improving the grammatical standard of this book. I am beholders to the members of staff of M.G.V.C. College, Muddebihal, for having provided an environment, conducive to hard work. I owe a debt of gratitude to my beloved wife Prof. (Smt.) Pushpa B. Unnibhavi for the help extended in preparing this book. Last but not least I am also thankful to Dr. K.R. Gupta, Honorary Advisor, Atlantic Publishers and Distributors (P) Ltd., New Delhi, for the interest evinced in bringing out this book.

CONTENTS

1

UNDERWRITING OF SHARES AND DEBENTURES

Meaning

The public company cannot get certificate to commerce business unless it gets the minimum subscription from the public. Therefore, in order to ensure the minimum subscription, public company would like to enter into underwriting arrangements.

The term 'underwriting' refers to a contract between the company and underwriter, whereby the underwriter, in return for a certain consideration, undertakes to take up the whole or a certain portion of shares or debentures which are not subscribed by the public. Underwriting is in the nature of guarantee or an insurance against the under-subscription or the possibility of inadequate subscription. **Gestenberg** quotes an English case in which the learned judge defines the underwriting as "an agreement entered into before the shares are brought before the public that in the event the public not taking up the whole of them or the number mentioned in the agreement, the underwriter will, for agreed commission, take an allotment of such part of the shares as the public has not applied for".[1] In other words, underwriting is an arrangement under which underwriter agreed to take up the whole or a portion of the offered shares or debentures which are not subscribed by the public for a certain remuneration.

Under this arrangement, generally the underwriter subscribes only those shares or debentures which are not subscribed by the public. For example, if the underwriter underwrites 5,000 shares issued by the company, he has to purchase only 2,000 shares if the public applied for 3,000 shares and 500 shares if the public applied for 4,500 shares and nothing if the public applied for 5,000 shares. Therefore, it is a guarantee given by the underwriter to

1. *Financial Organisation and Management,* p. 387.

subscribe to an agreed number of shares for remuneration called underwriting commission.

Underwriters. The persons who underwrite the shares or debentures issued by the company are known as underwriters. In other words, underwriters are those who are engaged in underwriting activities. Underwriters may be individuals or institutions such as partnership firms, joint stock companies, banks, specialised financial institutions (ICICI, IDBI, UTI, LIC) etc. They undertake themselves the responsibility of selling the shares or debentures to the public. They give the guarantee for selling the shares or debentures within a specified period of time. If some shares or debentures are unsold or unsubscribed, they will have to take up the unsubscribed portion of shares or debentures and pay for them.

Underwriters *Vs.* Brokers. The following are the main differences between underwriters and brokers.

1. Underwriters undertake themselves the responsibility of selling the shares or debentures of a company to an extent not taken up by the public. But, the brokers do not undertake the responsibility of subscribing the shares or debentures, but merely induce the customers to subscribe the shares or debentures of a company.

2. Since the underwriters undertake the responsibility of subscribing the shares or debentures, they undertake risk. But the brokers do not undertake any risk. Because, they do not undertake any responsibility to undertake unsubscribed shares or debentures.

3. Brokerage is to be paid to the broker for the service of placing the shares. On the other hand, the underwriting commission is to be paid to the underwriter for guaranteeing the subscription.

Underwriting Commission. The consideration payable to the underwriters for underwriting the shares or debentures is called underwriting commission. In other words, remuneration payable for the services rendered by the underwriters is known as underwriting commission. This commission is to be paid at a specified rate on the issue price of the whole of shares or debentures even if the public takes up all the shares or debentures offered by the company. But, no underwriting commission is payable to anyone on shares or debentures not offered to the public. The underwriters are entitled to a commission of 5% (maximum) of the issue price of the shares and 2½% (maximum) of the issue price of the debentures.

Sub-underwriting. An underwriter may appoint several underwriters working under him. Such underwriters are called as sub-underwriters. They are liable to the main underwriter and entitled to commission from the main underwriter. They are neither liable to the company nor are they entitled to any commission from the company. They are responsible only to the main underwriter. In order to minimise the risk, the underwriters appoint sub-underwriters. When there is a sub-underwriting, usually the company pays to the main underwriter over and above the underwriting commission an extra commission called over-riding commission.

Underwriting Agreement. The terms and conditions under which the underwriter agrees to underwrite the shares or debentures are embodied in a document called underwriting agreement (or contract). The underwriting agreement includes the following :

1. The number of shares which the underwriter agrees to underwrite and an undertaking by the underwriter to take up the shares which are not subscribed by the public.
2. The undertaking by the company that the terms of issue specified in the prospectus shall not be altered without the prior consent of the underwriter.
3. The underwriting commission shall be payable only on those shares which have been offered to the public.
4. The rate of commission payable to the underwriter for underwriting the shares or debentures.
5. The mode of payment of commission to underwriter.

Provisions of Companies Act Regarding Underwriting Commission

The main provisions of the Companies Act of 1956 in respect of underwriting commission are as follows :

1. The payment of underwriting commission must be duly authorised by the articles of association.
2. The commission payable to the underwriters for their service should not exceed 5% of the issue price of the shares or the amount authorised by the articles, whichever is less.
3. The commission payable to the underwriters on debentures for their service should not exceed $2\frac{1}{2}\%$ of the issue price of the debentures or the amount stated by the articles, whichever is less.
4. The amount or rate of commission and the number of shares and debentures which the underwriters have agreed to subscribe should be disclosed in the prospectus.
5. All sums paid or payable by way of underwriting commission, brokerage, etc. should be stated in the Balance sheet under the heading "Miscellaneous Expenditure and Losses".
6. A copy of contract relating to the payment of underwriting commission should be filed with the registrar of companies.

Advantages of Underwriting. Following are the main advantages of underwriting :

1. Underwriters are giving the guarantee for selling the shares or debentures. Therefore, the promoters will be free from the worries of arranging the necessary capital. They may concentrate their attention on the developmental activities of the company.

2. The company gets assurance from the underwriters for subscribing the entire capital. Therefore, it escapes from the danger of under capitalisation.

3. Underwriting creates public confidence. Hence, investors are in a safer position when they buy shares or debentures which have been underwritten.

4. Underwriters possess specialised skill and experience and they provide expert advice to make necessary changes in the price or form of the new shares or debentures.

5. When the shares or debentures are underwritten, the problem of issuing the shares or debentures at discount does not arise.

Type of Underwriting. The underwriting contract may be classified as below :

1. Joint Underwriting. When two or more underwriters jointly underwrite an issue of shares or debentures of a company in an agreed ratio, the underwriting will be called as joint underwriting.

2. Complete Underwriting. When the whole of the issue of shares or debentures of a company is underwritten either by a single underwriter or by two or more underwriters, it will be termed as complete underwriting.

3. Pure or Pre or Open Underwriting. It is an agreement whereby the underwriter agrees or underwriters agree to take up the shares or debentures of a company only that portion of shares or debentures not taken up by the public. In this case, the liability of underwriter arises only when the public is not subscribed in full.

4. Partial Underwriting. It is an agreement whereby an underwriter agrees to take up only a part or portion of issue of shares or debentures of company. For example, a company issues 60,000 shares of which 25,000 shares are underwritten by 'X' underwriter.

5. Firm Underwriting. It is a contract under which the underwriter agrees or underwriters agree to take up a certain number of shares or debentures definitely (firmly) for himself irrespective of the fact whether they are subscribed to by the public or not. In this case, the underwriter is bound to take up a specified number of shares or debentures underwritten by him in addition to the unsubscribed shares or debentures. For example, if the underwriter has firm underwritten 40,000 shares of the total issue of 1,00,000 shares, only 60,000 shares are available to the public even if there are applications for 70,000 shares.

Marked and Unmarked Application. When the issue of shares or debentures is underwritten, the underwriters issue the application forms to the public for subscribing the shares or debentures of the company. When the applications are issued to the public by the underwriters it is a common practice to put the seal or stamp on the application forms of the particular underwriter who has issued such forms. Those application forms which bear the underwriters' stamp are known as marked applications. This marking helps the company in identifying the application received through the various underwriters. This marking is useful in determining the amount of commission payable to each underwriter or broker as well as in fixing up the responsibility for the unsubscribed shares or debentures.

The applications received by the company directly from the public, which do not bear any seal or stamp of the underwriters are known as unmarked applications. In other words, the applications without any stamp or seal of the underwriters are called unmarked applications. The unmarked applications received by the company will be allocated among the underwriters in the ratio of shares or debentures underwritten and subscription of such applications will be deducted from the total issue in order to calculate the gross liability of underwriters.

Where the entire issue of shares or debentures of company is underwritten by only one underwriter, the distinction between marked and unmarked applications is of no significance. He will get the credit for all the applications whether they are marked or unmarked. When there are two or more underwriters, they will be given the credit by considering the marked applications.

Determination of Liability of the Underwriters under Different Circumstances

The liability of single underwriter or several underwriters would be determined on the basis of the nature of underwriting agreement. Therefore, the liability under different circumstances is discussed as below :

(a) When there is complete or total underwriting

The entire issue of shares or debentures may be underwritten by a single underwriter or several underwriters. Under such circumstances, the liability of single or several underwriters would be determined separately.

1. If the entire issue is underwritten by a single underwriter. In this case, he will be given the credit for all the applications whether marked or unmarked.

His liability will be equal to the number of shares/debentures underwritten by him minus the number of shares/debentures applied for from the public. It is shown in the statement as below :

Statement showing the liability of underwriter

His gross liability (*i.e.*, entire issue of shares or debentures underwritten)	xxxx
Less : Total applications received by the company from the public or underwriter	xxxx
Net liability of underwriter (*i.e.*, number of shares or debentures required to be taken up by the underwriter)	xxx

If the shares or debentures offered to the public are fully subscribed or over-subscribed by the public there will be no liability for the underwriter to take up any shares or debentures. However, he will be entitled to get the commission only on the issue price of the shares or debentures of the company.

2. If the entire issue is underwritten by the several underwriters. When the entire issue is underwritten by two or more underwriters in an agreed ratio, the following procedure is to be followed :

Step 1. Calculate the gross liability of each underwriter in the ratio in which he has underwritten the shares/debentures. Usually, this is given in the problem. Hence, it does not involve any calculation.

Step 2. Deduct the credit given to each underwriter in respective of unmarked applications from the gross liability of each underwriter *i.e.*, from step 1. This is to be done in the ratio of their gross liability.

Step 3. Deduct the marked applications of each underwriter from the remaining liability or each underwriter *i.e.*, from step 2.

Step 4. If surplus or over-subscription or minus figure remained in step 3, it should be transferred to other underwriters in the ratio of their gross liability and deducted from their respective liability.

If again surplus or over-subscription or minus figure arises to any underwriter or underwriters, that should be transferred to other underwriters and deducted from their respective liability. This process of transfer should be repeated until all the surpluses or over-subscriptions or minus figures are to be eliminated. The final balance left in each underwriter's account will be treated as net liability of each underwriter. This is shown in the statement as below :

Statement showing the liability of underwriters

	A	B	C
Gross liability of each underwriter	xxx	xxx	xxx
Less : Credit given to each underwriter in respect of unmarked applications	xxx	xxx	xxx
Balance	xxx	xxx	xxx
Less : Marked applications of each underwriter	xxx	xxx	xxx
Balance	xxx	xxx	xxx
Less : Surplus or over-subscription or minus figure (in the above balance) of any underwriter or underwriters transferred to other underwriters in the ratio of their gross liability.	xxx	xxx	xxx
Net liability (*i.e.*, the number of shares to be taken up by the underwriter)	xxx	xxx	xxx

If the marked applications exceed the number of shares/debentures or if the shares/debentures are fully subscribed or over-subscribed, the underwriter will be free from his liability.

(b) When there is partial underwriting

In the partial underwriting only a portion of the issue of shares/debentures is underwritten by the underwriter. The company itself becomes an underwriter for the remaining part of the issue which is not underwritten. The partial underwriting is also done by a single underwriter or the several underwriters. Therefore, the liability of single underwriter and several underwriters is determined separately.

1. If the partial issue is underwritten by single underwriter. In this case, the liability of a single underwriter will be ascertained as below :

Step 1. Calculate the gross liability of a single underwriter underwritten by him. Usually, it is given in the problem.

Step 2. Deduct the credit, if any, given to the underwriter in respect of surplus in the company's account for the unmarked applications (*i.e.,* if the credit given to the company for unmarked applications exceeds its liability, that surplus will be credited to underwriter) from the gross liability of underwriter *i.e.,* from step 1.

Step 3. Deduct the marked applications from the remaining liability of underwriter *i.e.,* from step 2. The final balance left in the underwriter's account will be treated as net liability of a single underwriter. This is shown in the statement as below :

Statement showing the liability of underwriter

	A	Company
Gross liability of underwriter and company	xxx	xxx
Less : Credit, if any, given in respect of surplus in the company's account for the unmarked applications	xxx	xxx
Balance	xxx	—
Less : Marked applications	xxx	—
Net liability of underwriter	xxx	—

If the marked applications of underwriter exceed his gross liability or if the shares or debentures are fully subscribed or over-subscribed, the underwriter will free from his liability.

2. If the partial issue is underwritten by the several underwriters. In this case, the liability of two or more underwriter will be determined as below :

Step 1. Calculate the gross liability of each underwriter. Usually, it is given in the problem.

Step 2. Deduct the credit, if any, given to each underwriter in respect of surplus in the company's account for the unmarked applications (*i.e.,* if the credit given to the company for the unmarked applications exceeds its liability, that surplus will be credited to each underwriter in the ratio of their gross liability) from the gross liability of each underwriter *i.e.*, from step 1.

Step 3. Deduct the marked applications from the remaining liability of each underwriter *i.e.,* from step 2.

Step 4. Transfer the surplus appeared in any underwriter's account to other underwriters in the ratio of their gross liability and should be deducted from their respective liability. The final balance left in each underwriter's account will be treated as net liability of each underwriter *i.e.,* the number of shares required to be taken up by each underwriter.

This is shown in the statement as below :

Statement showing the liability of underwriters

	A	B	C	Company
Gross liability of each underwriter and company	xxx	xxx	xxx	xxx
Less : Credit, if any, given in respect of surplus in the company's account for the unmarked applications	xxx	xxx	xxx	xxx
Balance	xxx	xxx	xxx	—
Less : Marked applications of each underwriter	xxx	xxx	xxx	—
Balance	xxx	xxx	xxx	—
Less : Surplus of any underwriter or underwriters transferred to other underwriters	xxx	xxx	xxx	—
Net liability of each underwriter	xxx	xxx	xxx	—

If the marked applications of any underwriter exceed his gross liability or if the shares or debentures are fully subscribed or over-subscribed, the underwriter will be free from his liabilities.

(c) When there is firm underwriting

When the underwriter agrees or underwriters agree to take up firm underwriting, it becomes an additional liability of the underwriter or underwriters. Hence, this must be added to the net liability ascertained under different circumstances discussed in the foregoing pages. If there is a firm underwriting in the problem, the liability of underwriter or underwriters is determined as below :

Step 1. Ascertain the net liability of single underwriter or several underwriters as ascertained in the complete underwriting by single underwriter or several underwriters and partial underwriting by single underwriter or several underwriters.

While calculating the net liability of single underwriter or several underwriters, firm applications must be taken into account. Generally, firm applications received from the single underwriter or several underwriters are treated as applications and added to the unmarked applications received from the public and as such they are treated as unmarked applications received from the public. On the other hand, if the instruction is given in the problem regarding the firm application should be treated as marked applications, then the firm applications should be treated as marked applications and added to the marked applications of underwriter or underwriters. Therefore, as regards the treatment of firm applications, it should be noted that unless we are specifically instructed that the firm application should be considered as marked applications, firm applications should always be considered as marked applications.

Step 2. Add the liability for firm underwriting to the net liability ascertained under complete underwriting (single or several) or partial underwriting (single or several) as the case may be. The final balance left in the underwriters' account will be treated as total liability of underwriter or underwriters *i.e.,* the number of shares/debentures required to be taken up by the underwriter or underwriters.

Illustration 1

(Total or complete underwriting by a single underwriter)

'A' company issued 20,000 shares of Rs. 25 each. These shares were underwritten by 'B'. However, the company received the applications for 15,000 shares only. Determine the liability of the underwriter.

Solution :

Statement showing the liability of underwriter

	Shares
Gross liability of underwriter (*i.e.,* entire issue)	20,000
Less : Total application received and credited to the underwriter	15,000
Net liability of underwriter	5,000

Illustration 2

(Total underwriting by several underwriters)

X Ltd., issued 30,000 equity shares of Rs. 10 each. The whole of the issue was underwritten as follows :

A–21,000 shares and B–9,000 shares

The public applied for 24,000 shares which included marked applications as follows :

A–15,000 shares and B–6,000 shares.

Determine the liability of underwriters.

Solution :

Statement showing the liability of underwriters

	A Shares	B Shares
Gross liability of each underwriter (as given in the problem)	21,000	9,000
Less : Credit given to each underwriter in respect of unmarked applications in their gross liability ratio of 7 : 3	2,100	900
Balance	18,900	8,100
Less : Marked applications of each underwriter (as given in the problem)	15,000	6,000
Net liability of each underwriter	3,900	2,100

Note : Unmarked applications are 3,000 (*i.e.,* total applications received minus marked applications of all underwriters *i.e.,* 24,000–21,000). They should be apportioned in the underwriters gross liability ratio *i.e.,* 21,000 : 9,000 = 7 : 3.

Illustration 3

Popular Ltd., issued 40,000 shares of Rs. 10 each for public subscription. The issue was underwritten as follows :

Sriram 25%, Raghu 50% and Ranga 25%

The company received a total of 30,000 applications of which marked applications are as follows :

Sriram 10,000, Raghu 15,000 and Ranga 5,000

Determine the liability of each underwriter.

Solution :

Statement showing the liability of each underwriter

	Sriram Shares	Raghu Shares	Ranga Shares
Gross liability of each underwriter (as given in the problem)	10,000	20,000	10,000
Less : Marked applications of each underwriter (as given the problem)	10,000	15,000	5,000
Net liability of each underwriter		5,000	5,000

Illustration 4

(Partial underwriting by single underwriter)

The Madras Motor Ltd., issued 28,000 shares of Rs. 100 each. 75% of the issue was underwritten by Rahim.

Applications for 21,000 shares were received in all by the company. Determine the liability of Rahim.

Solution :

Statement showing the liability of Rahim

	Rahim Shares	Company Shares
Gross liability of each underwriter & company (75% of the total issue *i.e.*, 28,000 × 75/100)	21,000	7,000
Less : Marked application (75% of the total applications received *i.e.*, 16,000 × 75/100)	12,000	—
Net liability of Rahim and Company	9,000	7,000

Note : (i) In this problem, there is no instruction regarding the marked applications. Therefore, it is assumed that 75% of the total number of applications received, are the marked applications.

(ii) The company column does not have any significance as far as liability is concerned. It is given just to verify whether there is surplus in the company's account or not. In this case there is no surplus.

Illustration 5

A Public Ltd. Company issued 50,000 shares of Rs. 100 each. 75% of the issue was underwritten by Singh. Applications for 35,000 shares were received in all, out of which marked applications were 20,000.

Determine the liability of Singh.

Solution :

Statement showing the liability of Singh

	Singh Shares	Company Shares
Gross liability of the underwriter and company	37,500	12,500
Less : Unmarked application credited to the company (35,000 – 20,000)	—	15,000
Balance	37,500	– 2,500
Less : Credit given to Singh in respect of surplus in the company's account for the unmarked applications	2,500	+ 2,500
Balance	35,000	—
Less : Marked applications	20,000	—
Net liability of Singh and Company	15,000	—

Illustration 6

(Partial underwriting by several underwriters)

A Company issued 1,00,000 shares of Rs. 10 each. These shares were underwritten as follows : X–30,000 shares, Y–50,000 shares.

The public applied for 70,000 shares. Determine the liability of X and Y.

(Bangalore April, 1991)

Solution :

Statement showing the liability of each underwriter

	X Shares	Y Shares	Company Shares
Gross liability	30,000	50,000	20,000
Less : Unmarked applications credited to the company (70,000 × 20/100)	—	—	14,000
Balance	30,000	50,000	6,000
Less : Marked applications	21,000	35,000	—
Net liability	9,000	15,000	6,000

Note : (i) In this problem, 80% of underwriting is related to X and Y and remaining 20% of underwriting is related to company. The company column does not have any significance as for as liability is concerned. It is given just to verify whether there is surplus in the company's account or not. But there is no surplus.

(ii) Out of 70,000 applications of shares, 14,000 shares are related to company (*i.e.,* 20%), 21,000 shares are related to X (*i.e.,* 30%) and 35,000 shares are related to Y. Applications which are not related to the underwriters are treated as unmarked applications and credited to the company and the applications which are related to underwriters are considered as marked applications and credited to the underwriters.

Illustration 7

Popular Ltd., issued 60,000 8% debentures of Rs. 100 each. 70% of the issue was underwritten by A and B in the ratio of 2 : 1. Applications for 50,000 debentures were received in all, out of which the marked applications were as follows : A–18,000 and B–9,500.

Determine the liability of the underwriters.

Solution :

Statement showing the liability of each underwriter

	A Debentures	B Debentures	Company Debentures
Gross liability	28,000	14,000	18,000
Less : Unmarked applications credited to the company (50,000 – 27,500)	—	—	22,500
Balance	28,000	14,000	– 4,500
Less : Credit given to underwriters in respect of surplus in the company's account for the unmarked applications in the ratio of their gross liability *i.e.,* 2 : 1	3,000	1,500	+4,500
Balance	25,000	12,500	—
Less : Marked applications	18,000	9,500	—
Net liability	7,000	3,000	—

Illustration 8

(Total underwriting by a single underwriter coupled with firm underwriting)

Blue Moon Ltd., issued 25,000 debentures of Rs. 1,000 each. The entire issue was underwritten by Bright Ltd. In addition to underwriting these debentures, Bright Ltd. made 'firm application' in the ordinary course for another 3,000 debentures. Applications for 24,000 debentures were received by the company in all. Determine the liability of Bright Ltd.

Solution :

Statement showing the liability of Bright Ltd.

	Debentures
Gross liability of the underwriter	25,000
Less : Total applications received by the company (Unmarked plus Marked plus Firm Applications as given in the problem)	24,000
Net liability under normal underwriting	1,000
Add : Liability for firm underwriting	3,000
Total liability of the underwriter	4,000

Note : In this case, if the issue is fully or over-subscribed by the public, then the liability of the underwriter will be limited to the extent of his firm applications.

Illustration 9

(Partial underwriting by a single underwriter coupled with firm underwriting)

The Madras Co. Ltd., issued 50,000 equity shares of Rs. 100 each. 75% of the issue was underwritten by Bangalore Co. Ltd. In addition to underwriting these shares, Bangalore Co. Ltd., made firm underwriting for 5,000 shares. Applications were received for 40,000 equity shares. The marked applications for shares were 25,000.

Calculate the liability of Bangalore Co. Ltd.

Solution :

Statement showing the liability of Bangalore Co. Ltd.

	Bangalore Co. Ltd. Shares	Company Shares
Gross liability	37,000	12,500
Less : Credit given to the company in respect of unmarked and firm applications (40,000–25,000)	—	15,000
	37,500	– 2,500
Less : Credit given to underwriter in respect of surplus in the company's account	2,500	+ 2,500
Balance	35,000	—
Less : Marked applications	25,000	—
Net liability under normal underwriting	10,000	—
Add : Liability under firm underwriting	5,000	—
Total liability of underwriter	15,000	—

Illustration 10

(Total underwriting by several underwriters coupled with firm underwriting)

A company issued 30,000 shares of Rs. 10 each. These shares were underwritten as follows :

X–18,000 shares; Y–7,500 shares; Z–4,500 shares.

In addition, there was a firm underwriting as follows :

X–2,400 shares; Y–900 shares; Z–3,000 shares. Total subscriptions received by the company (excluding firm underwriting and marked applications) were 4,500 shares.

Marked applications were : X–3,000 shares; Y–6,000 shares; Z – 1,500 shares. Determine the liability of the underwriters.

(Bangalore, November, 1993)

Solution :

Statement showing the liability of each underwriter

	X Shares	Y Shares	Z Shares
Gross liability of each underwriter	18,000	7,500	4,500
Less : Credit given to each underwriter in respect of unmarked applications and firm applications (4,500 + 6,300) in the ratio of their gross liability *i.e.,* 12 : 5 : 3	6,480	2,700	1,620
	11,500	4,800	2,880
Less : Marked applications of each underwriter	3,000	6,000	1,500
Balance	8,520	– 1,200	1,380
Less : Credit given to X and Z in respect of surplus in Y's account in the ratio of their liability *i.e.,* 18,000 : 4,500 or 4 : 1	960	+ 1,200	240
Net liability under normal underwriting	7,560	—	1,140
Add : Liability under firm underwriting	2,400	900	3,000
Total liability of each underwriter	9,960	900	4,140

Illustration 11

The following underwriting of shares takes place : P–10,000 shares; Q–8,000 shares and R–6,000 shares. In addition, there is a firm underwriting: P–1,000 shares, Q–1,200 shares and R–800 shares.

The issue consists of 24,000 shares. The shares applied for were 20,000. The following being the marked forms including firm underwriting, which is also regarded as marked forms.

P–5,000 shares; Q–3,500 shares and R–2,500 shares.

Show the allocation of liability of underwriters.

Solution :

Statement showing the liability of underwriters

	P Shares	Q Shares	R Shares
Gross liability of each underwriter	10,000	8,000	6,000
Less : Credit given to each underwriter in respect of unmarked applications (9,000) in their gross liability *i.e.,* 5 : 4 : 3	3,750	3,000	2,250
Balance	6,250	5,000	3,750
Less : Marked applications including firm applications of each underwriter	5,000	3,500	2,500
Net liability under normal underwriting	1,250	1,500	1,250
Add : Liability under firm underwriting	1,000	1,200	800
Total liability of each underwriter	2,250	2,700	2,050

Note : In this case, as per the instruction given in the problem, firm applications are considered as marked applications.

Illustration 12

(Partial underwriting by several underwriters)

Madan Ltd., issued 20,000 debentures of Rs. 100 each. 60% of the issue was underwritten by A and B in the ratio of 3 : 2. Applications for 15,000 debentures were received in all. The 'firm' and 'marked' applications of the underwriters are as below :

	Firm	Market
A	3,000	5,000
B	1,000	1,500

Determine the liability of each underwriter.

Solution :

Statement showing the liability of underwriters

	A Debentures	B Debentures	Company Debentures
Gross liability	7,200	4,800	8,000
Less : Credit given to company in respect of unmarked applications and firm applications (15,000 – 6,500)	—	—	8,500
Balance	7,200	4,800	–500
Less : Credit given to all underwriters in respect of surplus in the company's account in the ratio of their gross liability *i.e.,* 3 : 2	300	200	+500
Balance	6,900	4,600	—
Less : Marked applications	5,000	1,500	—
Net liability under normal underwriting	1,900	3,100	—
Add : Liability under firm underwriting	3,000	1,000	—
Total liability of each underwriter	4,900	4,100	—

Illustration 13

(Total underwriting by several underwriters)

A public limited company, with a capital of Rs. 10,00,000 divided into equity shares of Rs. 10 each, places its entire issue on the marked and the whole issue has been underwritten as follows :

P	30,000	shares	Q	35,000	shares
R	10,000	shares	M	15,000	shares
N	2,000	shares	O	8,000	shares

All the marked forms are to go in relief of the liability of the underwriters whose names they bear.

The applications received on the forms marked by the underwriters are :

P	25,000	shares	Q	23,500	shares
R	6,500	shares	M	1,000	shares
N	2,000	shares	O	7,000	shares

Applications for 20,000 equity shares are received on unmarked applications forms.

Calculate the liability of individual underwriters. In terms of the underwriting agreement, the relevant proportion is to be ascertained not in terms of the original liability ratio but after giving credit for marked forms.

(Adapted from C.A. Inter)

Solution :

Statement showing the liability of underwriters

	P Shares	Q Shares	R Shares	M Shares	N Shares	O Shares
Gross liability	30,000	35,000	10,000	15,000	2,000	8,000
Less : Credit given to each underwriter in respect of unmarked applications	2,857	6,572	2,000	8,000	—	571
Balance	27,143	28,428	8,000	7,000	2,000	7,429
Less : Marked applications of each underwriter	25,000	23,500	6,500	1,000	2,000	7,000
Net liability of each underwriter	2,143	4,928	1,500	6,000	—	429

Note: As per the instruction given in the problem, the unmarked applications for 20,000 shares are allocated among all the underwriters in the ratio of their gross liability after giving the credit for marked applications *i.e.,* in the ratio of 5,000 (30,000 – 25,000) : 11,500 (35,000 – 23,500) : 3,500 (10,000 – 6,500) : 14,000 (15,000 – 1,000) : 0 (20,000 – 20,000) : 1,000 (8,000 – 7,000).

Illustration 14

The Bangalore Battery Ltd., was formed with a capital of Rs. 10,00,000 in Rs. 10 each shares, the amount being issued to the public. The underwriting of these shares was as follows :

M : 35,000; N : 30,000; O : 20,000; P : 10,000; Q : 3,000; R : 2,000

All the marked application forms were to go in relief of the underwriters whose names they bore. The application forms marked by the underwriters were : M : 10,000; N : 22,500; O : 20,000; P : 7,500; Q : 5,000; R : Nil.

Applications for 20,000 shares were received on forms not marked.

Draw up a statement showing the number of shares each underwriter had to take up.

(A.C.S., Dec. 1980)

Solution :

Statement showing the liabilities of underwriters

	M Shares	N Shares	O Shares	P Shares	Q Shares	R Shares
Gross liability of each underwriter	35,000	30,000	20,000	10,000	3,000	2,000
Less : Credit given to each underwriter in respect of unmarked applications in the ratio of their gross liability *i.e.,* 35 : 30 : 20 : 10 : 3 : 2	7,000	6,000	4,000	2,000	600	400
Balance	28,000	24,000	16,000	8,000	2,400	1,600
Less : Marked application of each underwriter	10,000	22,500	20,000	7,500	5,000	Nil
Balance	18,000	1,500	- 4,000	500	– 2,600	1,600
Less : Credit given to M, N, P and R in respect of surplus of O's and Q's account (4,000 + 2,600) in the ratio of their gross liability *i.e.,* 35 : 30 : 10 : 2	3,000	2,571	+ 4,000	857	+2,600	172
Balance	15,000	–1,071	—	–357	—	1,428
Less : Credit given to M and R in respect of surplus in N's and P's account (1,071 + 357) in the ratio of their gross liability *i.e.,* 35 : 2	1,351	1,071	—	+357	—	77
Net liability of each underwriter	13,649	—	—	—	—	1,351

Accounting Entries as Regards Underwriting of Shares or Debentures

There are two stages in the accounting entries relating to underwriting of shares or debenture. In the first stage, normal entries relating to allotment of shares or debentures to the public are to be passed and in the second stage, entries relating to the underwriting agreement are be passed.

A. Entries relating to the allotment of shares or debentures to the underwriters

1. *Entry for the issue of shares or debentures at par :*

Underwriter's Account	Dr.	With the amount of shares/ debentures allotted to him.
To Share Capital/Debentures A/c		With amount of Shares/Debentures

2. *Entry for the allotment of shares/debentures at a discount*

Underwriter's Account	Dr.	With the net price of shares/ debentures issued.
Discount on Issue of Shares/Debentures A/c		With the amount of discount
To Share Capital/Debentures A/c		With the face value of shares/ debentures.

3. *Entry for the allotment of shares/debentures at a premium :*

Underwriter's Account	Dr.	With the amount of shares/ debentures plus premium.
To Share Capital/Debentures A/c		With the amount of shares/ debentures
To Shares/Debentures Premium A/c		With the amount of premium.

B. Entries relating to the underwriting agreement

1. *Entry for the underwriting commission payable to the underwriter :*

Commission on Issue of Shares/ Debentures A/c	Dr.	With the amount of commission.
To Underwriter's A/c		With the amount of commission due.

2. *Entry for the payment of commission to the underwriter :*

Underwriter's Account	Dr.	With the amount of commission paid.
To Bank or Shares or Debentures A/c		With the amount of cash or shares issued or debentures issued.

Note : Underwriting Commission will be paid either in cash, shares or debentures.

3. *Entry for the issue of shares/debentures in cash of under-subscription :*

If the shares or debentures are under-subscribed, the underwriter is forced to undertake the shares or debentures which are not subscribed by the public. In this case the entry will be :

Underwriter's Account	Dr.	With the amount of shares/debentures issued to him.
To Share Capital/Debentures A/c		

4. *Entry for receiving the payment on shares or debentures taken under contract:*

Bank Account	Dr.	With the final balance received from the underwriter.
To Underwriter's A/c		

Note: Instead of receiving cash from the underwriters for the shares or debentures taken by them and paying the commission to them; it is usual to settle the account for the difference between the two.

5. *Entry to transfer the discount on issue of shares/debentures and underwriting commission on issue of debentures/shares to 'Cost of Issue of Debentures/Shares Account' :*

If there is an underwriting commission on the issue of debentures/shares as well as discount on the issue of shares/debentures, the same should be transferred to the 'Cost of Issue of Debentures/Shares Account'. In this case, the entry will be :

Cost of Issue Debentures/ Shares Account	Dr.	With the amount of discount or commission.
To Discount/Commission on Issue of Debentures/Shares A/c		With the amount of discount/ commission.

Illustration 15

Reliance Computers Ltd., Mumbai, issues 550 debentures of Rs. 100 each at Rs. 95 and 4,000 shares of Rs. 10 each to the public. Ramesh & Co. has entered into an underwriting agreement with Reliance Computers for the subscription of the whole issue at commission of 2% on shares and 1% on debentures (nominal value). Cash was received for all the shares and debentures from the public except for 50 debentures. These were taken up by the underwriters. Underwriters paid the balance due. Pass the necessary entries in the books of Reliance Computers Ltd., and also prepare the Balance sheet.

(Adapted from Bangalore University)

Solution :

Journal Entries

Sl. No.	Particulars		L.F.	Dr. Rs.	Cr. Rs.
1.	Bank A/c (4,000 × 10)	Dr.		40,000	—
	To Share Capital A/c			—	40,000
	(Being the issue of 4,000 shares of Rs. 10 each to the public for cash)				
2.	Bank A/c	Dr.		47,500	—
	Discount on Issue of Debentures A/c	Dr.		2,500	—
	To Debentures' A/c			—	50,000
	(Being 500 debentures of Rs. 100 each issued for cash at a discount of Rs. 5 per debenture)				
3.	Ramesh and Co. A/c	Dr.		4,750	—
	Discount on the Issue of Debentures A/c	Dr.		250	—
	To Debentures' A/c			—	5,000
	(Being allotment of 50 debentures of Rs. 100 each at a discount of Rs. 5 per debenture not taken up by the public to the underwriters)				
4.	Commission on the Issue of Shares A/c	Dr.		800	—
	Commission on the Issue of Debentures A/c	Dr.		550	—
	To Ramesh and Co. A/c			—	1,350
	(Being commission due on 4,000 shares at 2% and on 550 debentures at 1%)				
5.	Bank A/c (4,750–1,350)	Dr.		3,400	—
	To Ramesh and Co. Account			—	3,400
	(Being the net amount due from the underwriters received)				
6.	Cost of the Issue of Debentures A/c	Dr.		3,300	
	To Discount on the Issue of Debentures A/c (2,500 + 250)			—	2,750
	To Commission on the Issue of Debentures A/c			—	550
	(Being the discount & commission on the issue of debentures transferred to the Cost of the Issue of Debentures A/c)				

Balance Sheet as on...

Liabilities	Rs.	Assets	Rs.
Shares Capital :		Current Assets :	
4,000 Shares of Rs. 10		Cash at Bank	
each fully paid	40,000	(40,000 + 47,500 + 3,400)	90,900
Secured Loans :		Miscellaneous Expenditure & Losses:	
550 Debentures of		Commission on the Issue of Shares	800
Rs. 100 each fully paid	55,000	Cost of the Issue of Debentures	3,300
	95,000		95,000

Illustration 16

X enters into a contract with Y Ltd. to undertake its 5,000 shares of Rs. 10 each in consideration of commission at 4%. He also enters into an agreement with Z to sub-underwrite 1,000 shares of Y Ltd. at a commission of 2%. The public subscribe for 2,000 shares only and subsequently the shares are taken up by X who sells his shares at a rate of Rs. 9 per share. The shares taken up by Z are sold at the rate of Rs. 10 per share. Expenses of underwriting amount to Rs. 500. Prepare underwriting account in the books of X.

(M.K.U., Oct. 1995)

Solution :

Dr. **Underwriting Account of Y Ltd.** Cr.

Liabilities	Rs.	Assets	Rs.
To Expenses	500	By Bank (Commission) (4% on Rs. 50,000)	2,000
To Bank (3,000 × 10) (Shares taken up by A)	30,000	By Bank (600 × 10) (Shares taken up by Z)	6,000
To Bank (2% on Rs. 10,000) (Commission paid to Z)	200	By Bank (2,400 × 9) (Shares taken by X sold at Rs. 9 per share)	21,600
		By Loss	1,100
	30,700		30,700

Notes : (1) Out of 5,000 shares, Z underwrites 1,000 shares. Then, out of 3,000 unsubscribed shares, Z should undertake 600 shares $\frac{(3,000 \times 1,000)}{5,000}$ of Rs. 10 each.

(2) Out of 3,000 shares not taken up, 600 shares are taken up by Z. The remaining balance of 2,400 shares are sold by X at Rs. 9 per share.

Illustration 17

A company limited offered for subscription 30,000 equity shares of Rs. 10 each. The whole issue was underwritten by B Co. Ltd. at an agreed commission of 5% payable as to 75% in fully paid shares and 25% in cash. In addition to underwriting of these shares, B Co. Ltd. also made a firm application in equity of 75,000 shares. 75% of the issue was obliged to take 25% of the shares underwritten. The shares in A Co. Ltd., were subsequently quoted at a discount of $12\frac{1}{2}\%$. Prepare the accounts showing the position as it would appear in the books of B Co. Ltd.

(Adapted from B.Com., Osmania)

Solution :

Dr. **Underwriting Commission Account** Cr.

	Rs.		Rs.
To Shares in A Co. Ltd., (Commission on 30,000 shares of Rs. 10 each in 5%)	15,000	By Bank (Commission) (25% of Rs. 15,000, *i.e.* 5% on Rs. 30,000)	3,750
		By Shares in A Co. Ltd. (75% of Rs. 15,000)	11,250
	15,000		15,000

Dr. **Shares in A Co. Ltd.** Cr.

	Rs.		Rs.
To Bank (7,500 × 10) (Unsubscribed portion *i.e.,* 25% of 30,000 shares taken up)	75,000.00	By Underwriting Commission	15,000.00
		By Profit and Loss A/c	5,156.25
To Bank (7,500 × 10) (Firm application taken up)	75,000.00	By Balance c/d	1,41,093.75
To Underwriting Commission (Shares issued for commission)	11,250.00		
	1,61,250.00		1,61,250.00

***Notes* : (1) Calculation of loss of shares**

Shares received as underwriting commission	11,250
Add : Unsubscribed portion of shares taken up (7,500 × 10)	75,000
Add : Shares on firm application taken up (7,500 × 10)	75,000
Value of shares on hand	1,61,250

A share of Rs. 10 is quoted at Rs. 8.75 (*i.e.,* 10 – 1.25). Therefore, shares of Rs. 1,61,250 will be valued at Rs. 1,41,093.75 (1,61,250 × 8.75/10).

Hence, the loss transferred to P & L A/c will be Rs. 5,156.25 (1,61,250 – 1,41,093.75 = 20,156.25 – 15,000).

Illustration 18

Export Ltd., incorporated on 1st January, 1997, issued a prospectus inviting application for 5,00,000 equity shares of Rs. 10 each at a premium of 10%.

The whole issue was fully underwritten by X, Y, A & B as follows :

X 2,00,000 shares A 1,00,000 shares

Y 1,50,000 shares B 50,000 shares

Applications were received for 4,50,000 shares of which marked applications were as follows :

X 2,20,000 shares A 1,10,000 shares

Y 90,000 shares B 10,000 shares

It was agreed that underwriters be paid commission at 5% on the issue price. You are required,

(a) to find out the liabilities of individual underwriters and

(b) to give necessary journal entries including for cash transactions.

(Adapted from C.A. Inter & Bangalore, April 1996 Mod.)

Solution :

(a) Statement showing the liabilities of underwriters

	X Shares	Y Shares	A Shares	B Shares	Total Shares
Gross liabilities of underwriters	2,00,000	1,50,000	1,00,000	50,000	5,00,000
Less: Credit given to each underwriter in respect of unmarked applications (4,50,000 – 4,30,000) in the ratio of gross liability *i.e.,* 4 : 3 : 2 : 1	8,000	6,000	4,000	2,000	20,000
Balance	1,92,000	1,44,000	96,000	48,000	4,80,000
Less: Marked applications of each underwriter	2,20,000	90,000	1,10,000	10,000	4,30,000
	– 28,000	54,000	–14,000	38,000	50,000
Less: Credit given to Y and B in respect of X's and A's Account in ratio of their gross liabilities *i.e.,* 3 : 1	+ 28,000	31,500	+14,000	10,500	—
Net liability of each underwriter	Nil	22,500	Nil	27,500	50,000

(b) Journal Entries

Sl. No.	Particulars	L.F.	Dr. Rs.	Cr. Rs.
1.	Bank Account Dr.		49,50,000	—
	To Equity Share Capital Account		—	45,00,000
	To Premium on the Issue of Shares A/c		—	4,50,000
	(Being 4,50,000 shares of Rs. 10 each issued for cash at a premium of Rs. 10 per share)			
2.	Y's Account Dr.		2,47,500	
	B's Account Dr.		3,02,500	—
	To Equity Share Capital Account		—	5,00,000
	To Premium on Issue of Shares A/c		—	50,000
	(Being allotment of 50,000 shares at Rs. 10 each at a premium of Rs. 10 per share not taken up by the public to Y and B in their net liability ratio *i.e.,* 9:11)			
3.	Commission on the Issue of Shares A/c Dr.		2,75,000	—
	To X's Account		—	1,10,000
	To Y's Account		—	82,500
	To A's Account		—	55,000
	To B's Account		—	27,500
	(Being commission of 5% due on 5,00,000 shares of Rs. 11 each)			
4.	Bank Account Dr.		4,40,000	—
	To Y's Account (2,47,500 – 82,500)		—	1,65,000
	To B's Account (3,02,500 – 27,500)		—	2,75,000
	(Being net amount due from the underwriters received)			
5.	X's Account Dr.		1,10,000	—
	A's Account Dr.		55,000	—
	To Bank Account		—	1,65,000
	(Being the commission due to the underwriters paid)			

Illustration 19

Sharma is an underwriter, who has agreed to underwrite the new issue of 25,000 shares of Rs. 10 each of Menaka Co. Ltd. For this work, the company agreed to give a commission of 10% to Sharma. It was also agreed that this commission was to be paid 75% in fully paid shares and the balance in cash. Further, Sharma had agreed to purchase another 3,000 shares as firm underwriting.

As the company did not receive sufficient demand for shares from the public, Sharma had taken up 40% of the total issued shares. Later it was found by Sharma that the shares of the company could be sold in the stock exchange at a profit of $12^1/_2$%, and he decided to show this profit suitably in the shares' account.

With the help of the above information, prepare journal entries and the shares' account in Sharma's books and journal entries in the books of the company.

(Adapted from Madras University & Bangalore April, 1992)

Solution :

Journal Entries in the Books of Menaka Co. Ltd.

Sl. No.	Particulars	L.F.	Dr. Rs.	Cr. Rs.
1.	Book Account Dr.		1,50,000	—
	To Share Capital Account		—	1,50,000
	(Being 60% of share capital received from the public)			
2.	Sharma's Account Dr.		1,00,000	—
	To Share Capital Account		—	1,00,000
	(Being shortfall in the public subscription 40% taken up by underwriters)			
3.	Sharma's Account Dr.		30,000	—
	To Share Capital Account		—	30,000
	(Being firm underwriting taken up by Sharma)			
4.	Underwriting Commission A/c Dr.		25,000	—
	To Sharma's Account		—	25,000
	(Being 10% of underwriting commission on Rs. 2,50,000 due)			
5.	Sharma's Account Dr.		18,750	—
	To Share Capital Account		—	18,750
	(Being commission of 75% of Rs. 25,000 paid by issuing fully paid shares)			
6.	Bank Account Dr.		1,42,500	—
	To Sharma's Account		—	1,42,500
	(Being net amount due from the underwriter received *i.e.,* 1,00,000 + 30,000 + 18,750 – 6,250 *i.e.,* 25,000 – 18,750)			

Journal Entries in the Books of Sharma

Sl. No.	Particulars	L.F.	Dr. Rs.	Cr. Rs.
1.	Shares in Menaka Co. Ltd. A/c Dr.		1,00,000	—
	To Menaka Co. Ltd. Account		—	1,00,000
	(Being the shares not taken over by public)			
2.	Menaka Co. Ltd. Account Dr.		25,000	—
	To Underwriting Commission A/c		—	25,000
	(Being the commission due)			
3.	Shares in Menaka Co. Ltd. A/c Dr.		30,000	—
	To Menaka Co. Ltd. A/c		—	30,000
	(Being firm underwriting taken over by Sharma)			
4.	Shares in Menaka Co. Ltd. A/c Dr.		18,750	—
	To Menaka Co. Ltd. A/c		—	18,750
	(Being commission of 75% of Rs. 25,000 received in the form of fully paid shares)			
5.	Menaka Co. Ltd. A/c Dr.		1,42,500	—
	To Bank Account		—	1,42,500
	(Being the net amount due to Menaka Co. Ltd. Paid)			
6.	Underwriting Commission A/c Dr.		28,125	—
	To Share Capital Account		—	25,000
	To Share Premium Account		—	3,125
	(Being the shares issued at a premium of 12.5%)			

Dr. **Shares in Menaka Co. Ltd.** Cr.

	Rs.			Rs.
To Menaka Co. Ltd.	1,00,000	By Underwriting Commission		25,000
To Menaka Co. Ltd.	30,000	By Menaka Co. Ltd. :		
To Menaka Co. Ltd.	18,750	Shares	1,48,750	
To Profit and Loss A/c	43,594	(1,00,000 + 30,000 + 18,750)		
(Profit)		Premium	18,594	1,67,344
		(12.5% on Rs. 1,48,750)		
	1,92,344			1,92,344

EXAMINATION QUESTIONS

(A) Answer the following questions in two sentences each :

(Each carrying two marks)

1. What do you mean by underwriting?
2. Who is underwriter?
3. What is the main function of underwriter?

(Bangalore, April 1992)

4. What is underwriting commission?
5. Write a note on underwriting commission.

(Bangalore, April 1994)

6. What is sub-underwriting?
7. What do you understand by underwriting agreement?
8. What do you mean by joint underwriting?
9. What is complete underwriting?

(Bangalore, April 1995)

10. What is pure underwriting?
11. What do you understand by partial underwriting?
12. What is firm underwriting?

(Bangalore, Nov. 1995)

13. What is meant by 'Marked Application'?

(Bangalore, April 1993)

14. Give the meaning of unmarked applications?

(Bangalore, Nov. 1993)

15. Give the meaning of marked and unmarked applications.

(Bangalore, Nov. 1994)

16. Distinguish between an underwriter and a broker.

(Bangalore, Nov. 1996)

17. Mention the maximum rate of commission payable for the underwriting of shares and debentures.
18. On what basis is the underwriting commission payable to the underwriters?

(B) Answer the following questions :

(Each carrying eight marks)

1. What are the contents of underwriting agreement?
2. What are the conditions as to payment of underwriting commission?
3. What are the advantages of underwriting?
4. What are the types of underwriting?
5. Determine the liability of underwriters when there is a complete underwriting.
6. Determine the liability of underwriters when there is partial underwriting.
7. X Co. Ltd., issued 20,000 equity shares of Rs. 10 each. The issue was underwritten as follows :

   A — 30%, B — 30% and C — 20%.

   However the company received applications for 16,000 shares only. Determine the liability of the respective underwriters.

Ans. : Net liability of underwriters : A – 1,200 shares, B – 1,200 shares and C – 800 shares.

8. A Company issued 10,000 shares of Rs. 10 each. These shares were underwritten as follows : A – 7,000 shares; B – 3,000 shares. The public applied for 8,000 shares which included marked applications as follows : A – 5,000 shares; B – 2,000 shares. Determine the liability of A and B.

   (Adapted from Mysore University)

Ans. : Net liability of underwriters : A – 1,300 shares and B – 700 shares.

9. Popular Ltd., issued 40,000 shares of Rs. 10 each for public subscription. The issue was underwritten as follows :

   Sriram – 25%, Raghu – 30% and Tilak – 25%. The Company received a total of 28,000 applications of which marked applications are as follows :

   Sriram – 8,000; Raghu – 6,000 and Tilak – 8,000.

   Determine the liability of each of the underwriters.

   (Bangalore, Oct. 1991)

Ans. : Net liability of underwriters : Sriram – 2,000 shares; Raghu – 6,000 shares and Tilak – 2,000 shares.

10. A company issued 20,000 shares of Rs. 10 each at par which were underwritten as follows :

    X – 10,000 shares; Y – 6,000 shares and Z – 4,000 shares. Applications were received for 18,000 shares which included marked applications as follows : X – 4,000 shares; Y – 2,000 shares and Z – 10,000 shares.

You are required to a prepare a statement showing how many more shares underwriters will have to take under the underwriting agreement.

(A.C.S., June 1994)

Note : Surplus in Z's account (6,400) is distributed to X and Y in the ratio of 10 : 6.

Ans. : Net liability of underwriters : X – 1,000 shares; Y – 1,000 shares and Z – Nil.

11. The following underwriting takes place : A – 5,000 shares; B – 3,000 shares and C – 2,000 shares.

In addition there is a firm underwriting : A – 1,000 shares; B – 500 shares and C – 1,500 shares.

The share issue is of 10,000 shares. Total subscription including firm underwriting was for 8,500 shares and the forms included the following marked forms : A – 2,000 shares; B – 1,000 shares and C – 1,000 shares.

Show the allocation of liability of the underwriters.

(M.K.U., Nov. 1997)

Ans. : Total liability of underwriters : A – 1,750 shares, B – 11,500 and C – 1,600 shares.

(C) Solve the Following Problems :

(Each carrying 15–16 marks)

1. Satara Sugars Limited incorporated on 1st January, 1987 issued a prospectus inviting applications for 20,000 equity shares of Rs. 10 each. The whole issue was fully underwritten by A, B and C as follows :

A – 10,000 shares, B – 6,000 shares and C – 4,000 shares.

Applications were received for 16,000 shares of which marked applications were as follows : A – 8,000 shares; B – 2,850 shares; C – 4,150 shares.

You are required to find out the liabilities of the individual underwriter.

(Adapted from C.A. Inter)

Ans. : Net liability of underwriters : A – 1,281 shares and B – 2,719 shares.

Hint : Surplus (350) in C's Account is distributed to A and B in the ratio of 5 : 3.

2. Able Ltd. has authorised capital of Rs. 50,00,000 divided into 1,00,000 equity shares of Rs. 50 each. The entire issue was underwritten as follows :

   X – 30,000 shares (Firm underwriting – 5,000 shares)

   Y – 15,000 shares (Firm underwriting – 2,000 shares)

   Z – 5,000 shares (Firm underwriting – 1,000 shares)

   Out of the total issue, 45,000 shares, including firm underwriting, were subscribed. The following were the marked forms :

   X – 16,000 shares; Y – 10,000 shares; Z – 4,000 shares.

   Calculate the liability of each underwriter.

   (Adapted from Company Secretaries)

Ans. : Total liability of underwriters : X – 9,667 shares; Y – 2,333 shares and Z – 1,000 shares.

Hint : Surplus (500) in Z's Account is credited to X & Y in the ratio of 2 : 1.

3. The following underwriting of shares takes place : A – 6,000; B – 2,500 shares and C – 1,500 shares.

   In addition, there is a firm underwriting : A – 800 shares; B – 300 shares and C – 1,000 shares.

   The issue consists of 10,000 shares. The total subscription including the firm underwriting was 7,100 shares.

   Applications include the following marked forms : A – 1,000 shares; B – 2,000 shares; C – 500 shares.

   Show the allocation of liability of underwriters.

   (Bangalore, April 1990)

Ans. : Total liability of underwriters : A – 3,320 shares; B – 300 shares and C – 1,380 shares.

Hint : Surplus (400) in B's Account credited to A & C in the ratio of 4 : 1.

4. Arunodaya Ltd., issued 2,00,000 shares of Rs. 10 each. The entire issue was underwritten as follows :

   Arun 1,00,000 shares (Firm underwriting 20,000 shares)
   Bharat 60,000 shares (Firm underwriting 10,000 shares)
   Uday 40,000 shares (Firm underwriting 10,000 shares).

   Shares applied for were 1,80,000, the following being the marked forms including firm underwriting, which are also regarded as marked forms.

   Arun 70,000 shares; Bharat 28,000 shares; Uday 32,000 shares.

   Calculate the liability of each underwriter.

   (I.C.S., June 1989)

Ans. : Total liability of underwriters : Arun – 23,700 shares, Bharat – 26,250 shares and Uday – 10,000 shares.

Hint : Surplus (2,000) in Uday's Account credited to Arun and Bharat in the ratio of 5 : 3.

5. Blue Bell Ltd., offered to the public, 5,000 7% Mortgage Debentures of Rs. 100 each at the issue price of Rs. 105. Eighty per cent of the issue was underwritten by M/s. Stock and Shares for a commission of 2½% of the price.

Applications were received from the public for 4,000 debentures which were fully allotted. Show how these transactions would appear in the balance sheet of the company.

(Adapted from My. Uni, B.Com., May 1978)

Ans. : Total of Balance sheet Rs. 5,04,000 and Underwriting Commission

$$\text{Rs. } 10{,}500 = \left(4{,}20{,}000\frac{25}{100}\right).$$

6. Company issued 10,000 shares of Rs. 100 each at par and 500 debentures Rs. 1,000 each at Rs. 950. The whole of the issue has been underwritten by P. Jones & Co. for a commission of 4% on shares and 2% on debentures (nominal value). The whole of the shares were applied for, but applications for 400 debentures were received. All the applications were accepted.

Give journal entries to record the above transactions and prepare the Balance Sheet at this stage, assuming that all amounts due have been received.

(C.A. Inter)

Ans. : Underwriting commission on issue of shares Rs. 40,000; Cost of the issue of debentures Rs. 35,000 (20,000 + 5,000 + 10,000); Total cash received Rs. 14,25,000 (10,00,000 + 3,80,000 + 45,000) and Total of Balance Sheet Rs. 15,00,000.

7. H Ltd., issues 1,000 equity shares of Rs. 100 each at Rs. 95; and 500, 12% debentures of Rs. 100 each at Rs. 95. The whole of the issue has been underwritten by M/s Chopra & Co. for the maximum commission allowed by law. The whole of the shares were applied for but only 400 debentures were applied for. All applications were accepted. Give journal entries and show the entries in the balance sheet assuming all amounts have been received.

(A.C.S., June 1996)

Ans. : Cost of Issue of shares Rs. 9,750 (4,750 + 5,000); Cost of Issues of Debentures Rs. 6,187.50 (5,000 + 1,187.50); Bank Rs. 1,36,562.50 and Balance Sheet Total Rs. 15,00,000.

8. X Co.Ltd. which carried on the business of underwriting shares, underwrote 15,000 shares of Rs. 10 each in a new issue made by A Co. Ltd. The agreed commission was 5% payable as to 70% in fully paid shares and the balance in cash. In addition to underwriting these shares, X Co. Ltd. made "firm application" in the ordinary course for another 2,500 shares.

The issue was not fully subscribed by the public and the underwriting company was obliged to take up 30% of the shares underwritten. The shares in A Co. Ltd. were consequently quoted at a discount of 12%.

Prepare necessary account showing the position in the books of X Co. Ltd.

(Adapted from Mysore University)

Ans. : Loss transferred to P& L A/c Rs. 9,030.

$$\left[75{,}250\ (i.e.,\ 45{,}000 + 25{,}000 + 5{,}250) - 66{,}220\left(i.e., \frac{75{,}250 \times 8.80}{10}\right)\right]$$

Balance in shares in A Co. Ltd. Rs. 66,220.

9. Krishna underwrites the new issue of 2,000 shares of Rs. 100 each of Rama Company Limited. The agreed commission was 5% payable as to 60% in cash and the rest in fully paid shares. The public subscribed for 800 shares and the rest had to be taken up by the underwriter. These shares were subsequently quoted in the marked at 15% discount.

Make necessary journal entires in the books of company and underwriter and prepare share account in the books of underwriter.

(B.Com., Rajasthan)

Ans. : In the books of Krishna : Loss transferred to P & L A/c Rs. 8,600 (Balancing figure); Shares in Rama Co. A/c Total Rs. 1,24,000 and Market value of shares in Rama Co. Ltd.

$$\text{Rs. } 1{,}05{,}400\left(1{,}24{,}000 \times \frac{85}{100}\right).$$

10. A Company made a public issue of 1,25,000 equity shares of Rs. 100 each, Rs. 50 payable on application. The entire issue was underwritten by four parties : A, B, C and D in the proportion of 30%, 25%, 25% and 20% respectively. Under the terms agreed upon, a commission of 2% was payable on the amounts underwritten.

A, B, C and D had also agreed on 'firm' underwriting of 4,000, 6,000, Nil and 15,000 shares respectively.

The total subscriptions, excluding firm underwriting, including marked applications were for 90,000 shares. Marked applications received were as under :

A – 24,000; B – 20,000; C – 12,000; D – 24,000

Ascertain the liability of the individual underwriter and and also show the journal entries that you would make in the books of the company. All working should form part of your answer.

(C.A. Inter, November 1987)

Ans. : Total liability including the liability in respect of firm underwriting :

	A	B	C	D
Firm treated as marked	4,000	6,000	10,000	15,000
Firm treated as unmarked	4,750	6,625	8,625	15,000

11. Bangalore House Building Association issued 1,00,000 Equity Shares of Rs. 100 each. P, Q, R and S underwrite the entire issue in the proportion of 40%, 30%, 20% and 10% respectively in consideration of commission in cash at 4%. They also apply firm for shares as follows :

P for 3,000 shares; Q for 2,000 shares; R for 2,000 shares and S for 3,000.

Besides the firm applications from the underwriters the public apply for 60,000 shares of which marked applications are as follows :

P – 10,000 shares; Q – 6,000 shares; R – 8,000 shares and S – 16,000 shares.

Show the number of shares to be taken up by each of the underwriters and also the commission receivable in cash.

(Bangalore, November 1994)

Ans. : Total liability including the liability in respect of firm underwriting : P – 17,000 shares; Q – 14,000 shares; R – 6,000 shares and S – 3,000 shares. Underwriting commission : P– Rs. 1,60,000; Q – Rs. 1,20,000; R – Rs. 80,000 and S – Rs. 40,000.

Total unmarked applications : 30,000 (60,000 – Marked applications 40,000 + 10,000 Firm underwriting). Surplus (9,000) of S credited to P, Q and R in the ratio of 4 : 3 : 2.

12. Gama Ltd. issued 10,000 6% Debentures of Rs. 100 each of a discount of 6%. Eighty per cent of the issue is underwritten by Bala and Co. for a commission of 2% on the issue price of Debentures. Public have applied for 7,500 Debentures. Determine the net liability of the underwriter and the company. Make an assumption that the whole money due has been received. Journalise the transactions in the Books of Gama Ltd.

(Bangalore, April 1995)

Ans. : Net liability of underwriter : 2,000 shares; Net liability of the company : 500 shares.

Marked Applications : Underwriter – 6,000 & Co. – 1,500.

Discount on the issue of debentures Rs. 57,000 (45,000 + 12,000).

Commission on the issue of debentures Rs. 15,040 (2% on Rs. 7,52,000).

Amount received from Bala & Co. Rs. 1,72,960 (1,88,000 – 15,040).

13. A company issues 10,000 equity shares of Rs. 100 each at par and 500 debentures of Rs. 1,000 each at Rs. 950. The whole of the issue has been underwritten by Jones & Co. for a commission of 4% on shares and 2% on debentures (nominal value). The whole of the shares were applied for, but applications for 400 debentures were received. All the applications were accepted. Give journal entries to record the above transactions, assuming that all amounts due have been received.

(Bangalore, November 1995)

Ans. : Bank A/c 14,25,000 (10,00,000 + 3,80,000 + 45,000)

Discount on the issue of debentures Rs. 25,000 (20,000 + 5,000)

Commission on the issue of shares Rs. 40,000.

Commission on the issue of debentures Rs. 10,000.

Net amount received from underwriters Rs. 45,000.

14. Ritika Ltd., a new company, went in for public issue of 1,00,000 shares of Rs. 100 each. The entire share issue was underwritten by A, B and C as follows :

A = 50,000 shares; B = 30,000 shares; C = 20,000 shares

In addition, there was firm underwriting as follows :
A = 10,000 shares; B = 7,500 shares; C = 7,500 shares.

The total subscription including firm underwriting was 80,000 shares and the forms included the following marked forms :

A = 15,000 shares; B = 20,000 shares; C = 7,500 shares.

Prepare statement showing allocation of liability.

(Bangalore, November 1996)

Ans. : Total liability including firm underwriting : A – 25,375 shares; B – 7,500 shares and C – 9,643 shares.

Unmarked Applications : 37,500 (80,000– Marked applications 42,500 *i.e.,* 15,000 + 20,000 + 7,500)

B's excess (1,250) transferred to A & C in the ratio of 5 : 2.

15. Embassy Limited issued 10,000 shares of Rs. 100 each at a premium of Rs. 20 per share. The entire issue was underwritten by A, B and C as follows :

A – 5,000 shares (Firm underwriting 1000 shares)

B – 3,000 shares (Firm underwriting 500 shares)

C – 2,000 shares (Firm underwriting 500 shares)

Public have applied for 9,000 shares. Following are the marked forms including firm underwriting :

A – 3,500 shares

B – 1,400 shares

C – 1,600 shares.

Determine the liability of each underwriter.

(Bangalore, April 1997)

Ans. : Net liability including firm underwriting : A – 1,187 shares; B – 1,313 shares and C – 500 shares.

Unmarked applications : 2,500 (9,000 – 6,500 marked applications *i.e.,* 3,500 + 1,400 + 1,600)

Surplus (100) of C credited to A and B in the ratio of 5 : 3.

******

2

VALUATION OF GOODWILL AND SHARES

VALUATION OF GOODWILL

Meaning and Definitions of Goodwill

Goodwill is the value of good name, reputation, wide connections and other advantages of a business which attracts more customers and brings excess earnings over and above the normal profits. In other words, it refers to the value of a business over and above the value represented by its tangible assets, such as land, buildings, machinery, furnitures, book debts, stock, cash etc. It means, it is an extra value attaching to a business over and above the value of its assets which are tangible in nature. It measures the capacity of a business to earn above the normal profits. It is always attached to the business, hence, it is born with the business, lives with business and dies with the business. It is not a fictitious asset. It is an intangible asset, as it has no physical existence and cannot be seen and touched. It is real asset and can be sold like any other asset. It is defined as the present value of a firm's anticipated excess earnings. The various definitions in respect of goodwill are given as below :

According to **Justice Lord Macnaghtan** "the goodwill is the benefit and advantage of good name, reputation and connection of a business. It is the attractive force which brings in customers".

Eric L. Kohler in his *A Dictionary for Accountants* defines goodwill as 'the present value of expected future income in excess of a normal return on the investments in tangible assets.'

According to **Prof. Dicksee** "When a man pays for goodwill, he pays for something which places him in the position of being able to earn more money than he would be able to do by his own unaided efforts."

According to **A.V. Adamson** "Goodwill has the characteristics of cement."

In the words of **Spicer and Pegler,** "Goodwill may be said to be that element arising from the reputation, connection or other advantages possessed by a business which enables it to earn greater profits than the return normally to be expected on the capital represented by the net tangible assets employed in the business."

Need for Valuation of Goodwill

The following are the circumstances under which the goodwill is to be valued and taken into account :

1. In the case of Individual :
   (a) For calculating the estate duty, death duty, etc. on the death of a person.
2. In the case of Sole -Trading Concern :
   (a) For selling the sole - trading concern.
   (b) For converting the sole - trading concern into a partnership firm.
3. In the case of Partnership Firm :
   (a) To change in thc profit sharing ratio of partners.
   (b) To take admission of a new partner.
   (c) On the retirement of a partner.
   (d) On the death of a partner.
   (e) On the amalgamation of partnership firm with another concern.
   (f) On the dissolution of a partnership firm.
   (g) For selling the partnership firm to a Joint Stock Company.
   (h) For calculating the taxes.
4. In the case of a Joint Stock Company :
   (a) For converting the private company into a public limited company.
   (b) For valuation of shares of a company.
   (c) On the amalgamation of a company.
   (d) On the absorption of a company.
   (e) On the external reconstruction of a company.
   (f) On the acquisition of a business.

For the above circumstances, the valuation of goodwill becomes necessary.

Factors Determining the Value of Goodwill

The following are the some of the main factors which determine or affect the value of goodwill of a firm :

1. Profitability. The profitability of a firm is the main factor determining the value of goodwill of a firm. If the profit earning capacity of a business is higher, the reputation or goodwill of the business is also higher and consequently, the business can enjoy more goodwill.

2. Rate of return. The rate of return on investments plays an important role in valuation of goodwill. If the investor gets a higher rate of return on his investment as compared with the rate of return prevailing in the market, the reputation of a concern will be higher and valuable. Consequently, the goodwill of such a concern will be more.

3. Capital required. If a concern requires low capital, the purchasers to purchase such a concern will be more in number and as such, the goodwill of such a concern will go up. On the other hand, if a concern requires huge capital, the purchasers to purchase such a concern will be less in number and hence, the goodwill of such a concern will be low.

4. Location factor. If the business is located in a favourable location *i.e.*, in a central or prominent locality, the earning capacity of a business will be more and as such, it can have more goodwill.

5. Time factor. The old, more established business, will enjoy more goodwill than a newly-started business.

6. Nature of business. A business which is dealing in essential goods, enjoys more goodwill than the one which is dealing in fashionable goods.

7. Courteous service. A business firm which renders courteous service to the customers, attracts more customers and consequently, it can enjoy more goodwill.

8. Efficiency of management. If the management of a business is efficient, it contributes to better profits and as such, the goodwill of such a concern will be higher and valuable.

9. Efficiency of employees. Efficient and skilled employees of a business contribute to higher profits and thereby, raise the value of its goodwill.

10. Other factors. Trade cycles, money market conditions, government policies, general economic conditions, political stability, etc., are other factors influencing the value of goodwill.

Methods of Valuation of Goodwill

The following are the main four methods of valuation of goodwill :

1. Simple-profits Method
2. Super-profits Method
3. Capitalisation Method
4. Annuity Method.

1. Simple-profit Method or Average Profit Method. Under this method, goodwill is valued on the basis of a certain number of years purchase (*i.e.*, times) of the average adjusted annual profits or average maintainable profits of the past few years. For example, if the average annual profits of a business for the last four years are Rs. 15,000 (*i.e.*,15,000 + 17,000 + 14,000 + 14,000 = 60,000 ÷ 4) and the goodwill is to be valued on the basis of three years' purchase of the average annual profits of last four years, the value of the goodwill of a business will be Rs. 45,000 (*i.e.*, 15,000 × 3).

In this connection, if may be noted that, if the average adjusted annual profits or average maintainable profits are not mentioned in the problem, average annual profits should be taken for the valuation of goodwill.

Steps involved under this method

The following are the steps involved for the valuation of goodwill under this method :

(i) First of all, the average adjusted annual profits or average maintainable profits should be ascertained. It is ascertained on the basis of average profits of the past few years. While ascertaining the average annual profits of the past few years, the profits of each of the past years should be adjusted for the non-operating profits or losses and exceptional, unusual, extra-ordinary or abnormal incomes of expenses of the year. Only operating, usual or normal profits of each of the past years should be taken into account. Non-operating profits or exceptional, unusual or abnormal incomes included in the profits of any past year should be deducted from the profits of that year and non-operating losses or exceptional, unusual or abnormal expenses included in the profits of any past year should be added to the profits of that year.

In this connection, it may be noted that some of the authors will not adjust the non-operating profits and losses in the profit of the past years.

(ii) After ascertaining the average annual profits of the past year, by taking into account the above instructions, the average maintainable profits for the future should be ascertained. This is to be ascertained on the basis of average profits of the past years plus changes likely to occur in the future. Therefore, the actual expenses and losses which are not likely to arise in the future should be added with the average normal operating profits and the expenses and losses that are likely to occur in the future should be deducted from the average normal operating profits, Similarly, provision for reasonable remuneration to the propritor or partner and provision for taxation should be deducted from the average normal operating profits. Preference dividend may also be deducted from the average profits while calculating the average maintainable profits for the future. But some authors will not adjust the preference dividend in the average profits.

(iii) While calculating the average profits of the past years, simple average or weighted average will be used. If the profits of the past years have been fluctuating, a simple average is used. If the profits of the past years show a rising trend or decreasing trend, appropriate weights are used giving the greater weightage for profits of the later year.

(iv) After calculating the average maintainable profits, the same has to be multiplied by a certain number of years' purchase to find out the value of goodwill of the business. If the number of years of purchase is not given in the problem, 1, 2 or 3 years' purchase should be applied for the downward trend of the past years profits and 5 years' purchase should be applied for the upward trend of the past years' profits.

2. Super-profits Method. Super profit means excess of actual average profits of the business over and above the normal profit excepted on the capital invested by the business. In other words, it is an actual average profit over and above the normal return. Under this method, goodwill can be valued by any of the following methods :

(i) Purchase of Super-profit Method. Under this method, the value of the goodwill is ascertained as follows :

Super-profits × Number of years' purchase.

For example. If the actual annual profits of a business is Rs. 25,000, the normal earning capacity is 10% on the capital invested, the capital investment is Rs. 2,00,000 and goodwill is agreed to be 3 years' purchase of super profit, then, the goodwill of the business would be :

Super-profits = Actual annual average profits – Normal return
= Rs. 25,000 – Rs. 20,000
= Rs. 5,000

Goodwill = Super profits × Number of years' purchase
= Rs. 5,000 × 3
= Rs. 15,000

(ii) Sliding-scale Valuation of Super-profit Method. This is only a slight variation of the first method. It is advocated by **A.E. Cutforth.** It is based on the logic that it is difficult to earn the super profits eventually or uniformly over a long span of period and it is not logical to purchase them in lump sum. Therefore, instead of multiplying the whole super-profit by a certain number of years, the super-profits of a business is divided into two or three divisions and each of these divisions is multiplied by different number of years' purchase in descending order from the first division. The total of the purchases of such divisions gives the value of goodwill. For instance, the super profit of a business is Rs. 20,000. It is divided into three divisions of Rs. 7,000, 5,000 and 8,000 respectively. The number of years' purchase to be applied for the different divisions or grades are 3, 2½ and ½ respectively. Then, the value of goodwill will be calculated as below :

First Rs. 7,000 of super-profits purchased over 3 years	21,000
Second Rs. 5,000 of super-profits purchased over 2½ years	12,500
Third Rs. 8,000 of super-profits purchased over ½ years	4,000
Goodwill of the business	37,500

Steps involved under this method

The following are the steps involved for the valuation of goodwill under this method :

(i) Calculation of capital employed at the end of the year. It can be calculated in two ways *i.e.*, either through assets side approach or through the liabilities side approach.

Asset side approach

Market value of tangible assets (other than goodwill, fictitious assets and non-trading assets)	xxxx
Less: Revised values of liabilities to outsiders	xxxx
Capital employed at the end of the year	xxxx

Liabilities side approach

Credit items belonging to shareholders such as —			
Equity share capital		xxxx	
Preference share capital		xxxx	
Reserves		xxxx	
Credit balance of P & L A/c		xxxx	xxxx
Add : Profit on revaluation of assets and liabilities			xxx
			xxxx
Less : Debit items belonging to shareholders such as —			
Debit balance of P & L A/c	xxx		
Preliminary expenses	xxx		
Underwriting commission	xxx		
Discount on issue of shares & debentures	xxx		
Advertising suspense, etc.	xxx	xxxx	
Goodwill (Book value)		xxxx	
Loss on revaluation of assets and liabilities		xxxx	xxxx
Capital employed at the end of the year			xxxx

Notes : (a) If the market values of assets are not given, the book values should be taken into account.

(b) If the goodwill is also acquired by payment, then, it should be taken into account.

(c) Non-trading assets such as investments in outside securities and fictitious assets such as underwriting commission, discount on issue of shares and debentures, preliminary expenses, advertising suspense, etc., should not be taken into account while considering the total values of tangible assets. Because, they are not real assets.

(d) The term capital employed for valuation of goodwill is generally taken from the point of the equity shareholders. Therefore, preference share capital should be deducted from the total capital employed while calculating the value of goodwill. But, some authors do not exclude preference share capital.

(ii) Calculation of average capital employed during the year. After calculating the capital employed at the end, the average capital employed during the year should be calculated. It can be ascertained in two ways :

(a) If the capital is employed at the beginning is given. In this case, average capital employed during the year is calculated as below :

$$\frac{\text{Capital employed at the beginning of the year} + \text{Capital employed at the end of the year}}{2}$$

(b) If the capital is employed at the beginning is not given. In this case, capital employed at the end of the year (as calculated in first step) minus half of the current year's profit will be the average capital employed during the year. For example, if the capital employed at the end of the year is Rs. 2,00,000 and the profit earned during the year is Rs. 40,000, the average capital employed during the year will be as below :

Capital employed at the end of the year — ½ of the current year profit
2,00,000 – 20,000 = 1,80,000

It can be proved as below :

Capital employed at the beginning = Capital employed at the end – Profit earned during the year
= 2,00,000 – 40,000
= Rs. 1,60,000

Average capital employed during the year

$$= \frac{\text{Capital at the beginning} + \text{Capital at the end}}{2}$$

$$= \frac{1{,}60{,}000 + 2{,}00{,}000}{2}$$

= Rs. 1,80,000

(iii) Calculation of normal return. After calculating the average capital employed during the year, the normal returns or profits or earnings should be calculated. Normal rate to return is that rate of earning which the investors in general expect on their investments. It can be calculated by applying the normal rate of return to the average capital employed during the year. For instance, if the normal rate of return is 12% and average capital employed during the year is Rs. 1,80,000, the amount of normal return will be Rs. 21,600. Usually, the normal rate of return is given in the problem; if it is not given, the reasonable rate may be taken as normal rate of return.

(iv) Calculation of average adjusted annual profit. It can be calculated in the same manner as in the case of first method *i.e.*, the average profit method.

(v) Ascertainment of super-profits. In can be ascertained by deducting the normal returns on the average capital employed during the year from the actual average adjusted annual profits. For instance, if the normal return is Rs. 21,600 and actual average adjusted annual profit is Rs. 41,600, super-profit will be Rs. 20,000.

(vi) Ascertainment of goodwill. It can be ascertained as below :

Super profit × Number of years' purchase

For instance, if the goodwill is agreed to be valued at 2 years' purchase of super-profit and the super-profit is Rs. 20,000, then, the amount of goodwill will be Rs. 40,000 (*i.e.*, 20,000 × 2).

3. Capitalisation Method

There are two methods of valuation of goodwill in the capitalisation method. They are as below :

(a) Capitalisation of average profits

(b) Capitalisation of super profits.

(a) Capitalisation of Average Profits. Under this method first of all, the total value of the business is ascertained by capitalising the average adjusted annual profits on the basis of normal rate of return. Secondly, the value of goodwill is to be ascertained by deducting the actual capital employed (net tangible assets *i.e.*, net assets other than goodwill) from the total value of the business (*i.e.*, capitalised value of the business). For example, if the actual capital employed in the business is Rs. 2,80,000, the normal rate of return is 12% and average adjusted annual profit is Rs. 36,000, the value of goodwill will be calculated as below :

(i) Capitalised value of business $= \dfrac{\text{Average adjusted annual profit}}{\text{Normal rate of return}}$

$$= \frac{36,000}{12\%} = \frac{36,000 \times 100}{12}$$

$$= \text{Rs. } 3,00,000$$

(ii) Value of goodwill = Capitalised value of business – Actual capital employed

$$= 3,00,000 - 2,80,000 = \text{Rs. } 20,000$$

Steps involved under this method

(i) Ascertain the average adjusted annual profit or average maintainable profit. It is prepared in the same manner as in the case of first method *i.e.*, the average profit method.

(ii) Capitalise this average profit at the normal rate of return. This will give total value or capitalised value of the business. This can be calculated with the help of following formula :

$$\frac{\text{Average Adjusted Annual Profit} \times 100}{\text{Normal Rate of Return}}$$

(iii) Find out the actual capital employed in the business *i.e.,* value of net tangible assets *i.e.*, assets less outside liabilities. This can be found out in the same manner as in the case of second method *i.e.,* super-profit method.

(iv) Deducted the actual capital employed from the capitalised value or total value of the business and the resulting balance is to be considered as the value of goodwill of the business.

(b) Capitalisation of super-profit. Under this method, the value of goodwill is directly found out by capitalising the super-profits on the basis of normal rate of return. It is calculated with the help of the following formula :

$$\text{Goodwill} = \frac{\text{Super-Profit} \times 100}{\text{Normal Rate of Return}}$$

For instance, if the super-profit of the business is Rs. 12,000 and the rate of return is 12%, the value of goodwill will be Rs. 1,00,000.

(12,000 × 100 ÷ 12).

Note : Ascertainment of super-profit under this method is the same as in the case of super-profit method.

(4) Annuity Method. Under this method, goodwill is calculated by taking into account the present value of super-profit for a certain number of years at a certain rate of interest. The super-profit is taken as the annuity and super-profit (annuity) is multiplied by the present value of a rupee. In this method, the super-profits of the business are capitalised to ascertain the goodwill. The super-profits of the business under this method are found out in the same manner as in the case of super-profits method. This method is based on the logic that the purchaser of the business has to pay out now for goodwill only the present value of super-profits calculated at an appropriate rate of interest. It means, the goodwill is the discounted value of the total amount calculated as per the purchase of super-profit method. The present value of annuity or super-profits will be found out by referring to the annuity table. The annuity table will give the present value of annuity for the given number of years and at the given rate of interest. Under this method, goodwill is calculated as below :

Goodwill = Super-profit × Annuity rate (*i.e.*, present value of rupee)

For instance, if the super-profit is Rs. 12,000 and the annuity of Re. 1 at 10% for 3 years is 2.48685, the value of goodwill will be Rs. 29,842.2 (*i.e.*, 12,000 × 2.48685).

If the present value of Re. 1 is not given in the problem, the present worth of annuity of Re. 1 for 'n' years at r% is obtained by the following formula :

$$\frac{1-\left(1+\frac{r}{100}\right)^{-n}}{\frac{r}{100}} \quad \text{OR} \quad \frac{1-\left(\frac{100}{100+r}\right)^{n}}{\frac{r}{100}}$$

Where 'r' is the per cent of interest per annum and 'n' is the number of years over which the payment is to be made. Suppose, the rate of interest is 10% and the payment of one rupee is to be made for 3 years annually, the present worth of rupee 1 would be :

$$\frac{1-\left(1+\frac{10}{100}\right)^{-3}}{\frac{10}{100}} \quad \text{OR} \quad \frac{1-(1.1)-3}{0.1} \quad \text{OR}$$

$$\frac{1-\frac{1}{(1.1)^3}}{10} \quad \text{OR} \quad \frac{1-\frac{1}{1.331}}{0.1} \quad \text{OR}$$

$$\frac{\frac{1.331-1}{1.331}}{0.1} \quad \text{OR} \quad \frac{\frac{0.331}{1.331}}{0.1} \quad \text{OR}$$

$$\frac{0.2486851}{0.1} = 2.48685$$

Comments on the methods of valuation of goodwill

Simple profits method is an easy method of calculation of goodwill, but, it does not indicate the real goodwill. Because, it ignores the capital employed in the business. Hence, it is not preferred generally.

Super-profit method is superior method of valuation of goodwill than simple profits method. Because, it gives due consideration for the capital employed in the business. It is generally adopted by the joint companies.

Capitalisation method gives the maximum value for goodwill. But, this method is not safe for one to follow. This method is useful to the seller and not useful to the buyer of the business.

Annuity method is not a popular method of valuation of goodwill. Because, it tries to be too exact in uncertain situations.

Illustration 1

A, B and C are equal partners in a partnership firm, decided to admit D as a partner. The goodwill of the firm was to be valued at 3 times the average profits for the last four years. The profits for the last four years were : Rs. 30,000, Rs. 24,000, Rs. 25,000 and Rs. 25,000.

Calculate the amount of goodwill of the firm and the amount to be contributed by D as his share of goodwill.

Solution :

(i) Average profits of the firm

(ii) Goodwill of the firm = Three times the purchase of average profits

$= 3 \times 26{,}000$

$= 78{,}000.$

(iii) D's share in goodwill (assuming he is an equal partner) : He has to contribute his share of goodwill of the firm. So, the amount of goodwill to be contributed by D will be : Rs. 19,500 (78,000 × 1/4)

Illustration 2

Comrade, Dost and Companion are equal partners in a partnership firm. 1 January 1999, Companion retired from the business. The goodwill of the firm be valued at three times the average profit of the last three years. The profits of the past three years were : 1996 Rs. 13,830, 1997 Rs. 32,000 and 1998 Rs. 20,170.

Calculate the retiring partner's share of goodwill.

Solution :

(i) Average profits of the firm = 66,000/3 = Rs. 22,000

(ii) Goodwill of the firm = Three times of average profits
= 22,000 × 3
= Rs. 66,000

(iii) Retiring partner's share = 1/3 of the goodwill
= 66,000 × 1/3
= Rs. 22,000.

Illustration 3

The net profits of a company after providing for taxation for the past five years are Rs. 64,000, Rs. 70,000, Rs. 75,000, Rs. 73,000 and Rs. 83,000. The capital employed in the business is Rs. 6,80,000 on which a reasonable rate of 10% is expected. Find out the value of goodwill of the business.

Solution :

(i) Average adjusted annual profits of the company $\frac{3,65,000}{5}$ = Rs. 73,000

(ii) Capitalised value of business = $\frac{\text{Average adjusted annual profit}}{\text{Normal rate of return}}$

$$= \frac{73,000}{10\%} = \frac{73,000 \times 100}{10}$$

= Rs. 7,30,000

(iii) Value of goodwill = Capitalised value of business – Annual capital employed

= 7,30,000 – 6,80,000
= Rs. 50,000

Illustration 4

The following particulars are available in respect of the business carried on by Wisehead :

1. Capital invested 50,000
2. Market rate of interest on investments 8%
3. Rate of risk return on capital invested in the business 2%
4. Remuneration from alternative employment of the proprietor (if not engaged in business) 3,600 p.a.
5. Trading results :
   1989 profit Rs. 12,200; 1990 profit Rs. 15,000;
   1991 Loss Rs. 2,000 and 1992 profit Rs. 21,000.

You are required to compute the value of goodwill on the basis of 3 years' purchase of super-profits of the business calculated on the average profits of the last four years.

(Adapted from Bangalore University)

Solution :

(i) Calculation of total profits of past years

	Rs.
Total profit of last 3 years (12,200 + 15,000 + 21,000)	48,200
Less : Trading loss of 1991	2,000
Total profits of past four years	46,200

(ii) Calculation of average profits

$$\frac{\text{Total profits}}{\text{Number of years}} = \frac{46,200}{4} = \text{Rs. } 11,550$$

(iii) Calculation of average maintainable profit

Average profits	11,550
Less : Remuneration of the proprietor	3,600
Average maintainable profit	7,950

(iv) Calculation of normal return

10% (8% + 2%) on capital invested of Rs. 50,000 = Rs. 5,000

(v) Calculation of super-profit

= Actual average maintainable profit – Normal return
= 7,950 – 5,000
= Rs. 2,950

(vi) Calculation of Goodwill = 3 years' purchase of super-profit
= 3 × 2,950
= Rs. 8,850

Note : The term capital invested given in the problem is taken to mean average capital employed during the years.

Illustration 5

A company desirous of selling its business to another company has earned an average past profit of Rs. 1,60,000 per annum and the same amount of profit is likely to be earned in future also, except that :

(i) Directors' fees of Rs. 12,000 per annum charged against such profits will not be payable by the purchasing company whose existing Board can manage the new business also.

(ii) Rent Rs. 28,000 per annum which had been paid by the Vendor Company will not be incurred in the future since the purchasing company own's its own premises and the necessary accommodation can be provided.

The net assets, other than goodwill, were Rs. 18,00,000 and it was considered that a reasonable return on investment in this type of business would be 10%.

(Adapted from M.K.U. B. Com.)

Solution :

(i) Calculation of average maintainable profits

		Rs.
Average annual profit		1,60,000
Add : Expenses not likely to be incurred in future :		
Directors' fees	12,000	
Rent	28,000	40,000
Average maintainable profit		2,00,000

(ii) Calculation of capitalised value of the business

$$= \frac{\text{Average Maintainable profit}}{\text{Normal rate of return}} = \frac{2,00,000}{10\%} = \frac{2,00,000 \times 100}{10}$$

= Rs. 20,00,000

(iii) Calculation of value of goodwill

Capitalised value of business – Annual capital employed

= 20,00,0000 – 18,00,000

= Rs. 2,00,000

Note : The amount of net assets other than goodwill is treated as the value of annual capital employed.

Illustration 6

The average profits of a business for the last 3 years amounted to Rs. 2,20,000, but on an adjustment of certain items being carried out for the purchase of goodwill valuation, the same were found to be Rs. 2,30,000 representing average normal profits. 7½% represented a fair commercial return on average capital employed. The book value of the capital employed worked out to be Rs. 13,45,000, but upon a proper valuation being made, the capital actually employed was ascertained to be Rs. 11,50,000. Valuing the goodwill on the basis of 5 years' super-profits, you are required to fix up the final value of goodwill.

(Adapted from C. A. Inter)

Solution :

(i) Normal return or profit or earning

7½% on average capital employed *i.e.*, 7½ % on

Rs. 11,50,000 = Rs. 86,250

(ii) Super-profit

= Average adjusted annual profit – Normal earnings

= Rs. 2,30,000 – Rs. 86,250

= Rs. 1,43,750

(iii) Value of goodwill

= Super-profit × Certain number of years' purchase

= Rs. 1,43,750 × 5

= Rs. 7,18,750

Note : The ascertained capital is treated as average capital employed.

Illustration 7

The following particulars are available in respect of the business carried on by Bankey Lal :

1. Profit earned by X : 1990 Rs. 50,000; 1991 Rs. 48,000; and 1992 Rs. 52,000.
2. Profit of 1991 is reduced by Rs. 5,000 due to stock destroyed by fire and profits of 1990 included a non-recurring income of Rs. 3,000.
3. Profit of 1992 include Rs. 2,000 income on investments.
4. The stock is not insured and it is thought prudent to insure the stock in future. The insurance premium is estimated at Rs. 500 p.a.
5. Fair remuneration to the proprietor (not taken in the calculation of profits) is Rs. 10,000 p.a.

You are required to compute the value of goodwill on the basis of 2 years' purchase of average profits of the last three years.

(Adapted from Madras, B.Com.)

Solution :

(i) Total profits of past 3 years :

		Rs.
1990 – Profits	50,000	
Less : Non-recurring income	3,000	47,000
1991 – Profits	48,000	
Add : Stock destroyed by fire	5,000	53,000
1992 – Profits	52,000	
Less : Interest on investments	2,000	50,000
	Total Profits	1,50,000

(ii) Actual average maintainable profit :

Average profits (1,50,000/3)		50,000
Less : Expenses likely to occur in future		
Insurance premium to be paid in future	500	
Remuneration to the proprietor	10,000	10,500
Average maintainable profit		39,500

(iii) Value of goodwill

= Average maintainable profit × 2 years' purchase

= Rs. 39,500 × 2

= Rs. 79,000.

Illustration 8

The following particulars are available in respect of the business carried by a trader :

1. Profit earned : 1990 Rs. 50,000; 1991 Rs. 60,000; 1992 Rs. 55,000.
2. Normal rate of profit 10%
3. Capital employed Rs. 3,00,000
4. Present value of annuity of one rupee for five years at 10% Rs. 3.78
5. The profit included non-recurring profits on an average basis of Rs. 4,000 out of which it was deemed that even non-recurring profits had a tendency of appearing at the rate of Rs. 1,000 p.a.

Calculate the value of goodwill on the basis of :

(a) 5 years' purchase of super-profit method.
(b) Annuity method
(c) Capitalisation of super-profit method.

(A.C.S. June, 1997)

Solution :

	Rs.	Rs.
(i) Total profits of past 3 years		
1990 – profits	50,000	
1991 – profits	60,000	
1992 – profits	55,000	1,65,000

(ii) Average profits

1,65,000/3 = Rs. 55,000

(iii) Average expected or maintainable profits

Average profits	55,000
Less : Non-recurring profit	4,000
	51,000
Add : Non-recurring profit having tendency of recurring profit	1,000
Average maintainable profits	52,000

(iv) Super-profits

Average maintainable profit – Normal earnings (*i.e.*, 10% on average capital employed of Rs. 3,00,000)

= Rs. 53,000 – 30,000 = Rs. 22,000

(a) Super-profit method :

Goodwill = Super-profits × 5 years' purchase

= Rs. 22,000 × 5

= Rs. 1,10,000

(b) Annuity method :

Goodwill = Super-profits × Annuity rate

= Rs. 22,000 × 3.78 = 83,160

(c) Capitalisation of super-profit method

$$\text{Goodwill} = \frac{\text{Super-profit}}{\text{Normal rate of return}} = \frac{22{,}000}{10\%}$$

$$= \frac{22{,}000 \times 100}{10} = \text{Rs. } 2{,}22{,}000$$

Note : Capital employed given in the problem is treated as average capital employed.

Illustration 9

Mr. Wiseman has invested a sum of 2,00,000 in his own business which is a very profitable one. The annual profit earned from his business is Rs. 45,000 which includes a sum of Rs. 10,000 received as compensation of a part of his business premises.

As an alternative to his engagement in his business he could have invested the money in long-term deposit with Bank earning a normal rate of interest of 10% and also could engage himself in employment thereby getting an annual salary income of Rs. 7,200.

Considering 2% as fair compensation for the risk involved in the business, calculate the value of goodwill of his business on capitalisation of super-profits at the normal rate of interest. Ignore taxation.

(Adapted from C. A. Inter)

Solution :

(i) Average maintainable profit

		Rs.
Average annual profit		45,000
Less : Compensation received (Abnormal item)	10,000	
Notional salary	7,200	17,200
Average maintainable profit		27,800

(ii) Super-profit

Average maintainable profits – Normal earnings (*i.e.*, 12% on Rs. 2,00,000 average capital employed)

= Rs. 27,800 – Rs. 24,000 = Rs. 3,800

(iii) Value of goodwill on capitalisation of super-profits method

$$\text{Goodwill} = \frac{\text{Super-Profit}}{\text{Normal rate of return}} = \frac{3{,}800}{10\%}$$

$$= \frac{3{,}800 \times 100}{10} = \text{Rs. } 38{,}000$$

Note : The invested amount is taken as average capital employed.

Illustration 10

A runs a Chemist's Shop. His net assets as on 31st March, 1999 amount to Rs. 20,00,000. After paying a rent of Rs. 45,000 a year and a salary of Rs. 30,000 to the chemist, he earns a profit of Rs. 2,10,000. His landlord, who happens to be an expert Chemist, is interested in purchasing the shop. 18% considered to be a reasonable return on the capital employed. The value of premises is Rs. 3,00,000. What can A expect as payment for goodwill?

(Adapted from C.A. Final)

Solution :

	Rs.
(i) Total capital employed	
Net assets or capital employed	20,00,000
Add : Value of premises which will now form part of capital employed in future (as the owner of the building is purchasing the business)	3,00,000
Capital employed in the business	23,00,000
(ii) Normal returns on the capital employed :	
18% on average capital employed of Rs. 23,00,000	4,14,000
(iii) Average adjusted annual profits :	
Profit earned	2,10,000
Add : Annual rent saved by the landlord (as the building belongs to the owner himself)	45,000
Add : Salary of the chemist not required to be paid in future (as the owner himself is an expert chemist)	30,000
	2,85,000
Less : Reasonable remuneration for the new proprietor as chemist (as he is engaged in his own business) (Assumed to be the same as what is paid to the chemist)	30,000
	2,55,000

(iv) Super-profit to the business. Excess of actual average adjusted profits (Rs. 2,55,000) over and above the normal returns (Rs. 4,14,000) is called super-profit. But, in this case, there is no excess of actual average adjusted profits. Hence, there is no super-profit.

(v) Value of goodwill. There is no super-profit and hence there is no goodwill.

Note : Net assets are taken as average capital employed.

Illustration 11

Arun purchased a business from Balan on April 1, 1993. Profits earned by Balan for the preceding years ending December 31 each year were :

1990 Rs. 50,000; 1991 Rs. 60,000; 1992 Rs. 54,000.

It was found out that profit for the year 1990 included a non-recurring item of Rs. 2,000 and the profit for the year 1992 was reduced by Rs. 3,000 due to an abnormal loss on account of a small fire in the shop. The properties of the business were not insured in the past, but it was thought prudent to insure the properties in the future and the premium was expected to be Rs. 500 per annum. Arun at the time of purchase of business was employed as a manager with Reny Ltd. at a monthly salary of Rs. 1,000. He intends to replace the manager of the business, who is at present paid a salary of Rs. 750 per month. The goodwill is estimated at 2 years' purchase of the average profits. Calculate the value of goodwill of the business.

(Poona University, April 1997)

Solution :

		Rs.	Rs.
(i)	**Average annual profits**		
	1990 – Profit	50,000	
	Less : Non-recurring profit	2,000	48,000
	1991 – Profit		60,000
	1992 – Profit	54,000	
	Add : Abnormal loss due to fire	3,000	57,000
	Total profit of past 3 years		1,65,000
	Average annual profit (1,65,000/3)		55,000
(ii)	**Average maintainable profits**		
	Average annual profit		55,000
	Less : Expenses to be incurred in future :		
	Insurance premium	500	
	Salary for the proprietor (1,000 × 12)	12,000	12,500
			42,500
	Add : Expenses not be incurred in future :		
	Salary for the manager (750 × 12)		9,000
	Average maintainable profit		51,500

(iii) Value of goodwill

Average maintainable profit × 2 years' purchase

= Rs. 51,500 × 2

= Rs. 1,03,000.

Illustration 12

Aruna Mills proposed to purchase the business carried on by Mr. Arvind. Goodwill for this purchase is agreed to be valued at three years' purchases of the weighted average profit of the past four years. The appropriate weights to be used are :

1990-91; 1991-92; 1992-93; 1993-94.

The profits for these years are : 1990-Rs. 30,300; 1991-Rs. 31,200; 1992-Rs. 36,000; 1993-Rs. 45,000. On a scrutiny of the accounts, the following matters are revealed :

(i) On 1st September, 1991, a major repair was made in respect of the plant incurring Rs. 19,000 which amount was charged to revenue. The said sum is agreed to be capitalised for goodwill calculation subject to adjustment of depreciation of 10% p.a. on diminishing balance method.

(ii) The closing stock of 1991 was overvalued by Rs. 3,600.

(iii) To cover management cost, an annual charge of Rs. 7,200 should be made for the purchase of goodwill valuation.

Compute the value of the goodwill of the firm.

(Adapted from C.A. Inter)

(i) Calculation of adjusted profits	Rs.	Rs.
1990 – Profits	30,300	
Less : Management expenses	7,200	23,100
1991 – Profits	31,200	
Less : Overvaluation of closing stock	3,600	
	27,600	
Add : Major repairs of plant charged to revenue, but to be treated as capital expenditure for valuation of goodwill	9,000	
	36,600	
Less : Depreciation to be provided on major repairs considered as a capital expenditure, but not provided before (9,000 × 10/100)	900	
	35,700	
Less : Management expenses	7,200	28,500

1992 – Profits	36,000	
Less : Depreciation (8,100 × 10/100)	810	
(*i.e.*, on diminishing balance)	35,190	
Add : Overvaluation of opening stock	3,600	
	38,790	
Less : Management expenses	7,200	31,590
1993 – Profits	45,000	
Less : Depreciation (7,290 × 10/100)	729	
	44,271	
Less : Management expenses	7,200	37,071

(ii) Calculation of weighted average profits

Year	Adjusted profits	Weight	Product
1990	23,100	1	23,100
1991	28,500	2	57,000
1992	31,590	3	94,770
1993	37,071	4	1,48,284
		10	3,23,154

Weighted average profits = 3,23,154/10 = Rs. 32,315.40

(iii) Calculation of value of goodwill

= Weighted average profit × 3 years' purchase

= 32,315.40 × 3 = Rs. 96,946.20 or Rs. 96,946

Illustration 13

The following is the balance sheet of Quality Traders, a concern owned by Sri Ramchandran, as at 30 April, 1996.

Balance Sheet

Liabilities	Rs.	Assets	Rs.
Creditors	76,080	Fixed Assets	1,80,000
Capital	3,28,000	Current Assets	2,44,080
Reserve	80,000	Investment of Shares	60,000
	4,84,080		4,84,080

The following net profits were earned which included a fixed income from investments of Rs. 4,000 p.a.

Year ended 30th April 1993 Rs. 64,000
Year ended 30th April 1994 Rs. 72,000
Year ended 30th April 1995 Rs. 86,000
Year ended 30th April 1996 Rs. 90,000

Standard rate of return on capital employment in such type of business is 8%.

Compute the amount of goodwill of the above business at three years' purchase of the average super-profits for four years assuming that each year's profit was immediately withdrawn in full by the proprietor.

(Adapted from C.A. Inter)

Solution :

(i) Calculation of Capital employed

	Rs.	Rs.
Fixed Assets	1,80,000	
Current Assets	2,44,080	4,24,080
Less : Creditors		76,080
Capital employed at the end of the year		3,48,000

(ii) Calculation of average capital employed

Capital employed at the end of the year	3,48,000
Less : ½ of the current year's operating profits (Profit Rs. 90,000 – Non-operating income *i.e.,* income from investment Rs. 4,000 = Rs. 86,000 × ½)	43,000
Average capital employed during the year	3,05,000

Note : Half of the current year's profit is capitalised. Assuming that profit earned eventually over the year, by the middle of the year, only half of the profit is employed and remaining half of the profit is not employed in the business. Hence, it is deducted.

(iii) Calculation of average adjusted annual profits

	Rs.	Rs.
1993 – Profits	64,000	
Less : Income from investment *i.e.,* non-operating income	4,000	60,000
1994 – Profits	72,000	
Less : Income from investment	4,000	68,000
1995 – Profits	86,000	
Less : Income from investment	4,000	82,000
1996 – Profits	90,000	
Less : Income from investment	4,000	86,000
Total profit of past your years		2,96,000

Average adjusted profit = 2,96,000/4 = Rs. 74,000

(iv) Calculation of super-profits

Average adjusted profits – Normal earnings (*i.e.,* 8% of average capital employed of Rs. 3,05,000)

= Rs. 74,000 – Rs. 24,400 = Rs. 49,600

(v) Calculation of value of goodwill

Super-profit × 3 years' purchase = Rs. 49,600 × 3 = Rs. 1,48,800

Illustration 14

Ascertain the value of goodwill of X Co. Ltd. from the following information.

Balance Sheet as on 31-12-1998

Liabilities	Rs.	Assets	Rs.
Share Capital :		Goodwill at Cost	35,000
25,000 Equity shares		Land and Buildings	1,00,000
of Rs. 10 each	2,50,000	Plant and Machinery	1,00,000
Profit and Loss Account	60,000	Stock	1,60,000
Sundry Creditors	90,000	Sundry Debtors	85,000
Bank Overdraft	60,000		
Provision for Taxation	20,000		
	4,80,000		4,80,000

The Company commenced operation in 1994. The profits earned before providing for taxation are : 1994 Rs. 62,000; 1995 Rs. 65,000; 1996 Rs. 70,000; 1997 Rs. 80,000; 1998 Rs. 1,00,000.

Dividends have been distributed from the profits of the first three years at the rate of 10% and from those of the next two years at the rate of 15% on the paid up capital. Assuming that income tax at the rate of 50% has been payable on these profits, ascertain the value of goodwill of the business.

(Adapted from Bangalore University)

Solution :

(i) Calculation of actual capital employed :

	Rs.	Rs.
Assets : Land and Buildings	1,00,000	
Plant and Machinery	1,00,000	
Stock and Machinery	1,60,000	
Sundry Debtors	85,000	4,45,000
Less : Liabilities :		
Sundry creditors	90,000	
Bank overdraft	60,000	
Provision for taxation	20,000	1,70,000
Actual capital employed at the end of the year		2,75,000

(ii) Calculation of average adjusted profits

Total profits of past five years	3,77,000
Average annual profits (3,77,000/5)	75,400
Less : 50% provision for taxation	37,700
Average adjusted profits	37,700

(iii) Calculation of normal rate of return

Average dividend paid = 10 + 10 + 10 + 15 + 15/5 = 12%

Assuming that normal rate of return is 12%

(iv) Calculation of capitalised value of business

$$= \frac{\text{Average adjusted annual profits}}{\text{Normal rate of return}} = \frac{37,700}{12\%}$$

$$= \frac{37,700 \times 100}{12} = \text{Rs. } 3,14,166$$

(v) Calculation of value of goodwill

= Capitalised value of business – Actual capital employed

= Rs. 3,14,166 – Rs. 2,75,000

= Rs. 39,166.

Illustration 15

Hamer Ltd. and Grace Ltd. propose to amalgamate.

Balance Sheet of Hamer Ltd. and Grace Ltd.
as on 31-12-1991

Liabilities	Hamer Rs.	Grace Rs.	Assets	Hamer Rs.	Grace Rs.
Share Capital :			Fixed Assets		
Equity share of			*Less* : Depreciation	4,00,000	1,00,000
Rs. 10 each	5,00,000	2,00,000	Investments (Face		
General Reserve	2,00,000	20,000	value Rs. 1,00,000		
Profit & Loss A/c	1,00,000	30,000	6% G.P. notes)	1,00,000	—
Current Liabilities	1,00,000	50,000	Current Assets	4,00,000	2,00,000
	9,00,000	3,00,000		9,00,000	3,00,000

Net profit (after taxation)	Hamer Ltd.	Grace Ltd.
1989	1,30,000	45,000
1990	1,25,000	40,000
1991	1,50,000	56,000

Goodwill for the purpose of amalgamation may be taken as 4 years' purchase of average super-profits trading on the basis of 15% normal profit on closing capital invested. The current assets of Hamer Ltd. are to be taken as Rs. 4,20,000 and that of Grace Ltd. as Rs. 2,10,000.

Ascertain the value of goodwill.

(Adapted from C.A. Inter)

Solution :

(i) Calculation of capital at the end of the year

		Hamer Ltd.	Grace Ltd.
Assets :	Fixed assets	4,00,000	1,00,000
	Current assets	4,20,000	2,10,000
		8,20,000	3,10,000
Less :	Current liabilities	1,00,000	50,000
	Capital employed	7,20,000	2,60,000
Alternative method :			
Equity Share Capital		5,00,000	2,00,000
General Reserve		2,00,000	20,000
Profit and Loss A/c		1,00,000	30,000
Increase in the value of current assets		20,000	10,000
		8,20,000	2,60,000
Less :	Investments	1,00,000	–
	Capital employed	7,20,000	2,60,000

(ii) Calculation of average adjusted annual profit

		Hamer Ltd.	Grace Ltd.
1989 – profit		1,30,000	45,000
1990 – profit		1,25,000	40,000
1991 – profit		1,50,000	56,000
Total profit of past three years		4,05,000	1,41,000
Average annual profits		1,35,000	47,000
Less :	Income from investments (6% on Rs. 1,00,000)	6,000	–
Average adjusted profit		1,29,000	47,000

(iii) Calculation of super-profits

Average adjusted profits – Normal earnings (*i.e.,* 15% on closing capital employed)

Hamer = 1,29,000–1,08,000 = Rs. 21,000

Grace = 47,000 – 39,000 = Rs. 8,000

(iv) Calculation of value of goodwill

Super-profit × 4 years' purchase

Hamer = 21,000 × 4 = Rs. 84,000

Grace = 8,000 × 4 = Rs. 32,000

Note : As per the instruction given in the problem, normal earning is calculated on the closing capital invested.

Illustration 16

The Balance Sheet of Toy Gun Manufacturing Co. Ltd. discloses the following financial position as at 31 March, 1997.

Balance Sheet as on 31-12-1997

Liabilities	Rs.	Assets		Rs.
Paid up Capital :		Goodwill at Cost		30,000
30,000 Equity share of		Land and Building at Cost		
Rs. 10 each fully paid	3,00,000	*Less :* Depreciation		1,75,000
Capital Reserve	60,000	Plant and Machinery at Cost		
Sundry Creditors	71,000	*Less :* Depreciation		90,000
Provision for Taxation	55,000	Stock as Cost		1,15,000
Profit and Loss A/c	26,000	Book Debts	98,000	
		Less : Provision for doubtful debts	3,000	95,000
		Cash at Bank		7,000
	5,12,000			5,12,000

Your are asked to value the goodwill of Toy Gun Manufacturing Co. Ltd. for which purpose the following information is supplied :

(a) Adequate provision has been made in the accounts for income tax and depreciation.

(b) Rate of income-tax may be taken at 50%.

(c) The average rate of dividend declared by the company for the past five years was 15 per cent.

(d) The reasonable return on capital invested in the class of business done by the company is 12%.

(Adapted from C.A. Inter)

Solution :

(i) Calculation of capital employed

		Rs.
Land and Buildings	1,75,000	
Plant and Machinery	90,000	
Stock	1,15,000	
Book Debts less Provision	95,000	
Cash at Bank	7,000	4,82,000
Less : Sundry Creditors	71,000	
Provision for Taxation	55,000	1,26,000
Capital employed at the end of the year		3,56,000

(ii) Calculation of average capital employed

Capital employed at the end of the year	3,56,000
Less : Half of the current year's profit	55,000
Average capital employed	3,01,000

Note : The given rate of income tax is 50% and provision for taxation is Rs. 55,000. It means, provision for taxation is half of the current year's profits. If half of the current year's profit is Rs. 55,000, the full profit of the current year will be Rs. 1,10,000 (55,000 × 2/1).

(iii) Calculation of average adjusted annual profits

	Rs.
Profit for the current year (As calculated above)	1,10,000
Less : Provision for taxation (50% of current year's profit)	55,000
Average adjusted annual profits	55,000

(iv) Calculation of super-profit

Adjusted annual profits – Normal earnings (*i.e.,* 12% on average capital employed of Rs. 3,01,000)

= Rs. 55,000 – Rs. 36,120 = Rs. 18,880

(v) Value of goodwill under super-profit method

Goodwill = Super-profit × 4 years' profit

= Rs. 18,880 × 4 = Rs. 75,520

Note : In this problem, the number of years' purchase is not given. Hence, it is assumed as 4 years' purchase.

(vi) Value of goodwill under capitalisation method

(a) Capitalisation of Average Profit Method

Goodwill = Capitalised value of the business – Actual capital employed

= 55,000 × 100/12 – Rs. 3,56,000

= Rs. 4,58,333 – Rs. 3,56,000 = Rs. 1,02,333

(b) Capitalisation of Super-profit Method

$$\text{Goodwill} = \frac{\text{Super-Profit} \times 100}{\text{Normal Rate of Return}} = \frac{18{,}880 \times 100}{12} = \text{Rs. } 1{,}57{,}333$$

Note : The normal rate of return of a business is 12%, but, the rate of dividend declared by the company is 15%. It indicates that the company has earned super-profit. Therefore, this problem has been solved under super-profit method.

Illustration 17

The net profits of a company after providing for taxation for the past five years were Rs. 40,000, Rs. 42,000, Rs. 45,000, Rs. 46,000 and Rs. 47,000.

The capital employed in the business is Rs. 4,00,000 on which a reasonable rate of return of 10% is expected. It is expected that the company will be able to maintain its super-profits for the next five years.

Calculate the value of goodwill on the basis of an annuity of super-profits taking the present value of an annuity of Re. 1 for five years at 10% interest as Rs. 3.78.

How could your answer differ if the goodwill is calculated by capitalising the excess of the annual average distributable profits over a reasonable return on capital employed on the basis of the same return of 10%?

(Adapted from C.A. Inter)

Solution :

(i) Calculation of Average Adjusted Annual Profits

	Rs.
First year profits	40,000
Second year profits	42,000
Third year profits	45,000
Fourth year profits	46,000
Fifth year profits	
Total profits for the past five years	

Average Annual Profits = 2,20,000/5 = Rs. 44,000

(ii) Calculation of Super-profits

Average Adjusted Annual Profits – Normal Earnings (*i.e.,* 10% on average capital employed)

= Rs. 44,000 – Rs. 40,000

= Rs. 4,000

Note : The capital employed given in the problem is taken as average capital employed.

(iii) Value of Goodwill under Annuity Method

Super-profit × Annuity Rate (*i.e.,* present value of rupee)
= Rs. 4,000 × 3.78
= Rs. 15,120

(iv) Value of Goodwill under Capitalisation Method

(a) Capitalisation of Average Profit Method :

Goodwill = Capitalised value of the business – Actual capital employed

= 44,000 × 100/10 – 4,00,000
= Rs. 4,40,000 – Rs. 4,00,000 = Rs. 40,000

(b) Capitalisation of Super-profit Method :

$$\text{Goodwill} = \frac{\text{Super-profit} \times 100}{\text{Normal Rate of Return}}$$

$$= \frac{4{,}000 \times 100}{10} = \text{Rs. } 40{,}000.$$

Illustration 18

Negotiation is going on for transfer of X Ltd., on the basis of the Balance Sheet and the additional information is as given below :

Balance Sheet of X Ltd. as on 31st March, 1998

Liabilities	Rs.	Assets	Rs.
Share Capital	10,00,000	Goodwill	1,00,000
(Rs. 10 fully paid up share)		Land and Buildings	3,00,000
Reserve and Surplus	3,50,000	Plant and Machinery	8,00,000
13% Debentures	1,05,000	Investment	1,00,000
Secured Loan	85,000	(To provide for replacement	
Sundry Creditors	2,10,000	of plant and machinery)	
		Raw Materials at Cost	1,00,000
		Work-in-Progress at Cost (Estimated)	60,000
		Finished Goods at Cost	40,000
		Book Debts	1,50,000
		Cash and Bank	50,000
		Discount on Debentures	20,000
		Underwriting Commission	30,000
	17,50,000		17,50,000

Profit before tax for 1997-98 amounted to Rs. 6,00,000 including Rs. 10,000 as interest on investment. However, an additional amount of Rs. 50,000 p.a. shall be required to be spent for the smooth running of the business.

Market values of Land and Buildings and Plant and Machinery are estimated at Rs. 9,00,000 and Rs. 10,00,000 respectively. In order to match the above figures further depreciation to the extent of Rs. 40,000 should be taken into consideration. Income tax rate may be taken at the 50%. Return on capital at the rate of 20% before tax may be considered normal for this business at the present stage.

For the purpose of determining the rate of return, profit for this year after the aforesaid adjustments may be taken as expected average profit. Similarly, the average trading capital employed is also to be considered on the basis of the position in this year.

It has been agreed that 4 years' purchase of super-profit shall be taken as the value of goodwill for the purpose of the deal.

You are required to calculate the value of goodwill of the company.

(Adapted from C.A. Final)

Solution :

(i) Calculation of Capital Employed at the end of the year

		Rs.
Land and Building	9,00,000	
Plant and Machinery	10,00,000	
Investments (these have been included because the purpose is to replace the Plant and Machinery)	1,00,000	
Raw Materials	1,00,000	
Work-in-progress	60,000	
Finished Goods	40,000	
Book Debts	1,50,000	
Cash and Bank	50,000	24,00,000
Less : 13% Debentures	1,05,000	
Secured Loan	85,000	
Sundry Creditors	2,10,000	4,00,000
Capital employed		20,00,000

(ii) Calculation of Average Capital Employed

Capital employed at the end of the year	20,00,000
Less : Half of the current year's profits of Rs. 2,30,000 [see (iii) below]	1,15,0000
Average capital employed	18,85,000

(iii) Calculation of Average Adjusted Annual Profits

Net profit before tax		6,00,000
Less : Additional depreciation	40,000	
Recurring expenses	50,000	
Non-operating income (Interest on investments)	10,000	1,00,000
		5,00,000
Less : Provision for taxation (50% of Rs. 5,40,000)		2,70,000
Average adjusted annual profits		2,30,000

Note : Additional depreciation is not deductible for calculating provision for taxation.

(iv) Calculation of Super-profits

Average Adjusted Annual Profits – Normal Earnings (*i.e.,* 10% on average capital employed of Rs. 18,85,000)

= Rs. 2,30,000 – Rs. 1,88,500 = Rs. 41,500.

Note : Since the tax rate is 50% and normal before tax rate is 20%, normal after tax rate will be 10% (20% – 10% *i.e.,* 50% of 20%).

(v) Calculation of Value of Goodwill = Super-profit × 4 years' Profit

= Rs. 41,500 × 4

= Rs. 1,66,000

VALUATION OF SHARES

Meaning and Definitions of Shares

A company's capital is divided into a large number of equal parts or units. Each part or unit is called a share. For example, the capital of a company may consist of Rs. 5 crores divided into parts or shares of Rs. 100 each. The person who is allotted such shares is called a shareholder of a company.

The **Companies Act, 1956** defines a share as "a share in the share capital of the company".

According to **Meig's W.B.**, the unit of corporate ownership is a share or stock.

Value of Shares

The following are the types of value of shares :

1. Par Value. A price equal to the nominal or face value of the share is called par value. It is mentioned in the Memorandum of the company. Less than the face value of a share is called discount and more than the face value of share is called premium.

2. Book Value. The amount of each share is mentioned in the books of accounts of a company, this amount is called as book value of share.

3. Cost Value. The price which a shareholder has to pay in order to purchase a share is called cost value of share. It includes market price, brokerage, etc.

4. Market Value. It means, it is a price that would be agreed to in an open and unrestricted market. In other words, it is a price for which a share is sold and purchased in the share market.

5. Capitalised Value. Average adjusted annual profits of the company is capitalised by the normal rate of return; it is called capitalised value of the shares. Capitalised value = Average adjusted annual profits × Normal rate of return. This amount is divided by the number of shares to find out the capitalised value of each share of a company.

6. Intrinsic Value. The amount of external liabilities is deducted from the realisable value of real assets, the balance is called intrinsic value of shares. This value is divided by the number of shares to find out the intrinsic value of each share.

7. Fair Value. The market value or yield value and intrinsic value of a share is divided by two, the resulting figure is called fair value of a share.

Need, Importance and Objectives of Valuation of Shares

Where the shares, debentures and other securities are quoted on recognised stock exchange, the stock exchange prices are generally taken as the basis for the valuation of shares, debentures and other securities. However, the stock exchange quotations are not generally acceptable, because, they are basically determined on interactions of demand and supply and business cycles. Therefore, stock exchange quotations do not reflect the true value of shares. The council of the London Stock Exchange has also expressed the same opinion. Similarly, the stock exchange quotations are not available for the shares of private companies and other unquoted shares.

On account of the above reasons, the need for valuation of shares of a company arises in the following purposes or circumstances :

1. For the assessment of estate duty, wealth tax and gift tax by tax authorities.
2. For purchase or sale of controlling shares (Holding company purpose).
3. For formulating amalgamation and absorption schemes.
4. For converting the shares from one class to another.
5. For advancing the loans on security of shares.
6. For assessing the value of assets of finance and investment trusts.
7. For determining the amount payable to the dissentient shareholders for the acquisition of their shares (Reconstruction purpose).
8. For compensating the shareholders on the acquisition of their shares by the Government.

9. For transferring the shares to the other party.
10. For issuing the bonus shares or making rights issue etc.

Factors Affecting the Valuation of Shares

Usually, the following factors affect the value of shares :

1. Nature of the business
2. Earning capacity of the business
3. Goodwill of the business
4. Investment with other business
5. Dividend declared by the business in the previous year
6. Possibility of competition
7. Demand and supply of shares
8. General economic conditions of the country
9. Possibility of progress in future
10. Number of shareholders
11. Net tangible assets of the business
12. Capital structure of the business
13. Qualifications, capacity and experiences of the directors
14. Scope of government control over the business
15. Position of peace and security in the business.

Methods of Valuation of Shares

The following methods are commonly adopted for the valuation of shares :

1. Net assets method
2. Yield or market value method
3. Earning capacity method
4. Fair value method

1. Net Assets Method. This method is also known as asset backing method, balance sheet method, capitalisation method, intrinsic value method or break-up value method. Under this method, the amount of net assets is divided by the number of issued shares to find out the value of each share. For instance, if the value of assets is Rs. 80,000, liabilities is Rs. 20,000 and the number of shares are Rs. 10,000, the value of each share would be Rs. 6 (60,000/10,000). This method aims at finding out the possible value of shares in the event of a company going into liquidation.

In order to find out the value of each share, the following procedure should be followed :

(i) To ascertain the value of the goodwill, as explained in the preceding pages.

(ii) To find out the realisable value of real assets. In this case, it must be remembered that fictitious assets such as preliminary expenses, debit balance in the Profit and Loss A/c etc., should be excluded. If the market value of assets is not given, the book value is taken as market value.

(iii) To find out the value of liabilities payable to the outsiders *i.e.,* external liabilities.

(iv) To find out the value of net assets. The value of net assets is the difference between the realisable value of assets and external liabilities.

(v) To find out the value of each share. In order to find out the intrinsic value of each share, the value of net assets should be divided by the number of issued shares.

Under this method, the intrinsic value of each share can be arrived as below :

Realisable Value of Real Assets :	
Goodwill (as ascertained)	xxxx
Other real or tangible assets such as land, building, plant and machinery, furniture, vehicles, patents and trade marks, investments, stock, debtors, bills receivable, prepaid expenses, outstanding expenses, cash in hand, cash at Bank etc. (Market value or present value)	xxxxx
	xxxxx
Less : Value of external Liabilities : Sundry creditors, bills payable, bank overdraft, debentures, outstanding debenture interest, premium on redemption of debentures, workmen's savings bank deposits, outstanding expenses, incomes received in advance outstanding dividends, provision for taxation etc.	xxxxx
Net Assets available	xxxxx

$$\text{Value of each share} = \frac{\text{Net Assets}}{\text{Number of shares held}} = \frac{\text{xxxxx}}{\text{xxxx}}$$

$$= \text{Intrinsic value of each share}$$

Alternative Procedure

Share capital of the company		xxxxx
Undistributed reserves and funds (All accumulated reserves)		xxxx
Profit and Loss A/c credit balance		xxx
		xxxxx
Less : All fictitious assets such as preliminary expenses, discount on issue of shares and debentures, underwriting commission, brokerage on shares etc.	xxxx	
Profit and Loss A/c debit balance	xxxx	xxxxx
		xxxxx
Add : Profits on revaluation of assets and liabilities		xxxx
		xxxxx
Less : Losses on revaluation of assets and liabilities		xxx
Net Assets available		xxxxx

$$\text{Value of each share} = \frac{\text{Net Assets}}{\text{Number of shares held}} = \frac{\text{xxxxx}}{\text{xxxx}}$$

= Intrinsic value of each share

Note : The goodwill should be taken into account, unless otherwise instructed, as it is realisable.

Determination of Value of Shares under Net Assets Method

When all shares belong to one class with equal paid up values, the value of each share will be calculated as below :

$$\text{Value of each share} = \frac{\text{Net Assets}}{\text{Number of shares held}}$$

But, if the shares are belonging to different classes such as equity and preference and of different denomination and paid-up values, the procedure of valuation is slightly different.

Valuation of Equity Shares

(i) When the values of equity shares are of different denominations. In this case the following procedure is to be followed to find out the value of each share of that class or denomination :

First Step. Ascertainment of net assets available for each class or denomination : It is ascertained as below :

Net Assets × Ratio of total paid up capital of each class of equity shareholders

Second Step. Ascertainment of value of each equity share of that class : It is ascertained as below :

$$\frac{\text{Net Assets available for each class of equity shareholders}}{\text{Number of equity shares of that class}}$$

Alternative Method

First Step. Ascertainment of value per rupee of the paid-up equity capital : It is ascertained as below :

$$\frac{\text{Net Assets available for all equity shareholders}}{\text{Total amount of paid up capital of all the equity shareholders}}$$

Second Step. Ascertainment of value of each equity share of each class or denomination : It is ascertained as below :

Value per rupee of the paid-up equity capital × Actual paid-up value per share of each class of equity shares.

(ii) When there are fully paid and partly-paid equity shares. In this case the following procedure is to be followed to find out the value of each fully paid and partly paid equity share :

First Step. Ascertainment of net assets including notional calls :

	Net assets available for equity shareholders	xxxxxx
Add :	Notional Calls (Uncalled Capital) (All categories of equity shareholders)	xxxx
	Net assets including notional calls	xxxxx

Second Step. Ascertainment of value of each fully paid equity share :

$$\frac{\text{Net assets including notional calls}}{\text{Total number of equity shares}}$$

Third Step. Ascertainment of value of each partly paid share :

Value of each fully paid equity share – Uncalled amount of the concerned partly paid equity share

(iii) When the preference shares have a priority as to payment of capital and arrears of dividend. In this case, the following procedure is to be followed to find out the value of each equity share.

First Step. Ascertainment of net assets available for equity share holders :

	Net assets available for all types of shareholders		xxxxx
Less :	Preference share capital	xxxxx	
	Arrears of preference dividend	xxxx	xxxxx
	Net assets available for equity shareholders		xxxxx

Second Step. Ascertainment of value of each equity share :

$$\frac{\text{Net assets available for equity shareholders}}{\text{Number of equity shares}}$$

(iv) When the preference shares have no priority for repayment of capital and dividend. In the case, the value of each equity share is ascertained as below :

Step 1. Ascertainment of net assets available for each kind of shareholders :

Preference shareholders = Net assets available for all shareholders × Ratio of total paid up capital of preference shareholders

Equity shareholders = Net assets available for all shareholders × Ratio of total paid up capital of equity shareholders.

Step 2. Ascertainment of value of each equity share :

$$\frac{\text{Net assets available for equity shareholders}}{\text{Number of equity shares}}$$

(v) When preference shares have priority for repayment of capital only. In this case, the value of each equity share is ascertained as below :

Step 1. Ascertainment of net assets available for equity shareholders :

	Net assets available for all shareholders	xxxxx
Less :	Preference share capital	xxxx
	Net assets available for equity shareholders	xxxxx

Step 2. Ascertainment of value of each equity share :

$$\frac{\text{Net assets available for equity shareholders}}{\text{Number of equity shares}}$$

(vi) When preference shares have no priority for capital but for arrears of dividends. In this case, the value of each equity share is ascertained as below :

Step 1. Ascertainment of net assets excluding arrears of dividend for all shareholders :

	Net assets available for all the shareholders	xxxxx
Less :	Arrears of preference dividend	xxxx
	Net assets excluding arrears of dividend	xxxxx

Step 2. Ascertainment of net assets available for each kind of shareholders :

Pref. shareholders = Net assets excluding arrears of dividend of all shareholders × Ratio of total paid up capital of pref. shareholders.

Equity shareholders = Net assets excluding arrears of dividend of all shareholders × Ratio of total paid up capital of equity shareholders.

Step 3. Ascertainment of value of each equity share :

$$\frac{\text{Net assets available for equity shareholders}}{\text{Number of equity shares}}$$

(vii) When there are participating preference shares. In this case, the value of each equity share is ascertained as below :

Step 1. Ascertainment of surplus assets available for all shareholders:

Net assets available for all the shareholders	xxxxx
Less : Preference share capital	xxxx
	xxxxx
Less : Equity share capital	xxxx
Surplus of assets available for all the shareholders	xxxxx

Step 2. Ascertainment of surplus assets available for each kind of shareholders :

Pref. shareholders = Surplus of assets available for all shareholders × Ratio of total paid up capital of pref. shareholders

Equity shareholders = Surplus of assets available for all shareholders × Ratio of total paid up capital of equity shareholders

Step 3. Ascertainment of value of each equity share :

$$\frac{\text{Surplus of assets available for equity shareholders}}{\text{Number of equity shares}}$$

Valuation of Preference Shares

In case of non-participating preference shares, the shares are to be valued at par. If they are having priority of payment of capital and dividend, their value will be increased or decreased due to increase or decrease in the rate of dividend.

In case of participating preference shares, any surplus remaining after payment to the equity shareholders will be distributed among the two categories of shareholders in the ratio of paid up amounts of equity and preference capital.

The following procedure is to be followed in order to find out the value of each preference share under the different circumstances.

(i) When the preference shares have priority for repayment of capital only. In this case, the value of each preference share is calculated as below :

$$\frac{\text{Total paid up preference share capital}}{\text{Number of preference shares}}$$

(ii) When the preferences shares have priority as to payment of capital and arrears of dividend. In this case, the value of each preference share-cum-dividend is calculated as below :

$$\frac{\text{Preference share capital + Arrears of dividend}}{\text{Number of preference shares}}$$

(iii) When the preference shares have no priority for capital but for arrears of dividends. In this case, the value of each preference share is ascertained as below :

Step 1. Ascertainment of net assets excluding arrears of dividend for all the shareholders :

Net assets available for all the shareholders	xxxxx
Less : Arrears of preference dividend	xxxx
Net assets excluding arrears of dividend	xxxx

Step 2. Ascertainment of net assets available for each kind of shareholders :

Pref. shareholders = Net assets available excluding arrears for dividend of all shareholders × Ratio of total paid up capital of pref. shareholders

Equity shareholders = Net assets available excluding arrears for dividend of all shareholders × Ratio of total paid up capital of equity shareholders

Step 3. Ascertainment of the value of each pref. share ex-dividend :

$$\frac{\text{Net assets available for pref. shareholders}}{\text{Number of preference shares}}$$

Step 4. Ascertainment of value of each pref. share-cum-dividend :

Value of each pref. share ex-dividend + Arrears of preference dividend

(iv) When preference shares have no priority for payment of capital and dividend. In this case, the value of each preference share is ascertained as below :

Step 1. Ascertainment of net assets available for each class of shareholders :

Pref. shareholders = Net assets available for all shareholders × Ratio of total paid up capital of pref. shareholders

Equity shareholders = Net assets available for all shareholders × Ratio of total paid up capital of equity shareholders

Step 2 : Ascertainment of value of each pref. share :

$$\frac{\text{Net assets available for preference shareholders}}{\text{Number of preference shares}}$$

(v) When there are participating preference shares. In this case, the value of each preference share is ascertained as below :

Step 1. Ascertainment of surplus assets available for all shareholders :

Net assets available for all the shareholders	xxxxx
Less : Preference share capital	xxxxx
	xxxxx
Less : Equity share capital	xxxxx
Surplus of assets available for all the shareholders	xxxxx

Step 2. Ascertainment of surplus assets available for each kind of shareholders :

Pref. shareholders = Surplus of assets available for all shareholders × Ratio of total paid up capital of pref. shareholders

Equity shareholders = Surplus of assets available for all shareholders × Ratio of total paid up capital of equity shareholders

Step 3. Ascertainment of value of each pref. share :

$$\frac{\text{Surplus of assets available for preference shareholders}}{\text{Number of preference shares}}$$

(2) Yield Method or Market Value Method

According to *'Henson's Dictionary of Commerce'* "Yield is the return on a security based on its current earnings in relation to its current price on the stock exchange or market." Yield is an effective rate of return or rate of income. When the value of share is found out on the basis of its yield *i.e.,* dividend, it is known as yield method. Under this method, expected rate of return is found out and it is compared with the normal rate of return. If expected rate of return is more than the normal rate of return, the paid up value of share will be increased proportionately. On the other hand, if the expected rate of return is lower than the normal rate of return, the market value of the share will be less than its paid up amount. For example, if the paid up amount of a share is Rs. 100, normal rate of return is 6% and expected rate of return is 9%, then, the value of share will be Rs. 150 (9/6 × 100). On the other hand, if the expected rate of return is 3%, its market value will be Rs. 50 (3/6 × 100) only.

The market value of the securities will be ascertained with the help of the following formula :

(A) (i) Capitalised profit = $\frac{\text{Average annual profit for equity dividend}}{\text{Normal rate of return on equity shares}} \times 100$

(ii) Market value of each equity share $= \dfrac{\text{Capitalised profit}}{\text{Number of equity shares}}$

or

(B) (i) Expected rate of return $= \dfrac{\text{Average annual profit for equity dividend}}{\text{Paid up equity share capital}} \times 100$

(ii) Market value of each equity share

$$= \frac{\text{Expected rate of return}}{\text{Normal rate of return}} \times \text{Paid up value of each share}$$

or

(C) Market value of each equity share $= \dfrac{\text{Dividend per share in rupees}}{\text{Normal rate of return}} \times 100$

or

(D) Market value of each equity share

$$= \frac{\text{Rate of dividend}}{\text{Normal rate of return}} \times \text{Paid up value per share}$$

While calculating the profits available for equity dividend, the following should be deducted from the average annual profits of the company : (i) taxes payable, (ii) transfer to reserve, (iii) transfer to various funds such as debenture redemption funds, etc., and (iv) dividend payable to preference shareholders.

Valuation of Equity Shares under Yield Method

(i) If the equity shares are different denominations. In this case, the following procedure is to be followed to calculate the value of each equity share.

First Step. Ascertainment of capitalised profit :

$$\frac{\text{Average annual profit for equity dividend}}{\text{Normal rate of return}} \times 100$$

Second Step. Ascertainment of market value per rupee of paid up equity capital :

$$\frac{\text{Capitalised profits}}{\text{Total of paid up equity capital of all categories of equity shareholders}}$$

Third Step. Ascertainment of market value per share of each category of equity share :

Market value per rupee of paid up capital × actual paid up value per share of each category of equity share

Alternative Method

First Step. Ascertainment of capitalised profits of each class of equity shareholders :

Capitalised profits × Ratio of total paid up capital of different classes of equity shareholders

Second Step. Ascertainment of market value of each equity share of that class :

$$\frac{\text{Capitalised profits of each class of equity shareholders}}{\text{Number of equity shares of that class}}$$

(ii) If there are fully paid and partly paid equity shares. In this case, the market value of each equity share of each class is calculated as below :

First Step. Ascertainment of capitalised profits :

$$\frac{\text{Average annual profit for equity dividend}}{\text{Normal rate of return}} \times 100$$

Second Step : Ascertainment of market value of each fully paid equity share :

$$\frac{\text{Capitalised profits}}{\text{Total of paid up equity capital of all categories of equity shares}} \times \text{Paid-up value of each fully paid equity share}$$

Third Step. Ascertainment of market value of each partly paid equity share :

$$\text{Market value of each fully paid equity shares} \times \frac{\text{Paid up amount of each partly paid equity share}}{\text{Paid up amount of each fully paid equity share}}$$

Alternative Method

First Step. Ascertainment of capitalised profits of fully paid and partly paid equity shares :

Capitalised profits × Ratio of total paid up capital of fully paid and partly paid equity shareholders

Second Step. Ascertainment of each fully paid equity share :

$$\frac{\text{Capitalised profits of fully paid equity shares}}{\text{Number of fully paid equity shares}}$$

Third Step. Ascertainment of each partly paid equity share :

$$\frac{\text{Capitalised profits of partly paid equity shares}}{\text{Number of partly paid equity shares}}$$

Valuation of Preference Shares under Yield Method

(i) If the preference shares are not participating. Non-participating preference shareholders are getting only fixed rate of dividend. Hence, the value of each non-participating share is calculated as below :

First Step. Ascertainment of capitalised profits :

$$\frac{\text{Dividend due to preference shareholders}}{\text{Normal rate of return on pref. shares}} \times 100$$

Second Step. Ascertainment of the value of each non-participating share :

$$\frac{\text{Capitalised profit of pref. shares}}{\text{Number of pref. shares}}$$

(ii) If the preference shares are participating. Participating preferences shareholders are getting usual dividend plus their share in the surplus profit. Hence, the value of each participating share is calculated as below :

First Step. Ascertainment of capitalised profits of pref. shares :

$$\frac{\text{Total dividend or profit due to pref. shareholders}}{\text{Normal rate of return on pref. shares}} \times 100$$

Second Step : Ascertainment of the value of each participating preference share :

$$\frac{\text{Capitalised profits of preference shares}}{\text{Number of preference shares}}$$

(3) Earning Capacity Valuation Method

Under this method average profits are estimated on the basis of past results and they are capitalised at the rate of normal return on the capital employed, having due regard to the risk involved and the current rate of interest on gilt-edged securities. Under this method, the valuation depends upon the comparison of the company's earning capacity and the normal rate of return on the capital employed. This method relates the value of share to the real efficiency, as measured by profitability of the company. The formula to calculate the value of the share is given as below :

$$\text{Value of share} = \frac{\text{Rate of earning}}{\text{Normal rate of return}} \times \text{Paid up value per share}$$

$$\text{Rate of Earning} = \frac{\text{Profit earned}}{\text{Capital employed}} \times 100$$

The capital employed for this purpose is the gross capital employed in the business including long-term borrowings.

The profit earned is profit before debenture interest, preference dividend, etc., but after income tax.

Gross Capital = Equity Share Capital + Pref. Share Capital + Reserves and Surplus + Debentures and Long-Term Borrowings

Profits for Equity Shareholders = Profits-Reasonable Transfers to reserves + Taxes + Abnormal items which may not be in future + Preference Dividend

Alternative Method

$$\text{Value of each equity share} = \frac{\text{Capitalised value of profits}}{\text{Number of equity shares}}$$

$$\text{Capitalised value of profits} = \frac{\text{Profits *}}{\text{Normal rate of return}} \times 100$$

*Profits here are the same as explained earlier.

Earning capacity valuation method is more appropriate for holding large blocks of shares. But, yield method of valuation is appropriate for valuing minority holdings.

(4) Fair Value Method

Fair value of share is a simple average of intrinsic value and yield value (market value) of such a share. Under this method, the total of intrinsic value of the share and the yield or market value of the share is to be ascertained and this total is divided by two in order to ascertain the fair value of the share. The formula for calculating the fair value of the share, therefore, is :

$$\text{Fair value of a share} = \frac{\text{Intrinsic value} + \text{Yield or Market Value}}{2}$$

The persons who are keenly interested in safety, prefer the asset valuation method and the persons who prefer the dividend, choose the yield method. On the other hand, if the persons are interested in both *i.e.*, safety as well ad dividend, they choose the fair value method. This method avoids the drawbacks of the two methods. But, in case of non-comparable figures, this method is not considered to be useful.

Illustration 1

X Co. Ltd., has 60,000 shares of Rs. 10 each. The profits of a company for the last four years are : Rs. 83,000; Rs. 87,000; Rs. 92,000, Rs. 98,000. The fair investment return is taken at 10%. Find out the value of the share by the yield method.

Solution :

Calculation of average annual profit

$$\frac{83{,}000 + 87{,}000 + 92{,}000 + 98{,}000}{4} = \frac{3{,}60{,}000}{4} = \text{Rs. } 90{,}000$$

Calculation of capitalised profits

$$\frac{\text{Average annual profit}}{\text{Normal rate of return}} \times 100 = \frac{90,000}{10} \times 100 = \text{Rs. } 9,00,000$$

Calculation of market value per share

$$\frac{\text{Capitalised profits}}{\text{Number of shares}} = \frac{9,00,000}{60,000} = \text{Rs. } 15.$$

Illustration 2

The authorised and paid up capital of a company consists of :

2,000, 10% preference shares of Rs. 100 each and 4,000 equity shares of Rs. 120 each, Rs. 100 per share called-up and paid-up.

X holds 2,500 equity shares in this company. The normal profit of the company is Rs. 60,000 and normal rate of return on equity shares is 10%. Calculate the value of X's shares by yield method.

Solution :

Calculation of profit for equity dividend :

Normal profit of the company	60,000
Less : Preference dividend (2,00,000 × 10/100)	20,000
Profit for equity dividend	40,000

Calculation of capitalised profits :

$$\frac{\text{Profit available for equity dividend}}{\text{Normal rate of return on equity shares}} \times 100$$

$$= \frac{40,000}{10} \times 100 = \text{Rs. } 4,00,000$$

Calculation of the value of one equity share :

$$\frac{\text{Capitalised profits}}{\text{Number of equity shares}} = \frac{4,00,000}{4,000} = \text{Rs. } 100$$

Calculation of the value of X's equity shares :

X's equity shares × Value of one equity share

2,500 × 100 = Rs. 2,50,000.

Illustration 3

A Co., Ltd., has 50,000 equity shares of Rs. 10 each Rs. 8 paid. The company transfers 10% of profit to general reserve every year. The expected profit (based on previous year's performance) before tax is Rs. 10,00,000 and the rate of tax is 65%. Normal rate of dividend is 16%. A Co. Ltd., 7% pref. share capital is Rs. 4,00,000 divided into share of Rs. 10 each. Find out the value of the share by the yield method.

(Bangalore, Oct. 1988)

Solution :

Calculation of profit for equity dividend

	The expected profit of the company	10,00,000
Less :	Tax (65% on Rs. 10,00,000)	6,50,000
		3,50,000
Less :	Transfer to general reserve (10%)	35,000
		3,15,000
Less :	Preference dividend (4,00,000 × 7/100)	28,000
	Profit for equity dividends	2,87,000

Calculation of expected rate of return

$$\frac{\text{Profit available for equity dividend}}{\text{Total paid up equity share capital}} \times 100$$

Calculation of the value of each equity share

$$\frac{\text{Expected rate of return}}{\text{Normal rate of return}} \times \text{Paid up value of each share}$$

$$= \frac{71.75 \times 8}{16} = \text{Rs. } 35.875$$

Illustration 4

Following is the position of X Co. Ltd.

Capital employed	1,50,00,000
(Paid up value of share is Rs. 100)	
Profit earned during the year	75,00,000
Actual dividend declared	40% of profits
Normal rate of earning	25%
Normal rate of dividend	10%

Calculate the value of shares under (i) Yield Method and (ii) Earning Capacity Valuation Method.

Solution :

(i) Yield Valuation Method

(a) *Calculation of the rate of dividend*

$$\text{Rate of dividend} = \frac{\text{Amount of dividend declared}}{\text{Amount of capital employed}}$$

$$= \frac{30,00,000}{1,50,00,000} \times 100 = 20\%$$

(b) *Calculation of the value of each share*

$$\text{Value per share} = \frac{\text{Rate of dividend}}{\text{Normal rate of dividend}} \times \text{Paid up value per share}$$

$$= \frac{20\%}{10\%} \times 100 = \text{Rs. } 200$$

(ii) Earning Capacity Valuation Method

(a) *Calculation of the rate of earning*

$$\text{Rate of earning} = \frac{\text{Profit earned}}{\text{Capital employed}} \times 100$$

$$= \frac{75,00,000}{1,50,00,000} \times 100 = 50\%$$

(b) *Calculation of the value of each share*

$$\text{Value per share} = \frac{\text{Rate of earning}}{\text{Normal rate of return}} \times \text{Paid up value of each share}$$

$$= \frac{50\%}{25\%} \times 100 = \text{Rs. } 200.$$

Illustration 5

The following particulars are available in relation to a company :

(a) Capital : 450 6% Preference shares of Rs. 100 each fully paid
4,500 Equity shares of Rs. 10 each fully paid

(b) External liabilities Rs. 7,500.

(c) Reserves and surplus Rs. 3,500.

(d) The average normal profit (after taxation) earned every year by the company Rs. 8,505.

(e) The normal profit earned on the market value of equity shares, fully paid, of the same type of companies is 9%.

Calculate the fair value of the share assuming that out of the total, assets worth Rs. 350 are fictitious.

(Adapted from B.Com. [Hons.] Calcutta)

Solution :

(A) Ascertainment of the value of the share under net assets method

Share Capital : Preference Share Capital	45,000	
Equity Share Capital	45,000	90,000
Reserves and Surplus		3,500

	Gross Assets available	93,500
Less :	Factitious assets	350
	Assets available to shareholders	93,150
Less :	Amount due to pref. shareholders	45,000
	Net assets available to equity shareholders	48,150

Intrinsic value of each equity share

$$= \frac{\text{Net ssets Available to Equity Shareholders}}{\text{Number of Equity Shares}}$$

$$= \frac{48{,}150}{4{,}500} = \text{Rs. } 10.70$$

(B) Ascertainment of the value of the share under Yeild Method :

Calculation of profit available to equity shareholders :

	Average profits (after tax)	8,505
Less :	Preference dividend (6% on Rs. 45,000)	2,700
	Profits available to equity shareholders	5,805

Calculation of capitalised profits :

$$\frac{\text{Average Annual Profit}}{\text{Normal Rate of Return}} \times 100 = \frac{5{,}805}{9} \times 100 = \text{Rs. } 64{,}500$$

Calculation of the market value of each equity share :

$$\frac{\text{Capitalised Profit}}{\text{Number of Equity Shares}} = \frac{64{,}500}{4{,}500} = \text{Rs. } 14.33$$

(C) Ascertainment of the value of the share under fair value method :

$$\text{Fair Value of Share} = \frac{\text{Intrinsic Value} + \text{Yield or Market Value}}{2}$$

$$= \frac{10.70 + 14.33}{2} = \text{Rs. } 12.51.$$

Illustration 6

From the following Balance Sheet, you are required to value the equity shares :

	Rs.		Rs.
2,000 6% Preference shares of of Rs. 100 each	2,00,000	Assets at Book Values	6,00,000
30,000 Equity shares of Rs. 10 each	3,00,000		
Liabilities	1,00,000		
	6,00,000		6,00,000

The market value of 50% of the assets is considered at 10% more than the book value and that of the remaining 50% at 5% less than book value. There was a liability of Rs. 5,000 which remained unrecorded. Assume preference shares have no priority as to the payment of capital or dividend.

(Bangalore, April 1987)

Solution :

Calculation of net assets for equity shareholders under net assets method

	Assets at book value (50%)	3,00,000	
Add :	10% increase	30,000	3,30,000
	Assets at book value (remaining 50%)	3,00,000	
Less :	5% decrease	15,000	2,85,000
	Market value of assets		6,15,000
Less :	Liabilities recorded (as per books)	1,00,000	
	Liabilities unrecorded	5,000	1,05,000
	Net assets available to all shareholders		5,10,000
Less :	Preference share capital		2,00,000
	Net assets available to equity shareholders		3,10,000

Calculation of value per equity share

$$\frac{\text{Net assets available to equity shareholders}}{\text{Number of equity shares}}$$

$$= \frac{3,10,000}{30,000} = \text{Rs. } 10.33$$

Calculation of value per perference share

(i) *Ascertainment of net assets available to preference shareholders*

Net assets available for all shareholders × Ratio of total paid-up capital of pref. shareholders

5,10,000 × 2/5 = Rs. 2,04,000

(ii) *Calculation of each preference share*

$$\frac{\text{Net assets available to preference shareholders}}{\text{Number of preference shares}}$$

$$= \frac{2,04,000}{2,000} = \text{Rs. } 102.$$

Illustration 7

From the information given below and the Balance Sheet of A Ltd. on 31 December, 1997, find the value of its equity shares by the intrinsic value method and the yield method.

(a) Company's prospects for 1998 are good;

(b) Buildings are now worth Rs. 3,50,000.

(c) Profits for the last three years have shown an annual increase of Rs. 50,000. The annual transfer to reserve is 25% of net profit.

(d) Preferential shares have preference as to capital and dividend.

(e) Normal rate of return expected is 15%.

Balance Sheet

Liabilities		Rs.	Assets	Rs.
1,000, 8% Preference shares of Rs. 100 each fully paid		1,00,000	Building	70,000
4,000 Equity shares of Rs. 100 each fully paid		4,00,000	Furniture	3,000
Reserves		1,50,000	Stock (Market Value)	4,50,000
Profit and Loss A/c :			Investment (at cost) (face value Rs. 4,00,000)	3,35,000
Balance on 1-1-97	80,000		Debtors	2,80,000
Add : Profit for 1997 (before transfer to reserve)	4,30,000	5,10,000	Bank	60,000
Creditors		48,000	Preliminary Expenses	10,000
		12,08,000		12,08,000

(Company Secretaries Center, June 1998)

Solution :

(A) Intrinsic Value Method :

(i) *Calculation of net assets available to equity shareholders*

Realisable value of real assets :	
Buildings	3,50,000
Furniture	3,000
Stock	4,50,000
Investments	3,35,000
Debtors	2,80,000
Bank	60,000
	14,78,000
Less : Value of external liabilities :	
Creditors	48,000
Net assets available for all shareholders	14,30,000
Less : Preference shares	1,00,000
Net assets available to equity shareholders	13,30,000

(ii) *Calculation of intrinsic value per share*

$$\frac{\text{Net assets available to equity shareholders}}{\text{Number of equity shares}} = \frac{13,30,000}{4,000} = \text{Rs. } 332.50$$

(B) Yield Method

(i) *Calculation of the expected rate of return*

$$\frac{\text{Profit available for equity dividend}}{\text{Total paid up equity shares capital}} \times = \frac{3,52}{4,00,00} \times 100 = 88\%$$

(ii) *Calculation of the value of each equity share*

$$\frac{\text{Expected rate of return}}{\text{Normal rate of return}} \times \text{Paid up value per share}$$

$$= \frac{88}{15} \times 100 = \text{Rs. } 586.66.$$

Illustration 8

From the following information pertaining to Plank Ltd., ascertain the value of shares if (A) only a few shares are to be sold and if (B) majority shares are to be sold.

(i) Share capital : 17,500 shares of Rs. 100 each fully paid.

(ii) Normal rate of return 10%.

(iii) Profits after tax and dividends :

Year	Profits	Dividend
1995	3,00,000	9%
1996	3,28,000	11%
1997	3,72,000	13%
1998	4,00,000	15%

Solution :

(A) Only a few shares are to be sold. In this case, the yield method of valuation is appropriate. The procedure to ascertain the value of share under the yield method is given as below :

(i) *Calculation of average rate of dividend*

$$\text{Average rate of dividend} = \frac{9\% + 11\% + 13\% + 15\%}{4} = 12\%$$

(ii) *Calculation of the value of each share*

$$\text{Value per share} = \frac{\text{Rate of dividend}}{\text{Normal rate of return}} \times \text{Paid up value per share}$$

$$= \frac{12\%}{10\%} \times 100 = \text{Rs. } 120$$

(B) Majority shares are to be sold. In this case, the earning capacity valuation method is appropriate. The procedure for ascertaining the value for share under this method is given as below :

(i) *Calculation of average profit earned*

$$\text{Average profit} = \frac{3,00,000 + 3,28,000 + 3,72,000 + 4,00,000}{4} = \text{Rs. } 3,50,000$$

(ii) *Calculation of the rate of earning*

$$\text{Rate of earning} = \frac{\text{Profit earned}}{\text{Capital employed}} \times 100 = \frac{3,50,000}{17,50,000} \times 100 = 20\%$$

(iii) *Calculation of the value per share*

$$\text{Value per share} = \frac{\text{Rate of earning}}{\text{Normal rate of return}} \times \text{Paid up value per share}$$

$$= \frac{20\%}{10\%} \times 100 = \text{Rs. } 200$$

Illustration 9

Following is the Balance Sheet of Sunrise Ltd., as at 31st December, 1998.

	Rs.		Rs.
Share Capital :		Land and Buildings	55,000
10,000 Shares of		Plant and Machinery at cost	65,000
Rs. 10 each	1,00,000	(Less Depreciation)	
General Reserve	20,000	Trade Marks	10,000
Taxation Reserve	30,000	Stocks	24,000
Workmen's Savings Accounts	15,000	Debtors	44,000
Profit and Loss Accounts	16,000	Cash at Bank	26,000
Sundry Creditors	49,000	Preliminary Expenses	6,000
	2,30,000		2,30,000

The Plant and Machinery is worth Rs. 60,000 and Land and Buildings have been valued at Rs. 1,20,000 by an independent valuer. Rs. 4,000 of the debts are bad. The profits of the company are as follows :

1996	Rs. 40,000
1997	Rs. 45,000
1998	Rs. 53,000

It is the company's practice to transfer 25% of the profits to Reserve. Ignoring taxation, find out the value of shares on the yield basis and also on the net assets basis. Similar companies give a yield of 10% on the market value of their shares. Goodwill may be taken to be worth Rs. 90,000.

(Andhra, Oct. 1999)

Solution :

(A) Net Assets Method

(i) *Calculation of the value of net assets available to shareholders*

		Rs.
Realisable value of real assets :		
Land and Buildings		1,20,000
Plant and Machinery		60,000
Trade Marks		10,000
Stock		24,000
Debtors	44,000	
Less : Bad debts	4,000	40,000
Cash		26,000
Goodwill		90,000
		3,70,000
Less : Value of external liabilities		
Sundry Creditors	49,000	
Workmen's Savings A/c	15,000	
Taxation Reserve	30,000	94,000
Net assets available to shareholders		2,76,000

(ii) *Calculation of the value of each share*

$$\text{Value of each share} = \frac{\text{Net assets available to shareholders}}{\text{Number of shares}}$$

$$= \frac{2,76,000}{10,000} = \text{Rs. } 27.60$$

(B) Yield method

(i) *Calculation of average annual profit for equity dividend*

Average annual profits $\left[\dfrac{40,000 + 45,000 + 49,000 \text{ } i.e. \text{ } 53,000 - 4,000 \text{ bad debts}}{3}\right]$	44,667
Less : 25% transferred to Reserve	11,167
Average annual profit available for equity dividend	33,500

(ii) *Calculation of capitalised profits*

$$\frac{\text{Average annual profits available for equity dividend}}{\text{Normal rate of return}} \times 100$$

$$= \frac{33,500}{10} \times 100 = \text{Rs. } 3,35,000$$

(iii) *Calculation of value of each share*

$$\frac{\text{Capitalised Profits}}{\text{Number of Shares}} = \frac{3,35,000}{10,000} = \text{Rs. } 33.50.$$

Illustration 10

Following is the balance sheet of X Company Ltd. as on 31st March, 1983.

	Rs.		Rs.
Share Capital :		Fixed Assets	4,00,000
6% Pref. share capital		Current Assets	2,48,000
of Rs. 10 each fully paid	2,00,000	Preliminary Expenses	10,000
Equity Shares of Rs. 10		Unwritten off Discount	5,000
each fully paid	3,00,000	Profit and Loss Account	27,000
General Reserve	5,000		
Debenture Redemption Fund	25,000		
Investment Fluctuation Fund	10,000		
5% Debentures	50,000		
Depreciation Fund	10,000		
Sundry Creditors	90,000		
	6,90,000		6,90,000

Current assets included investments Rs. 50,000, market price of which is Rs. 48,000. Debtors included in current assets are doubtful to the extent of Rs. 5,000 for which no provision has been made so far. Stock at the end did not include a return of Rs. 1,000 though transaction was properly recorded and posted.

Debenture interest is owing for one year and preference dividends are in arrears for two years. Assuming other assets are worth book values, you are required to value shares if any :

(a) Preference shares have priority both as to the payment of capital and arrears of dividend in the event liquidation takes place.

(b) Preference shares have no priority as capital and arrears of dividend.

(c) Preference shares have priority as to the payment of capital only.

(d) Preference shares have priority as to the payment of arrears of dividend only.

(M.K.U., April 1983)

Solution :

Calculation of value of net assets under Net Assets Method

			Rs.
Realisable value of real assets :			
	Fixed Assets	4,00,000	
	Less : Depreciation	10,000	3,90,000
	Current Assets		2,48,000
			6,38,000
Add :	Increase in the value of closing stock		1,000
			6,39,000
Less :	Fall in the Value of Investments	2,000	
	Provision for Doubtful Debts	5,000	7,000
			6,32,000
Less :	Value of external liabilities :		
	5% Debentures	50,000	
	Sundry Debtors	90,000	
	Debenture Interest (5% on 50,000)	2,500	1,42,500
Value of Net Assets available to all shareholders			4,89,500

(A) When preference shares have priority as to the repayment of capital as well as dividend

(i) *Calculation of net assets available to equity shareholders*

Net assets available to all shareholders		4,89,500
Less : Preference share capital	2,00,000	
Arrears of pref. dividend (6% for two years)	24,000	2,24,000
Net assets available to equity shareholders		2,65,500

(ii) *Calculation of the value of each equity share*

$$\frac{\text{Net assets available to equity shareholders}}{\text{Number of equity shares}} = \frac{2,65,500}{30,000} = \text{Rs. } 8.85$$

(B) When preference shares have no priority as to the repayment of capital and dividend

In this case, the preference shares and equity shares have equal rank. Therefore, the value of each share is calculated as below :

$$\frac{\text{Net assets available to equity shareholders}}{\text{Number of shares (Pref. \& equity both)}}$$

$$= \frac{4,89,500}{20,000 + 30,000} = \frac{4,89,500}{50,000} = \text{Rs. } 9.79$$

(C) When preference shares have priority as regards the repayment of capital only

(i) *Calculation of net assets available to equity shareholders*

	Net assets available to all shareholders	4,89,500
Less :	Preference share capital	2,00,000
	Net assets available to equity shareholders	2,89,500

(ii) *Calculation of value of each equity share*

$$\frac{\text{Net assets available to equity shareholders}}{\text{Number of equity shares}} = \frac{2{,}89{,}500}{30{,}000} = \text{Rs. } 9.65$$

(D) When preference shares have priority as regards the repayment of dividend only

(i) *Calculation of net assets available to equity shareholders*

	Net assets available to all shareholders	4,89,500
Less :	Preference share dividend for 2 years	24,000
	Net assets available to all shareholders	4,65,500

(ii) *Calculation of the value of each share*

$$\frac{\text{Net assets available to all shareholders}}{\text{Number of shares (Pref. \& equity both)}}$$

$$= \frac{4{,}65{,}500}{20{,}000 + 30{,}000} = \frac{4{,}65{,}500}{50{,}000} = \text{Rs. } 9.31$$

Illustration 11

Your client intends to invest not more than Rs. 15,000 in Equity Shares of Iron Foundry Ltd. and wants you to advise him the maximum number of shares he can expect to acquire with the said amount on the basis of the following information available to him.

	Rs.
Issued and paid up capital :	
6% Preference Shares of Rs. 100 each	5,00,000
Equity Shares of Rs. 10 each	3,00,000
	8,00,000

Average net profits of the business is Rs. 57,000.

Expected normal yield is 7% in case of such equity shares.

Total tangible assets (other than goodwill) Rs. 9,49,000 and total outside liabilities Rs. 95,000.

Goodwill is to be calculated at 5 years' purchase of the super-profits if any.

Show your workings in detail. Ignore income tax.

(Adapted from Calcutta B.Com. Hons.)

Solution :

Net Assets Method :

(i) *Calculation of net asset available to equity shareholders or capital employed by the equity shareholders*

	Rs.
Realisable value of assets	9,49,000
Less : Value of outside liabilities	95,000
Net assets available to all shareholders	8,54,000
Less : Preference share capital	5,00,000
Capital employed by the equity shareholders	3,54,000

(ii) *Calculation of Super-profit*

Average profit for all the shareholders	57,000
Less : Dividend for preference shareholders (6% on Rs. 5,00,000)	30,000
Profit available to equity shareholders	27,000
Less : Normal return (7% on Rs. 3,54,000) (7% of capital employed by equity shareholders)	24,780
Super-profit	2,220

(iii) *Calculation of Goodwill*

Super-profit × Number of Years Purchase

2,220 × 5 = Rs. 11,100

(iv) *Calculation of Value Per Share*

	Rs.
Net assets available to all the shareholders	8,54,000
Add : Goodwill	11,100
	8,65,100
Less : Preference share capital	5,00,000
Value of 30,000 equity shares	3,65,100

$$\therefore \text{ Value of each equity share } = \frac{3,65,100}{30,000} = \text{Rs. } 12.17$$

Hence, the number of shares the client can buy :

$$\frac{15,000}{12.17} = 1,233 \text{ (Approx.)}.$$

Illustration 12

The following details are ascertained in relation to the Prosperous Co. Ltd.

Capital :

10,000 'A' Equity shares of Rs. 10 each, fully paid	1,00,000
10,000 'B' Equity shares of Rs. 10 each, Rs. 7.50 per share paid	75,000
10,000 'C' Equity share of Rs. 10 each, Rs. 5 per share paid	50,000
General Reserve	1,20,000
External Liabilities	55,000
	4,00,000
Tangible Assets	4,00,000

The normal average profits (less tax) of the company are estimated to be Rs. 36,000 and the estimated rate for capitalisation purposes is 8%.

Calculate the value of each type of share by

(A) the Asset Backing Method

(B) the Earning Capacity Method.

(Adapted from Kolkata B.Com. Hons.)

Solution :

(A) Asset-Backing Method

(i) *Calculation of assets backing including notional calls for equity shareholders*

Market or present value of Assets :

Tangible Assets		4,00,000
Less : Value of External Liabilities		55,000
Net assets available for equity shareholders		3,45,000
Add : Notional calls (*i.e.,* uncalled capital) :		
'B' share at Rs. 2.50 (10,000 × 2.50)	25,000	
'C' share at Rs. 5 (10,000 × 5)	50,000	75,000
Assets backing including notional calls for equity shareholders		4,20,000

(ii) *Calculation of intrinsic value per equity share*

(a) Calculation of intrinsic value per fully paid equity share :

$$\frac{\text{Assets-backing including notional calls}}{\text{Total number of equity shares}} = \frac{4,20,000}{30,000} = \text{Rs. } 14$$

∴ Value of each 'A' share is Rs. 14.

(b) *Calculation of intrinsic value per partly paid equity share*

The intrinsic value per fully paid equity share – Uncalled amount per share

∴ Value of each 'B' share is Rs. 11.50 (Rs. 14-2.50)

Value of each 'C' share is Rs. 9.00 (Rs. 14-5)

(B) Earning Capacity Method

(i) *Calculation of capitalised value of profit*

$$\frac{\text{Profit}}{\text{Normal Rate of Return}} \times 100 = \frac{36{,}000}{8} \times 100 = \text{Rs. } 4{,}50{,}000$$

(ii) *Calculation of value per equity share*

(a) Calculation of the market value per fully paid equity share :

$$\frac{\text{Capitalised value of profits}}{\text{Total paid up equity capital of all categories of equity shares}} \times \text{Paid up value per fully paid equity share}$$

$$= \frac{4{,}50{,}000}{1{,}00{,}000 + 75{,}000 + 50{,}000} \times 10 = \frac{4{,}50{,}000}{2{,}25{,}000} \times 10 = \text{Rs. } 20.$$

∴ Value of each 'A' share is Rs. 20.

(b) *Calculation of the market value per partly paid equity share*

$$\text{Market value per fully paid equity share} \times \frac{\text{Paid up amount per partly paid equity share}}{\text{Paid up amount per fully paid equity share}}$$

∴ Value of each 'B' share is Rs. 15 (20 × 7.50 ÷ 10)

Value of each 'C' share is Rs. 10 (20 × 5 ÷ 10).

Illustration 13

Following is the Balance sheet of a Company :

Liabilities	Rs.	Assets	Rs.
Paid up Capital :		Goodwill	10,000
1,000 6% Preference shares		Fixed Assets	1,20,000
of Rs. 100 each fully paid	1,00,000	Investments	15,000
1,000 Equity shares of		Current Assets	2,50,000
Rs. 100 each fully paid	1,00,000	Preliminary Expenses	5,000
1,000 Equity shares of			
Rs. 100 each Rs. 40			
per share paid-up	40,000		
Reserve	20,000		
Profit and Loss A/c	40,000		
6% Debentures	10,000		
Sundry Creditors	90,000		
	4,00,000		4,00,000

The revaluation of assets was made as follows :

Fixed Assets Rs. 1,30,000, Investments Rs. 16,000 (Income from Investments Rs. 900). The average profit (less tax) of the last 3 years was Rs. 40,000. The normal return on capital employed for valuation of goodwill is 10%. The proposed dividend on equity shares is 10%. The dividend declared by the similar companies is 8%. Find out the value of equity shares, assuming goodwill is valued at 3 years' purchase of super-profits.

(Bombay, Oct. 1997)

Solution :

(A) Net Assets Method

(i) *Calculation of net assets available to all the shareholders*

	Realisable value of real assets :		
	Fixed assets		1,30,000
	Current Assets		16,000
	Current Assets		2,50,000
			3,96,000
Less :	Value of outside liabilities :		
	6% Debentures	10,000	
	Sundry Creditors	90,000	
	Proposed Dividend	14,000	1,14,000
			2,82,000

(ii) *Calculation of capital employed*

	Total assets		3,96,000
Less :	Non-trading asset— Investment		16,000
			3,80,000
Less :	Sundry Creditors	90,000	
	Proposed Dividend	14,000	1,04,000
	Capital employed in the business		2,76,000

(iii) *Calculation of super-profit*

	Average profit	40,000
Less :	Income from investments	900
		39,100
Add :	Interest on debentures	600
	Adjusted annual average profit	39,700
Less :	Normal return (10% on capital employed	27,600
	Super-profit	12,100

(iv) *Calculation of Goodwill*

Super-profits × Number of years purchase

12,100 × 3 = Rs. 36,300

(v) *Calculation value per equity share*

Net assets available to all the shareholders	2,82,000
Add : Goodwill	36,300
	3,18,300
Less : Preference share capital	1,00,000
Net assets available to equity shareholders	2,18,300
Add : Notional calls (*i.e.* uncalled capital) 1,000 Equity shares of Rs. 60 each	60,000
Value of 2,000 equity shares	2,78,300

∴ (a) Value of each fully paid equity share :

$$\frac{\text{Assets-backing including notional calls}}{\text{Total number of equity shares}}$$

$$= \frac{2,78,300}{2,000} = \text{Rs. } 139 \text{ (Approx.)}$$

Add : Ex-Dividend Rs. 10 (10% on Rs. 100)

Cum-Dividend Rs. 149

(b) Value of partly paid equity share :

Value of each fully paid equity share – Uncalled amount of each equity share

= 139 – 60 = Rs. 79

Add : Ex-Dividend Rs. 4 (10% on Rs. 40)

Cum-Dividend Rs. 83.

(B) Yield Method

(i) *Calculation of average annual profit available to equity shareholders :*

Average annual profit	40,000
Less : Preference share dividend	6,000
Average annual profit available for equity shareholders	34,000

(ii) *Calculation of value per equity share :*

(A) Calculation of value per fully paid equity share :

(a) Calculation of expected rate of return or dividend :

$$\frac{\text{Average annual profit available for equity dividend}}{\text{Paid up equity share capital}} \times 100$$

$$= \frac{34,000}{1,40,000} \times 100 = 24.29\%$$

(b) Calculation of value per equity share :

$$\frac{\text{Expected rate of return or dividend}}{\text{Normal rate of return or dividend}} \times \text{Paid up value per share}$$

$$= \frac{29.29\%}{8\%} \times 100 = \text{Rs. } 304 \text{(Approx.)}.$$

Alternate Method

(a) Calculation of capitalised profit :

$$\frac{\text{Average annual profit for equity dividend}}{\text{Normal rate of return or dividend on equity shares}} \times 100$$

$$= \frac{34{,}000}{8} \times 100 = \text{Rs. } 4{,}25{,}000$$

(b) Calculation of value per equity share :

$$\frac{\text{Capital profit}}{\text{Total paid up capital of all categories of equity shares}} \times \text{Paid up value per fully paid equity share}$$

$$= \frac{4{,}25{,}000}{1{,}40{,}000} \times 100 = \text{Rs. } 304 \text{ (Aprox.)}$$

(B) Calculation of value per partly paid equity share :

$$\text{Market value per fully paid share} \times \frac{\text{Paid up amount per partly paid equity share}}{\text{Paid up amount per fully paid equity share}}$$

$$= 304 \times \frac{40}{100} = \text{Rs. } 122 \text{ (Approx.)}.$$

Illustration 14

The share capital of a company consists of :

1,00,000, 5% Preference shares of Rs. 10 each.

2,00,000 Equity shares of Rs. 10 each.

The preference shareholders are entitled to participate in a share of the profits to the extent of a further 4% after payment of a dividend at 10% to the equity shareholders. Any further excess is available for equity shareholders.

The normal profit (less tax) of the company is Rs. 4,00,000 per annum.

The normal return applicable to the particular type of the company is 8% on the nominal value of equity shares and 8% on the nominal value of preference shares which are participating.

Find out the value each equity and each preference share.

(Adapted from Mysore University)

Solution :

In this problem, since the amount of assets and liabilities are given, the intrinsic value of each preference share and equity share can not be determined. Hence, we should find out directly the market value of each preference share and each equity share.

(A) Calculation of market value of each preference share

$$\frac{\text{Actual rate of dividend or rate of return payable to preference shareholders}}{\text{Normal rate of return on preference shares}} \times \text{Paid-up value per preference shares}$$

$$= \frac{9\ (5+4)}{8} \times 10 = \text{Rs. } 11.25$$

Note : Rate of Dividend = Normal 5% plus further 4% *i.e.* 9.

(B) Calculation of market value each of equity share

(i) *Calculation of profit available for dividend to equity shareholders*

Normal profit (less tax)	4,00,000
Less : Profit for dividend to preference shareholders (9% on 10,00,000)	90,000
Profit available to equity shareholders	3,10,000

(ii) *Calculation of expected rate of return*

$$\frac{\text{Profit available for divided to equity shareholder}}{\text{Total paid up equity share capital}} \times 100$$

$$= \frac{3,10,000}{20,00,000} \times 100 = 15.5\%$$

(iii) *Calculation of market value of each equity share*

$$\frac{\text{Expected rate of return on equity shares}}{\text{Normal rate of return on equity shares}} \times \text{Paid up value of each equity share}$$

$$= \frac{15 \cdot 5\%}{8\%} \times 10 = \text{Rs. } 19 \cdot 37.$$

Illustration 15

Following is the summarised balance sheet of Twinkle Star Ltd. as on 30th September, 1998 :

Liabilities		Rs.	Assets	Rs.
Share Capital :			Freehold Property	1,20,000
30,000 Equity Shares of			Plant	50,000
Rs. 10 each		3,00,000	Stock	3,10,000
Reserves and Surplus :			Debtors	2,03,000
General	1,20,000		Bank	1,17,000
Capital	40,000		Cash	1,700
P & L A/c	1,20,000	2,80,000		
Current Liabilities and Provisions :				
Creditors	93,700			
Income tax Payable	11,500			
Proposed Dividend	34,500			
Provision for Taxation	82,000	2,21,700		
		8,01,700		8,01,700

Net profit (before taxation) for the last three years ended :

30th September, 1996, Rs. 1,38,000; 30th September, 1997, Rs. 1,83,000; and 30th September, 1998, Rs. 1,97,000.

Freehold property was valued early in 1998 at Rs. 1,60,000. Average yield in this type of business is 15% on capital employed. You are required to find out the value of each equity share on the net assets basis (excluding goodwill) and on yield basis.

(Adapted from I.C.W.A.)

Solution :

(A) Intrinsic Value Method

(i) *Calculation of net assets available to equity shareholders :*

Realisable value of real assets :		
Freehold Property		1,60,000
Plant		50,000
Stock		3,10,000
Debtors		2,03,000
Bank		1,17,000
Cash		1,700
		8,41,700
Less : Value of external liabilities :		
Creditors	93,700	
Income tax payable	11,500	
Proposed dividend	34,500	
Provision for taxation	82,000	2,21,700
Value of net assets		6,20,000

(ii) *Calculation of value per share*

$$\frac{\text{Value of net assets available to equity shareholders}}{\text{Number of equity shares}}$$

$$= \frac{6,20,000}{30,000} = \text{Rs. } 20.67$$

(B) Yield Method

(i) *Calculation of profits available for dividend to equity shareholders*

Average profits $\left(\frac{1,38,000 + 1,83,000 + 1,97,000}{3}\right)$	1,72,667
Less : Income tax (assumed to be 50% of profit)	86,333
	86,334
Less : Transfer to reserve (assumed to be 20% of profit after taxation)	
Profit available for dividend to equity shareholders	17,267
	69,067

(ii) *Calculation of capitalised profit*

$$\frac{\text{Profit available for dividend to equity shareholders}}{\text{Rate of average yield in this type of business}} \times 100$$

$$= \frac{69,067}{15} \times 100 = \text{Rs. } 4,60,447$$

(iii) *Calculation of value per share*

$$\frac{\text{Capitalised profit}}{\text{Number of shares}} = \frac{4,60,447}{30,000} = \text{Rs. } 15 \cdot 35.$$

Illustration 16

The Balance sheet of Suraj & Co., Private Ltd., discloses the following financial position as on 30th September, 1998 :

Liabilities	Rs.	Assets	Rs.
Share Capital :		Goodwill at Cost	1,00,000
20,000 Equity share of		Land and Buildings	80,000
Rs. 10 each	2,00,000	Plant and Machinery	60,000
General Reserve	50,000	Stock-in-trade	2,40,000
Profit and Loss A/c	80,000	Sundry Debtors	1,64,000
Debentures	1,00,000	Cash at Bank	98,000
Sundry Creditors	3,12,000		
	7,42,000		7,42,000

You are asked to value the shares of the company for which purpose the following information is supplied :

(a) The above balance sheet does not provide for unassessed income-tax which is estimated at Rs. 37,000.

(b) The net profits, taxes paid and payable (including the provision for Rs. 37,000 stated above) and dividends paid during the last 5 years ended 30th September, 1998 were as follows :

Year End of 30th September	Net Profits Rs.	Taxes Rs.	Net Amount available for dividend
1994	62,000	30,000	32,000
1995	68,000	32,000	36,000
1996	73,000	35,000	38,000
1997	75,000	36,000	29,000
1998	80,000	37,000	43,000

(c) The company's shares are not quoted at the stock exchange.

(d) It is found that shares of similar concerns are quoted at the stock exchange at such price as earns 10% by way of dividend on their market value.

(e) It may be assumed that the company will be able to maintain its profit for the next 5 years.

(f) The valuation should be on the basis of the mean of the intrinsic values calculated by accepting the value of the goodwill as per Balance Sheet and calculating such goodwill on the basis of the present value of an annuity of the average expected profits for the coming 5 years, assuming interest at 10% p.a., given that the present value of one rupee p.a. for 5 years at 10% interest is Rs. 3.78.

(Adapted from C. A. Final and M.Com., Bangalore University)

Solution :

In this problem, the valuation of shares should be made on the basis of average (*i.e.,* mean) of intrinsic value calculated on the basis of value of goodwill given in the Balance Sheet and intrinsic value calculated on the basis of calculated goodwill. These two values are ascertained as below :

(1) Intrinsic Value of each share on the basis of goodwill in the Balance Sheet

(i) *Calculation of net assets available for equity shareholders :*

Realisable value of the assets :

Goodwill (as per Balance Sheet)	1,00,000
Land and Building	80,000
Plant and Machinery	60,000
Stock-in-trade	2,40,000
Sundry Debtors	1,64,000
Cash at Bank	98,000

		7,42,000
Less : Value of external liabilities :		
Debentures	1,00,000	
Sundry Debtors	3,12,000	
Provision for taxation (as given in the problem)	37,000	4,49,000
Net assets available to equity shareholders		2,93,000

(ii) *Calculation of intrinsic value per share*

$$\frac{\text{Net assets available to equity shareholder}}{\text{Number of equity shares}} = \frac{2,93,000}{20,000} = \text{Rs. } 14.65$$

(2) Intrinsic value of each share on the basis of calculated goodwill

(i) *Calculation of value of goodwill*

Average profit × Present value of one rupee

37,600 × 3.78 = Rs. 1,42,128

Note: $\text{Average profit} = \frac{1,88,000\ (32,000 + 36,000 + 38,000 + 39,000 + 43,000)}{5}$

(ii) *Calculation of net assets available for equity shareholders*

Realisable value of real assets :		
Goodwill (as calculated above)		1,42,128
Land and Building		80,000
Plant and Machinery		60,000
Stock-in-trade		2,40,000
Sundry Debtors		1,64,000
Cash at Bank		98,000
		7,84,128
Less : Value of external liabilities :		
Debentures	1,00,000	
Sundry Creditors	3,12,000	
Provision for taxation	37,000	4,49,000
Net assets available for equity shareholders		3,35,128

(iii) *Calculation of intrinsic value per share*

$$\frac{\text{Net Assets Available to Equity Shareholders}}{\text{Number of Equity Shares}}$$

$$= \frac{3,35,128}{20,000} = \text{Rs. } 16.75$$

(3) Intrinsic value of each share on the basis of average (*i.e.,* mean) of two intrinsic values

$$\frac{\text{Intrinsic value of each share on the basis of goodwill given in the Balance Sheet} + \text{Intrinsic value of each share on the basis of calculated goodwill}}{2}$$

$$= \frac{14.65 + 16.75}{2} = \frac{31.40}{2} = \text{Rs. } 15.70$$

Hence, intrinsic value of each share is Rs. 15.70.

EXAMINATION QUESTIONS

(A) Answer the following questions in two sentences each :

(Each carrying two marks)

(1) What do you mean by goodwill?

(2) Define goodwill. *(Bangalore, April 1988)*

(3) Enumerate the factors that affect the goodwill.

(4) What is normal rate of earnings?

(Bangalore, Oct. 1987)

(5) "Normal rate of return comprises of only return at Zero risk level." Is it false? *(Delhi, Oct. 1989)*

Ans. : False.

(6) How do you calculate the normal profit or earning?

(7) What is super-profit?

(8) What are the divisions of the super-profits methods?

(9) How do you calculate the goodwill under average profit method?

(10) Which method of valuing goodwill is commonly used in case of joint-stock companies?

(11) How do you ascertain the capitalised value of the business?

(12) Give the formula for calculating the value of goodwill under capitalisation of super-profit method.

(13) What is meant by annuity?

(14) What do you understand by annuity rate?

(15) How do you calculate the value of goodwill under annuity method?

(16) "The value of goodwill will be higher in case of purchase of super-profit method as compared to annuity method." Is it true?

(Delhi B. Com., April 1996)

Ans. : True.

(17) Define shares.

(18) What is capitalised value of shares?

(19) What do you mean by intrinsic value of shares?

(20) What is meant by fair value of shares?

(21) What is the need for valuing shares?

(22) Define the term 'yield'.

(23) What information is required for calculating the value of an equity share by yield method?

(24) How do you calculate the expected rate of return under yield method?

(25) What is the difference between yield method and earning capacity method?

(26) How do you calculate the rate of earning under the earning capacity method?

(27) How do you calculate the fair value of shares?

(28) The profit of the business for the past four years is Rs. 96,000. Calculate the average annual profit.

Ans. : Average annual profit Rs. 24,000.

(29) Actual annual average profits Rs. 30,000.

Normal earnings or profits Rs. 28,000.

Goodwill is agreed to be 4 years purchase of super-profits. Calculate the value of goodwill.

Ans. : Value of goodwill Rs. 8,000.

(30) Capital employed at the end Rs. 4,00,000

Profit earned during the year Rs. 80,000

Calculate the average capital employed.

Ans. : Average capital employed Rs. 3,60,000.

(31) Capital employed at the beginning of the year Rs. 3,50,000

Capital employed at the end of the year Rs. 4,00,000

Calculate the average capital employed.

Ans. : Average capital employed Rs. 3,75,000.

(32) Capital employed in the business Rs. 3,00,000

Normal rate of return 10%

Average adjusted annual profits Rs. 32,000

Calculate goodwill under capitalisation of average profits method.

Ans. : Value of goodwill Rs. 20,000.

(33) Super-profit of the business Rs. 30,000

Normal rate of profit 15%

Calculate goodwill under capitalisation of super-profit method.

Ans. : Value of goodwill Rs. 2,00,000.

(34) Super-profit of the business Rs. 4,000

Annuity of Re. 1 at five years at 10% interest Rs. 3.78

Calculate value of goodwill.

Ans. : Value of goodwill Rs. 15,120.

(35) Amount available for equity shareholders Rs. 2,80,500

Number of equity shares — 16,500

Calculate the value per equity share.

Ans. : Value per equity share Rs. 17.

(36) The paid up amount of a share is Rs. 120 and expected rate of return is 15% while normal rate of return is 18%. Calculate the value per share.

(M.K.U., Oct. 1992)

Ans. : Value per share Rs. 100.

(37) Profit earned during the year Rs. 3,21,300

Capital employed during the year Rs. 6,42,600

Calculate the rate of earning under earning capacity method.

Ans. : Rate of earning 50%.

(38) Intrinsic value per share Rs. 16.87

Yield value per share Rs. 18.23

Calculate fair value per share.

Ans. : Fair value per share Rs. 17.55.

(B) Answer the following questions :

(Each carrying 8 marks)

(1) Under what circumstance goodwill is valued?

(2) State the circumstances under which the need for valuation of goodwill arises in case of a joint stock company.

(3) Explain the factors to be considered for valuing the goodwill.

(M.K.U. Oct. 1993)

(4) What are the various methods of the valuation of goodwill?

(M.K.U. April, 1995)

(5) Explain the steps involved in the calculation of goodwill under average profit method.

(Poona B.Com., April 1996)

(6) What are the types of super-profit method?

(7) Mention the stages involved in the calculation of goodwill under super-profit method.

(Bangalore, Oct. 1988)

(8) What are the types of capitalisation method?

(9) Give the procedure for calculating the goodwill under annuity method.

(10) State the comments on the different methods of valuation of goodwill.

(11) Define goodwill. Explain the factors on which it is based and discuss the various methods which can be used in the valuation of goodwill.

(Kanpur, B.Com., Oct. 1996)

(12) Describe the concept of goodwill. Is it real or fictitious? Describe the factors on which it is based.

(Rajasthan, B.Com., April 1992)

(13) What are the circumstances under which shares are valued?

(14) What are the factors affecting the valuation of goodwill?

(15) What are the various methods of the valuation of shares?

(Kanpur, B.Com., April 1989)

(16) Describe and illustrate the yield valuation method of valuation of shares. *(Kanpur, B.Com., April 1991)*

(17) Explain procedure of valuation of equity shares under net asset method. *(M.K.U. B. Com., Oct. 1986)*

(18) How do you calculate value of preference shares under different circumstances in the net assets method? *(Bombay, April 1987)*

(19) State the procedure for valuating the equity shares under yield method.

(20) Enumerate the procedure of valuation of preference shares under yield method. *(Delhi, Oct. 1993)*

(21) Describe and illustrate the earning capacity method of the valuation of shares. *(I.C.W.A. Inter, 1994)*

(22) The average net profit adjusted for valuation of goodwill of the B. Co. Ltd., amounted to Rs. 2,26,045. The average profits (before adjustment) were Rs. 2,02,000. Six per cent represented a fair commercial return. The average "tangible" capital employed was Rs. 13,41,600, but upon valuations, the capital was valued at Rs. 14,40,000.

Assuming seven years' purchase, find out the value of the goodwill.

(Rajasthan, B.Com., 1988)

Ans. : Value of goodwill Rs. 9,77,515; Super-profits Rs. 1,39,645 and Normal earnings Rs. 86,400.

(23) Average normal profit of a company is Rs. 50,000. It is expected that for eight years company will go on making this profit.

Normal yield from similar company is 5%.

The present value of an annuity of one rupee for 8 years at 5% is 0.154722.

Capital employed is Rs. 3,00,000. Find out the value of goodwill according to annuity method.

Ans. : Value of goodwill Rs. 4,415; Super-profit Rs. 35,000 and Normal earnings Rs. 15,000.

(24) From the data given below calculate the goodwill of the company by the capitalization method.

(1) Normal rate of return applicable to the class of business carried on by the company 10%.

(2) Adjusted average profits of the preceding 5 years Rs. 30,000.

(3) Net assets employed in the company Rs. 2,00,000.

(Rajasthan, B.Com., April 1989)

Ans. : Capitalised value of the business Rs. 3,00,000 and the value of goodwill Rs. 1,00,000.

(25) State with reasons whether the following statement is correct or not :

Sunil-Sonal's financial position is as follows :

		Rs.
(a)	Sundry assets	9,27,342
(b)	Current liabilities	42,492
(c)	Average net profit of the last four years	1,20,500
(d)	Average capital employed	9,00,000
(e)	Partner's average annual remuneration	18,000
(f)	The goodwill valued at four years purchase of super-profit is	50,000

Therefore the expected rate of return is 15%.

(B.Com., Gujarat, 1975)

Ans. : Super-profit Rs. 12,500 $\left(50{,}000 \times \frac{1}{4}\right)$ Adjusted annual profit Rs. 1,02,500. Normal profit Rs. 90,000.

Note : The expected rate of return is 10% $\left(\frac{9{,}00{,}000}{90{,}000}\right)$ but not 15% as stated.

(26) A business is being carried on successfully for the last ten years. Mohan & Co., decided to purchase it for Rs. 80,000. It's profits for the last five years are : First year Rs. 12,000; Second year Rs. 10,000;

Third year Rs. 11,000; Fourth year Rs. 13,000 and Fifth year Rs. 12,000.

The management aspect of the business is looked after by the proprietor himself. He has neither taken any remuneration for his work, nor has been any record made in the books of account regarding it.

Find out the amount of goodwill if it is valued on the basis of three years' purchase of the average net profits of the last five years.

(Gujarat, Oct., 1995)

Ans. : Adjusted annual profit Rs. 53,000; Average adjusted annual profit Rs. 10,600 and value of goodwill Rs. 31,800.

***Note* :** Proprietor's remuneration for five years (Rs. 5000) at Rs. 1,000 per year (assumed) is deducted from the total profits.

(27) Average capital employed in Susheel Ltd., is Rs. 6,00,000. Its profits for the first four years are Rs. 65,000; Rs. 70,000; Rs. 75,000 and Rs. 80,000, respectively. It is expected that the company will maintain its super-profits in the next four years also. Take the present value on annuity of one rupee at 5% p.a. for four years is Rs. 2.82012. Fair return is expected to be 11%. Calculate goodwill according to annuity method.

(Gujarat, April 1997)

Ans. : Average annual profit Rs. 72,500; Normal profit Rs. 66,000; super-profits Rs. 6,500 and value of goodwill Rs. 18,331.

(28) Find out the Goodwill according to annuity method from the following particulars.

(i) Rate of interest is 10% p.a.

(ii) Expected super-profit is Rs. 50,000.

(iii) Expected period of super-profit is four years.

(M.K.U., Oct., 1997)

Ans. : Annuity rate Rs. 3.169865 and value of goodwill Rs. 1,58,493.

(29) Net profit to Mayank Ltd., after making provision for taxation for the last five years are :

Year	1982	1983	1984	1985	1986
	40,000	42,000	45,000	46,000	47,000

The capital employed in the business is Rs. 4,00,000; it is expected that the company will be able to maintain its super-profit for the next five years. Calculate goodwill according to annuity method after taking the present value of an annuity of one rupee for five years at 10% as Rs. 3.78. Fair return is expected at 10%.

(Delhi B.Com., Oct., 1989)

Ans. : Average annual profit Rs. 44,000; Normal earnings Rs. 40,000; Super-profit Rs. 4,000 and value of goodwill Rs. 15,120.

(30) From the following information calculate value of goodwill :

(i) Sundry assets of the firm are Rs. 22,50,800 and current liabilities are Rs. 93,625.

(ii) Average capital employed in the business is Rs. 18,00,000.

(iii) Rate of interest expected from capital having regard to the risk involved is 10%.

(iv) Net trading profits of the firm for the past three years were Rs. 3,22,800, Rs. 2,72,100 and Rs. 3,37,500.

(v) Fair remuneration to the partners for their services is Rs. 36,000 per annum. *(Bangalore, Oct. 1988)*

Ans. : Average annual profit Rs. 3,10,800; Average adjusted annual profit Rs. 2,74,800; Normal earnings Rs. 1,80,000; Super-profit Rs. 94,800 and value of goodwill Rs. 2,84,400.

(31) Sree Das holds 5,000 Equity Shares in Hindustan Ltd., the normal and paid up capital of which consists of :

(i) Rs. 20,000, Equity Shares of Re. 1 each.

(ii) Rs. 10,000, 5 per cent preference shares of Re. 1 each.

Note : The preference shares do not participate further in the profits.

It is ascertained—

The normal annual net profit of such a company is Rs. 5,000 and the normal return by way of dividend on the paid up value of Equity Share Capital for the type of business carried out by the company is 8 percent.

Sree Das requires you to value his shareholding based upon the above figures. *(Calcutta B. Com. Hons.)*

Ans. : Profit available for equity dividend Rs. 4,500; Capitalised profit Rs. 56,250 and value of Das's equity shares (5,000) Rs. 14,062.50.

(32) From the following information, calculate the value of equity share:

5,000, 6% Preference shares of Rs. 100 each	Rs. 5,00,000
40,000 Equity share of Rs. 10 each	Rs. 4,00,000
Expected profits per year before tax	Rs. 2,60,000
Rate of tax	50%

Transfer to General Reserve every year 20% of the profit after tax

Normal rate of earning 15%

(Rajasthan Oct., 1993)

Ans. : Profit available for equity dividend Rs. 74,000; Capitalised profit Rs. 4,93,333 and Market value per equity share Rs. 12.33.

Note : Transfer to general reserve Rs. 26,000 (20% on Rs. 1,30,000) and Tax Rs. 1,30,000.

(33) Following is the balance sheet of Self Made Company as at 31st March, 1987 :

Liabilities	Rs.	Assets	Rs.
Share Capital :		Fixed Assets	4,83,980
3,080 shares of Rs. 100 each	3,08,000	Preliminary Expenses	3,500
Reserve Fund	53,130	Stock	3,64,000
Employees Savings Account	31,780	Investment	2,84,900
Employees Security Deposit	7,560	(at market price)	
Workmen Compensation Fund	36,565	Cash and Bank Balance	4,31,760
Depreciation Fund	64,820		
Income-Tax	16,565		
Creditors	5,44,040		
Profit and Loss A/c	5,05,680		
	15,68,140		15,68,140

Depreciation fund is more by Rs. 7,560 than actual depreciation, find out the intrinsic value of the shares.

(Delhi, April 1989)

Ans. : Intrinsic value of each share Rs. 294.62; Net assets available to shareholders Rs. 9,07,435 and Amount of depreciation Rs. 57,260.

(C) Solve the following Problems :

(Each carrying 15-16 marks)

Valuation of Goodwill

(1) Mohan runs a Chemist's shop. His net assets on 31st December, 1980 amount to Rs. 20,00,000. After paying a rent of Rs. 20,000 a year and salaries of Rs. 15,000 to the Chemists, he earns a profit of Rs. 1,50,000. His landlord, who happens to be an expert Chemist, is interested in purchasing the shop. 8% is considered to be a reasonable return on the capital employed. The value of the building is Rs. 1,00,000. What can Mohan expect as payment for goodwill?

(C. A. Inter, May 1997)

Ans. : Average capital employed Rs. 21,00,000; Normal earnings Rs. 1,68,000; Average adjusted annual profit Rs. 1,70,000; Super-profits Rs. 2,000 and value of goodwill Rs. 2,000.

Notes : (i) Remuneration lost by the owner from the employment assumed to be Rs. 15,000 a year as what is paid to the Chemist.

(ii) One year's purchase of super-profit is taken as the value of goodwill.

(iii) Net assets are taken as average capital employed.

(2) From the following information, calculate the value of goodwill as per the super-profit method and the capitalisation method.

(i) Average capital employed in the business Rs. 6,00,000.

(ii) Net trading profits of the firm for the past three years were Rs. 1,07,600, Rs. 90,700 and Rs. 1,12,500.

(iii) Rate of interest expected from the capital having regard to the risk involved 12%.

(iv) Fair remuneration to the partners for their services Rs.12,000 per annum.

(v) Sundry assets of the firm Rs. 7,54,762, current liabilities Rs. 31,329.

(C.A. Inter, December 1996)

Ans. : (A) Super-profit method :
Average profits Rs. 1,03,600; Average adjusted profits Rs. 91,600; Super-profits Rs. 19,600 and the value of goodwill Rs. 58,800.

***Note* :** Fair remuneration to partners is deducted from the average profits to find out the average adjusted profits.

(B) Capitalisation Method :

(i) *Capitalisation of average Profit Method:*
Capitalised value of the business Rs. 7,63,333 and value of goodwill Rs. 39,900.

(ii) *Capitalisation of super-profit method :*
Value of goodwill Rs. 1,63,333.

(3) The Net profits of a business, after providing for taxation, for the past five years are : Rs. 80,000, Rs. 85,000, Rs. 92,000, Rs. 1,05,000 and Rs. 1,18,000. The capital employed in the business is Rs. 8,00,000. The normal rate of return expected in this type of business is 10%. It is expected that the company will be able to maintain its super-profit for the next 5 years. Calculate the value of goodwill on the basis of,

(a) 5 year's purchase of super-profit method.

(b) Annuity method, taking the present value of annuity of Re. 1 for five years at 10% as 3.78 and

(c) Capitalisation of super-profit method.

(M.K.U. April, 1989)

Ans. : Average profits Rs. 96,000; Normal earnings Rs. 80,000; Super-profits Rs. 16,000 and value of goodwill (a) Rs. 80,000 (b) Rs. 60,480 (c) Rs. 1,60,000.

***Note* :** The capital employed in the business is treated as average capital employed.

(4) Gery Ltd., proposed to purchase the business carried on by Success. Goodwill for this purpose was agreed to be valued at 3 years' purchase of the weighted average profits of the past four years. The appropriate weightages to be used are : 1980-81; 1981-82; 1982-83; 1983-84.

The profits for these years were : 1980-Rs. 81,000; 1981 Rs. 95,000; 1982-Rs. 1,20,000 and 1983-Rs. 1,50,000.

On a scrutiny of the accounts, the following were revealed :

(1) On June 30, 1982, a major repair was made in respect of machinery incurring Rs. 20,000 which amount was charged to revenue. The said sum is agreed to be capitalised for goodwill calculation subject to adjustment of depreciation of 10% per annum by the Reducing Balance Method.

(2) The closing stock for the year 1981 was undervalued by Rs. 5,000.

(3) To cover the management expenses, an annual charge of Rs. 10,000 should be made for the purpose of goodwill valuation. Compute the value of goodwill of the firm.

(Adapted from C.A.)

Ans. : Adjusted profits : 1980 Rs. 71,000; 1981 Rs. 90,000; 1982 Rs. 1,24,000 and 1983 Rs. 1,38,100; Average adjusted annual profits Rs. 1,17,540 and value of goodwill Rs. 3,52,620.

(5) From the following particulars, compute the value of Goodwill on Weighted Average Profit Basis, the weights being 1, 2, 3 for 1987, 1988, 1989 respectively.

Year	Profits Rs.
1987	17,000
1988	20,000
1989	21,000

The average capital employed in the business was Rs. 50,000 and Normal Return on capital employed in this business is considered to be 20%. The value of goodwill is assumed to be 3 years' purchase of super-profits.

(Calcutta, Oct. 1992)

Ans. : Average annual profits Rs. 20,000; Normal earning Rs. 10,000; Super-profits Rs. 10,000 and value of goodwill Rs. 30,000.

(6) A purchased business from B on 30th June 1988. Profits earned by B for the preceding 4 years ended on 31st December, each year were :

Years	Rs.
1985	4,10,000
1986	4,00,000
1987	4,20,000
1988	4,24,000

It was ascertained that profits of 1986 included a non-recurring item of Rs. 15,000 and profit of 1987 was reduced by Rs. 20,000 due to an extra-ordinary loss on account of theft. The properties were not insured and it was thought prudent to insure the business in future. The premium was estimated at Rs. 2,000 per annum. A, at the time of purchasing the business from B, was employed in Sure Co. Ltd., and was getting Rs. 5,000 per month. He intends to replace the manager of the business who, at present, is getting Rs. 3,500 per month. The goodwill is estimated at 2 years' purchase of the average profits.

Compute the value of Goodwill of the business.

(Calcutta April, 1993)

Ans. : Profits : 1985 Rs. 4,10,000; 1986 Rs. 3,85,000 (4,00,000 – 15,000); 1987 Rs. 4,40,000 (4,20,000 + 20,000) and 1988 Rs. 4,24,000; Average annual profits Rs. 4,14,750; Average adjusted annual profits Rs. 3,94,750 (16,59,000 – 62,000 [*i.e.,* 2,000 + 60,000] + 42,000) and value of goodwill Rs. 7,89,500.

(7) A company desirous of selling its business to another company has earned an average profit in the past of Rs. 1,50,000 per annum. It is considered that such average profit fairly represents the profit likely to be earned in the future, except that :

(a) Directors' fees Rs. 10,000 charged against such profits will not be payable by the purchasing company whose existing board can easily cope with the additional administrative work at present fees payable to the directors.

(b) Rent at Rs. 20,000 p.a. which had been paid by the vendor company will not be a charge in the future, since the purchasing company owns its own premises and can supply the accommodation necessary for the staff and equipment of the vendor company.

The value of the net tangle assets of the vendor company at the proposed date of sale was Rs. 15,00,000 and it was considered that a reasonable return on the capital invested, for the type commodity, was 10%.

The profit of the vendor company would in no way be affected by the sale of its business to the purchasing company and goodwill existed and was to be paid for on the basis that the vendor company was continuing enterprise. Calculate the value of goodwill by capitalisation of expected future net profits.

(Calcutta, Oct. 1996)

Ans. : Average maintainable profit Rs. 1,80,000 (1,50,000 + 10,000 + 20,000); Capitalised value of the business 18,00,000 and Value of goodwill Rs. 3,00,000.

(8) The balance sheet of X Ltd., as on 31-3-1988 is as follows :

Liabilities	Rs.	Assets	Rs.
8% 5,000 Pref. shares of		Goodwill	10,000
Rs. 10 each	50,000	Fixed assets	1,80,000
10,000 Equity shares of	1,00,000	Investments (5% Govt. loan)	20,000
Rs. 10 each		Current assets	1,00,000
Reserves (including provision		Preliminary expenses	10,000
for taxation Rs. 10,000)	1,00,000	Discount on debentures	5,000
8% Debentures	50,000		
Creditors	25,000		
	3,25,000		3,25,000

The average profit of the company (after deducting interest on debentures and taxes) is Rs. 31,000. The market value of the machinery included in fixed assets is Rs. 5,000 more.

Expected rate of return is 10%.

Evaluate the goodwill of the company at five times of the super-profits.

(B.Com., Gujarat, April 1988)

Ans. : Capital employed for equity shareholders Rs. 1,50,000 (2,85,000 – 85,000 = 2,00,000 – 50,000 *i.e.*, Pref. Share Capital); Average capital employed Rs. 1,37,000 (15,000 – 13,000 *i.e.*, 31,000 – 1,000 = Rs. 30,000; 4,000 Pref. dividend = 26,000 × ½); Average adjusted annual profits for equity shareholders Rs. 26,000 (31,000 – 1,000 = 30,000 – 4,000); Super-profits Rs. 12,300 and Value of goodwill Rs. 61,500.

(9) Following is the Balance Sheet of Sharad Ltd. for the year ending at 31st March, 1992 :

Liabilities		Rs.	Assets	Rs.
Capital :			Fixed Asset :	
10,000 shares of Rs. 10 each		1,00,000	Buildings	1,00,000
Reserve & Surplus :			Machinery	50,000
P & L A/c	10,000		Current Assets :	
Profit for 1991-92	80,000	90,000	Debtors	50,000
Secured Creditors :			Stock	40,000
7% Debentures		70,000	Cash	60,000
Current Liabilities :				
Creditors		40,000		
		3,00,000		3,00,000

Normal rate of return on average capital employed is 10%. Find out the value of goodwill on the basis of 2 year's purchase of super-profit. Buildings are revalued at Rs. 1,50,000 and Machinery at Rs. 40,000. All other assets are worth their book value.

(Poona, Oct. 1992)

Ans. : Capital employed Rs. 2,30,000 (3,40,000 – 1,10,000); Average capital employed Rs. 1,90,000 (2,30,000 – 40,000 *i.e.*, 80,000 × ½); Normal earnings Rs. 19,000; Super-profits Rs. 61,000 and Value of goodwill Rs. 1,22,000.

(10) The Balance Sheet of Mehta & Co. Private Ltd., discloses the following position on 31st December, 1983 :

Liabilities	Rs.	Assets	Rs.
Share Capital Subscribed :		Land and Buildings	3,00,000
50,000 Equity shares of		Plant and Machinery	5,00,000
Rs. 10 each fully paid	5,00,000	Stock	5,00,000
General Reserve	2,00,000	Sundry Debtors	3,00,000
Profit and Loss Account	50,000	Cash at Bank	1,00,000
5% Debentures	5,00,000		
Trade Creditors	4,50,000		
	17,00,000		17,00,000

It is proposed to convert Mehta & Co. Private Ltd., into a Public Limited Company, and for this purpose, you are asked to value the goodwill of this company. The following information is supplied to you :

1. The present market value of plant and machinery is Rs. 8,00,000.
2. The profits of the company for the last three years, after charging depreciation and taxation were as follows : 1981 Rs. 1,01,000, 1982 Rs. 1,50,000 and 1983 Rs. 1,72,000.
3. The reasonable return on capital invested in the class of business carried on by Mehta & Co., Private Ltd., is 8%.
4. It may be assumed that the company will be able to maintain its profits on an average for the next few years.

(Nagpur, Oct. 1997)

Ans. : Capital employed Rs. 10,50,000; Average capital employed Rs. 9,64,000 (10,50,000 – 86,000 *i.e.*, 1,72,000 × ½); Average adjusted annual profits Rs. 1,41,000; Super-profits Rs. 63,880 and Value of goodwill Rs. 1,91,640.

(11) The assets and liabilities of Silver Sands Ltd. as on 31st December, 1986 were as follows :

Liabilities	Rs.	Assets	Rs.
10,000 shares of Rs. 10 each fully paid	1,00,000	Land and Buildings	84,000
Profit and Loss Account	20,000	Plant and Machinery	60,000
Debentures	15,000	Furniture and Fittings	5,000
Trade Creditors	20,000	5% (tax fee) Govt. Bonds	10,000
Provision for Taxation	9,000	Stock	12,000
Proposed Dividend	15,000	Book debts	6,000
		Cash	2,000
	1,79,000		1,79,000

The net profits of the company after charging depreciation and taxes were as follows :

Year	Rs.
1982	17,000
1983	19,000
1984	18,000
1985	20,000
1986	19,000

On 31st December, 1986, land and buildings were revalued at Rs. 95,000, plant and machinery at Rs. 71,000 and furniture and fittings at Rs. 4,000.

10% represents a fair commercial rate of return on investment in the company.

Find out the value of goodwill basing it at five year's purchase of the average super-profits for the last five years.

(Bombay, Oct., 1991)

Ans. : Capital employed Rs. 1,31,000 (1,90,000 – 59,000); Average capital employed Rs. 1,21,750 (1,31,000 – 9,250 *i.e.,* 19,000 – 500 interest on investments = 18,500 × ½); Average adjusted annual profits Rs. 8,100 (90,500/5); Super-profits Rs. 5,925 and Value of goodwill Rs. 29,625.

Notes : (1) Govt. bonds are excluded while calculating the capital employed. Because, these are non-business investments.

(2) Interest on investment (*i.e.,* Rs. 500 *i.e.,* 10% on Rs. 10,000) is deducted from the profits of every year.

(12) Srikant is running a proprietary business whose assets and liabilities as on 31st March, 1985 are as under :

	Rs.	Rs.	Rs.
Current Assets :			
Stock on hand	30,000		
Sundry debtors less provision for doubtful debts	40,000		
Cash and bank balance	30,000	1,00,000	
Fixed Assets :			
Goodwill	20,000		
Plant and machinery less depreciation	40,000		
Land and building	40,000	1,00,000	2,00,000
Represented by :			
Current liabilities :			
Sundry creditors for goods	60,000		
Loans	40,000		
Liabilities for expenses	15,000		
	1,15,000		
Capital of Rama	85,000		2,00,000

Gavaskar is interested in buying the business. The average return from the particular line of business is estimated at 20%. The pre-tax profits of the latest five years, are found to be :

	Rs.
31st March 1981	40,000
31st March 1982	30,000
31st March 1983	32,000
31st March 1984	30,000
31st March 1985	33,000

Profits for the year ended 31st March, 1981 include a capital profit of Rs. 10,000 and for the year ended 31st March, 1985 are after adjustment of Rs. 7,500 being loss by fire. An average rate of 40% is payable as income-tax.

Ascertain the goodwill, payable by Gavaskar for the business, by capitalising the future maintainable post-tax profits on the basis of the past five years' average annual profits.

(Adapted from C.A.)

Ans. : Capital employed Rs. 65,000 (1,80,000 – 1,15,000); Total profit before tax Rs. 1,62,500; Average profit before tax Rs. 32,500; Average profit after tax Rs. 19,500 (32,500 – 13,000 *i.e.,* 40% on Rs. 32,500); Capitalised value of the business Rs. 97,500 and value of goodwill Rs. 32,500.

Notes : (i) Capital profit, which is an abnormal gain, is deducted from the profit to the concerned year.

(ii) Loss by fire, which is an abnormal loss, is added to the profit of the concerned year.

(13) Ascertain the value of goodwill of P. Co. Ltd. carrying on business as retail traders from the following information :

Balance Sheet on 31st December, 1988

Liabilities	Rs.	Assets	Rs.
Paid up Capital :		Goodwill at Cost	25,000
2,500 shares of Rs. 100 each	2,50,000	Land & Building at Cost	1,10,000
Profit & Loss Account	56,650	Plant & Machinery at cost	
Bank Over-draft	58,350	less Depreciation	1,00,000
Sundry Creditors	90,500	Stock at Cost	1,50,000
Provision for Taxation	19,500	Book Debts less Provision	
		for Doubtful Debts	90,000
	4,75,000		4,75,000

The company commenced operations in 1984 with a paid up capital as aforesaid of Rs. 2,50,000. The profits earned, before providing for taxation have been as : 1984 Rs. 61,000; 1985 Rs. 64,000; 1986 Rs. 71,500; 1987 Rs. 78,000 and 1988 Rs. 85,000.

You may assume that income-tax at the rate of 50% has been payable on these profits.

The average dividend paid by the company for the four years is 10%, which is taken as reasonable return expected on the capital invested in the business.

(Madras, April 1995)

Ans. : Average annual profit Rs. 71,900; Average adjusted annual profit Rs. 35,950 (*i.e.*, 71,900 – 35,950 *i.e.*, 50% income tax on Rs. 71,900); Capital employed Rs. 2,81,650; Capitalised value of the business Rs. 3,59,500 and Value of goodwill Rs. 77,850.

(14) X and Y are partners sharing profits and losses equally. It has been agreed that if a partner retires the other partner should be desire to carry on the business shall pay to the retiring partner his share by four equal half yearly instalments together with interest at 5 per cent annum with half-yearly rests. Goodwill is to be valued on the basis of five years of the average annual super-profits of the three preceding financial years, fixed assets being revalued for the purpose. The Balance Sheet of the firm as at 31st December, 1994 was as follows :

Liabilities	Rs.	Assets	Rs.
Creditors	9,160	Cash in hand	13,000
X's Capital A/c	22,420	Book Debts	10,200
Y's Capital A/c	16,650	Closing Stock	5,730
		Building	19,300
	48,230		48,230

Y retires on 1st January, 1995 and X decides to carry on the business. The profits for three years ended 31st December, 1994 were Rs. 13,500, Rs. 14,500 and Rs. 14,000. For the purpose of dissolution, building has been revalued at Rs. 24,800. No. interest on capital was charged and partners did not draw any salary. Show the computation of the value of goodwill.

Assume that normal management remuneration is Rs. 6,000 per annum and normal return on capital employed is 12 percent.

(Delhi, April 1995)

Ans. : Average annual profits Rs. 14,000; Adjusted average annual profits Rs. 8,000 (14,000 – 6,000 remuneration); Capital employed Rs. 44,570; Average capital employed Rs. 40,570 (*i.e.,* 44,570 – 4,000 *i.e.,* 14,000 – 6,000 remuneration = 8,000 × ½); Normal earnings Rs. 4,868; Super-profits Rs. 3,132 and Value of goodwill Rs. 15,660.

(15) Following is the Balance Sheet of Sharad Ltd., on the 31st Dec.,1994.

Liabilities		Rs.	Assets	Rs.
Share Capital :			Fixed Assets :	
10,000 6% cum. Pref. shares of Rs. 10 each		1,00,000	Building	3,00,000
			Machinery	5,00,000
20,000 Equity shares of Rs. 10 each		2,00,000	Motor Vehicles at Cost (Purchased Jan. 1, 1994)	50,000
Reserve and Surplus :				
Reserve		1,50,000	Investment (To provide for replacement of Plant & Machinery)	3,00,000
Profit & Loss A/c :				
Balance as per last B/s	15,000		Current Assets :	
Profit for 1994	1,15,000	1,30,000	Stock	50,000
Secured Loans :			Debtors	10,000
7% Debentures		7,00,000	Cash	40,000
Current Liabilities and Provisions :			Miscellaneous Expenses :	
Creditors		60,000	Underwriting Commission	60,000
Provision for Income-tax		60,000		
		14,00,000		14,00,000

Present value of Machine Rs. 4,00,000; Building Rs. 3,50,000; Bad Debts 5%. Market value of Investment Rs. 4,00,000. Market value of equity shares of Rs. 10 each in a similar company doing similar business is Rs. 25 each and the average dividend declared by that company during the previous five years was 20% without any fluctuations; but there has been fluctuations in the dividends of Sharad Ltd. Find out the value of goodwill after making your own assumptions.

(Calcutta, April 1997)

Ans. : Capital employed Rs. 4,55,000 (13,75,000 including investment– 8,20,000 = 5,55,000 – 1,00,000 pref. capital); Average Capital employed Rs. 4,05,000 (4,55,000 – 50,000 *i.e.,* current year profit of Rs. 1,00,000 [*i.e.,* 1,15,000 – Depreciation of Rs. 10,000 and Provision of Rs. 5000] × ½); Normal earnings Rs. 40,500; Super-profit Rs. 59,500 (1,00,000 – 40,500) and Value of goodwill Rs. 1,78,500.

Note : 20% dividend on Rs. 10 *i.e.,* a dividend of Rs. 2 per share; but this share of Rs. 10 is quoted at Rs. 25 in the market. Hence, on Rs. 25 a dividend is Rs. 2; therefore, on Rs. 100 a dividend is Rs. 8 (2 × 100/25). Hence, normal rate of return is 8%. But there is a fluctuation in the rate of dividend. Therefore, it is assumed that dividend will be somewhat high say, 10%.

Valuation of Shares

(16) The following particulars are available in relation to X Ltd.

(i) Capital, 450, 6% preference shares of Rs. 10 each fully paid and 4,500 equity shares of Rs. 10 each fully paid.

(ii) External liabilities Rs. 7,500.

(iii) Reserve and Surplus Rs. 3,500.

(iv) The average expected profit (after taxation) earned by the company Rs. 8,500.

(v) the normal profit earned on the Market Value of equity shares (fully paid) of the same type of companies is 9%.

(vi) 10% of the profits after tax each year is transferred to reserves.

Calculate the intrinsic value per equity share and the value per equity share according to yield basis. Assume that out of total assets, assets worth Rs. 350 are fictitious.

(C.S. (Inter), June 1989)

Ans. : **(A) Net Assets Method :** Net assets available for equity shares Rs. 48,150; Value per share Rs. 10.70.

(B) Yield Method : Net assets available for equity shareholders Rs. 4,950; expected rate of return 11% and value per share Rs. 12.22.

(17) The following details are obtained from the books of Sunrise Ltd. as on 30th June, 1993 :

	Rs.
Share Capital :	
10,000 Equity share of Rs. 10 each, fully paid up	1,00,000
10,000 Equity shares of Rs. 10 each Rs. 7.50 per share paid up	75,000
10,000 Equity shares of Rs. 10 each Rs. 5 per share paid up	50,000
General Reserve	50,000
Liabilities	1,25,000
Fixed Assets	1,80,000
Current Assets	2,20,000

The normal average profit (less tax) of the company is estimated at Rs. 30,000, and the estimated rate for capitalisation purpose is 10.

Calculate the value of each type of shares by :

(1) Assets backing method (excluding goodwill)

(2) Yield method.

(M.K.U., April 1994)

Ans. : (A) Net Assets Method : Assets backing including notional calls for equity shareholders Rs. 3,50,000 (2,75,000 + 75,000); Intrinsic value per fully paid share Rs. 11.67; Value per partly paid share Rs. 9.17 and Rs. 6.67.

(B) Yield Method : Capitalised profit Rs. 3,00,000; Value per fully paid equity share Rs. 13.33; Value per partly paid equity share Rs. 9.99 and Rs. 6.66.

(18) Following is the summarised Balance Sheet of a Company as at December, 31st 1998.

Liabilities	Rs.	Assets	Rs.
Share Capital :		Fixed Assets	38,00,000
10,000 5% Pref. shares of		Investments	10,25,000
Rs. 100 each fully paid	10,00,000	Current Assets :	
2,00,000 Equity shares of		Stock-in-Trade	5,72,000
Rs. 10 each fully paid	20,00,000	Sundry Debtors	
Reserves & Surplus :		*Less* : Provisions	12,78,000
General Reserve	15,00,000	Cash and Bank Balances	2,25,000
Profit & Loss A/c (Cr.)	12,00,000		
Secured Loan :			
6% Debentures	8,00,000		
Current Liabilities :			
Sundry Creditors	2,75,000		
Liabilities for Expenses	1,25,000		
	69,00,000		69,00,000

For purpose of valuation of Shares, Fixed Assets are to be depreciated by 10 per cent. Investments are to be taken at Rs. 10,80,000 and Sundry Debtors are to be further reduced by 5 percent.

Interest on Debentures is accrued due for 9 months and Preference Dividend for 1998 is also due; neither of these has been provided for in the balance Sheet.

Calculate the value of each Equity share.

(Calcutta, B.Com. Hons. Adapted)

Ans. : Amount of assets available to equity shareholders Rs. 42,25,100; Value of per equity share Rs. 21.13.

***Note* :** Interest on debentures Rs. 36,000 and preferences shares dividend Rs. 50,000.

(19) Calculate fair value of shares from the following particulars :

Balance Sheet

Liabilities	Rs.	Assets	Rs.
Capital :		Sundry Assets	2,50,000
500 7% Pref. shares of Rs. 10 each	5,000		
10,000 Equity shares of Rs. 10 each	1,00,000		
Reserves and Surplus	95,000		
Debentures	30,000		
Creditors	20,000		
	2,50,000		2,50,000

(i) Normal rate of return is 10%. (ii) Average normal profit of the company is Rs. 10,000 after tax. (iii) Transfer to reserve Rs. 300.

(M.K.U., Oct. 1992)

Ans. : (A) Net Assets Method : Amount of net assets available to equity shareholders Rs. 1,95,000 and Intrinsic value per share Rs. 19.50.

(B) Yield Method : Average profit available for equity shareholders Rs. 9,350; Capitalised profit Rs. 93,500 and value per equity share Rs. 9.35.

(C) Fair Value Method : Fair value per share Rs. 14.43.

(20) From the following particulars of the capital structure of a company, ascertain the value of each fully paid equity share under the asset backing and yield methods :

2,500 8% Preference shares of Rs. 100 each	2,50,000
40,000 Equity shares of Rs. 10 each	4,00,000
80,000 Equity shares of Rs. 10 each Rs. 8 paid	6,40,000
General Reserve	2,00,000
Profit and Loss (Credit balance)	1,50,000

Assume that the assets realise their book values in the event of the company's liquidation and that companies engaged in a similar business pay 10% return on capital. The average profits of the company are Rs. 2,00,000.

(Adapted from B.Com., Bangalore University)

Ans. : Assets Backing Method : Value per equity share Rs. 13; Yield Method: Value per equity share Rs. 15.

(21) On 31st Dec. 1994, the Balance Sheet of a Limited Company disclosed the following position :

Liabilities	Rs.	Assets	Rs.
Issued Capital in		Fixed Assets	5,00,000
Rs. 10 shares	4,00,000	Current Assets	2,00,000
Reserves	90,000	Goodwill	40,000
Profit & Loss A/c	20,000		
5% Debentures	1,00,000		
Current Liabilities	1,30,000		
	7,40,000		7,40,000

On 31st December, 1994, the fixed assets were independently valued at Rs. 5,50,000 and the goodwill at Rs. 50,000. The net profits for three years were :

1982 Rs. 51,600; 1983 Rs. 52,000; 1984 Rs. 51,650 of which 20% was placed to reserve, this proportion being considered reasonable in the industry in which company is engaged and where a fair investment return may be taken at 10 per cent. Compute the value of company's share by (a) the Asset Method and (b) the Yield Method.

(Delhi, April, 1995)

Ans. : (A) **Assets Method :** Value for share Rs. 14.25 (5,70,000/40,000)

(B) **Yield Method :** Average profit available to equity shareholders Rs. 41,400; Capitalised profit Rs. 4,14,000 and Value per share Rs. 10.35.

(22) The following is the Balance Sheet of a Company as on 31st Dec., 1986.

Liabilities	Rs.	Assets	Rs.
Share Capital :		Goodwill	50,000
Issued and subscribed :		Land and Buildings	1,00,000
8,000 8% Pref. shares		Plant and Machinery	1,00,000
of Rs. 10 each	80,000	Stock	50,000
10,000 Equity share of		Debtors	30,000
Rs. 10 each	1,00,000	Cash at Bank	4,000
8,000 Equity shares of			
Rs. 8 each paid	64,000		
Reserve Fund	50,000		
Profit and Loss A/c	30,000		
Creditors	10,000		
	3,34,000		3,34,000

For the purpose of valuation of shares, goodwill is to be taken at 4 years' purchase of super-profits and land and buildings are to be taken at the revalue of figure of Rs. 1,50,000. The average profits of the company after making provision for preference dividend of Rs. 6,400 are Rs. 80,000. Assume that 10% is a reasonable return on capital employed.

Ascertain the value of each fully paid up and partly paid up equity share.

(Adapted from B.Com., B'lore University)

Ans. : Value per fully paid equity share Rs. 26.44.
Value per partly paid equity share Rs. 22.44.

(23) The Balance Sheet of a Company was as follows :

Liabilities	Rs.	Assets	Rs.
Share Capital :		Goodwill	10,000
6% Preference shares of		Land and Buildings	1,00,000
Rs. 100 each fully paid	1,00,000	Machinery	2,00,000
3,000 Equity shares of		Stock	2,50,000
Rs. 100 each fully paid	3,00,000	Debtors	1,50,000
2,000 Equity shares of		Cash at Bank	90,000
Rs. 100 each, Rs. 50 per share called up and paid	1,00,000		
Reserves	1,00,000		
Profit & Loss A/c	80,000		
Sundry Creditors	1,20,000		
	8,00,000		8,00,000

The following assets have been revalued by an expert : Rs.

	Rs.
Land & Buildings	1,40,000
Machinery	1,80,000

In view of the nature of the business, it is considered that 10% is a reasonable return on capital employed. The Average profit is Rs. 84,000 after provision of Preference Share Dividend of Rs. 6,000. The basis of valuation of Goodwill is 3 years' purchase of the super-profits. Find out the value of Equity share. Ignore Tax.

(Bombay, April 1992)

Ans. : Capital employed Rs. 6,90,000; Super-profits Rs. 21,000; Goodwill Rs. 63,000; Net assets available to equity shareholders (Including notional calls) Rs. 7,53,000; Value of each fully paid equity share Rs. 150.60 and Value of each partly paid equity share Rs. 100.60.

(24) The following is the summarised Balance Sheet of S' and Co. Ltd. as at 31st December, 1985 :

Liabilities	Rs.	Assets	Rs.
Share Capital :		Fixed Assets	8,00,000
3,000 Equity shares of		Stock	2,00,000
Rs. 100 each	3,00,000	Debtors	2,00,000
7,000 8% Preference		Bank	50,000
shares of Rs. 100 each	7,00,000		
General Reserve	1,00,000		
Profit and Loss Account	1,00,000		
Creditors	50,000		
	12,50,000		12,50,000

The net profits of the company for the past five years before providing for taxation are :

Year	Rs.
1981	1,80,000
1982	2,00,000
1983	1,80,000
1984	1,50,000
1985	1,00,000

Another company engaged in the same line of business pays a dividend of 10% and its shares are quoted in the stock exchange at Rs. 11. Assuming a taxation provision of 50% of the profits and an appropriation of 10% of the balance of reserves, ascertain the value of each equity share of the company.

(Adopted from B.Com., Bangalore University)

Ans. : Value of each equity share Rs. 563.

(25) On 31st December, 1980; the Balance Sheet of a Limited Company disclosed the following position :

Liabilities	Rs.	Assets	Rs.
Issued Capital in Rs. 10 shares	4,00,000	Fixed Assets	5,00,000
Reserves	90,000	Current Assets	2,00,000
Profit and Loss Account	20,000	Goodwill	40,000
5 Per cent Debentures	1,00,000		
Current Liabilities	1,30,000		
	7,40,000		7,40,000

On 31st December, 1980 the fixed assets were independently valued at Rs. 3,50,000 and the goodwill at Rs. 50,000. The net profits for the three years were :

1978 Rs. 51,600; 1979 Rs. 52,000 and 1980 Rs. 51,650 of which 20 percent was placed to reserve this proportion being considered reasonable in the industry in which the company is engaged and where a fair investment return may be taken at 10 per cent.

Compute, the value of the company's shares by (a) the assets method, and (b) the yield method.

(C.A. Inter)

Ans. : (A) Assets Method : Intrinsic value per share Rs. 9.25 (3,70,000 ÷ 40,000).

(B) Yield Method : Average annual profit after reserve Rs. 41,400; Expected rate of return 10.35% and Value per share Rs. 10.35.

(26) Vivek want to buy all the shares of Nanda Ltd. Balance Sheet of Nanda Ltd., as on December 31, 1980.

Liabilities	Rs.	Assets		Rs.
Share Capital	6,00,000	Fixed assets :		
Reserves	1,00,000	Cost	10,00,000	
Profit & Loss A/c	25,000	*Less* : Dep.	2,70,000	7,30,000
8% Debentures	2,00,000	5% Govt. Securities		60,000
Sundry Creditors	80,000	Current Assets		2,70,000
Provision for Taxation	71,500	Preliminary Expenses		16,500
	10,76,500			10,76,500

The provision for taxation is only for the year and is at 55% of the Net Profits. Other companies in the same line of business show an income of 10% on capital employed.

Vivek seeks your advice as to the amount he should pay for the shares. Advise him suitably.

(B.Com., M.K.U., April 1983)

Ans. : Amount to be paid to buy the shares Rs. 6,30,000 (Approximately).

(27) The following is the Balance Sheet of a Company as at 31st Dec., 1985 :

Liabilities	Rs.	Assets	Rs.
Share Capital :		Goodwill	1,00,000
80,000 Equity shares		Land and Buildings	6,00,000
of Rs. 10 each	8,00,000	Plant and Machinery	3,00,000
1,000 6% Preference		Stock	1,50,000
shares of Rs. 100 each	1,00,000	Debtors	1,50,000
General Reserve	2,50,000	Cash	40,000
Creditors	1,00,000	Preliminary Expenses	10,000
5% Debentures	1,00,000		
	13,50,000		13,50,000

Normal return on capital employed for valuation of goodwill is 10%. The land and buildings are worth Rs. 7,00,000 and plant and machinery Rs. 2,80,000. Goodwill is to be valued on the basis of three years' purchase of super-profits. The profits and losses of the company for the past five years were :

	Profit	Loss
1981	1,80,000	—
1982	2,60,000	—
1983	—	40,000
1984	—	20,000
1985	1,30,000	—

Companies engaged in similar business pay 12% dividend on their equity shares. Ascertain the fair value of each equity share.

(Adapted from Bangalore University, B.Com.)

Ans. : Intrinsic value per equity share Rs. 12.75. Market value per equity share Rs. 10.00. Fair value per equity share Rs. 11.37.

(28) The following is the summarised Balance Sheet of Twinkle Star Ltd., as on 30th September, 1980 :

Liabilities		Rs.	Assets	Rs.
Share Capital :			Freehold Property	1,20,000
30,000 Equity shares of			Plant	50,000
Rs. 10 each		3,00,000	Stock	3,10,000
Reserves and Surplus :			Debtors	2,03,000
General	1,20,000		Bank	1,17,000
Capital	40,000		Cash	1,700
Profit and Loss	1,20,000	2,80,000		
Current Liabilities & Provisions				
Creditors	93,700			
Income tax payable	11,500			
Proposed dividend	34,500			
Provision for taxation	82,000	2,21,700		
		8,01,700		8,01,700

Net profit (before taxation) for the last three years ended 30th September, 1978, Rs. 1,38,000; 30th September, 1979, Rs. 1,83,000; and 30th September, 1980 Rs. 1,97,000. Freehold property was valued early in 1980 at Rs. 1,60,000. Average yield in this type of business is 15 percent on capital employed. You are required to find out the value of each equity share on the net assets basis (excluding goodwill) and on yield basis.

(Adapted from I.C.W.A.)

Ans. : Net Assets Method : Intrinsic value per share Rs. 20.67 (6,20,00/30,000)

Yield Method : Average profit Rs. 1,72,667; Income tax assumed to be 50% *i.e.* Rs. 86,333; Profit available for dividend to equity shareholders Rs. 86,334; Capitalised Profit Rs. 5,75,560 and Value per equity share Rs. 19.18.

(29) Balance Sheet of Weak Ltd., as on December, 31st 1997 :

Liabilities	Rs.	Assets	Rs.
Share Capital :		Sundry assets	5,10,000
10,000, 6% Preference shares		Discount on debentures	10,000
of Rs. 10 each fully paid	1,00,000	Preliminary expenses	30,000
30,000 Ordinary shares		Profit and Loss A/c	60,000
of Rs. 10 each fully paid	3,00,000		
Debenture Redemption Fund	30,000		
7% Debentures	50,000		
Depreciation Fund	30,000		
Sundry Creditors	1,00,000		
	6,10,000		6,10,000

The sundry assets are worth Rs. 5,25,000. One year's interest is owing on debentures and the dividends on preference shares are in arrears for two years. You are required to value the shares on the Net Assets Method. If :

(a) Preference shares have priority both as to the payment of capital and arrears of dividend, in the event of liquidation.

(b) Preference shares have no priority as to capital or arrears of dividend.

(c) Preference shares have priority as to payment of capital only.

(d) Preference shares have priority as to the payment of arrears of dividend only.

(B.Com., Andhra, April 1998)

Ans. : Intrinsic value per share (a) Rs. 8.65, (b) Rs. 9.29, (c) Rs. 9.05 and (d) Rs. 8.99.

(30) On 31st December, 1986 the Balance Sheet of Sunset Ltd. was as follows :

Liabilities	Rs.	Assets	Rs.
Share Capital :		Land and Buildings	2,20,000
Authorised and Issued :		Plant and Machinery	95,000
5,000 shares of Rs. 100		Stocks	3,50,000
each fully paid	5,00,000	Sundry Debtors	1,55,000
Profit and Loss Account	1,03,000		
Bank overdraft	20,000		
Creditors	77,000		
Provision for taxation	45,000		
Proposed dividend	75,000		
	8,20,000		8,20,000

The net profits of the company, after deducting all working charges and providing for depreciation and taxation, were as under :

Year	Rs.
1982	85,000
1983	96,000
1984	90,000
1985	1,00,000
1986	95,000

On 31st December, 1986 Land and Buildings were valued at Rs. 2,50,000 and Plant and Machinery at Rs. 1,50,000.

In view of the nature of the business, it is considered that 10% is a reasonable return on tangible capital.

Prepare a valuation of the company's shares, after taking into account, the revised values of fixed assets and your own valuation of goodwill based on five years' purchase of the annual super-profits.

(Adapted from C. A. Final)

Ans. : Average capital employed Rs. 6,40,500 (Assets Rs. 9,05,000 – Liabilities Rs. 2,17,000 + Half of current year's profit Rs. 47,500); Super-profits Rs. 29,150 (Average profit Rs. 93,200 – Normal rate of return Rs. 64,050); Goodwill Rs. 1,45,750 (29,150 × 5); Net assets available for shareholders Rs. 8,33,750 (Assets Rs. 10,50,750 (including goodwill) – Liabilities Rs. 2,17,000) and Intrinsic value per share Rs. 166.75.

(31) Under the articles of a Private Company dealing in wines and tobacco, you as an auditor, have to fix annually the fair value of the shares. At 31st March, 1989 company's position was as follows :

Liabilities		Rs.	Assets		Rs.
1,000, 14% Preference shares of Rs. 100 each fully paid up		1,00,000	Building at cost less depreciation		85,000
4,000 Equity shares of Rs. 100 each, fully paid up		4,00,000	Furniture at cost less depreciation		3,000
General Reserve		1,00,000	Stock in Trade (at Market Value)		4,50,000
Profit and Loss Account :			10% Government Securities at cost (face value Rs. 4,00,000)		3,75,000
Balance on 1st April, 88	30,000		Book Debts	3,00,000	
Profits for 1988-89 (Subject to tax)	5,30,000	5,60,000	*Less :* Provision for Bad and Doubtful Debts	20,000	2,80,000
Provision against :			Bank Balance		60,000
Buildings	10,000		Preliminary Expenses		10,000
Investment	45,000	55,000			
Creditors		48,000			
		12,63,000			12,63,000

You are given the following information :

(1) The company's prospects for 1989-90 are equally good.

(2) The buildings are now worth Rs. 5,65,000.

(3) Public Companies doing similar business show a profit earning capacity of 20 percent on market value of their shares.

(4) Profits for the past three years have shown an increase of Rs. 50,000 annually.

(5) Rate of tax is 50%.

(Adapted from C.A. Final and B.Com., Delhi)

Ans. : (A) **Net Assets Method :** Average capital employed Rs. 9,12,500 (Assets Rs. 13,58,000 – Liabilities Rs. 10,45,000 (Including provision for taxation *i.e.,* 50% on Rs. 5,30,000) + Half of the Profit after tax Rs. 1,32,500);

Average annual profit Rs. 4,80,000 $\left(\dfrac{4{,}30{,}000 + 4{,}80{,}000 + 5{,}30{,}000}{3}\right)$

Average adjusted annual profit Rs. 2,08,000; Super-profits Rs. 25,500; Goodwill Rs. 76,500; Net assets available to equity shareholders Rs. 13,51,500 (Assets 17,64,500 (including goodwill) – Liabilities Rs. 4,13,000) and Intrinsic value per share Rs. 337.87.

(B) **Yield Method :** Profit available to equity shareholders Rs. 2,26,000; Capitalised profit Rs. 11,30,000 and Market value per equity share Rs. 282.50.

(C) **Earning Capacity Method :** Capital employed Rs. 9,12,500; Profit earned Rs. 2,08,000; Rate of earning 22.79% and Value per equity share Rs. 113.95.

******

3

PROFIT OR LOSS PRIOR TO INCORPORATION

Meaning

A company comes into existence only from the date of its incorporation. Some times, a company may take over another running business from the date prior to its incorporation, normally from the beginning of the accounting year of the selling concern with a view to avoid preparation of final accounts upto the date of acquisition. For example, a company incorporated on 1st April, 1995, may agree to acquire another running business from 1st January, 1995, the date on which the accounting year of the vendor starts. If a company earned any profit from the date of purchase to the date of incorporation (*i.e.*, from 1-1-95 to 1-4-95) such profit is called as profit prior to incorporation. On the other hand, if a company suffered any loss from the date of purchase to the date of incorporation, such loss is called as loss prior to incorporation. Similarly, if a company earned any profit or suffered any loss from the date of incorporation upto the closing date of the first financial period (*i.e.*, from 1-4-95 to 31-12-95) such profit or loss is called post-incorporation profit or loss.

A company cannot legally earn profit or incur loss before it comes into existence. Therefore, any profit earned or any loss incurred by the company prior to incorporation cannot be treated as trading profit or loss of a company. It should be treated as capital profit or loss, because it is a profit or loss which is earned even before the company came into existence. Similarly, any profit earned or any loss suffered by the company after incorporation, it is treated as trading (*i.e.,* revenue) profit or loss.

Treatment. Profit prior to incorporation or pre-incorporation profit is a capital profit. Therefore, it cannot be credited to P & L A/c and cannot be used for distribution of dividend. But, the same is to be utilised :

(i) For writing off fictitious assets such as discount on issue of shares or debentures, underwriting commission, preliminary expenses etc.

(ii) For writing down goodwill or other fixed assets acquired.

(iii) Balance, if any, is to be transferred to capital reserve. The capital reserve will be shown on the liabilities side of the balance sheet under the heading 'Reserves and Surplus'.

Suppose, the company has pre-incorporation loss, in that case, such loss can be dealt in the following ways :

(i) It can be debited to goodwill account.

(ii) It can be debited against the profit after incorporation.

(iii) It can be debited to 'Loss Prior to Incorporation Account' which can be written off against any capital profits. Until this loss is completely written off, it will be shown as fictitious assets on the assets side of the balance sheet under the heading 'Miscellaneous Expenditure and Losses'.

Post-incorporation profit of a company is a trading profit. Hence, it should be credited to P & L Account and will be used for distribution as dividend. On the other hand, post-incorporation loss of a company is a trading loss. Hence, it should be debited to P & L Account of a company.

Ascertainment of Profit or Loss

In order to ascertain profit or loss prior to incorporation, stock taking and balancing of the accounts will have to be done on that date. But, it involves a lot of inconveniences. Therefore, to avoid this inconvenience, the profit and loss account is to be prepared for the whole accounting year dividing or allocating the common incomes and expenses between the two periods (*i.e.,* upto incorporation and after incorporation) to ascertain the profit prior to incorporation and after incorporation. The basis of allocation between the two periods is made on the following principles :

Sales Ratio. It means the ratio between the amount of sales made before incorporation and after incorporation. The following are apportioned as per sales ratio :

(i) Gross profit.

(ii) Variable expenses or expenses connected with sales, such as carriage outwards, advertisement, commission and brokerage, discount allowed, salesmen's salary, bad debts, etc.

Time Ratio. It means the ratio between the period prior to incorporation and after incorporation. Fixed expenses such as salary, wages, rent, rates, insurance, printing and stationery, postage and telegrams, depreciation, miscellaneous expenses etc. are apportioned between two periods on the basis of time of the respective periods.

Weighted Ratio. It is a ratio between the proportionate weights as regards the time and the number of employees prior to incorporation and after incorporation. In other words, it is a ratio calculated by taking into account the time as well as the number of employees engaged in prior to incorporation and after incorporation. It is also called weighted time ratio. It is calculated by assigning the proportionate weight as regards number of workers between the pre-incorporation and post-incorporation. While calculating the weighted ratio first we have to find out the time ratio and workers or employees ratio, then, workers ratio should be multified by the time ratio, the resulting figure will be weighted ratio. This ratio will be used while allocating the expenses like salary, wages etc. which do not remain constant (fixed) throughout the year due to change in the number of employees or workers. Hence, time ratio cannot be adopted in all cases in apportioning the expenses. While apportioning the expenses which do not remain constant over a period of time, the weighted ratio will be used. Both time and number of workers or employees should be considered in calculating the weighted ratio.

Expenses applicable to pre-incorporation period. All expenses wholly applicable to the period prior to incorporation need not be apportioned and they should be charged wholly to the pre-incorporation period. For example, interest on vendor's capital, interest on purchase consideration, vendor's salary etc.

Expenses applicable to post-incorporation. All expenses applicable to the period after incorporation should be charged wholly to the post-incorporation period. For example, managing directors' salary, directors' fees, discount on issue of shares, debenture interest written off, preliminary expenses written off, goodwill written off etc.

Expenses applicable to both the periods. Some expenses are applicable to both the periods. Such expenses are to be charged to the respective periods. For example, out of rent of Rs. 1,500, a sum of Rs. 500 is relating to the period prior to incorporation. It means, remaining amount of Rs. 1,000 is relating to the period after incorporation.

Rent and interest received. These incomes are to be apportioned between the two periods on the basis of time of the respective periods.

Audit fees. Audit fees may be considered in two ways. Auditor is appointed after incorporation. Therefore, audit fees may be charged after incorporation. Alternatively, as audit work is usually carried out for the whole period, audit fees may be charged between the two periods on the basis of the time of the respective periods.

Illustration 1

Ambica Co. Ltd. was incorporated on 1-7-1997 to take over the business of Arvind Co. Ltd. as from 1-4-1997. The company prepared its first final accounts on 31-3-1997. From the following information, calculate the sales ratio of pre-and post-incorporation periods.

(i) Sales from April 1997 to March, 1998 Rs. 4,20,000.

(ii) Sales for the month of April, twice the average sales; for the month of July and December ¼th of the average sales; sales for October ½ of the average sales and sales for February and March 1½ times of the averaged sales.

Solution :

Calculation of Sales Ratio

(a) Calculation of average sales per month $= \frac{4,20,000}{12}$ = Rs. 35,000

(b) Calculation of sales for each period

April	(2 times)	2 × 35,000	=	70,000	
May	(Average)	1 × 35,000	=	35,000	
June	(Average)	1 × 35,000	=	35,000	
	Sales prior to incorporation		=	1,40,000	1,40,000
July	(¼ times)	¼ × 35,000	=	8,750	
August	(Average)	1 × 35,000	=	35,000	
September	(Average)	1 × 35,000	=	35,000	
October	(½ times)	½ × 35,000	=	17,500	
November	(Average)	1 × 35,000	=	35,000	
December	(¼ times)	¼ × 35,000	=	8,750	
January	(Average)	1 × 35,000	=	35,000	
February	(1½ times)	1½ × 35,000	=	52,500	
March	(1½ times)	1½ × 35,000	=	52,500	
	Sales after incorporation			2,80,000	2,80,000
		Total sales			4,20,000

(c) Calculation of sales ratio of pre- and post-incorporation periods

Pre-incorporation period sales : post-incorporation periods sales

Rs. 1,40,000 : Rs. 2,80,000

Sales ratio = 1 : 2

Illustration 2

You are required to calculate the sales ratio for prior to incorporation and after incorporation periods from the following particulars :

(i) Date of incorporation— 1st April, 1997.

(ii) Period for financial accounts—January to December 1997.

(iii) Total sales for the year amounted to Rs. 6,00,000.

(iv) Sales for the month of January were equal to average sales and sales for March were 1½ times of the average sales, while the sales for July, August, September and October were only ¼th of the average and those for November and December 1¼ times of the average sales.

Solution :

Calculation of Sales Ratio :

(a) Calculation of average sales per month $= \frac{6,00,000}{12} =$ Rs. 50,000

(b) Calculation of sales for those months for which the information is given :

January	(Average)	1 × 50,000	=	50,000
March	(1½ times)	1½ × 50,000	=	75,000
July	(¼ times)	¼ × 50,000	=	12,500
August	(¼ times)	¼ × 50,000	=	12,500
September	(¼ times)	¼ × 50,000	=	12,500
October	(¼ times)	¼ × 50,000	=	12,500
November	(1¼ times)	1¼ × 50,000	=	62,500
December	(1¼ times)	1¼ × 50,000	=	62,500
	Total sales for the above months			Rs. 3,00,000

(c) Calculation of sales for the remaining months :

(i) Remaining months are – February, April, May and June.

(ii) Remaining unaccounted sales – Rs. 3,00,000 (*i.e.*, 6,00,000 – 3,00,000)

(d) Calculation of average sales for the remaining months :

$$\frac{\text{Remaining Sales}}{\text{Remaining months}} = \frac{3,00,000}{4} = \text{Rs. } 75,000 \text{ per month}$$

(e) Calculation of amount of sales prior to incorporation period :

January	Rs. 50,000
February	Rs. 75,000
March	Rs. 75,000
	Rs. 2,00,000

(f) Calculation of amount of sales after incorporation period :

Total sales – Pre-incorporation period sales

Rs. 6,00,000 – Rs. 2,00,000 = Rs. 4,00,000.

(g) Calculation of sales ratio prior to incorporation and after incorporation periods :

Prior to incorporation period : After incorporation period

Rs. 2,00,000 : Rs. 4,00,000

Sales Ratio 1 : 2.

Illustration 3

A company, incorporated on 1st April, 1997, took over a running business from 1st January, 1997. The company prepared its first final accounts of 31st December, 1997. From the following information, calculate the weighted time ratio and also divide the total wages in pre- and post-incorporation periods :

(i) Total wages Rs. 10,400.

(ii) Number of workers : Pre-incorporation period 15 and Post-incorporation period 60.

Solution :

Calculation of Weighted Time Ratio

Simple Time Ratio = Pre-incorporation period : Post-incorporation period

3 months : 9 months

1 : 3

Workers Ratio = Pre-incorporation period : Post-incorporation period

15 Workers : 60 Workers

1 : 4

Weighted Time Ratio = Pre-incorporation : Post-incorporation

Time ratio × Ratio Time ratio × Ratio

of workers : of workers

1 × 1 : 3 × 4

1 : 12

Pre-incorporation period wages Rs. 800 (10,400 × 1/13)

Post-incorporation period wages Rs. 9,600 (10,400 × 12/13)

Illustration 4

Envy Ltd. was incorporated on 30th June, 1997 to take over the business of Big & Co. Ltd., as from 1st January, 1997. The financial accounts of the business for the year ending 31st December, 1997 disclosed the following information :

Sales : January to June	75,000		
July to December	1,25,000	2,00,000	
Closing Stock		50,000	2,50,000
Less :			
Opening Stock		50,000	
Purchases		80,000	
Wages		5,000	1,35,000
Gross Profit			1,15,000
Less : Salaries		8,000	
Selling Expenses		2,400	
Directors' Remuneration		2,000	
Administrative Expenses		1,800	
Preliminary Expenses written off		1,400	
Miscellaneous Expenses		800	
Debenture Interest		500	
Depreciation		1,000	
Discount		1,600	
Commission		800	
Advertisement		1,200	21,500
Profit for the year			93,500

You are required to prepare a statement apportioning the balance of profit between the periods prior to and after incorporation for the year ended 31st December, 1997.

Solution :

Profit and Loss Account
For the period January 1 to December 31, 1997

	Prior	After		Prior	After
To Salaries (Time Ratio 1 : 1)	4,000	4,000	By Gross Profit (Sales Ratio 3:5)	43,125	71,875
To Selling Expenses (Sales Ratio 3 : 5)	900	1,500			
To Directors' Remuneration (After incorporation)	–	2,000			
To Administrative Expenses (Time Ratio 1 : 1)	900	900			
To Preliminary Expenses written off (After incorporation)	–	1,400			

(Contd.)

Profit and Loss Account (*Contd.*)

	Prior	After		Prior	After
To Miscellaneous Expenses (Time Ratio 1 : 1)	400	400			
To Debenture Interest (After-incorporation	–	500			
To Depreciation (Time Ratio 1 : 1)	500	500			
To Discount (Sales Ratio 3 : 5)	600	1,000			
To Commission (Sales Ratio 3 : 5)	300	500			
To Advertisement (Sales Ratio 3 : 5)	450	750			
To Net Profit transferred to Capital Reserve	35,075	–			
To Net Profit transferred to P & L Appropriation A/c	–	58,425			
	43,125	71,875		43,125	71,875

Notes :

	Pre-incorporation		Post-incorporation
(1) Time Ratio	January 1 to June 30	:	July 1 to December, 31
	6 months	:	6 months
	6	:	6
	1	:	1
(2) Sales Ratio	Rs. 75,000	:	Rs. 1,25,000
	3	:	5

Illustration 5

X. Ltd. which was incorporated on May 1, 1991, acquired a business on January 1, 1991. The first accounts were closed on September 30, 1991.

The gross profit for the period was Rs. 42,000.

Details of other expenses : General expenses Rs. 7,200; directors' remuneration Rs. 12,000; and preliminary expenses Rs. 2,000.

Rent upto June 30 was Rs. 6,000 per annum after which it was increased by 40%.

Salary of the manager, who, upon formation of the company had become a whole time director and whose remuneration has been given above, was agreed at Rs. 5,100 per annum.

The company earned a uniform gross profit. The sales upto September, 1991 were Rs. 98,000. The monthly average of sales for the first four months of the year was one-half of the remaining period.

Show the Profit and Loss Account and indicate how you would deal with the pre-incorporation results.

(C.A. Inter Nov. 1979 & B.Com., Kerala, April 1991)

Solution :

Profit and Loss Account for the year ended 30th Sept., 1991

	Prior	After		Prior	After
To General Expenses (Time Ratio 4:5)	3,200	4,000	By Gross Profit (Sales Ratio 2:5)	12,000	30,000
To Directors' Remuneration (After incorporation)	–	12,000			
To Rent (As stated in the problem)	2,000	3,100			
To Preliminary Expenses (After incorporation)	–	2,000			
To Managers' Salary (As stated in the problem)	1,700	–			
To Net profit transferred to Capital Reserve	5,100	–			
To Net Profit transferred to P & L Appropriation A/c	–	8,900			
	12,000	30,000		12,000	30,000

Notes : **(1) Time Ratio** = 4.5 (*i.e.*, 4 months prior, 5 months after)

(2) Sales Ratio : it is arrived as below.

As per the information given in the problem, the monthly average sales of pre-incorporation period are one-half of the monthly average sales of the post-incorporation period. It means, if the monthly average sales of pre-incorporation period are Re. 1, the monthly average sales of post-incorporation period will be Rs. 2. Like wise, if the total sales of pre-incorporation period for 4 months are Rs. 4 (*i.e.*, 1 × 4), the total sales of the post-incorporation period for five months will be Rs. 10 (*i.e.*, 2 × 5). Therefore, the sales ratio between the two periods will be 4 : 10 or 2 : 5.

(3) Allocation of Rent

Rent for the pre-incorporation period *i.e.*, upto May Rs. 2,000 (*i.e.*, 6000 × 4/12) Rent for the post-incorporation period will be :

(i)	For two months at Rs. 6,000 per annum (6,000 × 2/12)	Rs. 1,000
(ii)	For 3 months at Rs. 8,400 per annum (8,400 × 3/12)	Rs. 2,100
		Rs. 3,100

(4) Salary to the manager for the first 4 months = Rs. 1,700 (*i.e.*,5,100 × 4/12)

Illustration 6

Ashok Ltd. was incorporated on 1-8-1996 to take over the business of X. Co. Ltd., as a going concern as from 1-4-1996. The Profit and Loss Account of the company for the year ending 31-3-1997 was as follows :

	Rs.		Rs.
To Salary & Allowances	4,500	By Gross Profit	90,000
To Rent & Taxes	8,500	By Bad Debts realised	1,000
To Office Expenses	900		
To General Expenses	1,500		
To Formation Expenses	1,200		
To Discount on Sales	1,800		
To Bad Debts	1,300		
To Bank Charges	300		
To Carriage Outwards	990		
To Interest on Loans	330		
To Electricity	270		
To Interest to Vendors (upto 30-9-96)	900		
To Repairs to Building	1,500		
To Net Profit	67,010		
	91,000		91,000

The following is the further information.:

(i) The average monthly sales for the first 4 months during the year was Rs. 40,000 whereas the average monthly sales for the subsequent period was Rs. 70,000.

(ii) Rent was paid at Rs. 400 per month upto 1-8-1996 and thereafter it was increased by Rs. 200 per month.

(iii) Of the bed debts Rs. 1,300, Rs. 300 relate to debts created prior to incorporation and the realisation of bad debts was in respect of debts written off during 1995.

You are required to find out the profits prior to incorporation and to state the treatment thereof in the books of the company.

Solution :

Dr. **Profit and Loss Account for the year ending 31-3-1997** Cr.

	Prior	After		Prior	After
To Salary & allowances (1:2)	1,500	3,000	By Gross profit (2:7)	20,000	70,000
To Rent & rates (As stated in problem)	1,600	4,800	By Bad debts realised	1,000	—
To Rent & rates (1:2) (8,500 – 6,400)	700	1,400	(As stated in the problem)		
To Office expenses (1:2)	300	600			
To General expenses (1:2)	500	1,000			
To Formation expenses (After incorporation)	–	1,200			
To Discount on sales (2:7)	400	1,400			
To Bad debts (As stated in the problem)	300	1,000			
To Bank charges (1:2)	100	200			
To Carriage outwards (2:7)	220	770			
To Interest on loans	110	220			
To Electricity	90	180			
To Interest to vendors (4 months prior and 2 months after)	600	300			
To Repairs to building (1:2)	500	1,000			
To Net Profit transferred to Capital Reserve	14,080	—			
To Net Profit transferred to P & L Appropriation A/c	—	52,930			
	21,000	70,000		21,000	70,000

Notes : **(1) Time Ratio** = 1:2 (*i.e.*, 4 months prior & 8 months after *i.e.*, 4:8 or 1:2)

(2) Sales Ratio = Sales prior to incorporation (4 × 40,000) = 1,60,000

Sales after incorporation (8 × 70,000) = 5,60,000

i.e., 1,60,000 : 5,60,000 or 2:7

(3) Allocation of Rent & Rates

Total Rent & Rates		8,500
Less : Rent prior to incorporation (4 × 400)	1,600	
Rent after incorporation (8 × 600)	4,800	6,400
Balance of Rent & Rates allocated on time ratio		2,100

Illustration 7

Sarvottam Ltd., was incorporated on January 1, 1988, with an authorised capital of Rs. 50,000 and took over the running business of Uttam Bros. as from October 1, 1987. The following is the summarised Profit and Loss Account for the year ended September 30, 1988.

	Rs.	Rs.
Sales : Oct. 1, 1987 to Dec. 31, 1987	60,000	
Jan. 1, 1988 to Sept. 30, 1988	1,90,000	2,50,000
Cost of Sales for the year	1,54,000	
Administrative expenses	17,680	
Selling commission	8,750	
Goodwill written off	2,000	
Interest to vendors (loan repaid on Feb. 1, 1988)	3,730	
Distribution expenses (60% variable)	12,500	
Preliminary expenses	3,300	
Debenture interest	3,200	
Depreciation	4,440	
Directors' fees	1,000	2,10,600
Net profit		39,400

The company deals in only one product. The cost of sales per unit was reduced by 10% in the post-incorporation period, as compared to pre-incorporation period.

Prepare a statement showing the net profit of the pre-incorporation as well as the post-incorporation period, also showing the basis of apportionment.

(A.C.S., Dec. 1988)

Solution :

Sarvottam Ltd.

Statement showing the pre-incorporation and post-incorporation periods

	Basis of Allocation	Prior Rs.	After Rs.
Sales	As given	60,000	1,90,000
Less : Cost of sales	As calculated (*See* Note)	40,000	1,14,000
Gross profit		20,000	76,000
Less : Expenses :			
Administrative expenses	Time 1 : 3	4,420	13,260
Selling commission	Sales 6 : 19	2,100	6,650
Goodwill written off	After-incorporation	—	2,000
Interest to vendors	Time 3 : 1	2,797	933
Distribution expenses :			
Fixed	Time 1 : 3	1,250	3,750
Variable	Sales 6 : 19	1,800	5,700
Preliminary expenses	After-incorporation	—	3,300
Debenture interest	After-incorporation	—	3,200
Depreciation	Time 1 : 3	1,110	3,330
Director fees	After-incorporation	—	1,000
		13,477	43,123
Gross profit		20,000	76,000
Less : Expenses		13,477	43,123
		6,523	32,877

Notes : **(1) Time Ratio** = 1 : 3 (*i.e.,* 3 months prior & 9 months after *i.e.,* 3 : 9 or 1 : 3)

(2) Sales Ratio = Sales prior to incorporation : Sales after-incorporation
Rs. 60,000 : Rs. 1,90,000 = 6 : 19

(3) Interest to Vendors = 3 months prior : 1 month after = 3 : 1

(4) Calculation of ratio of cost of sales of two periods

Let cost of sales in the pre-incorporation period be Rs. 100.

Then, cost of sales in the post-incorporation period will be Rs. 90. (*i.e.*, Reduced by 10% *i.e.,* 100 – 10% of 100)

Therefore, the ratio of cost of sales between the two periods will be 60 : 171 (*i.e.,* 100 × 60,000 : 90 × 1,90,000). That means, the cost of sales of pre-incorporation period will be 1,54,000 × 60/231 = Rs. 40,000 and the cost of sales of post-incorporation period will be 1,54,000 × 171/231 = Rs. 1,14,000.

Illustration 8

Poornima Ltd. incorporated on April 1, 1983, with a capital of Rs. 50,000 in equity shares of Rs. 10 each took over the running business of Poornima as from January 1, 1983. The purchase price Rs. 20,000 was settled on July 1983, together with interest at 10% per annum by fully paid shares for Rs. 17,500 and the balance by cheque.

The company's Trial Balance as on December 31, 1983 was below :

	Rs.	Rs.
Cash & Bank balance (cash Rs. 180)	4,860	—
Share capital	—	22,500
Land and buildings	8,000	—
Fixtures	750	—
Cycles	1,000	—
Salaries	1,200	—
Purchases	48,500	—
Sales	—	45,000
Debtor and creditors	4,500	3,000
Rent from tenants	—	600
Rent, rates and taxes	300	—
Building up keep	150	—
Directors' fees	720	—
Sundry charges	120	—
Interest to vendor	1,000	—
	71,100	71,100

Prepare the final accounts for the year ending December 31, 1983, considering the following additional details :

(1) Stock at end Rs. 14,000.

(2) Bad debts Rs. 200 (including Rs. 50 on debtors taken over from vendor) to be written off.

(3) Sales above include sales upto April 1, 1983, Rs. 7,500.

(4) Provide for doubtful debts Rs. 250.

(5) Depreciate building 5% and cycles 20%.

(B.Com., M.K.U., April, 1984, Bangalore, April 1999)

Solution :

Poornima Ltd.
Trading and Profit and Loss Account for the year ended December 31, 1983

Dr. Cr.

	Rs.		Rs.
To Purchases	48,500	By Sales	45,000
To Gross profit c/d	10,500	By Closing stock	14,000
	59,000		59,000

	Prior	After		Prior	After
To Salaries (1 : 3)	300	900	By Gross Profit b/d (1 : 5)	1,750	8,750
To Rent rates & taxes (1 : 3)	75	225			
To Building up keep (1: 3)	38	112	By Rent (1: 3)	150	450
To Directors' fees (After)	—	720			
To Sundry charges (1 : 3)	30	90			
To Interest to vendors (3 : 3 or 1 : 1)	500	500			
To Bad debts (As stated in the problem)	50	150			
To Provision for doubtful debts (After)	—	250			
To Depreciation : Building 400, Cycles 200 = 600 (1 : 3)	150	450			
To Net profit transferred to Capital Reserve	757	—			
To Net Profit transferred to P & L Appropriation A/c	—	5,803			
	1,900	9,200		1,900	9,200

Balance Sheet of Poornima Ltd. as on December 31, 1983

Liabilities		Rs.	Assets		Rs.
Shares Capital :			**Fixed Assets:**		
Authorised :			Land and Buildings	8,000	
5,000 Equity shares of			*Less* : Dep. (5%)	400	7,600
Rs. 10 each		50,000	Fixtures		750
Issued, subscribed, called up			Cycles	1,000	
and paid up :			*Less* : Dep. (20%)	200	800
500 Equity shares of Rs. 10			**Investments, Assets, Loans**		
each issued to public			**and advances :**		
for cash as fully paid	5,000		Closing stock		14,000
1,750 Equity shares of			Sundry Debtors	4,500	
Rs. 10 each fully paid			*Less* : Bad Debts	200	
issued to vendors	17,500	22,500		4,300	
Reserves & Surplus :			*Less* : Provision for		
Capital Reserve		757	Doubtful Debts	250	4,050
(Pre-incorporation profit)			Cash at Bank		4,680
Profit & Loss Appropriation			Cash in hand		180
A/c credit balance		5,803	**Miscellaneous Expenditure**		
(Post-incorporation profit)			**& Losses**		—
Current Liabilities and					
Provisions :					
Sundry creditors		3,000			
		32,060			32,060

Notes : (1) Time Ratio = 1 : 3 (*i.e.,* 3 months prior : 9 months after *i.e.,* 3 : 9 or 1 : 3)

(2) Sales Ratio = 1 : 5 (*i.e.,* pre-sales : post-sales 7,500 : 37,500 = 1 : 5)

(3) Interest to Vendors = 3 months prior : 3 months after = 3 : 3 = 1 : 1.

(4) R.D.D. can be dealt in two ways. It is an expense connected with sales and hence, it can be allocated on sales ratio. Alternatively, as it is provided only at the end of the year and hence, it can be wholly charged to post-incorporation period. Here, it is charged to post-incorporation period.

Illustration 9

Rowlock Ltd. was incorporated on 1st October, 1988 to acquire Rocklock's mail order business, with effect from 1st June, 1988.

The purchases consideration was agreed at Rs. 35,000 to be satisfied by the issue on 1st December, 1988 to Rowlock or his nominee of :

20,000 ordinary shares of Re. 1 each, fully paid and Rs. 15,000 7% debentures.

The entries relating to the transfer were not made in the books which were carried on without a break until 31st May, 1989.

On 31st May, 1989 the trial balance extracted from the books showed the following :

	Rs.		Rs.
Sales	52,185	Directors' salary	1,000
Purchases	38,829	Debenture interest (gross)	525
Wrapping	840	Fixed assets	25,000
Postage	441	Current assets (other than stock)	9,745
Warehouse rent & rates	921		
Packing expenses	1,890	Current liabilities	4,162
Office expenses	627	Formation expenses	218
Stock on 31st May, 1988	5,261	Capital A/c Rocklock 31st May, 1988	29,450
		Drawings A/c – Rocklock	500

You are also to ascertain the following :

(1) Stock on 1st May, 1989 amounted to Rs. 4,946.

(2) The average monthly sales for June, July and August were one-half of those for the remaining months of the year. The gross profit margin was constant throughout the year.

(3) Wrapping, postage and packing expenses varied in direct proportion to sales, whilst office expenses were constant each month.

(4) Formation expenses are to be written off.

You are required to prepare the trading and profit and loss account for the year ended 31st May, 1989 apportioned between the periods before and after incorporation and balance sheet as on the date.

(C.A., Nov. 1989 & I.C.W.A., April 1990)

Solution :

Rocklock Ltd.
Trading and Profit and Loss Account
For the year ended May 31, 1989

Dr. Cr.

	Rs.		Rs.
To Opening stock	5,261	By Sales	52,185
To Purchases	38,829	By Closing stock	4,946
To Gross profit c/d	13,041		
	57,131		57,131

Rocklock Ltd.
Trading and Profit and Loss Account (*Contd.*)

	Prior	After		Prior	After
To Packing, postage and wrapping (5 : 16)	755	2,416	By Gross profit b/d (5:16)	3,105	9,936
To Warehouse rent and rates (5 : 16)	307	614			
To Office expenses (1 : 2)	209	418			
To Directors salary (After)	–	1,000			
To Debenture interest (After)	–	525			
To Formation expenses (After)	–	218			
To Net profit transferred to Goodwill	1,834	–			
To Net profit transferred to P & L Appropriation A/c	–	4,745			
	3,105	9,936		3,105	9,936

Balance Sheet of Rowlock Ltd. as at May 31, 1989

Liabilities	Rs.	Assets	Rs.
Shares Capital		**Fixed Assets:**	
Issued and paid up :		Goodwill	4,216
20,000 ordinary shares		Fixed assets	25,000
of Re. 1, fully paid	20,000	**Investments Current Assets,**	—
Reserves and Surplus :		**Loans and Advances :**	
P & L Appropriation A/c		Stock	4,946
Credit balance	4,745	Current assets	9,745
Secured Loans :		(Other than stock)	
7% Debentures	15,000	**Miscellaneous Expenditure**	
Unsecured Loans	—	**and Losses**	—
Current Liabilities and Provisions :			
Current liabilities	4,162		
	43,907		43,907

Notes : (1) Time Ratio = 1 : 2 (*i.e.,* 4 months prior : 8 months after *i.e.,* 4 : 8 or 1 : 2)

(2) Calculation of Sales Ratio :

1988	Pre-incorporation	Post-incorporation
June, July, August (one each) (*i.e.,* one is assumed as one-half)	3	—
September (two each) (*i.e.,* Double of one)	2	—
October to December (two each)	—	6
January to May (two each)	—	10
	5	16

Sales Ratio = 5 : 16.

(3) Calculation of Goodwill :

	Rs.
Excess of purchase consideration over capital (*i.e.,* Rs. 35,000 – Rs. 28,950)	6,050
Less : Pre-incorporation profit	1,834
Goodwill	Rs. 4,216

EXAMINATION QUESTIONS

(A) Answer the following questions in two sentences each :

(Each carrying two marks)

1. What is profit prior to incorporation?
2. What is profit after-incorporation?
3. What do you mean by loss prior to incorporation?
4. What do you mean by loss after incorporation?
5. What is the nature of profit prior to incorporation?
6. What is the nature of profit after incorporation?
7. How do you treat the profit prior to incorporation?
8. How do you treat the profit after incorporation?
9. What is sales ratio?

   (Karnataka, April 1999)
10. What is time ratio? Give an example.

    (Bangalore, April 1999)
11. Give the examples of expenses applicable to pre-incorporation profit.
12. Give the examples of expenses applicable to post-incorporation profit.
13. Why are profits prior to incorporation ascertained separately?

    (Karnataka, October 1997)
14. What is profit prior to incorporation? Why is it calculated?

    (Karnataka, April 1998)
15. What is weighted ratio?

    (Bangalore, April 1999).

(B) Answer the following question/problems :

(Each carrying 8 marks)

1. Give the meaning of pre-incorporation and post incorporation of profits. How are they ascertained?
2. How are pre-incorporation profits and post-incorporation profits treated in the books of accounts?
3. State the different steps you would take for apportioning the profits of a company between pre- and post-incorporation profits.

4. How do you ascertain the profits prior to incorporation?

5. Kumar Co. Ltd. was incorporated on 1-4-1996 to take over the business of Mohan Co. Ltd. as from 1-1-1996. The company prepared its first final accounts on 31-12-1996. From the following information, calculate sales ratio of pre- and post-incorporation periods.

(i) Sales from January, 1996 to December, 1996 Rs. 3,00,000.

(ii) Sales for the months January, February and September— ¼th of the average sales; sales for the months of March, June, November and December— 1½ times of average sales and sales for May twice of the average sales.

Ans. : Average Sales Rs. 25,000 (*i.e.,* 3,00,000 ÷ 12)
Sales Ratio = 1 : 5 (*i.e.*, Rs. 50,000 : 2,50,000).

6. A company, incorporated on 1st April, 1993, took over a running business from 1st January, 1993. The company prepared its first final accounts on 31st December, 1993. From the following information you are required to calculate the sales ratio of pre- and post-incorporation periods :

(a) Sales from January 1993-December, 1993— Rs. 3,60,000

(b) Sales for the month of January twice the average sales; for the month of February—equal to average sales; sales for four months from May to August—¼th of the average sale of each month; and sales for October and November three times the average sales.

(*A.C.S. Inter, April 1993*)

Ans. : Average Sales Rs. 30,000 (*i.e.,* 3,60,000 ÷ 12)
Sales Ratio = 7 : 17 (*i.e.,* 1,05,000 : Rs. 2,55,000)

7. 'A' Co. Ltd., incorporated on 1st April, 1997, took over a running business from 1st January, 1997. The company prepared its first final accounts on 31st December, 1997. From the following information, calculate the weighted time ratio and also divide the total wages in pre-and post-incorporation periods.

(i) Total wages Rs. 9,600.

(ii) Number of workers : Pre-incorporation period 10 and post-incorporation period 50.

Ans. : Weighted Time Ratio = 1 : 15
Pre-incorporation period wages Rs. 600
Post-incorporation period wages Rs. 9,000.

8. A company was incorporated on 30th June, 1983 to acquire the business of Mohan as from 1st January, 1983. The accounts for the year ended 31st December, 1983 disclosed the following :

(a) There was a gross profit of Rs. 2,40,000.

(b) The sales for the year amounted to Rs. 12,00,000 of which Rs. 5,40,000 were for the first six months.

(c) The expenses debited to the Profit and Loss Account included Directors' fees Rs. 15,000; Bad debts Rs. 3,600; Advertising Rs. 12,000 (under a contract amounting to Rs. 1,000 per month); Salaries and General expenses Rs. 64,000; Preliminary expenses written of Rs. 5,000; Donation to political party given by the company Rs. 5,000.

Prepare a statement showing the amount of profit made before and after incorporation.

(B.Com., Bangalore, April 1991)

Ans. : Time Ratio = 1 : 1 (*i.e.,* 6 months prior & 6 months after)
Sales Ratio = 9 : 11 (*i.e.,* Rs. 1,08,000 : Rs. 1,32,000)
Profit prior to incorporation Rs. 68,380
Profit after incorporation Rs. 67,020

Hint. Donation is chargeable after incorporation.

9. H. Co. Ltd., was incorporated on 1-5-1987. It acquired a running business as from 1-1-1987. The Profit and Loss A/c for the year ending 31-12-1987 was as under :

	Rs.		Rs.
To Salaries	40,000	By Gross Profit	2,00,000
To General Expenses	10,000		
To Carriage Outwards	15,000		
To Advertisement	20,000		
To Interest on Debentures	6,000		
To Directors' Fees	4,000		
To Audit Fees	5,000		
To Interest to Vendors (upto 30-6-1987)	10,000		
To Depreciation	20,000		
To Net Profit	70,000		
	2,00,000		2,00,000

The sales upto 1-5-1987 were Rs. 2,00,000 and from 1-5-1987 were Rs. 8,00,000.

Redraft the Profit and Loss A/c to show the profit prior to incorporation and after incorporation.

(Gulbarga, April 1992 & 1993)

Ans. : Profit prior to incorporation Rs. 1,333 and profit after incorporation Rs. 68,667.

Hints. (i) Sales ratio 1 : 4 & Time ratio 1 : 2.

(ii) Interest to vendors : Prior Rs. 6,667 & After Rs. 3,333.

(iii) Audit fees are allocated on time ratio.

10. XYZ Co. Ltd. was incorporated on 1-5-1990 to take over the business of Hind & Co. Ltd. as a going concern from 1-1-1990. The Profit and Loss Account for the year ending 31-12-1990 was as follows :

	Rs.		Rs.
To Salaries	48,000	By Gross Profit b/d	1,50,000
To Rent & Rates	15,000		
To Insurance	6,000		
To Electricity	4,800		
To Directors' Fees	2,000		
To Commission	5,000		
To Auditors' Fees	1,200		
To Advertisement	2,500		
To Office Expenses	4,200		
To Carriage on Sales	5,000		
To Bank Charges	1,500		
To Preliminary Expenses	3,500		
To Bad Debts	2,000		
To Interest on Debentures	3,000		
To Net Profit	46,300		
	1,50,000		1,50,000

The total turn over for the year ending 31-12-1990 was Rs. 10,00,000 divided into Rs. 4,00,000 for the period upto 1-5-1990 and Rs. 6,00,000 for the remaining period.

Ascertain the profit earned prior to and after incorporation of the company.

(Karnataka, April 1992)

Ans. Profit prior to incorporation Rs. 27,300 and profit after incorporation Rs. 19,000.

Hints. (i) Sales Ratio 2 : 3 and Time Ratio 1 : 2.

(ii) Audit fees are allocated on time ratio.

11. A. Co. Ltd. was incorporated on 1-7-1995 to take over the business of Ahmed as from 1-4-1995. The following was the Profit & Loss Account for the year ending 31-3-1996 :

	Rs.		Rs.
To Salaries	72,000	By Gross Profit	1,40,000
To Rent & Rates	3,600	By Net Loss	6,000
To Office Expenses	24,000		
To Commission on Sales	16,000		
To Free Samples	4,000		
To Audit Fees	2,000		
To Depreciation	8,000		
To Interest on Debentures	6,000		
To Directors' Fees	2,000		
To Formation Expenses	2,000		
To Printing & Stationery	4,000		
To Sundry Expenses	800		
To Bad Debts	1,600		
	1,46,000		1,46,000

Additional information

(a) Sales upto 1-7-1995 amounted to Rs. 1,50,000 and there after Rs. 2,40,000.

(b) Rent was paid at Rs. 200 per month.

(c) Bad debts upto 30-6-1995 were Rs. 400. Prepare a statement showing profit or loss prior to incorporation.

(*Karnataka, 1993 and April 1996*)

Ans. : Profit prior to incorporation Rs. 19,000 and loss after incorporation Rs. 25,000.

Hints. (i) Sales ratio 2 : 3 and Time ratio 1 : 3.

(ii) Rent Rs. 600 is before and Rs. 1,800 is after and rates Rs. 300 is before and 900 is after.

(iii) Bad debts Rs. 400 is prior and Rs. 1,200 is after.

(iv) Audit fees are allocated in time ratio.

12. R. & Co. Ltd., was formed on 1-4-1995 to take over business of M/s. Ram Traders w.e.f. 1-1-1995. The Profit & Loss Account of the company for the year ending 31-12-1995 is given below :

	Rs.		Rs.
To Salaries and Allowances	32,000	By Gross Profit	1,40,000
To Rent and Rates	7,000		
To Directors Fees	3,600		
To Commission to Agents	11,200		
To General Expenses	9,600		
To Advertising	2,800		
To Audit Fees	2,000		
To Debenture Interest	3,600		
To Depreciation	12,800		
To Interest to Vendors (upto 30-6-95)	2,000		
To Net Profit	53,400		
	1,40,000		1,40,000

Additional Information

(a) The average monthly sales for the first three months of 1995 was Rs. 32,000 and for the rest of the year was Rs. 64,000.

(b) Rent paid was Rs. 400 per month upto 31-3-95 and there after it was increased to Rs. 600 per month, Ascertain profit before and after incorporation.

(*Karnataka April, 1997*)

Ans. : Profit prior to incorporation Rs. 1,600 and After incorporation Rs. 51,800.

Hints. (i) Sales ratio 1 : 6 and Time ratio 1 : 3.

(ii) Rent Rs. 1,200 is prior and Rs. 5,400 is after. Rates Rs. 100 is prior and Rs. 300 is after.

(iii) Audit fees are allocated in time ratio.

(iv) Prior sales Rs. 96,000 (32,000 × 3) and after sales Rs. 5,76,000 (64,000 × 9).

13. Calculate Sales Ratio from the following :

X company was incorporated on 1-5-1992 and acquired a business with effect from 1-1-1992. Total sales from 1-1-1992 upto 31-12-1992 was Rs. 6,00,000.

Sales for January and February 1½ times the average monthly sales. Sales from March to July = ½ of average monthly sales. Sales for

August and September = ¼ of average monthly sales and sales from October to December = Double the average monthly sales.

(Bangalore, November 1993)

Ans. : Sales Ratio : 1 : 2 or 2,00,000 : 4,00,000.

Hint. Average monthly sales Rs. 50,000 (Rs. 6,00,000 ÷ 12); Sales of each month : Jan. & Feb.—75,000 each; March, April, May, June and July—25,000 each; Aug. & Sept.—12,500 each and Oct., Nov. & Dec.—1,00,000 each.

14. (1) A company had purchased a business on 1-1-1991. The company received its certificate of incorporation on 1-6-1991. The average monthly sales for the period before incorporation was 25% more than the average monthly sales for the period after incorporation. The total sales during the year was Rs. 6,62,500.

(2) There were 25 workers before incorporation and they were paid wages at Rs. 100 p.m. Later, there were 35 workers in the company and they were being paid at Rs. 125 per month per worker.

(3) Further the number of clients which was 12 before incorporation later increased to 15 after incorporation. The amount of salary also increased from Rs. 200 per month to Rs. 300 per month per clerk.

From the above, find out the Sales Ratio and the total amount of wages and salaries prior to and after incorporation.

(Bangalore, April 1993)

Ans. : Sales Ratio = 25 : 28 or 625:700 (125×5 : 100 × 7)
Prior Sales Rs. 3,12,500 and after Sales Rs. 3,50,000
Prior Wages Rs. 12,500 (25 workers × 5 months × 100 *i.e.,* rate)
After Wages Rs. 30,625 (35 workers × 7 months × 125 *i.e.,* rate)
Prior Salaries Rs. 12,000 (12 clerks × 5 months × 100 *i.e.,* rate)
After Salaries Rs. 31,500 (15 clerks × 7 months × 125 *i.e.,* rate)

Hint. Let the sales for the period after incorporation be 100 p.a. Therefore, sales for the period before incorporation will be 125 p.a. (*i.e.,* 100 + 25)

15. A Co. Ltd. was formed on 1-7-1996 to take over the business of "B" with effect from 1-4-1996. The following was the Profit and Loss Account of the company for the year ending 31-3-1997 :

	Rs.		Rs.
To Salaries	48,000	By Gross Profit	2,50,000
To Rent and Taxes	19,200		
To Office expenses	8,000		
To Electricity	4,000		
To Insurance	3,200		
To Directors' fees	7,000		
To Auditors' fees	4,800		
To Interest on loans	2,400		
To Advertisement	2,000		
To Commission on sales	4,000		
To Carriage outwards	2,500		
To Bank charges	800		
To Bad debts	1,500		
To Preliminary expenses	3,000		
To Depreciation	5,600		
To Net profit	1,34,000		
	2,50,000		2,50,000

The total turnover for the year ending 31-3-97 was Rs. 10,00,000 divided into Rs. 2,00,000 for the period up to 1-7-96 and Rs. 8,00,000 for the remaining period. Ascertain the profit prior to and after incorporation.

(*Karnataka, Oct. 1998*)

Ans. : Profit prior to incorporation Rs. 24,000 and after incorporation Rs. 1,10,000.

Hint. (i) Time Ratio = 1 : 3 and Sales Ratio = 1 : 4

(ii) Audit fees, Bank charges & Insurance are allocated on time ratio.

16. X company was incorporated on 1-4-98 and acquired a business with effect from 1-1-98. Total sales for the year 1998 was Rs. 7,20,000.

Sales for January and February was 1¼ times the average sales. Sales from March to July was 2/3 of the average sales. Sales for August and September was ¼ of the average monthly sales and sales for October and November was double the average monthly sales and the balance of sales in December. Calculate Sales ratio.

(*Bangalore, April 1999*)

Ans. : Average Sales Rs. 60,000; Sales prior to incorporation Rs. 1,90,000; Sales after incorporation Rs. 5,30,000 and Sales ratio = 19 : 53.

17. Ascertain the profit prior to and loss after incorporation from the below given additional information and Profit and Loss Account for the year ended 31-03-1996 :

(a) Nanda Co. Ltd. was incorporated on 1-7-1995 taking over the business of Vanajaxi Co. Ltd. as from 1-4-1995.

(b) Sales upto 1-7-1995 amounted to Rs. 3,20,000 and thereafter Rs. 4,80,000.

(c) Rent was paid Rs. 400 p.m.

(d) Bad debt upto 30-6-1995 was Rs. 800.

Profit and Loss Account for the year ending 31-3-1996

Dr. Cr.

Expenses	Amount	Incomes	Amount
To Salaries	1,44,000	By Gross Profit	2,80,000
To Rent and Rates	7,200	By Net Loss c/d	12,000
To Office expenses	48,000		
To Commission on sales	32,000		
To Free samples	8,000		
To Audit fees	4,000		
To Depreciation	16,000		
To Interest on Debentures	12,000		
To Directors' fees	4,000		
To Formation expenses	4,000		
To Printing and Stationery	8,000		
To Sundry expenses	1,600		
To Bad debts	3,200		
	2,92,000		2,92,000

(Karnataka, April 1999)

Ans. : Prior profit Rs. 38,000 and After Loss Rs. 50,000.

Hints. (i) Time Ratio = 1 : 3 (3 months prior of 9 months after) and Sales Ratio = 2 : 3 (Prior sales Rs. 3,20,000 & After sales Rs. 4,80,000).

(ii) Allocation of Rent of Rates :

Total Rent and Rates		7,200
Less : Rent and rates prior to incorporation	1,200	
Rent and rates after incorporation	3,600	4,800
Balance of Rent & Rates allocated on time ratio		2,400

(C) Solve the following problems :

(Each carrying 15/16 marks)

1. Ambica Co. Ltd. was incorporated on 1-4-1991 to take over the business of Aravind Co. Ltd. as from 1-1-1991. The following was the Profit & Loss Account of the latter company as on 31-12-1991:

	Rs.		Rs.
To Salaries & Wages	36,000	By Gross Profit	70,000
To Rent & Rates	1,800	By Net Loss	3,000
To Office Expenses	12,000		
To Commission on Sales	8,000		
To Advertisement	2,000		
To Audit Fees	1,000		
To Depreciation	4,000		
To Interest on Debentures	3,000		
To Directors' Fees	2,000		
To Printing & Stationery	2,400		
To Bad debts	800		
	73,000		73,000

Additional information

(a) Sales for the first three months amounted to Rs. 80,000 and Rs. 1,20,000 for the next nine months.

(b) Rent was paid at Rs. 100 per month.

(c) Bad debts include Rs. 200 upto 31-3-1991.

Prepare a statement showing profit or loss prior to and after incorporation.

(Karnataka, April 1993 & 1998)

Ans. : Profit prior to incorporation Rs. 9,500 and loss after incorporation Rs. 12,500.

Hints (i) Sales Ratio 2 : 3 and Time Ratio 1 : 3.

(ii) Bad Debts : Prior Rs. 200 and After Rs. 600.

(iii) Audit fees are allocated on time ratio.

2. X. Co. Ltd. was incorporated on 1-8-1995 to take over the business of M/s. X and Y as a going concern as from 1-4-1995. The profit and loss account of the company for the year ending 31-3-1996 was as follows :

	Rs.		Rs.
To Salaries & Allowances	60,000	By Gross Profit	2,00,000
To Rent & Taxes	23,000		
To General Expenses	7,200		
To Directors' Fees	3,000		
To Selling Expenses	4,000		
To Discount on Sales	1,000		
To Advertisement	3,000		
To Audit Fees	4,500		
To Formation Expenses	1,800		
To Miscellaneous Expenses	1,500		
To Interest on Debentures	1,400		
To Interest to Vendors (upto 30-9-1995)	6,000		
To Repairs to Buildings	1,200		
To Depreciation	2,400		
To Net Profit	80,000		
	2,00,000		2,00,000

The following is the further information

(a) Rent was paid at Rs. 1,000 per month upto 1-8-1995 and thereafter it was increased to Rs. 2,000 per month.

(b) The average monthly sales for the first 4 months during the year was Rs. 60,000, whereas the average monthly sales for the subsequent period was Rs. 70,000.

Prepare the statement showing profit prior to incorporation of the company.

(Karnataka, Oct. 1990)

Ans. : Profit prior to incorporation Rs. 23,000 and profit after incorporation Rs. 57,000.

Hints. (i) Sales Ratio 3 : 7 and Time Ratio 1 : 2

(ii) Allocation of Rent and Rates :

Total of Rent & Rates		23,000
Less : Prior rent (1,000 × 4)	4,000	
After rent (2,000 × 8)	16,000	20,000
Balance is allocated on time ratio		3,000

3. Ashok Ltd. was incorporated on 1st April to take over as from 1st January in the same year an existing business of Desai Bros. Under the agreement, all the profits made from 1st January are to belong to the company. The following balances appeared in the company's ledger as at 31st December :

	Rs.		Rs.
Share Capital	4,50,000	Preliminary Expenses	
Bank Overdraft	1,65,000	written off	8,000
Sundry Creditors	65,000	Salaries	48,000
Fixed Deposits	35,000	Rent Received	13,000
Freehold Land	50,000	Rates and Taxes	7,000
Building at Cost	1,30,000	Repairs to Building	3,000
Furniture	15,000	Miscellaneous Expenses	22,000
Transport Vehicles	35,000	Directors' Fees	2,400
Stock on 1st January	4,20,000	Interest to Vendors	17,500
Book Debts	95,000	(upto 30th June)	
Cash in hand	12,000	Purchases	7,70,000
		Sales	9,10,000
		Goodwill	3,100

Stock on 31st December amounted to Rs. 4,80,000. Bad debts amounting to Rs. 1,000 of which Rs. 500 related to book debts taken over by the company and a provision of Rs. 5,000 to be made for doubtful debts.

Depreciation has to be written off at 5% on buildings, 10% on furniture and 20% on vehicles.

Prepare : (a) Trading Account (b) Profit and Loss Account showing profit post and prior to incorporation of the company (assuring that the sales are evenly spread over throughout the year)

(Karnataka, Oct. 1988)

Ans. : Profit prior to incorporation Rs. 19,000 and Profit after incorporation Rs. 65,100.

Hint (i) Sales Ratio 1 : 3 and Time Ratio 1 : 3.

4. A company acquires a business as on 1st January, 1974, it being incorporated on the 1st May, 1974. The 1st accounts are drawn upto the 30th September, 1974.

The gross profit for the period is Rs. 56,000. The general expenses are Rs. 14,220, directors' fees Rs. 12,000 per annum; formation expenses Rs. 1,500.

Rent up to 30th June was Rs. 1,200 per annum, after which it was increased to Rs. 3,000 per annum.

Salary of the manager, who upon incorporation of the company was made a director, was Rs. 6,000 per annum (since incorporation included in directors' fees above).

Show Profit and Loss Account assuming that the net sales were Rs. 8,20,000 the monthly average of which for the first four months of 1974 being one half of that of the remaining period. The company earned a uniform profit. Interest and tax may be ignored.

(I.C.W.A., June 1976)

Ans. : Prior profit Rs. 7,280 and after profit Rs. 26,150.

Hints (i) Time ratio 4 : 5 (*i.e.*, 4 months prior and 5 months after)

(ii) *Calculation of Sales Ratio*

First 4 months sales (Say) 1.

∴ Subsequent sales will be 2.

No. of units = Prior 1 × 4 = 4
After 2 × 5 = 10 } *i.e.*, 4 : 10 or 2 : 5

(iii) *Allocation of Rent*

4 months at Rs. 100 = Rs. 400 (prior)
2 months at Rs. 100 = Rs. 200
3 months at Rs. 250 = Rs. 750 } Rs. 950 (After)

(iv) *Salary of the manager for the first four months*

Rs. 2,000 (6,000 × 4/12)

(v) *Directors' Fees* Rs. 5,000 (5 months at Rs. 1,000 PM).

5. The Fox Ltd. was incorporated on 1st April, 1980 for the purpose of taking over the business of the Sheep Stores as a going concern from 1st January, 1980. Purchase consideration will be paid on 31st December, 1980 and the vendors will be entitled to 50 per cent of the profits earned prior to incorporation in lieu of interest on unpaid purchase consideration. The summarised trading results on the basis of the accounts prepared for the year ended on 31st December, 1980 were as follows :

	Rs.		Rs.
Purchases (after adjusting stocks)	3,50,000	Sales (Jan.— March)	1,00,000
		Sales (April —Dec.)	4,00,000
Gross Profit	1,50,000		
	5,00,000		5,00,000
General Expenses	90,000	By Gross Profit	1,50,000
Directors' Fees	7,000		
Formation Expenses	3,000		
Net Profit	50,000		
	1,50,000		1,50,000

Prepare a statement showing the profit earned prior to and after incorporation and the amount due to the vendors. Gross profit should be apportioned on the basis of turnover and general expenses on time basis.

(Adapted from I.C.W.A.– Final)

Ans. : Prior profit Rs. 6,562-50 and After profit Rs. 39,687-50.

Hints (i) Sales Ratio 1 : 4 and Time Ratio 1 : 3

(ii) Calculation and allocation of vendor's share of profit :

Pre-incorporation profit (before charging vendors' share of profit) Rs. 7,500

(*i.e.,* Prior G/P Rs. 30,000–Prior Expenses Rs. 22,500)

Vendors' share of profit is 50% of Prior profit *i.e.,* Rs. 3,750

As purchase consideration was outstanding throughout the year, vendor's share of profit should be allocated between two periods on the basis of time *i.e.,* prior Rs. 937.50 and after Rs. 2,812.50.

6. The Tiger Ltd. was formed on 1st April to take over the business formerly carried on by Messrs. Brown and Smith as from 1st January. It was agreed that all profits made subsequent to this later date should belong to the company, but interest on the purchase consideration (Rs. 50,000) at the rate of 6% per annum should be paid to the vendors until the final settlement, which took place on 1st June.

The following was the profit and loss account, as prepared on 31st December for the year ending on that date.:

	Rs.		Rs.
Expenses of Management	3,050	Gross Trading Profit	20,000
Bad Debts	200		
Directors' Fees	1,000		
Interest to Vendors	1,250		
Preliminary Expenses written off	500		
Depreciation	1,000		
Balance being Net Profit	13,000		
	20,000		20,000

It was found that, of the bad debts written off, Rs. 100 related to debts take over by the company.

Apportion the profits between prior and subsequent incorporation, assuming that turnover is spread evenly over the year.

(Bangalore, Nov. 1997)

Ans. : Prior profit Rs. 3,137-50 and after profit Rs. 9,862-50.

Hints (i) The time ratio 1 : 3 (*i.e.,* 3 months prior & 9 months after).

(ii) The turnover is evenly spread through out the year, that means, gross profit can be straightaway apportioned on time ratio.

(iii) Interest to vendors : Prior (*i.e.,* for 3 months) Rs. 750 and after (*i.e.,* for 2 months) Rs. 500.

(iv) Bad debts : Prior Rs. 100 and after Rs. 100.

7. The Wolf Ltd. was incorporated on 1st January 1981 with an authorised capital consisting of 5,000 equity shares of Rs. 10 each to take over the running business of Sheep as from 1st October, 1980.

The following is the summarised Profit and Loss Account for the year ended 30th September, 1981 :

	Rs.	Rs.
Sales :		
1st October, 1980 to 31st December, 1980	6,000	
1st January, 1981 to 30th September, 1981	19,000	25,000
Cost of Sale for the year	16,000	
Administrative Expenses	1,768	
Selling Commission	875	
Goodwill written off	200	
Interest paid of Vendors (Loan repaid on 1st Feb., 1981)	373	
Distribution Expenses (60 per cent variable)	1,250	
Preliminary Expenses written off	330	
Debenture Interest	320	
Depreciation	444	
Directors' Fees	100	21,660
Net Profit		3,340

The company deals in one type of product. The unit cost of sales was reduced by 10 per cent in the post-incorporation period as compared to the pre-incorporation period in the year.

You are required to prepare a statement apportioning the net profit amount between pre-incorporation and post-incorporation periods showing the basis of apportionment.

(Adapted from A.C.S. Inter)

Ans. : Pre-incorporation profit Rs. 496 and post-incorporation profit Rs. 2,844.

Hints (i) Time ratio 1 : 3 and sales ratio 6 : 19.

(ii) Interest to vendors = Prior (*i.e.,* for 3 months) Rs. 280 and after (*i.e.,* 1 month) Rs. 93.

(iii) Cost of sales ratio 60 : 171 (*i.e.,* 100 × 6000 : 90 × 19,000) (prior cost of sales Rs. 4,156 and after cost of sales Rs. 11,844).

8. The Leopard Private Ltd. was incorporated on 1st July, 1981 with an authorised capital of Rs. 5,00,000 in equity shares of Rs. 10 each to take over as a going concern as from 1st April, 1981, the existing business of Buffalo Brothers. The agreement for taking over provided that all profits made from 1st April, 1981, should belong to the company. The purchase consideration of Rs. 2,00,000 together with interest at 8¾ per cent p.a. was satisfied on 1st October, 1981, by the allotment to the vendors, 17,500 equity shares fully paid and the balance in cash.

The Trial Balance of the company on 31st March, 1982 was as follows :

	Dr. Rs.	Cr. Rs.
Share Capital	—	2,25,000
Freehold Land at cost	25,000	—
Buildings at cost	65,000	—
Furniture at cost	7,500	—
Salaries	12,000	—
Purchases (including stock taken over)	4,85,000	—
Sales (including sales prior to incorporation Rs. 75,000)	—	4,50,000
Sundry Debtors	45,000	—
Sundry Creditors	—	30,000
Rent received	—	6,000
Rates and Taxes	3,000	—
Repairs	1,500	—
Directors Fees	1,200	—
Miscellaneous Expenses	7,200	—
Interest to Vendors	8,750	—
Cash in hand	1,800	—
Cash at Bank	48,050	—
	7,11,000	7,11,000

You are required to prepare the Profit and Loss Account of the company for the year ended 31st March, 1982, and a Balance Sheet as on that date after taking into account the following adjustments :

(a) Stock on 31-3-1982, Rs. 1,40,000.

(b) Bad debts Rs. 500 (Including Rs. 200 out of book debts taken over from the vendors) to be written off.

(c) Provision for doubtful debts to be made at Rs. 2,500.

(d) Depreciate buildings by 5% and furniture by 10%.

(Bangalore, April 1994, Mod. & Adapted from I.C.W.A. Inter)

Ans. : Pre-incorporation profit Rs. 7,500 and after incorporation profit Rs. 62,850.

Hints (i) Time Ratio 1 : 3 and Sales Ratio 1 : 5.

(ii) Interest to Vendors : Prior (*i.e.,* for 3 months) Rs. 4,375 and after (*i.e.,* for 3 months) Rs. 4,375.

(iii) Bad debts : Prior Rs. 200 and after Rs. 300.

9. A company was incorporated on 30th June, 1983 to acquire the business of Mohan as from 1st January 1983. The accounts for the year ended 31st December 1983 disclosed the following :

(a) There was a gross profit of Rs. 2,40,000.

(b) The sales for the year amounted to Rs. 12,00,000 of which Rs. 5,40,000 were for the first six months.

(c) The expenses debited to Profit and Loss Account included Directors' fees Rs. 15,000, Bad Debts Rs. 3,600, Advertising Rs. 12,000 (under a contract amounting to Rs. 1,000 p.m.), Salaries and general expenses Rs. 64,000, Preliminary Expenses written off Rs. 5,000 and Donation to Political Party given by the company Rs. 5,000.

Prepare a statement showing the amount of profit made before and after incorporation.

(*Bangalore April, 1991*)

Ans. : Profit Prior to incorporation Rs. 68,380 and After incorporation Rs. 67,020; Time Ratio = 1 : 1 or 6 months : 6 months; Sales Ratio = 9 : 11 or 5,40,000 : 6,60,000.

Hint Donation to political parties is chargeable after incorporation.

10. Navin Enterprises purchased from Navin his business on 1-1-1991. But Navin Enterprises was incorporated on 1-4-1991. Find out from the following details, the profits earned by the company prior to and after incorporation :

(a) From January 1991 to December 1991 total sales was Rs. 2,40,000. The trend of sales was as follows :

January and February = half the average sales for each month.

May, June, July and October = average sales for each month.

November and December = Half the sales for each month.

(b) Cost of goods sold Rs. 60,000.

(c) Salary and other expenses Rs. 6,000.

(d) Bad Debts Rs. 2,400.

(e) Interest for purchase consideration which was paid to Navin's old business on 1-8-1991 Rs. 2,100.

(f) Expenses exclusively related to the company Rs. 8,900.

(*Bangalore, April 1992*)

Ans. : Profit prior to incorporation Rs. 34,600 and after incorporation Rs. 1,26,000.

Gross profit Rs. 1,80,000 (Sales Rs. 2,40,000 – 60,000 cost of sales)

Sales Ratio = 5 : 19 or 50,000 : 1,90,000

Time Ratio = 1 : 3 or 3 months : 9 months.

Hints (i) Interest on purchase consideration : prior (*i.e.,* for three months) Rs. 900 and After (*i.e.,* for four months) Rs. 1,200.

(ii) Averages sales per month Rs. 20,000 (2,40,000 ÷ 12); Sales for eight months : Rs. 1,20,000 *i.e.,* Jan. & Feb.– 10,000 each.

May, June, July & Oct.—20,000 each; Nov. & Dec.—10,000 each.

Sales for remaining 4 months : Rs. 1,20,000 (2,40,000 – 1,20,000 sales for eight months).

Averages sales per month for these four months (*i.e.,* March, April, Aug. & Sept.) : Rs. 30,000 (1,20,000/4); Pre-incorporation sales Rs. 50,000 (10,000 + 10,000 + 30,000); Post-incorporation sale Rs. 1,90,000(2,40,000 – 50,000).

11. Shankar Pvt. Ltd. Co. took over the business of Shankar on 1-4-1991 and it was incorporated on 1-7-1991. The Profit & Loss Account of Shankar Pvt. Ltd. on 31-3-1992 was as follows :

	Rs.		Rs.
To Commission (Sales)	2,625	By Gross Profit	98,000
To Advertising	5,250	By Bad Debts realised	500
To M.D.'s remuneration	9,000		
To Depreciation	2,800		
To Salaries	18,000		
To Insurance	600		
To Preliminary Expenses written off	700		
To Rent and Taxes	3,000		
To Discount	350		
To Bad Debts	1,250		
To Net Profit	54,925		
	98,500		98,500

Further Details

(a) The average monthly sales after incorporation was twice the average monthly sales before.

(b) Rent, which was paid for the first three months at Rs. 200 per month, increased by Rs. 50 per month for the balance of the period.

(c) Bad Debts of Rs. 350 related only to the period after 1-9-1991 and the balance related to the sales made up 1-9-1991.

(d) The Bad Debts realised belonged to the Bad Debts which were written off in 1989.

Find out the profits before and after incorporation.

(*Bangalore, November 1992*)

Ans. : Profit prior to incorporation Rs. 6,951 and After incorporation Rs. 47,974.

Notes : (i) Let the sales per month before incorporation be 1. So, sales per month after incorporation will be 2.

∴ Sales Ratio will be 1 : 6 or 3 : 18 (1 × 3 : 2:9).

(ii) Time Ratio will be 1 : 3 or 3 months : 9 months.

(iii) Of the bad debts of Rs. 1,250, Rs. 350 is related to post incorporation period and remaining Rs. 900 is related upto 31-8-1991. This should be distributed between the two periods in the sales ratio for the period.

Prior sale is 1 × 3 = 3 (April, May, June)

After sale is 2 × 2 = 4 (July, August)

Bad Debts of Rs. 900 are allocated in the ratio of 3:4. Hence, prior bad debts are Rs. 386 (900 × 3/7) and after bad debts are Rs. 864 *i.e.*, 350 + 514 (900 × 4/7).

(iv) Prior rent is Rs. 600 (200 × 3) and after rent is Rs. 2,250 (250 × 9). The remaining part of rent and taxes of Rs. 150 (3,000–2,850) are to be allocated in the time ratio.

(v) Bad debts realised is related to prior-incorporation period.

12. Gajendra Ltd. was incorporated on 1-7-1994 to takeover the business of G.K. Enterprises as a going concern with effect from 1-4-1994. Their Profit & Loss Account for the year ended 31.3.1995 is as follows :

Opening Stock	60,000	Sales	1,50,000
Purchases	87,500	(upto 30-6-94 Rs. 50,000)	
Administration Expenses	9,000	Closing Stock	30,000
Director's Fee	1,500		
Selling Expenses	18,000		
Audit Fees	500		
Preliminary Expenses	1,500		
Net Profit	7,000		
	1,85,000		1,85,000

Prepare a statement showing the profit earned prior to and after incorporation.

(*Bangalore, November 1995*)

Ans. : Sales Ratio = 1:2 or 50,000 : 1,00,000.
Time Ratio = 1:3 or 3 months : 9 months.
Gross Profit Rs. 37,500 (Sales Rs. 1,50,000 + Closing Stock Rs. 35,000 – 1,47,500 Opening stock *i.e.,* Rs. 60,000 and purchases *i.e.,* 87,500)
Prior profit Rs. 4,125 and After profit Rs. 2,875.

13. Victory Ltd. was incorporated on May 1, 1994 to take over the business of Camlin Ltd., as a going concern from 1-1-1994. The Profit and Loss Account for the year ending on 31-12-1994 is follows :

	Rs.		Rs.
Rent and Taxes	24,000	Gross Profit	3,10,000
Insurance	6,000		
Electricity Charges	4,800		
Salaries	72,000		
Director's Fees	6,000		
Auditor's Fees	3,200		
Commission	12,000		
Advertisement	8,000		
Discount	7,000		
Office Expenses	15,000		
Carriage	6,000		
Bank Charges	3,000		
Preliminary Expenses	13,000		
Bad Debts	4,000		
Interest on Loan	6,000		
Net Profit	1,20,000		
	3,10,000		3,10,000

The total turnover for the year ending 31-12-94 was Rs. 10,00,000 divided into Rs. 3,00,000 for the period upto 1-5-94 and Rs. 7,00,000 for the remaining period.

Ascertain the profits earned prior to and post incorporation period.

(Bangalore, April 1997)

Ans. : Sales Ratio 3 : 7 or 30000 : 700000; Time Ratio 1 : 2 or 4 months : 8 months; Profit prior to Incorporation Rs. 38,300 and After Incorporation Rs. 81,700.

*****

4

AMALGAMATION

GENERAL CONCEPTS

Amalgamation

Meaning: It refers to the formation of a new company to purchase the business of two or more existing companies. When two or more existing companies carrying on similar type of business go into liquidation and form themselves into a new company to purchase their existing business, it is called amalgamation. The result of such amalgamation is that all the existing companies are going into liquidation and a new company is going to be formed. For instance, a new company 'C' Ltd. is to be formed to take over the assets and liabilities of 'A' Ltd. and 'B' Ltd. The shareholders and debentureholders of old companies may become the shareholders and debentureholders of new companies.

Objectives and Advantages

The following are the main objectives and advantages of amalgamation:

(1) Secures large scale economies.

(2) Eliminates the competition between the amalgamating companies.

(3) Reduces the cost of operation of the business unit.

(4) Earns more profit and declares higher rate of dividend.

Absorption

Meaning: When one existing company purchases (*i.e.,* absorbs) the business of other existing company or companies engaged in a similar business, it is called absorption. Under absorption no new company is formed. One company continues to exist whereas others go into liquidation. For instance, the existing company 'A' Ltd. takes over the business of 'B' Ltd. In this case, A Ltd. is absorbing company and 'B' Ltd. is absorbed company. A Ltd. continues to exist and B Ltd. goes into liquidation.

Objectives and Advantages

The following are the main objectives and advantages of absorption :

(1) Eliminates weaker units.

(2) Avoids duplication of plants.

(3) Encourages specialisation of work.

(4) Secures large scale production and economies.

External Reconstruction

Meaning. When an existing company which has suffered heavy losses goes into liquidation and in its place altogether new company is formed, it is called external reconstruction. External reconstruction is an arrangement under which an existing company goes into liquidation and a new company is formed to purchase the business of the company going into liquidation. For instance, 'Y' Ltd. is formed to take over the business of 'X' Ltd. Under this system, the weak company goes into liquidation and in its place a new company is formed. The assets and liabilities of weak company are revalued and transferred to a new company.

Objectives and Advantages

The following are the main advantages and objectives of external reconstruction :

(1) Changes the domicile of the company.

(2) Widens the sphere of operations.

(3) Raises fresh capital by issuing partly paid shares to the shareholders of old company in exchange for fully paid shares held by them in the old company.

(4) Compromises the creditors and debenturesholders to sacrifice a part of their claims along with the shareholders.

From the above discussion it is clear that in each of the three cases, the following differences are appeared :

(1) *Amalgamation* : Two or more liquidate and one formation

(2) *Absorption* : One or more liquidation and no formation

(3) *External Reconstruction* : One liquidation and one formation.

But, in each of the three cases, the following common factors are appeared:

(1) A company/companies goes/go into liquidation

(2) An existing company or a new company takes over the business of the company going into liquidation.

Legal Concept of Amalgamation or Accounting for Amalgamation (AS-14)

The above concepts have been modified by the Companies Act and Accounting Standard-14.

As per the Companies Act, 1956, the term amalgamation includes absorption. The same opinion has been accecpted by the various courts in our country. In *S.S. Somayajulu* V. *Hop Prudhommee and Co. Ltd.* amalgamation has been explained as "a state of things under which either two companies are joined so as to form a third entity or one is absorbed into or blended with another".[1] So as per these views, in case of amalgamation, a new company may not be formed. This legal meaning of amalgamation is also recognised by the Accounting Standard (AS)-14.

According to **Accounting Standard (AS)-14 "Accounting for Amalgamation", issued by the Institute of Chartered Accountants of India,** amalgamation means amalgamation pursuant to the provisions of the Companies Act, 1956 or any other statute which may be applicable to companies. As per this definition, amalgamation means, coming together of two or more companies to form a new company, or merging of two or more existing companies to form a new company, or taking over an existing company by a new company specially formed for the purpose. It means amalgamation includes amalgamation, absorption and external reconstruction. Therefore, the accounting for amalgamation, absorption and external reconstruction is just called **accounting for amalgamation.**

Accounting Standard-14 came into effect on 1st April, 1995. It is mandatory and not optional. It deals with accounting for all cases of amalgamation *i.e.*, amalgamation, absorption and external reconstruction.

Different Terms Used

Transferor Company : It means a company which is amalgamated into another company.

Transferee Company : It means a company into which a transferor Company is amalgamated.

Purchase Consideration : It means price payable by the transferee company to the shareholders of transferor company.

Taking over of Business : It means purchasing company takes over assets and liabilities of vendor company unless otherwise stated.

Reserves : As per AS-14 reserve means the portion of earnings, receipts or other surplus of enterprise (whether capital or revenue) appropriated by the management for a general or a specific purpose other than a provision for depreciation or diminution in the value of assets or for a known liability.

Dissentient Shareholders : They are the shareholders who have failed or refused to transfer their shares to the transferee company.

Types of Amalgamation

As per Accounting Standard-14, amalgamation is classified into two categories. They are :

1. Amalgamation in the nature of merger.
2. Amalgamation in the nature of purchase.

1. Amalgamation in the nature of merger : An amalgamation will be considered to be in the nature of merger when the following conditions are satisfied.

(i) All the assets and liabilities of the transferor company become, after amalgamation, the assets and liabilities of the transferee company.

(ii) Shareholders holding not less than 90% of the face value of the equity shares of the transferor company (other than equity shares held there in, immediately before the amalgamation, by the transferee company or its subsidiaries or their nominees) become equity shareholders of the transferee company by virtue of the amalgamation.

(iii) The consideration for the amalgamation receivable by those equity shareholders of the transferor company, who agree to become equity shareholders of the transferee company, is discharged by the transferee company wholly by the issue of equity shares in the transferee company, except that cash may be paid in respect of any fractional shares.

(iv) The business of the transferor company is intended to be carried on after amalgamation by the transferee company.

(v) No adjustment is intended to be made to the book value of the assets and liabilities of the transferor company when they are incorporated in the financial statement of the transferee company except to ensure uniformity of accounting policies.

In this type of amalgamation, there is a genuine pooling of assets and liabilities of the combining entities. In addition, the equity shareholders of the combining entities continue to have a proportionate share in the combined entity. It must be ensured that the resultant figures of assets, liabilities, capital and reserves more or less represent the sum of relevant figures of the amalgamating companies.

2. Amalgamation in the nature of purchase : When any one or more of the conditions specified above for amalgamation in the nature of merger is not satisfied, it is called amalgamation in the nature of purchase. In this type of amalgamation usually one company acquires another company and the equity shareholders of combining entities do not continue to have proportionate share in the equity of the combined entity and the business of the acquired company is not intended to be continued after the amalgamation.

Distinction between Merger and Purchase

Merger	Purchase
1. There is genuine merger or pooling of all assets, liabilities and shareholders' interest of amalgamating companies.	1. There is acquisition of business. Therefore, there is no genuine pooling of assets, liabilities and shareholders' interest of amalgamating company.
2. Not less than 90% of equity shareholders of transferor company become the equity shareholders of transferee company.	2. The shareholders of transferor company need not become equity shareholders of transferee company.
3. All assets and liabilities are transferred without revaluation (except for ensuring uniformity in accounting policies).	3. Takenover assets and liabilities may be revalued.
4. Purchase consideration is paid in equity shares only (except cash for fraction of share).	4. Purchase consideration may be paid in the form of shares, debentures and cash.
5. The business of transferor company is continued by the transferee company after amalgamation.	5. The business of transferor may or may not be continued by the transferee company after amalgamation.
6. The shareholders of transferor company have proportionate share in the equity of transferee company.	6. The shareholders of transferor company do not continue to have a proportionate share in the equity of transferee company.
7. Accounting method adopted in the books of transferee company is 'Pooling of Interests Method.'	7. Accounting method adopted in the books of transferee company is 'Purchase Method.'

Methods of Accounting for Amalgamation

The accounting method for amalgamatin in the books of transferor company is the same under both the methods of amalgamation (*i.e.,* merger and purchase). But, the accounting method for amalgamation in the books of transferee company is different depending upon the type of amalgamation.

There are two methods of accounting for amalgamation in the books of transferee company. They are :

1. Pooling of interests method
2. Purchase method.

1. Pooling of Interests Method

This method of accounting is applicable for amalgamatin in the nature of merger. According to Accounting Standard-14, the following factors should be taken into account while making the accounting entries in this method :

(i) In this case, the amalgamation is accounted for as if the separate businesses of the amalgamating companies were intended to be carried on by the transferee (i.e., amalgamated) company. Accordingly, only minimum changes are made in aggregating the individual financial statements of the amalgamating companies.

(ii) The assets, liabilities and reserves (whether capital or revenue arising on revaluation) of the transferor company should be recorded at their existing carrying amounts and in the same form as at the date of amalgamation. The balance of P & L A/c of the transferor company should be aggregated with the corresponding balance of the transferee company or transferred to general reserve, if any. This reflects the fact that the entries are simply merged together. No goodwill account should be accounted for.

(iii) The difference between the amount recorded as share capital issued (plus any additional consideration in the form of cash or other assets) and the amount of share capital of the trnasferor company should be adjusted against the reserves of transferee company.

(iv) If, at the time of amalgamation, the transferor company and the transferee company have conflicting (*i.e.,* different) accounting policies, a uniform set of accounting policies should be adopted after amalgamation. The effects of any changes in accounting policies on the financial statements of the transferee company should be appropriately disclosed [*i.e.,* reported in accordance wih the Accounting Standard (AS)-5 as "Prior Period and Extraordinary Items and Changes in Accounting Policies"]

2. Purchase Method

This method of accounting is applicable for amalgamation in the nature of purchase. According to Accounting Standard-14, the following factors should be considered while making the accounting entries in this method :

(i) In the books of transferee company the assets and liabilities of the transferor company should be incorporated at their existing carrying amount or the consideration should be allocated to individual identifiable assets and liabilities on the basis of their fair values.

(ii) The reserves (whether capital or revenue arising on revaluation) of the transferor company other than the statutory reserves should not be included in the financial statement of the transferee company.

(iii) Any excess of the purchase consideration over the value of net assets of the transferor company should be treated as goodwill and debited to goodwill account. On the other hand, if the purchase consideration is lower than the value of net assets acquired, the difference should be credited to capital reserve.

(iv) If it becomes necessary to carry forward any statutory reserve of the transferor company in the books of the transferee for legal compliance, it is accounted by debiting 'Adjustment Account' and crediting 'Statutory Reserve Account'.

(v) The Amalgamation Adjustment Account should be disclosed as a part of Miscellaneous Expenditure in the Balance Sheet. When the identity of statutory reserve is no longer required to be maintained, both Statutory Reserve Account and Amalgamation Adjustment Account should be reversed.

Distinction between the Pooling of Interests Method and Purchase Method

Pooling of Interests Method	Purchase Method
(1) It is applicable for amalgamation in the nature of purchase.	(1) It is applicable for amalgmation in the nature of purchase.
(2) All assets and liabilities of transferor company are recorded by the transferee company in its books of account.	(2) Only assets and liabilities taken over by the transferee company are recorded by the transferee company in its books of account.
(3) All reserves and profits are transferred to the books of transferee company without opening Amalgamated Adjustment A/c.	(3) Only statutory reserves are transferred by opening Amalgamated Adjustment A/c. Other reserves or profits are not transferred.
(4) It is total incorporation of financial figures.	(4) It is partial incorporation of financial figures.
(5) It is a complete aggregation of financial figures.	(5) It is only a partial aggregation of financial figures.

Contd.

(6) All assets and liabilities are recorded in the books of purchasing company at book values.	(6) Assets and liabilities are recorded in the books of purchasing company at fair values.
(7) Shares issued by the purchasing company as purchase consideration are valued at par value.	(7) Shares issued by the purchasing company as purchase consideration are valued at market price.
(8) The difference between purchase consideration and share capital of transferor company is adjusted in general reserve account or other reserve (*i.e.* profit or loss is revenue nature).	(8) The difference between the purchase consideration and the net assets taken over is treated as Goodwill or Capital Reserve (*i.e.,* Capital profit or loss).
(9) Amalgamation expenses paid by the transferee company is debited to Reserve A/c/ P & L A/c.	(9) Amalgamation expenses paid by the transferee company are charged to Goodwill A/c.
(10) Since all reserves are taken into account, Amalgamation Adjustment A/c does not appear in the books of transferee company.	(10) When the statutory reserves are required to be carried forward by the transferee company, Amalgamation Adjustment A/c appears in the books of transferee company.

Purchase Consideration

Meaning : Purchase consideration means the amount payable by the purchasing company to the vendor company for the assets taken over. As per the Accounting Standard (AS-14), consideration for amalgamation means the aggregate (*i.e.*, total) of the shares and other securities issued and the payment made in the form of cash or other assets by the transferee company to the shareholders of the transferor company.

From the above definition, it is clear that the payments made by the transferee company only to the shareholders of the transferor company constitute purchase consideration. But the direct payments made by the transferee company to the debentureholders or creditors of the transferor company do not constitute purchase consideration. For example, if the old debentureholders in the selling company are paid by issuing new debentures of purchasing company, new debentures issued to the old debentureholders do not constitute purchase consideration. But, if the shareholders in the selling company are paid by the purchasing company through debentures, these debentures form part of purchase consideration. Purchase consideration may be paid in the form of shares or debentures or in cash or other assets.

Calculation of Purchase Consideration

When the purchase price is specifically stated in the problem, the question of calculation of purchase consideration does not arise. In case the purchase consideration is not mentioned in the problem, it should be calculated. Calculation of purchase consideration would be the same, whatever may be the method of amalgamation. The following are the different methods of calculating purchase price :

(1) Net Assets Method
(2) Net Payment Method
(3) Combination of Net Assets and Total Payment Method
(4) A Lump Sum Method
(5) Intrinsic Value Method
(6) Shares Exchange Method.

1. Net Assets Method or Net Worth Basis : Under this method, the purchase consideration is arrived at by adding the agreed valued of assets taken over and deducting there from the agreed value of liabilities taken over by the purchasing company. It is given in the form of statement as below :

Statement showing the computation of purchase consideration under Net Assets Method.

	Rs.
Agreed values of assets taken over by the transferee company from the transferor company	****
Less : Agreed values of liabilities taken over by the transferee company from the transferor company	****
Net worth or purchase consideration	****

Here, net worth is considered as purchase consideration. Net assets represent the claims of only shareholders. The amount of purchase consideration paid by the transferee company to the shareholders of the transferor company may be in the form of preference shares or equity shares or in cash or other assets.

This method is useful when some form of payment is missing. While calculating the purchase consideration the following points should be noted :

(i) Only agreed value of those assets and liabilities which have been taken over by the purchasing company should be considered. But book value of these assets and liabilities should not be considered.

(ii) Assets and liabilities which are not taken over by the purchasing company should not be considered.

(iii) Fictitious assets and expenses such as preliminary expenses, discount on issue of shares or debentures, underwriting commission, advertising suspense etc., and the debit balance of P&L A/c appearing on the assets side of the B/S of the vendor company should not be considered.

(iv) Accumulated profits such as credit balance of P & L A/c, general reserve, dividend equalisation fund, insurance fund, sinking fund, contingency fund, investment fluctuations fund, share premium, capital reserves etc., appearing on the liabilities side of the B/S vendor company should not be considered. They should be transferred to shareholders account.

(v) Gratuity fund, provident fund, pension fund, workmen profit sharing fund etc., represent the liabilities to the employees. Therefore, if they are taken over by the purchasing company, they should be considered. But they should not be transferred to shareholder account since they are exclusive liabilities.

(vi) In case of workmen's compensation fund and accident fund, if there is no such liability, the entire amount represents accumulated profits and transferred to shareholders. In case there is any liability accrued on these funds, that part of the fund will be deemed to be liability and the balance treated as accumulated profit.

This method will be clear from the following example :

Balance Sheet of 'X' Co. Ltd. as at 31-12-1997

Liabilities	Rs.	Assets	Rs.
Share Capital :	1,00,000	Goodwill	20,000
8% Debentures	20,000	Buildings	50,000
General Reserve	10,000	Machinery	40,000
Bills Payable	5,000	Stock	25,000
Sundry Creditors	10,000	Debtors	10,000
Profit and Loss A/c	8,000	Cash	5,000
		Preliminary Expenses	3,000
	1,53,000		1,53,000

Calculate the purchase consideration under the following circumstances:

(A) 'Y' Co. Ltd. takes over the total assets and liabilities of Rs. 1,10,000 and Rs. 10,000 respectively of 'X' Co. Ltd.

(B) 'Y' Co. Ltd. takes over all assets and liabilities of 'X' Co. Ltd. at their book values.

(C) 'Y' Co. Ltd. agreed to take over the business of 'X' Co. Ltd. The agreed values of various assets and liabilities are—Goodwill Rs. 15,000; Buildings Rs. 40,000; Machinery Rs. 36,000; Stock at book value; Debtors subject to 5% reserve for doubtful debts; Bills Payable at book value and Creditors are taken over subject to 5% discount, but, Ltd. does not take over cash.

Solution :

Calculation of purchase consideration

(A) In this case purchase consideration will be Rs. 1,00,000
i.e., Net Assets = Value of assets taken over - value of liabilities taken over = Rs. 1,10,000 – Rs. 10,000 = Rs. 1,00,000

(B) In this case purchase consideration is as under :

		Rs.
Agreed value of assets taken over :		
Goodwill		20,000
Buildings		50,000
Machinery		40,000
Stock		25,000
Debtors		10,000
Cash		5,000
		1,50,000
Less : Agreed value of liabilities taken over :		
8% Debentures	20,000	
Bills Payable	5,000	
Sundry Creditors	10,000	35,000
Purchase consideration		1,15,000

(C) In this case purchase consideration is as under :

Agreed value of assets taken over :			
Goodwill			15,000
Building			40,000
Machinery			36,000
Stock			25,000
Debtors		10,000	
Less : R.D.D.		500	9,500
			1,25,500
Less : Agreed value of liabilities taken over :			
Bills Payable		5,000	
Sundry Creditors	10,000		
Less : Reserve for discount	500	9,500	14,500
Purchase consideration			1,11,000

Note : Debentures are not taken over by Y Co. Ltd.

(2) Net Payment Method :

Under this method, purchase consideration is ascertained by adding up the agreed value of shares and debentures allotted and cash paid by the purchasing company to the shareholders of the selling company. For example, if the purchasing company agrees to pay Rs. 50,000 in shares, Rs. 75,000 in debentures and Rs. 1,25,000 in cash to the shareholders of the selling company, the purchase consideration would be a sum of Rs. 2,50,000. Therefore, net payment that the purchasing company agrees to pay to the shareholders of selling company may comprise shares and other securities issued and payment made in the form of cash and other assets.

The following points should be noted while ascertaining the purchase consideration under this method :

(i) Assets and liabilities taken over by the purchasing company should not be considered.

(ii) Payments made by the purchasing company to the shareholders in the form of cash, shares or debentures should be taken into account.

(iii) When debentures and creditors are taken over by the purchasing company and directly discharged by the purchasing company, then such an amount should not be considered. Because, as per Accounting Standard-14, payments made by the transferee company to the persons other than the shareholders of the transferor company should not be treated as part of the purchase consideration.

(iv) Liquidation expenses of the transferor borne by the transferee are to be ignored.

(v) Any payment made by the purchasing company to some other party on behalf of the selling company should not be considered.

This method will be clear from the following example :

Balance Sheet of 'A' Ltd. as on 31-12-2009

Liabilities	Rs.	Assets	Rs.
Share Capital :		Building	1,70,000
1000 Equity shares of		Machinery	60,000
Rs. 100 each fully paid	1,00,000	Furniture	25,000
2000 Preference shares		Stock	38,000
of Rs. 100 each fully paid	2,00,000	Debtors	33,000
8% Debentures	1,00,000	Bills Receivable	87,000
General Reserve	20,000	Cash at Bank	20,000
Sundry Creditors	7,000	Cash on Hand	2,000
Workmen's Saving Bank	3,000		
Employees Profit Sharing Fund	5,000		
	4,35,000		4,35,000

Calculate the purchase consideration under the following circumstances :

(A) 'B' Co. Ltd. agrees to take over the business of 'A' Co. Ltd. Purchase price is to be satisfied by issue of 3000 shares of Rs. 100 each in 'B' Ltd. and the cash of Rs. 50,000.

(B) 'B' Co. Ltd. takes over the business of 'A' Ltd. B agrees to pay Rs. 50 per equity share and also 10 fully paid equity shares of Rs. 10 each at a market value of Rs. 15 each for every equity share held in 'A' Co. Ltd. It agrees to pay Rs. 15 per preference share and also issue 8 fully paid preference shares of Rs. 10 each at a premium of Rs. 5 per share for every preference share held in 'A' Ltd. It also agrees to pay cash for debentureholders at a premium of 10%.

(C) 'B' Co. Ltd. takes over the business of 'A' Co. Ltd. 'B' Co. Ltd. has agreed as under :

(i) To pay Rs. 30 per share in cash and to issue 5 equity shares of Rs. 100 each at a market value of Rs. 110 each it exchange for every 4 equity shares held in 'A' Co. Ltd.

(ii) To issue 8 preference shares of Rs. 100 each for every 10 preference shares held in 'A' Co. Ltd.

(iii) To issue mortgage debentures at Rs. 95 in lieu of debentures in 'A' Co. Ltd. which are redeemed at a premium of 10%.

(D) 'B' C. Ltd. agreed to take over the business of 'A' Co. Ltd. on the following basis :

(i) One equity share of Rs. 100 each at Rs. 120 per share fully paid in 'B' Co. Ltd. to be issued for every 2 equity shares in 'A' Co. Ltd.

(ii) Three equity shares of Rs. 100 each at Rs. 120 per share fully paid in 'B' Ltd. to be issued for every five preference shares in 'A' Ltd. and Rs. 50 per share in cash.

(iii) Debentureholders in 'A' Ltd. to be discharged at 10% premium by issue of 6% debentures in 'B' Ltd.

(iv) Rs. 5,000 for liquidation expenses.

Solution :

Calculation of purchase consideration :

(A) In this case purchase price is Rs. 3,50,000. Out of this amount Rs. 3,00,000 in the form of shares and balance Rs. 50,000 in cash.

(B) In this case the purchase consideration is arrived as below :

In cash	:	on equity shares (1000 × 50)	50,000
	:	on preference shares (2000 × 15)	30,000
In equity shares	:	(1000 × 10 ×15)	1,50,000
In preference shares	:	(2000 × 8 × 15)	2,40,000
		Purchase consideration	Rs. 4,70,000

Note : Payment to debentureholders does not form part of purchase consideration. It will be taken up by the purchasing company and then, discharged.

(C) In this case purchase consideration is ascertained as under :

In cash	:	on equity shares (1,000 × 30)	30,000
In equity shares	:	1,000 × 5/4 = 1250 shares × 110	1,37,500
In preference shares	:	2000 × 8/4 =1600 shares × 100	1,60,000
		Purchase consideration	3,27,500

Note : Issue of mortgage debentures is not included in the purchase consideration.

(D) In this purchase consideration is as under :

In equity shares	:	1,000 × 1/2 = 500 shares × 120	60,000
In preference shares	:	2,000 × 3/5 =1,200 shares × 120	1,44,000
In cash	:	2,000 shares × 50	1,00,000
		Purchase consideration	3,04,000

Note : Discharge of debentureholders and the liquidation expenses of vendor company are not considered as part of purchase consideration.

(3) Combination of Net Assets and Net Payment Method : Under this method purchase consideration is to be calculated as per both methods explained above. In this method firstly purchase price is calculated as per net assets method and further any payment agreed to be paid by the purchasing company is added. The total of such amount is treated as purchase consideration under this method.

(4) A Lump sum Method : In this case, a fixed amount is paid by the purchasing company to the vendor company to take over the business. Therefore, there is no question of calculating purchase consideration. For example, Q Co. Ltd. takes over the business of R Co. Ltd. for Rs. 7,00,000. In this case, purchase consideration is Rs. 7,00,000.

(5) Intrinsic Value Method : The value arrived at by dividing net value of assets of a company by the number of its equity shares is called intrinsic (*i.e.,* real) value. Under this method, intrinsic value is calculated as below :

Agreed value of assets taken over	****
Less: Agreed value of liabilities taken over	****
Net value of Assets	****

$$\text{Intrinsic value per share} = \frac{\text{Net Value of Assets}}{\text{Number of Equity Shares}}$$

If net value of assets is Rs. 6,00,000 (agreed value of assets taken over Rs. 16,00,000 – agreed value of liabilities taken over Rs. 10,00,000) and the number of shares of B Co. Ltd. are 50,000, then, intrinsic value per share would be Rs. 12 (Rs. 6,00,000 ÷ 50,000).

Under this method, purchase consideration is calculated on the basis of intrinsic value of shares of transferor company. For example, the paid-up share capital of B. Co. Ltd. consists of 50,000 equity shares of Rs. 10 each fully paid and the intrinsic value of each equity shares of B. Co. Ltd. is Rs. 12, then, the purchase consideration payable to B. Co. Ltd. would be Rs. 6,00,000 (50,000 × 12).

Sometimes intrinsic value of both the transferor and transferee company are given. In that case, the intrinsic values of both the companies are taken into account in calculating the purchase consideration. It can be dealt in the share exchange method.

(6) Shares Exchange Method : In this method, the purchase consideration is calculated on the basis of the ratio in which the shares of the purchasing company are to be exchanged for the shares of selling company. The ratio is determined on the basis of intrinsic value or agreed value of shares of each of the companies. For example :

	P Co. Ltd.		Q Co. Ltd.
Net value of assets	Rs. 10,00,000		Rs. 20,00,000
Number of shares	10,000		10,000
Intrinsic value per share	Rs. 100		Rs. 200
Share exchange ratio	1	:	2

If Q Co. Ltd. takes over P Co. Ltd., Q Co. Ltd. has to give one share in exchange of two shares in P Co. Ltd. It means Q Co. Ltd. has to give 5 thousand (*i.e.,* 10,000 ÷ 2) shares to take over the business of P Co. Ltd.

Another example is given as below :

Following is the Balance Sheet of X Ltd.

Liabilities	Rs.	Assets	Rs.
Share Capital : 10,000 Shares of Rs. 100 each	10,00,000	Sundry Assets	12,10,000
Debentures : 1,000 Debentures of Rs. 100 each	1,00,000		
General Reserve	50,000		
Creditors	60,000		
	12,10,000		12,10,000

Y Ltd. takes over the business of X Ltd. Y Ltd. has agreed as under :

(1) To pay Rs. 10 per share in cash and to issue 4 shares of Rs. 100 each at the market Value of Rs. 110 each in exchange for every 2 shares held in X Ltd.

(2) To issue 15% debentures at Rs. 95 in lieu of debentures in X Ltd. which are to be redeemed at a premium of 10%.

Calculate purchase consideration.

Solution :

Calculation of purchase consideration

Shareholders of X Ltd. :

(i)	In Cash (10,000 shares × Rs. 10)	1,00,000
(ii)	In Shares (4 shares for 2 shares then for 10,000 shares = $10,000 \times \frac{4}{2} = 20,000$ shares at Rs. 110 per share)	22,00,000
	Purchase consideration	23,00,000

Note : As per Accounting Standard - 14, payment to debentureholders does not form part of purchase consideration.

Accounting Entries for Amalgamation

In the books of Vendor Company or Selling Company :

Accounting entries to be passed for amalgamation in the books of vendor company is same under both the methods of amalgamation (*i.e.,* amalgamation in the nature of merger and amalgamation in the nature of purchase).

When the vendor company wound up, its all assets are disposed and all liabilities are paid and the surplus if any is to be distributed to shareholders. For this purpose an account called, 'Realisation Account', prepared to ascertain the profits or losses on realisation. Therefore, the following closing entries are to be passed in the books of vendor company to close the books:

Stage I : Entries to close all the accounts that appear in the Balance Sheet

(1) For transferring assets taken over by the purchasing company :

Realisation Account	Dr.	With total amount
To Individual Assets A/c		With book value

Notes : (i) If cash and bank balances are not taken over by the purchasing company, they should not be transferred to realisation account. Because they are in the realised form and they will not realise further. But other assets such as goodwill account and other intangible assets like trademarks, patent rights (which do not have any value) even if they are not taken over by the purchasing company should be transferred to the realisation account. Because they have to be realised by the selling company in some other way.

(ii) Fictitious such as preliminary expenses, discount on shares or debentures, debit balance in the P & L A/c etc., are not included in the definition of assets. They represent past losses. Hence, they should not be transferred to realisation account. They should be directly transferred to shareholders' account.

(2) For transferring the fictitious assets or the accumulated expenses and losses not yet written off :

Equity Shareholders' Account	Dr.	With total amount
To Preliminary Expenses A/c		With respective amounts as per Balance sheet
To Discount on Shares or Debentures A/c		
To Profit and Loss A/c (Dr. Balance)		
To Underwriting Commission A/c		
To Any Other Fictitious Assets A/c		

(3) For transferring the provisions against assets such as provision for bad debts, provision for discount on debtors, provision for depreciation etc. :

Individual Provision Against Assets A/c	Dr.	With the amount of each provision
To Realisation Account		With total amount

(4) For transferring the liabilities including debentures taken over by the purchasing company :

Individual Liabilities A/c	Dr.	With book value
To Realisation Account		With total amount

Notes :

(i) All those liabilities including debentures which are not taken over by the purchasing company are not to be transferred to realisation account. They are paid by the selling company directly.

(ii) Accumulated profits such as credit balance of P & L A/c, insurance fund, contingency reserve, plant replacement reserve, share premium, general reserve, sinking fund, dividend equalisation fund, development rebate reserve, capital redemption reserve, forfeited shares account, capital reserve, etc. are not be transferred to realisation account. These are profit items belonging to shareholders. Therefore, they should be directly transferred to shareholders' account.

(iii) All those liabilities which the purchasing company agrees to pay out are not to be transferred to realisation account.

(iv) Workmen's or employees' savings bank deposits, workmen's or employees' profit sharing fund, employees' pension fund, provident fund, superannuation fund, employees' security deposits etc., are the funds relating to workmen or employees. These are the funds payable by the employer to their employees. So, these are the liabilities for the vendor company. If these liabilities are taken over by the purchasing company, they should be transferred to realisation account at their book values. But, if these liabilities are not taken over by the purchasing company, they should be paid by the vendor company by debiting concerned liability account and crediting Cash or Bank Account.

(v) Any fund (*e.g.*, accident compensation fund) which partially represents liability and partially accumulated profits, then, that portion which represents a liability should be transferred to realisation account.

(5) For transferring provision against liability like provision for discount on creditors :

Provision for Liability A/c	Dr.	With the amount of provision for liabilities
To Realisation A/c		

(6) For transferring share capital and accumulated profits:

Share Capital A/c	Dr.	With respect amount as per Balance Sheet
General Reserve A/c	Dr.	
Dividend Equalisation Fund A/c	Dr.	
Share Premium A/c	Dr.	
Profit and Loss A/c	Dr.	
Accident Compensation Fund A/c	Dr.	
(To that extent it does not denote a liability)		
Share Forfeited A/c	Dr.	
Any Other Reserve or Fund A/c	Dr.	
To Equity Shareholders' A/c		With total amount

(7) For transferring the debentures not taken over by the purchasing company :

Debentures A/c	Dr.	With the book value
To Debentureholders' A/c		

Note : As per Accounting Standard-14, if the debentures are taken over by the purchasing company like other liabilities they should be transferred to Realisation Account at their book values.

Stage II : Entries for recording the purchase consideration

(1) For recording the purchase consideration due from the purchasing company :

Purchasing Company A/c	Dr.	With the amount of p.c. due.
To Realisation A/c		

(2) For receiving the purchase consideration from the purchasing company in the form of cash, shares or debentures :

Cash or Bank A/c	Dr.	With respective amounts
Shares in Purchasing Company A/c	Dr.	
Debentures in Purchasing Company A/c	Dr.	
To Purchasing Company A/c		With total amount

Stage III : Entries for recording the distribution of purchase Consideration

(1) For paying the liabilities not taken over :

Sundry Liabilities (Not taken over) A/c	Dr.	With total amount
To Cash or Bank A/c		With respective amounts
To Shares in Purchasing Company A/c		
To Debentures in Purchasing Company A/c		

Notes : The liabilities not taken over by the purchasing company will be paid by the Vendor Company. Any profit or loss on payment of such liabilities will be transferred to realisation account. The entry in this case will be :

(i) For loss on payment of liability :

Realisation A/c	Dr.	With the amount of loss if any
To Sundry Liabilities A/c		

(ii) For gain on payment of liability :

Sundry Liabilities A/c	Dr.	With the amount of profit if any
To Realisation A/c		

Alternatively, the liabilities not taken over can also be transferred on the credit side of the realisation account and when they are paid, the amount should be debited to the realisation account. Then, the profit or loss on such liabilities will be automatically adjusted.

(2) For selling the assets not taken over :

Cash or Bank A/c	Dr.	With total amount
To Sundry Assets (not taken over) A/c		With total amount

Note : The assets not taken over by the purchasing company will be sold by the vendor company. Any profit or loss on realisation of such assets will be transferred to realisation account. The entry in this case will be :

(i) *For loss on sale of assets :*

Realisation A/c	Dr.	With the amount of loss if any
To Sundry Assets A/c		

(ii) *For gain on sale of assets :*

Sundry Assets A/c	Dr.	With the amount of profit if any
To Realisation A/c		

Alternatively, the assets not taken over can also be transferred on the debit side of the realisation account and when they are realised, the realisation account itself should be credited, in that case the profit or loss on such sale will be automatically adjusted.

(3) For paying the liquidation expenses :

In this case, the Vendor Company can adopt any of the following three cases :

(A) When the expenses are borne by Vendor Company :

Realisation A/c	Dr.	With the amount
To Cash or Bank A/c		of expenses

(B) When the expenses are borne by the purchasing company:

No entry is to be passed in the books of transferor. Because, as the realisation expenses are paid by the transferee company it does not concern to the transferor. An entry for this should be passed in the books of transferee.

(C) When the expenses are borne by purchasing company are now paid by Vendor company, then reimbursed :

(i) *For payment of expenses* :

Purchasing Company A/c	Dr.	With the amount
To Bank or Cash A/c		of expenses paid

(ii) *For getting the expenses reimbursed* :

Bank or Cash A/c	Dr.	With the amount
To Purchasing Company A/c		recovered

Alternatively no entry may be passed in the books of vendor company. Since liquidation expenses are ultimately met only by the purchasing company and not by the vendor company.

(4) For adjustment of premium or discount to debentureholders and preference shareholders :

Realisation A/c	Dr.	With the amount of
To Debentureholders' A/c *or*		premium payable or
To Preference Shareholders' A/c		loss incurred

Reverse entry in case of discount earned or profit made.

(5) For discharging debentureholders :

Debentureholders' A/c	Dr.	With the total amount
To Cash or Bank A/c		With the respective
To Shares in Purchasing Co. A/c		amount
To Debentures in Purchasing Co. A/c		

(6) For closing realisation account :

Realisation A/c	Dr.	With the amount
To Equity Shareholders' A/c		of profit

Reverse entry in case of loss on realisation account.

(7) For paying shareholders :

(i)

Preference Shareholders' A/c	Dr.	With total amount
To Cash or Bank A/c		With amount of cash
To Shares in Purchasing Co. A/c		With amount of shares
To Debenture in Purchasing Co. A/c		With amount of deb.

(ii) Equity Shareholders A/c	Dr.	With total amount
To Cash or Bank A/c		With amount of cash
To Shares in Purchasing Co. A/c		With amount of shares
To Debentures in Purchasing Co. A/c		With amount of deb.

In the Books of Purchasing Company (Incorporating Entries)

As pointed out above, the accounting entries are same in both the methods of amalgamation in the books of vendor or transferor company. But in the books of purchasing company or transferee company, distinction is drawn towards the accounting entries between the pooling of interest method and purchase method. They are given as below:

Pooling of Interests Method

According to Para 31 of the Accounting Standard-14, when an amalgamation is considered to be an amalgamation in the nature of merger, it should be accounted for under the pooling of interest method. Under this method, the following entries have to be passed in the books of transferee company :

(1) For acquisition of business :

Business Purchase A/c	Dr.	With the amount of purchase consideration
To Liquidator of Transferor Company		

(2) For incorporation of assets liabilities and reserves :

Various Assets Accounts	Dr.	With their respective agreed or book values
Profit & Loss A/c	Dr.	With book balance (Dr.)
Fictitious Assets A/c	Dr.	With their respective agreed or book balances
Reserves Account *or*		
Capital Loss Account	Dr.	With balancing figure
To Various Liabilities Accounts (Including debentures)		With their respective agreed or book values
To Various Reserves Accounts		With their respective book balance
To Profit and Loss Account		With book balance (Cr.)
To Reserves Account *or* Capital Profit Account		With balancing figure or book value
To Business Purchase Account		With the amount of purchase consideration

Note : The difference between debits and credits is either debited or credited to Capital Loss or Profit A/c or Reserves A/c. In this method, neither Goodwill, nor Capital Reserve will arise.

(3) For adjustment of excess purchase consideration over share capital of transferor company :

General Reserve Account	Dr.	With the excess amount of purchase consideration over share capital
Other Reserve Account	Dr.	
Profit & Loss Account	Dr.	
To Capital Loss Account		

Note : **1.** The excess amount of purchase price over the paid-up share capital should be first adjusted against general reserve and then, other reserves and finally debited to the Profit and Loss Account.

Note : **2.** However, entry No. 2 and 3 can be combined by passing the following journal entry :

Each Asset Account	Dr.	Book value
To Each Liability Account		Book value
To Business Purchase Account		Purchase price

Note : The difference between debits and credits is either debited or credited to Reserves Account or P & L A/c.

(4) For settlement or payment of purchase consideration :

Liquidator of Vendor Company A/c	Dr.	With the amount of p.c.
Discount on Issue of Shares A/c	Dr.	With the amount of discount allowed on shares.
To Equity Share Capital A/c		With face value of equity shares issued.
To Preference Share Capital A/c		With face value of preference shares issued.
To Cash or Bank A/c		With the amount of cash payment made.

(5) For payment or re-imbursement of liquidation expenses of the vendor company :

General Reserve or Profit and Loss Account if there is not General Reserve	Dr.	With the amount of liquidation expenses.
To Cash *or* Bank Account		Cash paid for the same.

(6) For formation expenses of the transferee company :

Preliminary Expenses A/c	Dr.	With the amount of expenses incurred.
To Cash or Bank A/c		Cash paid for the same.

Purchase Method

This method of accounting is applicable for amalgamation in the nature of purchase. The following are the journal entries to be passed in the books of transferee company for the incorporation of the financial statement of the transferor company :

(1) For purchase consideration due :

Business Purchase Account	Dr.	With the amount of purchase consideration
To Liquidator of Transferor Company Account		

(2) For incorporation of assets, liabilities and reserves :

Various Assets Account (Other than Goodwill)	Dr.	With their respective agreed values
Goodwill Account	Dr.	With balancing figure
To Various Liabilities Account		With their respective agreed values
To Business Purchase Account		With purchase value
To Capital Reserve Account		With balancing figure

Note : 1. If the total credits exceed the total debits, the difference is treated as the value of goodwill and is debited to goodwill account. On the other hand, if the total debits exceed the total credits, the difference is considered as capital profit and is credited to capital reserve account.

Note : 2. If entry No. 1 and 2 are combined, then, the following one entry can also be passed by eliminating Business Purchase Account :

Individual Assets (taken over) A/c	Dr.	With agreed values
Goodwill A/c (Balancing fig. *i.e.,* if credit side exceeds debit side)	Dr.	The difference between credits and debits
To Individual Liabilities (taken over) A/c		With agreed values
To Vendor Co. A/c *or* Liquidator of Vendor Company A/c		With the amount of purchase consideration
To Capital Reserve A/c (Balancing fig. *i.e.*, if debit side exceeds credit side)		The difference between debits and credits

(3) Under this method, accounts relating to the profits and reserves are not transferred from the transferor company to the transferee company. However, there are certain statutory reserves, like Foreign Projects Reserves Account under Section 80 HHB and Reserve created under Section 80 HHD of the Income Tax Act of the transferor company are transferred and recorded in the books of transferee company for a prescribed period under law. The following journal entries passed in this regard.

(a) *For recording the statutory reserves of the Vendor Company :*

Amalgamation Adjustment Account	Dr.	With the amount of Statutory reserve
To Statutory Reserve A/c (by name)		

If the identity of the statutory reserve is no longer required to be maintained, then the above mentioned entry will be reversed for cancellation.

(b) *For cancellation of statutory reserve :*

Statutory Reserve Account (by name)	Dr.	With the amount of
To Amalgamation Adjustment A/c		statutory reserve

Note : Amalgamation Adjustment Account will be shown under the head Miscellaneous Expenditure Account.

(4) For making the payment of purchase consideration :

Vendor Co. A/c *or*		
Liquidator of Vendor Co. A/c	Dr.	With total amount
Discount on Issue of Shares/Debenture A/c	Dr.	With discount amount
To Share Capital A/c		With nominal value
To Share Premium A/c		With premium amount
To Debentures A/c		With nominal value
To Cash *or* Bank A/c		With amount of cash

If the shares or debentures have been issued at a premium or discount, the relevant premium or discount account should be credited or debited, as the case may be.

(5) For meeting the liquidation expenses of vendor company (if not included in the purchase consideration) :

Goodwill/Capital Reserve A/c	Dr.	With amount of
To Bank or Cash A/c		expenses paid

The amount of liquidation expenses will be debited to Goodwill or Capital Reserve A/c, as calculated under entry (1) discussed above.

(6) For formation expenses of the transferee if any

Preliminary Expenses Account	Dr.	Formation expenses.
To Cash or Bank Account		Expenses paid.

(7) For discharge of liability by the transferee company if any :

Concerned liability A/c	Dr.	With the amount of
To Share Capital/Debentures/ Bank Account (as the case may be)		respective liabilities

Treatment of Some Special Items

(1) Fictitious Assets : Assets which are not real or realisable are called fictitious assets. These are virtually not assets. These are the expenses and losses incurred in one accounting year, but carried forward to the subsequent period. Preliminary expenses (*i.e.,* expenses incurred for establishing a business), underwriting commission, discount on issue of shares and debentures, advertising expenses, debit balance in Profit and Loss A/c etc., are some of the examples of fictitious assets. These assets should not be considered in calculating the purchase consideration. Because they are not real assets and they do not represent real values. These assets should be transferred to the shareholders' account in the books of selling company by debiting the shareholders' account and crediting the concerned asset account. But, these assets should not be recorded in the books of purchasing company, as the purchasing company is not concerned with these assets.

(2) Trade and Non-trade Liabilities. Liabilities which are incurred by the concern on account of goods purchased on credit, are called trade liabilities. Trade liabilities include trade creditors and bills payable. All liabilities other than trade creditors and bills payable are called non-trade liabilities. If these liabilities (trade or non-trade liabilities) are taken over by the purchasing company, they should be transferred to realisation account at their book values. But if they are not taken over by the purchasing company, they should not be transferred to realisation account. They should be paid by the vendor company by debiting concerned liability account and crediting cash/shares/debentures account. The profit or loss arisen on the payment of such liabilities, should be transferred to realisation account.

(3) Goodwill and Capital Reserve. Goodwill refers to the value attached to a reputed business. It may be described as a value of all favourable attributes relating to a business enterprise such as favourable location, superiority of the products, customers attitude, absence of competition etc. In the books of purchasing company, it represents the excess amount paid to the vendor company over and above the value of net tangible assets acquired. In other words, purchase price less agreed value of net assets is treated as goodwill. On the other hand, capital reserve represents the surplus gained by paying less than the value of assets acquired. In other words, an agreed value of net assets less purchase price is treated as capital reserve.

In this context, the students should note that, for the purpose of calculating goodwill or capital reserve, the original amount of goodwill, if any appearing in the balance sheet of purchased company should be ignored.

(4) Fractions of Shares. Usually shares given as part of purchase consideration are to be distributed among the shareholders of vendor company at an agreed ratio of exchange. If this results any fractions while allotting shares, then the fractions of shares are to be satisfied in cash or by issuing fractional certificates. The calculation of equivalent amount of cash for fraction share is based on the market value of the share.

(5) Arrears of Dividend on Preference Shares of Vendor Company: Sometimes, arrears of preference dividend appear as contingent liability in the books of vendor company. In that case, it can be dealt in two ways. If the arrears of dividend on preference shares are required to be paid, they should be debited to Realisation Account and credited to preference shareholders' Account. On the other hand, if the arrears of dividend on preference shares are cancelled or not required to be paid at the time of selling the company, there cannot be any profit or loss arising from the cancellation of the same. Therefore, they should not be taken into account. As such, no entry should be passed in the books of selling company for the cancellation of arrears of preference dividend.

But in the books of purchasing company, no entry should be passed towards the arrears of preference dividend, whether they are required to be paid or not.

Illustration 1

The following are the abridged Balance Sheets of A Ltd. and B Ltd. as at 31st March, 2006 :

(In Rs. '000)

Liabilities	A Ltd.	B Ltd.	Assets	A Ltd.	B Ltd.
Equity Share Capital (Rs. 10 each)	24,000	9,000	Fixed Assets	33,000	14,190
			Current Assets	12,000	5,910
12% Pref. Share Capital (Rs. 100 each)	—	3,000			
General Reserve	13,830	2,940			
Statutory Reserve	1,170	375			
Profit and Loss A/c	1,689	1,065			
13% Debentures	—	750			
Current Liabilities	4,311	2,970			
	45,000	20,100		45,000	20,100

On April, 2006 A takes over B Ltd. on the following terms :

(i) A Ltd. will issue 10,50,000 equity shares of Rs. 10 each at par to the equity shareholders of B Ltd.

(ii) A Ltd. will issue 33,000 12% preference shares of Rs. 100 each at par to the preference shareholders of B. Ltd.

(iii) The debentures of B Ltd. will be converted into equal number of 14% debentures of the same denomination.

You are informed that the statutory reserves of B Ltd. are to be maintained for two more years. You are required to show the balance sheet of A Ltd. immediately after the above mentioned scheme of amalgamation has been implemented assuming that :

(a) The amalgamation is in the nature of merger, and

(b) The amalgamation is in the nature of purchase.

(Adapted from B.Com., Madras and B.B.M,. Bangalore)

Solution :

Calculation of purchase consideration

	Rs. in '000
In equity shares : 10,50,000 equity shares of Rs. 10 each	10,500
In preference shares : 33,000 preferences of Rs. 100 each	3,300
Purchase consideration	13,800

Notes: (i) Debentures of B Ltd. converted by A Ltd. does not form a part of purchase consideration. Therefore, these debentures are presumed to be taken over by the transferee company and then converted or discharged.

(ii) The amount of purchase consideration will be the same under both the methods of amalgamation.

(a) When the amalgamation is in the nature of merger

Balance Sheet of A Ltd. as on 1st April, 2006

Liabilities	Rs. in '000	Assets	Rs. in '000
Share Capital		**Fixed Assets**	47,190
34,50,000 Equity Shares of Rs. 10 each (24,00,000 + 10,50,000)	34,500	**Current Assets, Loans and Advances**	
33,000 Preference Shares of Rs. 100 each	3,300	(a) Current Assets	17,910
Reserves & Surplus		(b) Loans & Advances	—
General Reserve (Working Note)	14,970		
Statutory Reserve (11,70,000 + 3,75,000)	1,545		
Profit & Loss Account (16,89,000 + 10,65,000)	2,754		
Secured Loans			
14% Debentures	750		
Current Liabilities and Provisions			
(a) Current Liabilities	7,281		
(b) Provisions	—		
	65,100		65,100

Working Note :

Calculation of General Reserve

		Rs. in '000
Purchase consideration		13,800
Less : Share Capital of Vendor Company (*i.e.,* B Ltd.)		
Equity Share Capital	90,00,000	
12% Preference Share Capital	30,00,000	12,000
Excess being Capital loss		1,800

General Reserve : A Ltd.		13,830	
	B Ltd.	2,940	16,770
Less:	Capital loss		1,800
	Balance of general reserve shown in Balance Sheet.		14,970

(b) When the amalgamation is in the nature of purchase

Balance Sheet of A Ltd. as on 1st April, 2006

Liabilities	Rs. in '000	Assets	Rs. in '000
Share Capital		**Fixed Assets**	47,190
34,50,000 Equity Shares of		(3,30,00,000 + 1,41,90,000)	
Rs. 10 each	34,500	**Current Assets, Loans**	
33,000 Preference Share of		**and Advances**	
Rs. 100 each	3,300	(a) Current Assets	
Reserves and Surplus		(1,20,00,000 + 59,10,000)	17,910
General Reserve (only A Ltd.)	13,830	(b) Loans and Advances	Nil
Profit & Loss A/c (only A Ltd.)	1,689	**Miscellaneous Expenditure**	
Statutory Reserve	1,545	(a) Amalgamation	
(11,70,000 + 3,75,000)		Adjustment A/c	375
Capital Reserve	2,580	(Equal to Statutory	
(Working Note)		Reserve of B Ltd.)	
Secured Loans		(b) Other Miscellaneous	
14% Debentures	750	Expenditure	Nil
Current Liabilities and Provisions			
(a) Current Liabilities	7,281		
(b) Provisions	Nil		
	65,475		65,475

Working Note :

Calculation of Capital Reserve

Value of assets of B Ltd. takenover :		Rs. in '000
Fixed Assets		14,190
Current Assets		5,910
		20,100
Less : Value of liabilities takenover :		
13% Debentures	750	
Current liabilities	2,970	3,720
		16,380
Less : Purchase consideration		13,800
Capital Reserve		2,580

Illustration 2

The Balance Sheets of X Ltd. and Y Ltd. as at 31st March, 2009 are as under :

Liabilities	X Ltd.	Y Ltd.	Assets	X Ltd.	Y Ltd.
Equity Shares of Rs. 10 each	5,50,000	3,80,000	Buildings	2,00,000	1,50,000
9% Redeemable Pref. Shares of Rs. 100 each	30,000	—	Machinery	2,20,000	1,20,000
General Reserve	65,000	55,000	Furniture	12,000	15,000
Investment Allowance Reserve	—	8,000	Stock	1,80,000	1,50,000
Export Project Reserve	25,000	15,000	Debtors	2,00,000	40,000
Profit & Loss A/c	80,000	—	Bank	28,000	26,000
12% Debentures (Rs. 100 each)	40,000	30,000	Preliminary Expenses	—	10,000
Creditors	38,000	35,000	Profit and Loss A/c	—	20,000
Bills Payable	12,000	8,000			
	8,40,000	5,31,000		8,40,000	5,31,000

X Ltd. absorbed the business of Y Ltd. as a going concern on the following terms :

(1) X Ltd. will allot 40,000 equity shares of Rs. 10 each at a premium of 20% and cash Rs. 40,000.

(2) Debentureholders of Y Ltd. will be allotted new 12% debentures of equal amount in X Ltd.

(3) Liquidation expenses of Rs. 5,000 are to be paid by X Ltd.

You are informed that investment allowances reserve and export project reserve are required to be maintained for another one year. Give the necessary journal entries and ledger accounts in the books of Y Ltd. and show incorporating entries in the books of X Ltd. and opening Balance Sheet of X Ltd. under both the methods of amalgamation (*i.e.*, nature of merger and nature of purchase).

Solution :

Calculation of Purchase Consideration

	Rs.
In equity shares of X Ltd. 40,000 shares of Rs. 12 each	4,80,000
In cash	40,000
Purchase consideration	5,20,000

Notes : (i) Debentures issued to pay off old debentures do not form part of purchase consideration. It should be treated as debentures taken over and discharged by transferee company.

(ii) Liquidation expenses are directly paid by the purchasing company.

(iii) Journal entries to be passed in the books of transferor company will be the same under both the methods of amalgamation.

Journal Entries in the Books of Y Ltd. (Transferor Company)

Sl.No.	Particulars		L.F.	Dr. Rs.	Cr. Rs.
Stage I	**Entries to close all the accounts that appear in the Balance Sheet**				
1.	Realisation Account	Dr.		4,81,000	—
	To Building Account			—	1,50,000
	To Machinery Account			—	1,20,000
	To Furniture Account			—	15,000
	To Stock Account			—	1,50,000
	To Debtors Account			—	40,000
	To Bank Account			—	6,000
	(Being the above assets transferred to Realisation Account at their book values)				
2.	12% Debentures Account	Dr.		30,000	—
	Creditors Account	Dr.		35,000	—
	Bills Payable Account	Dr.		8,000	—
	To Realisation Account			—	73,000
	(Being the above liabilities transferred to Realisation Account at their book values)				
3.	Share Capital Account	Dr.		3,80,000	—
	General Reserve Account	Dr.		55,000	—
	Investment Allowance Reserve A/c	Dr.		8,000	—
	Export Project Reserve Account	Dr.		15,000	—
	To Equity Shareholders' Account			—	4,58,000
	(Being the above credit balances transferred to equity shareholders)				
4.	Equity Shareholders' Account	Dr.		50,000	—
	To Preliminary Expenses A/c			—	10,000
	To Profit & Loss Account			—	40,000
	(Being the above debit balances transferred to equity shareholders)				

Contd.

Sl. No.	Particulars	L.F.	Dr. Rs.	Cr. Rs.
Stage II	**Entries for recording the purchase consideration**			
5.	X Ltd. Account Dr.		5,20,000	—
	To Realisation Account		—	5,20,000
	(Being purchase consideration due from X Ltd.)			
6.	Shares in X Ltd. Account Dr.		4,80,000	—
	Bank Account		40,000	—
	To X Ltd. Account		—	5,20,000
	(Being purchase consideration received from X Ltd. in the form of equity share and cash)			
Stage III	**Entries for recording the distribution of purchase consideration**			
7.	Realisation Account Dr.		1,12,000	—
	To Equity Shareholders' Account		—	1,12,000
	(Being realisation profit transferred to equity shareholders' account)			
8.	Equity Shareholders' Account Dr.		5,20,000	—
	To Equity Shares in X Ltd. A/c		—	4,80,000
	To Bank Account		—	40,000
	(Being settlement of shareholders' account)			

Ledger Accounts

Realisation Account

Dr. Cr.

	Rs.		Rs.
To Buildings A/c	1,50,000	By 10% Debentures A/c	30,000
To Machinery A/c	1,20,000	By Creditors A/c	35,000
To Furniture A/c	15,000	By Bills Payable A/c	8,000
To Stock A/c	1,50,000	By X Ltd. A/c	5,20,000
To Debtors' A/c	40,000		
To Bank A/c	6,000		
To Equity Shareholders' A/c (Profit on Realisation) (Balancing figure)	1,12,000		
	5,93,000		5,93,000

Dr. **Equity Shareholders' Account** Cr.

	Rs.		Rs.
To Preliminary Expenses A/c	10,000	By Share Capital A/c	3,80,000
To Profit and Loss A/c	40,000	By General Reserve A/c	55,000
To Equity Shares in X Ltd. A/c	4,80,000	By Investment Allowances Reserve A/c	8,000
To Bank A/c	40,000	By Export Project Reserve A/c	15,000
		By Realisation A/c	1,12,000
	5,70,000		5,70,000

Dr. **X Ltd. Account** Cr.

	Rs.		Rs.
To Realisation A/c	5,20,000	By Equity Shares A/c	4,80,000
		By Bank A/c	40,000
	5,20,000		5,20,000

Incorporation Entries in the Books of Transferee Company

(A) Amalgamation in the nature of merger method

Journal Entries in the Book of X Ltd.

S. No.	Particulars	L.F.	Dr. Rs.	Cr. Rs.
1.	Business Purchase A/c Dr.		5,20,000	—
	To Liquidator of Y Ltd.		—	5,20,000
	(Being purchase consideration due to Y Ltd.)			
2.	Building Account		1,50,000	—
	Machinery Account		1,20,000	—
	Furniture Account		15,000	—
	Stock Account		1,50,000	—
	Debtors' Account		40,000	—
	Bank Account		26,000	—
	Preliminary Expenses A/c		10,000	—
	Profit and Loss Account		20,000	—
	Capital Loss Account (Balancing figure)		1,40,000	—
	To Business Purchase A/c		—	5,20,000
	To Creditors' Account		—	35,000
	To 12% Debentures Account		—	30,000
	To Bills Payable Account		—	8,000
	To Investment Allowance Reserve A/c		—	8,000
				Contd.

Sl. No.	Particulars	L.F.	Dr. Rs.	Cr. Rs.
	To Export Project Reserve A/c		—	15,000
	To General Reserve A/c		—	55,000
	(Being transfer of assets, liabilities, reserves, expenses and losses of Y Ltd. at their book values, the difference being placed in the capital loss account)			
3.	General Reserve A/c Dr.		1,20,000	—
	(65,000 + 55,000)			
	Profit and Loss A/c Dr.		40,000	—
	(Only required amount)			
	To Capital Loss A/c		—	1,60,000
	(1,40,000 + 20,000)			
	(Being excess of purchase consideration over paid up capital of Y Ltd. (*i.e.*, Rs. 5,20,000 – Rs. 3,80,000) Rs. 1,40,000 and debit balance of P & L A/c of Rs. 20,000 adjusted against General Reserve and other revenue profits)			
4.	Liquidators of Y Ltd. Account Dr.		5,20,000	—
	To Equity Share Capital A/c		—	4,00,000
	To Security Premium Account (20%)		—	80,000
	To Bank Account		—	40,000
	(Being Settlement of purchase consideration by the issue of 40,000 equity shares of Rs. 10 each at a premium of Rs. 2 per share and cash of Rs. 40,000)			
5.	12% Debentures of Y Ltd. A/c Dr.		30,000	—
	To 12% Debentures of X Ltd. A/c		—	30,000
	(Being redemption of debentures of Y Ltd. by the issue of new debentures of X Ltd.)			
6.	Profit and Loss Account Dr.		15,000	—
	To Bank Account		—	5,000
	To Preliminary Expenses Account		—	10,000
	(Being payment of liquidation expenses of Y Ltd.)			

Calculation Profit and Loss A/c Balance

			Rs.
	Purchase consideration		5,20,000
Less :	Share Capital of Vendor Company (Y Ltd.)		3,80,000
	Excess being Capital Loss		1,40,000
Add :	Debit balance of P & L A/c of Y Ltd.		20,000
	Balance of Capital Loss		1,60,000
Less :	Adjusted from General Reserve of Y Ltd.	55,000	
	Adjusted from General Reserve of X Ltd.	65,000	1,20,000
	Balance of Capital Loss		40,000
Less :	Adjusted from P & L A/c of X Ltd.		40,000
	Balance of Capital Loss		Nil
	Balance of P & L A/c of X Ltd. (80,000 – 40,000)		40,000
Less :	Liquidation Expenses Written off	5,000	
	Preliminary Expenses Written off	10,000	15,000
	Balance of Profit shown in Balance Sheet		25,000

Balance Sheet of X Ltd. (After Merger) as on 31st March, 2009

Liabilities	Rs.	Assets	Rs.
Share Capital		**Fixed Assets**	
Equity Shares of Rs. 10 each (5,50,000 + 4,00,000)	9,50,000	Building (2,00,000 + 1,50,000)	3,50,000
9% Redeemable Pref. Shares of Rs. 100 each	30,000	Machinery (2,20,000 + 1,20,000)	3,40,000
Reserves & Surplus		Furniture (12,000 + 15,000)	27,000
Security Premium	80,000		
Investment Allowance Reserve	8,000	**Current Assets**	
Export Project Reserve	40,000	Stock (1,80,000 + 1,50,000)	3,30,000
Profit & Loss A/c (80,000 – 55,000 *i.e.,* 40,000 + 5,000 + 10,000)	25,000	Debtors (2,00,000 + 40,000)	2,40,000
Secured Loans		Bank (28,000 + 26,000 – 45,000 *i.e.,* 40,000 + 5,000)	9,000
12% Debentures (40,000 + 30,000)	70,000		
Current Liabilities			
Creditors (38,000 + 35,000)	73,000		
Bills Payable (12,000 + 8,000)	20,000		
	12,96,000		12,96,000

(B) Amalgamation in the nature of purchase method

Journal Entries in the Books of X Ltd.

Sl. No.	Particulars	L.F.	Dr. Rs.	Cr. Rs.
1.	Business Purchase Account Dr.		5,20,000	—
	To Liquidator of Y Ltd.		—	5,20,000
	(Being purchase consideration due to Y Ltd.)			
2.	Buildings Account		1,50,000	—
	Machinery Account		1,20,000	—
	Stock Account		1,50,000	—
	Furniture Account		15,000	—
	Debtors Account		40,000	—
	Bank Account		26,000	—
	Goodwill Account (Balancing Figure)		92,000	—
	To 12% Debentures of Y Ltd. A/c		—	30,000
	To Creditors Account		—	35,000
	To Bills Payable Account		—	8,000
	To Business Purchase Account		—	5,20,000
	(Being the above assets and liabilities taken over at their agreed values, the excess of credits is charged to Goodwill Account)			
3.	Liquidator of Y Ltd. Account Dr.		5,20,000	—
	To Equity Share Capital A/c		—	4,00,000
	To Security Premium A/c		—	80,000
	To Bank Account		—	40,000
	(Being the purchase consideration paid in the form of shares and cash)			
4.	12% Debentures of Y Ltd. A/c Dr.		30,000	—
	To 12% Debentures of X Ltd. A/c		—	30,000
	(Being issue of new debentures of X Ltd. to discharge the debentures of Y Ltd.)			
5.	Amalgamation Adjustment A/c Dr.		23,000	—
	To Investment Allowances Reserve A/c		—	8,000
	To Export Project Reserve A/c		—	15,000
	(Being incorporation of statutory reserve of Y Ltd. to be maintained for one more year)			
6.	Goodwill Account Dr.		5,000	—
	To Bank Account		—	5,000
	(Being the payment of liquidation expenses)			

Calculation of Total Goodwill

				Rs.
	Purchase consideration			5,20,000
Less :	Value of assets taken over :			
	Building		1,50,000	
	Machinery		1,20,000	
	Furniture		15,000	
	Stock		1,50,000	
	Debtors		40,000	
	Bank		26,000	
	Excess being capital loss		5,01,000	
Less :	Value of liabilities takenover :			
	12% Debentures	30,000		
	Creditors	35,000		
	Bills Payable	8,000	73,000	4,28,000
	Goodwill of Y Ltd.			92,000
Add :	Liquidation expenses paid by the purchasing company			5,000
	Total Goodwill			97,000

Balance Sheet of X Ltd. as at 31st March, 2009

Liabilities	Rs.	Assets	Rs.
Share Capital		**Fixed Assets**	
Equity Shares of Rs. 10 each	9,50,000	Goodwill	97,000
9% Redeemable Pref. Shares		(92,000 + 5,000)	
of Rs. 100 each	30,000	Buildings	3,50,000
Reserves of Surplus		(2,00,000 + 1,50,000)	
General Reserve	65,000	Machinery	3,40,000
Security Premium	80,000	(2,20,000 + 1,20,000)	
Investment Allowance	—	Furniture	27,000
Reserve	8,000	(12,000 + 15,000)	
Export Project Reserve	40,000	**Current Assets**	
Profit and Loss A/c	80,000	Stock	3,30,000
Secured Loans		(1,80,000 + 1,50,000)	
12% Debentures	70,000	Debtors	2,40,000
(40,000 + 30,000)		(2,00,000 + 40,000)	
Current Liabilities		Bank	9,000
Creditors		(28,000 + 26,000 – 45,000	
(38,000 + 35,000)	73,000	*i.e.*, 40,000 + 5,000)	
Bills Payable		**Misc. Expenditure & Losses**	
(12,000 + 8,000)	20,000	Amalgamation Adjustment A/c	23,000
	14,16,000		14,16,000

Illustration 3

The following are the Balance Sheets of A Company Ltd. and B Company Ltd.

A Company Ltd.

Liabilities	Rs.	Assets	Rs.
Capital : 5,000 Shares of Rs. 10 each	50,000	Buildings	15,000
		Machinery	55,000
100, 6% Debentures of Rs. 100 each	10,000	Stock	8,000
		Debtors	7,000
Reserve Fund	17,000	Cash	1,500
Dividend Equalisation Fund	2,000		
Employees' Provident Fund	1,500		
Trade Creditors	5,000		
Profit and Loss A/c	1,000		
	86,500		86,500

B Company Ltd.

Liabilities	Rs.	Assets		Rs.
1,500 Shares of Rs. 20 each	30,000	Machinery		25,000
Trade Creditors	4,000	Stock		4,000
		Debtors	5,000	
		Less : Reserve	500	4,500
		Cash		500
	34,000			34,000

The two companies agree to amalgamate and form a new company called C Company Ltd. which takes over the assets and liabilities of both the companies. The assets of A Company Ltd. are taken over at a reduced valuation of 10% with the exception of buildings which is accepted at book value.

Both the companies are to receive 5% of the net valuation of their respective business as goodwill. The entire purchase price is to be paid by C Company Ltd. in fully paid shares of Rs. 10 each. In return for debentures in A Company Ltd., debentures of the same amount and denomination are to be issued by C Company Ltd.

Give journal entries to close the books of A Company Ltd. and B Company Ltd. and to open the books of C Company Ltd. and also show the opening Balance Sheet of C Company Ltd. whose Authorised Capital is Rs. 1,00,000 in Rs. 10 shares, assuming :

(a) that the amalgamation is in the nature of merger

(b) that the amalgamation is in the nature of purchase.

(Adopted from B.Com., Bombay and G.S. Inter Modified)

Solution :

Here, net assets method is used for calculalting the purchase consideration.

Calculation of purchase consideration payable to A Company Ltd.

			Rs.
Agreed Value of assets takenover :			
	Building (Book value)		15,000
	Machinery (55,000 – 5,500)		49,500
	Stock (8,000 – 800)		7,200
	Debtors (7,000 – 700)		6,300
	Cash (Book value)		1,500
	Total value of assets taken over		79,500
Less :	Agreed value of liabilities taken over :		
	Trade Creditors	5,000	
	Employees Provident Fund	1,500	
	6% Debentures	10,000	16,500
		Net Valuation	63,000
Add :	Goodwill (5% of net valuation) (63,000 × 5/100)		3,150
	Purchase consideration or Net value of assets		66,150

Note : Employees' provident fund is a liability

Calculation of purchase consideration payable to B Company Ltd.

			Rs.
Agreed Value of assets taken over :			
	Machinery		25,000
	Stock		4,000
	Debtors	5,000	
	Less: Reserve	500	4,500
	Cash		500
	Total value of assets taken over		34,000
Less:	Agreed value of liabilities taken over :		
	Trade creditors		4,000
		Net valuation	30,000
Add :	Goodwill (5% of net valuation) (30,000 × 5/100)		1,500
	Purchase consideration or Net value of assets		31,500

Journal Entries in the Books of A Company Ltd.
(Same under both methods)

Sl. No.	Particulars		L.F.	Dr. Rs.	Cr. Rs.
Stage I	**Entries to close all the accounts that appear in the Balance Sheet**				
1.	Realisation Account	Dr.		86,500	—
	To Buildings Account			—	15,000
	To Machinery Account			—	55,000
	To Stock Account			—	8,000
	To Debtors' Account			—	7,000
	To Cash Account			—	1,500
	(Being transfer of above assets to the realisation account at their book values)				
2.	Trade Creditors' Account	Dr.		5,000	—
	Employees' Provident Fund Account	Dr.		1,500	—
	6% Debentures Account	Dr.		10,000	—
	To Realisation Account			—	16,500
	(Being transfer of above liabilities to realisation account)				
3.	Share Capital Account	Dr.		50,000	—
	Reserve Fund Account	Dr.		17,000	—
	Dividend Equalisation Fund	Dr.		2,000	—
	Profit and Loss Account	Dr.		1,000	—
	To Equity Shareholders' A/c			—	70,000
	(Being transfer of above accounts to equity shareholders)				
Stage II	**Entries for recording the purchase consideration**				
4.	C Company Ltd. Account	Dr.		66,150	—
	To Realisation Account			—	66,150
	(Being purchase consideration due from C Company Ltd.)				
5.	Equity Shares in C Company Ltd. A/c	Dr.		66,150	—
	To C Company Ltd. Account			—	66,150
	(Being purchase consideration received from C Company Ltd. in the form of equity shares)				

Contd.

Stage III	**Entries for recording of distribution of purchase consideration**			
6.	Equity Shareholders' Account Dr.		3,850	—
	To Realisation Account		—	3,850
	(Being realisation loss transferred to equity shareholders account)			
7.	Equity Shareholders' Account Dr.		66,150	—
	To Equity Shares in C Company Ltd. A/c		—	66,150
	(Being distribution of shares among the shareholders)			

Journal Entries in the Books of B Company Ltd.
(Same under both the methods)

Sl. No.	Particulars	L.F.	Dr. Rs.	Cr. Rs.
Stage I	**Entries to close all the accounts that appear in the Balance Sheet**			
1.	Realisation Account Dr.		34,500	—
	To Machinery Account		—	25,000
	To Stock Account		—	4,000
	To Debtors Account (Gross Amount)		—	5,000
	To Cash Account		—	500
	(Being transfer of above assets to the realisation account at their book values)			
2.	Reserve for Bad Debts Account Dr.		500	—
	Trade Creditors Account Dr.		4,000	—
	To Realisation Account		—	4,500
	(Being transfer of above liabilities to realisation account)			
3.	Equity Share Capital Account Dr.		30,000	—
	To Equity Shareholders' A/c		—	30,000
	(Being the above credit balance transferred to equity shareholders' account)			
Stage II	**Entries for recording the purchase consideration**			
4.	C Company Account Dr.		31,500	—
	To Realisation Account		—	31,500
	(Being purchase consideration due from C Company Ltd.)			

Contd.

5.	Equity Shares in C Company Ltd. Dr. To C Company Ltd. Account (Being purchase consideration received from C Company Ltd. in the form of equity shares)		31,500 —	— 31,500
Stage III	**Entries for recording of distribution of purchase consideration**			
6.	Realisation Account Dr. To Equity Shareholders' Account (Being profit on realisation transferred to shareholders)		1,500 —	— 1,500
7.	Equity Shareholders' Account Dr. To Equity Shares in C Company Ltd. Account (Being distribution of shares among the shareholders)		31,500 —	— 31,500

Incorporation Entries in the Books of Transferee Companies

(A) Pooling of Interests Method (i.e., Nature of Merger)

Journal Entries in the Books of C Company Ltd.

Sl. No.	Particulars	L.F.	Dr. Rs.	Cr. Rs.
1.	Business Purchase Account Dr. (66,150 + 31,500) To Liquidator of A Company Ltd. A/c To Liquidator of B Company Ltd. A/c (Being purchase consideration payable to A Company Ltd. and B Company Ltd.)		97,650 — —	— 66,150 31,500
2.	Buildings Account Dr. Machinery Account Dr. Stock Account Dr. Debetors' Account Dr. Cash Account Dr. Capital Loss or Reserve Fund A/c (B.F.) Dr. To Employees' Provident Fund A/c To Trade Creditors' Account To 6% Debentures Account To Reserve Fund Account To Dividend Equalisation Fund A/c		15,000 55,000 8,000 7,000 1,500 16,150 — — — — —	— — — — — — 1,500 5,000 10,000 17,000 2,000

Contd.

	To Profit and Loss Account		—	1,000
	To Business Purchase Account		—	66,150
	(Being the incorporation of assets, liabilities, reserves and Profit & Loss A/c of A Company Ltd. and the difference between the purchase consideration and share capital [Rs. 66,150 – Rs. 50,000] debited to capital loss or reserve fund account.			
3.	Machinery Account Dr.		25,000	—
	Stock Account Dr.		4,000	—
	Debtors' Account (Gross Amount) Dr.		5,000	—
	Cash Account Dr.		500	—
	Capital Loss Account (B.F.) Dr.		1,500	—
	To Reserve for Bad Debts		—	500
	To Trade Creditors		—	4,000
	To Business Purchase Account		—	31,500
	(Being the incorporation of assets & liabilities of B Company Ltd. and the difference between purchase consideration and share capital [Rs. 31,500 – 30,000] debited to capital loss)			
4.	Reserve Fund Account Dr.		17,000	—
	P & L A/c (Only Required Amount) Dr.		650	—
	To Capital Loss A/c (16,150 + 1,500)		—	17,650
	(Being capital loss of A Company Ltd. and B Company Ltd. adjusted against reserve fund and revenue profits)			
5.	Liquidator of A Company Ltd. A/c Dr.		66,150	—
	Liquidator of B Company Ltd. A/c Dr.		31,500	—
	To Equity Share Capital A/c		—	97,650
	(Being the purchase consideration paid in the form of equity shares)			
6.	6% Debentures in A Company Ltd. A/c Dr.		10,000	—
	To 6% Debentures in C Company Ltd. A/c		—	10,000
	(Being the debentures in A Company Ltd. discharged by the issue of debentures in C Company Ltd.)			

Calculation of Profit and Loss Account Balance

			Rs.
	Purchase consideration (66,150 + 31,500)		97,650
Less :	Share Capital of Vendor Company (50,000 + 30,000) (*i.e.*, A Company Ltd. and B Company Ltd.)		80,000
	Excess being Capital Loss		17,650
Less :	Adjusted from Reserve Fund of A Company Ltd.	17,000	
	Adjusted from P & L A/c of A Company Ltd. (Only required amount)	650	17,650
	Balance of loss		Nil
	Balance of P & L A/c of A Company Ltd. (1,000 – 650)		350

Balance Sheet of C Company Ltd. as on ....

Liabilities	Rs.	Assets		Rs.
Share Capital		**Fixed Assets**		
9,765 Equity Shares of Rs. 10 each fully paid	97,650	Buildings		15,000
Reserve & Surplus		Machinery (55,000 + 25,000)		80,000
Dividend Equalisation Fund	2,000	**Current Assets**		
Profit and Loss A/c	350	Stock (8,000 + 4,000)		12,000
Secured Loans		Debtors (Gross)		
6% Debentures	10,000	(7,000 + 5,000)	12,000	
Current Liabilities		*Less* : Reserve for		
Trade Creditors (5,000 + 4,000)	9,000	Bad Debts	500	11,500
		Cash (1,500 + 500)		2,000
Employees' Provident Fund	1,500			
	1,20,500			1,20,500

(B) Purchase Method (*i.e.*, Nature of Purchase)

Journal Entries in the Books of C Company Ltd.

Sl. No.	Particulars		L. F.	Dr. Rs.	Cr. Rs.
1.	Business Purchase Account	Dr.		97,650	—
	To Liquidator of A Company Ltd. A/c			—	66,150
	To Liquidator of B Company Ltd. A/c			—	31,500
	(Being the purchase consideration payable)				
2.	Buildings Account	Dr.		15,000	—
	Machinery Account (49,500 + 25,000)	Dr.		74,500	—
	Stock A/c (7,200 + 4,000)	Dr.		11,200	—
	Debtors A/c (Gross Amount) (6,300 + 5,000)	Dr.		11,300	—

Contd.

	Cash A/c (1,500 + 500) Dr.		2,000	—
	Goodwill Account (Balancing figure) Dr.		4,650	—
	To Reserve for Bad Debts A/c		—	500
	To Trade Creditors Account (5,000 + 4,000)		—	9,000
	To Employees' Provident Fund A/c		—	1,500
	To 6% Debentures A/c		—	10,000
	To Business Purchase A/c		—	97,650
	(Being the incorporation of assets and liabilities taken over as per agreement)			
3.	Liquidator of A Company Ltd. A/c Dr.		66,150	—
	Liquidator of B Company Ltd. A/c Dr.		31,500	—
	To Equity Share Capital A/c		—	97,650
	(Being purchase consideration paid in the form of equity shares)			
4.	6% Debenures in A Company Ltd. A/c Dr.		10,000	—
	To 6% Debentures in C Company Ltd. Account		—	10,000
	(Being the debentures in A Company Ltd. discharged by the issue of debentures in C Company Ltd.)			

Balance Sheet of C Company Ltd. as on..........

Liabilities	Rs.	Assets		Rs.
Share Capital		**Fixed Assets**		
Authorised : 10,000 Equity Shares of Rs. 10 each	1,00,000	Goodwill (3,150 + 1,500)		4,650
		Buildings		15,000
Issued, Subscribed, Called up and Paid-up :		Machinery (49,500 + 25,000)		74,500
		Current Assets		
9,765 Equity Shares of Rs. 10 each fully paid	97,650	Stock (7,200 + 4,000)		11,200
Secured Loans		Debtors (Gross) (6,300 + 5,000)	11,300	
100, 6% Debentures of Rs. 100 each	10,000	*Less* : Reserve for Bad Debts	500	10,800
Current Liabilities		Cash (1,500 + 500)		2,000
Trade Creditors (5,000 + 4,000)	9,000			
Employees' Provident Fund	1,500			
	1,18,150			1,18,150

Illustration 4

A Ltd. and B Ltd. have agreed to amalgamate. A new company called 'C' Ltd. has been formed to take over the above concerns on 31-12-2009. The following are the agreed balance sheets of the two companies :

Balance Sheets as at 31-12-2009

Liabilities	A	B	Assets	A	B
Share Capital	55,000	60,000	Goodwill	—	25,000
General Reserve	—	15,000	Buildings	30,000	20,000
Profit & Loss A/c	—	5,000	Machinery	15,000	18,000
Creditors	28,000	20,000	Stock	12,000	10,000
Bills Payable	5,000	—	Debtors	22,000	19,000
			Cash	5,000	8,000
			Profit & Loss A/c	4,000	—
	88,000	1,00,000		88,000	1,00,000

Ascertain the purchase consideration payable to each of the above companies. Pass the journal entries and show the necessary accounts to close the books of vendor companies. Also pass the opening entries in the books of purchasing company and prepare the balance sheet of new company under both the methods of amalgamation.

Solution :

Calculation of Purchase Consideration (Net Assets Method)

	A Ltd. Rs.	B Ltd. Rs.
Agreed value of assets taken over :		
Goodwill	—	25,000
Buildings	30,000	20,000
Machinery	15,000	18,000
Stock	12,000	10,000
Debtors	22,000	19,000
Cash	5,000	8,000
Total value of assets taken over (A)	84,000	1,00,000
Agreed value of liabilities taken over :		
Creditors	28,000	20,000
Bills Payable	5,000	—
Total value of liabilities taken over (B)	33,000	20,000
Purchase Consideration (A) – (B)	51,000	80,000

Closing Entries in the Books of A Ltd.

(Same under both the methods)

Sl. No.	Particulars		L.F.	Dr. Rs.	Cr. Rs.
Stage I	**Entries to close all the accounts that appear in the Balance sheet :**				
1.	Realisation Account	Dr.		84,000	—
	To Buildings Account			—	30,000
	To Machinery Account			—	15,000
	To Stock Account			—	12,000
	To Debtors Account			—	22,000
	To Cash Account			—	5,000
	(Being transfer of above assets at book values to realisation account)				
2.	Shareholders' Account	Dr.		4,000	—
	To Profit & Loss Account			—	4,000
	(Being transfer of loss to shareholders)				
3.	Share Capital Account	Dr.		55,000	—
	To Shareholders' Account			—	55,000
	(Being share capital transferred to shareholders)				
4.	Creditors Account	Dr.		28.000	—
	Bills Payable Account	Dr.		5,000	—
	To Realisation Account			—	33,000
	(Being transfer of above liabilities to book values to realisation account)				
Stage II	**Entries for recording the purchase consideration**				
5.	C Ltd. Account	Dr.		51,000	—
	To Realisation Account			—	51,000
	(Being purchase consideration due from C Ltd.)				
6.	Shares in C Ltd. Account	Dr.		51,000	—
	To C Ltd. Account			—	51,000
	(Being purchase consideration received from C Ltd. in the form of shares)				

Contd.

Stage III	**Entries for recording of distribution of purchase consideration :**			
7.	Shareholders' Account	Dr.	51,000	—
	To Shares in C Ltd. Account		—	51,000
	(Being shareholders paid in the from of shares in C Ltd.)			

Ledger Accounts

Dr. **Realisation Account** Cr.

	Rs.		Rs.
To Building	80,000	By Creditors	28,000
To Machinery	15,000	By Bills Payable	5,000
To Stock	12,000	By C Ltd.	51,000
To Debtors	22,000	(*i.e.*, purchase consideration)	
To Cash	5,000		
	84,000		84,000

Dr. **C. Ltd. (Purchasing Co.) Account** Cr.

	Rs.		Rs.
To Realisation	51,000	By Shares in C Ltd.	51,000
	51,000		51,000

Dr. **Shareholders' Accounts** Cr.

	Rs.		Rs.
To Profit and Loss A/c	4,000	By Share Capital	55,000
To Shares in C Ltd.	51,000		
	55,000		55,000

Dr. **Shares in C Ltd.** Cr.

	Rs.		Rs.
To C Ltd.	51,000	By Shareholders	51,000
	51,000		51,000

Closing Entries in the Books of B Ltd.
(Same under both the methods)

Sl. No.	Particulars	L.F.	Dr. Rs.	Cr. Rs.
Stage I	**Entries to close all the accounts that appear in the Balance sheet**			
1.	Realisation Account Dr.		1,00,000	—
	To Goodwill		—	25,000
	To Building		—	20,000
	To Machinery		—	18,000
	To Stock		—	10,000
	To Debtors		—	19,000
	To Cash		—	8,000
	(Being transfer of above assets at book value to realisation account)			
2.	Share Capital Account Dr.		60,000	—
	General Reserve Account Dr.		15,000	—
	Profit and Loss Account Dr.		5,000	—
	To Shareholders' Account		—	80,000
	(Being transfer above accounts to shareholders)			
3.	Creditors Account Dr.		20,000	
	To Realisation Account		—	20,000
	(Being transfer of creditors to realisation account)			
Stage II	**Entries for recording the purchase consideration**			
4.	C Ltd. Account Dr.		80,000	—
	To Realisation Account		—	80,000
	(Being purchase consideration due from C Ltd.)			
5.	Shares in C Ltd. Account Dr.		80,000	—
	To C Ltd. Account		—	80,000
	(Being purchase consideration received from C Ltd. in the form of shares)			
Stage III	**Entries for recording of distribution of purchase consideration**			
6.	Shareholders' Account Dr.		80,000	—
	To Shares in C Ltd. Account		—	80,000
	(Being shareholders paid in the form of shares in C Ltd.)			

Ledger Accounts

Realisation Account

Dr.	Rs.		Cr. Rs.
To Goodwill	25,000	By Creditors	20,000
To Building	20,000	By C Ltd.	80,000
To Machinery	18,000	(*i.e.*, purchase consideration)	
To Stock	10,000		
To Debtors	19,000		
To Cash	8,000		
	1,00,000		1,00,000

C. Ltd. Account

Dr.	Rs.		Cr. Rs.
To Realisation	80,000	By Shares in C Ltd.	80,000
	80,000		80,000

Shareholders' Account

Dr.	Rs.		Cr. Rs.
To Shares in C Ltd.	80,000	By Share Capital	60,000
		By General Reserve	15,000
		By Profit & Loss Account	5,000
	80,000		80,000

Shares in C Ltd.

Dr.	Rs.		Cr. Rs.
To C Ltd.	80,000	By Shareholders	80,000
	80,000		80,000

(A) Purchase Method

Opening Entries in the Books of C Ltd.

Sl. No.	Particulars		L.F.	Dr. Rs.	Cr. Rs.
1.	Business Purchase A/c	Dr.		1,31,000	
	To Liquidator of A Company Ltd.			—	51,000
	To Liquidator of B Company Ltd.			—	80,000
	(Being purchase consideration payable to A Company Ltd. and B Company Ltd.)				
	Goodwill	Dr.		25,000	—
	Building A/c	Dr.		50,000	—
	Machinery A/c	Dr.		33,000	—

Contd.

	Stock A/c Dr.		22,000	
	Debtors A/c Dr.		41,000	
	Cash A/c Dr.		13,000	
	To Business Purchase A/c (51,000 + 80,000 Purchase consideration amount)		—	1,31,000
	To Creditors A/c		—	48,000
	To Bills Payable A/c		—	5,000
	(Being the above assets and liabilities taken over from A Ltd. and B Ltd. at their agreed values)			
2.	A Ltd. A/c and B Ltd. A/c Dr.		1,31,000	
	To Share Capital Account		—	1,31,000
	(Being purchase consideration paid to A Ltd. and B Ltd. in the form of shares)			

C Ltd. Balance sheet as on 31st December, 2009
(*i.e.,* Amalgamated New Balance Sheet)

Liabilities	Rs.	Assets	Rs.
Share Capital	1,31,000	**Fixed Assets**	
Current Liabilities		Goodwill	25,000
Creditors	48,000	Buildings	50,000
Bills Payable	5,000	Machinery	33,000
		Current Assets	
		Stock	22,000
		Debtors	41,000
		Cash	13,000
	1,84,000		1,84,000

(B) Pooling of Interests Method

Opening Entries in the Books of C Ltd.

Sl. No.	Particulars	L.F.	Dr. Rs.	Cr. Rs.
1.	Business Purchase Account Dr.		1,31,000	—
	To Liquidator of A Company Ltd.		—	51,000
	To Liquidator of B Company Ltd.		—	80,000
	(Being purchase consideration payable to A Company Ltd. and B Company Ltd.)			
2.	Buildings Account Dr.		30,000	—
	Machinery Account Dr.		15,000	—

Contd.

			Dr.	Cr.
	Stock Account	Dr.	12,000	—
	Debtors' Account	Dr.	22,000	—
	Cash Account	Dr.	5,000	—
	Profit and Loss Account	Dr.	4,000	—
	To Creditors' Account		—	28,000
	To Bills Payable Account		—	5,000
	To Capital Profit Account (B.F.)		—	4,000
	To Business Purchase Account		—	51,000
	(Being the incorporation of assets, liabilities and P & L A/c of A Company Ltd. and the difference between the purchase consideration and Share Capital (51,000 – 55,000) credited to Capital Profit Account)			
3.	Capital Profit Account	Dr.	4,000	—
	To P & L Account		—	4,000
	(Being debit balance of P & L A/c of A Company Ltd. adjusted against capital profit of A Company Ltd.)			
4.	Goodwill Account	Dr.	25,000	—
	Buildings Account	Dr.	20,000	—
	Machinery Account	Dr.	18,000	—
	Stock Account	Dr.	10,000	—
	Debtors' Account	Dr.	19,000	—
	Cash Account	Dr.	8,000	—
	Capital Loss Account (B.F.)	Dr.	20,000	—
	To General Reserve Account		—	15,000
	To Profit and Loss Account		—	5,000
	To Creditors' Account		—	20,000
	To Business Purchase Account		—	80,000
	(Being the incorporation of assets, liabilities, reserves and P & L A/c of B Company Ltd. and the difference between the purchase consideration and share capital (80,000 – 60,000) debited to Capital Loss Account)			
5.	General Reserve Account	Dr.	15,000	—
	Profit & Loss A/c	Dr.	5,000	—
	To Capital Loss Account		—	20,000
	(Being Capital loss of B Company Ltd. adjusted against general reserve and revenue profit of B Company Ltd.)			

Contd.

6.	A Company Ltd. & B Company Ltd. A/c Dr.		1,31,000	—
	To Share Capital Account		—	1,31,000
	(Being purchase consideration paid to A Company Ltd. and B Company Ltd. in the form of shares)			

Calculation of General Reserve and P & L A/c Balance

			Rs.
Purchase consideration (51,000 – 80,000)			1,31,000
Less :	Share Capital of Vendor Company (55,000 + 60,000)		1,15,000
	Excess being capital loss		16,000
Add :	P & L A/c of A Company Ltd. (Loss)		4,000
	Balance of loss		20,000
Less :	Adjusted from General Reserve A/c of B Co. Ltd.	15,000	
	Adjusted from P & L A/c of B Co. Ltd.	5,000	20,000
	Balance of loss		Nil
Balance in General Reserve A/c (15,000 – 15,000)			Nil
Balance in P & L A/c (5,000 – 5,000)			Nil

C Company Ltd. Balance Sheet as on 31st Dec., 2009
(*i.e.,* Amalgamated New Balance Sheet)

Liabilities	Rs.	Assets	Rs.
Share Capital	1,31,000	**Fixed Assets**	
(51,000 + 80,000)		Goodwill	25,000
Reserve and Surplus		Buildings	50,000
General Reserve	Nil	(30,000 + 20,000)	
(15,000 – 15,000)		Machinery	33,000
P & L A/c	Nil	(15,000 + 18,000)	
(5,000 – 5,000)		**Current Assets**	
Current Liabilities		Stock	22,000
Creditors	48,000	(12,000 + 10,000)	
(20,000 + 28,000)		Debtors	41,000
Bills Payable	5,000	(22,000 + 19,000)	
		Cash (5,000 + 8,000)	13,000
		Miscellaneous Expenditure and Loss	
		Profit & Loss A/c	Nil
		(4,000 – 4,000)	
	1,84,000		1,84,000

Illustration 5

X Co. Ltd. and Y Co. Ltd. decided to amalgamate their business and form a new company XY Co. Ltd. with an authorised capital of Rs. 15,00,000 divided into shares of Rs. 10 each.

Following are the two balance sheets :

Balance Sheets as on 31-12-2009

Liabilities	X Ltd.	Y Ltd.	Assets	X Ltd.	Y Ltd.
Equity Shares of Rs. 10 each	2,00,000	3,75,000	Goodwill	60,000	—
6% Debentures	—	1,00,000	Plant & Machinery	3,20,000	3,60,000
Reserve Fund	70,000	—	Stock	29,500	34,500
Sinking Fund	2,500	—	Debtors	42,750	24,500
Employees' Profit Sharing Fund	4,000		Cash at Bank	29750	21,000
Creditors	30,000	45,000	Profit & Loss A/c	—	80,000
Profit & Loss A/c	1,75,000	—			
	4,81,500	5,20,000		4,81,500	5,20,000

Following are the terms of agreement :

(1) X Co. Ltd. assets and liabilities are to be taken at book values except goodwill, plant and machinery and stock which are to be valued at Rs. 90,000, Rs. 3,00,000 and Rs. 32,000 respectively.

(2) Y Co. Ltd. assets except cash at Bank are valued at 10% less than the book and the liabilities are taken over at book figures. Prepare the balance sheet of the new company

(Adapted from Karnataka & Mysore Universities)

Solution :

Calculation of purchase consideration

			X Ltd.	Y Ltd.
Assets taken over :				
Goodwill			90,000	—
Plant & Machinery			3,00,000	3,24,000
Stock			32,000	31,050
Debtors			42,750	22,050
Cash at Bank			29,250	21,000
Total agreed value of assets taken over			4,94,000	3,98,100
Less : Liabilities taken over :	X Ltd.	Y Ltd.		
6% Debentures...	—	1,00,000		
Employers Profits Sharing Fund	4,000	—		—
Creditors	30,000	45,000	34,000	1,45,000
			4,60,000	2,53,100
Number of shares of Rs. 10 each issued			46,000	25,310

XY Ltd. Balance Sheet as on 31-12-2009

Liabilities		Rs.	Assets	Rs.
Share Capital			**Fixed Assets**	
Authorised 1,50,000 Shares of Rs. 10 each		15,00,000	Goodwill	90,000
Subscribed 71,310 Shares of Rs. 10 each fully paid		7,13,100	Plant & Machinery	6,24,000
Secured Loans			**Current Assets**	
Debentures		1,00,000	Stock	63,050
Current Liabilities			Debtors	64,800
Creditors	75,000		Cash at Bank	50,250
Employees Profit Sharing Fund	4,000	79,000		
		8,92,100		8,92,100

Hint : Amalgamation is in the nature of purchase.

Illustration 6

The Balance Sheets of X Co. Ltd. and Y Co. Ltd. as on 31st March, 2009 are as follows :

Liabilities	X Ltd. Rs.	Y Ltd. Rs.	Assets	X Ltd. Rs.	Y Ltd. Rs.
Share Capital			**Fixed Assets**		
Authorised Capital			Goodwill	80,000	—
Shares of Rs. 100 each	10,00,000		Fixed Assets	8,00,000	16,00,000
			Current Assets		
Shares of Rs. 10 each	—	20,00,000	Bank	—	2,00,000
			Other	9,00,000	6,60,000
Issued Capital fully paid	10,00,000	8,00,000			
Reserve & Surplus					
Capital Reserve	2,00,000	—			
General Reserve	70,000	8,00,000			
Secured Loans	—	5,00,000			
Unsecured Loan	2,00,000	—			
Current Liabilities and Provisions					
Sundry Creditors	3,10,000	3,60,000			
	17,80,000	24,60,000		17,80,000	24,60,000

It was proposed that X Co. Ltd. should be amalgamated in Y Co. Ltd. The following arrangement was accepted by both the companies :

(a) Goodwill of X Co. Ltd. is considered valueless.

(b) Arrears of depreciation in X Co. Ltd. amounted to Rs. 40,000.

(c) The holder of every 2 shares in X Co. Ltd. was to receive :

(i) As fully paid at par, 10 shares in Y Co. Ltd. and

(ii) So much cash as is necessary to adjust the right of shareholders of both the companies in accordance with the intrinsic value of the shares as per their balance sheets subject to necessary adjustments with regard to goodwill and depreciation in X Co. Ltd.'s Balance Sheet.

You are required to :

(a) Determine the composite of purchase consideration; and

(b) Show the Balance Sheet after amalgamation in the nature of purchase.

(Adapted from C.A. Inter & B. Com., Bangalore)

Solution :

Calculation of Intrinsic value of shares

X Company Ltd.

			Rs.
Agreed Value of assets taken over :			
	Fixed Assets	8,00,000	
Less:	Arrears of depreciation	40,000	7,60,000
	Current Assets		90,000
	Total value of assets taken over		16,60,000
Less :	Agreed value of Liabilities taken over :		
	Unsecured creditors	2,00,000	
	Sundry creditors	3,10,000	5,10,000
	Value of Net Assets		11,50,000
	Number of shares (Rs. 10,00,000 ÷ Rs. 100)		10,000
	Intrinsic value per share (Rs. 11,50,000 ÷ 10,000)		115

Y Company Ltd.

			Rs.
Agreed Value of assets taken over :			
	Fixed Assets		16,00,000
	Current Assets		8,60,000
	Total value of assets taken over		24,60,000
Less :	Agreed value of liabilities taken over :		
	Secured Loan	5,00,000	
	Sundry Creditors	3,60,000	8,60,000
	Value of Net Assets		16,00,000
	Number of shares (Rs. 8,00,000 ÷ 10)		80,000
	Intrinsic value per share (Rs. 1,60,000 ÷ 80,000)		20

Calculation of cash payable for every 2 shares

A shareholder of every two shares in X Co. Ltd. receives 10 shares in Y Co. Ltd. at their intrinsic value and difference in cash.

		Rs.
	Intrinsic value of 2 shares in X Co. Ltd. (2 × 115)	230
Less:	Intrinsic value of 10 shares in Y Co. Ltd. (2 × 20)	200
	Balance payable in cash for every 2 shares	30

Calculation purchase consideration

		Rs.
In Shares :	10 shares in Y Co. Ltd. for every 2 shares in X Co. Ltd., then, for 10,000 shares in X Co. Ltd. 10,000 × 10/2 = 50,000 shares in Y Co. Ltd.	
	50,000 shares in Y Co. Ltd. of Rs. 10 each issued at a premium of Rs. 10 per share (50,000 × 20)	10,00,000
In Cash :	Rs. 30 for every 2 shares in X Co. Ltd., then, for 10,000 shares in X Co. Ltd., cash payable will be (10,000 × 30/2)	1,50,000
	Purchase consideration	11,50,000

Balance Sheet of Y Co. Ltd. as on 31st March, 2009

Liabilities	Rs.	Assets	Rs.
Share Capital		**Fixed Assets**	
Authorised : 2,00,000 shares of Rs. 10 each	20,00,000	(8,00,000 + 16,00,000 – 40,000)	23,60,000
Issued and Subscribed		**Current Assets**	
1,30,000 shares of Rs. 10 each fully paid	13,00,000	Others (9,00,000 + 6,60,000)	15,60,000
(Of which 50,000 shares of Rs. 10 each issued for consideration other than cash)		Bank (2,00,000 – 1,50,000)	50,000
Reserves & Surplus			
Securities Premium (50,000 × 10)	5,00,000		
General Reserve (Y Co. Ltd.)	8,00,000		
Secured Loans (Y Co. Ltd.)	5,00,000		
Unsecured Loans (X Co. Ltd.)		2,00,000	
Current Liabilities			
Sundry Creditors (3,10,000 + 3,60,000)	6,70,000		
	39,70,000		39,70,000

Illustration 7

Ram Ltd. and Singh Ltd. agreed to amalgamate by transferring their undertaking to a new company styled as M/s Ramsingh Ltd. formed for that purpose. On the date of amalgamation the position of the two companies was as follow :

Liabilities	Ram Ltd.	Singh Ltd.	Assets	Ram Ltd.	Singh Ltd.
Share Capital :			Sundry Assets	4,00,000	3,00,000
Equity Shares of			Freehold Property	2,80,000	1,22,000
Rs. 10 each	6,00,000	4,00,000	Investments	40,000	40,000
5% Debentures	1,00,000	1,00,000	Debtors	2,60,000	1,50,000
Reserve Fund	—	50,000	Preliminary		
Surplus	50,000	25,000	Expenses	40,000	10,000
Mortgage Loan	50,000	—			
Creditors	2,20,000	47,000			
	10,20,000	6,22,000		10,20,000	6,22,000

The purchase consideration consisted of :

(a) The discharge of debentures in Ram Ltd. by the issue of equivalent amount of 6% debentures in Ramsingh Ltd.

(b) The assumption of the liabilities of both the companies; and

(c) The issue at a premium of 5 per share, of equity shares of Rs. 10 each in Ramsingh Ltd.

For the purpose of amalgamation the assets are to be valued as follows :

	Ram Ltd.	Singh Ltd.
Goodwill	1,00,000	75,000
Sundry Assets	4,10,000	2,80,000
Freehold property	3,00,000	1,00,000
Investments	40,000	50,000
Debtors	2,40,000	1,22,000

Pass the necessary journal entries in the books of amalgamated company to record the acquisition of business and prepare the amalgamated balance sheet of Ramsingh Ltd. Apply purchase method.

(Gulbarga, Oct. 1991)

Solution :

Calculation of purchase consideration

			Ram Ltd.	Singh Ltd.
			Rs.	Rs.
Agreed value of assets taken over :				
Goodwill			1,00,000	75,000
Sundry Assets			4,10,000	2,80,000
Freehold Property			3,00,000	1,00,000
Investments			40,000	50,000
Debtors			2,40,000	1,22,000
Total agreed value of assets taken over			10,90,000	6,27,000
Less : Agreed value of liabilities taken over :				
	Ram Ltd.	Singh Ltd.		
Debentures	—	1,00,000		
Mortgage Loan	50,000	—		
Creditors	2,20,000	47,000	2,70,000	1,47,000
Purchase consideration			8,20,000	4,80,000
Less : Paid by issue of debentures at par			1,00,00	—
Balance paid in shares at premium			7,20,000	4,80,000

Journal Entries in the Books of Ramsingh Ltd.

Sl. No.	Particulars		L.F.	Dr. Rs.	Cr. Rs.
1.	Goodwill Account	Dr.		1,75,000	—
	Sundry Assets Account	Dr.		6,90,000	—
	Freehold Property Account	Dr.		4,00,000	—
	Investments Account	Dr.		90,000	—
	Debtors Account	Dr.		3,62,000	—
	To 5% Debentures Account			—	1,00,000
	To Mortgage Loan Account			—	50,000
	To Creditors Account			—	2,67,000
	To Vendors' Account (*i.e.,* Ram Ltd. A/c & Singh Ltd. A/c 8,20,000 + 4,80,000)			—	13,00,000
	(Being entry to incorporate the assets and liabilities taken over as per agreement)				
2.	Vendors' Account	Dr.		13,00,000	
	To Share Capital Account			—	8,00,000
	To Share Premium Account			—	4,00,000
	To 6% Debentures Account			—	1,00,000
	(Being issue of 80,000 shares of Rs. 10 each at a premium of Rs. 5 per share and 6% debentures)				

Amalgamated Balance Sheet of Ramsingh Ltd.

Liabilities	Rs.	Assets	Rs.
Share Capital		**Fixed Assets**	
80,000 Equity Shares of		Goodwill	1,75,000
Rs. 10 each fully paid	8,00,000	Sundry Assets	6,90,000
Reserve & Surplus		Freehold Property	4,00,000
Share Premium	4,00,000	Investments	90,000
Secured Loans		**Current Assets**	
5% Debentures	1,00,000	Debtors	3,62,000
6% Debentures	1,00,000		
Mortgage Loan	50,000		
Current Liabilities			
Creditors	2,67,000		
	17,17,000		17,17,000

Illustration 8

P Co. Ltd. and Q Co. Ltd. agreed to amalgamate by transferring their undertakings to a new company PQ Co. Ltd. formed for that purpose on 31st December, 2009. Balance sheets of the respective companies were as under :

Liabilities	P. Ltd.	Q. Ltd.	Assets	P. Ltd.	Q. Ltd.
Share Capital	30,000	24,000	Furniture	9,000	6,300
Reserve	—	1,500	Debtors	14,400	18,000
Profit & Loss A/c	—	3,600	Bank	18,360	12,240
Creditors	12,900	7,440	Profit & Loss A/c	1140	—
	42,900	36,540		42,900	36,540

(i) The assets of P Co. Ltd. are taken at book values except furniture which is to be written down by Rs. 3,060.

(ii) Assets of Q Co. Ltd. are to be taken at book values except debtors which are considered to be worth Rs. 9,900.

(iii) The share capital of the combined company is to be 2,400 preference shares of Rs. 10 each fully paid and 500 ordinary shares of Rs. 45 each fully paid. The allocation of the shares is equal except that the surplus capital of P Co. Ltd. is to be satisfied in preference shares. The remaining purchase consideration is paid in cash.

Show the balances sheet of the new company as on 31st Dec., 2009 and the details of the exchange of shares. Apply purchase method.

(Adapted from Karnataka University)

Solution :

Calculation of purchase consideration

	P. Ltd.	Q. Ltd.
Revised value of assets taken over :		
Furniture	5,940	6,300
Debtors	14,400	9,900
Bank	18,360	12,240
Total value of assets taken over	38,700	28,440
Less : Liabilities taken over : Creditors	12,900	7,440
	25,800	21,000
Distribution of Shares		
Surplus Capital P. Ltd. Rs. 4,800 (*i.e.*, 25,800 – 21,000) should be paid in preference shares *i.e.*, 480 shares of Rs. 10 each	4,800	—
Remaining preference shares of 1920 should be distributed equally *i.e.*, 960 shares of Rs. 10 each to each company	9,600	9,600
Paid in preference shares	14,400	9,600
Part of purchase consideration should be paid in ordinary shares equally (*i.e.*, 250 shares of Rs. 45 each to each company)	11,250	11,250
Remaining amount of purchase consideration should be paid in cash	150	150
Total Rs.	25,800	21,000

Balance Sheet of PQ Ltd. as on 31-12-2009

Liabilities	Rs.	Assets	Rs.
Share Capital		**Fixed Assets**	
Preference Shares of Rs. 10		Furniture	12,240
each fully paid	24,000	**Current Assets**	
Ordinary Shares of Rs. 45		Debtors	24,300
each fully paid	11,250	Bank	30,300
Current Liabilities		(30,600 – 300)	
Creditors	20,340		
	66,840		66,840

Illustration 9

The following are the balance sheets of A Co. Ltd. and B C. Ltd. as on 31-12-2006. On that date they decided to amalgamate their business and form a new AB Co. Ltd. The authorised capital of AB Co. Ltd. will be Rs. 14,00,000 divided into 10,00,000 equity shares of Rs. 10 each and Rs. 4,00,000 12% preference shares of Rs. 100 each.

Liabilities	A Co.	B Co.	Assets	A Co.	B Co.
Share Capital :			Goodwill	60,000	55,000
Equity Shares of			Land & Buildings	1,50,000	1,90,000
Rs. 10 each	3,00,000	4,00,000	Plant & Machinery	1,00,000	1,50,000
Reserves & Surplus :			Stock	50,000	90,000
General Reserve	60,000	80,000	Debtors	70,000	80,000
Profit & Loss A/c	40,000	65,000	Bank	30,000	65,000
Current Liabilities :					
Creditors	40,000	60,000			
Bills Payable	20,000	25,000			
	4,60,000	6,30,000		4,60,000	6,30,000

The purchase consideration was agreed as under :

(i) A Co. Ltd.: The assets and liabilities were taken over at book values except :

(a) Land and Building values at Rs. 1,75,000 and

(b) Plant and Machinery at 10% less than the book value.

The consideration being :

(a) Equity shareholders of A Co. Ltd. will be paid cash of Rs. 5 per share and

(b) Four equity shares of Rs. 10 each in AB Co. Ltd. for every three shares in 'A' Co. Ltd.

(ii) B Co. Ltd. : All the assets except goodwill and bank balance be taken over at book values and the liabilities in respect of creditors only taken over, where bills payable were to be paid off before amalgamation by B Co. Ltd.

The consideration being :

The equity shareholders of B Co. Ltd. will receive :

(a) Rs. 1,00,000 12% preference shares of Rs. 100 each fully paid,

(b) Three equity shares of Rs. 10 each in AB Co. Ltd. in exchange for every four equity shares in B Co. Ltd. and

(c) The balance in cash.

Of the remaining equity shares of AB Co. Ltd. 20,000 equity shares were issued to public and the cash was duly received.

Pass the journal entries in the books of new company and prepare the amalgamated balance sheet of the new company. Apply purchase method.

(Adapted from Karnataka & Poona)

Solution :

Calculation of purchase consideration of A Co. Ltd.

In cash : Rs. 5 per share, then for shares 30,000 × 5	1,50,000
In equity shares : 4 shares for 3 shares, then for 30,000 shares *i.e.,* 30,000 × 4/3 = 40,000 shares of Rs. 10 each *i.e.,* 40,000 × 10	4,00,000
Purchase consideration	5,50,000

Calculation of purchase consideration of B Co. Ltd.

Agreed value of assets taken over :	
Land and Buildings	1,90,000
Plant & Machinery	1,50,000
Stock	90,000
Debtors	80,000
Total value of assets taken over	5,10,000
Less : Agreed value of liabilities taken over :	
Creditors	60,000
Purchase consideration	4,50,000

Allocation of purchase consideration

In equity shares : 3 shares for 4 shares, then for 40,000 shares *i.e.,* 40,000 × 3/4 = 30,000 shares of Rs. 10 each *i.e.,* 30,000 × 10	3,00,000
In preference shares : 1,000 shares of Rs. 10 each	1,00,000
In cash : Remaining balance paid in cash	50,000
Total Rs.	4,50,000

Journal Entries in the Books of AB Co. Ltd.

Sl. No.	Particulars	L.F.	Dr. Rs.	Cr. Rs.
1.	Goodwill Account (Balancing Figure) Dr.		1,95,000	—
	Land and Building Account Dr.		3,65,000	—
	Plant and Machinery Account Dr.		2,40,000	—
	Stick Account Dr.		1,40,000	—
	Debtors Account Dr.		1,50,000	—
	Bank Account Dr.		30,000	—
	To Vendors Account		—	10,00,000
	To Creditors Account		—	1,00,000
	To Bills Payable Account		—	20,000
	(Entry to incorporate the assets and liabilities taken over as per agreement)			

Contd.

2.	Vendors' Account	Dr.	10,00,000	
	To Equity Share capital			7,00,000
	To Preference Share capital			1,00,000
	To Cash			2,00,000
	(Issue of 70,000 *i.e.*, 40,000 + 30,000 equity shares of Rs. 10 each, 1,000 preference shares of Rs. 100 each and the balance paid in cash in satisfaction of purchase consideration)			
3.	Cash Account	Dr.	2,00,000	
	To Equity Share Capital			2,00,000
	(Cash received on issue of 20,000 shares to public at Rs. 10 each in full)			

Balance Sheet of AB Co. Ltd. as on 31-12-2006

Liabilities	Rs.	Assets	Rs.
Share Capital		**Fixed Assets**	
Authorised		Goodwill	1,95,000
1,00,000 Equity Shares		Land & Buildings	3,65,000
of Rs. 10 each	10,00,000	Plant & Machinery	2,40,000
4,000 12% Preference		**Current Assets**	
shares of Rs. 100 each	4,00,000	Stock	1,40,000
Subscribed and Paid up :		Debtors	1,50,000
90,000 Equity Shares of		Bank	30,000
Rs. 10 each fully paid.			
(40,000+30,000+20,000)	9,00,000		
1,000 12% Preference			
Shares of Rs. 100 each			
fully paid	1,00,000		
Current Liabilities			
Creditors	20,000		
Bills Payable	20,000		
	11,20,000		11,20,000

Illustration 10

The following were the Balance Sheets of B Ltd. and D Ltd. as on 31st March, 2006 :

Rs. in '000

Liabilities	B. Ltd.	D. Ltd.	Assets	B. Ltd.	D. Ltd.
75,000 13% Preference			Goodwill	—	250
shares of Rs. 100 each	7,500	—	Freehold Premises	12,000	—
30,00,000 Equity Shares			Machinery	34,510	—
of Rs. 10 each	30,000	—	Furniture & Fixtures	1,120	750
5,00,000 Equity Shares			Trade Marks	100	—
of Rs. 10 each	—	5,000	Stock	12,800	5,010
Capital Reserve	9,600	—	Debtors	4,340	1,170
General Reserve	12,400	1,450	Bills Receivable	—	100
Profit & Loss A/c	1,150	220	Cash at Bank	2,230	220
12% Debentures	5,000	—			
Creditors	1,450	830			
	67,100	7,500		67,100	7,500

On the above mentioned date, B Ltd. and D Ltd. agreed to amalgamate their business unit and formed a new company named BD Ltd. for the purpose. The merger took place on the following terms :

(i) BD Ltd. allotted to B Ltd. 75,000 14% fully paid preference shares of Rs. 100 each and 45 lakh fully paid equity shares of Rs. 10 each to satisfy the claims of B Ltd.'s preference shareholders and equity shareholders respectively. It also agreed to convert 12% debentures of B Ltd. into 13% debentures of identical amount.

(ii) BD Ltd. allotted to D Ltd. 5,50,000 fully paid equity shares of Rs. 10 each to be distributed among D Ltd.'s shareholders in full satisfaction of their claims.

Expenses on the liquidation of the two companies Rs. 10,000 were borne by BD Ltd. In addition to this, the preliminary expenses of BD Ltd. totalled Rs. 88,000.

You are required to : (i) Prepare in columnar from important ledger accounts pertaining to B Ltd. and D Ltd. (ii) Pass journal entries in the books of BD Ltd. and (iii) Draw BD Ltd.'s balance sheet after all the transactions have been recorded.

(Adapted from ACS and B.Com., B.U.)

Solution :

Purchase Consideration of B Ltd.	**Rs. in '000'**
Preference Shares : 75,000 × 100	7,500
Equity Shares : 45,00,000 × 10	45,000
Purchase Consideration	52,500

Purchase consideration of D Ltd. Rs. in '000

	Rs. in '000
Equity Shares : 5,50,000 × 10	5,500
	5,500

Note : Debentures do not form part of purchase consideration under AS-14. It is assumed that it is taken over by the purchasing company and then, discharged.

Ledger Accounts

Dr. **Realisation Account** Cr.

	B. Ltd. Rs. in '000	D. Ltd. Rs. in '000		B. Ltd. Rs. in '000	D. Ltd. Rs. in '000
To Goodwill	—	250	By 12% Debentures	5,000	—
To Freehold Premises	12,000	—	By Creditors	1,450	830
To Machinery	34,510	—	By BD Ltd. (Purchase consideration)	52,500	5,500
To Furniture & Fixtures	1,120	750			
To Trade Marks	100	—	By Equity Shareholders' A/c (Loss transferred)	8,150	170
To Stock	12,800	5,010			
To Debtors	4,340	1,710			
To Cash at Bank	2,330	220			
To Bills Receivable	—	100			
	67,100	7,500		67,100	7,500

Dr. **BD Ltd. Account** Cr.

	B. Ltd. Rs. in '000	D. Ltd. Rs. in '000		B. Ltd. Rs. in '000	D. Ltd. Rs. in '000
To Realisation A/c (Purchase consideration)	52,500	5,500	By 14% Preference Shares in BD Ltd. A/c	7,500	—
			By Equity Shares in BD Ltd. A/c	45,000	5,500
	52,500	5,500		52,500	5,500

Dr. **14% Preference Shares in BD Ltd. Account** Cr.

	B. Ltd. Rs. in '000	D. Ltd. Rs. in '000		B. Ltd. Rs. in '000	D. Ltd. Rs. in '000
To 14% Preference Shares in BD Ltd. A/c	7,500	—	By 13% Preference Share Capital	7,500	—
	7,500	—		7,500	—

Dr. **Equity Shares in BD Ltd. Account** Cr.

	B. Ltd. Rs. in '000	D. Ltd. Rs. in '000		B. Ltd. Rs. in '000	D. Ltd. Rs. in '000
To Realisation A/c (Loss)	8,150	1,170	By Equity Share Capital	30,000	5,000
To Equity Shares Ltd. A/c (Settlement)	45,000	5,500	By Capital Reserve	9,600	—
			By General Reserve	12,400	1,450
			By P & L Account	1,150	220
	53,150	6,670		53,150	6,670

In the Books of BD Ltd.
Journal Entries

Sl. No.	Particulars		L.F.	Dr. Rs. in '000	Cr. Rs. in '000
1.	Business Purchase Account	Dr.		58,000	—
	To Liquidator of B Ltd. Account			—	52,500
	To Liquidator of D Ltd. Account			—	5,500
	(Being Purchase consideration payable to Liquidator of B Ltd.)				
2.	Goodwill Account	Dr.		250	—
	Freehold Premises Account	Dr.		12,000	—
	Machinery Account	Dr.		34,510	—
	Furniture & Fixtures Account	Dr.		1,870	—
	Trade Marks Account	Dr.		100	—
	Stock Account	Dr.		17,810	—
	Debtors Account	Dr.		5,510	—
	Cash at Bank Account	Dr.		2,450	—
	Bills Receivable Account	Dr.		100	—
	To Capital Reaserve A/c (Balancing figure)			—	9,320
	To 12% Debentures (B Ltd.) Account			—	5,000
	To Creditors Account			—	2,280
	To Business Purchase Account			—	58,000
	(Being incorporation of assets, liabilities and reserves of B Ltd. and D Ltd. at book values, the excess of purchase consideration over share capitals of B Ltd. and D Ltd. adjusted against General Reserve, Profit & Loss A/c and finally against Capital Reserve)*				

Contd..

3.	12% Debentures (B Ltd.) Account Dr. To 13% Debentures Account (BD Ltd.) (Being discharge of 12% Debentures of B Ltd. by issue of 13% Debentures of BD of Ltd.)	5,000 —	— 5,000
4.	Liquidator of B Ltd. Account Dr. Liquidator of D Ltd. Account Dr. To 14% Preference Share Capital A/c To Equity Share Capital Account (Being issue of 75,000 14% fully paid pref. shares of Rs. 100 each and 45 lakh fully paid equity shares of Rs. 10 each to take over the business of B Ltd. and issue of 5,50,000 fully paid equity shares of Rs. 10 each to takeover the business of D Ltd.)	52,500 5,500 — —	— — 7,500 50,500
5.	Capital Reserve Account Dr. To Bank Account (Being payment of expenses on the liquidation of B Ltd. and D Ltd. debited to capital reserve)	10 —	— 10
6.	Preliminary Expenses Account Dr. To Bank Account (Being payment of preliminary expenses)	88 —	— 88

Note : *Combined journal entry has been passed in direct and summary manner

Calculation of Capital Reserve Account Balance

		Rs. in '000'	Rs. in '000'
	Purchase Consideration : B Ltd.	52,500	
	D. Ltd.	5,500	58,000
Less :	Share Capital : B Ltd. (75 ,00,000 + 3,00,00,000)	37,500	
	D. Ltd.	5,000	42,500
	Excess being Capital loss		15,500
Less :	Adjusted from general reserve :		
	B Ltd.	12,400	
	D Ltd.	1,450	13,850
	Balance of Capital loss		1,650
Less :	Adjusted from P & L A/c : B Ltd.	1,150	
	D Ltd.	220	1,370
	Balance of Capital loss		280
Less :	Adjusted from Capital Reserve (only required amount)		280
	Balance of loss		Nil

		Rs. in '000
Balance in Capital Reserve Account (96,00,000 – 2,80,000)		9,320
Less :	Liquidation expenses written off	10
	Balance of Capital Reserve shown in the Balance Sheet	9,310

Calculation of Cash at Bank Balance

		Rs. in '000	Rs. in '000
	Cash at Bank of B Ltd.		2,230
	Cash at Bank of D Ltd.		220
			2,450
Less :	Liquidation expenses	10	
	Preliminary expenses	88	98
		Balance of Cash at Bank	2,352

Balance Sheet of B D Ltd. as at 31st March, 2009

Liabilities	Rs. in '000	Assets	Rs. in '000
Share Capital		**Fixed Assets**	
Authorised	Nil	Goodwill	250
Issued and subscribed :		Freehold Premises	12,000
75,000 14% Preference		Machinery	34,510
Shares of Rs. 100 each,		Furniture & Fixtures	1,870
paid up	7,500	Trade Marks	100
5,50,000 Equity Shares of		**Current Assets, Loans**	
Rs. 10 each, fully paid-up	50,500	**and Advances**	
(45,00,000 + 5,50,000 × 10)		(a) Current Assets :	
Reserves and Surplus		Stock	17,810
Capital Reserve	9,310	Debtors	5,510
Secured Loans		Cash at Bank	2,352
13% Debentures	5,000	(b) Loans & Advances :	
Current Liabilities and		Bills Receivable	100
Provisions		**Miscellaneous Expenditure**	
(a) Current Liabilities :		Preliminary expenses	88
Creditors	2,280		
(b) Provisions	Nil		
	74,590		74,590

Illustration 11

The following are the balance sheets of X Co. Ltd. and Y Co. Ltd. as on 31-12-2009.

Liabilities	X Co. Ltd.	Y Co. Ltd.	Assets	X Co. Ltd.	Y Co. Ltd.
Share Capital			**Fixed Assets**		
Authorised :			Goodwill	75,000	—
Shares of Rs. 10 each	25,00,000	—	Buildings	2,75,000	75,000
Issued & Subscribed :			Machinery	5,00,000	2,00,000
Shares of Rs. 10 each	12,50,000	4,00,000	Furniture	25,000	12,500
Reserve & Surplus			**Investments**		
General Reserve	1,50,000	25,000	Shares in A Co.	1,25,000	—
Secured Loans			Govt. Securities	—	75,000
Debentures	2,50,000	—	**Current Assets,**		
Unsecured Loans	—	1,00,000	**Loans & Advances**		
Current Liabilities			Stock	4,50,000	87,500
& Provisions			Debtors	1,25,000	45,000
Creditors	1,00,000	—	Bills Receivable	25,000	15,000
Staff Provident Fund	—	20,000	Bank	1,00,000	40,000
Bills Payable	—	5,000	Cash	50,000	—
	17,50,000	5,50,000		17,50,000	5,50,000

X Co. Ltd. agrees to absorb the business of Y Co. Ltd. as on 31-12-2009 and to take over the assets and liabilities at their balance sheet values in exchange for which it is to issue 5 shares of Rs. 10 each for every 4 shares of Rs. 10 each in the Y Co. Ltd. The expenses of absorption of Rs. 5,000 be paid by X Co. Ltd.

Pass the closing entries and show the ledger accounts in the books of Y Co. Ltd. and opening entries in the books of X Co. Ltd. and show the new balance sheet under purchase method.

Solution :

Calculation of purchase consideration payable to Y Co. Ltd.

In shares : For every 4 shares of Y Co. Ltd.,

5 shares of X Co. Ltd. are given at Rs. 10 per share

$$\left(\frac{40,000 \times 5 \times 10}{4}\right) \qquad 5,00,000$$

Rs. 5,00,000 is the purchase consideration.

Closing Entries in the Books of Y Co. Ltd.

Sl. No.	Particulars		L.F.	Dr. Rs.	Cr. Rs.
Stage I	**Entries to close all the accounts that appear in the Balance sheet**				
1.	Realisation Account	Dr.		5,50,000	—
	To Buildings Account			—	75,000
	To Machinery Account			—	2,00,000
	To Furniture Account			—	12,500
	To Govt. Securities Account			—	75,000
	To Stock Account			—	87,500
	To Debtors Account			—	45,000
	To Bills Receivables Account			—	15,000
	To Bank Account			—	40,000
	(Being transfer of assets at their book values)				
2.	Share Capital Account	Dr.		4,00,000	—
	General Reserve Account	Dr.		25,000	—
	To Shareholders' Account			—	4,25,000
	(Being transfer of share capital and general reserve to shareholders)				
3.	Unsecured Loans	Dr.		1,00,000	—
	Staff Provident Fund	Dr.		20,000	—
	Bills Payable	Dr.		5,000	—
	To Realisation Account				
	(Being liabilities transferred to realisation account at their book values)			—	1,25,000
Stage II	**Entries for recording the purchase consideration**				
4.	X Co. Ltd. Account	Dr.		5,00,000	—
	To Realisation Account			—	5,00,000
	(Being purchase consideration due from X Co. Ltd.)				
5.	Shares in X Co. Ltd. Account	Dr.		5,00,000	—
	To X Co. Ltd. Account			—	5,00,000
	(Being purchase consideration received in the form of shares)				
Stage III	**Entries for recording of allotment of purchase consideration**				
6.	Realisation Account	Dr.		75,000	—
	To Shareholders' Account			—	75,000
	(Being transfer of realisation profit to shareholders)				
7.	Shareholders' Account	Dr.		5,00,000	—
	To Shares in X Co. Ltd.			—	5,00,000
	(Being distribution of shares among shareholders)				

Ledger Accounts in the Books of Y Ltd.

Realisation Account

Dr.	Rs.		Cr. Rs.
To Buildings	75,000	By Unsecured Loans	1,00,000
To Machinery	2,00,000	By Staff Provident Fund	20,000
To Furniture	12,500	By Bills Payable	5,000
To Govt. Securities	75,000	By X Co. Ltd.	5,00,000
To Stock	87,500	(Purchase	
To Debtors	45,000	consideration)	
To Bills Receivable	15,000		
To Bank	40,000		
To Shareholders (Profit)	75,000		
	6,25,000		6,25,000

Shareholders' Account

Dr.	Rs.		Cr. Rs.
To Shares in X Co. Ltd.	5,00,000	By Share Capital	4,00,000
		By General Reserve	25,000
		By Realisation A/c (Profit)	75,000
	5,00,000		5,00,000

X. Co. Ltd. Account

Dr.	Rs.		Cr. Rs.
To Realisation A/c	5,00,000	By Share in X Co. Ltd.	5,00,000
	5,00,000		5,00,000

Shares in X Co. Account

Dr.	Rs.		Cr. Rs.
To X Co. Ltd.	5,00,000	By Shareholders'	5,00,000
	5,00,000		5,00,000

Opening Entries in the Books of X Co. Ltd.

Sl. No.	Particulars		L.F.	Dr. Rs.	Cr. Rs.
1.	Buildings Account	Dr.		75,000	—
	Machinery Account	Dr.		2,00,000	—
	Furniture Account	Dr.		12,500	—
	Government Securities Account	Dr.		75,000	—
	Stock Account	Dr.		87,500	—
	Debtors Account	Dr.		45,000	—
	Bills Receivables Account	Dr.		15,000	—
	Bank Account	Dr.		40,000	—
	Goodwill A/c (Balancing figure)	Dr.		75,000	—
	To Unsecured Loans A/c			—	1,00,000
	To Staff Provident Fund A/c			—	20,000
	To Bills Payable A/c			—	5,000
	To Liquidator of Y Co. Ltd.			—	5,00,000
	(Being entry to incorporate the assets and liabilities taken over and the excess of liabilities over assets is treated as goodwill)				
2.	Liquidator of Y Co. Ltd. A/c	Dr.		5,00,000	—
	To Share Capital Account			—	5,00,000
	(Being issue of 50,000 shares of Rs. 10 each fully paid in satisfaction of purchase consideration)				
3.	Goodwill A/c	Dr.		5,000	—
	To Bank A/c			—	5,000
	(Being liquidation expenses of Y Co. Ltd. paid)				

Balance Sheet of X Co. Ltd. as on 31-12-2006 (After absorption)

Liabilities	Rs.	Assets	Rs.
Share Capital		**Fixed Assets**	
Authorised :		Goodwill (75,000 + 75,000 + 5,000)	1,55,000
2,50,000 Shares of Rs. 10 each	2,50,000	Buildings	3,50,000
Issued & Subscribed :		Machinery	7,00,000
1,75,000 Shares of Rs. 10 each fully paid	17,50,000	Furniture	37,500

(*Contd.*.)

Reserve & Surplus :		**Investments :**	
General Reserve	1,50,000	Shares in A Co. Ltd.	1,25,000
Secured Loans :		Govt. Securities	75,000
Debentures	2,50,000	**Current Assets, Loans**	
Unsecured Loans	1,00,000	**and Advances**	
Current Liabilities and		Stock	5,37,500
Provisions		Debtors	1,70,000
Creditors	1,00,000	Bills Receivable	40,000
Staff Provident Fund	20,000	Bank	1,40,000
Bills Payable	5,000	Cash (50,000 – 5,000)	45,000
	23,75,000		23,75,000

Note : It is assumed that liquidation expenses of Rs. 5,000 are directly paid by X Co. Ltd.

Illustration 12

The assets and liabilities of Moti Ltd. and Choti Ltd on 31st December, 2009 were as follows :

Liabilities	Moti Ltd.	Choti Ltd.	Assets	Moti Ltd.	Choti Ltd.
Authorised Capital :			Goodwill	4,000	—
Divided into shares			Land	8,000	4,000
of Re. 1 each	1,00,000	40,000	Buildings	30,000	10,000
Issued Capital :			Machinery	20,000	4,000
Divided into paid up			Debtors	10,000	8,000
shares of Re. 1 each	50,000	32,000	Stock	16,000	10,000
General Reserve	—	2,000	Cash	4,000	—
Profit and Loss A/c	16,000	—	Furniture	—	2,000
Debentures	20,000	—			
Creditors	6,000	4,000			
	92,000	38,000		92,000	38,000

Moti Ltd. agreed to purchase from Choti Ltd. the following assets at these valuation : Land Buildings at book values; Machinery less 10%; Furniture at Rs. 1,800; Debtors less 5% Stock in Trade less 20%. It is also agreed to give Rs. 16,000 for goodwill and to allot 40,000 shares for purchase consideration with a cash payment for the balance. The shares of Moti Ltd. are quoted on exchange at Rs. 1.25 per share, Choti Ltd. agreed to pay off its own creditors and for the purpose sell sufficient shares allotted by Moti Ltd. at the market rate of Rs. 1.25 per share. Give journal entries to close the books of Choti Ltd. and show the Balance Sheet of Moti Ltd. after the completion of purchase under purchase method.

(Adapted from Mysore, University)

Solution :

Calculation of purchase consideration

	Rs.
Agreed values of assets taken over :	
Land (Book value)	4,000
Buildings (book value)	10,000
Machinery (4,000 – 400)	3,600
Furniture (Agreed value)	1,800
Debtors (8,000 – 400)	7,600
Stock (10,000 – 2,000)	8,000
Goodwill (Agreed value)	16,000
Less : Liabilities taken over	Nil
Purchase consideration	51,000

The purchase consideration is settled as below :	Rs.
In the form of shares (40,000 × 1.25)	50,000
In the form of cash (Balance)	1,000
	51,000

Closing Entries in the Books of Choti Ltd.

Sl. No.	Particulars		L.F.	Dr. Rs.	Cr. Rs.
Stage I	**Entries to close all the accounts that appear in the Balance Sheet**				
1.	Realisation Account	Dr.		38,000	—
	To Land Account			—	4,000
	To Buildings Account			—	10,000
	To Machinery Account			—	4,000
	To Debtors Account			—	8,000
	To Stock Account			—	10,000
	To Furniture Account			—	2,000
	(Being transfer of assets taken over)				
2.	Share Capital Account	Dr.		32,000	—
	General Reserve Account	Dr.		2,000	—
	To Shareholders' Account			—	34,000
	(Being above items transferred to shareholders)				

(Contd..)

Stage II	**Entries for recording the purchase consideration**			
3.	Moti Ltd. Account Dr.		51,000	—
	To Realisation Account		—	51,000
	(Being purchase consideration due from Moti Ltd.)			
4.	Bank Account Dr.		1,000	—
	Shares in Moti. Ltd. Account Dr.		50,000	—
	To Moti Ltd. Account		—	51,000
	(Being purchase consideration received in the form of cash and shares)			
5.	Bank Account Dr.		3,000	—
	To Shares in Moti Ltd. Account		—	3,000
	(Being cash received from the sale of 2,400 shares allotted by Moti Ltd. at Re. 1.25 per share)			
Stage III	**Entries for recording of allotment of purchase consideration**			
6.	Creditors' Account Dr.		4,000	—
	To Bank Account		—	4,000
	(Being payment of creditor not taken over)			
7.	Realisation Account Dr.		13,000	—
	To Shareholders' Account		—	13,000
	(Being profit on realisation transferred to shareholders)			
8.	Shareholders' Account Dr.		47,000	—
	To Shares in Moti Ltd. Account		—	47,000
	(Being payment of shareholders in the form of shares)			

	Calculation of amount paid to creditors :	
	Amount payable to creditors	4,000
Less :	Cash received from the purchasing company towards purchase consideration	1,000
	Amount of cash required for paying the creditors	3,000

The vendor company has to sell sufficient number of shares to collect Rs. 3,000. Therefore, for collecting Rs. 3,000 the vendor company has to sell

2,400 shares of Rs. 1.25 each. But the vendor has sold 2,400 shares of Rs. 1.25 each. Therefore, there is no profit or loss on the sale of 2,400 shares. If there is a profit or loss on the sale of 2,400 shares, that should be transferred to realisation account.

Moti Ltd. Balance Sheet as on 31-12-2009

Liabilities	Rs.	Assets	Rs.
Share Capital :		Goodwill (4,000 + 16,000)	20,000
Authorised :		Land (8,000 + 4,000)	12,000
1,00,000 Shares		Buildings (30,000 + 10,000)	40,000
of Re. 1 each	1,00,000	Machinery (20,000 + 3,600)	23,600
Issued, Subscribed,		Furniture	1,800
Called-up and Paid up :		Stock (16,000 + 8,000)	24,000
90,000 (50,000 + 40,000)		Debtors (10,000 + 7,600)	17,600
Shares of Re. 1 each fully		Cash	3,000
paid	90,000	(Balance Rs. 4,000	
Share Premium	10,000	Less : cash paid towards	
(40,000 × 0.25)		purchase consideration	
Profit and Loss A/c :		Rs. 1,000)	
Credit Balance	16,000		
Debentures	20,000		
Creditors	6,000		
	1,42,000		1,42,000

Illustration 13

The following is the Balance Sheet of Weak Ltd. as at 30th June, 2009.

Liabilities	Rs.	Assets	Rs.
Share Capital :		Goodwill	35,000
2,000 Shares of		Land & Building	85,000
Rs. 100 each	2,00,000	Plant & Machinery	1,60,000
Reserve Fund	20,000	Stock	55,000
5% Debentures	1,00,000	Cash at Bank	34,000
Loan from 'A'	40,000	Discount on Debentures	6,000
(a director)		Debtors	65,000
Sundry Creditors	70,000		
Employee Savings Bank A/c	10,000		
	4,40,000		4,40,000

The business of the company is taken over by Strong Ltd. as on that date on the following terms :

(a) The Strong Ltd. to take over all the assets except cash, the assets to be valued at their book values less 10% except goodwill which was to be valued at 4 years' purchase of the excess of average (five years) profits over 8% of the combined amount of share capital and reserves.

(b) The Strong Ltd. to take over trade creditors and employees savings bank account which were subject to a discount of 5%.

(c) The purchase consideration was to be discharged in cash to the extent of Rs. 1,50,000 and the balance in fully paid equity shares of Rs. 10 each valued at Rs. 12.50 per share.

(d) The average of the 5 years' profits was Rs. 30,100. The expenses of liquidation amounted to Rs. 4,000. Show the necessary accounts in the books of Weak Ltd. and the Journal entries in the books of Strong Ltd. Amalgamation is in the nature of purchase.

(Adapted from S.U. and B.U.)

Solution :

Calculation of purchase consideration

		Rs.
Agreed value of assets taken over :		
(*i.e.*, 10% less than book values)		
Land and Buildings		76,500
Plant and Machinery		1,44,000
Debtors	65,000	
Less : Provision	6,500	58,500
Stock		49,500
Goodwill		50,000
		3,78,500
Less : Liabilities taken over : Creditors	70,000	
Employees Saving Bank Account	10,000	
	80,000	
Less : Reserve for discount	4,000	76,000
Purchase consideration		3,02,500

The purchase consideration is settled as below :	Rs.
In the form of cash	1,50,000
Balance paid in fully paid equity shares	1,52,500
	3,02,500
Number of shares to be issued *i.e.*, 1,52,500 ÷ 12,50	12,200

Note : Value of goodwill is calculated as below :

Goodwill is to be valued at 4 times the excess of average profits of 5 years over 8% of the total of share capital and reserves *i.e.,* 4 (Average profits less 8% capital plus reserve)

Therefore, 5 years average profits as given	Rs. 30,100
Less : 8% of capital + reserve *i.e.,* 8 × 2,20,000/100	Rs. 17,600
Excess of five years profits	12,500

Goodwill is 4 times of this excess of Rs. 12,500

Hence, value of goodwill is Rs. 50,000 (*i.e.,* 12,500 × 4)

Ledger Accounts in the Books of Weak Ltd.

Realisation Account

Dr.	Rs.		Cr. Rs.
To Goodwill	35,000	By Sundry Creditors	70,000
To Land & Building	85,000	By Employees Savings Bank Account	10,000
To Plant & Machinery	1,60,000	By Strong Ltd. (Purchase considerations)	3,02,500
To Stock	55,000	By Shareholders (Loss transferred)	21,500
To Debtors	65,000		
To Bank (expenses)	4,000		
	4,04,000		4,04,000

Shareholders' Account

Dr.	Rs.		Cr. Rs.
To Realisation A/c (Loss)	21,500	By Share Capital	2,00,000
To Shares in Strong Co. Ltd.	1,52,500	By Reserve Fund	20,000
To Discount on Debentures	6,000		
To Bank	40,000		
	2,20,000		2,20,000

Strong Ltd. Account

Dr.	Rs.		Cr. Rs.
To Realisation A/c (Purchase price)	3,02,500	By Bank	1,50,000
		By Shares	1,52,500
	3,02,500		3,02,500

5% Debentures' Account

Dr.	Rs.		Cr. Rs.
To Bank	1,00,000	By Balance b/d	1,00,000
	1,00,000		1,00,000

Dr. **A's Loan Account** Cr.

	Rs.		Rs.
To Bank	40,000	By Balance b/d	40,000
	40,000		40,000

Dr. **Bank Account** Cr.

	Rs.		Rs.
To Balance b/d	34,000	By Realisation (expenses)	4,000
To Strong Ltd.	1,50,000	By Debentures	1,00,000
		By A's Loan	40,000
		By Shareholders	40,000
	1,84,000		1,84,000

Journal Entries in the Books of Strong Ltd.

Sl. No.	Particulars	L. F.	Dr. Rs.	Cr. Rs.
1.	Land and Account A/c Dr.		76,500	—
	Plant and Machinery A/c Dr.		1,44,000	—
	Stock Account (65,000 – 6,500)		58,500	—
	Debtors Account		49,500	—
	Goodwill Account		50,000	—
	To Sundry Creditors (70,000—3,500)		66,500	—
	To Employees Savings Bank A/c (10,000 – 500)		—	9,500
	To Weak Ltd. A/c (purchase consideration)		—	3,02,500
	(Being the assets and liabilities taken over at agreed values and purchase price payable to Weak Ltd.)			
2.	Weak Ltd. A/c Dr.		3,02,500	—
	To Share Capital A/c		—	1,22,000
	To Share Premium A/c		—	30,500
	To Bank Account		—	1,50,000
	(Being payment of cash Rs. 1,50,000 and issue of 12,200 shares of Rs. 10 each at Rs. 12.50 per share)			

Illustration 14

A Ltd. agrees to absorb the business of B Ltd. The following is the balance sheet of B Ltd. as on 31-12- 2008.

Liabilities	Rs.	Assets		Rs.
Shares Capital :		Buildings		50,000
5,000 shares of Rs. 20 each	1,00,000	Machinery		35,000
Reserves	15,000	Stock		15,000
Profit & Loss Account	5,000	Debtors	22,000	
Creditors	10,000	*Less* : Provision for D.D.	2,000	20,000
		Cash		10,000
	1,30,000			1,30,000

A Ltd. took over all the assets and liabilities of B Ltd. except the cash of Rs. 5,000 which is retained to provide for liquidation expenses, income-tax and to satisfy any dissentient shareholders.

The purchase consideration is the allotment to the shareholders in B Ltd. of one share of Rs. 100 each as Rs. 40 per share paid up at the market value of Rs. 60 per share in A Ltd. for every two shares in B Ltd.

The Liquidator of B. Ltd. made the following payments out of retained amount of Rs. 5,000 :

	Rs.
(a) Liquidation expenses	500
(b) Income-tax	1,000
(c) Dissentient shareholders holding 150 shares	3,500

Show the necessary accounts in the books of B Ltd. and give the opening entries in the books A Ltd. under polling of interests method.

(Adapted from ICWA, Inter & B.Com., Andhra University)

Calculation of purchase consideration

	Rs.
1 share for 2 shares, then, for 5,000 Shares	
i.e., 5,000 × 1/2 = 2,500 Shares	
of market value of Rs. 60 each (2500 × 60)	1,50,000
Purchase consideration	1,50,000

In the Books of B Ltd.

Realisation Account

Dr.	Rs.	Cr.	Rs.
To Building Account	50,000	By Provision for Doubtful Debts A/c	2,000
To Machinery Account	35,000	By Creditors A/c	10,000
To Stock Account	15,000	By A Ltd. Account (Purchase Consideration)	1,50,000
To Debtors Account	22,000		
To Cash Account (10,000 – 5,000)	5,000		
To Cash Account (Expenses)	500		
To Cash Account (Income-tax)	1,000		
To Dissentient Shareholders' Account	500		
To Shareholders' Account (Balancing figure) (Realisation Profit transferred)	33,000		
	1,62,000		1,62,000

A Ltd. Account

Dr.	Rs.	Cr.	Rs.
To Realisation Account	1,50,000	By Shares in A Ltd.	1,50,000
	1,50,000		1,50,000

Dissentient Shareholders' Account

Dr.	Rs.	Cr.	Rs.
To Cash Account	3,500	By Shareholders' A/c (150 × 20)	3,000
		By Realisation A/c (Profit)	500
	3,500		3,500

Shareholders' Account

Dr.	Rs.	Cr.	Rs.
To Dissentient Shareholders (transferred *i.e.,* 150 × 20)	3,000	By Share Capital A/c	1,00,000
To Shares in A Ltd.	1,50,000	By Reserves A/c	15,000
		By Profit & Loss A/c	5,000
		By Realisation A/c (Profit)	33,000
	1,53,000		1,53,000

Dr. **Cash Account** Cr.

	Rs.		Rs.
To Balance b/d	5,000	By Realisation A/c (Expenses)	500
		By Realisation A/c (Income-tax)	1,000
		By Dissentient Shareholders' A/c	3,500
	5,000		5,000

Opening Entries in the Books of A Ltd.

Sl.No.	Particulars		L.F.	Dr. Rs.	Cr. Rs.
1.	Business Purchase Account	Dr.		1,50,000	—
	To Liquidator of B Ltd.			—	1,50,000
	(Being purchase consideration due to B Ltd.)				
2.	Buildings Account	Dr.		50,000	—
	Machinery Account	Dr.		35,000	—
	Stock Account	Dr.		15,000	—
	Debtors Account	Dr.		22,000	—
	Cash Account	Dr.		5,000	—
	Capital Loss Account (B.F.)	Dr.		55,000	—
	To Provision for Doubtful Debts A/c			—	2,000
	To Creditors Account			—	10,000
	To Profit and Loss A/c			—	5,000
	To Reserve Account			—	15,000
	To Business Purchase A/c			—	1,50,000
	(Being transfer of assets, liabilities, reserves and profit of B Ltd. at their agreed values, the difference being placed in Capital Loss A/c)				
3.	General Reserve Account	Dr.		15,000	—
	Profit & Loss Account	Dr.		5,000	—
	To Capital Loss Account			—	20,000
	(Being part of excess paid over paid-up share capital adjusted against general reserve and revenue profits)				
	Alternative combined entry in the place of entries Nos, 2 and 3				
	Buildings Account	Dr.		50,000	—
	Machinery Account	Dr.		35,000	—

Contd.

			Dr.	Cr.
	Stock Account Dr.		15,000	—
	Debtors Account Dr.		22,000	—
	Cash Account (10,000 – 5,000) Dr.		5,000	—
	General Reserve P & L A/c Dr.		35,000	—
	To Provision for Doubtful Debts A/c		—	1,50,000
	To Creditors Account		—	2,000
	To B Ltd. Account		—	10,000
	(Being transfer of assets & liabilities of B Ltd. at their book or agreed values, excess of purchase consideration over paid up capital is debited General Reserve A/c and Profit & Loss A/c)			
4.	B Ltd. Account Dr.		1,50,000	—
	To Share Capital A/c		—	1,00,000
	To Share Premium Account		—	50,000
	(Being issue of 2,500 shares of Rs. 100 each, Rs. 40 paid-up at a premium of Rs. 40 per share in satisfaction of purchase consideration)			

Illustration 15

The X Bank has on 30th June, 2007 an issued capital of 50,000 shares of Rs. 100 each, Rs. 60 paid. Its reserves amounted to Rs. 40,00,000. The Z Bank takes over the business of the X Bank on 30th June, 2007, on the basis of allotment of one share in the Z Bank for every three shares in X Bank. The Share Capital of the Z Bank consists of 2,00,000 shares of Rs. 100 each, Rs. 70 paid-up. The shares are quoted at Rs. 450 in the market but the issue is to be recorded at par. The reserves of the Z Bank were Rs. 1,00,00,000.

On 31st December, 2007 the shareholders of the Z Bank were paid dividend for the whole of the year 2007 at the rate of Rs. 40 per share. Journalise the entries in the books of the Z Bank Ltd.

Solution :

Calculation of purchase consideration

For every three shares, one share is given. So for 50,000 shares, the number of shares to be given will be 50,000 × 1/3 = 16,666 2/3. As shares cannot be given in fraction, the shareholders of the company should be given only 16,666 shares. The amount equivalent of fraction share will be paid in cash. Hence, purchase consideration is —

In the form of shares : 16,666 shares × Rs. 70	11,66,620
In the form of cash : 2/3 share × Rs. 450	300
	Rs. 11,66,920

Balance Sheet of X Bank as on 30th June, 2007

(To find out the agreed value of the assets)

Liabilities	Rs.	Assets	Rs.
Share Capital 50,000 Shares of Rs. 100 each, Rs. 60 paid	30,00,000	Sundry Assets (Balancing figure)	70,00,000
Reserves	40,00,000		
	70,00,000		70,00,000

Journal Entries in the Books of Z Bank

Sl. No.	Particulars	L.F.	Dr. Rs.	Cr. Rs.
1.	Sundry Assets Account Dr.		70,00,000	—
	(Agreed value of assets taken over)			
	To X Bank Account (Purchase consideration)		—	11,66,920
	To Capital Reserve (Balancing figure *i.e.,* the difference between debits and credits)		—	58,33,080
	(Being incorporation of assets taken over is transferred to Capital Reserve A/c)			
2.	Liquidator of X Bank Account Dr.		11,66,920	—
	To Share Capital Account		—	11,66,620
	To Cash Account		—	300
	(Being purchase consideration paid in the form of cash and shares at par)			
3.	Capital Reserve Account Dr.		3,33,320	—
	Profit and Loss Account Dr.		83,33,320	—
	To Dividend to Shareholders' Account		—	86,66,640
	(Being the dividend at the rate of 40 per share declared on 2,16,666 (2,00,000 + 16,666) shares partly out of capital reserve and partly out of profits)			
4.	Dividends to Shareholders' Account Dr.		86,66,640	—
	To Bank Account		—	86,66,640
	(Being dividend paid to shareholders)			

Notes : (i) The agreed value of sundry assets taken over is arrived at by preparing the Balance Sheet of the selling company on the date of sale.

(ii) Dividend on 16,666 shares for 6 months *i.e.,* from Jan, 2007 to June, 2007 amounting to Rs. 3,33,320 (*i.e.,* 16,666 × 40 × 6/12) has to be declared out of capital reserve and not out of current year's profit. Because, the payment of dividend for that period relates to the purchase of business. Therefore, dividend of Rs. 3,33,320 is declared out of the capital reserve and the remaining dividend Rs. 83,33,320 (*i.e.,* 86,66,640 – 3,33,320) is declared out of profits.

Treatment of Mutual Dealings

Some times, there may be mutual dealings between the vendor company and the purchasing company. Mutual dealings or inter company dealings may be as below :

(1) Mutual or Inter Company Debts : If one company purchases or sells goods on credit, or accepts or draws bills of exchange or receives or advances loans to other company, such an amount owned by one company to the other company are called 'inter company debts'. Such debts should be eliminated by passing the appropriate entries in the books of purchasing company. But, in the books of vendor company, no special treatment is required for the mutual debts. Only usual entries should be passed in the books of vendor company for the assets and liabilities including these inter company debts. But, in the books of purchasing company first usual entries have to be passed for incorporating the assets and liabilities including the inter company debts taken over from the vendor company. Then, the following additional entries have to be passed for the set off of inter company debts :

(i) For set off of inter company debtors and creditors :

Creditors' A/c	Dr.	With the amount of debtors
To Debtors' A/c		and creditors set-off

(ii) For set-off inter company bills receivable and bills payable :

Bills Payable A/c	Dr.	With the amount of
To Bills Receivable A/c		B/R and B/P set-off

(iii) For set-off on inter company loans given and loans borrowed:

Loans Borrowed (Payable) A/c	Dr.	With the amount of loans
To Loans Advanced (Receivable) A/c		advanced and borrowed set-off

Note : From the above entries the debtors and creditors, the bills receivable and bills payable, the loans borrowed and loans advanced are reduced by the inter company debts.

For example : If the debtors of one company include some amount, say Rs. 5,000 due from the other company, this will be eliminated or cancelled by passing the following entry in the books of the purchasing company.

Creditors' Account	Dr.	5,000	—
To Debtors' Account		—	5,000

(2) Inter Company Unrealised Profit. When one company sold the goods to another company at a profit and a portion of such goods remained unsold as closing stock, that portion of goods will naturally be included some margin of profit. The amount of such profit included in unsold goods or in closing stock is termed as 'unrealised profit'. Such unrealised profit should be recorded in the books of vendor and purchasing companies.

In the books of vendor company, no additional entry is required to be passed for the unrealised profit. Only usual entries have been passed for the transfer of assets and liabilities. But, in the books of purchasing company, an additional entry for elimination of unrealised profit should be passed in addition to the usual entries for incorporation of assets and liabilities. The entry will :

(a) If the amalgamation is in the nature of merger :

General Reserve *or* P & L Account	Dr.	With the amount of
To Stock Account		unrealised profit

(b) If the amalgamation is in the nature of purchase :

Goodwill or Capital Reserve A/c	Dr.	With the amount of
To Stock A/c		unrealised profit

Note : This entry will reduce the value of stock and at the same time value of the goodwill will be increased or value of the capital reserve will be decreased.

(3) Inter Company Holdings : When one company holds the shares in another company, it is called inter company holdings or inter company investments.

Inter company holdings may take place in any of the following forms :

(A) When purchasing company holds shares in the vendor company.

(B) When vendor company holds shares in the purchasing company.

(C) When both companies hold shares in each other.

The accounting treatment in each of the above situations has been explained as below :

(A) When Purchasing Company Holds Shares in Vendor Company: When the purchasing company holds shares in the vendor company, the purchase consideration payable to the vendor company will be proportionately reduced. For example, if X Ltd. acquires the business of Y Ltd. at an agreed value of Rs. 4,00,000 and if X Ltd. holds 25% of the shares of Y Ltd. then the purchase price payable of Y Ltd. would be only Rs. 3,00,000 (*i.e.,* 75% of Rs. 4,00,000). Because, 25% of Rs. 4,00,000 already belongs to X Ltd.

The following points should be kept in mind while passing the accounting entries in such a situation.

(i) *In the books of vendor company, the following procedure should be followed :* The purchasing company is debited with full price, but credited with only what is received in respect of outsiders. This leaves a debit balance representing the amount still receivable from the purchasing company. Similarly, only the outside shareholders are to be paid from the shareholders account, the balance remaining in that account represents the amount payable to the purchasing company. This is an amount neither receivable nor payable and will be closed by the following entry :

Shareholders' A/c	Dr.
To Purchasing Company's A/c	

(ii) *In the books of Purchasing Company, the following procedure should be followed :* The usual entries for taking over the assets and liabilities have to be passed. Then, if the question of setting the amount due to the liquidator of vendor company arises, the payment should be shown only in respect of the amount due to outsiders and for the remaining balance, the shares in the vendor company are surrendered by crediting the account. The entry for this will be :

Liquidator of Vendor Company A/c	Dr.	With full purchase price
To Share Capital/Deb./Bank A/c		With the amount payable to outsiders
To Shares in the Vendor Co. A/c		With the amount due to Purchasing Co.

When the purchasing company cancels or revalues its investments or shares in the vendor company before acquisition. The profit or loss on such cancellation or revaluation will be transferred to capital reserve or goodwill account. The profit should be transferred to capital reserve account and the loss should be transferred to goodwill account. The entry for this will be :

For Profit : Investment in Shares of Vendor Co. A/c	Dr.
To Capital Reserve/P & L A/c	
For Loss : Goodwill A/c	Dr.
To Investments in Shares of Vendor Co. A/c	

(B) When Vendor Company Holds Shares in the Purchasing Company : When the vendor company holds shares in the purchasing company, the purchase consideration is to be calculated as below :

(i) *Net Assets Method :* In this case, do not take into consideration, the vendor company investments in shares of the purchasing company while calculating the net assets taken over by the purchasing for the purpose of calculating the purchase consideration.

(ii) *Net or Total Payment Method :* In this case, first find out the total number of shares to be issued to the vendor company as purchase consideration. Then, deduct the number of shares already held by the vendor company from the total number of shares agreed to be issued and ascertain the number of new shares to be issued to the vendor company as purchase consideration. Thereafter, multiply the number of new shares to be issued to the vendor company by an agreed value of each new share. The result will be the amount of purchase consideration.

The following points should be kept in mind while passing the accounting entries in such a situation :

(i) *In the books of vendor company, the following procedure is to be followed :* The investment of vendor company in shares of the purchasing company's is not taken over by the purchasing company. Therefore, vendor company investment in the purchasing company (given on the assets side of the B/S) should not be transferred to realisation account. It should be transferred to 'Shares Account'. When investment is revalued, there may be profit or loss on revaluation. The profit or loss on the revaluation of investment should be transferred to shareholders account.

(ii) *In the books of purchasing company, the following procedure is adopted :* The purchasing company cannot buy the investment of vendor company. Therefore, the vendor company's investments in the shares of purchasing company should be excluded while passing the entry for incorporation of assets and liabilities taken over from the vendor company.

(C) When Both Companies Hold Shares in Each Other : When the shares are mutually held, the purchase consideration should be calculated as below :

(1) Net or Total Payment Method : Under this method, purchase consideration is calculated as below :

(i) Ascertain the number of shares to be issued to outside shareholders of vendor company.

(ii) Ascertain the number of shares due to the purchasing company as a shareholder of vendor company.

(iii) Add the shares ascertained under (i) and (ii) to get the total number of shares.

(iv) From the total under (iii) deduct the number of shares already held by the vendor company in the purchasing company and find out the balance of shares.

(v) Multiply the balance of shares as calculated above with the issue price and the resultant figure is the amount of purchase consideration.

(2) Net Assets Method : Under this method, the purchase consideration has to be calculated by simultaneous or algebraic equations. Because, the value of share of one company affects the value of share of other company.

The following steps are necessary in this situation :

(i) Ascertain the total value of assets of each company (except its investment or the shares of other company) by algebraic equations.

(ii) From the total value of assets of vendor company deduct the proportionate value of assets which belongs to the purchasing company on account of its holdings in the vendor company.

(iii) From the above amount, ascertain the number of shares required to be issued for satisfying the purchase consideration.

(iv) From the above number of shares deduct the number of shares already held by the vendor company in the purchasing company. The balance of shares represents the purchase consideration.

(v) Finally, the above balance of shares should be multiplied by the issue price of shares of purchasing company. The resulting amount is treated as the purchase consideration.

When there are cross holdings, the same accounting procedure is adopted in the books of vendor company as in case of the vendor company holds shares in the purchasing company and the purchasing holds shares in the vendor company and in the books of purchasing company, the same accounting procedure is followed as in case of the vendor company holds shares in the purchasing company and the purchasing company holds shares in the vendor company.

Illustration 16

Red Ltd. agreed to absorb the business of Blue Ltd. as on 31-12-2006 and to take over the assets and liabilities, in exchange for which it is to issue one share at the market value of Rs. 120 each for every three shares in the Blue Ltd. The following were the balance sheets on the above date :

Liabilities	Red Ltd.	Blue Ltd.	Assets	Red Ltd.	Blue Ltd.
Share Capital :			Goodwill	25,000	10,000
Shares of Rs. 100			Buildings	40,000	16,000
each fully paid	1,50,000	—	Machinery	70,000	10,000
Shares of Rs. 30 each			Stock	25,000	20,000
fully paid	—	30,000	Debtors	30,000	11,000
Reserve Fund	30,000	10,000	Cash	10,000	3,000
Dividend Equalisation					
Fund	5,000	—			
Creditors	15,000	30,000			
	2,00,000	70,000		2,00,000	70,000

Stock of Blue Ltd. includes goods valued at Rs. 10,000 purchased from Red Ltd. which company invoiced goods at cost plus 25%. The debtors of Red Ltd. included Rs. 5,000 due from Blue Ltd.

Show the accounts to close the books of Blue Ltd. Pass the opening entries in the books of Red Ltd. and prepare the balance sheet after absorption under amalgamation in the nature of purchaser and merger.

(Adapted from Gulbarga University and Andhra University Modify)

Solution :

Calculation of purchase consideration

For every 3 shares, 1 share is given.

So, for 1,000 shares, the number of shares to be given will be :

$\frac{1,000 \times 1}{3} = 333\frac{1}{3}$. As shares cannot be given in fraction, the shareholders of the selling company should be given only 333 shares. For 1/3 share, cash must be paid.

In shares : 333 shares × Rs. 120	39,960
In Cash : 1/3 share × Rs. 120	40
Total payment of purchase consideration	40,000

In the Books of Blue Ltd.

Realisation Account

Dr.	Rs.		Cr. Rs.
To Goodwill	10,000	By Creditors	30,000
To Buildings	16,000	By Red Ltd.	40,000
To Machinery	10,000	(Purchase consideration)	
To Stock	20,000		
To Debtors	11,000		
To Cash	3,000		
	70,000		70,000

Shareholders' Account

Dr.	Rs.		Cr. Rs.
To Shares in Red Ltd.	39,960	By Share Capital	30,000
To Cash	40	By Reserve Fund	10,000
	40,000		40,000

Red Ltd. Account

Dr.	Rs.		Cr. Rs.
To Realisation A/c	40,000	By Shares in Red Ltd.	39,960
(Purchase consideration)		By Cash	40
	40,000		40,000

(A) Amalgamation in the nature of purchase (Purchase Method)

Opening Entries in the Books of Red Ltd.

Sl. No.	Particulars		L.F.	Dr. Rs.	Cr. Rs.
1.	Goodwill Account	Dr.		10,000	—
	Buildings A/c	Dr.		16,000	—
	Machinery A/c	Dr.		10,000	—
	Stock A/c	Dr.		20,000	—
	Debtors A/c	Dr.		11,000	—
	Cash A/c	Dr.		—	3,000
	To Creditors A/c			—	30,000
	To Blue Ltd. (purchase consideration)			—	40,000
	(Being the above assets and liabilities taken over from Blue Ltd.)				
2.	Blue Ltd. A/c	Dr.		40,000	—
	To Share Capital A/c (333 × 100)			—	33,300
	To Share Premium A/c (333 × 20)			—	6,660
	To Cash A/c			—	40
	(Being the purchase consideration paid in the form of cash and shares at premium)				
3.	Creditors (of Blue Ltd.) A/c	Dr.		5,000	—
	To Debtors (of Red Ltd.) A/c			—	5,000
	(Being inter company debt *i.e.,* debtors and creditors set off)				
4.	Goodwill A/c	Dr.		2,000	—
	To Stock A/c			—	2,000
	(Being the unrealised profit included in stock debited to goodwill account)				

Balance Sheet of Red Ltd. (after Absorption) as on 31-12-2006

Liabilities	Rs.	Assets	Rs.
Share Capital :		Goodwill	37,000
1,833 (1,500 + 333) Shares		(25,000 + 10,000 + 2,000)	
of Rs. 100 each fully paid	1,83,300	Buildings	56,000
Reserve Fund	30,000	Machinery	80,000
Dividend Equalisation Fund	5,000	Stock	43,000
Share Premium	6,660	(25,000 + 20,000 – 2,000)	
Creditors	40,000	Debtors	36,000
(15,000 + 30,000 – 5,000)		(30,000 + 11,000 – 5,000)	
		Cash	12,960
		(10,000 + 3,000 – 40)	
	2,64,960		2,64,960

Notes : (i) Unrealised profit on the unsold stock is calculated as below :
Goods are supplied by the Red Ltd. at cost + 25% profit. Therefore, the invoice price (selling price) will be 125 (*i.e.,* 100 + 25). If invoice price is 125, the profit is 25, then for Rs. 10,000 unsold stock (goods), the profit is Rs. 2,000 (10,000 × 25/120). For elimination of this unrealised profit, Rs. 2,000 is deducted from the stock of Blue Ltd. and added to the goodwill.

(ii) Inter company debts Rs. 5,000 are deducted from the debtors of Red Ltd. as well as creditors of Blue Ltd.

(B) Amalgamation in the nature of merger (Pooling of Interests Method)

Opening Entries in the Books of Red Ltd.

Sl. No.	Particulars		L.F.	Dr. Rs.	Cr. Rs.
1.	Business Purchase Account	Dr.		40,000	—
	To Liquidator of Blue Ltd. A/c			—	40,000
	(Being purchase consideration payable to Blue Ltd.)				
2.	Goodwill Account	Dr.		10,000	—
	Building Account	Dr.		16,000	—
	Machinery Account	Dr.		10,000	—
	Stock Account	Dr.		20,000	—
	Debtors Account	Dr.		11,000	—
	Cash Account	Dr.		3,000	—
	Capital Loss Account (Balancing figure)	Dr.		10,000	—
	To Creditors Account			—	30,000
	To Reserve Fund Account			—	10,000
	To Business Purchase Account			—	40,000
	(Being incorporation of assets, liabilities and reserve and the difference between the purchase consideration and paid up share capital (40,000 – 30,000) Rs. 10,000 debited to Capital Loss A/c)				
3.	Reserve Fund Account	Dr.		10,000	—
	To Capital Loss Account			—	10,000
	(Being excess of purchase consideration over paid up capital (Rs. 10,000) adjusted against reserve fund)				
4.	Blue Ltd. Account	Dr.		40,000	—
	To Share Capital Account			—	33,300
	To Share Premium Account			—	6,660
	To Cash Account			—	40
	(Being purchase consideration paid in the form of cash and shares at premium)				

(Contd..)

			Dr.	Cr.
5.	Creditors (of Blue Ltd.) A/c	Dr.	5,000	—
	To Debtors (of Red Ltd.) A/c		—	5,000
	(Being inter company debt i.e., debtors and creditors set off)			
6.	Reserve Fund (Red Ltd.) A/c	Dr.	2,000	—
	To Stock Account		—	2,000
	(Being the unrealised profit included in stock debited to Reserve Fund Account)			

Calculation of Reserve Fund Balance

		Rs.
	Purchase Consideration	40,000
Less :	Paid-up Share Capital of Blue Ltd.	30,000
	Excess being Capital Loss	10,000
Less :	Reserve Fund of Blue Ltd. adjusted	10,000
	Capital loss	Nil
	Reserve Fund of Red Ltd.	30,000
Less :	Unrealised Profit Adjusted	2,000
	Reserve Fund shown in Balance Sheet	28,000

Balance Sheet of Red Ltd. as on 31-12-2006

Liabilities	Rs.	Assets	Rs.
Share Capital		**Fixed Assets**	
1833 (1,500 + 333) shares		Goodwill	35,000
of Rs. 100 each fully paid	1,83,300	(25,000 + 10,000)	
Reserves & Surplus		Buildings	56,000
Reserve Fund 30,000		Machinery	80,000
Less : Unrealised Profit 2,000	28,000	**Current Assets**	
Dividend Equalisation Fund	5,000	Stock	43,000
Share Premium	6,660	(25,000 + 20,000 – 2,000)	
Current Liabilities		Debtors	36,000
Creditors	40,000	(30,000 + 11,000 – 5,000)	
(15,000 + 30,000 – 5,000)		Cash	12,960
		(10,000 + 3,000 – 40)	
	2,62,960		2,62,960

Illustration 17

Following are the balance sheets of A Ltd. and B Ltd. as on 31-3-2007.

A Ltd.

Liabilities	Rs.	Assets	Rs.
Share Capital :		Fixed Assets	30,00,000
40,000 Equity Shares		Investments	50,00,000
of Rs. 100 each	40,00,000	Current Assets	65,00,000
General Reserve	30,00,000		
Current Liabilities	30,00,000		
	1,00,00,000		1,00,00,000

B Ltd.

Liabilities	Rs.	Assets	Rs.
Share Capital :		Goodwill	50,000
20,000 Equity Shares		Fixed Assets	3,50,000
of Rs. 50 each	10,00,000	Current Assets	14,00,000
General Reserve	5,00,000		
Current Liabilities	1,00,000		
Provision for Tax	1,00,000		
Proposed Dividend	1,00,000		
	18,00,000		18,00,000

B Ltd. is to be absorbed by A Ltd. on the following terms :

(1) B Ltd. declares a dividend of 10% before absorption for the payment of which it is to retain sufficient amount of cash.

(2) The net worth of B Ltd. is valued at Rs. 14,50,000.

(3) The purchase consideration is satisfied by the issue of fully paid-up shares of Rs. 100 each in A Ltd.

Following further information is also to be taken into consideration :

(a) A Ltd. holds 5,000 shares of B Ltd. at the cost of Rs. 3,00,000.

(b) The stocks of B Ltd. include items valued at Rs. 1,00,000 purchased from A Ltd. (cost to A Ltd. Rs. 75,000).

(c) The creditors of B Ltd. include Rs. 50,000 due to A Ltd.

Show ledger accounts in the books of B Ltd. to give effect to the above and journal entries in the books of A Ltd. and also the Balance Sheet of A Ltd. after the completion of the absorption. Apply purchase method.

(Adapted from C.A. Inter)

Solution :

Calculation of purchase consideration

The purchase consideration is given as Rs. 14,50,000. Therefore, we need not calculate the purchase consideration. But, the actual purchase consideration payable by A Ltd. is only that portion of the total purchase consideration which is payable to outside shareholders. This is calculated as below :

Total number of shares held by B. Ltd. is 20,000. Out of this, shares held by A Ltd. are 5,000 and shares held by outside shareholders are 15,000 (20,000 – 15,000). Therefore, the actual purchase consideration payable is Rs. 10,87,500 $\left(i.e., \dfrac{15,000 \times 14,50,000}{20,000}\right)$. This amount is given in the form of shares.

Ledger Accounts in the Books of B Ltd.

Realisation Account

Dr.	Rs.		Cr. Rs.
To Goodwill	50,000	By Current Liabilities	1,00,000
To Fixed Assets	3,50,000	By Provision for Tax	1,00,000
To Current Assets (Excluding proposed dividends of Rs. 1,00,000)	13,00,000	By A Ltd. (Purchase consideration)	14,50,000
		By Shareholders A/c (Loss transferred)	50,000
	17,00,000		17,00,000

Shareholders' Account

Dr.	Rs.		Cr. Rs.
To Realisation A/c (Loss on realisation)	50,000	By Share Capital	10,00,000
		By General Reserve	5,00,000
To Shares in A Ltd.	10,87,500		
To A Ltd. A/c (Final balance transferred)	3,62,500		
	15,00,000		15,00,000

A Ltd.'s Account

Dr.	Rs.		Cr. Rs.
To Realisation A/c (Total purchase consideration)	14,50,000	By Shares in Ltd.	10,87,500
		By Shareholders' A/c (Transfer of final balance)	3,62,500
	14,50,000		14,50,000

Shares in A Ltd. Account

Dr.	Rs.		Cr. Rs.
To A Ltd.'s A/c	10,87,500	By Shareholders' A/c	10,87,500
	10,87,500		10,87,500

Current Assets Account

Dr.	Rs.		Cr. Rs.
To Balance b/d	14,00,000	By Realisation A/c	13,00,000
		By Proposed Dividend	1,00,000
	14,00,000		14,00,000

Note: Proposed dividend is paid off. Therefore, there is no liability by way of proposed dividend. Hence, it is not transferred to realisation account.

Journal Entries in the Books of A Ltd.

Sl. No.	Particulars		L.F.	Dr. Rs.	Cr. Rs.
1.	Fixed Assets A/c	Dr.		3,50,000	—
	Current Assets A/c	Dr.		13,00,000	—
	To Current Liabilities A/c			—	1,00,000
	To Provision for Tax A/c			—	1,00,000
	To B Ltd.'s A/c			—	14,50,000
	(Total purchase consideration)				
	(Being the above assets and liabilities taken over from B Ltd.)				
2.	B Ltd.'s A/c	Dr.		14,50,000	—
	To Share Capital A/c			—	10,87,500
	(Actual p.c. satisfied in shares)				
	To Share in B Ltd. A/c			—	3,62,500
	(Balancing figure)				
	(Being purchase consideration settled)				
3.	Shares in B Ltd. A/c	Dr.		62,500	—
	(3,62,500 – 3,00,000)				
	To Capital Reserve A/c			—	62,500
	(Being the transfer of final balance *i.e.,* profit on cancellation transferred to capital reserve account)				
4.	Creditors' Account	Dr.		50,000	—
	To Debtors' Account			—	50,000
	(Being inter company debtors and creditors eliminated)				

Contd.

5.	Capital Reserve Account Dr. To Stock Account (1,00,000 – 75,000) (Being the unrealised profit included in stock debited to capital reserve account)	25,000 —	 25,000
6.	Bank or Cash Account Dr. To Profit & Loss Account (Being the share of [*i.e.,* 1/4 or 5,000/20,000] proposed dividend received from B Ltd. credited to P & L A/c)	25,000 —	— 25,000

Balance Sheet of A Ltd. as on 31-3-2007

Liabilities	Rs.	Assets		Rs.
Share Capital :		Fixed Assets	30,00,000	
Issued and Paid up : 50,875(40,000 + 10,875)		Additions during the year	3,50,000	33,50,000
Equity Shares of Rs. 100 each fully paid	50,87,500	Investments (5,00,000 – 3,00,000)		2,00,000
Capital Reserve (62,500 – 25,000)	37,500	Current Assets		77,50,000
General Reserve	30,00,000			
Profit & Loss A/c	25,000			
Current Liabilities	30,50,000			
Provision for Taxation	1,00,000			
	1,13,00,000			1,13,00,000

Notes : (i) **Current assets are calculated as below :**

			Rs.
	Current Assets of A. Ltd.		65,00,000
Add :	Current assets taken over from B Ltd.		13,00,000
	Dividend received from B Ltd. 1/4 in of proposed dividend)		25,000
			78,25,000
Less :	Inter company debts eliminated	50,000	
	Unrealised profit eliminated from Stock	25,000	75,000
	Current assets shown in the Balance Sheet		77,50,000

(ii) **Current liabilities are calculated as below :**

	Current liabilities of A Ltd.	30,00,000
Add :	Current liabilities taken over from B Ltd.	1,00,000
		31,00,000
Less :	Inter company debts eliminated	50,000
	Current liabilities shown in the Balance sheet	30,50,000

Illustration 18

Balance Sheets of A Ltd. and B Ltd. are given below as at 31-12-2006.

Liabilities	A. Ltd.	B. Ltd.	Assets	A. Ltd.	B. Ltd.
Share Capital :			Sundry Assets	3,10,000	6,00,000
(Rs. 10)	2,00,000	4,00,000	Loan to B Ltd.	30,000	—
Reserves and Surplus	40,000	1,00,000	5,000 Shares in		
7% Debentures (Rs. 100)	1,00,000	—	B Ltd.	50,000	—
Loan from A Ltd.	—	30,000			
Other liabilities	50,000	70,000			
	3,90,000	6,00,000		3,90,000	6,00,000

B Ltd. takes over A Ltd. on the following terms :

(a) B Ltd. will issue sufficient number of shares at Rs. 11 each and pay 50 paise cash per share held by members of A. Ltd.

(b) 7% Debentures of A Ltd. are to be paid at 8% premium by issue of sufficient number of 8% debentures of B Ltd. at Rs. 100.

Show the Ledger Accounts in the books of A Ltd. and Journal Entries in the books of B Ltd. Also draft the balance sheet of B Ltd. after absorption.

Apply purchase mathod.

(Adapted from A.C.S. Inter)

Solution :

Calculation of purchase consideration

In cash : 20,000 shares × 50 paise	10,000
In Shares : 20,000 – 5,000 = 15,000 Outside shares × Rs. 11	1,65,000
(Out of 20,000 shares, 5,000 shares are held by B Ltd.)	
Purchase Consideration	1,75,000

Note : Payment made to debentureholders should not be treated as part of purchase consideration.

Ledger Accounts in the Books of A Ltd.

Realisation Account

Dr. Cr.

	Rs.		Rs.
To Sundry Assets	3,10,000	By Other Liabilities	50,000
To Loan to B Ltd.	30,000	By Debentures A/c	1,00,000
		By B Ltd. A/c (Purchase consideration)	1,75,000
		By Shares in B Ltd. (Profit on revaluation *i.e.*, 55,000 – 50,000)	5,000
		By Shareholders' A/c (Loss transferred)	10,000
	3,40,000		3,40,000

B Ltd.'s Account

Dr.	Rs.		Cr. Rs.
To Realisation A/c (Purchase consideration)	1,75,000	By Cash Account	10,000
		By Shares in B Ltd.	1,65,000
	1,75,000		1,75,000

Shareholders' Account

Dr.	Rs.		Cr. Rs.
To Realisation A/c (Loss)	10,000	By Share Capital A/c	2,00,000
To Cash Account	10,000	By Reserves & Surplus A/c	40,000
To Shares in B Ltd. A/c (50,000 + 1,65,000 + 5,000)	2,20,000		
	2,40,000		2,40,000

Shares in B Ltd. Account

Dr.	Rs.		Cr. Rs.
To Balance b/d	50,000	By Shareholders' A/c (Shares distributed)	2,20,000
To B Ltd.	1,65,000		
To Realisation A/c (Profit on revaluation of shares)	5,000		
	2,20,000		2,20,000

Note : Special treatment is not necessary in the books of A Ltd. as regards inter company debt *i.e.,* Loan of Rs. 30,000.

Journal Entries in the Books of B Ltd.

Sl. No.	Particulars	L.F.	Dr. Rs.	Cr. Rs.
1.	Business Purchase Account Dr.		1,75,000	—
	To Liquidator of A Ltd. Account		—	1,75,000
	(Being purchase consideration due to A Ltd.)			
2.	Sundry Assets A/c Dr.		3,10,000	—
	Loan to B Ltd. A/c Dr.		30,000	—
	To Other Liabilities A/c		—	50,000
	To Debentures Accounts		—	1,08,000
	To Business Purchase Account (*i.e.,* purchase consideration)		—	1,75,000
	To Capital Reserve A/c (Bal. Figure)		—	7,000
	(Being the above assets and liabilities taken over from A Ltd.)			

Contd.

			Dr. (Rs.)	Cr. (Rs.)
3.	Liquidator of A Ltd.'s A/c Dr.		1,75,000	—
	To Cash A/c		—	10,000
	To Share Capital A/c (1,65,000 × 10/11)		—	1,50,000
	To Share Premium A/c (1,65,000 × 1/11)		—	15,000
	(Being the purchase consideration paid in the form of cash and shares at premium)			
4.	Loan from A Ltd. A/c Dr.		30,000	
	To Loan to B Ltd. A/c			30,000
	(Being inter company debt cancelled)			
5.	Debentures in A Ltd. A/c Dr.		1,08,000	
	To Debentures A/c		—	1,08,000
	(Being debentures discharged)			

Balance Sheet of B Ltd. as on 31-12-2006

Liabilities	Rs.	Assets	Rs.
Share Capital : 55,000 (40,000 + 15,000) Shares of Rs. 10 each fully paid	5,50,000	Sundry Assets (6,00,000 + 3,10,000 = 9,10,000 – 10,000 cash)	9,00,000
Reserve and Surplus	1,00,000		
Capital Reserves	7,000		
Share Premium (15,000 × 1)	15,000		
8% Debentures	1,08,000		
Other liabilities (50,000 + 70,000)	1,20,000		
	9,00,000		9,00,000

Illustration 19

The following Balance Sheets of B Ltd. and A Ltd. as at 31st March, 2007 are given to you :

Liabilities	A. Ltd.	B. Ltd.	Assets	A. Ltd.	B. Ltd.
Share Capital :			Fixed Assets	12,60,000	20,000
Fully paid-up shares			Sundry Debtors	2,30,000	1,80,000
of Rs. 100 each	15,00,000	5,00,000	Stock	3,80,000	2,10,000
General Reserve	2,00,000	1,00,000	1,000 Shares in		
Profit and Loss A/c	1,60,000	10,000	A Ltd.	1,50,000	—
Current Liabilities	2,00,000	3,90,000	3,000 Shares in		
			B Ltd.	—	5,00,000
			Cash at Bank	40,000	90,000
	20,60,000	10,00,000		20,60,000	10,00,000

A Ltd. traded in raw materials which were required by B Ltd. for manufacture of its products. Of the stock B Ltd. Rs. 1,00,000 represented purchases made from A Ltd. which company made a profit of 20% on the selling price. B Ltd. Owed Rs. 50,000 to A Ltd. in this respect. It was decided that B Ltd. should absorb A Ltd. by issuing 5 shares of Rs. 100 each at a premium of 10% for every 4 shares of A Ltd.

Give the ledger accounts in the books of A Ltd. and journal entries in the books of B Ltd. under purchase method.

(Adapted from ICWA Inter)

Solution :

Calculation of purchase consideration

Number of shares to be issued to outside shareholders of A Ltd. (5,000 – 1,000 = 4,000 × 5/4)	5,000
Add : Number of shares due to B Ltd. (which however will not be issued *i.e.,* 1,000 × 5/4)	1,250
	6,250
Less : Shares already held by A Ltd. in B Ltd.	3,000
Net number of shares constituting purchase consideration	3,250

Therefore, the amount of purchase consideration = Number of shares to be issued to A Ltd. × Issue price per share,

i.e., 3,250 × Rs. 110 = Rs. 3,57,500.

But the actual amount of purchase consideration payable will be :

	Rs.
Total amount of purchase consideration	3,57,500
Less : Amount due to B for 1,250 shares (*i.e.,* 1,250 × 110)	1,37,500
Portion of purchase consideration payable actually	2,20,000

Ledger Accounts in the Books of A Ltd.

Dr. **Realisation Account** Cr.

	Rs.		Rs.
To Fixed Assets A/c	20,000	By Current Liabilities A/c	3,90,000
To Sundry Debtors A/c	1,80,000	By B Ltd. Account (Total purchase consideration)	3,57,500
To Stock Account	2,10,000		
To Bank Account	90,000		
To Shares in B Ltd. A/c (Loss on revaluation of shares *i.e.,* 5,00,000 – 3,30,000)	1,70,000		
To Shareholders' A/c (Profit transferred)	77,500		
	7,47,500		7,47,500

Dr. **B Ltd.'s Account** Cr.

	Rs.		Rs.
To Realisation A/c (Total purchase consideration)	3,57,500	By Shares in B Ltd. (Actual p.c. received)	2,20,000
		By Shareholders' A/c (Set off of final balance)	1,37,500
	3,57,500		3,57,500

Dr. **Shareholder's Account** Cr.

	Rs.		Rs.
To B Ltd. (Transferred to B Ltd.'s A/c)	1,37,500	By Share Capital	5,00,000
		By General Reserve	1,00,000
To Shares in B Ltd.		By Profit & Loss A/c	10,000
(Shares distributed)	5,50,000	By Realisation A/c (Loss)	77,500
	6,87,500		6,87,500

Dr. **Shares in B Ltd. Account** Cr.

	Rs.		Rs.
To Balance b/d	5,00,000	By Realisation A/c (Loss on revaluation of shares)	1,70,000
To B Ltd.'s A/c (Shares actually received)	2,20,000		
		By Shareholders' A/c (Distribution of shares)	5,50,000
	7,20,000		7,20,000

Calculation of Loss on Revaluation of Shares

		Rs.
	Cost of 3,000 shares held by A Ltd. in B Ltd.	5,00,000
Less :	Revised value of 3,000 shares (3,000 × 110)	3,30,000
	Loss on revaluation of shares	1,70,000

This loss is debited to realisation account credited to shares in B Ltd. account.

Journal Entries in the Books of B Ltd.

Sl. No.	Particulars		L.F.	Dr. Rs.	Cr. Rs.
1.	Sundry Assets A/c			20,000	—
	Sundry Debtors A/c	Dr.		1,80,000	—
	Stock A/c	Dr.		2,10,000	—
	Bank A/c	Dr.		90,000	—
	Goodwill A/c (Balancing figure)	Dr.		2,47,500	—
	To Current Liabilities A/c				3,90,000
	To A Ltd.'s A/c (Purchase consideration)			3,57,500	—
	(Being the above assets and liabilities taken over)				
2.	A Ltd.'s A/c	Dr.		3,57,500	—
	To Share Capital A/c (2,000 × 100)			2,00,000	—
	To Share Premium A/c (2,000 × 10)			20,000	—
	To Investment in Shares of A Ltd. (Balancing figure)			—	1,37,500
	(Being 2,000 shares of Rs. 10 each at a premium of Re. 1 per share are issued in satisfaction of purchase consideration to out side shareholders and the balance transferred to investment in shares of A Ltd. account)				
3.	Goodwill Account (1,50,000 – 1,37,500)	Dr.		12,500	—
	To Investments on Shares of A Ltd. A/c			—	12,500
	(Being the loss on cancellation of investments on shares of A Ltd. debited to Goodwill A/c)				
4.	Creditors' Account	Dr.		50,000	—
	To Debtors 'Account			—	50,000
	(Being inter company debt eliminated)				
5.	Goodwill Account	Dr.		20,000	—
	To Stock Account			—	20,000
	(Being the unrealised profit *i.e.,* $\frac{1,00,000 \times 20}{100}$ included in stock debited to Goodwill A/c				

***Note* :** Calculation of loss on cancellation of investments on shares of A Ltd. :

	Cost of investment on shares of A Ltd.	1,50,000
Less :	Present value of investment on shares of A Ltd.	1,37,500
	Loss on cancellation of investments	12,500

Illustration 20

X Ltd. and Y Ltd. are two companies carrying on business in the same line of activity. Their balance sheets as on December 31, 2006, are given below :

Balance Sheets

Liabilities	X. Ltd.	Y. Ltd.	Assets	X. Ltd.	Y. Ltd.
Fully Paid up Equity Shares of Rs. 10 each	6,00,000	2,00,000	Land and Buildings	1,00,000	—
General Reserve	4,00,000	2,00,000	Plant & Machinery	7,00,000	3,00,000
Secured Loans	6,00,000	1,00,000	Investments	1,00,000	—
Current Liabilities	6,00,000	4,00,000	Stocks	9,00,000	4,00,000
			Debtors	3,00,000	1,00,000
			Cash at Bank	1,00,000	1,00,000
	22,00,000	9,00,000		22,00,000	9,00,000

The two companies decide to amalgamate into XY Ltd. The following further information is given :

(1) X Ltd. holds 8,000 shares in Y Ltd. at Rs. 12.50 each.

(2) All assets and liabilities of two companies except investments, are taken over by XY Ltd.

(3) Each share in Y Ltd. is valued at Rs. 25 for the purpose of the amalgamation.

(4) Shareholders in X Ltd. and Y Ltd. are paid off by issuing to them a sufficient number of equity shares of Rs. 10 each in XY Ltd. as fully paid up at par.

(5) Each share in X Ltd. is valued at Rs. 15 for the purpose of amalgamation.

Show journal entries to close the books of both the companies under purchase method.

(Adapted from C.A. Inter)

Solution :

Calculation of purchase consideration

X Ltd. : In shares 60,000 shares × Rs. 15	9,00,000
Number of equity shares allotted 9,00,000/10	90,000 Shares
Y Ltd. : Number of share in Y Ltd.	20,000
Less : Shares already held by X Ltd.	8,000
Shares held by the outsiders	12,000
Agreed value of shares Rs. 25	

Hence, purchase consideration will be (12,000 × 25) Rs. 3,00,000

Number of equity shares to be allotted 3,00,000/10 = 30,000 Shares

Closing Entries in the Books of X Ltd.

Sl. No.	Particulars	LF	Dr. Rs.	Cr. Rs.
Stage I	**Entries to close all the accounts that appear in the Balance Sheet**			
1.	Realisation A/c Dr.		22,00,000	
	To Land and Buildings A/c		—	1,00,000
	To Plant and Machinery A/c		—	7,00,000
	To Investment A/c		—	1,00,000
	To Stock A/c		—	9,00,000
	To Debtors A/c		—	3,00,000
	To Cash at Bank A/c		—	1,00,000
	(Being transfer of above assets at book values to realisation account)			
2.	Secured Loans A/c Dr.		6,00,000	—
	Current Liabilities A/c Dr.		6,00,000	—
	To Realisation A/c		—	12,00,000
	(Being transfer of above liabilities at book values to realisation account)			
3.	Share Capital A/c Dr.		6,00,000	—
	General Reserve A/c Dr.		4,00,000	—
	To Shareholders' A/c		—	10,00,000
	(Being transfer of above items to shareholders' account)			
Stage II	**Entries for recording the purchase consideration**			
4.	XY Ltd. A/c Dr.		9,00,000	—
	To Realisation A/c		—	9,00,000
	(Being purchase consideration due from XY Ltd.)			
5.	Shares in XY Ltd. A/c Dr.		9,00,000	
	To XY Ltd. A/c		—	9,00,000
	(Being purchase consideration received from XY Ltd. in the form of shares)			
Stage III	**Entries for recording of distribution of purchase consideration**			
6.	Shareholders' A/c Dr.		1,00,000	—
	To Realisation A/c		—	1,00,000
	(Being loss on realisation transferred to shareholders' account)			*Contd.*

7.	Shareholders' A/c Dr.		9,00,000	
	To Shares in XY Ltd. A/c		—	9,00,000
	(Being shareholders' paid in the form of shares in XY Ltd.)			

Closing Entries in the Books of Y Ltd.

Sl. No.	Particulars	L.F.	Dr. Rs.	Cr. Rs.
Stage I	**Entries to close all the accounts that appear in the Balance Sheet**			
1.	Realisation A/c Dr.		9,00,000	—
	To Plant & Machinery Account		—	3,00,000
	To Stock Account		—	4,00,000
	To Debtors Account		—	1,00,000
	To Cash at Bank Account		—	1,00,000
	(Being transfer of above assets at book values to realisation account)			
2.	Secured Loans Account Dr.		1,00,000	—
	Current Liabilities Account Dr.		4,00,000	—
	To Realisation Account		—	5,00,000
	(Being transfer of above liabilities at book values to realisation account)			
3.	Share Capital Account Dr.		2,00,000	—
	General Reserve Account Dr.		2,00,000	—
	To Shareholders' Account		—	4,00,000
	(Being transfer of above items to shareholders' account)			
Stage II	**Entries for recording the purchase consideration**			
4.	XY Ltd. Account Dr.		3,00,000	
	To Realisation Account		—	3,00,000
	(Being purchase consideration due from XY Ltd.)			
5.	Shares in XY Ltd. Account Dr.		3,00,000	—
	To XY Ltd. Account		—	3,00,000
	(Being purchase consideration received from XY Ltd. in the form of shares)			

(Contd..)

Stage III	**Entries for recording of distribution of purchase consideration :**		
6.	Shareholders' Account Dr.	1,00,000	—
	To Realisation Account	—	1,00,000
	(Being loss on realisation transferred to shareholders' account)		
7.	Shareholders' Account Dr.	3,00,000	—
	To Shares in XY Ltd. Account	—	3,00,000
	(Being shareholders' paid in the form of shares in XY Ltd.)		

External Reconstruction

In external reconstruction, companies are undergo financial reconstruction and assets and liabilities are revalued. Therefore, it is similar to amalgamation in the nature of purchase. Under this method, since the transferor company is replaced by the transferee company, there is no pooling of interests. Hence, problems relating to external reconstruction are solved under 'Purchase Method'.

Illustration 21

The Good Luck Stores Limited, Bombay, having proved unsuccessful resolves by Special Resolution to wind-up for the purpose of reconstruction and sale to the New Fashions Ltd.; newly formed company for the purpose. The balance sheet of the Good Luck Stores Ltd. at the date of the confirmatory resolution was as follows :

Balance Sheet

Liabilities	Rs.	Assets		Rs.
Share Capital :		Land and Buildings		4,50,000
1,00,000 Equity Shares		Machinery and Plant		2,40,000
of Rs. 10 each fully paid	10,00,000	Sundry Debtors	1,05,000	
Sundry Creditors	30,000	*Less* : R.D.D	5,000	1,00,000
Bills Payable	20,000	Stock		50,000
Contingent Liability :		Cash at Bank		10,000
Workmen Compensation		Profit and Loss A/c		2,00,000
Claim Rs. 4,000				
	10,50,000			10,50,000

The scheme of reconstruction assented to buy all the parties was as follows :

(1) The new company to take over all the assets of old company but not the liabilities.

(2) The new company was to purchase to goodwill of the business and assets of the old company for the sum of Rs. 8,00,000 payable as to Rs. 7,00,000 by issue of 1,40,000 equity shares of Rs. 10 each with Rs. 5 per share credited as paid up and as to Rs. 1,00,000 in cash.

(3) The members of the new company were to pay in cash the balance of Rs. 5 per share due upon the shares issued to them.

(4) The expense of reconstruction amounted to Rs. 3,000. Workmen compensation claim was settled at Rs. 2,000.

No further shares were issued beyond those forming part of the purchase consideration as stated above.

(A) Pass journal entries to close the books of Good Luck Stores Limited. Also give necessary ledger accounts, and

(B) Pass opening entries and give an opening balance sheet in the books of the New Fashions Ltd.

(Adapted from Shivaji University)

Solution :

In the Books of Good Luck Stores Ltd.
Journal Entries

Sl. No.	Particulars	L.F.	Dr. Rs.	Cr. Rs.
Stage I	**Entries to close all the accounts that appear in the Balance sheet :**			
1.	Realisation A/c Dr.		8,55,000	—
	To Land and Buildings A/c		—	4,50,000
	To Machinery and Plant A/c		—	2,40,000
	To Sundry Debtors A/c		—	1,05,000
	To Stock Account		—	50,000
	To Bank Account		—	10,000
	(Being transfer of above assets at book value to realisation account)			
2.	Reserve for Doubtful Debts A/c Dr.		5,000	—
	To Realisation Account		—	5,000
	(Being transfer of R.D.D. to realisation A/c			
3.	Shareholders' Account Dr.		2,00,000	—
	To Profit & Loss Account		—	2,00,000
	(Being debit balance of P & L A/c transferred to shareholders' account)			
4.	Equity Share Capital Account Dr.		10,00,000	—
	To Shareholders' Account		—	10,00,000
	(Being balance of share capital account transferred to shareholders' account)			*(Contd..)*

			Dr.	Cr.
Stage II	**Entries for recording the purchase consideration**			
5.	The New Fashions Ltd. A/c Dr.		8,00,000	—
	To Realisation Account		—	8,00,000
	(Being purchase consideration due from New Fashions Ltd.)			
6.	Shares in the New Fashions Ltd. A/c Dr.		7,00,000	—
	Bank Account Dr.		1,00,000	—
	To The New Fashions Ltd. A/c		—	8,00,000
	(Being purchase consideration received from The New Fashion Ltd. in the form of shares and cash)			
Stage III	**Entries for recording the distribution of purchase consideration**			
7.	Realisation Account Dr.		5,000	—
	To Bank Account (3,000 + 2,000)		—	5,000
	(Being payment of reconstruction expenses and workmen compensation claim)			
8.	Sundry Creditors Account Dr.		30,000	—
	Bills Payable Account Dr.		20,000	—
	To Bank Account		—	50,000
	(Being repayment of above liabilities)			
9.	Shareholders' Account Dr.		55,000	—
	To Realisation Account		—	55,000
	(Being loss on realisation transferred to shareholders' account)			
10.	Shareholders' Account Dr.		7,45,000	—
	To Shares in The New Fashions Ltd.		—	7,00,000
	To Bank Account		—	45,000
	(Being shareholders' paid in the form of shares and cash)			

Ledger Accounts

Dr. **Realisation Account** Cr.

	Rs.		Rs.
To Land and Buildings	4,50,000	By R.D.D.	5,000
To Machinery and Plant	2,40,000	By The New Fashions Ltd. (Purchase consideration)	8,00,000
To Stock	50,000		
To Sundry Debtors	1,05,000	By Shareholders' Account (Loss transferred to shareholders)	55,000
To Bank	10,000		
To Bank (3,000 + 2,000) (*i.e.,* Reconstruction expenses and workmen compensation claim)	5,000		
	8,60,000		8,60,000

Dr. **The New Fashions Ltd. Account** Cr.

	Rs.		Rs.
To Realisation	8,00,000	By Shares in the New Fashions Ltd.	7,00,000
		By Bank	1,00,000
	8,00,000		8,00,000

Dr. **Shares in The New Fashions Ltd. Account** Cr.

	Rs.		Rs.
To The New Fashions Ltd.	7,00,000	By Shareholders' A/c	7,00,000
	7,00,000		7,00,000

Dr. **Shareholders' Account** Cr.

	Rs.		Rs.
To Realisation (Loss)	55,000	By Share Capital	10,00,000
To Profit & Loss A/c	2,00,000		
To Shares in The New Fashions Ltd.	7,00,000		
To Bank	45,000		
	10,00,000		10,00,000

Dr. **Bank Account** Cr.

	Rs.		Rs.
To Balance b/d	10,000	By Realisation (transfer)	10,000
To The New Fashions Ltd.	1,00,000	By Sundry Creditors	30,000
		By Bills Payable	20,000
		By Realisation (expenses and claim)	5,000
		By Shareholders' (Balance transferred)	45,000
	1,10,000		1,10,000

Note : Actual amount paid regarding workmen compensation claim is recorded in the books of accounts but not the original amount.

Opening Entries in the Books of The New Fashions Ltd.

Sl. No.	Particulars		L.F.	Dr. Rs.	Cr. Rs.
1.	Land and Building A/c	Dr.		4,50,000	—
	Machinery and Plant A/c	Dr.		2,40,000	—
	Sundry Debtors A/c	Dr.		1,05,000	—
	Stock Account	Dr.		50,000	—
	Bank Account	Dr.		10,000	—
	To Reserve for Doubtful Debts A/c			—	5,000
	To Good Luck Stores Ltd. Account (Purchase consideration)			—	8,00,000
	To Capital Reserve A/c (Bal. figure)			—	50,000
	(Being the above assets and liabilities taken over from the selling company at their agreed values)				
2.	Good Luck Stores Ltd. A/c	Dr.		8,00,000	—
	To Equity Share Capital A/c			—	7,00,000
	To Bank Account			—	1,00,000
	(Being shares issued and cash paid to venders in settlement of purchase price)				
3.	Equity Share Final Call Account	Dr.		7,00,000	—
	To Equity Share Capital Account			—	7,00,000
	(Being final call of Rs. 5 per share called on 1,40,000 shares issued as partly paid shares to the vendors)				
4.	Bank Account	Dr.		7,00,000	—
	To Equity Shares Final Call A/c			—	7,00,000
	(Being cash received for final call)				

The New Fashions Ltd. Balance Sheet

Liabilities	Rs.	Assets		Rs.
Share Capital :		Land and Buildings		4,50,000
1,40,000 Shares of Rs. 10		Machinery and Plant		2,40,000
each partly paid *i.e.,* Rs. 5		Stock		50,000
and balance *i.e.,* Rs. 5		Debtors	1,05,000	
received in cash	14,00,000	*Less* R.D.D	5,000	1,00,000
Capital Reserve	50,000	Bank		6,10,000
	14,50,000			14,50,000

Note : Calculation of Bank Balance :

	Rs.
Balance taken over from vendors	10,000
Add : Cash received from final call	7,00,000
	7,10,000
Less : Cash paid to vendors	1,00,000
Balance as shown in the Balance Sheet	6,10,000

Illustration 22

Zigma Ltd. was formed to take over the business of Stigma Ltd. The following was the balance sheet of Stigma Ltd. on the date of purchase.

Balance Sheet as at 31-12-2006

Liabilities	Rs.	Assets	Rs.
Share Capital :		Buildings	3,20,000
10,000 Equity Shares		Plant	2,40,000
of Rs. 50 each	5,00,000	Stock	1,60,000
3% Debentures	2,00,000	Debtors	48,000
Creditors	1,50,000	Cash	2,000
Bank Overdraft	20,000	Profit & Loss A/c	1,00,000
	8,70,000		8,70,000

(a) The capital of Zigma Ltd. is to be Rs. 10,00,000 consisting of 1,00,000 shares of Rs. 10 each.

(b) Zigma Ltd. agreed to issue 5 shares of Rs. 10 each credited with Rs. 7 per share for every share held in stigma Ltd. The shareholders are to pay the balance of Rs. 3 per share in cash and the same has been duly collected by Zigma Ltd.

(c) The debentureholders are to be issued 4% debentures in Zigma Ltd. sufficient to discharge the debentures to Stigma Ltd. at a premium of 10%.

(d) Bank overdraft and creditors were taken over by Zigma Ltd. and the assets at the following values :

Buildings Rs. 3,00,000; Plant Rs. 2,00,000; Stock Rs. 1,25,000; Debtors Rs. 40,000 and Cash Rs. 2,000.

(e) The expenses of liquidation of Rs. 2,000 were paid by Zigma Ltd.

Prepare realisation account and shareholders' account in the books of Stigma Ltd. and the balance sheet of Zigma Ltd.

(Adapted from B.Com.,Karnataka University)

Solution :

Calculation of purchase consideration

	Rs.
50,000 (10,000 × 5/1) shares are issued as Rs. 7 paid up	3,50,000
Total	3,50,000

Note : Payment made to debentures does not form part of purchase consideration.

In the books of Stigma Ltd.

Dr. **Realisation Account** Cr.

	Rs.		Rs.
To Buildings	3,20,000	By Creditors	1,50,000
To Plant	2,40,000	By Debentures	2,00,000
To Stock	1,60,000	By Bank Overdraft	20,000
To Debtors	48,000	By Zigma Ltd.	3,50,000
To Cash	2,000	(Purchase consideration)	
		By Shareholders (Loss transferred)	50,000
	7,70,000		7,70,000

Dr. **Shareholders' Account** Cr.

	Rs.		Rs.
To Profit and Loss A/c	1,00,000	By Share Capital	5,00,000
To Realisation (Loss)	50,000		
To Shares in Zigma Ltd.	3,50,000		
	5,00,000		5,00,000

Opening Entries in the Books of Zigma Ltd.

Sl. No.	Particulars		L.F.	Dr. Rs.	Cr. Rs.
1.	Building A/c	Dr.		3,00,000	—
	Plant A/c	Dr.		2,00,000	—
	Debtors A/c	Dr.		40,000	—
	Stock A/c	Dr.		1,25,000	—
	Cash A/c	Dr.		2,000	—
	Goodwill A/c (Balancing figure)	Dr.		73,000	—
	To Creditors A/c			—	1,50,000
	To Debentures A/c			—	2,20,000
	To Bank Overdraft A/c			—	20,000
	To Stigma Ltd. A/c (Purchase consideration)			—	3,50,000
	(Being the above assets and liabilities taken over from the selling company at their agreed values)				
2.	Stigma Ltd. A/c	Dr.		3,50,000	—
	To Share Capital (50,000 × 7)			—	3,50,000
	(Being purchase consideration paid in the form of shares)				
3.	Cash Account	Dr.		1,50,000	—
	To Share Capital Account			—	1,50,000
	(Being call amount received on 50,000 shares at Rs. 3 per share)				
4.	Goodwill Account	Dr.		2,000	—
	To Bank Account *or* Cash Account			—	2,000
	(Being expenses of liquidation are paid as agreed)				
5.	3% Debentures in Stigma Ltd. A/c	Dr.		2,20,000	—
	To 4% Debentures in Zigma Ltd. A/c			—	2,20,000
	(Being debentures discharged)				

Balance Sheet of Zigma Ltd. As on 31-12-2006

Liabilities	Rs.	Assets	Rs.
Share Capital :		**Fixed Assets**	
Authorised :		Goodwill (73,000 + 2,000)	75,000
1,00,000 Shares of Rs. 10 each	1,00,000	Building	3,00,000
Subscribed and paid up :		Plant	2,00,000
50,000 Shares of Rs. 10 each		**Current Assets**	
fully paid		Stock	1,25,000
(3,50,000 + 1,50,000)	5,00,000	Debtors	40,000
Secured Loan		Cash	1,50,000
4% Debentures	2,20,000	(2,000 + 1,50,000 – 2,000)	
Current Liabilities			
Creditors	1,50,000		
Bank Overdraft	20,000		
	8,90,000		8,90,000

Illustration 23

The creditors and shareholders having agreed upon a scheme of reconstruction the United Trading Co. Ltd. went into voluntary liquidation. The balance sheet on the date of reconstruction stood as follows :

Liabilities	Rs.	Assets	Rs.
Share Capital :		Goodwill	40,000
25,000 Shares of		Buildings	95,000
Rs. 10 each	2,50,000	Plant	1,05,000
Reserve Fund	27,000	Stock	50,000
5% Debentures	1,00,000	Debtors	60,000
Creditors	40,000	Bank	2,000
		Profit & Loss Account	65,000
	4,71,000		4,71,000

The following are the terms of reconstruction :

(a) The new company called National Trading Company Ltd. be formed with a capital of Rs. 5,00,000 in 50,000 shares of Rs. 10 each.

(b) The new company is to take over from the above company, the stock and debtors at 20% less than book values and building and plant at Rs. 77,000 and Rs. 1,00,000 respectively.

(c) The debentureholders were to be satisfied by the issue of 6% debentures of Rs. 1,50,000 in the new company in exchange for the old debentures.

(d) The new company is to take over the creditors. The creditors agreed to receive Rs. 35,000 from the new company in full settlement of their accounts.

(e) The shareholders agreed to receive 25,000 shares of Rs. 10 each credited with Rs. 5 per share paid up from the new company. They further agreed to pay a call of Rs. 2.50 per share immediately to the new company.

(f) The balance at bank was utilised in payment of reconstruction expenses.

Prepare realisation expenses and shareholders account in the books of United Trading Co. Ltd. and the balance sheet of the new company assuming that the call money is duly received.

(Adapted from B.Com., Bangalore University)

Solution :

Calculation of purchase consideration

Issue of 25,000 Shares as Rs. 5 paid up	1,25,000
Total Rs.	1,25,000

Note : Payments made to debentureholders do not form part of purchase consideration.

In the Books of United Trading Co. Ltd.

Dr. **Realisation Account** Cr.

	Rs.		Rs.
To Goodwill	40,000	By Creditors	40,000
To Building	95,000	By Debentures	1,00,000
To Plant	1,05,000	By National Trading Co. Ltd.	1,25,000
To Stock	50,000	(Purchase consideration)	
To Debtors	60,000	By Shareholders	87,000
To Bank (Expenses)	2,000	(Loss transferred)	
	3,52,000		3,52,000

Dr. **Shareholders' Account** Cr.

	Rs.		Rs.
To Realisation A/c (Loss)	87,000	By Share Capital	2,50,000
To Profit and Loss A/c	65,000	By Reserve Fund	27,000
To Share in National Trading Company Ltd.	1,25,000		
	2,77,000		2,77,000

Balance Sheet of National Trading Company Ltd.

Liabilities	Rs.	Assets	Rs.
Share Capital		**Fixed Assets**	
Authorised :		Goodwill	45,000
50,000 Shares of Rs. 10 each	5,00,000	Building	77,000
Subscribed and Paid up :		Plant	1,00,000
20,000 shares of Rs. 7.50		**Current Assets**	
(5 + 2.50) each fully paid up		Stock (50,000 – 10,000)	40,000
(1,25,000 + 62,500)	1,87,500	Debtors (60,000 – 12,000)	48,000
Secured Loans		Cash	27,500
6% Debentures	1,50,000		
	3,37,500		3,37,500

Notes : (i) Calculation of Goodwill :

	Rs.
Agreed value of Liabilities taken over (35,000 + 1,00,000 + 1,75,000 *i.e.,* P. C.)	3,10,000
Less : Agreed values of Assets taken over (77,000 + 1,00,000 + 40,000 + 48,000)	2,65,000
Value of Goodwill	45,000

(ii) Calculation of Cash :

Balance as per Balance Sheet	2,000
Less : Utilised for reconstruction expenses	2,000
	Nil
Add : Cash received from call (25,000 × 2,50)	62,500
	62,500
Less : Cash paid to creditors	35,000
Balance of cash	27,500

Illustration 24

The Balance Sheet of Z Ltd. as on 31-3-2006 was as follows :

Liabilities	Rs.	Assets	Rs.
Share Capital :		Goodwill	80,000
50,000 Shares of		Building	1,80,000
Rs. 10 each	5,00,000	Plant	2,00,000
Contingency Reserve	10,000	Stock	1,20,000
5% Debentures	2,00,000	Debtors	90,000
Staff Provident Fund	30,000	Bank	10,000
Creditors	1,00,000	Profit & Loss A/c	1,60,000
	8,40,000		8,40,000

The shareholders and creditors decided as follows :

(a) A new company namely A Ltd. be formed with a capital of Rs. 10,00,000 divided into shares of Rs. 10 each.

(b) The new company is to take over creditors and staff provident fund and all assets (except Cash at Bank) at 25% less than book value of such assets.

(c) The debentureholders of Z Ltd. are to be satisfied by issuing 8% debentures in A Ltd. of Rs. 1,50,000 at par.

(d) The creditors have agreed to accept 75% of their claims in full satisfaction from new company.

(e) The shareholders are to be issued 30,000 equity shares in A Ltd. as fully paid.

(f) The liquidation expenses were paid by Z Ltd. Rs. 10,000.

(g) A Ltd. issued 20,000 shares to public at par and received the amount. Underwriting commission and brokerage amounted to Rs. 10,000.

Required

(1) Realisation account and shareholders account in the books of Z Ltd.

(2) Balance sheet of A Ltd. after implementing above decisions.

(Adapted from B. Com. Karnataka University)

Solution :

Calculation of purchase consideration

Issue of 30,000 equity shares of Rs. 10 each	3,00,000
Total Rs.	3,00,000

Note : Payment made to debentureholders does not form part of purchase consideration.

In the Books of Z Ltd.

Realisation Account

Dr. Cr.

	Rs.		Rs.
To Goodwill	80,000	By Staff Provident Fund	30,000
To Building	1,80,000	By Creditors	1,00,000
To Plant	2,00,000	By 5% Debentureholders	2,00,000
To Stock	1,20,000	By A Ltd.	3,00,000
To Debtors	90,000	(Purchase consideration)	
To Bank (Expenses)	10,000	By Shareholders	50,000
		(Loss transferred)	
	6,80,000		6,80,000

Shareholders' Account

Dr.	Rs.		Cr. Rs.
To Realisation A/c (Loss)	50,000	By Share capital	5,00,000
To Profit & Loss A/c	1,60,000	By Contingency Reserve	10,000
To Shares in A Ltd.	3,00,000		
	5,10,000		5,10,000

Balance Sheet of A Ltd. as on 31-3-2006

Liabilities	Rs.	Assets	Rs.
Share Capital		**Fixed Assets**	
Authorised :		Goodwill	1,12,500
1,00,000 Shares of Rs. 10 each	10,00,00	Building (1,80,000 – 45,000)	1,35,000
Issued & Subscribed		Plant (2,00,000 – 50,000)	1,50,000
50,000 shares of Rs. 10 each	5,00,000	**Current Assets**	
Secured Loans		Stock (1,20,000 – 30,000)	90,000
8% Debentures	1,50,000	Debtors (90,000 – 22,500)	67,500
Current Liabilities			
Staff Provided Fund	30,000	Bank (2,00,000 – 85,000)	1,15,000
		Miscellaneous Expenditure	
		Underwriting Commission & Brokerage (*i.e.,* Miscellaneous expenditure not written off)	10,000
	6,80,000		6,80,000

Notes : **(i) Calculation of value of Goodwill**

		Rs.
Agreed value of Liabilities taken over (30,000 + 75,000 + 1,50,000 + 3,00,000)		5,55,000
Less : agreed value of assets taken over (1,35,000 + 1,50,000 + 90,000 + 67,500)		4,42,500
Value of Goodwill	Rs.	1,12,500

(ii) Calculation of Balance of Bank

		Rs.
Cash received on issue of 20,000 shares at Rs. 10 each in full		2,00,000
Less : Payment made to creditors (*i.e.,* 75% of Rs. 1,00,000)	75,000	
Underwriting Commission and Brokerage	10,000	85,000
Balance of Bank	Rs.	1,15,000

(iii) Alternatively underwriting commission can be debited to goodwill account.

Illustration 25

The following was the balance sheet of Thin Ltd. as on 31-12-2006.

Liabilities	Rs.	Assets	Rs.
Share Capital :		Goodwill	40,000
5,000 6% Preference Shares		Patents	15,000
of Rs. 10 each fully paid	50,000	Sundry Assets	1,64,500
15,000 Equity Shares of		Bank	500
Rs. 10 each fully paid	1,50,000	Profit & Loss A/c	28,000
6% Debentures	30,000	Preliminary Expenses	2,000
Sundry Creditors	20,000		
Preference Dividends in arrears for four years			
	2,50,000		2,50,000

The following scheme of reconstruction was agreed upon :

(1) A new company called Thick Ltd. was to be formed to take over the business with an authorised capital of Rs. 3,25,000 in equity shares of Rs. 10 each.

(2) One equity share Rs. 5 paid up in the new company to be issued for every equity share in Thin Ltd.

(3) Arrears of dividend to be cancelled.

(4) Two equity shares of Rs. 5 paid up in the new company to be issued for every preference share in Thin Ltd.

(5) Debentureholders to receive 3,000 equity shares fully paid in the new company in fully satisfaction of their claims.

(6) Creditors to be taken over by the new company.

(7) The remaining unissued shares to be taken up by the directors and paid in full.

(8) The new company to take over all assets (except patents) subject to writing down sundry assets by Rs. 35,000.

(9) Patents realised Rs. 1,000.

(10) Liquidation expenses amounted to Rs. 1,000.

Close the books of Thin Ltd. and open the books of Thick Ltd. (only journal entries need be given) and prepare the balance sheet of Thick Ltd. on the basis of the above scheme.

(Adapted from Mysor University)

Solution :

Calculation of purchase consideration

In partly paid equity shares :

		Rs.
(a)	10,000 (5,000 × 2/1) shares of Rs. 5 paid up (payment made to preference shareholders)	50,000
(b)	15,000 (15,000 × 1/1) shares of Rs. 5 paid up (payment made to equity shareholders)	75,000
	Total	1,25,000

Note : Payment made to debentureholders does not form part of purchase consideration.

Closing Entries in the Books of Thin Ltd.

Sl. No.	Particulars	L.F.	Dr. Rs.	Cr. Rs.
Stage I	**Entries to close all the accounts that appear in the Balance Sheet**			
1.	Realisation A/c Dr.		2,20,000	–
	To Goodwill A/c		–	40,000
	To Patents A/c		–	15,000
	To Sundry Assets A/c		–	1,64,500
	To Bank Account		–	500
	(Being transfer of assets to Realisation A/c)			
2.	Sundry Creditors' A/c Dr.		20,000	–
	Debentures A/c Dr.		30,000	–
	To Realisation A/c		–	50,000
	(Being transfer of creditors to debentures and Realisation A/c)			
3.	Equity Shareholders' A/c Dr.		30,000	–
	To Profit and Loss A/c		–	28,000
	To Preliminary Expenses A/c		–	2,000
	(Being transfer of above accounts to Equity Shareholders' A/c)			
4.	Cumulative Pref. Share Capital A/c Dr.		50,000	–
	To Pref. Shareholders' A/c		–	50,000
	(Being transfer of preference share capital to preference shareholder)			
5.	Equity Share Capital A/c Dr.		1,50,000	–
	To Equity Shareholders' A/c		–	1,50,000
	(Being transfer of equity share capital to equity shareholders)			

(Contd.)

			Dr.	Cr.
Stage II	**Entries for recording the purchase consideration**			
6.	Thick Ltd.'s A/c	Dr.	1,25,000	–
	To Realisation A/c		–	1,25,000
	(Being purchase consideration due from Thick Ltd.)			
7.	Equity Shares in Thick Ltd. A/c	Dr.	1,25,000	
	To Thick Ltd. A/c			1,25,000
	(Being purchase consideration received from Thick Ltd. in the form of equity shares)			
8.	Bank Account	Dr.	1,000	–
	To Realisation A/c		–	1,000
	(Being realisation of patent not taken over)			
State III	**Entries for recording the distribution of purchase consideration**			
9.	Realisation Account	Dr.	1,000	–
	To Bank Account		–	1,000
	(Being realisation expenses paid)			
10.	Equity Shareholders' Account	Dr.	45,000	–
	To Realisation Account		–	45,000
	(Being realisation loss transferred to equity shareholders' account)			
11.	Preference Shareholders' A/c	Dr.	50,000	–
	To Partly Paid Equity Shares in Thick Ltd. A/c		–	50,000
	(Being preference shareholders paid in the form of partly paid shares in Thick Ltd.)			
12.	Equity Shareholders' Account	Dr.	75,000	–
	To Partly Paid Equity Shares in Thick Ltd. A/c		–	75,000
	(Being equity shareholders' paid in the form of partly paid shares in Thick Ltd.)			

Note : When the arrears of preference dividend are cancelled, there cannot be any profit or loss arising from the cancellation of the same. Therefore, no entry is necessary in the books of selling company.

Opening Entries in the Books of Thick Ltd.

Sl. No.	Particulars		L.F.	Dr. Rs.	Cr. Rs.
1.	Sundry Assets A/c (1,64,500 – 35,000)	Dr.		129500	–
	Bank Account	Dr.		500	–
	Goodwill (Balancing figure)	Dr.		45,000	–
	To Sundry Creditors A/c			–	20,000
	To Debentures A/c			–	30,000
	To Thin Ltd.'s A/c (P.C.)			–	1,25,000
	(Being the above assets and liabilities taken over at their agreed values)				
2.	Thin Ltd.'s Account	Dr.		1,25,000	–
	To (Partly paid) Share Capital A/c			–	1,25,000
	(Being purchase consideration paid in the form of partly paid shares)				
3.	Bank Account	Dr.		45,000	–
	To (Fully paid) Share Capital A/c			–	45,000
	(Being the remaining 4,500 [*i.e.,* Total shares 32,500 – 28,000 *i.e.,* 3,000 + 10,000 + 15,000 shares issued to selling company] unissued shares issued as fully paid to directors for cash)				
4.	Debentures in Thin Ltd. A/c	Dr.		30,000	–
	To Fully paid share Capital A/c			–	30,000
	(Being debentures paid)				

Balance Sheet of Thick Ltd. as on 31-12-1996

Liabilities		Rs.	Assets		Rs.
Share Capital			**Fixed Assets**		
Authorised :			Goodwill		45,000
32,500 equity shares of Rs. 10 each		3,25,000	Sundry Assets		1,29,500
Issued & Subscribed :			**Current Assets**		
32,500 Equity Shares of Rs. 10 each		3,25,000	Bank :		
Called up & Paid up :			Bank Balance	500	
7,500 (3,000 + 4,500) Equity shares of Rs. 10 each fully paid up	75,000		Amount received from directors, on 4,500 shares	45,000	45,500
25,000 (10,000 + 15,000) Equity shares of Rs. 10 each Rs. 5 paid up	1,25,000	2,00,000			
Current Liabilities					
Sundry Creditors		20,000			
		2,20,000			2,20,000

Illustration 26

The balance sheet of Child Ltd. was as follows :

Balance Sheet as at 31st December, 2006

		Rs.		Rs.
Authorised & Issued Capital			**Fixed Assets**	
5,000 $6^1/_2$ Pref. Shares of			Patents	24,500
Rs. 10 each fully paid		50,000	Freehold Property	60,000
6,000 Equity Shares of			**Current Assets**	
Rs. 10 each fully paid		60,000	Stock	18,000
5% Debentures	10,000		Debtors	12,000
Add : Interest	2,000	12,000	Cash	500
Creditors		8,000	Profit & Loss A/c	15,000
		1,30,000		1,30,000

The following scheme was passed and sanctioned :

(1) Parent Ltd. to be formed to take over the business.

(2) One share of Rs. 5 each fully paid in the new company to be issued for every three equity shares in the old company.

(3) Three shares of Rs. 5 each fully paid in the new company to be issued for every five preference shares in the old company.

(4) Debentureholders to be taken over by Parent Ltd.

(5) The creditors to receive 80% of the sums due to them in fully paid shares of Rs. 5 each in the new company in full settlement.

(6) Patents and Profit and Loss Account to be written off.

(7) Arrears of preference dividend to be cleared by issuing one Rs. 5 fully paid share in Parent Ltd. for every twenty shares held in the old company.

(8) Any balance available by the scheme to be used in writing down the freehold property.

Give the opening journal entries and prepare the initial balance sheet of Parent Ltd.

(Adapted from Mysor University and Bangalore University)

Solution :

Calculation of purchase consideration

	Rs.	Mode
1. Payment made to equity shareholders 6,000 × 1/3 = 2,000 shares × Rs. 5)	10,000	In shares

2. Payment made to preference shareholders :	Rs.	Rs.	Mode
(a) Towards their capital (5,000 × 3/5 = 3,000 shares × Rs. 5)	15,000		In shares
(b) Towards arrears of pref. dividend (5,000 × 1/20 = 250 shares × Rs. 5)	1,250	16,250	In shares
Total		26,250	In shares

Opening Journal Entries in the Books of Parent Ltd.

Sl. No.	Particulars	L.F.	Dr. Rs.	Cr. Rs.
1.	Freehold Property A/c (Balancing figure) Dr.		14,150	—
	Stock A/c Dr.		18,000	—
	Debtors A/c Dr.		12,000	—
	Cash A/c Dr.		500	—
	To Debentures A/c		—	10,000
	To Accrued Interest A/c		—	2,000
	To Creditors' Account		—	6,400
	To Child Ltd.'s A/c (P.C.)		—	26,250
	(Being the above assets and liabilities taken over from the selling company at their agreed values. The value of freehold property is the balancing figure since it is to be adjusted)			
2.	Child Ltd.'s A/c Dr.		26,250	—
	To Share Capital A/c		—	26,250
	(Being purchase consideration paid in shares)			
3.	Creditors' Account Dr.		6,400	—
	To Shares in Parent Ltd. A/c		—	6,400
	(Being creditors paid in the form of shares 8000 × 80/100)			

Balance Sheet of Parent Ltd. as on 31-12-2006

Liabilities	Rs.	Assets	Rs.
Share Capital		**Fixed Assets**	
3,265 (2625 + 640) shares		Freehold Property	14,150
of Rs. 10 each fully paid	32,650	**Current Assets**	
Secured Loans		Stock	18,000
5% Debentures	10,000	Sundry Debtors	12,000
Accrued Debentures Interest	2,000	Cash	500
	44,650		44,650

Illustration 27

The following is the summarised Balance Sheet as on 31, March, 2006 of Baharat Ltd.

Liabilities		Rs.	Assets	Rs.
Share Capital			Goodwill	2,00,000
Authorised, issued and fully paid-up :			Tangible Fixed Assets	12,00,000
			Balance at Bank	10,000
25,000 12% Cumulative Pref.			Other Current Assets	4,60,000
Shares of Rs. 20 each		5,00,000	Preliminary Expenses	20,000
6,00,000 Equity Shares of			Profit & Loss Account	2,60,000
Rs. 20 each		12,00,000		
10% Debentures	2,00,000			
Interest thereon	20,000	2,20,000		
Creditors		2,30,000		
		21,50,000		21,50,000

Note : The dividend on the preference shares in arrears is Rs. 1,80,000.

The following scheme of external reconstruction was agreed to by all parties and the necessary sanction obtained.

A new company Navbharat Ltd. was to be registered with a capital of 1,50,000 shares of Rs. 10 each to acquire as from April 1, 2006 the undertaking and assets of the old company for a consideration to be satisfied partly in cash and partly in shares of the new company to implement the following terms :

(1) The new company to assume the old company's debenture liability by issuing to the holders corresponding debentures in the new company, together with one fully paid equity share in the new company for every Rs. 10 of interest in arrears.

(2) The creditors of the old company agree to forego 10% of the amount due to them, the balance to be paid in each by Navbharat Ltd. immediately.

(3) The preference shareholders in the old company to receive two fully paid equity shares in the new company for each share held in the old company; further the arrears of preference dividend to be satisfied by the issue of one fully paid equity share in the new company for every Rs. 50 due (Ignore corporate dividend tax).

(4) The equity shareholders in the old company to receive one fully paid equity share in the new company for every three shares held.

(5) Cost amounting to Rs. 20,000 to be borne by the new company.

It was agreed that current assets should be taken into the new company's books at the values in the old company's books (except that stock was to be reduced by Rs. 10,000): goodwill was to be eliminated and the tangible fixed assets were valued at Rs. 7,23,000.

The new company allotted 30,000 equity shares at par for cash to some of the old shareholders of Bharat Ltd.

You are required to give :

(a) in the old company's books, necessary ledger accounts.

(b) in respect of the new company :

(i) journal entries to record all the transactions and

(ii) a summarised balance sheet.

(B.Com. Madras University and Guwahati University)

Solution :

Calculation of purchase consideration

		Rs.	Mode of Payment
1. Payment made to Preference Shareholders :			
50,000 (25,000 × 2) Shares of Rs. 10 each	5,00,000		
Arrears of Preference Dividend (1,80,000 × 10/50)	36,000	5,36,000	In Equity Shares
2. Payment made to Equity Shareholders : 20,000 (60,000 ÷ 3) Shares of Rs. 10 each		2,00,000	In Equity Shares
		7,36,000	In Equity Shares

In the Books of Bharat Ltd.

Dr. **Realisation Account** Cr.

	Rs.		Rs.
To Goodwill	2,00,000	By 10% Debentures	2,00,000
To Other Fixed Assets	12,00,000	By Outstanding Interest on Debentures	20,000
To Balance at Bank	10,000	By Creditors	2,30,000
To Other Current Assets	4,60,000	By New Bharat Ltd. (purchase consideration)	7,36,000
To Preference Shareholders (Arrears of Preference Dividend)	36,000	By Equity Shareholders' A/c (Loss transferred)	7,20,000
	19,06,000		19,06,000

Dr. **Nav Bharat Ltd.** Cr.

	Rs.		Rs.
To Realisation Account	7,36,000	By Equity Shares in Nav Bharat Ltd.	7,36,000
	7,36,000		7,36,000

Dr. **Equity Shares in Nav Bharat Ltd.** Cr.

	Rs.		Rs.
To Nav Bharat Ltd.	7,36,000	By Pref. Shareholders' A/c	5,36,000
		By Equity Shareholders' A/c	2,00,000
	7,36,000		7,36,000

Dr. **Preference Shareholders' Account** Cr.

	Rs.		Rs.
To Equity Shares in Nav Bharat Ltd. A/c	5,36,000	By 12% Cumulative Pref. Share Capital	5,00,000
		By Realisation A/c (Arrears of Dividend)	36,000
	5,36,000		5,36,000

Dr. **Equity Shareholders' Account** Cr.

	Rs.		Rs.
To Preliminary Expenses	20,000	By Equity Share Capital A/c	12,00,000
To Profit and Loss A/c	2,60,000		
To Realisation A/c	7,20,000		
To Equity Shares in Nav Bharat Ltd.	2,00,000		
	12,00,000		12,00,000

Dr. **Cash Book (Bank Column)** Cr.

	Rs.		Rs.
To Balance b/d (Business Purchase A/c)	10,000	By Capital Reserve A/c (Expenses)	20,000
To Equity Share Capital A/c (Allotment of Shares)	3,00,000	By Creditors	2,07,000
		By Balance c/d	83,000
	3,10,000		3,10,000

In the Books of Nav Bharat Ltd.
Journal Entries

Sl. No.	Particulars		L.F.	Dr. Rs.	Cr. Rs.
1.	Business Purchase Account	Dr.		7,36,000	—
	To Liquidator of Bharat Ltd. A/c			—	7,36,000
	(Being purchase consideration due to Bharat Ltd.)				
2.	Tangible Fixed Assets Account	Dr.		7,23,000	—
	Balance at Bank Account	Dr.		10,000	—
	Other Current Assets Account	Dr.		4,50,000	—
	To 10% Debentures Account			—	2,20,000
	To Creditors' Account			—	2,07,000
	To Business Purchase Account			—	7,36,000
	To Capital Reserve Account (Balancing figure)			—	20,000
	(Being transfer of assets and liabilities at their agreed value, the difference being placed in capital reserve account)				
3.	Liquidator of Bharat Ltd. Account	Dr.		7,36,000	—
	To Equity Share Capital Account			—	7,36,000
	(Being issue of 73,600 equity shares of Rs. 10 each fully paid to Bharat Ltd. in satisfaction of purchase consideration)				
4.	10% Debentures (Bharat Ltd.) Account	Dr.		2,20,000	—
	To 10% Debentures Account			—	2,00,000
	To Equity Share Capital Account			—	20,000
	(Being issue of 10% debentures in discharge of principal amount and 2,000 equity shares of Rs. 10 each in discharge of outstanding interest)				
5.	Bank Account	Dr.		3,00,000	—
	To Equity Share Capital Account			—	3,00,000
	(Being issue of 30,000 equity shares at Rs. 10 each at par for cash)				
6.	Creditors' Account	Dr.		2,07,000	—
	To Bank Account			—	2,07,000
	(Being creditors paid)				
7.	Capital Reserve Account	Dr.		20,000	—
	To Bank Account			—	20,000
	(Being cost of scheme paid)				

Balance Sheet of Nav Bharat Ltd.
as on April, 2006

Liabilities	Rs.	Assets	Rs.
Share Capital		**Fixed Assets**	
Authorised :		Tangible Fixed Assets	7,23,000
1,50,000 Equity Shares		**Current Assets**	
of Rs. 10 each fully paid	15,00,000	Balance at Bank	83,000
Issued & Subscribed		Other Current Assets	4,50,000
1,05,600 Equity Shares			
of Rs. 10 each fully paid	10,56,000		
Secured Loans			
10% Debentures	2,00,000		
	12,56,000		12,56,000

Calculation of Equity Shares

	Rs.
Equity Shares issued to satisfy Shareholders	7,36,000
Equity Shares issued to discharge debenture interest	20,000
Equity Shares allotted for cash	3,00,000
Total Equity Shares	10,56,000

EXAMINATION QUESTIONS

(A) Answer the following questions in two sentences each :

(*Each carrying two marks*)

1. What is amalgamation of companies? *(Kar., April 1996)*

2. Give the meaning of amalgamation with an example. *(B'lore, April 1997)*

3. Under what circumstances you favour amalgamation of companies? *(B'lore, Oct. 1991)*

4. Mention two important causes for amalgamation of two companies. *(B'lore, Nov. 1992)*

5. State any two objectives of amalgamation. *(B'lore, April 1996 & 1998)*

6. What do you mean by absorption of a company? *(Kar., April 1997)*

7. Give the meaning of absorption with an example. *(B'lore, April 1995)*

8. State any two objectives of absorption.

9. Mention two causes for absorption.

10. Distinguish between amalgamation and absorption. *(B'lore, November 1994)*

11. What do you mean by external reconstruction? *(Kar., Oct. 1998)*

12. Give the meaning of external reconstruction. *(B'lore, Nov. 1995)*

13. Mention the two objectives of external reconstruction.

14. State any two advantages of external reconstruction.

15. Bring out the difference between the absorption and external reconstruction. *(B'lore, April 1983)*

16. What is purchase consideration?

17. How do you compute purchase consideration payable to selling company? *(Kar., April 1996)*

18. Name the methods of calculation of purchase consideration.
(B'lore, Nov. 1993)

19. How do you treat depreciation fund while computing purchase consideration?
(B'lore, April 1991)

20. How do you treat the following in the case of amalgamation of companies :

(a) Workers savings deposits.

(b) Workmen's compensation fund.
(Kar., April 1997)

21. What is amalgamation adjustment account?
(Kar., April 2004)

22. When will you recommend a company to undergo external reconstruction?
(Kar., April 1996)

23. How do you treat liquidation expenses and formation expenses paid by purchasing company in its books?
(B'lore, Nov. 1981)

24. How do you ascertain the goodwill or capital reserve in the books of purchasing company?
(B'lore, April 1983)

25. What is capital reserve? *(B'lore, Nov. 1983)*

26. Give two journal entries recorded in the purchasing company for acquisition of business.
(B'lore, April 1984)

27. What are the different means by which purchase consideration can be discharged?

28. How do you deal with fraction shares in arriving at purchase consideration?

29. What is amalgamation of companies? Name the types of amalgamation recommended by Accounting Standard-14.
(Kar., Oct. 2004)

30. What is business purchase account?

31. What are fictitious assets? Why are they not considered in computing purchase consideration?

32. How do you treat assets not taken over by the purchasing company?
(Mysore, April 1996)

33. How do you settle a liability not taken over by the purchasing company when there is insufficient cash?

(Gulbarga, Oct. 1991)

34. What are inter company debts? *(Kuvempu, Oct. 1993)*

35. What do you understand by unrealised profit?

36. What are inter company holdings. *(Mangalore, Oct. 1994)*

37. What do you understand by the purchase consideration? How is it calculated? *(Kar., Oct. 1997)*

38. How will you treat the workmen's compensation fund on amalgamation of companies.

(Kar., Oct. 1997)

39. What is amalgamation of companies? Give two advantages of amalgamation.

(Kar. Oct., 1998)

40. What do you mean by inter companies owings ?

(Kar. April, 2005)

(B) Answer the following questions :

(Each carrying eight marks)

1. What are the advantages amalgamation of companies?

2. What do you understand by the term purchase consideration? How is it calculated under different methods?

(Kar., Oct. 1998)

3. State the advantages of external reconstruction?

4. What are the differences between amalgamation, absorption and external reconstruction?

5. What are inter company holdings? How are they dealt with in the books of purchasing and vendor company?

6. How do you treat the following while computing purchase consideration under net assets method :

(a) Workmen's compensation fund

(b) Insurance fund

(c) Depreciation fund

(d) Workmen's savings bank or employees savings bank deposit.

(e) Reserve for taxation or provision for taxation

(f) Preliminary expenses

(g) Workmen's profit sharing fund.

7. What are the entries relating to amalgamation in the books of vendor company under pooling of interests methods?

8. What are the conditions for amalgamation in the nature of merger ? *(Kar., April 2004)*

Simple Problems

9. A Ltd. takes over the business of B Ltd. The share capital of B Ltd. consists of 5,000 shares of Rs. 10 each fully paid. There are also 8% debentures of Rs. 50,000. A Ltd. agrees to pay Rs. 5 and also to issue 6 fully paid shares of Rs. 10 each at a market value of Rs. 15 each for every 5 shares held in Y Ltd. It also agrees to pay cash for debentureholders at a discount of 5%.

   Calculate purchase consideration.

Ans. : Purchase consideration Rs. 95,000

Note : Distribution of purchase consideration :

	Rs.
In shares (5,000 × 5/6 × 15)	90,000
In cash : on share (5,000 × 5/5)	5,000
	95,000

Note : Payments to debentureholders do not form part of purchase consideration.

10. Star Ltd. agrees to absorb the business of Light Ltd. as on 31-3-2006. The share capital of Light Ltd. consists of 4,500 equity shares of Rs. 100 each fully paid and 2,500 preference shares of Rs. 100 each fully paid. There are debentures of Rs. 75,000 of Rs. 100 each. Star Ltd. has agreed as under :

    (a) To issue 2 equity shares of Rs. 100 each for every share held in Light Ltd.

    (b) To pay Rs. 10 per share in cash and to issue 3 preference shares of Rs. 100 each at the market value of Rs. 120 each in exchange for every 5 preference shares held in Light Ltd.

    (c) To issue mortgage debentures at Rs. 95 in lieu of debentures in Light Ltd. which are to be redeemed at a premium of 10%.

    Ans. : Purchase consideration Rs. 11,05,000.

    Note : Distribution of purchase consideration :

In equity shares (4,500 × 2 × 10)	9,00,000
In cash (2,500 × 10)	25,000
In preference shares (2,500 × 3/5 × 120)	1,80,000
Total Rs.	11,05,000

11. X Ltd. absorbs the business of Y Ltd. The share capital of Y Ltd. includes 20,000 equity shares of Rs. 10 each fully paid and 8%, 10,000 pref. shares of Rs. 10 each fully paid. There are also 9% debentures of Rs. 1,00,000. X Ltd. has agreed the following terms:

(a) Equity shareholders to be given 6 equity shares of Rs. 10 each of X Ltd. issued at 10% premium against 5 shares surrendered.

(b) 8% preference shareholders are to be paid at 10% premium by 9% preference shares of Rs. 10 of X Ltd. issued at par.

(c) 9% Debentureholders are to be paid at 8% premium by 10% debentures of X Ltd. issued at 10% discount.

Ans. : Purchase consideration Rs. 3,74,000.

Note : Distribution of purchase consideration

	Rs.
In equity shares (20,000 × 6/5 × 10 = 2,40,000 + 24,000)	2,64,000
In preference shares (10,000 × 10 = 1,00,000 + 10,000)	1,10,000
	3,74,000

12. A Ltd. sells its business to B Ltd. as on 31-12-2006 on which date its Balance Sheet was as under :

Liabilities	Rs.	Assets	Rs.
Share Capital	2,00,000	Goodwill	50,000
Reserve Fund	50,000	Plant & Machinery	1,50,000
Profit and Loss A/c	20,000	Furniture	35,000
Debentures	1,00,000	Stock	83,000
Creditors	30,000	Bills Receivable	4,500
		Debtors	27,500
		Cash	50,000
	4,00,000		4,00,000

B Ltd. agreed to take over the assets (exclusive of cash and goodwill) at 10% less than book value, to pay Rs. 75,000 for goodwill and to take over debentures.

Calculate the purchase consideration and pass journal entries in the books of 'B' Ltd.

Ans. : Purchase consideration Rs. 2,45,000 (Assets Rs. 3,45,000 minus Liability Rs. 1,00,000).

13. The Balance Sheet of X Co. Ltd. on 1-1-2006 was as follows :

Liabilities	Rs.	Assets	Rs.
Capital :		Building	7,00,000
90,000 Ordinary shares		Patents	2,00,000
of Rs. 10 each	9,00,000	Stock	3,25,000
50,000 Pref. shares		Debtors	1,60,000
of Rs. 10 each	5,00,000	Cash	25,000
5% Debentures	1,00,000	Profit & Loss A/c	2,20,000
Interest Outstanding on above	20,000		
Sundry Creditors	1,10,000		
	16,30,000		16,30,000

On 1-7-2006 'Y' company agreed to absorb 'X' Co. Ltd. on the following terms :

(a) 2 shares of Rs. 5 each fully paid in 'Y' Co. Ltd. to be issued for every 3 shares in 'X' Co. Ltd.

(b) 6 shares of Rs. 5 each fully paid in 'Y' Co. Ltd. to be issued for every 5 preference shares in 'X' Co. Ltd.

(c) Debentureholders to be paid in full in ordinary shares of Rs. 5 each and for the interest outstanding in cash.

(d) The creditors to receive 75% of sums due to them in fully paid shares of Rs. 5 each and 50% of the balance in cash in full settlement.

(e) Absorption expenses of Rs. 1,000 should be paid.

Calculate purchase consideration.

Ans. : Purchase consideration Rs. 6,00,000.

Note : Distribution of purchase consideration :

To the Ordinary shareholders (2 × 90,000 × Rs. 5/3)	3,00,000
To the Pref. shareholders (50,000 × 6/5 × Rs. 5)	3,00,000
	6,00,000

14. The following is the Balance Sheet of Mr. Shyam, a sole trader as at 31-12-2006. Progressive Ltd. was formed to take over Shyam's business. It has an authorised capital of Rs. 5,00,000 divided into 25,000 equity shares of Rs. 10 each and 2,500, 6% preference shares of Rs. 100 each.

Balance Sheet of Mr. Shyam as at 31-12-2006

Liabilities	Rs.	Assets	Rs.
Bills Payable	3,500	Cash	4,500
Creditors	6,400	Fixed Assets	95,000
Capital	1,32,100	Debtors	7,500
		Stock	35,000
	1,42,000		1,42,000

The purchase price was agreed at Rs. 1,75,000. This is to be paid as follows : Rs. 50,000 in fully paid equity shares and Rs. 50,000 in fully paid preference shares, Rs. 30,000 in debentures and the balance in cash. The remaining shares were issued to be public and fully paid for. Give journal entries and prepare Balance Sheet in the books of the company after acquisition.

(Adapted from B.Com., Bangalore University)

Ans. : Goodwill Rs. 42,900; Cash balance Rs. 3,59,500 and Balance Sheet Total Rs. 5,39,900.

(C) Solve the following Problems :

(Each carrying 15/16 Marks)

1. The Popular Ltd. and the Famous Ltd. have agreed to amalgamate. A New Company 'Wonderful Ltd.' has been formed with an authorised capital of 3,00,000 shares of Rs. 10 each, to take over the combined concerns as on 31-12-2006.

After negotiation, the assets of the two companies have been agreed as shown in the following Balance Sheets :

Liabilities	Popular	Famous	Assets	Popular	Famous
Share Capital :	—	—	Goodwill	—	50,000
Shares of Rs. 10 each	10,00,000	5,00,000	Buildings	5,00,000	3,00,000
Reserve Fund	—	50,000	Machinery	3,10,000	2,50,000
Profit & Loss A/c	50,000	50,000	Stock	1,50,000	20,000
Creditors	80,000	50,000	Debtors	1,20,000	20,000
			Bank	50,000	10,000
	11,30,000	6,50,000		11,30,000	6,50,000

Show how the amount payable to each company is arrived at and prepare the amalgamated Balance Sheet of the new company under purchase method.

(Adapted from B.Com., K.U.D.)

Ans. : Purchase consideration : Popular Rs. 10,50,000 (*i.e.*, 11,30,000 – 80,000); Famous Rs. 6,00,000 (*i.e.*, 6,50,000 – 50,000); Wonderful Ltd. Balance Sheet Total Rs. 17,80,000.

Illustration 2

The following are the balance sheets of P Ltd. and S Ltd. as on 31st March, 2006 :

Liabilities	P Ltd.	S Ltd.
	Rs.	Rs.
Equity share capital (Rs. 10 each)	5,00,000	3,00,000
14% Preference share capital (Rs. 100 each)	2,20,000	1,70,000
General Reserve	50,000	25,000
Export Profit Reserve	30,000	20,000
Investment Allowance Reserve	—	10,000
Profit and Loss Account	75,000	50,000
13% Debentures (Rs. 100 each)	50,000	35,000
Current Liabilities	65,000	50,000
	9,90,000	6,60,000
Assets		
Land and Buildings	2,50,000	1,55,000
Plant and Machinery	3,25,000	1,70,000
Furniture and Fittings	57,500	35,000
Investments	1,25,000	95,000
Stock	90,000	1,03,000
Debtors	72,500	52,000
Cash and Bank	70,000	50,000
	9,90,000	6,60,000

P Ltd. takes over S Ltd. on 1st April, 2006. P Ltd. discharges purchase consideration as below :

(a) Issued 35,000 equity shares of Rs. 10 each at par to the equity shareholders of S Ltd.

(b) Issued 15% preference shares of Rs. 100 each to discharge the preference shares of S Ltd. at 10% premium.

(c) The debentures of S Ltd. will be converted into equivalent number of debentures of P Ltd.

(d) The Statutory reserve of S Ltd. (Export Profit Reserve and Investment Allowances Reserve) are to be maintained for three more years.

You are required to show the balance sheet of P Ltd. assuming that :

(a) The amalgamation in the nature of merger

(b) The amalgamation in the nature of purchase.

(Adapted from B.Com., Hons., Delhi)

Ans. : (a) Amalgamation in the nature of merger: purchase consideration Rs. 5,37,000 (3,50,000 + 1,70,000 + 17,000); General Reserve Rs. 8,000; Profit and Loss A/c Rs. 1,25,000; Share Capital Rs. 12,57,000 (8,50,000 + 2,20,000 + 1,87,000) and B/S Total Rs. 16,50,000.

(b) Amalgamation in the nature of purchase: purchase consideration Rs. 5,37,000; General Reserve Rs. 50,000; Capital Reserve Rs. 38,000; P & L A/c Rs. 75,000; Amalgamation Adjustment A/c (Equal to Statutory Reserve) Rs. 30,000 and B/S Total Rs. 16,80,000.

Illustration 3

X Ltd. absorbs Y Ltd. for a consideration of Rs. 20,00,000 to be satisfied in fully paid equity shares of Rs. 10 each. The balance sheets of both companies on 31st March, 2006 were as follows :

Balance Sheets as on 31st March, 2006

Liabilities	X Ltd.	Y Ltd.	Assets	X Ltd.	Y Ltd.
Share Capital			**Fixed Assets**		
Equity shares of			Premises	20,00,000	14,00,000
Rs. 10 each	20,00,000	15,00,000	Plant & Equipment	13,00,000	10,00,000
Reserves & Surplus			Furniture	3,00,000	1,00,000
General Reserve	8,00,000	1,50,000	**Current Assets**		
Development			Stock	5,00,000	3,00,000
Rebate Reserve	1,00,000	50,000	Debtors	3,00,000	2,00,000
Export Profit Reserve	3,00,000	2,00,000	Bills Receivable	2,00,000	1,00,000
P & L Account	6,00,000	3,00,000	Bank	2,00,000	1,00,000
Current Liabilities	10,00,000	10,00,000			
	48,00,000	32,00,000		48,00,000	32,00,000

Note : Development Reserve and Exports Profit Reserve are required to be continued.

(a) Close the books of Y Ltd. (only ledger accounts)

(b) Pass journal entries and draw up balance sheet of X Ltd. after absorption under merger method.

(B.Com., Osmania Adapted)

Ans. : Realisation Loss Rs. 2,00,000; General Reserve Rs. 7,50,000; P & L A/c Rs. 6,00,000; B/s Total Rs. 80,00,000.

4. The following are the Balance Sheets of Week Ltd. and Meek Ltd. as on 31-12-2009 on which date they have agreed to amalgamate and form a new company called Strong Co. Ltd.

Balance Sheets

Liabilities	Week Ltd. Rs.	Meek Ltd. Rs.	Assets	Week Ltd. Rs.	Meek Ltd. Rs.
Share Capital :			Goodwill	20,000	—
Shares of			Buildings	1,50,000	1,85,000
Rs. 100 each	2,00,000	3,00,000	Machinery	60,000	1,00,000
Reserve Fund	30,000	—	Stock	30,000	20,000
P & L Account	10,000	—	Debtors	15,000	10,000
Creditors	60,000	60,000	Bank	25,000	5,000
			P & L Account	—	40,000
	3,00,000	3,60,000		3,00,000	3,60,000

The Strong Co. Ltd. is incorporated with an authorised capital of Rs. 10,00,000 divided into 1,00,000 equity shares of Rs. 10 each.

Prepare the amalgamated balance sheet under pooling of interests method.

(B.Com., Calicut Adapted)

Ans. : Purchase consideration :

Week Ltd. (3,00,000 – 60,000) Rs. 2,40,000

Meek Ltd. (3,20,000 – 60,000) Rs. 2,60,000

General Reserve & P & L A/c Balance Rs. Nil (30,000 + 10,000 – 40,000); B/S Total Rs. 6,20,000.

5. The following are the Balance Sheets of X Ltd. and Y Ltd. which agree to amalgamate their business and form a new company styled as X Y Co. Ltd. with a registered capital of Rs. 50,00,000 divided into 50,000 equity shares of Rs. 100 each.

Liabilities	X. Ltd.	Y. Ltd.	Assets	X. Ltd.	Y. Ltd.
Share Capital :	—	—	Goodwill	1,00,000	7,50,000
Shares of Rs. 100 each	10,00,000	8,00,000	Buildings	3,00,000	2,50,000
Reserves	1,80,000	—	Investments	5,00,000	3,00,000
Profit & Loss A/c	2,00,000	—	Machinery	5,00,000	4,00,000
8% Debentures	1,50,000	—	Stock	1,50,000	1,00,000
Public Deposits	—	4,00,000	Debtors	80,000	60,000
Creditors	2,00,000	1,00,000	Bank	1,50,000	70,000
Bills Payable	50,000	30,000	P & L A/c	—	75,000
	17,80,000	13,30,000		17,80,000	13,30,000

Prepare statement showing the purchase consideration payable to the shareholders of each of these companies and the Balance Sheet of amalgamated company. Apply purchase mathod.

(Adapted from B.Com., K.U.D.)

Ans. : Purchase consideration : X Ltd. Rs. 13,80,000 (*i.e.,* 17,80,000 – 4,00,000); Y Ltd. Rs. 7,25,000 (*i.e.,* 12,50,000 – 5,30,000); XY Co. Ltd. Balance Sheet Total Rs. 30,35,000.

6. The balance sheets of A Ltd. and B Ltd. are given below. They decided to amalgamate and form a new company called C Ltd. and G. Ltd. decided to issue fully paid shares of Rs. 50 each.

Liabilities	A Ltd.	B Ltd.	Assets	A Ltd.	B Ltd.
Share Capital :			Goodwill	—	10,000
Shares of Rs. 10 each	2,50,000	2,00,000	Buildings	75,000	75,000
Reserve Fund	—	50,000	Machinery	90,000	1,00,000
Profit & Loss A/c	—	10,000	Stock	95,000	45,000
Sundry Creditors	41,000	30,000	Debtors	—	35,000
			Cash at Bank	11,000	25,000
			P & L A/c	20,000	—
	2,91,000	2,90,000		2,91,000	2,90,000

Pass the journal entries to close the books of A Ltd. and B Ltd. and prepare the Balance Sheet of C Ltd. under purchase arrangement.

(Adapted from B.Com., Gulbarga University)

Ans. : Purchase consideration : A Ltd. Rs. 2,30,000 (*i.e.,* 2,71,000 – 41,000); B Ltd. Rs. 2,60,000 (*i.e.,* 2,90,000 – 30,000); Share Capital Rs. 4,90,000 & C Ltd. B/S Total Rs. 5,61,000.

7. The balance sheets of A Ltd. and B Ltd. as on 31st March 2006 were as follows :

Liabilities	A Ltd.	B Ltd.	Assets	A Ltd.	B Ltd.
Share Capital :			Buildings	50,000	30,000
Equity Shares of	1,50,000	90,000	Machinery	65,000	34,000
Rs. 10 each			Stock	50,500	36,000
General Reserve	4,000	9,000	Debtors	18,000	21,600
Export Project Reserve	6,000	4,000	Bank	14,500	10,400
(Statutory)			Preliminary Expenses	—	2,000
Investment Allowance					
Reserve	—	2,000			
P & L Account	15,000	12,000			
13% Debentures	10,000	7,000			
(Rs. 100 each)					
Creditors	10,000	8,000			
Bills Payable	3,000	2,000			
	1,98,000	1,34,000		1,98,000	1,34,000

A Ltd. absorbed B Ltd. on the following terms :

(1) A Ltd. shall issue 10,000 equity shares of Rs. 10 each at a premium of 10% and cash Rs. 10,000.

(2) Debentureholders of B Ltd. will be issued new 15% debentures of equivalent amount in A Ltd.

(3) Export Project Reserve and Investment Allowance Reserve are required to be maintained for 3 more years.

(4) Absorption expenses Rs. 4,500 are to be paid by A Ltd.

Required :

(i) Computation of purchase consideration due to B Ltd.

(ii) Journal entries and ledger accounts in the books of B Ltd.

(iii) Incorporation entries in the books of A Ltd., and

(iv) Balance sheet of A Ltd. (after absorption).

Assume the conditions of amalgamation in the nature of merger have been fulfilled.

(Adapted from C.A. Inter)

Ans. : Purchase Consideration :

In Equity Shares (10,000 × 11)	1,10,000
In Cash	10,000
Total Rs.	1,20,000

Realisation profit Rs. 5,000; Share premium Rs. 10,000; General Reserve Rs. Nil; P & L A/c Rs. 3,500; Debentures Rs. 17,000 and Balance Sheet Total Rs. 3,15,500.

8. X Co. Ltd. and Y Co. Ltd. decided to amalgamate their business and form a new XY Co. Ltd. with an authorised capital of Rs. 15,00,000 divided into shares of Rs. 10 each. Following are the two balance sheets.

Balance Sheets
as at 31-12-2006

Liabilities	X Ltd.	Y Ltd.	Assets	X Ltd.	Y Ltd.
Share Capital :			Goodwill	60,000	—
Equity Shares of Rs. 10 each	2,00,000	3,75,000	Plant & Machinery	3,20,000	3,60,000
			Stock	29,500	34,500
6% Debentures	—	1,00,000	Debtors	42,750	24,500
Reserved Fund	72,500	—	Cash at Bank	29,250	21,000
Profit & Loss Account	1,75,000	—	Profit & Loss Account	—	80,000
Creditors	34,000	45,000			
	4,81,500	5,20,000		4,81,500	5,20,000

The following are the terms of agreement :

(1) X Co. Ltd. assets and liabilities are to be taken over at book values except goodwill, plant & machinery and stock which are to be valued at Rs. 90,000, Rs. 3,00,000 and Rs. 32,000 respectively.

(2) Y. Co. Ltd. assets except cash at bank are valued at 10% less than book values and the liabilities are taken over at book figures.

Prepare the balance sheet of the new company under purchase method.

(Adapted from B.Com., K.U.D.)

Ans. : Purchase consideration : X Ltd. Rs. 4,60,000 (*i.e.,* 94,000 – 34,000)
Y Ltd. Rs. 2,53,100 (*i.e.,* 3,98,100 – 1,45,000)
XY Co. Ltd. Balance Sheet Total Rs. 8,92,100.

9. Chand Ltd. and Star Ltd. decided to amalgamate their business on 31-12-2006 and form a new company Chand Star Ltd. with an authorised capital of Rs. 1,20,00,000 divided into shares of Rs. 40 each. The following are the balance sheets of the above companies as on 31-12-2006

Liabilities	Chand Ltd.	Star Ltd.	Assets	Chand Ltd.	Star Ltd.
Share Capital :	—	—	Goodwill	4,80,000	
Shares of Rs. 40 each	16,00,000	30,00,000	Machinery	25,60,000	28,80,000
Reserve Fund	5,80,000	—	Stock	2,36,000	2,76,000
Profit & Loss Account	14,00,000	—	Debtors	3,42,000	1,96,000
Debentures	—	8,00,000	Cash at Bank	2,34,000	1,68,000
Creditors	2,72,000	3,60,000	Profit & Loss Account	—	6,40,000
	38,52,000	41,60,000		38,52,000	41,60,000

The following are the terms of amalgamation :

(1) The assets and liabilities of Chand Ltd. are to be taken over at book values except goodwill, machinery and stock which are to be valued at Rs. 7,20,000, Rs. 24,00,000 and Rs. 2,56,000 respectively.

(2) The assets of Star Ltd. are to be taken over except cash at bank and debtors valued at 10% more than their book values and the liabilities, cash at bank and debtors are taken over at book values.

Prepare the amalgamated balance sheet of the new company. Apply purchase method.

(Adapted from B.Com., Gulbarga University)

Ans. : Purchase consideration : Chand Ltd. Rs. 36,80,000 (*i.e.,* 39,52,000 –2,72,000); Star Ltd. Rs. 26,75,600 (*i.e.,* 38,35,600 – 11,60,000)
Chand Star Co. Ltd. Balance Sheet Total Rs. 63,55,600.

10. The two companies Abad Ltd. and Nabad Ltd. agreed to amalgamate and form a new company Kamyab Ltd. On the date of amalgamation the balance sheets of the two companies were as follows :

Balance Sheet as on 31-12-2006

Liabilities	Abad Ltd.	Nabad Ltd.	Assets	Abad Ltd.	Nabad Ltd.
Share Capital :			Sundry Assets	60,000	31,000
Equity Shares of Rs. 10 each	75,000	25,000	Freehold Property	3,000	—
10% Debentures	—	3,000	Debtors	18,000	5,000
Reserves	—	2,000	Investments	13,000	3,000
Mortgage Loan Secured by Freehold Property	5,000	—	Bank	10,000	2,000
Creditors	4,000	10,000			
Profit & Loss A/c	20,000	1,000			
	1,04,000	41,000		1,04,000	41,000

The purchase consideration consisted of :

(a) The assumption of the liabilities of both the companies.

(b) The discharge of the debentures in Nabad Ltd. by the issue of Rs. 3,500 15% debentures in Kamyab Ltd.

(c) The issue at a premium of Rs. 5 per share of equity shares of Rs. 10 each in Kamyab Ltd.

For the purpose of the transfer, the assets are to be revalued as follows :

	Abad Ltd.	Nabad Ltd.
Sundry Assets	65,000	35,000
Freehold Property	5,000	—
Debtors	17,100	4,500
Investments	14,900	4,000
Goodwill	11,000	4,000

Prepare the realisation account and shareholders account in the books of Abad Ltd. and Nabad Ltd. to give effect to the above transactions. Also prepare the amalgamated Balance Sheet of Kamyab Ltd. under purchase method.

(Adapted from B.Com., Gulbarga University)

Ans. : Purchase consideration :

	Abad Ltd.	Nabad Ltd.
Value of assets taken over	1,23,000	49,500
Less : Liabilities taken over	9,000	10,000
Purchase consideration	1,14,000	39,500
Less : Paid by 15% debentures at premium	—	3,500
P.C. paid in shares at premium	1,14,000	36,000
No. of shares of Rs. 10 at Rs. 5 premium	7,600	2,400

Kamyab Ltd. Balance Sheet Total Rs. 1,72,500.

11. The following are the balance sheets of A Ltd. and B Ltd. as on 31-3-2006.

Liabilities	A Ltd.	B Ltd.	Assets	A Ltd.	B Ltd.
Share Capital :			Sundry Fixed		
Equity shares of			Assets	2,70,000	1,40,000
Rs. 10 each	3,00,000	1,50,000	Sundry Debtors	80,000	60,000
Reserve & Surplus :			Stock	50,000	40,000
Reserve Fund	60,000	40,000	Cash at Bank	10,000	6,000
Workmen's			Bills Receivable	15,000	4,000
Compensation Fund	—	10,000			
Current Liabilities :					
Sundry Creditors	60,000	40,000			
Bills Payable	5,000	10,000			
	4,25,000	2,50,000		4,25,000	2,50,000

Both the companies have agreed to amalgamate and form C Ltd. which will take over all the assets and liabilities of both companies.

(a) The shareholders of A Ltd. are issued four (4) shares of Rs. 10 each at Rs. 2 per share in exchange for three (3) shares in A Ltd.

(b) The assets and liabilities of B Ltd. are to be taken over at book values subject to 5% provision on debtors and bills receivable and 10% depreciation on sundry fixed assets. Goodwill of B Ltd. was valued at Rs. 25,000.

Compute the purchase consideration due and prepare the Balance Sheet of C Ltd. under purchase method.

(Adapted from B.Com., K.U.D.)

Ans. : Purchase consideration :

A Ltd. Rs. 4,80,000 (*i.e.,* 30000 × 4/3 × 12)

B Ltd. Rs. 2,07,800 (*i.e.,* 2,57,800 – 50,000)

Share Capital Rs. 6,07,800; Share Premium Rs. 80,000;

Goodwill Rs. 1,45,000 & C Ltd. Balance Sheet Total Rs. 8,02,800

Note : Workmen's compensation fund is transferred to shareholders.

12. The following are the balance sheets of X Ltd. and Y Ltd. as on 31-3-2008 when they decided to amalgamate and form a new company, namely Z Ltd :

Liabilities	X. Ltd.	Y. Ltd.	Assets	X. Ltd.	Y. Ltd.
Share Capital :			Fixed Assets :		
Equity shares of			Land & Building	4,20,000	1,50,000
Rs. 10 each	7,00,000	2,50,000	Plant	3,80,000	1,10,000
9% Pref. shares			Investments	—	—
of Rs. 100 each	—	2,50,000	Current Assets :		
Reserve & Surplus :			Stock	1,00,000	1,20,000
General Reserve	1,10,000	—	Debtors	70,000	1,50,000
Profit & Loss A/c	70,000	—	Bills Receivable	25,000	30,000
Secured Loans	—	1,00,000	Bank	65,000	40,000
Current Liabilities :			Profit & Loss A/c	—	80,000
Creditors	1,40,000	50,000			
Bills Payable	40,000	30,000			
	10,60,000	6,80,000		10,60,000	6,80,000

The purchase consideration was agreed upon as under :

For X Ltd.

5 equity shares of Rs. 10 each in Z Ltd. in exchange for 4 equity shares in X Ltd. at 20% premium for taking over assets and liabilities except its bills payable which are to be paid off before amalgamation.

For Y Ltd.

(a) The secured loans of Y Ltd. would be discharged by issuing an equal amount of 8% debentures in Z Ltd. at 10% discount.

(b) The holders of 9% preference shares in Y Ltd. would be allotted 3 12% preference shares of Rs. 100 each in X Ltd. in exchange for every 4 preference shares in Y Ltd.

(c) The equity shareholders would be allotted sufficient equity shares of Rs. 10 each in Z Ltd. to cover the balance on their accounts after writing off plant by 10% and providing 5% on debtors and Rs. 5,000 for workers compensation.

Prepare the statement of purchase consideration and the balance sheet of Z Ltd. under purchase method.

(Adapted from B.Com., K.U.D.)

Ans. : Goodwill Rs. 1,70,000

Z Ltd. Balance Sheet Total Rs. 17,81,500.

Purchase consideration :

X Ltd. : Rs. 10,50,000 (87,500 shares of Rs. 12 each *i.e.,* 10 + 2 Premium)

Y Ltd. : Rs. 4,06,500. This is arrived as below :

(a) In preference shares : For 4 shares, 3 shares are given at Rs. 100 each (2,500 × 3/4 × 100) 1,87,500

(b) In equity shares : It is arrived as below :

Value of Assets taken over			5,81,500
(1,50,000 + 99,000 + 1,20,000 + 1,42,500 + 30,000 + 40,000)			
Less : Liabilities taken over :			
Creditors	50,000		
Bills payable	30,000		
Workers' compensation	5,000		
Preference shareholders	1,87,500		
Debentureholders	90,000	3,62,500	2,19,000
Purchase consideration			4,06,500

13. Two companies *viz.*, Honey Ltd. and Moon Ltd. carrying on similar business decided to amalgamate as on and from 1st Jan. 2007.

Their respective agreed Balance Sheets were as follows :

Liabilities	Honey Ltd.	Moon Ltd.	Assets	Honey Ltd.	Moon Ltd.
Share Capital :			Fixed Assets :		
Shares of Rs. 100 each	75,000	50,000	Goodwill	30,000	15,000
Reserve and Surplus :			Freehold Land	12,000	—
General Reserve	5,500	—	Plant & Machinery	19,500	25,000
Profit and Loss A/c	2,000	2,500	Investments	—	—
Secured Loans	—	—	Current Assets		
Unsecured Loans	—	—	Loans & Advances:		
Current Liabilities and			Stock	15,000	12,000
Provisions :			Debtors	8,000	6,000
Creditors	3,500	3,500	Cash in Hand and		
Depreciation Provision	—	2,500	at Bank	1,500	500
	86,000	58,500		86,000	58,500

In the case of Honey Ltd., which has been in existence for several years, plant and machinery has been regularly depreciated, but in the case of Moon Ltd. which commenced business only 1st January, 2005, plant and machinery stands at cost and depreciation has been provided by means of depreciation provision.

It is agreed that the combined company which is to be called Honey, Moon Ltd. shall take over the assets (including goodwill) and discharge the liabilities of each company on the basis of figures in their respective balance sheets as shown above.

The capital of the Honey-Moon Ltd. was Rs. 2,00,000 divided into 10,000 ordinary shares of Rs. 10 each and 10,000 6% cumulative preference shares of Rs. 10 each.

The Honey Moon Ltd. issued 1,500 shares for cash and agreed to allot to each shareholder in Honey Ltd. and Moon Ltd. five ordinary and five preference shares of Rs. 10 each fully paid, and to discharge the balance in cash.

Draw up the Balance Sheet of the Honey-Moon Ltd. after the above transactions have been completed and show what each shareholder in Honey Ltd. and Moon Ltd. would receive in shares in the new company and in cash. Apply purchase method.

(Adapted from Karnataka University)

Ans. : Purchase consideration: Honey Ltd. Rs. 82,500 (*i.e.* 86,000 – 3,500) Moon Ltd. Rs. 52,500 (*i.e.,* 58,500 – 6,000);

Share Capital Rs. 1,40,000 (*i.e.,* equity Rs. 77,500 (*i.e.,* 3,750 + 2,500 + 1,500 = 7,750 × 10 each) + Preference Rs. 62,500);

Cash in hand and at Bank Rs. 7,000 (*i.e.,* 1,500 + 500 + 15,000 – 10,000);

Honey-Moon Ltd. Balance Sheet Total Rs. 1,47,000

Note : Settlement of purchase consideration :

	Honey Ltd.	Moon Ltd.
Purchase consideration	82,500	52,500
No. of shares issued	750	500
Value of every share	110 $\left(\frac{82,500}{750}\right)$	105 $\left(\frac{52,500}{500}\right)$
Value of every share (*i.e.,* 110 and 105) held will be settled as below :		
(a) In the form of ordinary shares (5 ordinary shares of Rs. 10 each)	50	50
(b) In the form of preference shares (5 preference shares of Rs. 100 each)	50	50
(c) In the form of cash (balance)	10	5

14. On 31st March, 2006 the balance sheet of X Ltd. stood as follows :

Liabilities	Rs.	Assets	Rs.
Share Capital :		Plant and Machinery	16,10,000
1,50,000 Equity Shares of		Furniture and Fixtures	1,94,400
Rs. 10 each, fully paid	15,00,000	Stock	7,05,500
Securities Premium	1,50,000	Debtors	1,98,440
General Reserve	6,25,500	Cash at Bank	1,13,200
Profit & Loss Account	1,85,300		
Creditors	3,60,740		
	28,21,540		28,21,540

On this date, X Ltd. took over the business of Y Ltd. for Rs. 6,60,000 payable in the form of its fully paid equity shares of Rs. 10 each at par, shareholders of Y Ltd. getting 110 shares of X Ltd. for every 100 shares held in Y Ltd. The scheme of amalgamation also provided that 3,000 11% Debentures of Y Ltd. would be converted into equal number of 12% Debentures of X Ltd. of Rs. 100 each. The balance sheet of Y Ltd. on the date of the amalgamation was as follows :

Liabilities	Rs.	Assets	Rs.
Share Capital :		Machinery	5,50,000
60,000 Equity Shares of		Furniture	1,35,200
Rs. 10 each, fully paid	6,00,000	Stock	3,15,800
Capital Reserve	13,000	Debtors	1,29,300
Foreign Projects Reserve		Cash at Bank	68,260
(Statutory Reserve)	9,700	Preliminary Expenses	6,100
General Reserve	75,350		
Profit & Loss Account	24,130		
3,000 11% Debentures			
of Rs. 100 each	3,00,000		
Creditors	1,82,480		
	12,04,660		12,04,660

You are required to pass journal entries in the books of X Ltd. and draw X Ltd.'s balance sheet immediately after the take over, assuming the amalgamation is the nature of merger.

(Adapted from C.S. Inter)

Ans. : Share Capital Rs. 21,60,000; General Reserve Rs. 6,64,980; P & L A/c Rs. 1,85,300; B/S Total Rs. 40,26,200 & Preliminary Expenses Rs. 6,100.

15. A Ltd. agrees to absorb the business of B Ltd. as on 31-12-2006 to take over the assets and liabilities at the balance sheet values and to issue fully paid shares of Rs. 10 each. The following are the balance sheets of the two companies :

Balance Sheets
as on 31-2-2006

Liabilities	A Ltd.	B Ltd.	Assets	A Ltd.	B Ltd.
Share Capital	3,00,000	1,00,000	Goodwill	60,000	10,000
General Reserve	50,000	20,000	Buildings	90,000	—
P & L Account	20,000	10,000	Machinery	80,000	45,000
Creditors	30,000	40,000	Stock	70,000	65,000
Bills Payable	—	15,000	Debtors	50,000	40,000
			Cash	50,000	25,000
	4,00,000	1,85,000		4,00,000	1,85,000

Pass the closing entries and show the necessary ledger accounts in the books of B Ltd. and pass the opening entries in the books of A Ltd. and show the new balance sheet under pooling of interests method.

(Adapted from B.Com., Bharathiar)

Ans. : Share Capital Rs. 4,30,000; General Reserve Rs. 50,000; Profit & Loss A/c Rs. 20,000 and Balance Sheet Total Rs. 5,85,000.

16. The following were the balance sheets of P Ltd. and V Ltd. as 31st March, 2006 :

Liabilities	P Ltd. (Rs. in lakhs)	V Ltd. (Rs. in lakhs)	Assets	P Ltd. (Rs. in Lakhs)	V Ltd. (Rs. in Lakhs)
Equity Share Capital (Fully paid shares of Rs. 10 each)	15,000	6,000	Land and Buildings	6,000	—
			Plant & Machinery	14,000	5,000
Securities Premium	3,000	—	Furniture, Fixtures & Fittings	2,304	1,700
Foreign Projects Reserve	—	310	Stock	7,862	4,041
General Reserve	9,500	3,200	Debetors	2,120	1,020
Profit & Loss Account	2,870	825	Cash at Bank	1,114	609
12% Debentures	—	1,000	Bills Receivable	—	80
Bills Payable	120	—	Cost of Issue of Debentures	—	50
Sundry Creditors	1,080	463			
Sundry Provisions	1,830	702			
	33,400	12,500		33,400	12,500

All the bills receivable held by V Ltd. were P Ltd.'s acceptances. On 1st April, 2006 P Ltd. took over V Ltd. in an amalgamation in the nature of merger. It was agreed that in discharge of consideration for the business, P Ltd. would allot three fully paid equity shares of Rs. 10 each at par for every two shares held in V Ltd. It was also agreed that 12% debentures in V Ltd. would be convered into 13% debentures in P Ltd. of the same amount and denomination. Expenses of amalgamation amounting to Rs. 1 lakh were borne by P Ltd.

You are required to :

(i) Pass journal entries in the books of P Ltd. and

(ii) Prepare P Ltd.'s balance sheet immediately after the merger.

(Adapted from C.A. Inter)

Ans. : Purchase consideration Rs. 9,000 lakhs; P & L A/c Rs. 3,695 lakhs; Share Capital Rs. 24,000 lakhs; Cost of issue of Debentures Rs. 50 lakhs; Bills payable Rs. 40 lakhs; Bills Receivable Rs. Nil, B/S Total Rs. 45,819 lakhs and General Reserve Rs. 9,669.

17. Two companies Ram Ltd. and Raj Ltd. amalgamate and form a new company Ram Raj Ltd. Following are the Balance Sheets of the two companies :

Liabilities	Ram Ltd.	Raj Ltd.	Assets	Ram Ltd.	Raj Ltd.
Paid up Capital	50,000	40,000	Cash	24,000	4,000
Shares of Rs. 10 each			Debtors	40,000	44,000
P & L A/c	14,000	8,400	Stock	20,000	12,000
Debentures	20,000	—	Goodwill	6,000	—
Creditors	6,000	11,600			
	90,000	60,000		90,000	60,000

The average profits of Ram Ltd. and Raj Ltd. have been Rs. 10,000 and Rs. 6,000 respectively. Ram Raj Ltd. agrees with the two companies to take over the concerns for Rs. 1,20,000 discharge all liabilities, to pay Rs. 24,000 in cash and the balance in shares at face value. Debtors of both the companies are to be written off by 10% before being taken over. The profit on conversion should be shared between the two companies as per the ratio of average profits stated above. Cash and shares should be apportioned between them in the same ratio as the total purchase price is shared.

You are required to :

(a) Allocate purchase consideration between Ram and Raj and show its discharge.

(b) Prepare only Realisation A/c in Ram Ltd. and Raj Ltd., and Amalgamated Balance Sheet of Ram Raj Ltd. under purchase method.

(Adapted from B.Com., Bangalore University)

Ans. : Realisation profit : Ram Rs. 3,250 and Raj Rs. 4,350; Balance Sheet total Rs. 1,33,600

Note : Purchase consideration as per Net Assets Method :

	Rs.
Ram Ltd. (Assets Rs. 86,000 – Liabilities Rs. 26,000)	60,000
Raj Ltd. (Assets Rs. 60,000 – Liability Rs. 11,600)	48,400
Total	1,08,400
Profit on conversion :	
Purchase consideration actually paid	1,20,000
Less : Purchase consideration actually payable	1,08,400
Profit on conversion	11,600

This profit on conversion is to be shared in the ratio of 5 : 3 (*i.e.,* 10,000 : 6,000). Therefore, Ram gets Rs. 7,250 and Raj gets Rs. 4,350. So, Purchase consideration payable to Ram Ltd. is Rs. 67,250 (*i.e.,* 60,000 + 7,250) and Raj Ltd. is Rs. 52,750 (*i.e.,* 48,400 + 4,350).

Distribution of purchased consideration

To be satisfied in cash :	Ram Ltd.	Raj Ltd.
Ram: Rs. 24,000 × 6,725/12,000	13,450	—
Raj : Rs. 24,000 × 5,275/12,000	—	10,550
To be satisfied in shares (Balancing figure)	53,800	42,200
	67,250	52,750

18. X Ltd. agreed to absorb the business of Y Ltd. as on 31-3-2006 and to take over the assets and liabilities at their balance sheet values in exchange for which it is to issue 6 shares of Rs. 10 each for every 5 shares of Rs. 10 each in Y Ltd. The expenses of absorption of Rs. 5,000 shall be paid by X Co. Ltd. Balance Sheets of both the companies are as follows :

Balance Sheet of X Ltd. as at 31-3-2006

Liabilities	Rs.	Assets		Rs.
Share Capital		**Fixed Assets**		
Authorised : 2,00,000		Goodwill	50,000	
shares of Rs. 10 each	20,00,000	Buildings	2,50,000	
Issued & Subscribed		Plant	2,00,000	5,00,000
1,20,000 Shares of	12,00,000	**Investments**		
Rs. 10 each		Government Securities		3,00,000
Reserve & Surplus		**Current Assets**		—
General Reserve	1,00,000	**Loans & Advances**		
Current Liabilities &		Stock	4,00,000	
Provisions :		Debtors	1,50,000	
Creditors	1,50,000	Bank	1,00,000	6,50,000
	14,50,000			14,50,000

Balance Sheet of Y Ltd. as on 31-3-2006

Liabilities		Rs.	Assets		Rs.
Share Capital			**Fixed Assets**		
60,000 Shares of			Buildings	1,00,000	
Rs. 10 each		6,00,000	Plant	1,50,000	2,50,000
Reserve & Surplus			**Investments**		
Reserve Fund		20,000	Govt. Securities		2,00,000
Current Liabilities &			**Loans & Advances**		
Provisions			Stock	1,20,000	
Creditors	50,000		Debtors	1,50,000	
Bills Payable	80,000	1,30,000	Bank	30,000	3,00,000
		7,50,000			7,50,000

Show the journal entries in the books of both the companies and the opening balance sheet of X Ltd. after absorption. Apply purchase method.

(Adapted from B.Com., K.U.D.)

Ans. : Purchase consideration Rs. 7,20,000 (*i.e.,* 6/5 × 60,000 × 10)
Realisation Profit Rs. 1,00,000 (*i.e.,* 8,50,000 – 7,50,000);
Goodwill Rs. 1,55,000 (1,00,000 + 50,000 + 5,000);
Bank Balance Rs. 1,25,000.
New Balance Sheet Total Rs. 23,00,000.

Note : Absorption expenses of Rs. 5,000 are directly paid by X Co. Ltd.

19. The following are the balance sheets of X Co. Ltd. and Y Co. Ltd. as on 31-3-2006 :

Liabilities	X Ltd.	Y Ltd.	Assets	X Ltd.	Y Ltd.
Share Capital :			Goodwill	30,000	10,000
Equity Shares			Buildings	2,00,000	1,00,000
of Rs. 10 each	5,00,000	2,00,000	Machinery	3,00,000	1,50,000
8% Pref. Shares			Stock	90,000	50,000
of Rs. 100 each	1,00,000	1,00,000	Sundry Debtors	1,20,000	1,15,000
9% Debentures	1,00,000	1,00,000	Cash & Bank Bal.	30,000	10,000
General Reserve	20,000	10,000	Preliminary Exps.	10,000	5,000
Sundry Creditors	60,000	30,000			
	7,80,000	4,40,000		7,80,000	4,40,000

X Co. Ltd. absorbs Y Co. Ltd. on the following terms :

(a) Equity shareholders are to be given 6 equity shares of Rs. 10 each of X Co. Ltd. issued at 10% premium against 5 shares held in Y Co. Ltd.

(b) 8% preference shareholders are to be paid at 10% premium by 9% preference shares of Rs. 10 each of X Co. Ltd. issued at par.

(c) 9% debentureholders are to be paid at 8% premium by 10% debentures of X Co. Ltd. issued at 10% discount.

(d) Rs. 5,000 cash is retained by Y Co. Ltd. for liquidation expenses.

(e) Buildings of Y Co. Ltd. are taken over at Rs. 1,50,000.

Prepare the necessary ledger accounts in the books of Y Co. Ltd. and the journal entries in the books of X Co. Ltd. under purchase method.

(Adapted from B.Com., Gulbarga University)

Ans. : Purchase consideration :

	Rs.
In Equity Shares (6/5 × 20,000 × 11 *i.e.,* 10 + 1 premium)	2,64,000
In Preference Shares (1,00,000 + 10% premium *or* 11,000 × 10)	1,10,000
Total	3,74,000

Realisation Profit Rs. 59,000 and Goodwill Rs. 72,000 (*i.e.,*30,000 + 42,000).

20. Chota Co. Ltd. was agreed to be absorbed by Mota Co. Ltd. on 30-6-2006 on which date the balance sheet of Chota Co. Ltd. was as follows :

Liabilities	Rs.	Assets	Rs.
45,000 shares (Rs. 10)	4,50,000	Land & Buildings	3,50,000
General Reserve	3,00,000	Furniture	30,000
Profit & Loss Account	1,40,000	Machinery	5,60,000
5% Debentures	1,10,000	Stock	80,000
Dividend Equalisation Fund	20,000	Debtors	36,000
Creditors	40,000	Cash	4,000
	10,60,000		10,60,000

Mota Co. Ltd. having decided to acquire all the assets and liabilities of Chota Co. Ltd. valued the assets as follows :

It was decided to acquire the current assets at book value and fixed assets at the following values :

Land and Buildings Rs. 4,00,000; Furniture Rs. 20,000; Machinery Rs. 6,00,000; Goodwill Rs. 60,000.

The purchase consideration is payable half in shares and the balance in cash.

Prepare the necessary ledger accounts in the books of Chota Co. Ltd. and pass the journal entries in the books of Mota Co. Ltd. under purchase method.

(Adapted from B.Com., Mysore University)

Ans. : Purchase consideration Rs. 10,50,000 (In Shares Rs. 5,25,000 + In Cash Rs. 5,25,000); Realisation Profit Rs. 1,40,000.

21. The following is the balance sheet of Karnataka Traders Ltd. as on 31-12-2006 :

Liabilities	Rs.	Assets	Rs.
Share Capital :		Land & Buildings	1,25,000
Equity Shares of		Plant & Machinery	1,25,000
Rs. 10 each	2,00,000	Work-in-progress	30,000
6% Debentures	1,00,000	Stock	60,000
Creditors	30,000	Furniture	2,500
Reserve Fund	25,000	Sundry Debtors	35,000
Employees Savings Bank A/c	20,000	Bank Balance	2,500
Surplus	5,100	Cash	100
	3,80,100		3,80,100

The company is absorbed by Sunshine Co. Ltd. on the above date. The consideration for absorption is discharge of the debentures at a premium of 5% taking over liabilities and a payment of Rs. 7 in cash and one share of Rs. 5 in Sunshine Co. Ltd. at a market value of Rs. 8 per share in exchange for one share in Karnataka Traders Ltd. The cost of liquidation of Rs. 5,000 is to be met by the purchasing company.

Prepare necessary ledger accounts in the books of Karnataka Traders Ltd. to close the books. Pass necessary entries in the books of sunshine Co. Ltd. to record the above. Apply purchase method.

(*Adapted from B. Com. K.U.D.*)

Ans. : Purchase consideration :

	Rs.
In shares (2,000 × 8)	1,60,000
In cash : For shares (20,000 × 7)	1,40,000
Total	3,00,000

Realisation profit Rs. 69,900.

Note : Cost of liquidation is paid by the purchasing Company by debiting goodwill account.

22. The assets of Laxmi Ltd. are purchased by Jayalaxmi Ltd. The purchase consideration was as follows :

(1) A payment in cash at Rs. 50 for every share in the Laxmi Ltd.

(2) A further payment in cash at Rs. 110 for every debenture of Rs. 100 each in Laxmi Ltd. which the debentureholders have agreed to accept in full discharge of their debentures.

(3) An exchange of three shares of Jayalaxmi Ltd. of Rs. 20 each at the market value of Rs. 40 each for every share in the Laxmi Ltd.

The following was the balance sheet of Laxmi Ltd. when it was absorbed.

Liabilities	Rs.	Assets	Rs.
Share Capital :		Buildings	60,000
1,000 Shares of Rs. 100		Machinery	30,000
each fully paid	1,00,000	Furniture	8,000
Profit & Loss Account	20,000	Stock	22,000
Workman's Compensation		Sundry Debtors	20,000
Fund	10,000	Bills Receivable	15,000
10% Debentures	20,000	Cash	15,000
Workmen's Savings Deposits	5,000		
Employees Profit Sharing Fund	3,000		
Sundry Creditors	12,000		
	1,70,000		1,70,000

Show the necessary accounts to close the books of Laxmi Ltd. and pass the necessary entries in the books of Jayalaxmi Ltd. under purchase method.

(Adapted from B.Com., K.U.D.)

Ans. : Purchase Consideration

	Rs.
In Cash : For Shares (1,000 × 50)	50,000
In Shares : 3/1 × 1,000 = 3,000 × 4	1,20,000
Total	1,70,000

Realisation Profit Rs. 20,000; Goodwill Rs. 22,000 (1,70,000 – 1,48,000).

Notes : (i) Debenture are paid by the purchasing company in cash Rs. 22,000.

(ii) Employees profit sharing fund and workmen's saving deposits are also liabilities.

23. The Karnataka Cements Ltd. is absorbed by Andhra Cements Ltd. the consideration being the assumption of the liabilities, the discharge of the debenture debt at a premium of 5% by the issue of the 6% debentures in the Andhra Cements Ltd. and a payment in cash of Rs. 30 per share and the exchange of three Rs. 10 shares in the Andhra Cements Ltd. at an agreed value of Rs. 15 per share for every share in the Karnataka Cements Ltd.

Balance Sheet of Karnataka Cement Ltd.

Liabilities	Rs.	Assets	Rs.
Share Capital :		Goodwill	2,50,000
Shares of Rs. 50 each	30,00,000	Land & Buildings	7,65,000
5% Debentures	15,00,000	Machinery	22,00,000
Sundry Creditors	2,00,000	Plants	50,000
Workmen's Profit		Patterns	25,000
Sharing Fund	1,00,000	Stock	10,60,000
Accident Compensation Fund	50,000	Debtors	4,50,000
General Reserve	3,20,000	Investments	50,000
Profit & Loss A/c	30,000	Cash at Bank	3,50,000
	52,00,000		52,00,000

Pass the journal entries to close the books of Karnataka Cements Ltd. and also to open the books of Andhra Cements Ltd. under purchase method.

(Adapted from B.Com., Gulbarga University)

Ans. :		Rs.
	Purchase consideration	
	In Cash : For Share (60,000 × 30)	18,00,000
	In Shares : 3/1× 60,000 = 1,80,000 × 15	27,00,000
	Total	45,00,000

Realisation of Profit Rs. 11,00,000

24. The following are the balance sheets of May Co. Ltd. and Fair Co. Ltd. as at 31st March, 2006.

Balance Sheet of May Co. Ltd.

Liabilities	Rs.	Assets	Rs.
Share Capital :		Goodwill	1,00,000
Issued and Subscribed :		Land and Buildings	18,00,000
8,000 7% Preference Shares		Machinery and Plant	5,00,000
of Rs. 100 each	8,00,000	Furniture & Fittings	2,00,000
10,00,000 Equity Share of		Stock	9,00,000
Rs. 10 each	10,00,000	Debtors	4,00,000
General Reserve	8,00,000	Bank	50,000
Profit & Loss Account	4,00,000		
8% Debentures	5,00,000		
Creditors	2,00,000		
Bills Payable	1,00,000		
Provident Fund	1,00,000		
Provision for Tax	50,000		
	39,50,000		39,50,000

Balance Sheet of Fair Co. Ltd.

Liabilties	Rs.	Assets	Rs.
Share Capital :		Goodwill	1,00,000
Issued and Subscribed :		Land and Buildings	15,00,000
5,000 8% Preference shares of Rs. 100 each	5,00,000	Machinery and Plant	3,40,000
		Furniture & Fittings	3,00,000
90,000 Equity shares of Rs. 10 each	9,00,000	Stock	5,00,000
		Debtors	2,00,000
General Reserve	5,00,000		
Profit & Loss Account	3,00,000		
9% Debentures	2,00,000		
Creditors	2,00,000		
Bank Overdraft	1,00,000		
Provident Fund	2,00,000		
Provision for Tax	40,000		
	29,40,000		29,40,000

The above companies were engaged in a similar business. They decided to amalgamate and form a new company, 'Mayfair' Company Ltd., from 1-4-2006 The following were the terms agreed upon by both the companies :

(a) The Mayfair Company Ltd. to have an authorised capital of Rs. 2,50,00,000 divided into 1,50,000 8% preference shares of Rs. 100 each and 10,00,000 equity shares of Rs. 10 each.

(b) The Mayfair Co. Ltd. agrees to take over all the assets and liabilities of both the companies at the values stated in the respective balance sheets.

(c) The shareholders of each of the companies were to be allotted 4,00,000 equity shares and 3,00,000 equity shares of Rs. 10 each, respectively. This includes claims of preference shareholders.

(d) The Mayfair Co. Ltd. agrees to discharge the debentures of both the companies by the issue of 10% debentures.

(e) The Mayfair Co. Ltd. issued to the public 1,00,000 preference shares and 1,00,000 equity shares which were duly taken up and paid for.

(f) The Mayfair Co. Ltd. incurred Rs. 50,000 formation expenses.

(g) Liquidation expenses of May Co. Ltd. amounted to Rs. 10,000 and those of Fair Co. Ltd. amounted to Rs. 8,000.

Journalise the transactions in the books of May Co. Ltd., Fair Co. and also Mayfair Co. Ltd. Prepare the balance sheet of Mayfair Co. Ltd. after putting through the above scheme of amalgamation under merger method.

(Adapted from I.C.W.A. Inter)

Ans. : Purchase consideration: May Co. Ltd. Rs. 40,00,000 and Fair Co. Ltd. 30,00,000; Realisation Profit: May Co. Ltd. Rs. 10,00,000 and Fair Co. Ltd. Rs. 8,00,000; Shareholders A/c Total: May Co. Ltd. Rs. 32,00,000 and Fair Co. Ltd. Rs. 25,00,000; Share Capital: Pref. Share Capital Rs. 1,00,00,000 and Equity Share Capital Rs. 80,00,000; General Reserve Rs. Nil; P & L A/c (Debit) Rs. 18,00,000; Provision for Tax Rs. 90,000 and Balance Sheet Total Rs. 1,96,90,000.

25. The Bangalore Co. Ltd. decided to sell its business to the Karnataka Co. Ltd. as on 31-12-2006. On that date its balance sheet was as follows :

Liabilities	Rs.	Assets	Rs.
Share Capital :		Goodwill	4,000
20,000 Shares of Re. 1 each	20,000	Buildings	15,000
Reserve Fund	5,000	Machinery	1,500
Profit & Loss A/c	2,000	Stock	3,500
5% Debentures	10,000	Sundry Debtors	4,000
Trade Creditors	3,000	Bills Receivable	2,000
		Cash	10,000
	40,000		40,000

The Karnataka Co. Ltd. agreed to take over the assets (exclusive of goodwill and cash) at the amounts stated in the above balance sheet to discharged the liabilities to trade creditors and to pay Rs. 10,000 for goodwill.

The purchase price was to be discharged by the allotment to the Bangalore Co. Ltd. of 1,200 shares of Rs. 10 each in the capital of the Karnataka Co. Ltd. at Rs. 12.50 per share and the balance in cash.

The Bangalore Co. Ltd. went into voluntary liquidation and the expenses of liquidation amounted Rs. 300.

Prepare (i) Realisation Account, (ii) Karnataka Co. Ltd. Account, (iii) Shareholders Account and (iv) Cash Account. Apply purchase method.

(Adapted from B.Com., Karnataka & Gulbarga University)

Ans. : Purchase consideration Rs. 33,000 (*i.e.,* Agreed value of Assets Rs. 36,000 – 3,000 Agreed value of liabilities)

	Rs.
In the form of shares (25/2 × 1200)	15,000
In the form of cash balance (*i.e.,* 33,000 – 15,000)	18,000
Total	33,000

Realisation profit Rs. 5,700.

***Note* :** Debentures are paid by Vendor Company.

26. G Ltd. has been absorbed by D Ltd. with effect from 1-1-2006. The consideration was that D Ltd. was :

(a) to take over the assets and liabilities except debentures of G Ltd. at their balance sheet values.

(b) to pay cash at Rs. 110 for every debenture in G Ltd.

(c) to pay cash at Rs. 80 for every share in the G Ltd.

(d) to issue 5 shares of D Ltd. of Rs. 100 each at market price (quoted in the market at Rs. 180) for every share in the G. Ltd.

Balance Sheet of G Ltd. as on 31-12-2006.

Liabilities	Rs.	Assets	Rs.
Share Capital		**Fixed Assets**	
2,000 shares of	12,00,000	Goodwill	1,00,000
Rs. 600 each		Land & Buildings	5,00,000
Reserves & Surplus		Plant & Machinery	3,00,000
General Reserve	2,00,000	Furniture	50,000
Insurance Fund	50,000	Plants	50,000
Profit & Loss A/c	50,000	**Investments**	
Secured Loans		Govt. securities	3,00,000
5,000 6% Debentures of Rs. 100 each	5,00,000	**Current Assets, Loans & Advances**	
Current Liabilities &		Loans	2,00,000
Provisions		Stock	5,00,000
Sundry Creditors	2,00,000	Sundry Debtors	2,00,000
Staff Provident Fund	50,000	Cash at Bank	1,00,000
Bills Payable	50,000		
	23,00,000		23,00,000

Show the necessary accounts in the ledger of G Ltd. and give opening entries in the books of D Ltd. Apply purchase method.

(Adapted from B.Com., Kanpur, Andhra, Madurai & Bangalore)

Ans. : Purchase consideration :

	Rs.
In cash : For shares (2,000 × 80)	1,60,000
In shares : 5/1 × 2,000 = 10,000 shares × Rs. 180	18,00,000
Total	19,60,000

Realisation profit Rs. 4,60,000.

Note : Staff provident funds is also liability.

27. The following was the Balance Sheet of General Co. Ltd. as on 30-6-2006 on which date it was absorbed try Premier Co. Ltd. :

Liabilities		Rs.	Assets	Rs.
Share Capital :			Goodwill	40,000
5,000 5% Pref. shares			Land & Buildings	3,00,000
of Rs. 50 each		2,50,000	Machinery	3,00,000
1,50,000 Equity shares			Patents	1,30,000
of Rs. 5 each		7,50,000	Stock	4,20,000
Debentures of Rs. 100 each			Sundry Debtors	3,00,000
redeemable at the option			Cash at Bank	60,000
of the company at Rs. 105		1,20,000		
General Reserve		90,000		
Sundry Creditors		3,20,000		
Profit & Loss Account :				
As per Last B/S	2,000			
Profit for the year	18,000	20,000		
		15,50,000		15,50,000

(1) The Premier Co. Ltd. took over the assets only and the consideration for absorption was :

(a) Payment of cash sufficient to discharge the debenture debt and the liability to sundry creditors.

(b) Payment of cash of Rs. 1.50 for each equity share in General Co. Ltd.

(c) Allotment of one fully paid equity share of Re. 1 each (market value Rs. 1.75) in its capital to the holders of every 2 equity shares in General Co. Ltd.

(d) Five fully paid 6% preference shares of Rs. 10 each (value at par) in its capital duly allotted to the holders against 1 preference share of General Co. Ltd.

(2) Dividend due for the year on preference shares to be paid to them.

(3) The General Co. Ltd. met its own liquidation expenses Rs. 5,250.

(4) The Premier Co. Ltd. took over the assets in its books at the revalued figures appreciating buildings by Rs. 16,500 and depreciating machinery, stock and patents by Rs. 21,000, Rs. 36,000 and Rs. 30,000 respectively and creating a provision for bad debts at $2^1/_2$% on debtors.

Show the necessary accounts in the ledger of General Co. Ltd. and pass the opening entries in the journal of Premier Co. Ltd. under purchase method.

(Adapted from B.Com., K.U.D.)

Ans. : Purchase consideration

	Rs.
Preference shares : 5/1 × 5,000 = 25,000 shares × Rs. 10	2,50,000
In Equity shares : 1/2 ×1,50,000 = 75,000 shares × Rs. 1.75	1,31,250
In cash : For Equity shares (1,50,000 × 1.50)	2,25,000
Total	6,06,250

Realisation Loss Rs. 5,09,000; Capital Reserve Rs. 3,79,750 & Balance of P & L transferred to Equity shareholders Rs. 7,500 (*i.e.*, Balance Rs. 20,000 – Rs. 12,500 dividend payable to Preference shareholders).

Note : Received value of assets should be incorporated in the opening entries of the purchasing company.

28. The following is the balance sheet of ABC Co. Ltd. on December 31, 2006 :

Liabilities	Rs.	Assets	Rs.
Capital :		Land & Buildings	1,20,000
20,000 Shares of		Plant and Machinery	1,50,000
Rs. 10 each	2,00,000	Work-in-progress	30,000
Debentures	1,00,000	Stock	60,000
Sundry Creditors	30,000	Furniture and Fittings	2,500
Reserve Fund	25,000	Sundry Debtors	25,000
Workmen's Compensation		Cash at Bank	12,500
Fund	10,000	Cash in Hand	100
Dividend Equalisation Fund	10,000		
P & L Appropriation A/c	5,100		
Depreciation Provision :			
Land & Buildings	20,000		
	4,00,100		4,00,100

The company is absorbed by XYZ Co. Ltd. on the above date. The consideration for the absorption is the discharge of the debentures at a premium of 5 per cent, taking over the trade liability and a payment of Rs. 7 in cash and one share of Rs. 5 in XYZ Co. Ltd. at the market value of Rs. 8 per share in exchange for one share in ABC Co. Ltd. The cost of liquidation Rs. 500 is to be met by the purchasing company.

Pass Journal entries in the books of both the companies. Show how the purchase price is arrived at. Apply purchase method.

(Adapted from B.Com., Kanpur, Andhra, Madurai & Bangalore)

Ans. : Purchase consideration :

	Rs.
In cash : For debentures (1,00,000 + 5% Premium)	1,05,000
For shareholders (20,000 shares × Rs. 7)	1,40,000
In shares : 20,000 shares × Rs. 8	1,60,000
Total	4,05,000

Realisation profit Rs. 49,900 and Goodwill Rs. 54,900.

Note : Share capital reserve fund, workmen's compensation fund, dividend equalisation fund & P & L Appropriation A/c should be transferred to shareholders account.

29. The following is the balance sheet of Chetana Ltd. as on 31-12-2006

Liabilities	Rs.	Assets	Rs.
Share Capital :		Land & Buildings	3,00,000
20,000 Shares of		Plant & Machinery	3,50,000
Rs. 25 each	5,00,000	Investments	97,500
Reserve Fund	75,000	Furniture & Fixtures	13,700
Dividend Equalisation Fund	67,000	Stock	1,02,500
Workmen's Compensation		Sundry Debtors	1,06,300
Fund	73,100	Cash at Bank	30,100
Debentures	2,00,000		
Sundry Creditors	85,000		
	10,00,100		10,00,100

The company is absorbed by Parag Ltd. on the above date. The purchase consideration was the discharge of debentures at a premium of 10% taking over of the liabilities in respect of sundry creditors and the payment of Rs. 15 in cash and issue of two shares of Rs. 10 each in Parag Ltd. at the market value of Rs. 15 per share in exchange for one share in Chetana Ltd.

The cost of liquidation of Rs. 3,500 is met by the purchasing company, Parag Ltd. valued land and buildings at 10% more and investments at Rs. 67,970.

Prepare realisation account and shareholders account in the books of Chetana Ltd. and pass the opening entries in the books of Parag Ltd. under purchase method.

(Adapted from B.Com., K.U.D.)

Ans. : Purchase consideration :

In cash : For shares (20,000 shares × Rs. 15)	3,00,000
In shares : 2/1 × 20,000 = 40,000 shares × Rs. 15	6,00,000
Total	9,00,000

Realisation Profit Rs. 1,84,900 and Goodwill Rs. 2,07,930 (2,04,430 + 3,500 expenses paid).

Notes : (i) Liquidation expenses are debited to goodwill.

(ii) Revalued figures should be taken only in the books of purchasing company.

30. A Ltd. and B Ltd. doing business in the same field, decided to amalgamate to avoid unnecessary competitions and secure economy in production and marketing. Following were the Balance Sheets as on 31st December 2006.

Liabilities	A. Ltd.	B. Ltd.	Assets	A. Ltd.	B. Ltd.
Share Capital :			Goodwill	—	1,00,000
Equity shares of			Land & Buildings	15,30,000	8,10,000
Rs. 10	10,00,000	5,00,000	Plant & Machinery	4,80,000	2,40,000
8% Preference			Furniture & Fittings	30,000	26,000
shares of Rs. 10	5,00,000	3,00,000	Investments	20,000	10,000
10% Debentures of			Stock	3,05,000	1,87,000
Rs. 100	5,00,000	—	S. Debtors	1,25,000	69,000
8% Debentures of			Bills Receivable	19,000	11,000
Rs. 100	—	2,50,000	Cash and Bank	74,000	38,000
Reserve Fund	1,60,000	1,10,000	Miscellaneous	63,000	33,000
P & L A/c	70,000	50,000			
Workmen's S B A/c	1,30,000	—			
Other Liabilities	2,86,000	3,14,000			
	26,46,000	15,24,000		26,46,000	15,24,000

The amalgamation was effected on 1-1-2006. The purchase consideration payable by the new company AB Ltd. was as follows :

For A Ltd.

(a) Equity shareholders to get one equity share of Rs. 10 each in AB Ltd. valued at Rs. 12 per share, for every equity share in A Ltd.

(b) 8% Preference shareholders to get 10% preference shares in AB Ltd. equal to their claim.

(c) 10% Debentureholders to get sufficient 12.5% debentures of AB Ltd. so as to get the same amount of interest as they were getting in A Ltd.

For B Ltd.

(a) 4 Equity shares of Rs. 10 each in AB Ltd. valued at Rs. 12 per share for every 5 equity shares in B Ltd.

(b) 8% Preference shareholders to get 90% of their claim in 10% preference shares in AB Ltd. in full satisfaction.

(c) 8% Debentureholders to get sufficient 12.5% debentures of AB Ltd. so as get the same amount of interest as they were getting in B Ltd.

AB Ltd. took over all the assets and liabilities of both companies at their book values except Land and Buildings, Plant and Machinery and Stock of

A Ltd. which were taken over at Rs. 18,50,000, Rs. 3,20,000 and Rs. 2,80,000 respectively investments of B Ltd. at Rs. 16,000. The liquidation expenses of A Ltd. came to Rs. 13,000 and that of B Ltd. to Rs. 9,000. Balance of Cash and Bank was transferred to AB Ltd.

The authorised capital of AB Ltd. is 2,50,000 equity shares of Rs. 10 each and 1,00,000, 10% preference of Rs. 10 each.

Prepare purchase consideration statements and opening Balance Sheet of AB Ltd. under purchase method.

(Adapted from B.Com., Bangalore University)

Ans. : Purchase consideration :

	A Ltd.	B Ltd.
In equity shares	12,00,000	4,80,000
In preference shares	5,00,000	2,70,000
Total	17,00,000	7,50,000

B/S Total Rs. 40,93,000; Share premium Rs. 2,80,000; Capital reserve Rs. 3,53,000; Cash and Bank Rs. 90,000; Equity share capital Rs. 14,00,000 (10,00,000 + 4,00,000) and Preference share capital Rs. 7,70,000 (5,00,000 + 2,70,000); Realisation profit (A Ltd.) Rs. 33,000; Realisation loss (B Ltd.) Rs. 1,47,000.

31. On 31st March 2006 Thin Ltd. was absorbed by Thick Ltd. The latter taking over all the assets and liabilities of the former at book values. The consideration for the business was fixed at Rs. 4,00,000 to be discharged by the transferee company in the form of its fully paid equity shares of Rs. 10 each, to be distributed among the shareholders of the transferor company, each shareholder getting two shares for every share held in the transferor company. The balance sheets of the two companies as on 31st March, 2006 stood as under :

Liabilities	Thick Ltd. Rs.	Thin Ltd. Rs.
Share Capital :		
Authorised	15,00,000	5,00,000
Issued and Subscribed :		
Equity shares of Rs. 10 each, fully paid	9,00,000	2,00,000
General Reserve	1,80,000	50,000
Profit and Loss Account	20,502	12,900
Workmen's Compensation Fund	12,000	9,000
Sundry Creditors	58,567	30,456
Staff Provident Fund	10,200	4,000
Provision for taxation	12,300	5,000
	1,93,5961	3,11,356

Assets		
Goodwill	2,00,000	60,000
Plant and Machinery	4,12,000	1,00,000
Furniture	80,000	30,000
Stock-in-trade	2,65,500	60,000
Sundry Debtors	2,21,200	46,000
Prepaid insurance	—	700
Income tax refund claim	—	6,000
Cash in hand	869	356
Cash at bank	14,000	8,300
	11,93,569	3,11,356

Amalgamation expenses amounting to Rs. 1,000 were paid by Thick Ltd. You are required to :

(i) prepare realisation account and equity shareholder's account in the books of Thin Ltd.

(ii) pass the necessary journal entries in the books of Thin Ltd. and

(iii) prepare the balance sheet of Thick Ltd. after the amalgamation in the nature of merger.

(Adapted from C.S. Inter)

Ans. : Realisation profit Rs. 1,28,100; Share Capital Rs. 13,00,000; General Reserve Rs. 41,900; P & L A/c Rs. 20,502; Balance Sheet Total Rs. 15,03,925.

Note : (i) Prepaid insurance and income tax refund claim should be shown on the asset side of the Balance Sheet under the heading Loans and Advances.

(ii) Provision for taxation and staff provident fund should be shown on the liability side of the Balance Sheet under the heading 'Provisions'.

32. The following are the Balance Sheets of S Ltd. and P Ltd. as on 31st March, 2006.

Liabilities	S Ltd.	P Ltd.	Assets	S Ltd.	P Ltd.
Shares of Rs. 10 each	4,20,000	6,00,000	Premises	2,00,000	5,00,000
Reserves	1,00,000	1,50,000	Plant	2,60,000	1,90,000
Insurance fund	20,000	10,000	Investments	40,000	—
Secured loan	40,000	—	Debtors	1,20,000	1,00,000
8% Bonds	—	1,00,000	Stock	60,000	70,000
Creditors	1,00,000	1,00,000	Bank	—	90,000
			Goodwill	—	10,000
	6,80,000	9,60,000		6,80,000	9,60,000

P Ltd. absorbed S Ltd. on the following terms :

(a) P Ltd. shall give 4 shares of Rs. 10 each at Rs. 15 per share for every shares in S Ltd.

(b) P Ltd. shall pay sufficient cash to enable S Ltd. to discharge its secured loan at a premium of 25%.

(c) The creditors of S Ltd. included Rs. 10,000 due to P Ltd.

(d) P Ltd. had valued investments of S Ltd. at Rs. 50,000.

Prepare

(a) Realisation A/c and Shareholders A/c in the books of S Ltd.

(b) Journal entries in the books of P Ltd., and

(c) Balance Sheet of P Ltd. after acquisition. Apply purchase method.

(Adapted from B.Com., K.U.D.)

Ans. : Purchase consideration

In shares (4 × 42,000/3 = 56,000 shares × Rs. 15)	8,40,000
	Rs. 8,40,000

Realisation profit or loss-Nil; Shareholders Account Total Rs. 8,40,000; Goodwill Rs. 3,10,000 (10,000 + 3,00,000 B.F.); Share premium Rs. 2,80,000; Creditors Rs. 1,90,000; Debtors Rs. 2,10,000; Bank Rs. 40,000 and Balance Sheet Total Rs. 18,90,000.

Note : Debentures are discharged by the purchasing company at a premium (40,000 + 10,000) in the form of cash.

33. Mohanjadaro Ltd. acquired the business of Harappa Ltd. as on 31-12-2006. The Balance Sheet of Harappa Ltd. as on 31-12-2006 was as follows :

Liabilities	Rs.	Assets	Rs.
Share Capital :		Land & Buildings	2,00,000
1,000 6% Preference		Plant	1,00,000
shares of Rs. 100 each	1,00,000	Stock	2,00,000
20,000 Equity shares		Debtors	50,000
of Rs. 10	2,00,000	Bank	35,000
Reserve	20,000	Preliminary Expenses	10,000
7% Debentures	1,00,000	Discount on Debentures	5,000
Profit & Loss Account	30,000		
Creditors	1,50,000		
	6,00,000		6,00,000

The purchase consideration was agreed as under :

(1) Preference shareholders of Harappa Ltd. were to be allotted 8% preference shares of Rs. 1,10,000.

(2) Equity shareholders to be allotted six equity shares of Rs. 10 each issued at a premium of 10% and Rs. 3 in cash for every five shares held.

(3) 7% debentures of Harappa Ltd. to be paid at a premium of 8% by the issue of 9% debentures at a discount of 10%.

(4) The assets were revalued as follows :

Land & Buildings Rs. 2,50,000, stock Rs. 2,20,000 and debtors at book value subject to a provision of 5% for doubtful debts.

(5) Debtors of Harappa Ltd. included Rs. 10,000 due from Mohanjadaro Ltd.

(6) Liquidation expenses were Rs. 5,000.

Write up the necessary accounts in the books of Harappa Ltd. Also pass the journal entries in the books of Mohanjadaro Ltd. recording the acquisition of Harappa Ltd.

(Adapted from B.Com., Mangalore University)

Ans. : Purchase consideration :

In cash : for shares (3/5 × 20,000)	12,000
In preference shares : 8% preference shares	1,10,000
In equity shares; 6/5 × 20,000 = 24,000 Shares × Rs. 11	2,64,000
Total	3,86,000

Realisation Profit Rs. 36,000; Capital Reserve Rs. 8,500.

Notes : (i) Liquidation expenses are paid by vendor company.

(ii) Inter company debts Rs. 10,000 are eliminated.

(iii) Revised value of assets should be incorporated;

(iv) Debentures are discharged by the purchasing company at a premium *i.e.,* 1,00,000 + 8,000 = 1,08,000.

34. Ajanta agreed to acquire the business of Elora Ltd. as on 31-12-2006.

Liabilities	Rs.	Assets	Rs.
Share Capital :		Land & Buildings	3,00,000
1,000 10% Preference		Machinery	1,50,000
shares of Rs. 100 each	1,00,000	Furniture	45,000
40,000 Equity shares	4,00,000	Stock	2,00,000
of Rs. 10		Debtors	1,00,000
Reserve Fund	60,000	Cash & Balances	45,000
Profit & Loss Account	40,000	Preliminary Expenses	60,000
8% Debentures	2,00,000		
Creditors	80,000		
Employees Savings Bank Deposits	20,000		
	9,00,000		9,00,000

The consideration payable by Ajanta Ltd. agreed was as follows :

(1) To take over all the assets and trade liabilities.

(2) To allot 1,100 12% preference shares of Rs. 100 each as fully paid in Ajanta Ltd. to be issued to preference shareholders of Elora Ltd.

(3) To pay cash at Rs. 3 per share for every equity shares in Elora Ltd.

(4) To issue 15% debentures of Rs. 100 each at par in Ajanta Ltd. to discharge 8% debentures of Elora Ltd. at a discount of 5%.

(5) To issue 5 equity shares of Rs. 10 each in Ajanta Ltd. (quoted in the market at Rs. 12.50 per share) as fully paid for every 4 equity shares held in Elora Ltd. Debtors of Elora Ltd. included Rs. 20,000 due from Ajanta Ltd.

The realisation expenses amounted to Rs. 10,000. Prepare the ledger accounts in the books of the absorbed company. Also pass the journal entries in the books of absorbing company to incorporate the business of absorbed company. Apply purchase method.

(Adapted from B.Com., Gulbarga University)

Ans. : Purchase consideration :

	Rs.
In cash : 40,000 shares × Rs. 3	1,20,000
In equity shares : 40,000 × 5/4 = 50,000 shares Rs. 12.50 each	6,25,000
In pref. shares : 1,100 shares × Rs. 100	1,10,000
Total	8,55,000

Realisation profit Rs. 2,75,000; Goodwill Rs. 2,85,000.

Notes **:** (i) Inter company debts Rs. 20,000 are eliminated from the purchasing company.

(ii) Debentures are discharged by the purchasing company at a discount *i.e.*, 2,00,000 – 10,000 = Rs. 1,90,000.

(iii) Realisation expenses are borned by vendor company.

(iv) Preliminary expenses are transferred to shareholders.

(v) Employees Savings Bank deposits are not trade liabilities. They are to be paid by the vendor company.

35. Agumbe Ltd. is absorbed by Sampage Ltd. on the following terms :

(1) Sampage Ltd. should take over the liabilities and assets of Agumbe Ltd.

(2) Sampage Ltd. has to pay the purchase price as under :

(a) The cost of absorption (as part of purchase consideration) not exceeding Rs. 8,000.

(b) To pay cash for repayment of 'B' debentures of Agumbe Ltd. at a premium of 5%.

(c) To discharge 'A' debentures of Agumbe Ltd. at a premium of 10% by the issue of 6% debentures in Sampage Ltd.

(d) To pay at the rate of Rs. 15 per share in cash and allotment of one 7% preference shares of Rs. 100 each and five equity shares of Rs. 100 each at a market value of Rs. 140 per share for every four shares in Agumbe Ltd.

The actual cost of absorption comes to Rs. 10,000. The creditors of Agumbe Ltd. include Rs. 50,000 due to Sampage Ltd.

The following is the balance sheet of Agumbe Ltd. on the date of absorption.

Liabilities	Rs.	Assets	Rs.
Share Capital :		Fixed Assets	33,50,000
Shares of Rs. 100 each	20,00,000	Goodwill	4,00,000
Reserve Fund	3,00,000	Sinking Fund Investments	1,00,000
Sinking Fund	1,00,000	Stock	3,60,000
Accident Compensation Fund	2,50,000	Debtors	1,30,000
Provident Fund	2,50,000	Bank	1,00,000
'A' Debentures	4,00,000		
'B' Debentures	10,00,000		
Creditors	1,40,000		
	44,40,000		44,40,000

Give the necessary ledger account in the books of Agumbe Ltd. and pass the opening entries in the books of Sampage Ltd. under purchase method.

(Adapted from B.Com., Mangalore University)

Ans. : Purchase Consideration :

	Rs.
In Cash : 20,000 shares × Rs. 15	3,00,000
In equity shares : 20,000 × 5/4 = 25,000 shares Rs. 140	35,00,000
In pref. shares : 20,000 × 1/4 = 5,000 shares × Rs. 100	5,00,000
Total	43,00,000

Realisation profit Rs. 16,48,000 & Goodwill Rs. 21,48,000 (43,00,000 – 21,60,000 + 8,000 Cost of absorption)

Note : (i) Inter company debts of Rs. 50,000 are eliminated from the purchasing company.

(ii) Debentures are discharged by the purchasing company.

(iii) Entries of cost of absorption are :

			Dr.	Cr.
(a) For receiving cash :	Cash A/c	Dr.	8,000	–
	To Sampage Ltd. A/c		–	8,000
(b) For payment of Expenses:	Realisation A/c	Dr.	10,000	–
	To Cash A/c		–	10,000

36. The following are the balance sheets of S Ltd. and P Ltd. as on 31-3-2006 :

Liabilities	S Ltd.	P Ltd.	Assets	S Ltd.	P Ltd.
Share Capital :			Fixed Assets :		
Shares of Rs. 10 each	2,00,000	3,00,000	Land & Buildings	1,00,000	2,50,000
Reserve & surplus :			Plant & machinery	1,30,000	95,000
Reserve Fund	60,000	80,000	Investments :		
Work Compensation			6% Debentures in		
Fund	20,000	—	P Ltd. (at Par)	20,000	—
Secured Loans :			Current Assets :	—	—
6% Debentures	—	50,000	Loans & Advances :		
Current Liabilities &			Debtors	60,000	50,000
Provisions :			Stock	30,000	70,000
Creditors	60,000	50,000	Bank	—	15,000
	3,40,000	4,80,000		3,40,000	4,80,000

P Ltd. absorbed S Ltd. on the following terms :

(a) P. Ltd. shall give one share of Rs. 15 each at Rs. 20 per share for every two shares in S Ltd.

(b) The creditors of S Ltd. included Rs. 10,000 due to P Ltd.

(c) The stock of S Ltd. consisted to goods worth Rs. 20,000 bought from P Ltd. on which the latter had made a profit of 20% on sales.

(d) The land & building and plant & machinery of S Ltd., were taken over at Rs. 1,20,000 and Rs. 1,00,000 respectively.

Prepare (i) Realisation Account and Shareholders Account in the books of S Ltd., (ii) Journal entries relating to acquisition in the books of P Ltd. and (iii) Balance Sheet of P Ltd. after absorption. Apply purchase method.

(Adapted from B.Com., K.U.D.)

Ans. : Purchase Consideration :

In shares : 20,000 × 1/2 = 10,000 shares × Rs. 20 = 2,00,000;

Realisation Loss Rs. 80,000; Balance Sheet Total Rs. 7,76,000;

Capital Reserve Rs. 66,000 (70,000 – 4,000 unrealised profit).

Notes : (i) Work compensation fund is accumulated profit.

(ii) Inter company creditors and debtors Rs. 10,000 and debentures Rs. 20,000 are eliminated from both sides of the balance sheet.

(iii) Unrealised profit of Rs. 4,000 (*i.e.,* 20% of Rs. 20,000) is deducted from stock and debited to capital reserve account.

37. Y Ltd. is absorbed by X Ltd. on 31-12-2006 on which date their balance sheets stood as follows :

Liabilities	X Ltd.	Y Ltd.	Assets	X Ltd.	Y Ltd.
Share Capital :			Machinery	90,000	65,000
Shares of Rs. 10			Investments :		
each fully paid	2,00,000	1,00,000	2,000 shares of		
Reserve Fund	80,000	30,000	X Ltd. at cost	—	25,000
Creditors	20,000	20,000	Stock	1,40,000	15,000
			Debtors	60,000	40,000
			Cash at Bank	10,000	5,000
	3,00,000	1,50,000		3,00,000	1,50,000

X Ltd. has agreed to issue 3 shares of Rs. 10 each at a premium of Rs. 5 per share for every 2 shares of Y Ltd.

Show the necessary ledger accounts in the books of Y Ltd. and the journal entries in the books of X Ltd. and also prepare the balance sheet of X Ltd. after absorption. Apply purchase method.

(Adapted from B.Com., M.K.U.)

Ans. : Purchase consideration :

Number of shares to be issued to the shareholders of Y Ltd. (10,000 × 3/2) 15,000

Less : Number of shares held by Y Ltd. in the shares of X Ltd. 2,000

Number of new shares to be issued by X Ltd. to Y Ltd. 13,000

Therefore, the amount of purchase consideration = Number of new shares to be issued to Y Ltd. X issue price per share *i.e.,* 13,000 shares × Rs. 15 = Rs. 1,95,000;

Realisation profit Rs. 95,000; Goodwill Rs. 90,000; Share premium Rs. 65,000 and Balance Sheet Total Rs. 5,15,000.

Note : Appreciation in the value of 2,000 shares of Rs. 5,000 (30,000 – 25,000) is credited to realisation account and debited to shares in X Ltd. account.

38. A Ltd. is to absorb B Ltd. by issuing 5 shares of Rs. 10 each at a premium of 10% for every 4 shares held in B Ltd. On the date of absorption the balance sheets were as under :

Liabilities	A Ltd.	B Ltd.	Assets	A Ltd.	B Ltd.
Share Capital :			Fixed Assets	4,00,000	2,00,000
Shares of Rs. 10 each	5,00,000	3,00,000	Investments :		
General Reserve	50,000	40,000	6,000 share in B Ltd.	80,000	—
Creditors	1,00,000	60,000	5,000 share in A Ltd.	—	60,000
			Current Assets	1,70,000	1,40,000
	6,50,000	4,00,000		6,50,000	4,00,000

You are required to show (a) the important ledger accounts in the books of B Ltd. and (b) the acquisition entries in the books of A Ltd. Under purchase method.

(Adapted from B.Com., Bombay University)

Ans. : Purchase consideration :

Shares to be issued to outsiders (30,000 – 6,000 = 24,000 × 6/4)	30,000
Shares due to A Ltd. (6,000 × 5/4)	7,500
	37,500
Less : Deduct shares already held by B Ltd.	5,000
Net number of shares constituting purchase consideration	32,500
∴ Purchase Consideration will be (32,500 × 11)	3,57,500
But, the actual purchase consideration payable will be :	
Total amount of purchase consideration	3,57,500
Less : Amount due to B for 7,500 shares (7,500 ×11)	82,500
Portion of purchase consideration actually payable	2,75,000

Realisation profit Rs. 77,500; Goodwill Rs. 72,500 and Share premium Rs. 25,000.

Note : Loss on revaluation of 5,000 shares of Rs. 5,000 (60,000 – 55,000) is debited to Realisation Account and credited to Shares in A Ltd. Account.

39. A Ltd. is absorbed by B Ltd. On that date, the balance sheet of A Ltd. is as follows :

Liabilities	Rs.	Assets		Rs.
20,000 Equity Shares of Rs. 100 each	20,00,000	Machinery		30,00,000
General Reserve	14,00,000	Patents		3,50,000
12% Debentures	4,00,000	Investments		2,50,000
Creditors	1,40,000	Stock		2,00,000
Staff Provident Fund	2,00,000	Debtors	4,00,000	
Workmen's Accident Compensation Fund (estimated liability Rs. 10,000)	50,000	*Less*: Provision	40,000	3,60,000
		Bank		30,000
	41,90,000			41,90,000

The consideration for absorption is as follows :

(i) Payment of Rs. 15 per equity share in cash.

(ii) Allotment of one 14% preference share of Rs. 100 each in B Ltd. for every 4 equity shares held in A Ltd.

(iii) Allotment of 5 equity shares of Rs. 100 each in B Ltd. for every 4 equity shares held A Ltd.

The creditors of A Ltd. include Rs. 50,000 due by A Ltd. to B Ltd. The cost of liquidation amounts to Rs. 10,000. Close the books of A Ltd. and give opening entries in the books of B Ltd. under merger method.

(Adapted from B.Com., Hons., Delhi)

Ans. : Purchase consideration (Cash Rs. 3,00,000 + Shares Rs. 5,00,000 + Rs. 25,00,000) = Rs. 33,00,000; Realisation Loss Rs. 1,50,000; Capital Reserve Rs. 1,40,000 (Workmen's Accident Compensation Fund Rs. 10,000); Shareholders' Account Total Rs. 34,40,000.

40. The Pig Iron Company agrees to absorb the business of the Iron Ore Company Ltd. and to take over the assets and liabilities at their balance sheet values in exchange for which it is to issue 12 shares of Rs. 10 each for every share of Rs. 100 each in the Iron Ore Company Ltd. The expenses of absorption Rs. 10,000 will be paid by the Pig Iron Company Ltd. On the date of absorption, *i.e.* 31st March, 2006 the balance sheets of the two companies were as under :

The Iron Ore Company Ltd.

	Rs.			Rs.
5,000 Equity Shares		Land & Buildings		3,00,000
of Rs. 100 each	5,00,000	Machinery & Plant		2,00,000
General Reserve	35,000	Sundry Debtors	55,000	
Bills Payable	35,000	*Less :* Provision	5,000	50,000
Creditors	40,000	Stock		25,000
		Bank		35,000
	6,10,000			6,10,000

The Pig Iron Company Ltd.

	Rs.		Rs.
1,00,000 Equity Shares of		Land & Buildings	5,00,000
Rs. 10 each	10,00,000	Machinery & Plant	3,00,000
General Reserve	80,000	Goodwill	1,00,000
Creditors	1,00,000	Stock	60,000
		Debtors	1,20,000
		Bank	1,00,000
	11,80,000		11,80,000

Show the journal entries in the books of the Pig Iron Company Ltd. and prepare its opening balance sheet under pooling of interest method.

(Adapted from B.Com., Pondichery)

Ans. : Purchase consideration Rs. 6,00,000 (5,000 × 12 × 10); Share Capital Rs. 1,60,000; General Reserve Rs. 5,000 (1,15,000 – 1,10,000 *i.e.*, 1,00,000 + 10,000); Bank Rs. 1,25,000 (1,35,000 – 10,000); Balance Sheet Total Rs. 1,78,000.

41. Hosiery Ltd. and Darn Ltd. propose to amalgamate. Their Balance Sheets as on 31st December, 2006 were :

Liabilities	Hosiery Ltd. Rs.	Darn Ltd. Rs.	Assets	Hosiery Ltd. Rs.	Darn Ltd. Rs.
Share Capital			Fixed Assets	4,00,000	1,00,000
Equity Shares of			(*Less* depreciation)		
Rs. 10 each	5,00,000	2,00,000	Investments	1,00,000	
Reserves & Surplus			(face value)		
General Reserve	2,00,000	20,000	(Rs. 1,00,000 6%		
Profit & Loss A/c	1,00,000	30,000	Tax free G.P. Notes)		
Current Liabilities			**Current Assets**		
Creditors	1,00,000	50,000	Stock	2,00,000	1,30,000
			Debtors	1,70,000	60,000
			Cash & Bank balances	30,000	10,000
	9,00,000	3,00,000		9,00,000	3,00,000

Net profit (after taxation)

	Hosiery Ltd. Rs.	Darn Ltd. Rs.
2003	1,30,000	45,000
2004	1,25,000	40,000
2005	1,50,000	56,000

Goodwill may be taken at four years' purchase of average super trading profits on the basis of 15% trading profits on closing capital invested. The stock of Hosiery Ltd. and Darn Ltd. to be taken at Rs. 2,04,000 and Rs. 1,42,000 respectively for the purpose of amalgamation. Weft Ltd. was formed for the purpose of amalgamation of both the companies.

Advise Weft Ltd. on the scheme of exchange of shares of that purpose. Draft the Balance Sheet of Weft Ltd. under nature of purchase.

(Adapted from C.A. Inter Revision Test)

Ans. : Capital Employed : H – Rs. 7,00,000 (8,00,000 – 1,00,000) and D– Rs. 2,50,000; Trading profit; H – Rs. 1,29,000 (1,35,000 – 6000 Non-trading profit *i.e.* 6% on Rs. 10,000) and D– Rs. 47,000; Super profits; H – Rs. 24,000 (1,29,000 – 1,05,000 *i.e.,* 15% of Capital employed) and D – Rs. 9,500 (47,000 – 37,500); Goodwill : H – Rs. 96,000 and D – Rs. 38,000. Share Capital Rs. 12,00,000; Balance Sheet total Rs. 13,50,000 and Intrinsic value of Shares : H – Rs. 18 & D – Rs. 15.

42. The following is the balance sheet of B. Com. Ltd. as on 31-12-2006:

Liabilities	Rs.	Assets	Rs.
Shares Capital :		Building	90,000
20,000 shares of Rs. 10		Machinery	80,000
each fully paid	2,00,000	Stock	70,000
Creditors	1,50,000	Debtors	50,000
		Profit & Loss Account	60,000
	3,50,000		3,50,000

The shareholders resolved as follows :

(1) That the company be liquidated and a new company called A Company Ltd. be formed with an authorised capital of 50,000 shares of Rs. 10 each to take over the assets and liabilities of B Co. Ltd.

(2) That the assets be valued as under :
Building Rs. 1,00,000; Machinery Rs. 80,000; Stock Rs. 50,000; Debtors Rs. 40,000.

(3) That 20,000 shares of Rs. 10 each be issued to the shareholders of B Co. Ltd. as Rs. 6 per share paid up.

(4) That the balance of Rs. 4 per share shall be paid by the shareholders.

(5) The creditors be paid 1/3 of their amount in cash and the balance by the issue of 12% debentures.

Prepare the necessary ledger accounts in the books of B Co. Ltd. and the opening balance sheet of A Co. Ltd. after passing the journal entries in its books.

(Adapted from B.Com., Karantaka & Gulbarga University)

Ans. : Purchase Consideration Rs. 1,20,000 (20,000 shares × Rs. 6 paid up)

Realisation Loss Rs. 20,000; Bank Balance Rs. 30,000 (*i.e.,* 80,000 *i.e.,* 20,000 shares × Rs. 4 paid up minus Rs. 50,000 paid to creditors).

Balance Sheet Total Rs. 3,00,000.

Notes : (i) Since the net value of assets at revised value and purchase consideration are equal, there is no goodwill nor capital reserve.

(ii) 5% debentures of Rs. 1,00,000 (*i.e.,* issued to satisfy the creditors) will appear in the new balance sheet.

43. The Unlucky Ltd. having proved unsuccessful, decided to wind up its affairs and to reconstruct itself by forming a new company called Lucky Ltd. The following was the balance sheet on the date of reconstruction :

Liabilities	Rs.	Assets	Rs.
Share Capital :		Buildings	75,000
20,000 shares of Rs. 10		Machinery	50,000
each fully paid	2,00,000	Stock	40,000
Loan from Bank	2,000	Debtors	30,000
Creditors	10,000	Cash	5,000
Bills Payable	8,000	Profit & Loss Account	20,000
	2,20,000		2,20,000

The following are the terms of reconstruction :

(1) The new company is to take over all the assets of the old company but not the liabilities.

(2) The capital of the new company is to be Rs. 5,00,000 in shares of Rs. 5 each.

(3) The new company is to issue 50,000 shares of Rs. 5 each credited with Rs. 3 per share as paid up and also to pay Rs. 25,000 in cash on account of purchase consideration.

(4) The balance of Rs. 2 per share due by the members of the new company is to be paid on application and allotment and same has been duly collected in full.

(5) The expenses of reconstruction amounted to Rs. 5,000. Show the necessary accounts to close the books of the old company and prepare the balance sheet of the new company.

(Adapted from B.Com., K.U.D.)

Ans. : Purchase Consideration : Rs. 1,75,000 (*i.e.,* in Cash Rs. 25,000 + 1,50,000. In Shares *i.e.,* 50,000 Shares of Rs. 3 paid up)
Realisation Loss Rs. 30,000; Capital Reserve Rs. 25,000 and Balance Sheet Total Rs. 2,75,000.

***Note* :** Expenses of reconstruction is borned by Vendor Company.

44. The Moon Co. Ltd. having proved unsuccessful decided to wind up its affairs and to reconstruct itself by forming a new company called the Sun Co. Ltd. The following was the balance sheet of the Moon Co. Ltd. as on the date of reconstruction.

Liabilities	Rs.	Assets	Rs.
Share Capital :		Land & Buildings	4,50,000
1,00,000 Equity Shares		Plant & Machinery	2,40,000
of Rs. 10 each fully paid	10,00,000	Sundry Debtors	1,00,000
Sundry Creditors	30,000	Stock	50,000
Bills Payable	20,000	Cash	10,000
		Profit & Loss Account	2,00,000
	10,50,000		10,50,000

The following are the terms of reconstruction :

(1) The Sun Co. Ltd. is to take over all the assets of the Moon Co. Ltd. and not the liabilities.

(2) The capital of the Sun Co. Ltd. is to be Rs. 15,00,000 in equity shares of Rs. 10 each.

(3) The Assets of the Moon Co. Ltd. are purchased for 8,00,000 payable by the allotment of 70,000 shares of Rs. 10 each fully paid and Rs. 1,00,000 in cash.

(4) The Sun Co. Ltd. issued the remaining 80,000 equity shares of Rs. 10 each to the public and has been duly collected in full.

(5) The expenses of the reconstruction amounted to Rs. 5,000.

Show the necessary ledger accounts in the books of the Moon Co. Ltd. and prepare the balance sheet of the Sun Co. Ltd. after giving effect to the above.

(Adapted from B.Com., Gulbarga University)

Ans. : Purchase consideration : Rs. 8,00,000 (In shares Rs. 7,00,000 + 1,00,000 in cash) as stated in the problem.

Realisation Loss Rs. 55,000; Capital Reserve Rs. 50,000 & Balance Sheet Total Rs. 15,50,000.

Note : Realisation expenses and liabilities are borned by Vendor Company.

45. Amar Ltd. was incorporated with an authorised capital of Rs. 10,00,000 divided into shares of Rs. 100 each to take over the business of Raj Ltd. on 1-1-2005. The following was the position of Raj Ltd :

Balance Sheet as on 1-1-2005

Liabilities	Rs.	Assets		Rs.
Share Capital :		Buildings		1,00,000
2,000 shares of		Machinery		80,000
Rs. 100 each	2,00,000	Goodwill		20,000
General Reserve	50,000	Investments		60,000
Surplus	40,000	Stock		1,00,000
5% Debentures	1,00,000	Sundry Debtors	1,20,000	
Employees Security Deposits	10,000	*Less :* Provision	6,000	1,14,000
Sundry Creditors	85,000	Cash at Bank		26,000
Bills Payable	15,000			
	5,00,000			5,00,000

The terms of agreement were as follows :

(1) The Amar Ltd. is to issue 3 shares of Rs. 100 each for every 2 shares in Raj Ltd.

(2) The Amar Ltd. is to issue 6% debentures & pay cash of Rs. 10,000 to discharge the 5% debentures at 10% premium.

(3) The Amar Ltd. is to pay cash of Rs. 5 for every share in Raj Ltd.

(4) The realisation expenses amounted Rs. 4,000 and are to be paid by Raj Ltd.

(5) The Amar Ltd. issued 1,000 shares of Rs. 100 each at par to the public and were fully subscribed.

Prepare the necessary ledger accounts to close the books of Raj Ltd. and also the opening balance sheet of Amar Ltd.

(Adapted from B.Com., K.U.D.)

Ans. : Purchase consideration :

	Rs.
In cash : 2,000 shares of Rs. 5 each	10,000
In shares : 2,000 × 3/2 = 30,000 shares × Rs. 100	3,00,000
Total	3,10,000

Realisation Profit Rs. 16,000; Balance Sheet Total Rs. 61,00,000; Goodwill Rs. 50,000 and Cash Balance Rs. 1,06,000 (*i.e.,* 26,000 + 1,00,000 – 20,000 paid to Shareholders and Debentureholders)

Note : Debentures discharged at a premium (1,00,000 + 10,000) by the purchasing company..

46. Balance Sheet of Small Ltd. was as follows :

Liabilities	Rs.	Assets		Rs.
Issued Capital :		Goodwill		1,00,000
6% Rs. 10 Pref. shares	1,20,000	Building		1,10,000
Rs. 10 Equity shares	80,000	Plant		90,000
Debentures	1,00,000	Stock		83,000
Creditors	82,000	Debtors	70,000	
General Reserve	84,000	*Less* : RBD	3,500	66,500
P & L A/c	20,000	Bills Receivable		4,000
		Cash		32,500
	4,86,000			4,86,000

A new company called the Big Ltd. was floated to purchase the business of the above concern. All the assets except cash and creditors were to be transferred to the new venture.

The purchase price was :

(1) The allotment of eleven 5% preference shares of Rs. 10 each fully paid for each ten preference shares held.

(2) Twenty equity shares of Rs. 10 each credited as Rs. 9 paid for each 16 equity shares held.

(3) And sufficient debentures to enable the existing debentureholders to be satisfied at a premium of 5% on their holding by the issue of debentures in the new company.

The expenses of winding up of Small Ltd. were Rs. 7,500. Show the ledger accounts in the books of Small Ltd. and the journal entries in the books of the purchasing company.

(Adapted from Mysore University)

Ans. : Purchase consideration :

	Rs.
In pref. shares : 12,000 × 11/10 × 10	1,32,000
In equity shares : 8,000 × 20/16 × 9	90,000
Total	2,22,000

Realisation Loss Rs. 69,000; Debentures premium Rs. 5,000; Excess amount payable to Preference shareholders Rs. 12,000; Cash used : For realisation expenses Rs. 7,500 and the balance paid to Equity shareholders Rs 25,000 and Goodwill Rs. 3,500 (*i.e.*, 4,12,500 – 3,57,000).

Note : Debentures are discharge separately.

47. Given below is the Balance Sheet of Hard Luck Ltd. as at 31st March, 2006 :

Balance Sheet

Liabilities	Rs.	Assets	Rs.
40,000 Shares of Rs 10		Land & Buildings	3,20,000
each fully paid	4,00,000	Plant & Machinery	1,30,000
Creditors	3,00,000	Stock	70,000
		Debtors	1,20,000
		Cash	500
		Preliminary Expenses	5,000
		Profit & Loss Account	54,500
	7,00,000		7,00,000

The following scheme of reconstruction was arranged :

(1) The company to go into liquidation and a new company called Good Luck Ltd. with an authorised capital of Rs. 8,00,000 to be formed to take over the assets and liabilities.

(2) Preferential creditors of Rs. 10,000 included in the above Balance Sheet are to be paid in full.

(3) Unsecured creditors to receive either (a) 5% of their claim in cash or (b) 6% debentures in the new company equivalent to their claims at par.

(4) Shareholders in Hard Luck Ltd. to be allotted one share in new company of Rs. 10 each, Rs. 5 paid for every existing share held by them.

(5) Reconstruction costs amounting to Rs. 6,000 to be paid by Hard Luck Ltd. from cash made available by the new company.

Half of the unsecured creditors in value opted for immediate cash payment for which purpose necessary cash was made by the new company, which made a call of Rs. 5 each on the partly paid shares allotted as aforesaid. The new company valued all assets (except land & buildings) taken over from Hard Luck Ltd. at par.

Prepare the balance sheet of the new company after the above transactions are concluded.

(Adapted from ACS, MKU & Bangalore, University)

Ans. : Purchase consideration :

In shares : 40,000 × 5 = 2,00,000

Value of Building (Balancing Fig.) Rs. 1,13,000 (*i.e.*,4,33,500–3,20,500);

Cash Balance Rs. 1,12,000 (500 + 2,00,000 – 88,500) and Balance Sheet Total Rs. 5,45,000; Reconstruction Expenses debited Goodwill A/c which is merged in the value of building.

Note : Journal Entry to discharge preferential and unsecured creditors

Creditors Account	Dr.	2,27,500	—
To 6% Debentures A/c (2,90,000 × 1/2)		—	1,45,000
To Cash Account		—	82,500
(2,90,000 × ½ × 50/100 = 72,500 + 10,000)			

48. The following was the balance sheet of Unlucky Ltd. as on 31-3-2009 :

Liabilities	Rs.	Assets	Rs.
Share Capital :		Goodwill	30,000
5,000 Equity shares of		Building	40,000
Rs. 20 each fully paid	1,00,000	Machinery	65,000
3,000 Cumulative Pref.		Stock	25,000
shares of Rs. 20		Debtors	15,000
each fully paid	60,000	Cash	5,000
Debentures	40,000	Preliminary Expenses	3,000
Creditors	10,000	Profit & Loss Account	27,000
	2,10,000		2,10,000

Note : Arrears of cumulative preference share dividends Rs. 6,000.

The scheme of reconstruction as agreed upon by all the parties was as under :

(1) A new company to be formed called Lucky Ltd. with an authorised capital of Rs. 3,00,000 all in equity shares of Rs. 10 each.

(2) Two equity shares, as Rs. 5 paid up in the new company to be issued for every one equity share in the old company.

(3) Four equity shares as Rs. 5 paid up in the new company to be issued for every preference share in the old company.

(4) Debentureholders to be allotted 4,000 equity shares as fully paid in the new company.

(5) Arrears of preference share dividend to be cancelled.

(6) Creditors to be taken over by the new company.

(7) The remaining equity shares to be issued to public and duly collected in full.

(8) The assets of the old company to be taken over subject to writing down the value of machinery by Rs. 5,000.

Show the necessary accounts in the books of old company and the opening entries in the books of new company.

(Adapted from B.Com., K.U.D.)

Ans. : Purchase consideration :

	Rs.
To equity shareholders : 5,000 × 2/1 × 5	50,000
To Pref. shareholders : 3,000 × 4/1 × 5	60,000
	1,10,000

Realisation loss Rs. 20,000; Goodwill Rs. 15,000; Balance Sheet Total Rs. 2,00,000 and Cash Balance Rs. 45,000 (5,000 + 40,000 received from public).

Note : No entry is necessary for the cancellation of arrears of cumulative preference dividend.

49. On 31-3-2006 the balance sheet of Vivek Ltd. was as follows :

Liabilities	Rs.	Assets	Rs.
Authorised & Issued capital :		Goodwill	40,000
6,000 6% Pref. shares		Patents	25,000
of Rs. 10 each fully paid	60,000	Sundry Other Assets	1,64,500
15,000 Equity shares of		Cash	500
Rs. 10 each fully paid	1,50,000	Preliminary Expenses	2,000
6% Debentures	30,000	Profit & Loss Account	28,000
Creditors	20,000		
	2,60,000		2,60,000

The preference dividend is in arrears for four years.

The following scheme of reconstruction was agreed upon :

(a) A new company called "Naveen Ltd." to be formed with an authorised capital of Rs. 3,50,000 all in equity shares of Rs. 10 each.

(b) Two equity shares as Rs. 5 per share paid in the new company to be issued for every three equity shares in the old company.

(c) Five equity shares of Rs. 5 per share paid in the new company to be issued for every three preference shares in the old company.

(d) An issue of 500 equity shares of Rs. 10 as fully paid to be made to satisfy the arrears of preference dividend.

(e) The discharge of debenture debt at a discount of 5% by the issue of 8% debentures in the Naveen Ltd.

(f) To pay cost of liquidation Rs. 1,500.

(g) Naveen Ltd. made a call of Rs. 5 per share on the partly paid equity shares and the call amount was received in full.

Show the necessary accounts to close the books of Vivek Ltd. and pass the necessary entries in the books of Naveen Ltd. Also prepare the balance sheet of Naveen Ltd.

(Adapted from B.Com., Mysore University)

Ans. : Purchase consideration

	Rs.
In shares : For equity shareholders (15,000 × 2/3 × 5)	50,000
For Pref. shareholders (6,000 × 5/3 × 5)	50,000
For arrears of dividend (500 × 10)	5,000
Total	1,05,000

Realisation Loss Rs. 70,000; Capital Reserve Rs. 35,000; Share Capital Rs. 2,05,000 and Balance Sheet Total Rs. 2,88,500.

Notes : (i) Debentures are discharged by the purchasing company at a discount (*i.e.* 30,000 – 1,500 = 28,500).

(ii) Liquidation expenses are paid separately.

50. The following is the Balance Sheet of X Co. Ltd. as on 31st December, 2006 :

Liabilities	Rs.	Assets	Rs.
12,000 Shares of Rs. 10 each fully paid	1,20,000	Land and Buildings	1,00,000
		Plant and Machinery	40,000
Sundry Creditors	30,000	Stock	15,000
Bank Overdraft	28,000	Sundry Debtors	22,000
		Profit and Loss A/c	1,000
	1,78,000		1,78,000

The company went into voluntary liquidation and the assets were sold to Y Co. Ltd. for Rs. 1,50,000 payable as to Rs. 60,000 in cash and Rs. 90,000 in the form of 12,000 shares of Rs. 10 each of Y Co. Ltd. at Rs. 7.50 per share paid to the shareholders of X Co. Ltd. The creditors and Bank overdraft are not be taken over. The expenses of liquidation were Rs. 2,000 to be paid by the vendor company. In the Books of X Co. Ltd. prepare Realisation A/c., Shareholders A/c, Cash A/c, Sundry Creditors A/c, Bank Overdraft A/c and Y Co. Ltd. A/c. Also pass opening entries in the Books of Y Co. Ltd.

(Adapted from B.Com., Bangalore University)

Ans. : Purchase consideration : Rs. 1,50,000.

Realisation loss Rs. 29,000; Equity Shareholders' A/c Total Rs. 1,20,000; Bank A/c Total Rs. 60,000; Capital Reserve (Balancing figure) Rs. 27,000.

Note : Bank overdraft of Rs. 28,000 should be credited to Bank A/c.

51. The Balance Sheet of Unsound Ltd. stood as below on 31st May, 2009 :

Liabilities	Rs.	Assets	Rs.
Share Capital :		Profit and Loss Account	10,800
2,000 Equity shares of		Cash	2,000
Rs. 20 each fully paid up	40,000	Preliminary Expenses	1,200
1,200 10% Cumulative Pref.		Machinery	26,000
shares of Rs. 20 each		Stock	10,000
fully paid up	24,000	Debtors	6,000
Mortgage debentures	16,000	Goodwill	12,000
Sundry creditors	4,000	Building	16,000
	84,000		84,000

On the date of the above Balance Sheet, on the preference shares, the dividend was in arrears for one year.

The following scheme of reconstruction was agreed upon by all the concerned parties :

(a) A new company called "Ray of Hope Ltd.", to be formed with an authorised capital of Rs. 1,20,000 consisting of equity shares of Rs. 10 each.

(b) For every one equity share in the old company, two equity shares as Rs. 5 paid up in the new company to be issued.

(c) For each preference share in the old company, four equity shares in the new company with Rs. 5 paid up per share, to be issued.

(d) Debentureholders were to be get 1,600 equity shares in the new company as fully paid up.

(e) Arrears of dividend on the preference shares to be cancelled and hence to be foregone by the preference shareholder.

(f) Creditors' liability to be assumed by the new company.

(g) The balance of equity shares to be issued to public and collected in full.

(h) The assets of the old company are to be taken over by the new company subject to the condition that the value of the machinery be reduced by Rs. 2,000.

Prepare the necessary accounts in the books of Unsound Ltd. and pass the necessary journal entries in the books of Ray of Hope Ltd.

(Adapted from B.Com., K.U.D.)

Ans. : Purchase consideration :

	Rs.
In equity shares : For equity shareholders (4,000 × 5)	20,000
For preference shareholders (4,800 × 5)	24,000
Total	44,000

Realisation loss Rs. 8,000; Goodwill Rs. 6,000 (B.F.) and Cash received from the public by the issue of shares Rs. 16,000 (1,600 shares [12,000 – 10,400 *i.e.,* 4,000 + 4,800 + 1600] of Rs. 10 each.

Notes : (i) There is no need for passing the journal entry for cancellation of cumulative preference dividend. Because, there cannot be any profit or loss arising from cancellation of the same. It appears as a contingent liability by way of footnote under the balance sheet.

(ii) Debentures are discharged by the purchasing company by the issue of 1,600 equity shares of Rs. 10 each.

******

5

INTERNAL RECONSTRUCTION

Meaning

The term reconstruction refers to reorganisation of capital structure of a company. Such a reconstruction becomes necessary to improve the financial position of the company. Reconstruction is divided into two parts, one is external reconstruction and another is internal reconstruction. External reconstruction is explained in the previous chapter and internal reconstruction is to be discussed in this chapter.

Internal reconstruction means rearrangement of capital structure of a company to infuse new life in the company without going into liquidation. In other words, it is a process of altering or reducing the share capital and claims of the shareholders, debentureholders and creditors of the company with their consent. It is the internal rearrangement of the affairs of the company by writing off the accumulated losses, reducing the share capital or revaluation of assets without going into liquidation. When a company is over capitalised or suffered huge losses or has over valued fixed assets, instead of going into liquidation it may enter into the process of internal reconstruction.

Internal reconstruction differs from external reconstruction. The main differences between the two are :

(1) In the case of internal reconstruction, no company is liquidated. But in the case of external reconstruction, one company is liquidated.

(2) In the case of internal reconstruction, the existing company is continued with certain arrangements. But in the case of external reconstruction, the existing company is going into liquidation and new company is formed with almost the same shareholders.

(3) Internal reconstruction is a slow and tedious process. Because, approval of all shareholders, creditors and the confirmation by the court are required to start the scheme. But, external reconstruction cannot be carried out by the confirmation of the

court. It is carried out by the decision of the shareholders. Therefore, it is a speed process.

(4) In internal reconstruction debentureholders, creditors and bank overdraft may continue. But in external reconstruction they may not continue, they will have to be settled.

Forms of Internal Reconstruction

The following are the two important forms of internal reconstruction :

(i) Alternation of share capital

(ii) Reduction of share capital.

(I) Alternation of share capital

Alternation of share capital means rearrangement of share capital of the company. The Companies Act has used the words "Alternation proper" for alternation of share capital. Such alternation can be done under the provisions of Sections 94, 95 and 97 of the Companies Act. The company can make the alteration by merely altering the conditions of its memorandum of association, if it is authorised by its articles. The term alteration of share capital or alteration of proper includes the following :

(a) Increase of share capital. The share capital of a company can be increased by issue of new shares. For the issue of new shares, the same journal entries are to be passed as in the case of issue of shares of a company.

(b) Conversion fully paid shares into stock. A company can convert its fully paid-up shares into stock. The entry required for the conversion of shares into stock will be :

Share Capital Account	Dr.	With the amount of shares
To Stock Account		converted into stocks

(c) Reconversion of stocks into shares. A company can reconvert the stocks into shares. The entry required for the conversion of stocks into shares will be :

Stock Account	Dr.	With the amount of stocks
To Share Capital A/c		reconverted into shares

(d) Cancellation of unissued shares. A company can cancel the unissued shares to decrease the share capital. For the cancellation of unissued shares, no journal entry is required. Just the details of the share capital will be changed *i.e.*, the authorised share capital will be reduced by the amount cancelled unissued shares.

(e) Consolidation of shares. In this case, shares of smaller denominations are to be converted into shares of larger denominations. Here, the paid-up share capital remains the same but the number of shares is to be reduced. Journal entry in respect of such conversion will be :

Share Capital Account Dr. (Smaller value, say, Rs. 10) To Share Capital Account (Higher value, say Rs. 10)		With the amount of shares of smaller value converted into shares of higher value

(f) Sub-division of shares. In this case, shares of larger denominations are to be converted into shares of smaller dominations. Journal entry in respect of such conversion will be :

Share Capital Account Dr. (Higher value, say Rs. 10) To Share Capital Account (Smaller value, say Rs. 10)		With the amount of shares of higher value converted into shares of smaller value

Illustration 1

Show the journal entries for the following transactions :

(i) Conversion of 10,000 equity shares of Rs. 10 each fully paid into equity stock.

(ii) Conversion of 30,000 equity shares of Rs. 10 each fully paid into Rs. 3,10,000 stock on the basis of Rs. 105 of stock for every 10 fully paid shares of Rs. 10 each.

(iii) Conversion of equity stock of Rs. 5,25,000 into 52,500 equity shares of Rs. 10 each.

(iv) Cancellation of unpaid amount of Rs. 30,000 in respect of 10,000 equity shares of Rs. 10 each, Rs. 7 called and paid-up.

(v) Sub-division of 20,000 equity shares of Rs. 10 each fully paid into shares of Rs. 2 each fully paid.

(vi) Consolidation of 10,000 equity shares of Rs. 10 each fully paid into 1,000 shares of Rs. 100 each.

Solution :

Journal Entries

Date/ Sl. No.	Particulars	L.F.	Debit Rs.	Credit Rs.
(i)	Equity Share Capital A/c Dr.		1,00,000	—
	To Equity Stock A/c		—	1,00,000
	(Being conversion of fully paid equity shares into equity stock)			
(ii)	Equity Share Capital A/c Dr.		3,00,000	—
	Discount on Stock A/c Dr.		10,000	—
	To Equity Stock A/c		—	3,10,000
	(Being conversion of 30,000 fully paid equity shares of Rs. 10 each into Rs. 3,10,000 stock)			*Contd.*

(iii)	Equity Stock A/c Dr.	5,25,000	—
	To Equity Share Capital A/c	—	5,25,000
	(Being conversion of equity stock into equity shares of Rs. 10 each)		
(iv)	Equity Share Capital (Partly called) A/c Dr.	70,000	—
	To Equity Share Capital (Fully called) A/c	—	70,000
	(Being cancellation of unpaid amount and the partly paid-up shares of Rs. 10 each, Rs. 7 paid up become shares of Rs. 7 each fully paid-up)		
(v)	Equity Share Capital (Rs. 10) A/c Dr.	2,00,000	—
	To Equity Share Capital (Rs. 2) A/c	—	2,00,000
	(Being sub-division of 20,000 fully paid equity shares of Rs. 10 each into 1,00,000 shares of Rs. 2 each fully paid)		
(vi)	Equity Share Capital (Rs. 10) A/c Dr.	1,00,000	—
	To Equity Share Capital (Rs. 100) A/c	—	1,00,000
	(Being consolidation of 10,000 shares of Rs. 10 each into 1,000 shares of Rs. 100 each)		

(II) Reduction of Share Capital

Reduction of capital means the process of reducing the capital of members and some times, the claims of the creditors and the debenture-holders. The reduced amount is utilised for writing off the accumulated losses, fictitious assets and the overvalued portion of fixed assets. The process of returning the excess share capital to the members is also called as reduction of capital.

Legal Provisions Relating to Capital Reduction

The company can reduce its share capital according to the provisions laid down in Sections 100 to 105 of the Companies Act, 1956. The important provisions are given as below :

(a) No company is empowered to reduce the share capital unless and until it is authorised by its Articles of Association.

(b) Share capital of the company can be reduced by a special resolution. The capital reduction requiring a special resolution can take the following forms :

(i) by reducing or extinguishing the liability of the members for uncalled liability; or

(ii) by writing off or cancelling any paid-up capital which is lost or unrepresented by available assets; or

(iii) by paying off capital which is in excess of the requirements of the company; or

(iv) in any other way approved by the court.

(c) The court usually confirms the second type of reduction without consulting the creditors because their interests are in no way affected by such reduction.

(d) Creditors interests are affected by the first and third type of reductions. Hence, the court in these cases will confirm only after consulting them. If some creditors are unwilling to give their consent, the company will have to settle their claims.

(e) The court may order the use of the words 'and reduced' after the name of the company and also publish reasons for reduction in local newspapers.

(f) The order of the court has to be filed with the registrar.

(g) Where capital reduction involves the variation of rights of different classes of shares, consent of the holders of at least ¾th of the shares concerned is to be obtained before reduction is affected.

(h) Holder of at least 1/10th of issued share capital affected by the variation may apply to the court within 21 days after the consent is obtained or resolution is passed for the cancellation of such variation. The decision of the court is final.

Accounting Entries. The following entries are required for various forms of reduction of capital :

1. Reducing the liability of members for the uncalled capital. When the uncalled capital on shares is reduced or cancelled, the paid up capital is not affected. The partly paid shares now become fully paid shares. The following entry is to be passed for closing the partly paid share capital account and for opening the fully paid share capital account :

Share Capital (Partly paid-up) A/c	Dr.	With in amount of paid-up capital
To Share Capital (Fully paid-up) A/c		

2. Paying off paid up capital which is in excess of the needs of the company. When a company finds that it has a surplus capital, it may decide to reduce it by returning the extra capital to shareholders. The following entries have to be passed for such refund :

(a) For transferring the extra or excess capital to Shareholders' Account :

Share Capital Account	Dr.	With the amount to be refunded
To Shareholders' Account		

(b) For paying the cash to the shareholders :

Shareholders' Account	Dr.	With the amount of cash refunded
To Bank Account		

3. Creditors and debentureholders are sacrificing a part of their claims. Some times creditors and debentureholders may agree to sacrifice a part of their claims. When they are sacrificed a part of their claims, the claims of creditors and debentureholders should be reduced. In such a case, the entry will be :

Creditors' Account	Dr.	With the amount of their claims reduced
Debentureholders' Account	Dr.	
To Capital Reduction A/c *or* Reconstruction A/c *or* Reorganisation A/c		With the total of amount of claims reduced

Note : When the creditors and debentureholders sacrifice a part of their claims, some accountants prefer to use "Reconstruction Account or Reorganisation Account" and when the shareholders sacrifice a part of their claims, they prefer to use "Capital Reduction Account". But others desire to use "Capital Reduction Account" in all cases.

4. Writing off of or cancellation of paid-up capital which is lost. It means cancelling or writing off that part of the paid up capital which is not represented by tangible assets. In such a case, accumulated losses such as debit balance of profit and loss account, fictitious assets like underwriting commission, preliminary expenses, discount on issue of shares and debentures and over valued assets, goodwill, advertising suspense, unrecorded liabilities etc., are to be written off against share capital. It involves two steps, viz., (i) Reduction of share capital and (ii) Writing off of losses or utilisation of capital reduction amount. The entries for these steps are given as below :

(i) For reducing the share capital :

(a) When same shares are continued :

Share Capital Account	Dr.	With the amount of capital reduced
To Capital Reduction A/c		

(b) When old shares are cancelled and new shares are issued :

Share Capital (Old) A/c	Dr.	With the amount of old capital
To Share Capital (New) A/c		With the amount of new capital
To Capital Reduction A/c		With the amount of capital reduced

(ii) For writing off of losses or utilisation of capital reduction amount

Capital Reduction Account	Dr.	With the amount credited in Capital Reduction A/c
To Profit and Loss A/c		
To Preliminary Expenses A/c To Underwriting Commission A/c To Discount on Shares and Debentures Account		The respective amounts should always be written off if the amount is sufficient
To Goodwill Account		
To Overvalued Assets Account		As per scheme.
To Liabilities, hither to unrecorded, brought into account		With the amount of unrecorded liabilities brought into account.
To Capital Reserve Account		Balance left in the capital reduction A/c after eliminating the accumulated losses.

Capital reduction amount represents the sacrifice made by the shareholders, debentureholders, creditors etc. This sacrifice is utilised for eliminating the accumulated losses, intangible assets, overvaluation of assets etc. If there is any appreciation in the value of some assets, the same should be credited to the capital reduction account. Similarly, if there are any reconstruction expenses and any contingent liabilities such as arrears of preference dividends etc., they should be debited to the capital reduction account. But no entry should be passed for the cancellation of any contingent liability. After making all the adjustments, if there is a balance left in the Capital Reduction or Reconstruction Account, that balance should be transferred to Capital Reserve Account. The capital reserve account will appear in the balance sheet on the liability side.

Reorganisation through surrender of shares

Some times, internal reconstruction may take place by surrender of shares. Under this method, shares are sub-divided into shares of smaller denominations and shareholders are asked to surrender (give back) a part of them to the company to facilitate the capital reorganisation. Such surrendered shares are utilised for the purpose of reducing or extinguishing debentures and trade liabilities. The amount of shares surrendered and the claims foregone by creditors and debentureholders are transferred to capital reorganisation account, which will be utilised to write off losses, etc., in the same way as capital reduction account.

Illustration 2

Pass the journal entries under the following circumstances :

(i) 2,500 shares of Rs. 10 each are reduced to shares of Rs. 6 each.

(ii) 5,000, 6% preference shares of Rs. 10 each are cancelled and the same number of 7% preference shares of Rs. 5 each are issued.

(iii) 10,000 equity shares of Rs. 10 each, Rs. 7 called up. The company extinguishes the uncalled capital on its shares.

(iv) 20,000 equity shares of Rs. 10 each fully paid. The company's shares capital is much in excess of its requirements and hence, it decides to refund Rs. 2 per share to the shareholders.

Solution :

Journal Entries

Date/ Sl. No.	Particulars	L.F.	Debit Rs.	Credit Rs.
(i)	Share Capital Account Dr.		10,000	—
	To Capital Reduction A/c		—	10,000
	(Being 2,500 shares of Rs. 10 each reduced by Rs. 4 each)			
(ii)	6% Preference Share Capital A/c Dr.		50,000	—
	To 7% Preference Share Capital A/c		—	25,000
	To Capital Reduction A/c		—	25,000
	(Being 6% preference shares of Rs. 10 each cancelled and 7% preference shares of Rs. 5 each issued and the difference credited to capital reduction account)			
(iii)	Equity Share Capital Account (Rs. 10) Dr.		70,000	—
	To Equity Share Capital A/c (Rs. 7)		—	70,000
	(Being uncalled capital cancelled and partly paid shares become fully paid shares)			
(iv)	(a) Equity Share Capital Account (Rs. 10) Dr.		2,00,000	—
	To Equity Share Capital A/c (Rs. 8)		—	1,60,000
	To Sundry Equity Shareholders' A/c		—	40,000
	(Being conversion of share capital and money due to shareholders)			
	(b) Sundry Equity Shareholders' A/c Dr.		40,000	—
	To Bank A/c		—	40,000
	(Being payment of money to equity shareholders)			

Note : In this case, old share of Rs. 10 has now converted into Rs. 7 fully paid share. Therefore, there exists no account for Rs. 10 share. Hence, it is cancelled by debiting it and a new account for Rs. 7 share is created by crediting it.

Illustration 3

Following are the extracts from the Balance Sheet of 'Unsuccessful Ltd.,' as on 31-12-2005.

Balance Sheet

Liabilities	Rs.	Assets	Rs.
12% Debentures of Rs. 120 each	2,40,000		
Creditors	65,000		

Under the scheme of reconstruction, the debentureholders agree to accept 13% debentures of Rs. 2,00,000 in full satisfaction of their claims and the creditors agree to reduce their claims by Rs. 15,000.

The amount so available is to utilise for wiping out the accumulated losses of Rs. 40,000, to write down patents Rs. 5,000, goodwill Rs. 6,000 and preliminary expenses Rs. 4,000.

Pass the journal entries to give the effect to the above.

Solution :

Journal Entries

Dates/ Sl. No.	Particulars		L.F.	Debit Rs.	Credit Rs.
1.	12% Debentures A/c	Dr.		2,40,000	—
	Creditors' A/c	Dr.		15,000	—
	To 13% Debentures A/c			—	2,00,000
	To Capital Reduction A/c			—	55,000
	or Reconstruction Account				
	(Being sacrifice made by debentureholders and creditors adjusted to capital reduction account)				
2.	Capital Reduction A/c	Dr.		55,000	—
	To Profit and Loss A/c			—	40,000
	To Patents A/c			—	5,000
	To Goodwill A/c			—	6,000
	To Preliminary Expenses			—	4,000
	(Being capital reduction amount utilised to wipe out accumulated loss and to write down the value of assets)				

Illustration 4

On the reconstruction of a company, the following terms were agreed upon :

The shareholders to receive in lieu of their present holding (viz., 50,000 shares of Rs. 10 each) the following :

(a) Fully paid equity shares equal to 2/5th of their holding.

(b) 5% preference shares fully paid to the extent of 1/5th of the above new equity shares.

(c) Rs. 60,000, 6% second debentures.

An issue of Rs. 50,000, 5% first debentures was made and allotted, payment for the same having been received in cash.

The goodwill which stood at Rs. 3,00,000 was written down to Rs. 1,50,000.

The plant and machinery which stood at Rs. 1,00,000 were written down to Rs. 75,000.

The freehold and leasehold premises which stood at Rs. 1,50,000 were written down to Rs. 1,25,000.

Make the journal entries in the books of the company necessitated by the above reconstruction.

(Adapted from My. Uni. & Bangalore, April 1993)

Solution :

Journal Entries

Date/ Sl. No.	Particulars	L.F.	Debit Rs.	Credit Rs.
1.	Old Share Capital A/c (50,000 × 10) Dr.		5,00,000	—
	To New Equity Share Capital A/c (5,00,000 × 2/5)		—	2,00,000
	To 5% Preference Share Capital A/c		—	40,000
	(1/5th of New Equity Shares of Rs. 2,00,000)			
	To 6% Second Debentures A/c		—	60,000
	To Capital Reduction A/c		—	2,00,000
	(Balancing figure *i.e.*, 5,00,000 – 3,00,000)			
	(Being the issue of new equity shares of Rs. 2,00,000, pref. shares of Rs. 40,000 and 6% second debentures of Rs. 60,000 in lieu of the existing shares of Rs. 5,00,000)			
2.	Bank A/c Dr.		50,000	—
	To 5% First Debentures A/c		—	50,000
	(Being the issue of 5% debentures for cash)			

Contd.

3.	Capital Reduction A/c Dr.		2,00,000	—
	To Goodwill A/c		—	1,50,000
	To Plant & Machinery A/c		—	25,000
	To Freehold and Leasehold Premises A/c		—	25,000
	(Being the capital reduction amount utilised to written off the above assets)			

Illustration 5

The reconstruction of Improving Ltd. was carried out on the following terms :

(a) The shareholders holding 2,00,000 shares of Rs. 10 each were to receive (i) 2/5th of their holding in fully paid equity shares of Rs. 10 each; and (ii) 1/5th of their holding in 6% preference shares of Rs. 10 each fully paid, in cancellation of old shares.

(b) Apply the credit balance of General Reserve of Rs. 80,000 for reconstruction purpose.

(c) The goodwill which stood at Rs. 3,80,000 was to be written off fully.

(d) The plant and premises which stood at Rs. 9,00,000 and Rs. 7,00,000 respectively were to be reduced by 30% each.

(e) Expenses of reconstruction amounted to Rs. 12,500.

Pass the journal entries and show the Old Equity Share Capital A/c and Capital Reduction A/c.

Solution :

Journal Entries

Date/ Sl.No.	Particulars	L.F.	Debit Rs.	Credit Rs.
1.	Old Share Capital A/c Dr.		2,00,000	—
	To New Equity Share Capital A/c (20,00,000 × 2/5)		—	8,00,000
	To 6% Preference Share Capital A/c— (20,00,000 × 1/5)		4,00,000	
	To Capital Reduction A/c		—	8,00,000
	(Being the issue of new equity shares of Rs. 8,00,000 and 6% preference shares of Rs. 4,00,000 in lieu of cancellation of old shares and the difference credited to Capital Reduction A/c)			
				Contd.

			Dr.	Cr.
2.	Capital Reduction A/c	Dr.	8,00,000	—
	General Reserve A/c	Dr.	80,000	—
	To Reconstruction Expenses A/c		—	12,500
	To Goodwill A/c		—	3,80,000
	To Plant A/c		—	2,70,000
	To Premises A/c		—	2,10,000
	To Capital Reserve A/c		—	7,500
	(Being the above assets written off against capital reduction and general reserve and the remaining balance carried to capital reserve)			

Old Share Capital Account

Dr.	Rs.	Cr.	Rs.
To New Equity Share Capital	8,00,000	By Balance b/d	20,00,000
To 6% Pref. Share Capital	4,00,000		
To Capital Reduction (20,00,000 – 12,00,000)	8,00,000		
	20,00,000		20,00,000

Capital Reduction Account

Dr.	Rs.	Cr.	Rs.
To Reconstruction Expenses	12,500	By Old Share Capital A/c (Old share capital transferred to Capital Reduction A/c)	8,00,000
To Goodwill	3,80,000		
To Plant	2,70,000		
To Premises	1,37,500		
	8,00,000		8,00,000

Note : Remaining part of premises amount of Rs. 72,500 (2,10,000 – 1,37,500) is to be written off against general reserve.

Illustration 6

The Paid-up Capital of Bangalore Company Ltd. is Rs. 5,00,000 and it includes 2,000, 5% Cumulative Preference Shares of Rs. 100 each and 30,000 Ordinary Shares of Rs. 10 each.

Because of heavy losses, the company has decided to reduce the burden of its capital and has secured the required permission :

(i) Reduction in the value of Patents by Rs. 70,000, Machinery by Rs. 17,000 and Equipment by Rs. 2,000.

(ii) Cancellation of the balance of loss of Rs. 1,98,000 shown on the Profit and Loss Account.

(iii) Writing down the balance of Research Expenditure A/c by using the balance remaining in the Capital Reduction A/c (The Research Expenditure is shown in the Balance Sheet at Rs. 79,000).

The approved scheme of Capital Reduction is as follows :

(a) In exchange for every five 5% Preference Shares, issue of three 4% Preference Shares of Rs. 100 each and 20 Ordinary Shares of Rs. 2 each.

(b) Issue of one Ordinary Share of Rs. 2 each in payment of arrears of Preference Shares dividend of Rs. 10 (The total arrears of Preference Share Dividend is Rs. 30,000. The dividend has not yet been declared).

(c) Issue of one new Ordinary Share of Rs. 2 each in exchange for every five old Ordinary Shares.

Draft suitable journal entries.

(Bangalore, Nov. 1992)

Solution :

In the Books of Bangalore Company Ltd.

Journal Entries

Date/ Sl.No	Particulars	L.F.	Debit Rs.	Credit Rs.
1.	5% Preference Share Capital A/c Dr.		2,00,000	—
	To 4% Preference Share Capital A/c (3/5 × 2,000 × Rs. 100)		—	1,20,000
	To Ordinary Share Capital Account (20/5 × 2,000 × Rs. 2)		—	16,000
	To Capital Reduction A/c		—	64,000
	(Being the issue of new pref. shares of Rs. 1,20,000 and ordinary shares of Rs. 16,000 in lieu of cancellation of old pref. shares and the difference credited to capital reduction a/c)			
2.	Capital Reduction A/c Dr.		6,000	—
	To Ordinary Share Capital A/c (2/10 × 30,000)		—	6,000
	(Being the issue of ordinary shares in payment of arrears of preference dividend)			

(Contd.)

			Dr.	Cr.
3.	Ordinary Share Capital A/c (Old) Dr.		3,00,000	—
	To Ordinary Share Capital A/c (New)		—	12,000
	To Capital Reduction A/c		—	2,88,000
	(Being the issue of one ordinary share of Rs. 2 each in exchange for every 5 old ordinary shares)			
4.	Capital Reduction A/c Dr. (Rs. 64,000 – Rs. 6,000 + Rs. 2,88,000)		3,46,000	—
	To Patents A/c		—	70,000
	To Machinery A/c		—	17,000
	To Equipments A/c		—	2,000
	To Profit and Loss A/c		—	1,98,000
	To Research Expenditure A/c		—	59,000
	(Being the capital reduction amount utilised to written off the above assets as per the scheme of reconstruction)			

Note : Dividend is not declared. Hence, no entry is necessary for cancelling the arrears.

Illustration 7

The following are the balances of Rejeshwari Ltd., as at 31st Dec., 1996 :

	Rs.
Capital : 10,000 6% cumulative preference shares of Rs. 10 each	1,00,000
16,000 equity shares of Rs. 10 each	1,60,000
Share premium account	30,000
Creditors	26,000
Goodwill	10,000
Patent and trade marks	21,000
Freehold property at cost	70,000
Depreciation thereon	14,000
Plant and Machinery at cost	1,40,000
Depreciation thereon	30,000
Stock on 31st December, 1996	24,000
Debtors	15,000
Profit and Loss A/c (Dr.)	55,000
Preliminary expenses	25,000

A scheme for reduction of capital was passed by the court on the following terms :

(i) Preference shares to be reduced to Rs. 9 per share.

(ii) Equity shares to be reduced to Re. 1.25 per share.

(iii) The share premium account and intangible assets to be written off.

(iv) Plant and machinery to be revalued at Rs. 50,000.

(v) One equity share of Re. 1.25 to be issued for each Rs. 10 of gross preference dividend arrears, which is in arrears since January 1993.

Draft journal entries and the revised balance sheet.

(Poona and M.K.U.)

Solution :

Journal Entries

Date/ Sl.No.	Particulars	L.F.	Debit Rs.	Credit Rs.
1.	Preference Share Capital A/c (10,000 × 1) Dr.		10,000	—
	Equity Share Capital A/c (16,000 × 8.75) Dr.		1,40,000	—
	To Capital Reduction A/c		—	1,50,000
	(Being 10,000 preference shares of Rs. 10 each reduced by Re. 1 (10 – 9) per share and 16,000 equity shares of Rs. 10 each reduced by Rs. 8.75 (10 – 1.25) per share as per scheme)			
2.	Preference Share Dividend A/c Dr.		3,000	—
	To Equity Share Capital A/c		—	3,000
	(Being the issue of 2,400 equity shares of Re. 1.25 each in payment of preference shares dividend in arrears)			
3.	Capital Reduction A/c Dr.		1,50,000	—
	Share Premium A/c Dr.		30,000	—
	To Profit and Loss A/c		—	55,000
	To Preliminary Expenses A/c		—	25,000
	To Preference Share Dividend A/c		—	3,000
	To Goodwill A/c		—	10,000
	To Patents and Trade Marks A/c		—	21,000
	To Plant and Machinery A/c		—	60,000
	To Capital Reserve A/c		—	6,000
	(Being the amount of sundry assets written off and the balance carried to capital reserve account)			

Balance Sheet of Rajeshwari Ltd.
as on 31st Dec., 1996 (and Reduced)

Liabilities	Rs.	Assets		Rs.
Share Capital :		Freehold Property		
10,000 6% Cumulative		at cost	70,000	
Pref. Shares of Rs. 10 each	90,000	*Less* : Depreciation	14,000	56,000
16,000 Equity Shares of		Plant and Machinery		50,000
Re. 1.25 each	20,000	Stock		24,000
2,400 Equity Shares of		Debtors		15,000
Re. 1.25 each	3,000			
(Issued in repayment of Pref. Shares Dividend)				
Capital Reserve	6,000			
Creditors	26,000			
	1,45,000			1,45,000

***Note* :** **Calculation of Preference Share Dividend**

4 years preference share dividend arrears Rs. 24,000

But, for every Rs. 10, a share of Re. 1.25 is to be issued

i.e., Rs. Rs. share

10 : 24,000 : 1 = 2,400 shares × Re. 1.25

= Rs. 3,000.

As it is contingent liability, only the amount actually paid is to be recorded.

Illustration 8

X Co. Ltd. had the following balance sheet as at 31-3-1997

Liabilities	Rs.	Assets	Rs.
5,000 Equity Shares of		Fixed Assets	3,00,000
Rs. 100 each	5,00,000	Goodwill	90,000
6% Debentures	2,00,000	Patents	50,000
Profit Prior to Incorporation	10,000	Stock	1,00,000
Creditors	1,50,000	Debtors	1,00,000
		Profit and Loss A/c	2,20,000
	8,60,000		8,60,000

The following scheme of reconstruction was adopted :

(i) Each share was to be reduced to a share of Rs. 20 each.

(ii) Each shareholder was to subscribe newly equal to half the number of shares already held by him and pay immediately in cash for the new shares acquired.

(iii) All fictitious assets including goodwill and patents were to be eliminated.

(iv) A provision of 5% on debtors for doubtful debts was to be created.

(v) Fixed assets were to be written down by Rs. 40,000.

Give the necessary journal entries to record the above and prepare the revised balance sheet after reconstruction.

(Bangalore University)

Solution :

Journal Entries

Date/ Sl.No.	Particulars	L.F.	Debit Rs.	Credit Rs.
1.	Equity Share Capital A/c (50,000 × 8) Dr.		4,00,000	—
	To Capital Reduction A/c		—	4,00,000
	(Being amount reduced transferred to capital reduction account)			
2.	Bank A/c Dr.		50,000	—
	To Share Application & Allotment A/c		—	50,000
	(Being application and allotment money on 2,500 shares at Rs. 20 each received)			
3.	Share Application and Allotment A/c Dr.		50,000	—
	To Share Capital A/c		—	50,000
	(Being application and allotment money received from the shareholders, transferred to share capital account)			
4.	Profit Prior to Incorporation A/c Dr.		5,000	—
	To Capital Reduction A/c		—	5,000
	(Being deficit amount required for writing off the assets transferred)			
5.	Capital Reduction A/c Dr.		4,05,000	—
	To Profit and Loss A/c		—	2,20,000
	To Goodwill A/c		—	90,000
	To Patents A/c		—	50,000
	To Provision for Doubtful Debts A/c		—	5,000
	To Fixed Assets A/c		—	40,000
	(Being assets written off or written down as per the scheme of reconstruction)			

Balance Sheet of X Co. Ltd.

As on 31-3-1997 (and Reduced)

Liabilities	Rs.	Assets		Rs.
Share Capital :		Fixed Assets		2,60,000
5,000 Equity shares of		(3,00,000 – 40,000)		
Rs. 20 each fully paid	1,00,000	Stock		1,00,000
2,500 Equity shares (New)		Debtors	1,00,000	
of Rs. 20 each fully paid	50,000	*Less* : Reserve for		
6% Debentures	2,00,000	Doubtful Debts	5,000	95,000
Profit Prior to Incorporation	5,000	Bank		50,000
(10,000 – 5,000)				
Creditors	1,50,000			
	5,05,000			5,05,000

Illustration 9

The following is the Balance Sheet of Bright Ltd. on 31-12-1997 :

Liabilities	Rs.	Assets	Rs.
Authorised Capital :		Patents as Cost	8,50,000
10,000 Pref. shares of		Leasehold Premises	1,30,800
Rs. 100 each	10,00,000	Plant & Machinery	42,200
10,000 Equity shares of		Sundry Debtors	76,500
Rs. 100 each	10,00,000	Stock-in-Trade	55,000
Subscribed Capital :		Discount on Shares	18,000
7,500 Pref. shares of		Profit and Loss A/c	1,15,000
Rs. 100 each fully paid	7,50,000	Cash in hand	500
5,000 Equity Shares of		Preliminary Expenses	12,000
Rs. 100 each fully paid	5,00,000		
Sundry Creditors	30,000		
Bank Overdraft	20,000		
	13,00,000		13,00,000

The company suffered heavy losses and was not getting on well. The following scheme of reconstruction was adopted :

(i) The preference shares be reduced to an equal number of fully paid shares of Rs. 50 each.

(ii) The equity shares be reduced to an equal number of shares of Rs. 25 each.

(iii) The amount available be used to write off Rs. 30,800 of the lease-hold premises, Rs. 15,000 off stock, 20% off plant and machinery and sundry debtors; and the balance available off patents.

Journalise the transactions and prepare the balance sheet after the reconstruction has been carried out.

(Karnataka University)

Solution :

Journal Entries in the Book Bright Ltd.

Date/ Sl.No.	Particulars	L.F.	Debit Rs.	Credit Rs.
1.	Preference Share Capital A/c Dr.		3,75,000	—
	To Capital Reduction A/c		—	3,75,000
	(Being the amount reduced transferred to capital reduction account)			
2.	Equity Share Capital A/c Dr.		3,75,000	—
	To Capital Reduction A/c		—	3,75,000
	(Being the amount reduced transferred to capital reduction account)			
3.	Capital Reduction A/c Dr.		7,50,000	—
	To Discount on Issue of Shares A/c		—	18,000
	To Preliminary Expenses A/c		—	12,000
	To Profit Loss A/c		—	1,15,000
	To Leasehold Premises A/c		—	30,800
	To Stock A/c		—	15,000
	To Plant and Machinery A/c		—	8,440
	To Provision for Doubtful Debts A/c		—	15,300
	To Patents A/c (Balancing figure)		—	5,35,460
	(Being the assets and losses written off or written down as per the scheme)			

Note : Discount on issue of shares, preliminary expenses and losses should be written off even though the problem does not state like that.

Balance Sheet of Bright Ltd.
as on 31-12-1997 (and reduced)

Liabilities	Rs.	Assets		Rs.
Share Capital :		Patents	8,50,000	
Authorised :		*Less* : Reduced under		
10,000 Pref. shares of		Scheme	5,35,460	3,14,540
Rs. 50 each	5,00,000	Lease-hold Premises	1,30,800	
10,000 Equity shares of		*Less* : Reduced under		
Rs. 25 each	2,50,000	scheme	30,800	1,00,000
Subscribed :		Plant & Machinery	42,200	
7,500 Pref. shares of		*Less* : Reduced under		
Rs. 50 each fully paid	3,75,000	scheme	8,440	33,760
5,000 Equity shares of		Sundry Debtors	76,500	
Rs. 25 each fully paid	1,25,000	*Less*: Provision	15,300	61,200
Sundry Creditors	30,000	Stock-in-Trade	55,000	
Bank Over Draft	20,000	*Less:* Reduced	15,000	40,000
		Cash on hand		500
	5,50,000			5,50,000

Illustration 10

The Balance Sheet of Ideal Trading Co. Ltd. Mumbai as at 31st October, 1997 was as follows :

Liabilities	Rs.	Assets	Rs.
Share Capital :		Plant & Machinery	3,60,247
10,000 Pref. shares of		Land and Buildings	10,676
Rs. 10 each fully paid	1,00,000	Steamer	16,645
20,000 ordinary shares		Furniture	12,994
of Rs. 10 each fully paid	2,00,000	Investment	13,481
Debentures	1,20,000	Stock-in-Trade	13,705
Creditors	14,552	Debtors	9,366
Bills Payable	558	Cash at Bank	13,521
General Reserve	10,882	Cash in hand	134
Profit and Loss A/c	4,777		
	4,50,769		4,50,769

A scheme of reconstruction of the company was approved by the court, according to which preference shares were to be written off by Rs. 4 per share and ordinary shares by Rs. 6 per share. The amount so available was to be utilised for writing off the following assets :

		Rs.
(i)	Plant and Machinery	1,57,201
(ii)	Buildings	676
(iii)	Investments	6,261
(iv)	Steamer	4,045
(v)	Furniture	3,372

The general reserve should be extinguished and the difference should be adjusted to profit and loss account.

Draft journal entries and prepare the balance sheet after carrying out the terms of reconstruction.

(Karnataka University)

Solution :

Journal Entries in the books of Ideal Co. Ltd.

Date/ Sl. No.	Particulars		L. F.	Debit Rs.	Credit Rs.
1.	Preference Share Capital A/c	Dr.		40,000	—
	Ordinary Share Capital A/c	Dr.		1,20,000	
	To Capital Reduction A/c			—	1,60,000
	(Being the amount reduced transferred to capital reduction account)				
2.	General Reserve Account	Dr.		10,882	—
	Profit and Loss Account	Dr.		673	—
	To Capital Reduction Account			—	11,555
	(Being general reserve and part of the profit transferred to capital reduction account as per the scheme)				
3.	Capital Reduction A/c	Dr.		1,71,555	—
	To Plant and Machinery A/c			—	1,57,201
	To Buildings A/c			—	676
	To Investments A/c			—	6,261
	To Steamer A/c			—	4,045
	To Furniture A/c			—	3,372
	(Being assets written down as per the scheme)				

Balance Sheet of Ideal Trading Co. Ltd. Bombay as on 31st October, 1997 (and Reduced)

Liabilities	Rs.	Assets		Rs.
Share Capital :		Plant & Machinery	3,60,247	
10,000 Pref. Shares of		*Less* : Reduced	1,57,201	2,03,046
Rs. 6 each fully	60,000	Land and Building	10,676	
20,000 Ordinary Shares		*Less* : Reduced	676	10,000
of Rs. 4 each fully paid	80,000	Steamer	16,645	
Debentures	1,20,000	*Less* : Reduced	4,045	12,600
Creditors	14,552	Furniture	12,994	
Bills Payable	558	*Less* : Reduced	3,372	9,622
Profit and Loss A/c	4,104	Investments	13,481	
(4,777 – 673)		*Less* : Reduced	6,261	7,220
		Stock in Trade		13,705
		Debtors		9,366
		Cash at Bank		13,521
		Cash in hand		134
	2,79,214			2,79,214

Note : Total amount to be written of as per the scheme is Rs. 1,71,555. But, the amount of capital reduced is Rs. 1,60,000. Therefore, still Rs. 11,555 are required to make good the deficit. Hence, the entire reserve of Rs. 10,882 and the profit of Rs. 673 should be transferred to capital reduction account.

Illustration 11

The Balance Sheet of Improving Ltd. as at 31st December, 1997 was as follows :

	Rs.			Rs.
Share Capital :		Goodwill at Cost		15,000
2,000 5% Cumulative Pref.		Freehold Premises		2,00,000
Shares of Rs. 100 each	2,00,000	Plant & Machinery		3,00,000
4,000 Equity Shares of		Stock-in-trade		50,000
Rs. 100 each	4,00,000	Debtors		40,000
5½ 1st Mortgage Debentures	1,00,000	Profit & Loss A/c :		
Bank Overdraft	50,000	Balance on 1-1-1997	3,00,000	
Creditors	1,00,000	*Less* : Profit for the year	60,000	2,40,000
		Cash		5,000
	8,50,000			8,50,000

The company business was passed through a depression and the worse seems to have been over. The following scheme of reconstruction is adopted with the consent of all and approved by the court :

(i) The preference shares to be reduced to Rs. 75 per share fully paid, but the rate of dividend be increased to 8%.

(ii) The equity shares be reduced to Rs. 40 per share fully paid.

(iii) The debentureholders took over stock in trade and book debts in full satisfaction of the amount due to them.

(iv) the goodwill account is to be eliminated.

(v) The value of freehold premises is to be increased by 30%.

(vi) The value of plant and machinery is to be depreciated by $33\,^1/_3$.

(vii) Expenses of reconstruction amounted to Rs. 3,000.

(viii) The issue of 2,000 equity shares to the public for cash.

(ix) The repayment of bank overdraft.

(B.Com., Gulbarga and Mysore)

Solution :

Journal Entries in the Books of Improving Ltd.

Date/ Sl. No.	Particulars	L.F.	Debit Rs.	Credit Rs.
1.	Preference Share Capital A/c Dr.		50,000	—
	(2,000 × 25)			
	Equity Share Capital A/c (4,000 × 60) Dr.		2,40,000	—
	To Capital Reduction A/c		—	2,90,000
	(Being the reduction of pref. share capital by Rs. 25 per share and equity share capital Rs. 60 per share)			
2.	Debentures A/c Dr.		1,00,000	—
	To Debentureholder's A/c		—	1,00,000
	(Being the debentures transferred to debentureholders' account)			
3.	Debentureholders' A/c Dr.		1,00,000	—
	To Stock-in-trade A/c		—	50,000
	To Debtors A/c		—	40,000
	To Capital Reduction A/c		—	10,000
	(Being stock and debtors taken over by debentureholders in full satisfaction of their claims)			

(*Contd.*)

			Rs.	Rs.
4.	Freehold Premises A/c	Dr.	60,000	—
	To Capital Reduction A/c		—	60,000
	(Being the appreciation in the value of freehold premises taken into account)			
5.	Reconstruction Expenses A/c	Dr.	3,000	—
	To Cash A/c		—	3,000
	(Being the payment of reconstruction expenses)			
6.	Capital Reduction A/c	Dr.	3,60,000	
	To Profit and Loss A/c		—	2,40,000
	To Reconstruction Expenses A/c		—	3,000
	To Goodwill A/c		—	15,000
	To Plant & Machinery A/c		—	1,00,000
	To Capital Reserve A/c (Balancing figure)		—	2,000
	(Being the above losses written off and the balance of capital reduction account transferred to capital reserve account)			
7.	Cash Account (2,000 × 40)	Dr.	80,000	—
	To Equity Share Capital A/c		—	80,000
	(Being cash received on the issue of 2,000 shares to the public)			
8.	Bank Overdraft A/c	Dr.	50,000	—
	To Cash A/c		—	50,000
	(Being bank overdraft paid)			

Balance Sheet of Improving Ltd., (and Reduced) as on 31st December, 1997

Liabilities	Rs.	Assets		Rs.
Share Capital :		Freehold Premises	2,00,000	
2,000, 8% Cumulative Pref.		*Add* : Appreciation	60,000	2,60,000
shares of Rs. 75 fully paid	1,50,000	Plant & Machinery	3,00,000	
6,000 (4,000 + 2,000) Equity		*Less* : Depreciation	1,00,000	2,00,000
shares of Rs. 40 each fully paid	2,40,000	Cash :		
Capital Reserve	2,000	Old Balance	5,000	
Creditors	1,00,000	*Add* : From issue of shares	80,000	
			85,000	
		Less : Reconstruction Expenses and Bank overdraft	53,000	32,000
	4,92,000			4,92,000

Illustration 12

The following was the balance sheet of XYZ Co. Ltd. before reconstruction :

Liabilities	Rs.	Assets	Rs.
Issued and Paid-up Capital :		Building	4,00,000
12,000, 7% Pref. Shares of		Plants & Machinery	2,68,000
Rs. 50 each	6,00,000	Trade Mark & Goodwill	3,18,000
15,000 Equity Shares of		Stock	4,00,000
Rs. 50 each	7,50,000	Debtors	3,28,000
Loan	5,73,000	Preliminary Expenses	11,000
Sundry Creditors	2,07,000	Profit and Loss A/c	4,40,000
Liabilities	35,000		
	21,65,000		21,65,000

The company is now earning profit but short of working capital and a scheme of reconstruction has been approved by both classes of shareholders and sanctioned by the court. The scheme is :

(1) The equity shareholders have agreed that their Rs. 50 shares to be reduced to Rs. 2.50 per share.

(2) They have also agreed to subscribe in cash for three new equity shares of Rs. 2.50 each.

(3) The preference shareholders have agreed to cancel the arrears of dividend and to accept four new 5% preference shares of Rs. 10 each for every preference share they held plus six new equity shares of Rs. 2.50 each fully paid.

(4) Loan creditors of Rs. 1,50,000 have agreed to convert their loans in to shares of Rs. 10 each and 12,000 new equity shares of Rs. 2.50 each.

(5) The directors have agreed to subscribe in cash for additional 40,000 new equity shares of Rs. 2.50 fully paid.

(6) Of the cash received by the issue of new shares, Rs. 2,00,000 is to be used to reduce the loan due by the company.

The amount available to be applied to write off preliminary expenses, profit and loss account, debit balance and to write off plant and machinery by Rs. 35,000. The balance is to be used to write off the value of trade marks and goodwill.

Show the journal entries to put through the scheme and prepare the Balance Sheet of the company after reconstruction.

(Bangalore University)

Solution :

Journal Entries in the Books of XYZ Co. Ltd.

Date/ Sl.No.	Particulars	L.F.	Debit Rs.	Credit Rs.
1.	Equity Share Capital A/c (15,000×47.50) Dr.		7,12,500	—
	To Capital Reduction A/c		—	7,12,500
	(Being the amount reduced transferred to capital reduction account)			
2.	Bank A/c (15,000 × 3 × 2.50) Dr.		1,12,500	—
	To Equity Share Capital A/c		—	1,12,500
	(Being the issue of 3 equity shares of Rs. 2.50 each for each existing share for cash)			
3.	7% Preference Share Capital A/c Dr.		6,00,000	—
	To 5% Pref. Share Capital A/c (12,000 × 4 × 10)		—	4,80,000
	To Capital Reduction A/c		—	1,20,000
	(Being the issue of 5% pref. share of Rs. 4,80,000 to the existing 7% pref. share of Rs. 6,00,000)			
4.	Bank A/c (12,000 × 6 × 2.50) Dr.		1,80,000	—
	To Equity Share Capital A/c		—	1,80,000
	(Being the issue of 6 equity shares of Rs. 2.50 each for each existing pref. share)			
5.	Loan A/c Dr.		1,50,000	—
	To Equity Share Capital A/c (12,000×2.50)		—	30,000
	To 5% Preference Share Capital A/c		—	1,20,000
	(Being the issue of equity and pref. shares to satisfy part of the loan creditors)			
6.	Bank A/c (40,000 × 2.50) Dr.		1,00,000	—
	To Equity Share Capital A/c		—	1,00,000
	(Being the issue of 40,000 equity shares of Rs. 2.50 each to directors for cash)			
7.	Loan A/c Dr.		2,00,000	—
	To Bank Account		—	2,00,000
	(Being cash paid to satisfy further part of loan creditors)			

Contd.

			Rs.	Rs.
8	Capital Reduction A/c (7,12,500 + 1,20,000)	Dr.	8,32,500	—
	To Profit and Loss A/c		—	4,40,000
	To Preliminary Expenses A/c		—	11,000
	To Plant and Machinery A/c		—	35,000
	To Trade Marks and Goodwill A/c		—	3,18,000
	To Capital Reserve A/c (Balancing figure)		—	28,500
	(Being the above assets written off and the balance is transferred to capital reserve account)			

Reconstructed Balance Sheet of XYZ Co. Ltd., as on ....

Liabilities	Rs.	Assets	Rs.
Share Capital :		Buildings	4,00,000
1,84,000 Equity Share of Rs. 2.50 each fully paid	4,60,000	Plant & Machinery (2,68,000 – 35,000)	2,33,000
60,000, 5% Pref. Shares of Rs. 10 each fully paid	6,00,000	Stock	4,00,000
Capital Reserve	28,500	Cash at Bank (1,12,500 + 1,80,000 + 1,00,000 – 2,00,000)	1,92,500
Loan (5,73,000 – 3,50,000 *i.e.,* 1,50,000 + 2,00,00)	2,23,000		
Sundry Creditors	2,07,000		
Liabilities	35,000		
	15,53,500		15,53,500

Notes : (i) Arrears of preference share dividend is contingent liability. As such, cancellation of arrears of preference share dividend is not a gain to the company. Therefore, no entry should be passed for the cancellation of any contingent liability.

(ii) The total number of equity and preference shares are arrived as below :

Equity Shares :	Issued to existing equity shareholders for cash (15,000 × 3)	45,000
	Issued to existing pref. shareholders for each (12,000 × 6)	72,000
	Issued to loan creditors	12,000
	Issued to directors for cash	40,000
	Existing equity shares (as per old B/S)	15,000
	Total	1,84,000
Pref. Shares :	Issued to existing pref. shareholders in cancellation of their holdings (12,000 × 4)	48,000
	Issued to loan creditors (1,20,000/10)	12,000
	Total	60,000

Illustration 13

The Dull Star Company Limited decided to reconstruct its affairs by a special resolution and with the sanction of the court, on the following lines :

(a) The equity shares to be reduced to an equal number of fully paid up shares of Rs. 3 each.

(b) The preference shares to be reduced to an equal number of fully paid shares of Rs. 80 each.

(c) The preference shareholders agreed to forego 50% of the arrears of dividend and receive equity shares for the balance.

(d) The 'A' debentureholders agreed to receive 40% of the interest amount due to them in preference shares and the balance in cash.

(e) The 'B' debentureholders agreed to buy a part of the freehold property of the book value of Rs. 2,00,000 for Rs. 2,50,000 in part settlement of their claims and receive cash for interest due to them.

(f) The directors agreed to waive off the entire amount due to them.

(g) The amount made available to the company by the acceptance of the above scheme was to be utilised in writing down freehold property to the extent possible after eliminating goodwill and the fictitious assets from the books, writing down the plant and machinery by Rs. 80,000 stock by Rs. 20,000, patent to Rs. 1,00,000 and creating a provision of Rs. 30,000 on sundry debtors.

(h) The company decided to provide itself with Rs. 1,00,000 liquid cash for working capital requirements by raising a loan from the State Finance Corporation on the security of its plant and machinery.

On the date of reconstruction *i.e.,* on 31st December, 1997, the balance sheet of the Dull Star Co. Ltd. was as follows :

Liabilities	Rs.	Assets	Rs.
Share Capital :		Goodwill	2,00,000
1,00,000 Equity Shares of		Plant & Machinery	10,00,000
Rs. 10 each	10,00,000	Freehold Property	15,00,000
10,000, 6% Cumulative Pref.		Furniture & Fixtures	1,00,000
Shares of Rs. 10 each	10,00,000	Patents Rights	2,00,000
5% 'A' Debentures	5,00,000	Stock	1,00,000
6% 'B' Debentures	8,00,000	Debtors	2,50,000
Interest Accrued :		Cash	3,000
'A' Debentures	25,000	Advertising Suspense	50,000
'B' Debentures	48,000	Profit and Loss A/c	80,000
Directors Loan	10,000		
Creditors	1,00,000		
Arrears of Pref. dividend			
Rs. 1,20,000	—		
	34,83,000		34,83,000

Pass the journal entries to give effect to the above and prepare the Balance Sheet of the Dull Star Co. Ltd., after reconstruction.

Solution :

Journal Entries in the Books of Dull Star Co. Ltd.

Date/S.No.	Particulars	L.F.	Debit Rs.	Credit Rs.
1.	Equity Share Capital A/c (1,00,000×7) Dr.		7,00,000	—
	To Capital Reduction Account		—	7,00,000
	(Being the amount reduced transferred to capital reduction account)			
2.	6% Cumulative Pref. Share Capital A/c Dr.		2,00,000	—
	To Capital Reduction A/c		—	2,00,000
	(Being the amount reduced transferred to capital reduction account)			
3.	Capital Reduction A/c (1,20,000 × ½) Dr.		60,000	—
	To Equity Share Capital A/c		—	60,000
	(Being the issue of 2,000 equity shares of Rs. 3 each to satisfy 50% of the arrears of preference share dividend)			
4.	Accrued Interest on 'A' Debentures A/c Dr.		25,000	—
	To Pref. Share Capital A/c (25,000 × $^{40}/_{100}$)		—	10,000
	To Cash Account (25,000 – 10,000)		—	15,000
	(Being the accrued interest on 'A' Debentures satisfied partly in 125 pref. shares of Rs. 80 each and partly in cash)			
5.	Accrued Interest on 'B' Debentures A/c Dr.		48,000	—
	To Cash A/c		—	48,000
	(Being the accrued interest on 'B' Debentures paid in cash)			
6.	'B' Debentures A/c Dr.		2,50,000	—
	To 'B' Debentureholders A/c		—	2,50,000
	(Being 'B' debentures of Rs. 2,50,000 transferred to 'B' debentureholders account)			
7.	'B' Debentureholders A/c Dr.		2,50,000	—
	To Freehold Property A/c		—	2,00,000
	To Capital Reduction A/c (Profit on sale of property)		—	50,000
	(Being freehold property of Rs. 2,00,00 sold to 'B' debentureholders for Rs. 2,50,000)			

(*Contd.*)

			Dr.	Cr.
8.	Directors' Loan A/c	Dr.	10,000	—
	To Capital Reduction A/c		—	10,000
	(Being loan amount waived by directors)			
9.	Cash A/c	Dr.	1,00,000	—
	To Loan from State Finance Corporation A/c		—	1,00,000
	(Being loan borrowed from S.F.C.)			
10.	Capital Reduction Account (7,00,000 + 2,00,000 + 50,000 + 10,000 – 60,000)	Dr.	9,00,000	—
	To Profit and Loss A/c		—	80,000
	To Advertising suspense A/s		—	50,000
	To Goodwill A/c		—	2,00,000
	To Patents A/c (2,00,000 – 1,00,000)		—	1,00,000
	To Plant & Machinery A/c		—	80,000
	To Stock Account		—	20,000
	To Reserve for Doubtful Debts A/c		—	30,000
	To Freehold Property A/c (Balance)		—	3,40,000
	(Being the above assets written off as per the scheme)			

Reconstructed Balance Sheet of the Dull Star Co. Ltd. as on 31st December, 1997

Liabilities	Rs.	Assets		Rs.
Share Capital :		Plant and Machinery	10,00,000	
1,20,000 (1,00,000 + 20,000)		*Less* : Written off	80,000	9,20,000
Equity Shares of Rs. 3		Freehold Property	15,00,000	
each fully paid	3,60,000	*Less* : Sold to 'B' Debenture holders	2,00,000	
10,125 (10,000 + 125)			13,00,000	
6% Cum. Pref. Shares of Rs. 80 each fully paid	8,10,000	*Less* : Written off	3,40,000	9,60,000
5% 'A' Debentures	5,00,000	Furniture & Fixtures		1,00,000
6% 'B' Debentures	5,50,000	Patent Rights	2,00,000	
(8,00,000 – 2,50,000)		*Less* : Written off	1,00,000	1,00,000
Loan from State Finance		Stock	1,00,000	
Corporation	1,00,000	*Less* : Written off	20,000	80,000
Creditors	1,00,000	Debtors	2,50,000	
		Less : R.D.D.	30,000	2,20,000
		Cash (3,000 + 1,00,000– 63,000)		40,000
	24,20,000			24,20,000

Note : Half of arrears of preference share dividend foregone by the preference shareholders. No entry should be passed as it results neither in a profit nor in a loss. Similarly, the directors agreed to forego the entire amount of loan. This is a gain for the company. Therefore, this amount should be credited to capital reduction account.

Illustration 14

The Balance Sheet of A Ltd. as at 31st December, 1997 is as follows :

Liabilities	Rs.	Assets	Rs.
Authorised & Issued Capital :		Fixed Assets	14,30,000
8,000 shares of Rs. 100 each	8,00,000	Stock -in-trade	80,000
6% Debentures	14,00,000	Debtors	30,000
Interest accrued on the above	70,000	Investments	17,000
Trade Creditors	4,50,000	Cash	1,03,000
Income Tax due	10,000	Profit and Loss A/c	10,70,000
	27,30,000		27,30,000

The following scheme of reorganisation was approved and confirmed by the court :

(1) Each share shall be sub-divided into twenty fully paid equity shares of Rs. 5 each.

(2) After sub-division, each shareholder shall surrender to the company 95% of its holding for the purpose of re-issue of debentureholders and creditors so far as required and otherwise for cancellation.

(3) Of the surrendered shares, 46,000 shares of Rs. 5 each shall be converted into 8% participating preference shares of Rs. 5 each fully paid.

(4) Debentureholders' claim to be reduced to Rs. 2,30,000. This will be satisfied by the issue to them of 46,000 participating preference shares of Rs. 5 each fully paid.

(5) The liability of Income-tax is to be satisfied in full.

(6) The claims of unsecured creditors shall be reduced by 80% and the balance shall be satisfied by allotting them equity shares of Rs. 5 each fully paid from the shares surrendered.

(7) Shares surrendered and not issued shall be cancelled.

Journalise the various entries to be made and prepare the Balance Sheet after reorganisation, assuming that the tax liability is not paid.

(Adapted from Bangalore University)

Solution :

Journal Entries in the Books of A Ltd.

Date/S.No.	Particulars	L.F.	Debit Rs.	Credit Rs.
1.	Equity Share Capital A/c (Rs. 100) Dr.		8,00,000	—
	To Equity Share Capital A/c (Rs. 5)		—	8,00,000
	(Being the sub-division of 8,000 shares of Rs. 100 each into 1,60,000 [*i.e.*, 8,000 × 20] shares of Rs. 5 each)			
2.	Equity Share Capital A/c Dr.		7,60,000	—
	To Surrendered Share A/c		—	7,60,000
	(Being the surrender of 95% of the shareholding to the company)			
3.	Surrendered Shares A/c Dr.		2,30,000	—
	To 8% Participating Pref. Share Capital A/c		—	2,30,000
	(Being the conversion of 46,000 surrendered shares into 8% participating shares so as to issue to the debentureholders)			
4.	Surrendered Shares A/c Dr.		90,000	—
	To Equity Share Capital A/c		—	90,000
	(Being the conversion of surrendered shares into equity capital so as to satisfy the creditors)			
5.	Surrendered Shares A/c Dr.		4,40,000	—
	To Capital Reduction A/d		—	4,40,000
	(Being the cancellation of shares surrendered [*i.e.,* 7,60,000 – 3,20,000 *i.e.,* 2,30,000 + 90,000] but not issued)			
6.	6% Debentures A/c Dr.		14,00,000	—
	Interest on Debentures A/c Dr.		70,000	—
	Sundry Creditors A/c Dr.		4,50,000	—
	To Capital Reduction A/c		—	19,20,000
	(Being the cancellation of liabilities on their reduction)			
7.	Capital Reduction A/c* Dr.		23,60,000	—
	To Profit and Loss A/c		—	10,70,000
	To Capital Reserve A/c (B.F.)		—	12,90,000
	(Being the debit balance of P & L A/c written off and the balance is transferred to capital reserve account)			

***Note** : It may be even Capital Re-organisation A/c instead of Capital Reduction A/c.

A Ltd. Reconstructed Balance Sheet as on 31-12-97

Liabilities	Rs.	Assets	Rs.
Share Capital :		Fixed Assets	14,30,000
46,000 Preference Shares		Investments	17,000
of Rs. 5 each	2,30,000	Stock-in-trade	80,000
26,000 Equity Shares		Debtors	30,000
of Rs. 5 each	1,30,000	Cash	1,03,000
Capital Reserve	12,90,000		
Liability of Income Tax	10,000		
	16,60,000		16,60,000

Note : Equity Shares consist of 8,000 unsurrendered shares and 18,000 shares issued to creditors.

EXAMINATION QUESTIONS

(A) Answer the following questions in two sentences each :

(Each carries Two marks)

(1) What do you mean by internal reconstruction ?

(2) What are the forms of internal reconstruction ?

(3) What is alternation of share capital ?

(4) What is capital reduction ? When is it prepared ?

(Bangalore, Nov. 1981, May 1982 and Oct. 1991)

(5) Under what circumstance do you prepare the capital reduction account ? What is its main purpose ?

(Bangalore, April 1993)

(6) What is the use of the capital reduction account ?

(Bangalore, Nov. 1993)

(7) Distinguish between internal reconstruction and external reconstruction.

(Bangalore, April 1986 and 1994)

(8) What journal entry do you pass when the uncalled capital on shares is reduced ?

(B) Answer the following questions :

(Each carries Eight marks)

(1) What is internal reconstruction ? What are the differences between internal reconstruction and external reconstruction ?

(2) Explain the different forms of internal reconstruction.

(3) Give the journal entries for alteration of share capital.

(4) Give the journal entries for reduction of share capital.

Simple Problems :

(5) On reconstruction of a company, the following terms were agreed upon :

(a) The shareholders holding 1,00,000 shares of Rs. 10 each were to receive (i) 2/5th of their holding in fully paid equity shares of Rs. 10 each; and (ii) 1/5th of their holding in 5% preference shares of Rs. 10 each fully paid, in cancellation of old shares.

(b) Apply the credit balance of general reserve of Rs. 30,000 for reconstruction purpose.

(c) The goodwill stood at Rs. 3,00,000 was to be written off fully.

(d) The plant and premises which stood at Rs. 2,00,000 and Rs. 3,00,000 respectively were to be reduced by 25% each.

Pass journal entries in the books of the company.

(Karnataka, April 1997)

Ans. : Capital Reserve Rs. 5,000 and Total Capital Reduction Rs. 4,30,000.

(6) Sanjog Company Ltd., passed necessary resolution and received sanction of the court for the reduction of its share capital by Rs. 2,50,000 for the purposes enumerated here under :

(a) to write off the debit balance of profit and loss account Rs. 1,05,000.

(b) to reduce the value of investments to market value by writing off Rs. 40,000.

(c) to reduce the value of plant and machinery by Rs. 45,000 and of goodwill by Rs. 20,000.

The reduction was made by converting 25,000 preference of Rs. 20 each fully paid to the same number of preference shares of Rs. 15 each fully paid and by converting 25,000 equity shares of Rs. 20 each and Rs. 15 paid up into 25,000 equity shares of Rs. 10 each fully paid.

(Adapted from Bombay University)

Ans. : Capital Reserve Rs. 40,000 and Total Capital Reduction Rs. 2,50,000.

(7) The reconstruction of Picking-up Ltd., having a paid up capital of Rs. 5,00,000 in shares of Rs. 10 each was carried out on the following terms :

The shareholders to receive in lieu of their present holding the following :

(a) Fully paid ordinary shares to the extent of $^{2}/_{5}$th of their holding.

(b) 6% fully paid preference shares to the extent of $^{1}/_{5}$th of the above ordinary shares.

(c) Rs. 60,000 5% debentures.

The goodwill which stood at Rs. 3,25,000 was written down to Rs. 1,50,000; Plant which stood at Rs. 90,000 was written down to Rs. 75,000; Freehold premises which stood at Rs. 1,10,000 were written down to Rs. 1,00,000.

Pass the necessary journal entries and prepare capital reduction account.

(Adapted from Mysore University)

Ans. : Total Capital Reduction Rs. 2,00,000.

(8) The position of a company on 31-12-1997 was as follows :

Liabilities :

(1)	20,000 equity shares of Rs. 100 each	20,00,000
(2)	1,000, 6% debentures of Rs. 1000 each	10,00,000
(3)	Interest due on debentures	1,20,000
	Total liabilities	31,20,000

The book value of all the fixed assets and current assets of the company was Rs. 9,40,000. The following was the scheme approved by the court :

(a) The existing shares to be converted into shares of Rs. 5 each and 90% of theses new shares to be surrendered by the shareholders.

(b) The total amount due to the debentureholders to be satisfied as follows :

(i) Issue of new 8% debentures for Rs. 4,90,000.

(ii) Issue of new equity shares of Rs. 5 each for Rs. 2,50,000 (out of the surrendered shares).

(c) Shares surrendered and not issued to the debentureholders to be cancelled.

(d) Accumulated losses should be written off.

Draft suitable journal entries for the above details.

(Adapted from Bangalore University)

Ans. : Surrendered shares A/c credit balance transferred to capital reduction account Rs. 16,50,000; Accumulated losses written off Rs. 19,10,000 and Total Capital Reduction Rs. 21,60,000.

Notes :

(i) **Capital Reduction Account**

To New 8% Debentures	2,50,000	By Old 6% Debentures	5,10,000
To Accumulated Losses	19,10,000	By Surrendered Shares A/c	16,50,000
	21,60,000		21,60,000

(ii) Surrendered Shares Account

To New Equity Share Capital A/c	2,50,000	By Old Equity Share Capital A/c	19,00,000
To Capital Reduction A/c	16,50,000		
	19,00,000		19,00,000

(iii) The amount of fictitious or accumulated losses is Rs. 21,80,000 (31,20,000 – 9,40,000). But, the amount available in capital reduction account is only Rs. 19,10,000. Therefore, that much amount is written off against accumulated losses.

(9) The following is the Balance Sheet of X Ltd., when it was decided to reconstruct the same :

Liabilities	Rs.	Assets	Rs.
Share Capital :		Goodwill	10,000
10,000 Equity Shares of		Other fixed assets	90,000
Rs. 10 each fully paid	1,00,000	Stock in trade	25,000
10,000, 7% Pref. shares of		Debtors	30,000
Rs. 10 each fully paid	1,00,000	Profit and Loss A/c	45,000
	2,00,000		2,00,000

It was resolved that equity capital of Rs. 10 each be reduced to fully paid shares of Rs. 6 each and 7% preference shares of Rs. 10 each be reduced to 7½% fully paid preference shares of Rs. 7 each. Number of shares in each case remained the same.

It was further resolved that the amount so available be used for writing off the loss, goodwill account and as far as possible other fixed assets. There were preference share dividends in arrears for the past three years and it was decided to cancel the same. Draft the journal entries for effecting the above scheme of reconstruction.

(Bangalore, Oct. 1991)

Ans. : Amount available for writing off fixed assets Rs. 15,000; Total Capital Reduction Rs. 70,000; Balance Sheet Total Rs. 1,30,000.

(10) X Co. Ltd., had the following Balance Sheet as at 31-31-1998 :

Liabilities	Rs.	Assets	Rs.
5,000 Equity Shares of		Fixed Assets	3,00,000
Rs. 100 each	5,00,000	Goodwill	90,000
6% Debentures	2,00,000	Patents	50,000
Profit prior to incorporation	10,000	Stock	1,00,000
Creditors	1,50,000	Debtors	1,00,000
		Profit and Loss A/c	2,20,000
	8,60,000		8,60,000

The following scheme of reconstruction was adopted :

(i) Each share was to be reduced to a share of Rs. 20 each.

(ii) Each shareholder was to subscribe newly, equal to half the number of shares already held by him and pay immediately in cash for the new shares acquired.

(iii) All fictitious assets including goodwill and patents were to be eliminated.

(iv) A provision of 5% on debtors for doubtful debts was to be created.

(v) Fixed assets were to be written down by Rs. 40,000.

Give the necessary journal entries to record the above scheme.

(Adapted from Karnataka University)

Ans. : Total Capital Reduction Rs. 4,05,000 (*i.e.,* Rs. 4,00,000 [5,000 × 80] on shares plus Rs. 10,000 profit prior to incorporation to make up the required amount).

(11) The following scheme of reconstruction has been approved for Divya Ltd. :

(1) The shareholders to receive in lieu of their present holding of 60,000 shares of Rs. 10 each fully paid. The following :

(a) Fully paid new equity shares equal to 1/5 of their present holding.

(b) 8% preference shares fully paid to the extent of ½ of the above new equity shares, and

(c) Rs. 60,000, 80% second debentures.

(2) the debentureholders total claim of Rs. 75,000 to be reduced to Rs. 25,000. This will be satisfied by the issue of 250, 8% preference shares of Rs. 100 each fully paid.

(3) An issue of Rs. 50,000, 6% first debentures was made and allotted, payment for the same having been received in cash.

(4) The goodwill which stood at Rs. 3,00,000 was written down to Rs. 75,000 and machinery which stood at Rs. 1,00,000 was written down to Rs. 75,000.

(5) The freehold premises which stood at Rs. 1,75,000 was written down by Rs. 75,000.

Pass the necessary journal entries in the books of Divya Ltd., for the scheme of reconstruction.

(Mysore, Oct. 1985)

Ans. : Capital Reserve Rs. 85,000 and Total Capital Reduction Rs. 4,10,000.

Note : Capital reduction is calculated as below :

Shareholder's present holding *i.e.*, 60,000 × 10		6,00,000
Less : Issue of new equity shares (6,00,000 × 1/5)	1,20,000	
Issue of preference shares (1,20,000 × 1/2)	60,000	
Issue of second debentures	60,000	2,40,000
		3,60,000
Less : Sacrifice by the old debentureholders (75,000–25,000)		50,000
Total Capital reduction		4,10,000

(12) The following agreement was made in the reconstruction of a company.

The shareholders had agreed to receive the following in exchange for 50,000 shares of Rs. 10 each held by them :

(a) Fully paid Equity Shares up to the extent of 2/5 of the present holding.

(b) 5% Preference Shares, to the extent of 1/5 of the above new Equity Shares.

(c) 6% Debentures of Rs. 60,000.

Further, 5% Debentures for Rs. 50,000 had been issued to the Public and the company has received the amount in cash.

Goodwill of Rs. 3,00,000 was reduced to Rs. 1,50,000, Machinery was reduced from Rs. 1,00,000 to Rs. 75,000 and Leasehold Premises reduced from Rs. 1,50,000 to Rs. 1,25,000.

Give necessary journal entries.

(Bangalore Uni., Second Year B.Com., 1993 April [1989-90 onwards])

Ans. : Capital reducation amount total Rs. 2,00,000 (*i.e.*, 5,00,000 – 3,00,000 *i.e.*, 2,00,000 + 40,000 + 60,000).

(C) Solve the following problems :

(Each carries 15/16 marks)

(1) The following is the Balance Sheet of Vinod Ltd. as on 31-12-1995:

Liabilities	Rs.	Assets	Rs.
Share Capital :		Goodwill	40,000
30,000 Preference Shares of		Buildings	2,70,000
Rs. 10 each	3,00,000	Machinery	1,20,000
30,000 Ordinary Shares of		Patents	50,000
Rs. 10 each	3,00,000	Stock	30,000
Creditors	70,000	Debtors	1,00,000
Bills Payable	30,000	Cash	10,000
		Preliminary Expenses	20,000
		Profit and Loss Account	60,000
	7,00,000		7,00,000

The following scheme of reconstruction is approved :

(a) That the equity shares be reduced to an equal number of fully paid shares of Rs. 5 each.

(b) That the preference shares be reduced to an equal number of fully paid shares of Rs. 7 each.

(c) The amount so available is utilised as follows :

(i) Goodwill, preliminary expenses and Profit and Loss Accounts are to be written off completely.

(ii) Rs. 50,000 to be written off buildings, Rs. 30,000 to be written off machinery, Rs. 50,000 to be written off stock, a provision for doubtful debts to be made at 5% of debtors and the balance available be utilised to write off patents.

Pass the journal entries to give effect to the above and show the balance sheet of the company after reconstruction.

(Gulbarga, Oct. 1993)

Ans. : Total Capital Reduction Rs. 2,40,000 (*i.e.*, 1,50,000+ 90,000); Balance Sheet Total Rs. 4,60,000 and Patents written off by Rs. 30,000 (B.F.).

(2) The following is the Balance Sheet of Nirma Ltd. as on 31-12-1988.

Liabilities	Rs.	Assets	Rs.
Capital :		**Fixed Assets**	
Authorised :		Goodwill	50,000
6,000, 9% Pref. Shares		Freehold Property	3,50,000
of Rs. 100 each	6,00,000	Plant and Machinery	6,00,000
10,000 Equity shares of		**Current Assets**	
Rs. 100 each	10,00,000	Stock-in-trade	1,70,000
Issued & Paid up		Debtors	2,10,000
4,000, 9% Pref. Shares		Profit & Loss Account	3,80,000
of 100 each fully paid	4,00,000		
8,000 Equity Shares of			
Rs. 10 each fully paid	8,00,000		
Secured Loans			
6% Debentures	2,40,000		
Bank Overdraft	1,10,000		
Current Liabilities	2,10,000		
	17,60,000		17,60,000

The following scheme of reconstruction was approved by the court and was given effect to :

(1) The preference shares and the equity shares were reduced to Rs. 80 and Rs. 50 per share fully paid up respectively.

(2) The debentureholders agreed to receive 2,000 preference shares in full satisfaction of their dues.

(3) The goodwill account and the debit balance of profit and loss account were written off.

(4) Freehold property and plant and machinery were depreciated by 20% and 10% respectively.

Pass the journal entries to give effect to the above arrangements and prepare the revised balance sheet after reconstruction.

(Karnataka, April 1989 & 1998)

Ans. : Total Capital reduction Rs. 5,60,000 (*i.e.*, 80,000 + 4,00,000 + 80,000) and Balance Sheet Total Rs. 12,00,000.

(3) Rao & Co. Ltd. had the following Balance Sheet as at 30-6-1997 :

Liabilities	Rs.	Assets	Rs.
1,500, 8% Pref. Shares of		Goodwill	40,000
Rs. 100 each	1,50,000	Land & Buildings	2,00,000
3,000 Equity Shares of		Patents	70,000
Rs. 100 each	3,00,000	Stock	1,00,000
Profit Prior to Incorporation	15,000	Debtors	80,000
9% Debentures	1,00,000	Profit and Loss A/c	95,000
Creditors	20,000		
	5,85,000		5,85,000

The following scheme of reconstruction was adopted :

(1) 8% preference shares were to be reduced to a share of Rs. 50 each.

(2) Equity shares were to be reduced to a share of Rs. 40 each.

(3) Debentureholders have agreed to accept 900, 10% debentures of Rs. 100 each in full satisfaction of their claims.

(4) All the fictitious assets including goodwill and patents were to be eliminated.

(5) Land and buildings be reduced by 20% and stock by 25%.

(6) A provision of 10% on debtors for doubtful debts was to be created.

Pass the journal entries and prepare the balance sheet after reconstruction has been carried out.

(Karnataka, April 1988)

Ans. : Total Capital Reduction Rs. 2,78,000 (*i.e.*, 75,000 + 1,80,000 + 10,000 + 13,000 from profit prior to incorporation only) and Balance Sheet Total Rs. 3,07,000.

(4) The following is the Balance Sheet of X Co. Ltd. as on 31-3-1982.

Liabilities	Rs.	Assets	Rs.
Authorised Capital :		Goodwill	6,000
20,000 Shares of Rs. 10 each	2,00,000	Buildings	30,000
Issued Capital :		Machinery	24,000
8,000 Shares of Rs. 10 each	80,000	Stock	10,000

(Contd.)

Bank Overdraft	4,000	Sundry Debtors	15,000
Sundry Creditors	10,000	Cash	1,000
Bills Payable	6,000	Profit & Loss A/c	9,000
		Preliminary Expenses	5,000
	1,00,000		1,00,000

The following scheme of reconstruction was adopted :

(1) The shares be reduced to an equal number of fully paid shares of Rs. 6 each.

(2) The amount so available to be used to write off goodwill, preliminary expenses and profit and loss account balances completely and to depreciate buildings by Rs. 5,000; machinery by Rs. 4,000 and to provide for writing off bad debts Rs. 1,000.

(3) The company is to issue 500 shares of Rs. 6 each for cash to raise the necessary amount to pay off the Bank Overdraft.

Pass the necessary journal entries to record the above and prepare the balance sheet of the company after reconstruction has been carried out.

(Karnataka, Oct. 1983)

Ans. : Total Capital Reducation Rs. 32,000 (8,000 × 4); Capital Reserve Rs. 2,000 and Balance Sheet Total Rs. 69,000.

Note : Bank Overdraft is fully paid Rs. 4,000 (*i.e.,* Rs. 1,000 Cash balance plus Rs. 3,000 by issue of shares).

(5) The Balance Sheet of A Ltd. on 31-12-1982 is as under :

Liabilities	Rs.	Assets		Rs.
Authorised Capital :		Goodwill		30,000
2,000, 8% Pref. Shares of		Freehold Property		2,50,000
Rs. 100 each	2,00,000	Machinery		3,00,000
10,000 Equity Shares of		Stock		75,000
Rs. 100 each	10,00,000	Cash		10,000
Subscribed Capital :		Debtors		85,000
2,000, 8% Pref. Shares of		Preliminary Expenses		20,000
Rs. 100 each	2,00,000	Profit & Loss A/c :		
5,000 Equity Shares of		Balance on 1-1-1982	2,00,000	
Rs. 100 each	5,00,000	*Less* : Profit for the year	40,000	1,60,000
10% Debentures	1,00,000			
Bank Overdraft	40,000			
Creditors	90,000			
	9,30,000			9,30,000

The business was passed through a depression and the worse seems to have been over. The following scheme of reconstruction is adopted with the consent of all and approved by the court :

(i) The preference shares be reduced to Rs. 75 per share fully paid, but the rate of dividend be increased to 15%.

(ii) The equity shares be reduced to Rs. 50 per share fully paid.

(iii) The debentureholders to take over the stock-in-trade in full satisfaction of the amount due to them.

(iv) The amount available be used to write off goodwill, preliminary expenses, profit and loss account balance and depreciate freehold property and machinery by 10% and write off bad debts Rs. 10,000.

(v) The issue of 2,000 equity shares to the public for cash.

(vi) The repayment of bank overdraft.

Pass journal entries to give effect to the above arrangement and prepare the revised balance sheet thereafter.

(Gulbarga, April 1983)

Ans. : Total Capital Reduction Rs. 3,25,000 (*i.e.,* 50,000 + 2,50,000 – 25,000 *i.e.,* 1,00,000 – 75,000); Capital Reserve Rs. 50,000; Cash Rs. 70,000 and Balance Sheet Total Rs. 6,40,000.

(6) The Balance Sheet of Mohan Ltd. as on 31-12-1984 was as follows :

Liabilities	Rs.	Assets	Rs.
Authorised Capital :		Goodwill	90,000
Pref. Shares of Rs. 10 each	1,00,000	Land and Building	1,40,000
Equity Shares of Rs. 10 each	5,00,000	Machinery	37,500
Paid up Capital :		Furniture	15,000
Preference Shares	50,000	Profit & Loss A/c	1,25,000
Equity Shares	2,50,000	Preliminary Expenses	1,000
General Reserve	20,000		
6% Debentures of Rs. 100 each	20,000		
Bank Overdraft	28,500		
Creditors	40,000		
	4,08,500		4,08,500

The capital reduction shame approved by the court is as under :

(1) Holders of 6% debentures of Rs. 100 each are to be given 9% debentures of Rs. 50 each and preference shares of Rs. 10 each of equal amount for the remaining amount of Rs. 50.

(2) The value of all the preference shares including those given to debentureholders as shown above is to be reduced to Rs. 6 and dividend rate is to be increased to 9%.

(3) The value of equity shares be reduced by 80% of its face value.

(4) The existing equity shareholders are to purchase additional equity shares of Rs. 60,000 for cash, to pay off the full amount of bank overdraft and 75% of the creditors.

(5) Machinery and furniture are to be written off in proportion of their book values with the help of general reserve and capital reduction amount.

Pass the necessary journal entries in the books of the company to record the above transactions and also prepare the balance sheet after such changes.

(Mangalore, April 1985 Mod.)

Ans. : Total Capital Reduction Rs. 2,24,000 (Pref. Shares Rs. 24,000 + Equity Shares Rs. 2,00,000) (Excluding general reserve utilised); Cash Rs. 1,500 and Balance Sheet Total Rs. 1,66,000.

Notes : (i) Machinery and furniture are written down in the ratio of 5 : 2 respectively *i.e.,* Rs. 20,000 and Rs. 8,000.

(ii) General reserve is utilised to write off the assets as per the scheme.

(7) The following was the Balance Sheet of progressing Ltd. as on 31st Dec., 1987.

Liabilities		Rs.	Assets		Rs.
Authorised Capital :			Goodwill		10,000
20,000, Equity Shares of			Land and Buildings		20,500
Rs. 10 each		2,00,000	Machinery		50,850
Issued Subscribed and			Preliminary Expenses		1,500
Paid-up Capital :			Stock		10,275
12,000 Equity shares of			Book Debts		15,000
Rs. 10 each	1,20,000		Cash at Bank		1,500
Less : Calls in arrears			Profit and Loss A/c :		
(Rs. 3 per share on			Balance as per last		
3,000 shares)	9,000	1,11,000	Balance Sheet	22,000	
Sundry Creditors		15,425	*Less* : Profit for the year	1,200	20,800
Provision for Taxes		4,000			
		1,30,425			1,30,425

A valuation of machinery reveals that it is overvalued by Rs. 10,000. It is proposed to write down this asset to its true value to extinguish the deficiency in the Profit and Loss Account and to write off Goodwill and Preliminary Expenses by the adoption of the following course :

(1) Forfeit the shares on which the call is outstanding.
(2) Reduce the paid up capital by Rs. 3 per share.
(3) Re-issue the forfeited shares of Rs. 5 per share.
(4) Utilise the provision for taxes, if necessary.

All the above were duly put into action. You are required to give the necessary journal entries and the Balance Sheet of the company after carrying out the terms of the scheme.

(Adapted from Mysore University & Bangalore, April 1997)

Ans. : Total Capital Reduction Rs. 42,300 (*i.e.*, equity shares Rs. 27,000 (12,000 – 3,000 = 9,000 shares of Rs. 3 each) plus credit balance in forfeited shares account Rs. 15,000 (*i.e.*, 3,000 × 5) plus provision for taxes utilised Rs. 3,000); Cash Balance Rs. 16,500 (1,500 + 15,000); Share Capital Rs. 84,000 (12,000 × 7) and Balance Sheet Total Rs. 1,03,125.

Note : (1) Amount required to write off various assets is Rs. 42,300 (20,800 + 1,500 + 10,000). But the actual balance in capital reduction account is Rs. 42,000. Therefore, the required amount of Rs. 300 is transferred from provision for taxes account to capital reduction account.

(2) **Forfeited Shares Account**

To Capital Reduction	15,000	By Equity Share Capital	21,000
To Equity Share Capital (Discount allowed on issue of forfeited share *i.e.*, 3,000 × 2)	6,000	(Amount received on forfeited shares *i.e.*, 3,000 × 7)	
	21,000		21,000

(8) On 31-12-1982 the following balances appearing in the books of Diewalk Co. Ltd. :

Share Capital :		
9,000, 7% Cumulative Pref. Shares of Rs. 100 each	—	9,00,000
1,65,000 Equity Shares of Rs. 10 each	—	16,50,000
Share Premium Account	—	2,40,000
Freehold Premises	15,00,000	—
Plant & Machinery	9,00,000	—
Depreciation Fund :		
For Freehold Premises	—	3,00,000
For Plant & Machinery	—	1,95,000
Goodwill	2,00,000	—

(Contd.)

Stock	2,00,000	–
Sundry Debtors	1,25,000	–
Preliminary Expenses	1,00,000	–
Profit & Loss Account	5,00,000	–
Sundry Creditors	–	2,40,000
	35,25,000	35,25,000

Dividends on preference shares are in arrears as from 1-4-1979. The following terms were settled under a duly appropriated capital reduction scheme :

(a) Preference shares to be reduced to Rs. 80 each and equity shares to Rs. 5 each.

(b) Share premium account is to be written off and depreciation fund account be adjusted to the respective assets.

(c) A liability for the arrears of dividends be created first and then one Rs. 5 equity shares be issued on exchange for every Rs. 10 of gross arrears of preference dividends.

(d) All intangible assets be written off.

(e) Stock be depreciated by 10% and provision for doubtful debts be created at 20% of debtors.

(f) Freehold premises be reduced to Rs. 10,00,000 and the balance on Capital Reduction Account be used for reducing plant & machinery.

Pass journal entries to implement the above scheme and prepare Balance Sheet.

(Karnataka Oct., 1982)

Ans. : Total Capital Reduction Rs. 11,50,500; Plant & Machinery written off by Rs. 1,05,500; Freehold premises written off by Rs. 2,00,000 and Balance Sheet Total Rs. 18,79,500.

Note : Capital reduction is calculated as below :

On Equity Shares (1,65,000 × 5)	8,25,000
On Pref. Shares (9,000 × 20)	1,80,000
Share Premium transferred	2,40,000
	12,45,000
Less : Dividend adjusted (63,000 × 3)	1,89,000
	10,56,000
Add : Dividend sacrificed $\left(1,89,000 \times \frac{5}{10}\right)$	94,500
Total Capital Reduction	11,50,500

(9) The following is the Balance Sheet of Ajit And Co. Ltd. as at 31-12-1989 :

Liabilities	Rs.	Assets	Rs.
Share Capital :		Goodwill	40,000
Authorised :		Building	90,000
1,00,000 Equity Shares of		Machinery	3,75,000
Rs. 10 each	10,00,000	Patents	45,000
2,000, 12% Pref. shares of		Furniture	30,000
Rs. 100 each	2,00,000	Stock	1,45,000
Subscribed & Paid up :		Debtors	90,000
50,000 Equity shares of		Cash at Bank	10,000
Rs. 10 each	5,00,000	Preliminary Expenses	30,000
1,000, 12% Pref. Shares of		Profit and Loss Account	1,55,000
Rs. 100 each	1,00,000		
9% Debentures	2,50,000		
Secured Loan	75,000		
(mortgaged on building)			
Creditors (unsecured)	85,000		
	10,10,000		10,10,000

The company suffered heavy losses and was not getting on well. The board of directors in the meeting of creditors and shareholders decided to adopt the following scheme of reconstruction :

(a) Equity shares of Rs. 10 each be reduced to Rs. 3 per share paid up and further agreed to pay a call money of Rs. 2 per share. The amount was received from all shareholders.

(b) 12% preference shares of Rs. 100 each were reduced by Rs. 25 per share.

(c) 9% debentureholders have agreed to accept new 11% debentures of the amount of Rs. 2,25,000 by concelling the old debentures.

(d) Secured loan amount was paid at 80% of their claims. For this purpose mortgaged building was sold for Rs. 95,000.

(e) The amount available as a result of the above scheme of capital reduction is utilised to write off :

(1) All the fictitious assets including goodwill and patents,

(2) The remaining assets were revalued as follows :

Machinery less by 20%

Furniture less by 25%

Stock was valued at Rs. 1,10,000

Provision on debtors at 5% be created.

Pass the journal entries to give effect to the above in the books of the company and prepare the new balance sheet.

(Karnataka, April 1991)

Ans. : Capital Reserve Rs. 28,000; Cash Balance Rs. 1,45,000 (10,000 + 1,00,000 + 95,000 – 60,000) ; Total Capital Reduction Rs. 4,20,000 and Balance Sheet Total Rs. 6,63,000.

Notes : (i) Capital reduction includes equity shares Rs. 3,50,000; Pref. Shares Rs. 25,000; Debentures Rs. 25,000; Secured loan Rs. 15,000 and Profit on building Rs. 5,000.

(ii) Profit on sale of building may also be credited directly to capital reserve.

(10) The position of Noble Ltd. on 31st March, 1987 was as follows :

20,000 Equity shares of Rs. 100 each	20,00,000
1,000, 6% Debentures of Rs. 1,000 each	10,00,000
Interest on above	1,20,000
Creditors	5,00,000
Fixed Assets	20,00,000
Current Assets	6,50,000

The fixed assets on that date were revalued as Rs. 9,60,000 and current assets at Rs. 4,80,000.

The following steps were taken with the approval of all concerned :

(1) The shares were subdivided into shares of Rs. 5 each and 90% of the shares were surrendered.

(2) The total claims of the debentureholders were reduced to Rs. 4,90,000 and in consideration of this, they were also allotted shares (out of the surrendered shares) amounting to Rs. 2,50,000.

(3) The creditors agreed to reduce their claims to Rs. 3,00,000, ½ of which was satisfied by the issue of equity shares out of those surrendered.

(4) The shares surrendered but not reissued were cancelled.

Draft journal entries and give the balance sheet of the company after the reconstruction.

(Adapted from Mysore University, April 1981)

Ans. : Total capital reduction Rs. 23,80,000; Capital Reserve Rs. 2,00,000; P & L A/c to be written off as per old B/S Rs. 9,70,000 (*i.e.*, Liabilities Rs. 36,20,000 – Rs. 26,50,000 assets); Share Capital Rs. 5,50,000 (Rs. 2,00,000 + 3,50,000 = 5,50,000 *i.e.*, 1,10,000 equity shares of Rs. 5 each) and Balance Sheet Total Rs. 14,40,000.

Notes : (i)

Dr. **Surrendered Shares Account** Cr.

	Rs.		Rs.
To Equity Share Capital (Rs. 5) (issue of Rs. 2,50,000 equity shares to debenture-holders and Rs. 1,00,000 to creditors out of surrendered shares)	3,50,000	By Equity Share Capital (Rs. 5) (Surrender of 90% equity shares of Rs. 5 each)	18,00,000
To Capital Reduction/ Reconstruction (Transfer of remaining surrendered shares cancelled)	14,50,000		
	18,00,000		18,00,000

(ii)

Dr. **Capital Reduction or Reconstruction Account** Cr.

	Rs.		Rs.
To P & L A/c (36,20,000 – 26,50,000)	9,70,000	By 6% Debentures (6,30,000 – 1,20,000)	5,10,000
To Fixed Assets (20,00,000 – 9,60,000)	10,40,000	By Outstanding Interest on Debenture	1,20,000
To Current Assets (6,50,000 – 4,80,000)	1,70,000	By Creditors (5,00,000 – 2,00,000)	3,00,000
To Capital Reserve (Balance transferred)	2,00,000	By Surrendered Shares	14,50,000
	23,80,000		23,80,000

(11) The following is the Balance Sheet of Weak Ltd. as on 31st December, 1986.

Liabilities	Rs.	Assets	Rs.
13% Cumulative Pref. Shares of Rs. 100 each	1,00,000	Fixed Assets	15,00,000
		Current Assets	35,00,000
Equity Shares of Rs. 10 each	7,00,000	Profit & Loss Account	3,00,000
8% Debentures	3,00,000		
Current Liabilities	39,00,000		
Provision for Taxation	3,00,000		
	53,00,000		53,00,000

The following scheme of re-organisation is sanctioned :

(1) Fixed assets are to be written down by $33^1/_3$%.

(2) Current assets are to be revalued at Rs. 27,00,000.

(3) Preference shareholders decide to forego their right to arrears of dividend which are in arrears for three years.

(4) The taxation liability is settled at Rs. 4,00,000.

(5) One of the creditors of the company, to whom the company owes Rs. 25,00,000, decides to forego 50% of this claim. He is allotted 1,00,000 equity shares of Rs. 5 each in part satisfaction of the balance of his claim.

(6) The rate of interest on debenture is increased to 11%. The debentureholders surrender their existing debentures of Rs. 100 each and exchange the same for fresh debentures of Rs. 75 each.

(7) All existing equity shares are reduced to Rs. 5 each.

(8) All preference shares are reduced to Rs. 75 each.

Pass journal entries and show the balance sheet of the company after giving effect to the above.

(Bangalore Nov., 1994)

Ans. : Total Capital Reduction or Reconstruction Rs. 16,00,000 (Equity shares Rs. 3,50,000 + Pref. Shares Rs. 25,000 + Creditors Rs. 12,50,000 + 8% Debentures Rs. 75,000 + Additional Provision for taxation Rs. 1,00,000); Provision for Taxation Rs. 4,00,000 (3,00,000 + 1,00,000); Share Capital Rs. 9,25,000 (Equity Rs. 8,50,000 + Pref. Rs. 75,000); 11% Debentures Rs. 2,25,000 (3,000 × 75) and Balance Sheet Total Rs. 37,00,000.

Note : Arrears of preference dividend is a contingent liability. Therefore, the arrears of pref. dividend foregone by the pref. shareholder is not a gain to the company. Hence, no entry should be passed for the arrears of pref. dividend foregone or cancelled by the pref. shareholders.

(12) The Balance Sheet of The Awakened Ltd. on 31 December, 1986 was as follows :

Liabilities	Rs.	Assets		Rs.
Capital :		Cash		50,000
18,000 Shares of Rs. 100		Goodwill		1,00,000
each Rs. 50 paid	9,00,000	Machinery		2,00,000
Debentures	4,50,000	Stock		50,000
Interest Due on Debentures	50,000	Debtors		1,50,000
Creditors	5,50,000	P & L Account	15,00,000	
		Less : Profit for 1986	1,00,000	14,00,000
	19,50,000			19,50,000

The machinery is worth only rupees one lakh. The company having become profit earning, the directors are anxious to construct the company, and both the debentureholders and the creditors are prepared to forego a reasonable part of their claims. The uncalled capital is to be called in full. Give a scheme of reconstruction which is in your opinion most equitable and pass the necessary journal entries and show the reconstructed Balance Sheet.

(Adapted from Mysore University)

Ans. : Share Capital Rs. 2,70,000 (18,000 × 15); Cash Balance Rs. 9,50,000 (50,000 + 9,00,000); Balance Sheet Total Rs. 12,50,000 and Capital Reduction of Reconstruction Rs. 16,00,000 (*i.e.*, shareholders Rs. 15,30,000 + Debentureholders Rs. 33,333 + Creditors Rs. 36,667).

Note : The total amount of losses to be written off is Rs. 16,00,000 (*i.e.,* P & L A/c Rs. 14,00,000 + Goodwill Rs. 1,00,000 + Dep. on Machinery Rs. 1,00,000). The major part of the entire amount of losses should be borne by the shareholders and reasonable part should be borne by the debentureholders and creditors. Therefore, the shareholders should forego a major part of their share capital *i.e.*, say; 85% of their share capital *i.e.*, 15,30,000 (18,00,000 × $^{85}/_{100}$). The remaining part Rs. 70,000 (16,00,000 – 15,30,000) should be borne by the debentureholders and creditors in the ratio of the total amount due to them *i.e.,* 10 : 11 or 5,00,000 : 5,50,000. Hence, the amount to be foregone by the debentureholders will be Rs. 33,333 and creditors will be Rs. 36,667.

(13) The following is the balance sheet of Pickwick Ltd. as on 31-12-1993 :

Liabilities	Rs.	Assets	Rs.
Share Capital :		Goodwill	1,94,000
30,000 Pref. Shares of		Buildings	3,13,000
Rs. 10 each	3,00,000	Machinery	1,56,000
40,000 Ordinary Shares of		Debtors	64,000
Rs. 10 each	4,00,000	Stock	1,05,000
Reserve Fund	22,000	Bank	6,600
9% Debentures	1,50,000	Profit & Loss Account	1,94,000
Creditors	1,60,600		
	10,32,600		10,32,600

The company suffered heavy losses and found that goodwill was worthless and the assets were overvalued to the following extent :

Building Rs. 53,000, Machinery Rs. 46,000 and Stock Rs. 13,000. A provision for doubtful debts at 5% was necessary.

The following scheme of reconstruction was adopted :

(a) The creditors to accept 9% debentures to the extent of half of their dues and the balance to be paid six months after date.

(b) The preference shares to be reduced to Rs. 5 each.

(c) The assets to be reduced to the revalued figures and the debits balance to profit and loss account to be wiped out.

(d) The ordinary shares be reduced to shares of Re. 1 each. Draft the journal entries to give effect to the above scheme and prepare the reconstructed balance sheet.

(Karnataka, April 1985)

Ans. : Total Capital Reduction Rs. 5,10,000 (Pref. Shares Rs. 1,50,000 + Ordinary Shares Rs. 3,60,000); Capital Reserve Rs. 6,800; Reserve Fund Rs. 22,000; Debentures Rs. 2,30,300; Creditors Rs. 80,300 and Balance Sheet Total Rs. 5,29,400.

(14) The following is the Balance Sheet of P. Ltd. as on 31-12-1990 :

Liabilities	Rs.	Assets	Rs.
Share Capital :		Goodwill	60,000
2,000, Pref. Shares of		Buildings	1,10,000
Rs. 100 each	2,00,000	Machinery	80,000
2,000, Equity Shares of		Patents	40,000
Rs. 100 each	2,00,000	Stock	80,000
10% Debentures	1,00,000	Debtors	50,000
Bank Overdraft	10,000	Cash	1,10,000
Creditors	50,000	Preliminary Expenses	20,000
Bills Payable	40,000	Profit & Loss Account	50,000
	6,00,000		6,00,000

The following scheme of reconstruction is sanctioned :

(a) The preference shares be reduced to an equal number of shares of Rs. 50 each fully paid.

(b) The equity shares be reduced to an equal number of shares of Rs. 60 each fully paid.

(c) The debentureholders to take over the stock in full satisfaction of the amount due to them.

(d) The amount so available is utilised to write off goodwill, patents, preliminary expenses and profit & loss account completely. Rs. 10,000 to be written off; buildings and the balance available is used to write off machinery.

(e) The bank overdraft is repaid.

Pass the journal entries and show the balance sheet of the company after giving effect to the above.

(Gulbarga, April 1986 & 1996)

Ans. : Total Capital Reduction Rs. 2,00,000 (Pref. Shares Rs. 1,00,000 + Equity Shares Rs. 80,000 + Debentureholders Rs. 20,000); Machinery written off by Rs. 20,000 and Balance Sheet Total Rs. 3,10,000.

(15) The position of Darbar Co. Ltd. on 31st March, 1988 was as follows :

Liabilities	Rs.	Assets	Rs.
20,000 Equity Shares of		Goodwill	80,000
Rs. 10 each fully paid	2,00,000	Land & Building	1,75,000
15,000, 7% Pref. Shares of		Plant & Machinery	3,25,000
Rs. 10 each fully paid	1,50,000	Patents & Designs	54,000
13,000, 5% Pref. Shares of		Furniture & Fittings	15,000
Rs. 10 each Rs. 5 paid	65,000	Investments	75,000
5% Debenture Stock	1,50,000	Sundry Debtors	4,15,000
5% Debenture of Rs. 100 each	3,00,000	Cash in hand & at Bank	20,000
Sundry Creditors	4,50,000	Profit and Loss A/c	1,75,500
Interest Due on debentures	19,500		
	13,34,500		13,34,500

The following scheme of reconstruction was submitted and approved by the court :

(a) Equity shares of Rs. 10 each were reduced to the denomination of Rs. 5 each fully paid.

(b) 7% Preference shares of Rs. 10 each fully paid were reduced to 6% preference shares of Rs. 10 each, Rs. 6 per share paid.

(c) 5% Preference shares of Rs. 10 each, Rs. 5 paid per share, were reduced to 4½% preference shares of Rs. 10 each, Rs. 3 paid per share.

In view of the unsatisfactory state of affairs of the company, the Debentureholders agreed to forego the interest due to debentures. The company meanwhile recovered as damages a sum of Rs. 45,000 from a third party and it was decided to utilise this sum to write off the capital losses. The reconstruction expenses were Rs. 2,250.

Make the Journal Entries recording the transactions and draw up the Balance Sheet there after.

(Shivaji, May 1980 and Bangalore, April 1996)

Ans. : Total Capital Reduction Rs. 2,50,500; Share Capital 2,29,000 (1,00,000 + 90,000 + 39,000); and Balance Total Rs. 11,29,000.

Note :

Dr. **Capital Reduction Account** Cr.

	Rs.		Rs.
To Reconstruction Expenses	2,250	By Equity Share Capital	1,00,000
To Profit and Loss A/c	1,75,500	By 7% Pref. Share Capital	60,000
To Goodwill	72,750	By 5% Pref. Share Capital	26,000
(Balance written off)		By Interest on Debentures	19,500
		By Bank (Amount recovered as damages)	45,000
	2,50,500		2,50,500

(16) The position of a company on 31-12-1991 was as follows :

Liabilities	Rs.
(1) 20,000 Equity shares of Rs. 100 each	20,00,000
(2) 1,000, 6% Debentures of Rs. 100 each	10,00,000
(3) Interest Due on Debentures	1,20,000
Total Liabilities	31,20,000

The Book value of all the Fixed Assets and Current Assets of the company was Rs. 9,40,000. The following was the scheme approved by the court :

(a) The existing shares to be converted into shares of Rs. 5 each and 90% of these new shares to be surrendered by the shareholders.

(b) The total amount due to the debentureholders to be satisfied as follows :

(i) Issue of new 8% Debentures for Rs. 4,90,000.

(ii) Issue of new equity shares of Rs. 5 each for Rs. 2,50,000. (Out of the surrendered Shares)

(c) Shares surrendered and not issued to the debentureholders to be cancelled.

(d) Accumulated losses to be written off.

Draft suitable journal entries for the above details.

(Bangalore Univ., Second Year B.Com., April 1992 (1989-90 onwards))

Ans. : Accumulated losses of the company Rs. 21,80,000 (*i.e.*, total liabilities Rs. 31,20,000 – total assets Rs. 9,40,000); Capital reduction amount total Rs. 21,80,000 (6,30,000 + 15,50,000).

Note :

Dr. **Surrendered Shares Account** Cr.

	Rs.		Rs.
To Equity Share Capital	2,50,000	By Equity Share Capital	18,00,000
To Capital Reduction	15,50,000		
	18,00,000		18,00,000

(17) Following is the Balance Sheet of Venus Ltd.:

Balance Sheet as on 31-12-1997

Liabilities	Rs.	Assets	Rs.
Preference Share Capital :		Buildings	50,000
15,000 Shares of Rs. 5	75,000	Stock	1,00,000
Ordinary Share Capital :		Debtors	1,15,000
30,000 Shares of Rs. 5	1,50,000	Investments	35,000
Debentures	50,000	Deficiency	75,000
Loan Creditors	25,000		
(Secured by Investments)			
Trade Creditors	75,000		
	3,75,000		3,75,000

The company was reconstructed on the following lines :

1. Loan creditors are to be paid off by selling investments which realised Rs. 35,000.
2. Trade creditors agree to accept preference shares of Rs. 5 to the extent of two-thirds of their dues in full satisfaction.
3. The preference shares are to be reduced to shares of Rs. 3 each fully paid.
4. The ordinary shares are to be reduced to shares of Rs. 3 each and shareholders are to pay Rs. 2 per share making the shares again Rs. 5 fully paid.

Prepare Capital Reduction Account and the Reconstructed Balance Sheet of Venus Ltd.

(Bangalore Univ., Second Year B.Com., Nov. 1996 [1989-90 onwards])

Ans. : Reconstructed Balance Sheet Total Rs. 3,35,000; Capital Reserve Rs. 60,000 (Trade Creditors Rs. 25,000 + Pref. Shares Rs. 50,000 + Ordinary Shares Rs. 60,000 – Deficiency Rs. 75,000); Capital Reduction A/c Total Rs. 1,35,000; Bank Balance Rs. 70,000 (Investments Rs. 35,000 + Ordinary Share Capital Rs. 60,000 – Loan Creditors Rs. 25,000). No. of preference shares 25,000 (*i.e.*, No. of Shares before reconstruction 15,000 + No. of Share issued to creditors 10,000).

(18) The following is Balance Sheet of Shiva Ltd. as on 31-12-1997 :

Liabilities	Rs.	Assets	Rs.
30,000 Pref. Shares of		Goodwill	97,000
Rs. 5 each	1,50,000	Buildings	1,56,500
40,000 Ordinary Shares of		Machinery	78,000
Rs. 5 each	2,00,000	Debtors	32,000
Reserve Fund	11,000	Stock	52,500
9% Debentures	75,000	Bank	3,300
Creditors	80,300	Profit and Loss	97,000
	5,16,300		5,16,300

The company suffered heavy losses and found that goodwill was worthless and that assets were overvalued to the following extent :

Buildings Rs. 26,500; Machinery Rs. 23,000; Stock Rs. 6,500. A provision for doubtful debt at 5% was necessary.

The following schemes of reconstruction was adopted :

(a) The creditors to accept 9% debentures to the extent of half their dues and their balance to be paid six months after date.

(b) The preference shares to be reduced to Rs. 2.50 each.

(c) The assets to be reduced to the revalued figures and profit and loss account debit balance be wiped out.

(d) Ordinary share be reduced to Re. 0.50 each.

Draft the Journal Entries for giving effect to the above scheme and prepare the reconstructed Balance Sheet.

(Karnataka, April 1998)

Ans. : Total Capital Reduction Rs. 2,55,000; Capital Reserve (B.F.) Rs. 3,400; 9% Debentures Rs. 1,15,150 (75,000 + 40,150 issued to creditors); Creditors Rs. 40,150 and Balance Sheet Total Rs. 2,64,700.

Hint : Goodwill and profit and loss account balance are wiped out.

******

6

LIQUIDATION OF COMPANIES

Meaning and Definition

A company comes into existence through a legal process and as such, it can come to an end only through the process of law. The legal process by which a company is come to an end, is called 'liquidation or winding up'. It is a legal process by which a company closes its business and disposes of its assets to pay off its liabilities. When a company is wound up (*i.e.,* closed down), its assets are realised or disposed off, liabilities are paid off and surplus if any, is distributed among the members (*i.e.,* shareholders) in accordance with their rights.

According to **Prof. Gower** "Winding up of a company is the process whereby its life is ended and its property administered for the benefit of its creditors and members. An administrator called a liquidator, is appointed and takes control of the company, collects its assets, pay its debts and finally distributes any surplus among the members in accordance with their rights."

The company need not be wound up only on the grounds of insolvency or bankruptcy. Even a solvent (financially sound) company may be wound up on attaining its objects of formation. The following are the main reasons for the winding up of a company :

(1) When the company has become insolvent.

(2) When the company has been sold to another company.

(3) When the company has fulfilled the objects of formation.

(4) When the company has found it impossible to fulfil its main objects.

Modes of Liquidation or Winding up

There are three types or methods of liquidation, they are :

(1) Voluntary winding up.

(2) Winding up under the supervision of the court.

(3) Compulsory winding up.

(1) Voluntary Winding up. When the members and creditors of a company come to a compromise and decide to dissolve their company without the interference of the court, it is called voluntary winding up. Voluntary winding up takes place in the following circumstances :

(i) When the duration of the company is expired.

(ii) When the objects of the company are completed.

(iii) When the company passes a special resolution for the voluntary winding up.

There are two types of voluntary winding up namely : (i) Members voluntary winding up and (ii) Creditors voluntary winding up. When a company is solvent and capable to pay off its liability in full, the company can wind up by the members themselves without consulting the creditors. Such a winding up is called 'Members voluntary winding up'. In the case of 'members voluntary winding up', the board of directors of the company must make a declaration of solvency of the company and file it with the registrar along with the statement of company's assets and liabilities. When a company is not solvent, the company will be wound up by the decision taken at the meeting of the creditors which is convened by the company. Such a winding up is called creditors voluntary winding up.

(2) Voluntary Winding up under the Supervision of the Court. When a company is being wound up voluntarily either by the members or the creditors, the members or the creditors of the company request the court to pass an order for winding up under the supervision of the court, such a winding up is called voluntary winding up under the supervision of the court. In this case, the company should pass a special resolution for the voluntary winding up and present the application to the court to pass an order for winding up under the supervision of the court on the ground of fraud or irregularities in the voluntary winding up. Then, the court may pass an order that the voluntary winding up of a company should be under its supervision. When the court passes such an order, it can exercise full control over the company. The court passes such an order to protect the interests of the company, members and creditors.

(3) Compulsory Winding up. Winding up of a company by an order of the court is known as compulsory winding up. The court will issue the order of winding up only if a written petition for winding up is made to it. The petition for winding up may be made by the company itself or by the creditors or by the contributories (*i.e.,* members) or by the registrar of companies or by the central government. After the receipt of the petition from the above parties, the court studies the reasons for winding up and if the court is convinced that it is just and proper that the company should be wound up, it will issue the order for the same. Compulsory winding up takes place in the following circumstances :

(i) The company has passed a special resolution that it should be wound up by the court.

(ii) If the company has failed to hold the statutory meeting or file the statutory report.

(iii) If the number of members falls below the statutory minimum limit.

(iv) If the company is unable to pay its debts.

(v) If the company fails to commence business within one year of incorporation or if it suspends its business for one year.

(vi) If the object of the company is fraudulent.

(vii) If the court is of the opinion that it is just and equitable that the company should be wound up.

Liquidator

The person who is appointed to liquidate or wind up the affairs of the company, is called liquidator. He will carry out the necessary formalities of liquidation in accordance with the provisions of the companies act. He has to consult with the members and creditors of a company. He is entitled to receive remuneration for his services.

In case of voluntary winding up, the liquidator is appointed by the members or the creditors depending upon the members or the creditors voluntary winding up. In case of winding up under the supervision of the court, the liquidator is appointed by the members or by both the members and creditors. In this case, the court can appoint new liquidator in the place of liquidator appointed by the members or creditors or the court can appoint an additional liquidator. The liquidator appointed by the court may together carry on the liquidation proceedings. In case of compulsory winding up, the official liquidator attached to the high court, functions as liquidator of the company.

The liquidator, whether appointed by the members or by the creditors or by the court, performs the following mainfunctions :

(i) He realises all the assets of the company.

(ii) He collects the amounts due from the contributories.

(iii) He distributes the sale of assets and the amount collected from the contributories in the following order :

(a) Secured creditors upto their claims or upto the amount realised from the sale of assets held by them, whichever is less.

(b) His remuneration.

(c) Cost and expenses of winding up.

(d) Preferential creditors.

(e) Debentures or other creditors holding a floating charge.

(f) Unsecured creditors.

(g) Surplus if any, among the shareholders as per their rights.

(iv) He submits the records of receipts and payments to the company in case of voluntary winding up and to the court in case of compulsory winding up.

Contributories

The term 'Contributory' means any person liable to contribute to the asset of the company in the event of its being wound up. It includes present as well as past shareholders. The contributories are classified into two lists—List-'A' which includes the present members of the company as appearing in register of members. List-'B' which includes the past members who have ceased to be the members within one year from the date of commencement of winding up. The liability of past shareholders arises only when the present members are unable to bring the required contributions and debts incurred by the company. The liability of past shareholders is limited to the extent of the amount remaining unpaid on their shares only to meet the debts created during their membership.

Steps in the Accounting Procedure of Liquidation

The following are the mains steps to be followed in the accounting procedure of winding up :

(a) Statement of Affairs and Deficiency/Surplus Account. This is prepared and submitted by the officers and directors to the official liquidator in case of compulsory liquidation and to the Registrar of Companies in case of voluntary liquidation.

(b) Liquidator's Final Statement of Account. This is prepared and submitted by the liquidator to the court in case of compulsory liquidation and to the company in case of voluntary liquidation.

Each of these stages or steps is being explained in the following pages.

(A) Statement of Affairs and Deficiency/Surplus Account

Statement of Affairs

When a company is wound up by an order of court or when the official liquidator has been appointed by the court as provisional liquidator, the officers and directors of the company must submit a statement of affairs within 21 days of passing the winding up order or within such extended time, not exceeding 3 months, as the official liquidator or the court may permit. The statement should be submitted to the liquidator. The statement should contain the following particulars :

(1) The assets of the company.
(2) The debts and liabilities of the company.
(3) The particulars of secured and unsecured creditors
(4) The particulars of debtors and the amount likely to be realised from them.
(5) Other information as may be prescribed by the central government or official liquidator may require.

The statement of affairs must be prepared in the prescribed form and must be verified by an affidavit and signed by one or more of the directors and manager, secretary or other chief officers of the company. The simplified form of the statement of affairs is given below :

STATEMENT OF AFFAIRS AS ON.......

Assets					Estimated realisable Value Rs.
Assets not specifically pledged (As per list "A")					
Cash in hand/Cash at Bank					xxxx
Trade Debtors					xxxx
Bills Receivable					xxxx
Stock-in-Trade					xxxx
Loans and Advances					xxxx
Freehold/Leasehold property					xxxx
Land and Building					xxxx
Plant, Machinery, Furniture, Fittings etc.					xxxx
Other property, other assets etc.					xxxx
Assets specifically pledged (As per List 'B')					
	(a) Estimated realisable values Rs.	(b) Due to secured creditors Rs.	(c) Deficiency ranking as unsecured Rs.	(d) Surplus carried to last column Rs.	
Freehold property	xxx	xxx	xxx	xxx	
--------------------	xxx	xxx	xxx	xxx	
--------------------	xxx	xxx	xxx	xxx	
	xxx	xxx	xxx	xxx	
Estimated surplus from Assets specifically pledged					xxx
Estimated total assets available for preferential creditors, debenture-holders secured by floating charge and unsecured creditors (carried forward)					xxxx

Summary of Gross Assets

Gross realisable value of assets specifically pledged	xxxx	
Other assets	xxxx	
Gross Assets	xxxx	

Gross Liabilities	Liabilities		
Rs.	(to be deducted from surplus or added to deficiency)		
xxxx	**Secured Creditors** (As per List 'B') to the extent to which claims are estimated to be covered by assets specifically pledged		–
xxxx	**Preferential creditors** (As per list 'C')		xxxx
	Estimated balance of assets available for debenture holders secured by a floating charge and unsecured creditors		xxxx
xxxx	**Debentureholders secured by a floating charge** (As per List 'D')		xxxx
	Estimated Surplus/Deficiency as regards "Debentureholders"		xxx
	Unsecured Creditors (As per List 'E')		
xxx	(i) Estimated unsecured balance of claims of creditors partly secured on specific assets	xxx	
xxx	(ii) Trade creditors	xxx	
xxx	(iii) Bills payable	xxx	
xxx	(iv) Outstanding/other creditors	xxx	x x x
xxxx	Estimated Surplus/Deficiency as regards **"Creditors"** (Difference between gross assets and gross liabilities)		xxx
	Issued and Called up Capital		
	Preference Share Capital (As per List 'F')	xxxx	
	Equity Share Capital (As per List 'G')	xxxx	xxxxx
	Estimated Surplus/Deficiency as regards "Contributories" (As per List 'H')		xxxx

Lists to be attached to the statement of Affairs

List 'A' gives a complete list of assets which are not specifically pledged to any of the creditors.

List 'B' gives a list of assets which are specifically pledged either to fully secured or partly secured creditors.

List 'C' is a list of preferential creditors and the amount due.

List 'D' is a list of debentureholders having a floating charge.

List 'E' contains the names of unsecured creditors and the amount due.

List 'F' gives a list of preference shareholders and shares held by them.

List 'G' gives a list of equity shareholders and the shares held by them.

List 'H' is a statement showing how the deficiency or surplus in the statement of affairs has been brought about.

Procedure in the preparation of Statement of Affairs

(1) Take all the assets, which are not specifically pledged at their realisable values.

(2) Add to the above assets, any surplus expected from securities in the hands of the creditors.

(3) From the total as obtained by adding 1 and 2, first deduct preferential creditors, then creditors having a floating charge and then unsecured creditors.

(4) After having deducted the unsecured creditors, deduct from the remaining surplus (or add to the deficiency) the amount of share capital.

(5) The balance left will be the surplus or deficiency.

Deficiency/Surplus Account (As per List 'H')

The deficiency or surplus stated in the statement of affairs has to be proved by another statement called "Deficiency or Surplus Account". This statement was previously in the form of a ledger account. But now the items contributing to deficiency are listed first, followed by items reducing deficiency. The difference between the totals is the deficiency or surplus. This must tally with the amount of deficiency or surplus stated in the statement of affairs. The prescribed form is given below.

List 'H' Deficiency or Surplus Account

Items contributing to Deficiency or Reducing Surplus :	Rs.	Rs.
1. Excess (if any) of capital and liabilities over assets	xxx	
2. Net dividends and bonuses declared during the period from..............20........ to the date of statement	xxx	
3. Net trading losses (after charging items shown in note below) for the same period.	xxx	
4. Losses other than trading losses written off or for which provision has been made in the books during the same period.	xxx	
5. Estimated losses now written off or for which provision has been made for the purpose of preparing the statement.	xxx	
6. Other items contributing to Deficiency or reducing surplus.	xxx	xxxx
7. Excess (if any) of assets over capital and liabilities	xxx	

Contd.

Items contributing to Deficiency or Reducing Surplus :		
8. Net trading profits (after charging items shown in note below) for the period from ....20...... to the date of statement.	XXX	
9. Profit and income other than trading profits during the same period.	XXX	
10. Other items reducing deficiency or contributing to surplus	XXX	XXXX
Deficiency or **Surplus** (as shown by the Statement of Affairs)		XXX

Note as to Net Trading Profits and Losses

		Rs.
1. Provisions for depreciation, renewals or diminution in value of fixed assets		XXX
2. Charges for Indian Income-tax and other Indian Taxation on profits		XXX
3. Interest on debentures and other fixed loans		XXX
4. Payments to directors made by the company and required by the law to be disclosed in the accounts		XXX
5. Exceptional or non-recurring expenditure	XXX	
Less : Exceptional or non-recurring receipts	XXX	XXX
6. Balance, being other trading profits or losses		XXX
Net trading profits or losses as shown in Deficiency or Surplus Account above		XXX

Note : In the case of members voluntary winding up, the statement of affairs and deficiency/surplus account should be prepared and submitted by the board of directors to the registrar of joint stock companies. But, it is to be prepared on the same lines as in the case of compulsory winding up.

Illustration 1

The following information is extracted from the books of Vikram Limited company on 31st Dec., 1996 on which date a winding up order was made :

	Rs.
Equity share capital, 40,000 shares of Rs. 10 each	4,00,000
10% Preference share capital, 6,000 shares of Rs. 100 each	6,00,000
Calls in arrears on equity shares (estimated to produce Rs. 4,000)	8,000
9% First Mortgage Debentures, secured by a floating charge on the whole of the assets of the company	4,00,000
Creditors fully secured (value of shares in 'A' Ltd. Rs. 80,000)	70,000
Creditors partly secured (value of shares in 'B' Ltd. Rs. 40,000)	80,000
Preferential Creditors	15,000
Bank overdraft secured by a second charge on the whole of the assets of the company	40,000

Unsecured creditors		5,20,000
Estimated liability on bills discounted		20,000
Freehold Land and Buildings (estimated to produce Rs. 3,91,000)		3,30,000
Plant and Machinery (estimated to produce Rs. 1,06,000)		1,50,000
Fixtures and Fittings (estimated to produce Rs. 15,000)		25,000
Stock-in-Trade (estimated to produce Rs. 1,19,350)		1,44,000
Book Debts :	Rs.	
Good	75,000	
Doubtful (estimated to produce 40%)	15,000	
Bad	9,000	99,000
Cash in hand		4,050

You are required to prepare a Statement of Affairs.

(B. Com., M.K.U. Nov., 1997)

Solution :

VIKRAM LIMITED

Statement of Affairs as on December 31, 1996

Assets	Estimated Realisable Value
Assets not specifically pledged (As per list 'A')	Rs.
Cash in hand	4,050
Trade Debtors (Rs. 75,000 + 6,000)	81,000
Unpaid Calls	4,000
Stock-in-Trade	1,19,350
Freehold Land and Buildings	3,91,000
Plant & Machinery	1,06,000
Fixtures and Fitting	15,000
	7,20,400

Assets specifically pledged (As per List 'B')

	Estimated realisable value	Due to secured creditors	Deficiency ranking as unsecured	Surplus carried to last column
	Rs.	Rs.	Rs.	Rs.
Shares in 'A' Ltd.	80,000	70,000	–	10,000
Shares in 'B' Ltd.	40,000	80,000	40,000	–
	1,20,000	1,50,000	40,000	10,000

Estimated surplus from assets specifically pledged	10,000
Estimated total assets available for preferential creditors, debenture holders secured by floating charge and unsecured creditors (b/fd)	7,30,400

Contd

Summary of Gross Assets

Gross realisable value of assets specifically pledged	1,20,000
Other assets	7,20,400
Gross Assets	8,40,400

Gross Liabilities	Liabilities (To be deducted from surplus or added to deficiency as the case may be)		
1,10,000	**Secured creditors** (As per List 'B') to the extent to which claims are estimated to be covered by assets specifically pledged		–
15,000	**Preferential Creditors** (As per List 'C')		15,000
	Estimated balance of assets available for debenture holders secured by a floating charge and unsecured creditors		7,15,400
4,00,000	**Debentures holders secured by a floating charge** (As per list 'D')		4,00,000
			3,15,400
40,000	**Bank overdraft secured by a second floating charge** (As per list 'D')		40,000
			2,75,400
	Estimated Surplus/Deficiency as regards **Debenture Holders and Bank**		
	Unsecured Creditors (As per List 'E')		
	(i) Estimated unsecured balance of claims of creditors partly secured on specific assets	40,000	
	(ii) Unsecured creditors	5,20,000	
5,80,000	(iii) Liability on bills discounted	20,000	5,80,000
11,45,000	Estimated deficiency as regards **'creditors'**, being the difference between gross liabilities and gross assets		3,04,600
	Issued and Called up Capital		
	6,000 10% Preference shares of Rs. 100 each fully paid up (As per List 'F')		6,00,000
	40,000 Equity shares of Rs. 10 each fully paid up (As per List 'G')	4,00,000	
	Less : Irrecoverable unpaid calls	4,000	3,96,000
	Estimated deficiency as regards members or contributories (as per List 'H')		13,00,600

Illustration 2

Shri S. Somashekar is appointed liquidator of a company in voluntary liquidation on 1st July, 1996, and the following balances are extracted from the books on that date :

	Rs.		Rs.
Capital :		Machinery	30,000
16,000 Shares of 5 each	80,000	Lease hold properties	40,000
Reserve for Bad Debts	10,000	Stock in trade	1,000
Debentures	50,000	Book Debts	60,000
Bank Overdraft	18,000	Investments	6,000
Liabilities for purchases	20,000	Calls in Arrears	5,000
		Cash in hand	1,000
		Profit & Loss A/c	35,000
	1,78,000		1,78,000

The machinery is valued at Rs. 60,000, the leasehold properties at Rs. 73,000, investments at Rs. 4,000, Stock in Trade at Rs. 2,000, bad debts are Rs. 2,000, doubtful debts are Rs. 4,000, estimated to realise Rs. 2,000. The Bank overdraft is secured by deposit of title deeds of leasehold properties. Preferential creditors for taxes and wages Rs. 1,000. Telephone rent owing is Rs. 80. You are required to make out (1) Statement of Affairs as regards creditors and contributories and (2) Deficiency or Surplus Account.

(B.Com., Madras, Nov. 1996)

Solution :

S. Somashekar

Statement of Affairs as on July 1, 1996

Assets	Estimated Realisable Value
Assets not specifically pledged (As per List 'A')	Rs.
Cash in hand	1,000
Trade Debtors (60,000 – 4,000 *i.e.*, 2,000 + 2,000 *i.e.*, 4,000 – 2,000)	56,000
Calls in Arrears	5,000
Investments	4,000
Stock	2,000
Machinery	60,000
	1,28,000

Contd.

Assets specifically pledged (As per List 'B')

	(a) Estimated realisable value	(b) Due to secured creditors	(c) Deficiency ranking as unsecured	(d) Surplus carried to last column	
	Rs.	Rs.	Rs.	Rs.	
Leasehold properties	73,000	18,000	–	55,000	
Estimated surplus from assets specifically pledged					55,000
Estimated total assets available for preferential creditors, debenture holders secured by a floating charge and unsecured creditors (b/fd)					1,83,000

Summary of Gross Assets

Gross realisable value of assets specifically pledged	73,000	
Other assets	1,28,000	
	2,01,000	

Gross Liabilities	Liabilities (To be deducted from surplus or added to deficiency as the case may be)		Rs.
18,000	**Secured Creditors** (As per List 'B') to the extent to which claims are estimated to be covered by assets specifically pledged.		—
1,000	**Preferential Creditors** (A per List 'C')		1,000
	Estimated balance of assets available for debenture-holders secured by a floating charge and unsecured creditors		1,82,000
50,000	**Debentureholders secured by a floating charge** (As per List 'D')		50,000
	Estimated Surplus as regards 'Debentureholders'		1,32,000
20,080	**Unsecured Creditors** (As per List 'E')		
	(i) Liabilities for purchases	20,000	
	(ii) Telephone Rent Outstanding	80	20,080
89,080	Estimated Surplus as regards 'Creditors'		1,11,920
	Issued and Called up Capital		
	16,000 Shares of Rs. 5 each (As per List 'F' & 'G')		80,000
	Estimated Surplus as regards Contributories' (As per List 'H')		31,920

Surplus Account (List 'H')

			Rs.	Rs.
Items Reducing Surplus :				
Excess of Capital and Liabilities over assets *i.e.,* Profit and Loss Account			35,000	
Estimated losses now written off or for which provision has been made for the purpose of preparing the statement :		Rs.		
Investments (Rs. 6,000 – Rs. 4,000)		2,000		
Preferential creditors for Taxes & Wages		1,000		
Telephone rent outstanding		80	3,080	38,080
Items Contributing to Surplus :				
Machinery (60,000 – 30,000)			30,000	
Leasehold property (73,000 – 40,000)			33,000	
Stock (2,000 – 1,000)			1,000	
Debtors : Provision for Bad Debts		10,000		
Less : Bad Debts	2,000			
Doubtful Debts	2,000	4,000	6,000	70,000
Surplus as shown by the Statement of Affairs				31,920

(B) Liquidator's Final Statement of Account

When the affairs of the company are fully wound up, the liquidator is required to prepare an account of winding up known as 'Liquidator's Final Statement of Account' showing how the winding up has been conducted. It is prepared on the basis of receipts and payments made by him. It is nothing but a summary of 'Cash Book'. Receipts of cash from various accounts are to be recorded on the debit side or left hand side and payments of cash to various accounts are to be recorded on the credit side or right hand side of the statement. This statement is also called the "Liquidator's Statement of Receipts and Payments" or "Liquidator's Statement of Account" or "Liquidator's Account to the Court". It is prepared and submitted by the liquidator to the court in case of compulsory winding up and to the company in case of voluntary winding up *i.e.,* he submits it to that party who appointed him. It is prepared in the form prescribed by the Companies Act. The liquidator has to record the following items on the debit side of the statement:

(1) Amount realised on sale of assets and any surplus from the secured creditors.

(2) Amount received from delinquent directors and other officers of the company.

(3) Amount received from the contributories.

The liquidator has to record the payments on the credit side of the statement in the following order :

(1) Cost of winding up— it includes legal charges, liquidator's remuneration, auctioneer's and Valuer's charges, cost of possession and maintenance of assets, cost of notice in gazette and news papers, incidental outlay etc.

(2) Preferential creditors.

(3) Creditors having floating charge, *e.g.,* debentures having floating charge.

(4) Unsecured creditors.

(5) Returns to contributories— (a) Preference shareholders with arrears of dividends. (b) Equity shareholders.

If the amount available with the liquidator is exhausted after paying, say, creditors having floating charge, payments will not be made to the unsecured creditors, preference shareholders and equity shareholders.

Form of Account. The form of account prescribed by the Supreme Court is given as below :

Form No. 156

(See Rule 329)

Companies Act, 1956

*Here state whether the winding-up is a members' or creditor's voluntary winding-up or winding-up under the supervision of the court. If under the supervision of the court, mention the number of the petition in which the order was made and the date of order.

*Strike out what does not apply.

Liquidator's Statement of Account of the Winding-up

(Members'/Creditors' Voluntary Winding up)

(Pursuant to section 497/509)

1. Name of the company ..... Ltd.
2. Nature of proceedings :
3. Date of commencement of the winding up :
4. Name and address of the liquidator :

Statement showing how the winding up has been conducted and the property of the company that has been disposed of from..........20...... .

(Commencement of winding up) to ....20..... . (close of winding up)

Receipts	Estimated value Rs.	Value realised Rs.	Payments	Payments Rs.
Assets :			**Legal Charges**	
Cash at Bank			Liquidator's Remuneration	
Cash in hand			where applicable	
Marketable Securities			% on Rs....realised	--------
Bills Receivable			% on Rs....distributed	--------
Trade Debtors			Total	
Loans and Advances			(By Whom fixed --------)	
Stock-in-Trade			Auctioneers & Valuers Charges	
Work-in-progress			Cost of Possession and	
Freehold Property			Maintenance of Estate	
Lease hold Property			Gazette and Newspapers	
Plant & Machinery			Incidental Outlay	
Furniture, Fittings, Utensils, etc.			(Establishment charges and other expenses of liquidation)	
Patents, Trade Marks etc.			Total Costs of Charges	
Investments other than Marketable Securities			(i) Debentureholders : Payment of Rs. .... per Rs. ...... debenture	
Surplus from Securities			Payment of Rs. .... per Rs. .... debenture	
Unpaid calls at Commencement of winding up			(ii) Creditors :	
Amounts received from calls on Contributories made in winding-up.			.... *Preferential .... *Unsecured Dividend(s) .... p. in the rupee on Rs.	
Receipts per Trading Account			(The estimate of the amount expected to rank for dividend was Rs. ....)	
Other properties, viz.,				
....			(iii) Returns to Contributories :	
....			.... **per rupee .... share........	
Total				
Less: Payment to redeem securities			...... ** P. per rupee....... **share	
Cost of execution			...... P. per rupee	
Payments per Trading Account			**Share	
			Add : Balance	
Net Realisations				

* State the number; preferential creditors need not be separately shown if all creditors have been paid in full.

** State nominal value and class of shares.

(1) The following assets estimated to be of the value of Rs....have proved to be unrealisable (Give details of the assets which have proved to be unrealisable)

(2) Amount paid into the companies Liquidation Account in respect of :

(a) Unclaimed dividends payable to creditors in the winding up. Rs..........

(b) Other unclaimed distributions in the winding up Rs..........

(c) Moneys held by the company in trust in respect of dividends or other sum due before the commencement of the winding up to any person as a member of the company. Rs. ....

(3) Add here any remarks the liquidators thinks desirable :

(Sd.)

Dated this.....day of..........20..... Liquidator

I declare that the above statement is true and contains a full and accurate account of the winding up from the commencement to the close of the winding up.

(Sd.)

Dated this......day of.........20...... Liquidator

A simplified form of statement is given as below :

Liquidator's Final Statement of Account

Receipts	Amount	Payments	Amount
To Cash in hand	xxx	By Cost of Winding up	xxx
To Cash at Bank	xxx	By Liquidator's Remuneration	xxx
To Assets Realised	xxx	By Debentureholders (with interest payable)	xxx
To Surplus from Secured Creditors	xxx	By Preferential Creditors	xxx
To Calls in Arrears Recovered	xxx	By Unsecured Creditors	xxx
		By Preference Shareholders	xxx
To Calls made and realised from Contributories	xxx	By Equity Shareholders	xxx
		By Deferred Shareholders	xxx
Total	xxxx	Total	xxxx

Explanation of certain terms

(1) Secured Creditors. The creditors who are holding security of assets of the company, are called 'Secured Creditors'. If such assets are realised by the secured creditors themselves, then, they will hand over the surplus proceeds to the liquidator after deducting their amounts from the sale proceeds. On the other hand, if those assets are realised by the liquidator, he will pay the amount to the secured creditors out of the sale proceeds and keeps the surplus proceeds. In both the cases, the liquidator has to record only the surplus proceeds on the receipts side of the liquidator's account as "Surplus from secured creditors". In this case, the secured creditors will not appear on the payment side of liquidator's accounts as "payments to secured creditors". But, if the amount of sale proceed is insufficient to pay secured creditors, then, they become partly secured creditors. These partly secured creditors will be treated as unsecured creditors to that extent.

(2) Preferential Creditors. These are the unsecured creditors who have priority payment over other unsecured creditors. Under section 530 of the Companies Act, 1956, the following items are treated as preferential creditors or preferential payments :

(i) All Govt. and Local Authority dues due and payable within 12 months before the date of commencement of winding up of the company.

(ii) Any compensation, lay off or retrenchment, which has become due to the workmen under the Industrial Disputes Act within 12 months before the date of commencement of winding up.

(iii) Four months' all wages and salaries due and payable to the employees of the company within 12 months before the date of commencement of winding up to a maximum of Rs. 1,000 per employee.

(iv) All accrued holiday remuneration becoming payable to any employee on the termination of his services on account of winding up.

(v) All contributions payable by the company as an employer of any person under the Employees' State Insurance Act, 1948 or any other law in force during 12 months before winding up, except where the company is wound up for the purpose of amalgamation or reconstruction.

(vi) All amounts due in respect of any compensation or liability under Workmen's Compensation Act, 1923.

(vii) All sums due to any employee from a provident fund, a pension fund, a gratuity fund or any other fund for the welfare of the employees maintained by the company.

(viii) Expenses of investigation payable by the company.

(ix) Advances received from any person for the purpose of making the preferential payments in respect of wages, salaries and accrued holiday remuneration.

(3) Debentureholders. Unless otherwise stated, the debenture holders should be treated as creditors secured by floating charge. Therefore, they should be paid immediately after the preferential creditors. If the interest is due on debentures or any other creditors, it should be paid upto the date of payment if the company is solvent. On the other hand, if the company is insolvent, it should be paid only upto the date of winding up.

(4) Receiver for Debentureholders or Mortgages. A receiver is an independent person appointed by the court or by the debenture holders. If the debentureholder has empowered to appoint a 'Receiver', he can appoint the 'Receiver' on happening of a specified event. This power may be stated in the debenture deed itself. If no such power is not given in the debenture deed, the debentureholder will have to apply to the court for the appointment of the 'Receiver'. Such a 'Receiver' (Whether appointed by the court or the debentureholder) will realise the assets. Out of sales proceeds, he meets his own expenses and remuneration. The balance of sale proceeds is used to make the payment to the debentureholders or the mortgagee by whom he is appointed. After making the payment to the debenture holders, if there is any surplus left, the same is handed over to the liquidator for making the payments to the debentureholders, if there is any surplus left, the same is handed over to the liquidator for making the payments to others like unsecured creditors (other than preferential creditors) and contributories.

When a 'Receiver' is appointed, two statement of accounts will have to be prepared :

(i) *Receiver's Statement of Account :* It is prepared by the 'Receiver' in the same manner as the Liquidator's Statement of Account.

(ii) *Liquidator's Statement of Account :* It is prepared by the liquidator on the completion of 'Receiver's Statement of Account'.

(5) Unsecured Creditors. The creditors who are not holding any securities of the company, are called 'Unsecured Creditors'. If the amount is sufficient, they will be paid at prorata, (*i.e.,* in proportion to the amount held by them) as per their rights.

(6) Calls-in-Arrears and Calls-in-Advance. If the shares are partly paid, the liquidator has to make a call in order to repay the creditors and preference shareholders. If the shareholders have paid different amounts on the same class of shares (equity or preference), the liquidator has to make the calls to the shareholders who have paid previously less amount, for the required amount only.

If some shareholders have paid the calls money in advance, they should be paid before returning the respective share capitals.

(7) Arrears of Preference Dividends. The question of payment of dividend will arise only in case of cumulative preference shares, but not in case of non-cumulative preference shares. Unless otherwise stated, preference shares are to be presumed as cumulative. The following points should be borne in mind regarding payment of arrears of dividend :

(i) Arrears of dividend should be paid only upto the date of liquidation.

(ii) If dividend is declared but not paid, it becomes a debt and is to be paid before any repayment of capital.

(iii) If dividend is in arrears and not declared, it is to be paid only after repayment of equity share capital in full.

(iv) If the Articles of Association of company state that the arrears of dividend on preference shares are to be paid before anything paid to equity shareholders, the payment of dividend is to be made accordingly. If there are no provisions in the articles regarding the payment of arrears preference dividend, arrears should be paid only after repayment of equity capital.

(8) Calls on Partly paid Shares. If the available cash is insufficient to pay the claims of others, calls should be made to shareholders to collect the necessary amount, though it is not stated in the problem.

While collecting the amount from the shareholders having same rights, first we should collect the amount from those shareholders who have paid less to equalise the paid up capital of the shareholders. Then, the required amount should be collected from all the shareholders equally.

(9) Repayment of Capital. If the surplus amount is available after paying all the outside liabilities, it should be paid to all the three types of shareholders.

(i) *Preference Shareholders :* All preference shares should be considered as non-participating preference shares, unless they are specifically stated as participating preference shares. If it is specifically stated that the preference shares are participating preference shares and there remains surplus after payment of preference shareholders and equity shareholders, the preference shareholders are entitled to share in surplus amount along with equity share holders. If the preference shareholders are non-participating, all cash available after payment of preference shareholders is paid to equity shareholders.

(ii) *Equity and Deferred Shareholders :* After having paid all the claims of preference shareholders, the surplus amount available should be distributed between the ordinary or equity shareholders and the deferred shareholders in the proportion of their total paid up capitals, unless the preference shareholders are participating preference shareholders. If there are participating preference shareholders, then, they share in surplus as explained above. If there are no participating preference shareholders and deferred shareholders, the entire surplus should be paid to the equity shareholders.

While distributing the amount to the shareholders having same rights, first we should pay the amount to those shareholders who have paid more to equalise the claims of the shareholders. Then, the available surplus amount should be distributed among all the shareholders equally.

(10) Liquidator's Remuneration. It is fixed by the party who appointed him. It is generally paid in the form of commission based on the assets realised and payments made to unsecured creditors or shareholders. Some times a fixed amount may be given as remuneration with or without the above mentioned commission. While calculating such commission, the following points should be kept in mind :

(i) He gets the commission at an agreed percentage on the free assets (*i.e.,* assets which are not specifically pledged) realised by him. If the assets are specifically pledged and if they are realised by the concerned creditors himself, the liquidator will be allowed commission only on the amount of surplus realised from such creditor and not on the total value of assets realised. If such assets are realised by the liquidator and not by the creditor, the liquidator will get the commission on the full amount of assets realised. If it is not clearly stated in the problem as to who realises the securities held by the secured creditors, it is better to assume that the securities given to secured creditors are realised by the liquidator.

(ii) Unless otherwise stated, he is not entitled for the commission on cash and bank balance and calls in arrears or fresh calls recovered.

(iii) If the liquidator's remuneration is based on the amount paid to unsecured creditors, preferential creditors are also taken into account because they are also unsecured creditors.

(iv) If the amount available is sufficient to pay unsecured creditors and the liquidator's remuneration in full, then, the following procedure is followed for the calculation of remuneration :

$$\text{Liquidator's Remuneration} = \frac{\begin{array}{c}\text{Amount due to} \\ \text{unsecured Creditors}\end{array} \times \begin{array}{c}\text{Rate of} \\ \text{Remuneration}\end{array}}{100}$$

If the amount available is not sufficient (*i.e.,* in case of deficiency) to pay unsecured creditors/shareholders and the liquidator's remuneration in full, then, the liquidator's remuneration is calculated as follows :

$$\text{Liquidator's Remuneration} = \frac{\text{Amount due to unsecured Creditors/Shareholders} \times \text{Rate of Remuneration}}{100 + \text{Rate of Remuneration}}$$

For instance

Creditors to be paid	Rs. 4,50,000
Commission to be given on the amount paid to creditors	5%
Total amount available	Rs. 3,15,000

The liquidator's remuneration to be paid will be :

$$\text{Rs. } 15{,}000 \text{ } i.e., \text{ } 3{,}15{,}000 \times \frac{5}{105} = \text{Rs. } 15{,}000.$$

(11) Undistributed Profits or Losses. If there are any undistributed profit or losses in the Balance Sheet of the company, they should not be considered while preparing the liquidator's final statement of account.

(12) Double Entry. As the liquidator's final statement of account is only a statement, there is no question of double entry.

Illustration 1

The Oltra Optimist Ltd. went into liquidation. Its assets were realised for Rs. 85,000. Cash on hand was Rs. 2,000, Rs. 855 were spent as costs of liquidation. Debentureholders were paid Rs. 49,000 together with interest, preferential creditors were paid in full.

Unsecured creditors including preferential creditors of Rs. 8,000 amounted to Rs. 54,000. The liquidator is entitled to a remuneration of 2½% on the amount realised (excluding the cash in hand) and at 3% on the amount distributed to the unsecured creditors.

Find out the amount of remuneration payable to liquidator.

Solution :

Calculation of Liquidator's Remuneration

2½% on assets realised	$\left(\frac{85{,}000 \times 5}{100 \times 2}\right)$	Rs. 2,125
3% on amount distributed to unsecured creditors		
Liquidator's Total Remuneration	$\left(\frac{35{,}020 \times 3}{103}\right)$	Rs. 1,020
		Rs. 3,145

Note : Amount available for distribution to unsecured creditors is given as below :

		Rs.
Total amount available for distribution (Including cash on hand)		87,000
Less : Liquidation expenses	855	
Part of Liquidator's Remuneration	2,125	
Debentureholders	49,000	51,980
Amount available to unsecured creditors		35,020

Illustration 2

The Unpopular Co. Ltd. went into voluntary liquidation. The assets realised Rs. 2,25,000 excluding amount realised by sale of securities held by the secured creditors. The following was the position :

Share Capital : 2,500 Shares of Rs. 100 each	2,50,000
Secured creditors (Securities realised Rs. 35,000)	22,000
Debentures having a floating charge on the assets of the company	1,54,000
Preferential Creditors	11,000
Unsecured Creditors	1,71,000
Liquidation expenses	2,000
Liquidator's remuneration	5,500

Prepare the liquidator's final statement of account and state the percentage of payments made to unsecured creditors.

Solution :

Unpopular Co. Ltd.

Liquidator's Final Statement of Account

Receipts		Rs.	Payments	Rs.
To Assets Realised		2,25,000	By Liquidation Expenses	2,000
To Surplus from secured creditors :			By Liquidator's Remuneration	5,500
Securities Realised	35,000		By Debentureholders having floating charge	1,54,000
Less : Paid	22,000	13,000	By Preferential creditors	11,000
			By Unsecured creditors at 38.3% (Approx.) (*i.e.* Balancing figure)	65,500
		2,38,000		2,38,000

Note : Unsecured creditors of Rs. 1,71,000 will get only Rs. 65,500. Since creditors have not been paid in full, there is no question of paying to shareholders.

Illustration 3

The Vinayak Co. Ltd. went into voluntary liquidation on 1-4-1997 on which date dividend on preference shares were in arrears for 4 years. The subscribed capital of the company consisted of—

(i) 2,000 7% Preference shares of Rs. 100 each fully paid.

(ii) 3,000 Equity shares of Rs. 100 each Rs. 60 paid up.

Cash on hand was Rs. 2,000 and assets were realised for Rs. 3,00,000. The expenses of liquidation amounted to Rs. 1,750. The liquidator is entitled to a remuneration of Rs. 8,000 and a commission of 4% on the amount of capital and dividend paid to preference shareholders. The liquidator has paid the liabilities of Rs. 58,000.

Prepare the liquidator's final statement of account.

Solution :

Liquidator's Final Statement of Account

Receipts	Rs.	Payments		Rs.
To Cash on hand	2,000	By Liquidation Expenses		1,750
To Assets Realised	3,00,000	By Liquidator's Remuneration :		
To Calls made on		Fixed	8,000	
3,000 Equity shares	31,990	Commission	10,240	18,240
(Only required amount)		(4% on Rs. 2,56,000)		
		By Liabilities		58,000
		By Preference Shareholders :		
		Capital	2,00,000	
		Dividend	56,000	2,56,000
	3,33,990			3,33,990

Note : Only deficit amount has been collected from the equity shareholders.

Illustration 4

X Ltd. went into Voluntary liquidation on 31-3-1991 when its position was as follows :

2,000 6% Preference shares of Rs. 100 each fully paid.

1,000 Equity shares of Rs. 100 each fully paid.

1,000 Equity shares of Rs. 100 each Rs. 60 per share paid up.

Calls-in-arrears	6,000
Calls-in-advance	4,000
Total assets realised	3,00,000
Sundry Creditors : Secured	40,000
Sundry Creditors : Unsecured	20,000
Sundry Creditors : Preferential	8,000

There are arrears of preference dividend for one year. Preference shareholders have priority as to dividend and repayment of capital.

The liquidator made the necessary calls on the partly paid shares and received the same in full.

Prepare the liquidator's final statement of account.

(K.U.D., B.Com., April 1994)

Solution :

Liquidator's Final Statement of Account

Receipts		Rs.	Payments		Rs.
To Assets realised	3,00,000		By Preferential creditors		8,000
Less: Paid to secured			By Unsecured creditors		20,000
creditors	40,000	2,60,000	By Calls-in-advance		4,000
To Calls-in-arrears		6,000	By Preference shareholders :		
To Calls on partly paid shares :			Capital	2,00,000	
1,000 Shares at Rs. 9 each		9,000	Dividend	12,000	2,12,000
			By Fully paid Equity Shareholders at Rs. 31 per share		31,000
		2,75,000			2,75,000

Note : To equalise the paid up capital of the shareholders, Rs. 9 are called on partly paid shareholders and Rs. 31 are paid to fully paid shareholders.

Illustration 5

Chaduranga Co. Ltd. went into voluntary liquidation on 1-1-1997 on which date dividend on preference shares were in arrears for two years. The subscribed capital of the company consisted of :

45,000 6% Preference shares of Rs. 10 each fully paid.

30,000 Equity shares of Rs. 10 each Rs. 8 paid up.

20,000 Equity shares of Rs. 10 each Rs. 7 paid up.

The cash at Bank was Rs. 3,000 and assets were realised for Rs. 2,15,000. The expenses came to Rs. 4,584. The liquidator is entitled to a commission of 3% on the amount paid to preference shareholders as capital and the liabilities amounted to Rs. 1,20,000.

Prepare liquidator's final statement of account.

Solution :

Liquidator's Final Statement of Account

Receipts	Rs.	Payments	Rs.
To Cash at Bank	3,000	By Liquidation Expenses	4,584
To Assets realised	2,15,000	By Liquidator's Commission	
To Calls made on		3% on Rs. 2,07,200	6,216
30,000 Equity shares at Rs. 2 each	60,000	By Liabilities	1,20,000
20,000 Equity shares at Rs. 3 each	60,000	By Preference Shareholders	2,07,200
	3,38,000		3,38,000

Note : Calculation of Commission

		Rs.
Total amount available		3,38,000
Less : Liquidation expenses	4,584	
Liabilities	120,000	1,24,584
Amount available for Pref. share & Commission to liquidator		2,13,416

Since the available amount is insufficient, the liquidator's commission is calculated as below :

$$\text{Liquidator's Commission} = \frac{2,13,416 \times 3}{103} = \text{Rs. } 6,216$$

Illustration 6

The cash left with liquidator after realising all assets and after paying all liabilities but before any call and return of capital is Rs. 1,84,000. The issued share capital of a company is composed of :

1,000 6% Preference shares of Rs. 100 each fully paid.

40,000 'A' Equity shares of Rs. 10 each fully paid.

30,000 'B' Equity shares of Rs. 10 each Rs. 8 paid up.

20,000 'C' Equity shares of Rs. 5 each Rs. 3 paid up.

The preference dividends were in arrears for four years. Assume Articles include the provision relating to payment of preference dividend in priority to the equity capital. You are required to prepare liquidator's final statement of account making necessary calls.

Solution :

Liquidator's Final Statement of Account

Receipts	Rs.	Payments		Rs.
To Cash balance left	1,84,000	By Pref. shareholders :		
To Calls made on 20,000 'C' Equity Shares at Re. 1 each (which are Rs. 3 paid up)	20,000	Capital	1,00,000	
		Dividends	24,000	1,24,000
		By 'A' Equity shareholders on 40,000 shares at Rs. 2 per share		80,000
	2,04,000			2,04,000

Note : In order to equalise the paid up value, Re. 1 per share is to be called on share holders who are paid Rs. 3 on their shares and Rs. 2 per share are to be returned to shareholders who are paid Rs. 10 on their shares.

10 = 10 paid up – 2 Returned = 8

10 = 8 paid up = 8

5 = 3 paid up – 1 called = 4

Another method of calculation is also given as below :

Calculation of total deficiency or loss

The amount payable to shareholders is as under :

	Rs.
1,000 6% Preference shares of Rs. 100 each fully paid	1,00,000
40,000 'A' Equity shares of Rs. 10 each fully paid	4,00,000
30,000 'B' Equity shares of Rs. 10 each Rs. 8 paid up	2,40,000
20,000 'C' Equity shares of Rs. 5 each Rs. 3 paid up	60,000
Arrears of Dividend	24,000
Total amount payable	8,24,000
Less : Cash available	1,84,000
Total deficiency	6,40,000

Percentage of loss to be suffered by equity shareholders :

$$\frac{\text{Total Deficiency}}{\text{Total Equity Capital (Nominal Value)}} \times 100$$

$$\frac{6{,}40{,}000}{4{,}00{,}000 + 3{,}00{,}000 + 1{,}00{,}000} \times 100 = 80\%$$

Hence, deficiency per share is 80%

For 40,000 'A' Equity shares Rs. 10 paid up

Less : Deficiency Rs. 8 *i.e.*, Rs. 2 per share to be returned

For 30,000 'B' Equity shares Rs. 8 paid up

Less : Deficiency Rs. 8

For 20,000 'C' Equity shares Rs. 3 paid up

Less : Deficiency Rs. 4 *i.e.,* Re. 1 per share to be collected.

Illustration 7

The Fast Ltd. went into voluntary liquidation on 31-12-1997 on which date its position was as follows :

7,000 7% Preference shares of Rs. 10 each (Arrears of dividend for 1 year)	70,000
12,000 Equity shares of Rs. 10 each Rs. 8 paid	96,000
Profit & Loss Account	11,000
General Reserve	20,000
9% Debentures (having floating charge)	20,000
Unsecured creditors (Rs. 8,000 preferential)	48,000
Assets realised	2,80,000
Cash at Bank	2,000

Cost of liquidation amounted to Rs. 2,980. The interest on debentures was due for one year to the date of winding up. The liquidator is entitled to a remuneration at 3% on realisation of assets and 4% on distribution to unsecured creditors. The preference shareholders have preferential right as to capital and dividend. They have also right to receive ¼th of the surplus remaining after repaying the equity share capital.

Prepare the liquidator's final statement of account.

Solution :

Liquidator's Final Statement of Account

Receipts	Rs.	Payments		Rs.
To Cash at Bank	2,000	By Cost of Liquidation		2,980
To Assets realised	2,80,000	By Liquidator's Remuneration :		
		3% on 2,80,000	8,400	
		4% on 48,000	1,920	10,320
		By Debentureholders	20,000	
		Interest thereon	1,800	21,800
		By Preferential creditors		8,000
		By Unsecured creditors		40,000
		By Preference shareholders :		
		Capital	70,000	
		Dividends	4,900	74,900
		By Equity shareholders		96,000
		By Distribution of Surplus		
		¼th to Pref. shareholders		7,000
		¾th to Equity shareholders		21,000
	2,82,000			2,82,000

Illustration 8

The Quick Ltd. went into liquidation on 31-12-1997 to which date its share capital and liabilities were as follows :

4,000 Equity shares of Rs. 100 each, Rs. 65 called	2,60,000	
Calls received in advance	4,000	2,64,000
6,000 Equity shares of Rs. 100 each Rs. 80 called	4,80,000	
Calls received in advance	30,000	
	5,10,000	
Less : Calls unpaid	12,000	4,98,000
Debentures (having floating charge)		35,000
Interest on debentures		3,500
Unsecured creditors (Rs. 15,000 preferential creditors)		75,000
Assets realised		4,00,000
Cost of Liquidation		9,500

The liquidator is entitled to a commission of 3% on assets realised and 4% on amount distributed to unsecured creditors.

Prepare liquidator's final statement of account, assuming that the calls unpaid were duly collected.

Solution :

Liquidator's Final Statement of Account

Receipts	Rs.	Payments		Rs.
Assets Realised	4,00,000	By Cost of Liquidation		9,500
Calls unpaid Received	12,000	By Liquidator's Remuneration :		
		3% on 4,00,000	12,000	
		4% on 75,000	3,000	15,000
		By Debenture	35,000	
		Add : Interest	3,500	38,500
		By Preferential Creditors		15,000
		By Unsecured Creditors		60,000
		By Calls-in-advance (4,000 + 30,000)		34,000
		By Equity shareholders : on 4,000 shares at Rs. 15 per share		60,000
		on 6,000 shares Rs. 30 per share		1,80,000
	4,12,000			4,12,000

Illustration 9

The Capital of the Datar Company Limited was as follows :

(1) 4,000 Equity shares of Rs. 100 each fully paid;

(2) 3,000 Equity shares of Rs. 100 each Rs. 80 per share paid up;

(3) 1,000 Preference shares of Rs. 100 each fully paid (these shares have preference as to Capital) and,

(4) 1,000 Deferred shares of Rs. 100 each, Rs. 80 per share paid up (these shares, under the articles are to be paid after satisfying the claims of equity shareholders).

The various creditors amounted in all to Rs. 1,00,000 including the liquidator's remuneration Rs. 2,500. The liquidator made a call of the remaining Rs. 20 on the deferred shares which was paid in full. He also realised all the assets amounting to Rs. 1,91,000.

A call of Rs. 15 per share was made on the equity shares which were partly paid up. This was paid in full with the exception of that on 100 shares.

Prepare the liquidator's account showing the return to the shareholders.

(B.Com., Bangalore, May 1994)

Solution :

Liquidator's Final Statement of Account

Receipts		Rs.	Payments	Rs.
To Assets Realised		1,91,000	By Liquidator's Remuneration	2,500
To Calls made on			By Creditors	97,500
3,000 Equity shares at			By Preference shareholders	1,00,000
Rs. 15 per share	45,000		By Equity shareholders :	
Less : Call in arrears	1,500	43,500	On 4,000 fully paid	
(100 × Rs. 15)			share at Rs. 10 each	40,000
To Call made on			On 6,900 partly paid	
1,000 Deferred shares at			shares at Rs. 5 each	14,500
Rs. 20 per share		20,000		
		2,54,500		2,54,500

Note : The available amount of Rs. 54,500 (40,000 + 14,500) is distributed to equity shareholders as below :

Available Cash	54,500
Less : Rs. 5 per share is returned on 4,000 shares (To reduce them to Rs. 95 paid up)	20,000
Balance	34,500
Less : Rs. 5 per share is returned on 6,900 shares	34,500
(Balance is equally distributed among all shareholders except those who are in default)	Nil

Illustration 10

Bekar Limited went into voluntary liquidation. The details regarding liquidation are as follows :

Share Capital :

1. 2000 8% Preference shares of Rs. 100 each (fully paid up)
2. Class-A 2,000 Equity shares of Rs. 100 each (Rs. 75 paid up)
3. Class-B 1,600 Equity shares of Rs. 100 each (Rs. 60 paid-up)
4. Class-C 1,400 Equity shares of Rs. 100 each (Rs. 50 paid-up)

Assets including machinery realised Rs. 4,20,000. Liquidation expenses amount to Rs. 15,000.

Bekar Limited has borrowed a loan of Rs. 50,000 from Patel Brothers against the mortgage of machinery (which realised Rs. 80,500). In the books of the company, salaries of four clerks for four months at a rate of Rs. 300 per month and salaries of four peons for three months at a rate of Rs. 15 per month, are outstanding. In addition to this, the company's books show the creditors worth Rs. 87,400. Prepare liquidator's statement of receipts and payments.

(Gujarat, B.Com., 1995)

Solution :

Liquidator's Final Statement of Account

Receipts	Rs.	Payments	Rs.
To Assets Realised (4,20,000 – 80,500)	3,39,500	By Expenses of Liquidation	15,000
		By Preferential Creditors	5,800
To Surplus from Secured Creditors (80,500 – 50,000)	30,500	By Unsecured Creditors	88,200
		By Preference Shareholders	2,00,000
To Calls made on 1,400 Class-C Equity shares of Re. 1 per share	1,400	By Equity Shareholders : 2,000 class-A Equity shares at Rs. 24 each	48,000
		1,600 Class-'B' Equity shares at Rs. 9 each	14,400
	3,71,400		3,71,400

Notes :(1) Calculation of Preferential Creditors

	Rs.
Salary of Clerks : For 4 clerks of Rs. 1,200. Each restricted to Rs. 1,000 per employee	4,000
Salary of peons : For 4 peons at Rs. 450 each	1,800
Total	5,800

(2) Unsecured creditors include salary of clerks Rs. 800 which is not treated as preferential creditors.

(3) Adjustment of rights of contributories :

This can be worked out in different methods and the student can adopt any method which he finds convenient.

Calculation of Surplus

	Rs.
Assets Realised	4,20,000
Less : Outside claims (15,000+5,800+50,000+88,200)	1,59,000
Balance available to all shareholders	2,61,000
Less : Preference share holders claims	2,00,000
Balance available to equity shareholders	61,000

I. Method on the basis of paid up amount :

	Rs.
Class-'A' 2,000 Equity shares at Rs. 75 paid up Amount returned Rs. 24 (*i.e.,* now Rs. 51 paid)	48,000
Class-'B' 1,600 Equity shares at Rs. 60 paid up Amount returned Rs. 9 (*i.e.,* now Rs. 51 paid)	14,400
Surplus available	62,400
Less : Class-'C' 1,400 Equity shares at Rs. 50 paid up Amount called Re. 1 (*i.e.,* now Rs. 51 paid)	1,400
Surplus available	61,000

II. Method on the basis of total deficiency or loss :

	Rs.
Class-'A' 2,000 Equity shares at Rs. 75 paid up	1,50,000
Class-'B' 1,600 Equity shares at Rs. 60 paid up	96,000
Class-'C' 1,400 Equity shares at Rs. 50 paid up	70,000
Total to be returned	3,16,000
Less : Surplus available (as shown above)	61,000
Total deficiency for 5,000 equity shares	2,55,000

Hence, Deficiency per share is Rs. 51 $\left(i.e., \frac{2,55,000}{5,000}\right)$

	A's Shares	B's Shares	C's Shares
Paid up amount	Rs. 75	Rs. 60	Rs. 50
Deficiency per share	Rs. 51	Rs. 51	Rs. 51
Net amount receivable or returnable	Rs. 24	Rs. 9	– Rs. 1

From the above it is clear that Rs. 24 and Rs. 9 should be returned to 'A' shareholders and 'B' shareholders respectively and Re. 1 should be recovered from 'C' shareholders.

III. Method on the basis of full calls receivable :

	Rs.
Class-'A' 2,000 Equity shares (Rs. 75 paid up) Rs. 25 called	50,000
Class-'B' 1,600 Equity shares (Rs. 60 paid up) Rs. 40 called	64,000
Class-'C' 1,400 Equity shares (Rs. 50 paid up) Rs. 50 called	70,000
Total receivable	1,84,000
Add : Surplus available	61,000
Balance refundable to 5,000 equity shares	2,45,000

Hence, refundable on each share is Rs. 49 $\left(i.e., \frac{2,45,000}{5,000}\right)$

	A's Share	B's Share	C's Share
Amount to be returned	Rs. 49	Rs. 49	Rs. 49
Amount to be collected	Rs. 25	Rs. 40	Rs. 50
Net amount to be returned or collected	Rs. 24	Rs. 9	– Re. 1

Illustration 11

X Co. Ltd. went into voluntary liquidation on 1-1-1990. The following was the position on that date.

Liabilities		Rs.	Assets	Rs.
Share Capital :			Goodwill	50,000
Equity shares of Rs. 10 each		3,00,000	Building	50,000
Sundry Creditors :			Machinery	90,000
(a) Secured against			Furniture	60,000
machinery	65,000		Stock	68,500
(b) Creditors having			Debtors	82,000
lien on stock	75,000		Cash at Bank	4,500
(c) Preferential	25,000		Profit & Loss Account	1,51,000
(d) Unsecured	91,000	2,56,000		
		5,56,000		5,56,000

The liquidator was appointed to carry out the process of liquidation.

The secured creditors exercised their claims against the securities offered :

Machinery was sold at Rs. 70,000; Stock realised at 30% only.

The liquidator realised the remaining assets as under :

Building	Rs. 30,000	Furniture	Rs. 27,000
Debtors	Rs. 60,250	Cash at Bank	Rs. 4,500

The liquidation expenses amounted to Rs. 1,465.

The liquidator's remuneration was agreed as follows :

(a) 2% commission on assets realised; and

(b) 3% commission on the amount paid to unsecured creditors.

Prepare the liquidators final statement of account.

(B.Com., K.U.D., April 1992)

Solution :

Liquidator's Final Statement of Account

Receipts		Rs.	Payments		Rs.
To Assets Realised			By Liquidation Expenses		1,465
Buildings	30,000		By Liquidator's Remuneration :		
Debtors	60,250		2% on Rs. 1,26,750 = 2535		
Furniture	27,000		(1,21,750 + 5,000)		
Cash at Bank	4,500	1,21,750	3% on Rs. 1,19,175 = 3575		6,110
To Surplus from Securities :			By Preferential Creditors		25,000
Machinery Realised	70,000		By Unsecured Creditors		94,175
Less : Paid	65,000	5,000			
Stock Realised	20,550				
Less : Paid	20,550	—			
(Remaining creditors are treated as unsecured					
		1,26,750			1,26,750

Note : (i) Calculation of 3% Commission or Remuneration :

Total Unsecured Creditors :	Rs.
Unsecured creditors as given in B/s	91,000
Unsatisfied partly secured creditors	
(75,000 – 20,550)	54,450
Preferential creditors	25,000
(Included for calculation of commission)	
Total unsecured creditors	1,70,450

The total amount payable to unsecured creditors is Rs. 1,70,450. But the available amount for the above creditors and commission) is Rs. 1,22,750 (*i.e.,* 1,26,750 *Less* 1,465 *Less* 2,535). Since the amount available is insufficient, the commission is calculated as below :

$$1,22,750 \times \frac{3}{103} = \text{Rs. } 3,575$$

(ii) The liquidator has realised cash at Bank and hence, this amount is also included for calculation of his 2% remuneration.

(iii) Machinery and stock are realised by creditors. Hence, they should not be considered for calculation of 2% commission of liquidator.

Illustration 12

Balance Sheet of Bubles Ltd. as on 31-12-1984. From this, prepare Liquidator's Statement of Account.

Liabilities	Rs.	Assets	Rs.
Paid up Capital :		Fixed Assets :	
1,000 6% Preference shares		Land & Buildings	2,00,000
of Rs. 100 each	1,00,000	Plant & Machinery	2,20,000
2,000 Equity shares of		Current Assets :	
Rs. 100 each fully paid	2,00,000	Stock	1,00,000
3,000 Equity shares of		Debtors	1,00,000
Rs. 100 each Rs. 50 paid	1,50,000	Cash at Bank	30,000
Secured Loan :		Misc. Expenditures :	
6% Debentures (Floating		Profit & Loss A/c	1,00,000
Charge on all assets)	1,00,000		
Others : (Mortgage on			
Land and Building)	1,00,000		
Current Liabilities :			
Sundry Creditors	90,000		
Income-tax	10,000		
	7,50,000		7,50,000

The company went into liquidation on 1-1-1985. The preference dividends were in arrears for the 3 years. The arrears are payable on liquidation. The assets were realised as follows :

Land & Building	Rs. 2,40,000	Stock	Rs. 70,000
Plant & Machinery	Rs. 1,80,000	Debtors	Rs. 60,000

The expenses of liquidation amounted to Rs. 8,000. The liquidator is entitled to a commission at 2% on all assets realised and 3% on amounts distributed to unsecured creditors. All payments were made on 30th June, 1985.

(Bangalore, B.Com., Oct. 1985 & April 1994)

Solution :

Liquidator's Statement of Account

Receipts		Rs.	Payments		Rs.
To Cash at Bank		30,000	By Expenses of Liquidation		8,000
To Assets Realised			By Remuneration of Liquidators:		
Plant & Machinery	1,80,000		2% on Rs. 5,50,000 =11,000		
Stock	70,000		(3,10,000 + 2,40,000)		
Debtors	60,000	3,10,000	3% on Rs. 1,00,000 = 3,000		14,000
To Surplus from Secured			By Debentures	1,00,000	
Creditors :			*Add* : Interest	3,000	1,03,000
Land and Buildings	2,40,000		(For 6 months)		
Less : Paid	1,00,000	1,40,000	from 1-1-84 to 30-6-84)		
			By Preferential Creditors		10,000
			(Income tax)		
			By Unsecured Creditors		90,000
			By Pref. Shareholders :		
			Capital	1,00,000	
			Dividend	18,000	1,18,000
			By Equity Shareholders :		
			On 2,000 shares		
			Rs. 57.40 each		1,14,800
			On 3,000 shares		
			Rs. 7.40 each		22,200
		4,80,000			4,80,000

Note **:** First Rs. 50 is paid to 3,000 equity shareholders to equalise their paid up value. Remaining amount is paid to all the equity shareholders equally.

Illustration 13

The Solvent Co. Ltd. went into liquidation on 31st Dec., 1990. Its Balance Sheet on that date was as under :

Liabilities		Rs.	Assets	Rs.
Share Capital :			Goodwill	40,000
Paid up Capital :			Building	90,000
20,000 shares of Rs. 10 each			Plant	1,00,000
Rs. 8 called up	1,60,000		Stock	8,600
Less : Calls-in-arrears	4,000	1,56,000	Debtors	27,700
Debentures		50,000	Cash	8,000
Interest on Debenture due		2,500	Profit and Loss A/c	1,13,700
Pref. Creditors for tax		18,500		
Secured Creditor secured on plant		63,000		
Unsecured Creditors		86,500		
Bank Overdraft (unsecured)		9,000		
Bills Payable		2,500		
		3,88,000		3,88,000

The liquidator realised the assets as follows :

Buildings	Rs. 42,500	Plant	Rs. 48,000
Debtors	Rs. 27,100	Stock	Rs. 10,400

Liquidation expenses amounted to Rs. 430. Liquidator's remuneration was at 3% on amount of assets realised (except on calls) and 2% on amount paid to unsecured creditors. Assume the payment was made on 31st March, 1991.

Prepare the liquidators final statement of account.

(My. U., B.Com. & K.U.D., April 1989 Mod.)

Solution :

Liquidator's Final Statement of Account

Receipts		Rs.	Payments		Rs.
To Cash in hand		8,000	By Liquidation Expenses		430
To Assets Realised :			By Liquidator's Remuneration		
Buildings	42,500		3% on Rs. 1,28,000		
Stock	10,400		(80,000 + 48,000) =	3,840	
Debtors	27,100	80,000	2% on Rs. 73,142 =	1,463	5,303
To Surplus from secured Creditors :			By Debentureholders :		
Plant Realised	48,000		Debentures	50,000	
Less : Paid	48,000	—	Interest	3,125	
To Calls-in-arrears		4,000	(2,500 + 625 for free months)		53,125
To Calls made on—			By Pref. Creditors for Tax		18,500
20,000 shares at			By Unsecured Creditors		54,642
Rs. 2 per share		40,000			
		1,32,000			1,32,000

Note : (i) Calculation of 2% Remuneration :

Total unsecured creditors :	Rs.
Unsecured creditors (as given)	86,500
Bills payable	2,500
Bank overdraft	9,000
Unsatisfied unsecured creditors (63,000 – 48,000)	15,000
Preferential creditors	18,500
Total amount by unsecured creditors	1,31,500

But, the available amount for the above creditors and commission is Rs. 74,605 [1,32,000 – 57,395 (430 + 3,840 + 53,125)] since the amount available is insufficient, the commission is calculated as below :

$$74{,}605 \times \frac{2}{102} = \text{Rs. } 1{,}463.$$

(ii) Interest on debentures is paid till the date of payment.

Illustration 14

Fair Deal Ltd. went into voluntary liquidation on 31-3-1991 on which date its position was as under :

Share Capital :

3,000 6% Preference shares of Rs. 50 each (preference dividend due for 3 years)	1,50,000
6,000 Equity shares of Rs. 50 each Rs. 25 paid	1,50,000

Liabilities :

Mortgage on Machinery	15,000
Trade Creditors	35,000
Bills payable	20,000
Preferential claims for salaries & wages	3,000
Government tax owing	1,050

Assets Realised :

Machinery	35,000
Other assets	1,72,000

The cost of liquidation and legal expenses amounted to Rs. 1,500 and Rs. 500 respectively.

The liquidator is entitled to a remuneration of Rs. 6,000 plus 5% commission on amount paid to the preference shareholders as capital and dividend and 5% commission on the total amount collected (including calls on shares).

Prepare the liquidator's final statement of account.

(B.Com., K.U.D., Oct. 1991)

Solution :

Liquidator's Final Statement of Account

Receipts		Rs.	Payment		Rs.
To Assets Realised		1,72,000	By Legal expenses		1,500
To Surplus from secured creditors :			By Liquidation expenses		500
Machinery realised	35,000		By Remuneration to liquidator :		
Less : Paid	15,000	20,000	Fixed	6,000	
To Call on 6,000 Equity shares (required amount only)		75,000	5% on Rs. 2,82,000 (1,72,000+35,000+75,000)	14,100	
			5% on Rs. 1,77,000	8,850	28,950
			By Preferential Creditors (3,000 + 1,050)		4,050
			By Unsecured Creditors (35,000 + 20,000)		55,000
			By Preference Shareholders :		
			Capital	1,50,000	
			Dividend	27,000	1,77,000
		2,67,000			2,67,000

Note : Calculation of 5% commission on the amount collected :

Total amount payable in all is Rs. 2,63,250 [*i.e.,* 1,500 + 500 + 6,000 + 10,350 (*i.e.,* 5% commission on Rs. 1,72,000 and Rs. 35,000) + 8,850 + 4,050 + 55,000 +1,77,000] plus 5% commission on calls. But, the amount available before collecting the calls is Rs. 1,92,000. Therefore, the deficit amount *i.e.,* Rs. 71,250 plus 5% commission on calls should be collected. Rs. 71,250 is 95% of the amount collected. Therefore, the extra 5% is to be collected to pay off commission. Hence, the amount to be collected is Rs. 75,000.

$$\left(i.e., \ 71{,}250 \times \frac{100}{95}\right)$$

Illustration 15

The following is the Balance Sheet of Olympus Ltd. as on 31st August, 1994

Liabilities	Rs.	Assets	Rs.
Issued Capital :		Sundry Assets	4,79,000
1,000, 7% Preference shares		Buildings	1,00,000
of Rs. 100 each fully paid	1,00,000	Preliminary expenses	10,000
1,500 Equity shares of		Profit and Loss Account	33,500
Rs. 100 each, Rs. 95 paid	1,42,500		
5% Debentures	2,00,000		
Loan on Mortgage	80,000		
Bank Account	25,000		
Creditors including Rs. 55,000 for the assessed tax	75,000		
	6,22,500		6,22,500

The mortgage was secured on the Buildings and the Debentures were secured by floating charge on the "Sundry Assets". The debenture holders appointed a 'Receiver' who took charge of the 'Sundry Assets' amounting to Rs. 3,15,000. A 'Liquidator' was also appointed as the company went into voluntary liquidation. The 'Receiver' realised the assets for Rs. 2,95,000 and his costs and remuneration were Rs. 1,500 and Rs. 2,000 respectively. Rs. 90,000 was realised from buildings and Rs. 1,45,000 from the sale of the remaining 'Sundry Assets'. The Bank had the Guarantees of the Directors amounting to Rs. 22,000 which was duly honoured by them. The costs of liquidation were Rs. 3,000 and the liquidator's remuneration amounted to Rs. 1,250. Prepare the accounts of the Receiver and the Liquidator.

(B.Com. Osmania)

Solution :

Receiver's Receipts and Payments Account

Receipts		Rs.	Payments	Rs.
To Assets Realised		2,95,000	By Cost of Receiver	1,500
To Buildings	90,000		By Remuneration of Receiver	2,000
Less : Mortgage Paid	80,000	10,000	By Preferential Payments (Income tax)	55,000
			By Debentureholders	2,00,000
			By Balance transferred to liquidator	46,500
		3,05,000		3,05,000

Note : Preferential Creditors have legal preference of payment over debenture holders.

Liquidator's Final Statement of Account

Receipts	Rs.	Payments	Rs.
To Surplus received from Receiver	46,500	By Cost of Liquidation	3,000
		By Liquidator's Remuneration	1,250
To Remaining Sundry Assets Realised	1,45,000	By Unsecured Creditors (20,000 + 25,000)	45,000
		By Preference Shareholders	1,00,000
		By Equity Shareholders at Rs. 28.17 per share approximately	42,250
	1,91,500		1,91,500

***Note* :** Though the bank had guarantees for Rs. 22,000, the full amount of Rs. 25,000 is paid to them as there is sufficient cash.

Illustration 16

In a liquidation which commenced on April 2, 1995, certain creditors could not receive payment out of the realisation of assets and out of the contributions from 'A' list of contributories. The following are the details of certain transfers which took place in 1994 and 1995.

Shareholders	Numbers of shares transferred	Date of ceasing to be members	Creditors remaining unpaid and outstanding at the date of ceasing to be member
A	100	Feb. 1, 1994	Rs. 3,000
B	500	May 1, 1994	Rs. 4,200
C	400	Aug. 1, 1994	Rs. 5,100
D	300	Oct. 1, 1994	Rs. 5,400
E	200	Jan. 1, 1995	Rs. 6,000

All the shares were Rs. 10 each, Rs. 5 paid up. Ignoring expenses, remuneration to liquidator etc. Show the amount to be realised from the various persons listed above.

(C.A. Inter, 1995)

Solution :

Statement of Liabilities of 'B' List Contributories

Date of ceasing to be members	Creditors outstanding on the date of ceasing to be member Rs.	Share of liability by the contributories				Amount payable by contributories Rs.
		B 500 shares Rs.	C 400 shares Rs.	D 300 shares Rs.	E 200 shares Rs.	
1-5-94	4,200	1,500	1,200	900	600	4,200
1-8-94	900	–	400	300	200	900
1-10-94	300	–	–	180	120	300
1-1-95	600	–	–	–	600	80*
	Total A	1,500	1,600	1,380		1,520
Amount unpaid on shares B		2,500	2,000	1,500	1,000	
Contribution under A restricted to unpaid amount on shares (B)		1,500	1,600	1,380	1,000	

*The Liability against 'E' is Rs. 1,520. But, his unpaid amount on shares is Rs. 1,000 only. He will not contribute any thing more than Rs. 1,000. Hence, the loss of Rs. 520 will have to be suffered by these creditors.

Working Notes

(i) 'A' does not enter the list of 'B' contributories, since he transferred his shares prior to one year preceding the date of winding up.

(ii) Rs. 4,200 outstanding on 1-5-1994 will have to be contributed by B, C, D and E in the ratio of 5 : 4 : 3 : 2 *i.e.,* in the ratio of number of shares held by them.

(iii) Debts incurred between 1-5-1994 to 1-8-1994 are Rs. 900. The same will be contributed by C, D and E alone in the ratio of 4 : 3 : 2, as the debt were contracted after 'B' ceased to be a member.

(iv) The incremental liability of Rs. 300 from 1-8-1994 to 1-10-1994 will be contributed by 'D' and 'E' alone in the ratio of 3 : 2, as the liability was contracted after 'C' ceased to be a member.

(v) The incremental liability of Rs. 600 from 1-10-1994 to 1-1-1995 will be contributed by 'E' only, as the liability was contracted after 'D' ceased to be a member.

EXAMINATION QUESTIONS

(A) Answer the following questions not exceeding 4 lines each :

(Each Carries 2 Marks)

(1) What do you mean by liquidation of companies?

(2) What is voluntary winding up?

(3) What is winding up under the supervision of the court?

(4) What do you understand by compulsory winding up?

(5) Who is 'liquidator'?

(6) What is statement of affairs? How is it prepared?

(7) Who is a list 'A' contributory and list 'B' contributory?

(B.Com., M.K.U., Nov. 1992)

(8) What is liquidator's statement of account?

(B.Com., Bangalore, April 1984 & K.U.D. April 1996)

(9) What are the rights of debenture holders in respect of interest arrears in the event of liquidation of a company?

(B.Com., K.U.D., April 1996)

(10) How do you treat the undistributed profits and losses while preparing the liquidators final statement of account?

(B.Com., Shivaji, Oct. 1991)

(11) Who is the 'Receiver' for debentureholders? What are his duties?

(B.Com., Poona, Oct. 1992)

(12) What are the points to be considered while paying the arrears of dividend?

(B.Com., Osmania, April 1991)

(13) What is liquidator's final statement of account?

(Karnataka, Oct. 1997 & April 1998)

(14) What do you mean by liquidation of a company? Mention two types of liquidation.

(Karnataka, Oct. 1998)

(15) What are contributories in the liquidation of a company.

(Karnataka, April 1999)

(B) Answer the following questions/problems :

(Each carries 8 marks)

(1) What are preferential creditors under the Indian companies Act?

(B.Com., Mysore, April 1974)

(2) What are the functions of liquidator?

(3) What points do you consider while paying the arrears of preference dividend?

(B.Com., Osmania, Oct. 1989)

(4) How do you treat the following items in the liquidator's statement of account?

(a) Call-in-advance

(b) Calls-in-arrears

(c) Arrears of preference dividend

(d) Interest on debentures

(e) Surplus available after the repayment of all liabilities and capital.

(C.A. Inter, May 1986)

(5) The liquidator of a company in voluntary liquidation is entitled to a remuneration of 3% on the amount realised (excluding the cash in hand) and 2% on the amount distributed to the unsecured creditors. Unsecured creditors including preferential creditors of Rs. 5,000 amounted to Rs. 40,000.

Debentureholders were paid Rs. 51,875 together with interest. Preferential creditors were paid in full. Rs. 510 were spent as costs of liquidation.

Cash on hand was Rs. 1,000 and assets realised Rs. 79,000. Find out liquidator's total remuneration.

(B.Com., Saurashtra, April 1984)

Ans. : Liquidator's Total Remuneration Rs. 2,865

$$\left(i.e., 2{,}370 + 495\ i.e., 25{,}245 \times \frac{2}{102}\right)$$

(6) The Efficient Co. Ltd. went into voluntary liquidation. Its assets realised Rs. 1,75,000 excluding the amount realised by sale of securities held by secured creditors. The following was the position of the company.

Share capital : 1,000 Shares of Rs. 50 each	50,000
Secured creditors (Securities realised Rs. 20,000)	17,500
Preferential creditors	3,000

Unsecured creditors	70,000
Debentures (having floating charge on the assets)	1,25,000
Liquidation expenses	2,500
Liquidator's remuneration	3,750

Prepare the liquidator's final statement of account and state the percentage of payment made to unsecured creditors.

(B.Com., Gulbarga, Oct. 1990)

Ans. : Total of liquidator's final statement of account Rs. 1,77,500.

Amount distributed to unsecured creditors Rs. 43,250 at 61.79%

$\left(i.e., 43,250 \times \frac{100}{70,000}\right)$ approximately.

(7) The position of X Co. Ltd. (in liquidation) was as under :

Issued Capital :

2,000 6% Preference shares of Rs. 100 each fully paid.
(dividend for one year is in arrears)

1,000 Equity shares of Rs. 100 each fully paid

1,000 Equity shares of Rs. 75 each Rs. 60 called

Calls-in-arrears Rs. 8,000

Calls-in-advance Rs. 12,000

Cash in hand Rs. 2,18,500

Articles provide priority to preference shareholders as to dividend and capital.

Prepare the liquidator's final statement of account assuming that the necessary call amount is duly received.

(B.Com., K.U.D., Oct. 1992)

Ans. : Total of liquidator's final statement Rs. 2,34,000.

Calls made on partly called equity shares Rs. 7,500 (Rs. 7.50 per share)

Repayment to preference shareholders Rs. 2,12,000.

Repayment to fully paid equity shares Rs. 10,000 (Rs. 10 per share)

(8) The following particulars relate to a limited company which has gone into voluntary liquidation. You are required to prepare the liquidator's final statement of account allowing for his remuneration at 2% on the amount realised, 2% on the amount distributed to unsecured creditors other than preferential creditors.

Preferential creditors	10,000
Unsecured creditors	32,000
Debentures	10,000

The assets realised the following sums :

Land and Buildings	20,000
Plant and Machinery	18,650
Fixtures and Fittings	1,000

The liquidation expenses amounted to Rs. 1,000.

(B.Com., Bangalore, April 1991)

Ans. : Total of liquidator's final statement of account Rs. 39,650. Liquidators Remuneration Rs. 1,143 (*i.e.,* 793 + 350 *i.e.,* 17,857 × 2/102); Amount distributed to unsecured creditors Rs. 17,507.

(9) The Ultra Optimist Ltd. went into liquidation. Its assets realised by sale of securities held by the secured creditors. The following was the position :

	Rs.		Rs.
Share capital : 1,000 shares of Rs. 100 each		Debentures having a floating charge on assets of the company	2,50,000
Secured creditors (Securities realised Rs. 40,000)	35,000	Liquidation Expenses	5,000
Preferential creditors	6,000	Liquidator's remuneration	7,500
Unsecured creditors	1,40,000		

Prepare the liquidator's final statement of account.

(B.Com., [Hons.] Delhi, 1974)

Ans. : Total of liquidator's final statement of accounts Rs. 3,55,000. Amount paid to unsecured creditors Rs. 86,500.

(10) The Moon Co. Ltd. went into voluntary liquidation on 31-3-87 on which date its capital consisted of :

(a) 12,000 preference shares of Rs. 10 each fully paid.

(b) 15,000 equity shares of Rs. 10 each fully paid.

The assets realised Rs. 1,80,000; the expenses of liquidation amounted to Rs. 11,200; Unsecured Creditors were Rs. 75,000 and Preferential creditors Rs. 5,000. The liquidator's remuneration was fixed at 4% Commission on assets realised and 2% Commission on the amount distributed to shareholders.

Preference shares carry preferential right as to payment of capital.

Prepare the liquidator's final statement of account.

(B.Com., K.U.D., Oct. 1983 & April 1988)

Ans. : Total of liquidator's final statement of account Rs. 1,80,000. Liquidator's remuneration Rs. 8,800 (*i.e.,* 7,200 + 1,600 *i.e.,* 81,600 × 2/102); Amount distributed to preference shareholders Rs. 80,000.

(11) The Share Capital of A Ltd. at the time of liquidation consisted of :

(i) 1,000 5% Preferences of Rs. 100 each fully paid.

(ii) 2,500 Equity shares of Rs. 10 each fully paid.

(iii) 1,500 Equity shares of Rs. 10 each Rs. 7 paid up.

(iv) Rs. 37,500 6% debentures holding floating charge.

(v) Rs. 4,500 preference claims.

(vi) Rs. 12,500 unsecured creditors.

(vii) Rs. 6,000 liquidator's remuneration.

(viii) The liquidator realised Rs. 1,60,000.

Prepare the liquidator's statement of account.

(Karnataka, Oct. 1997)

Ans. : Total of liquidator's final statement of account Rs. 1,63,000
Calls made on partly paid equity shares Rs. 3,000 (Rs. 2 per share)
Repayment to fully paid equity shares Rs. 2,500 (Re. 1 per share).

(12) The Ashok Company Ltd. went into voluntary liquidation on 31-12-1996 when the state of affairs was as follows :

Unsecured creditors stood at Rs. 40,000 including preferential creditors of Rs. 5,000. Secured creditors, secured on plant & machinery stood at Rs. 20,000. Cash in hand was Rs. 1,000. The liquidator realised plant and machinery for Rs. 15,000 and the other assets realised Rs. 10,000. The liquidation expenses amounted to Rs. 1,000 and the liquidator's remuneration was fixed at 4% of the amount realised including cash balance and 2% of the amount distributed to unsecured creditors including preferential creditors.

Prepare liquidator's final statement of account showing the dividend paid to unsecured creditors.

(Bangalore, Nov. 1995 & Karnataka, Oct. 1997)

Ans. : Total of liquidator's final statement of account Rs. 11,000. Liquidator's remuneration Rs. 1,216 (*i.e.,* 1,040 + 176 *i.e.,* 8,960 × 2/102); Amount distributed to unsecured creditors Rs. 8,784.

(C) Solve the following Problems :

(Each carries 15/16 marks)

(1) The following particulars are extracted from the books of the Unfortunate Ltd. on 31st December, 1987, on which day, a winding up order was made :

		Rs.
20,000 Equity shares of Rs. 10 each Rs. 5 paid up		1,00,000
20,000 Preference shares Rs. 10 each fully paid up		2,00,000
5% First Mortgage Debentures secured by a floating charge upon the whole assets of the company exclusive of uncalled capital		1,50,000
Fully Secured Creditors (value of Securities Rs. 35,000)		30,000
Partly Secured Creditors (value of securities Rs. 10,000)		20,000
Preferential Creditors		6,000
Bills Payable		1,00,000
Unsecured Creditors		70,000
Bank Overdraft		10,000
Bills Receivable in hand		15,000
Bills discounted (of which Rs. 10,000 are bad)		40,000
Book Debts : Good	10,000	
Doubtful	7,000	
(Estimated to produce 50 paise in a Rupee)		
Bad	6,000	23,000
Land and Buildings (Estimated to produce Rs. 1,00,000)		1,50,000
Machinery (Estimated to produce Rs. 2,000)		5,000
Cash in Hand		100

Prepare Statement of Affairs as regards (1) Creditors (b) Contributories.

(Adapted from Karnataka U., B.Com.)

Ans. : Deficiency as regards Creditors Rs. 1,80,400
Deficiency as regards Contributories Rs. 4,80,400.

(2) On January 31, 1987 a compulsory order for winding-up was made against Unsafe Limited, the following particulars being disclosed :

	Book value	Estimated to produce
	Rs.	Rs.
Cash in hand	100	100
Debtors	4,000	3,600
Land and Buildings	60,000	48,000
Furniture and Fixtures	20,000	20,000
Unsecured Creditors	20,000	

Debentures :

Secured on Land and Buildings	42,000
Secured on floating charge	10,000
Preferential Creditors	6,000
Share capital (3,200 shares of Rs. 100 each)	3,20,000

Estimated liability for bills discounted was Rs. 6,000—estimated to rank at Rs. 6,000. Other contingent liabilities were Rs. 12,000—estimated to rank at Rs. 12,000.

The company was formed on the 1st day of January, 1984; and has suffered losses of Rs. 3,13,900.

Prepare statement of affairs and deficiency account.

(Adapted from C.A. Final)

Ans. : Deficiency as regards Creditors Rs. 24,300

Deficiency as regards Contributories Rs. 3,44,300.

(3) The Badluck Co. Ltd. went in to voluntary liquidation with the following liabilities :

Liabilities :

Trade Creditors		4,80,000
Bank overdraft		3,00,000
Capital : 1,50,000 preference shares of Rs. 10 each.		
Rs. 7 per shares called up		10,50,000
1,50,000 Equity shares of Rs. 10 each		
Rs. 9 per share called up	13,50,000	
Less : Calls in arrears	30,000	13,20,000
Calls in advance received :		
On Preference shares	3,60,000	
On Equity shares	60,000	4,20,000

The assets realised Rs. 30,00,000. Prepare the liquidator's final statement of account allowing Rs. 30,000 for expenses of liquidation. The preference shares have no prior right as to refund of capital.

(Gulbarga, Oct. 1987 & Bangalore, Nov. 1994)

Ans. : Total of liquidator's final statement of account Rs. 30,30,000

Amount paid to Preference shareholders Rs. 7,50,000 (5 × 1,50,000)

Amount distributed to Equity shareholders Rs. 10,50,000 (7 × 1,50,000)

Note : Calls-in-arrears are collected and calls-in-advance are refunded.

(4) Ambica Ltd. went in to voluntary liquidation on 31-12-1990. The following information is available to the liquidator :

Sundry creditors Rs. 75,660 including Rs. 8,160 being preferential creditors. 6% debentures Rs. 80,000 on which interest paid upto 30-6-1989.

The assets realised as follows :

Stock Rs. 84,000; Machinery Rs. 60,600 and Cash in hand stood at Rs. 500.

The debentureholders were paid off on 31-7-1991 with interest. The secured creditors realised the securities of building and handed over the surplus of Rs. 3,000 to the liquidator. The cost of liquidation come to Rs. 1,899.

The liquidator is entitled to a remuneration at 2% on the amount realised and 2% on the amount distributed to unsecured creditors.

Prepare the liquidator's final statement of account.

(Bangalore, Nov. 1995 & Karnataka & Mysore, April 1993)

Ans. : Total of liquidator's final statement of account Rs. 1,48,100. Liquidator's remuneration Rs. 4,051 (*i.e.,* 2,952 + 1,099 *i.e.,* 56,049 × 2/102)

Amount paid up to unsecured creditors Rs. 46,790.

Notes : (i) Cash on hand is not included in assets realised for calculation of commission.

(ii) Interest is paid to debentureholders for 1½ years.

(5) On 30th June, 1986, the liquidator of Hard Luck Ltd. having a share capital issued of 50,000 preference shares of Re. 1. each fully paid without priority as to capital, 80,000 ordinary shares of Re. 1 each. 90 paise per share paid and 1,20,000 ordinary shares of Re. 1 each, 75 paise per share paid up had a cash balance of Rs. 16,450.

On 31st December 1986, he had realised the remaining assets amounting to Rs. 31,000 of which Rs. 20,000 was in respect of secured creditors of Rs. 14,000. All the costs of liquidation were Rs. 2,700.

The creditors other than secured creditors were :

	Rs.
Trade creditors	47,400
Gas Board for gas supplied	140
Salary of clerk for six months	1,380
Directors' fees for four months	2,000

Out of the above dues, a dividend to the unsecured creditors of 62.5 paise in the rupee had already been paid as well as the amount due to the preferential creditors in respect of preferential claim.

Prepare the Liquidators Final Receipts and Payments Account.

(Adapted from My. U., B.Com.)

Ans : Total of liquidator's final statement of account Rs. 39,450 & Calls made on 1,20,000 ordinary shares at paise 5 per share Rs. 6,000.

Notes : (i) Amount distributed to unsecured creditors Rs. 18,750. This is arrived as below :

	Rs.	Rs.
Trade Creditors	47,400	
Gas Board for gas supplied	140	
Salary of clerks for 2 months $\left(1{,}380 \times \frac{2}{6}\right)$	460	
Directors' fees	2,000	50,000
Less : Payment already made to unsecured creditors at the rate of 62.5 paise		31,250
Balance of unsecured creditors paid		18,750

(ii) Salary of clerk for 4 months *i.e.,* 920 is preferential. But the preferential creditors have already been paid. Hence, payment need not be made now to preferential creditors.

(iii) Here, the preference shares do not have priority. That means, the Preference shares & Equity shares have the same right. Hence, the amount of paid up capital to be foregone or sacrificed by all types of shareholders should be equalised. The amount of paid up capital that has to be foregone by all types of shareholders per share is to be fixed at 80 paise. Hence, amount distributed to preference shareholders is Rs. 10,000 (50,000 × 0.20) and to equity shareholders is Rs. 8,000 (80,000 × 0.10).

(6) The Well-done Mining Co. Ltd. went into voluntary liquidation on 1st January, 1987, as its mines had reached. Such a state of depletion that it became too costly to excavate further minerals. The liquidator, whose remuneration is 3% on realisation of assets and 2% on distribution to shareholders, realised all the assets. The following was the position of the company on 31st December, 1986 :

	Rs.
Cash on realisation of assets	5,00,000
Expenses of Liquidation	9,000
Unsecured creditors (including salaries and wages for one month prior to liquidation, Rs. 6,000)	68,000

5,000 6% Preference shares of Rs. 30 each (dividend paid up to 31st December, 1985)	1,50,000
10,000 Equity shares of Rs. 10 each Rs. 9 per share called and paid up	90,000
General Reserve as at 31st December, 1986	1,20,000
Profit and Loss Account as at 31st December, 1986	20,000

Under the Articles of Association of the company, the preference shareholders have the right to receive one-third of the surplus remaining after repaying the equity share capital.

(Adapted from My. U., B.Com.)

Ans. : Total of liquidator's final statement of account Rs. 5,00,000.
Liquidator's remuneration Rs. 23,000 (Rs. 15,000 *i.e.,* 2% on Rs. 5,00,000 + Rs. 8,000 *i.e.,* 4,08,000 × 2/102)
Surplus amount paid to preference shareholders Rs. 50,333.
Surplus amount paid to equity shareholders Rs. 1,00,667.

Note : Creditors for salaries and wages, viz., Rs. 6,000 preferential creditors.

(7) Laxmi Co. Ltd. went into voluntary liquidation on 1-1-1989. The following was the position on that date :

Share Capital :

(a) 3,000 12% Preference shares of Rs. 100 each fully paid.

(b) 50,000 Equity shares of Rs. 10 each fully paid

(c) 40,000 Equity shares of Rs. 10 each Rs. 8 paid up.

(d) 30,000 Equity shares of Rs. 10 each Rs. 6 paid up.

Dividend on preference shares was in arrears for one year. The preference shareholders have priority over the equity shareholders as regards capital and dividend.

Liabilities :

Mortgage on building	65,000
Preferential creditors	15,000
Unsecured creditors	7,20,000
Assets realised :	
Building	75,000
Other assets	10,11,000

Liquidation expenses amounted to Rs. 4,440 Liquidator's remuneration :

(1) 1% commission on assets realised.

(2) 2% commission on amount paid to unsecured creditors.

Prepare liquidator's final statement of account.

(Karnataka, April 1991)

Ans. : Total of liquidator's final statement of account Rs. 11,51,000.
Liquidators remuneration Rs. 25,560 (10,860 + 14,700)
Amount collected from calls Rs. 1,30,000 (40,000 shares of Re. 1 each and 30,000 shares of Rs. 3 each)
Amount paid to preference share holders Rs. 3,36,000 (3,00,000 + 36,000)
Amount returned to fully paid equity shares holders Rs. 50,000 (50,000 × 1)

(8) The following particulars related to the Badluck Ltd. which went into voluntary liquidation on 31-12-1982 :

4,000 8% Preference shares of Rs. 100 each.	4,00,000
2,000 Equity shares of Rs. 100 each Rs. 75 paid up	1,50,000
6,000 Equity shares of Rs. 100 each Rs. 60 paid up	3,60,000
5% Debentures (having floating charge on all assets)	2,00,000
Creditors	2,90,000

The liquidator realised the assets as follows :

Land and Buildings	2,40,000
Plant and Machinery	4,00,000
Patents	60,000
Stock	1,20,000
Debtors	1,60,000

The dividend on preference shares was in arrears for two years which was to be paid on liquidation as per Articles of the company. The interest on debentures was due for the year 1982. The creditors include Rs. 1,00,000 loan on mortgage of land and buildings and Rs. 30,000 preferential creditors.

The expenses of liquidation amounted to Rs. 19,800. The liquidator is entitled to a commission at 5% on the assets realised and 2% on the amount distributed among the creditors. All payments were made on 30-6-1983.

Prepare the liquidator's final statement of account.

(Gulbarga, April 1984, 1987 Mod. & 1989)

Ans. : Total of liquidator's final statement of account Rs. 9,50,200.
Liquidator's remuneration Rs. 54,800 (*i.e.,* 49,000 *i.e.,* 5% on Rs. 9,80,000 + 5,800 *i.e.,* 2% on Rs. 2,90,000). Amount collected from calls Rs. 70,200 (*i.e.,* 6,000 Shares at Rs. 11.70 each).
Amount paid to equity shareholders Rs. 6,600 (*i.e.,* 2,000 Shares at Rs. 3.30 each)

(9) The Capital of the Unfortunate Ltd. (in voluntary liquidation), consists of 2,000 preference shares of Rs. 100 each fully paid up, 8,000 Ordinary Shares of Rs. 100 each fully paid up, 6,000 ordinary shares of Rs. 100 each, Rs. 80 per share paid up and 2,000 Deferred Shares of Rs. 100 each, Rs. 80 per share paid up. Under the Articles of Association, the preference shares have priority as to repayment of capital over the ordinary shares, and the ordinary shares have priority over the deferred shares.

The cost of liquidation including the liquidator's remuneration amounted to Rs. 14,000 and the creditors amounted to Rs. 1,78,000.

The assets realised Rs. 3,74,000. The call made by the liquidator on the deferred shareholders for the adjustment of the rights of shareholders (as between themselves) was fully paid. A call of Rs. 15 per share was made on the partly paid ordinary shareholders, which was duly paid, with the exception of that on 200 shares which was irrecoverable.

Prepare the liquidator's final statement of account.

(Adapted from Bangalore University)

Ans. : Total of liquidator's final statement of account Rs. 5,01,000.

Amount collected from calls Rs. 1,27,000 (*i.e.,* 2,000 deferred shares at Rs. 20 each plus 5,800 (6,000 – 200) partly paid equity shares at Rs. 15 each).

Amount paid to Ordinary shareholders who are fully paid Rs. 40,000 (*i.e.,*8,000 × 5). The remaining cash of Rs. 69,000 returned to 13,800 (8,000 + 5,800) ordinary shares.

Note : 200 partly paid ordinary shareholders who failed to pay the cash of Rs. 15 per share, lose their rights to receive any refund of capital.

(10) The Hubli Co. Ltd. went into voluntary liquidation on 31-12-1988. Its balance sheet on that date was as under :

Liabilities		Rs.	Assets	Rs.
Share Capital :			Goodwill	20,000
10,000 Shares of Rs. 10 each of which Rs. 8 per share called up	80,000		Building	45,000
			Plant	50,000
			Stock	4,300
Less : Calls unpaid	2,000	78,000	Debtors	13,850
Debentures		25,000	Cash	1,500
Preferential Creditors		9,250	Profit and Loss Account	56,850
Secured Creditors (secured on plant)		31,500		
Unsecured Creditors		43,250		
Bank Overdraft (unsecured)		4,500		
		1,91,500		1,91,500

The liquidator realised the assets as under :

Building	21,250
Plan	24,000
Stock	5,200
Debtors	13,550

The liquidation expenses amounted to Rs. 217. The liquidator's remuneration was agreed at 3% on the amount of assets realised and 2% on the amount paid to unsecured creditors.

Prepare the liquidator's final statement of account.

(Karnatak, April 1989 & 1998)

Ans. : The liquidator's final statement of account Rs. 63,500. Liquidator's remuneration Rs. 2,633 (Rs. 1,920 *i.e.* 3% on Rs. 64,000 plus Rs. 713 *i.e.,* 36,363 × 2/102)

Amount paid to unsecured creditors Rs. 35,650 including preferential creditors.

Amount collected from calls Rs. 20,000 (*i.e.* 10,000 × 2).

(11) The Secure Co. Ltd. went into voluntary liquidation on 31-12-1984 when the following balance sheet was prepared :

Liabilities	Rs.	Assets	Rs.
Share Capital :		Goodwill	50,000
Authorised :		Freehold Property	48,000
30,000 Shares of Rs. 10 each	3,00,000	Plant & Machinery	65,500
Subscribed & Paid up :		Debtors	64,820
19,500 Shares of Rs. 10 each	1,95,000	Stock	56,800
Sundry Creditors :		Cash	2,500
Preferential Creditors	24,200	Profit & Loss Account	98,680
Partly Secured Creditors	55,310		
Unsecured Creditors	99,790		
Bank Overdraft (unsecured)	12,000		
	3,86,300		3,86,300

The liquidators realised the assets as follows :

Leasehold property which was used in the first instance to pay the partly secured creditors pro-rate	35,000
Plant and Machinery	51,000
Stock	39,000
Sundry Debtors	58,500
Cash	2,500

The expenses of liquidation amounted to Rs. 1,000 and the liquidators remuneration was agreed at 2½% on the amount realised including cash in hand and 2% on the amount paid to unsecured creditors.

Prepare the liquidator's final statement of account.

(Gulbarga, Oct. 1982, 1984 & 1985 & Bangalore, April 1992)

Ans. : Total of liquidator's final statement of account Rs. 1,51,000
Liquidator's remuneration Rs. 7,500 (Rs. 4,650 *i.e.,* 2½% on Rs. 1,86,000 plus Rs. 2,850 *i.e.,* 1,45,350 × 2/102)
Amount paid to unsecured creditors Rs. 1,18,300.

(12) The following is the Trial Balance of Bombay Co. Ltd., on 1-4-1994, on which date the dividends on preference shares were in arrears for three years :

	Dr.	Cr.
	Rs.	Rs.
Share Capital :		
3,000 Equity shares of Rs. 100 each Rs. 50 per share paid up	–	1,50,000
1,500, 6% preference shares of Rs. 100 each fully paid up	–	1,50,000
Secured Loans against Machinery	–	15,000
Preferential Creditors	–	4,050
Machinery	1,50,000	–
Other Assets	1,95,000	–
Profit & Loss Account	29,050	–
Unsecured Creditors	–	35,000
Bills Payable	–	20,000
	3,74,050	3,74,050

The Company went into voluntary liquidation. Liquidator realised the assets as follows :

(a) Machinery Rs. 35,000; and (b) other assets Rs. 1,72,000. The liquidation expenses amounted to Rs. 2,760. The liquidator is entitled to a remuneration of Rs. 6,000 and a commission at 5% on the amount paid to preference shareholders as capital and dividends and 5% on the amount collected by him.

Prepare liquidator's final statement of account.

(Karnataka, April 1996 Old)

Ans. : Total of liquidator's final statement of account Rs. 2,67,800.
Liquidator's remuneration Rs. 22,990 (*i.e.,* Rs. 10,350 *i.e.,* 5% on 2,07,000 plus Rs. 8,850 *i.e.,* 5% on 1,77,000 plus Rs. 3,790 *i.e.,* on 5% on 75,800).
Amount collected from calls Rs. 75,800 (*i.e.,* Rs. 22.27 per share on 3,000 equity shares).

Note : Calculation of 5% Commission on the amount collected :

Amount to be collected on partly paid shares :

Amount needed for distribution except 5% commission on calls (2,760 + 10,350 + 8,850 + 4,050 + 35,000 + 2,000 + 1,77,000)	Rs. 2,64,010
Less : Amount available before collecting calls (1,72,000 + 20,000)	Rs. 1,92,000
Amount to be collected except 5% commission on calls	72,010

Therefore, deficit amount *i.e.,* 72,010 plus 5% commission on calls should be collected. Rs. 72,010 is 95% of the amount collected. Hence, the extra 5% is to be collected to pay off commission. So, the amount to the collected is Rs. 75,800 (*i.e.,* 72,010 × 100/95).

(13) The Fast Ltd. went into voluntary liquidation on 31-12-1987 on which date its balance sheet was as follows :

Liabilities	Rs.	Assets	Rs.
Share Capital :		Goodwill	15,000
10,000 Equity shares of		Building	25,000
Rs. 10 each fully paid	1,00,000	Machinery	30,000
Bank Overdraft (unsecured)	20,000	Stocks	45,000
Sundry Creditors :		Debtors	34,000
Preferential	4,000	Cash	1,000
Unsecured	56,000	Profit & Loss Account	50,000
Partly secured (building)	20,000		
	2,00,000		2,00,000

The liquidator realised the assets as follows :

Building	Rs. 12,000
Machinery	Rs. 25,000
Stock	Rs. 30,000
Debtors	Rs. 13,000
Cash	Rs. 1,000

The expenses of liquidation came to Rs. 4,600 and the liquidator's remuneration was fixed at 4% on the amounts realised (excluding cash) and 2% on the distribution made to unsecured creditors.

Prepare the liquidator's final statement of account.

(Gulbarga, Oct. 1988)

Ans. : Total of liquidator's final statement of account Rs 69,000.

Liquidator's Remuneration Rs. 4,400 (Rs. 3,200 *i.e.,* 4% on Rs. 80,000 plus Rs. 1,200 *i.e.,* 61,200 × 2/102)

Amount paid to unsecured creditors Rs. 56,000 excluding preferential creditors.

Note : Rs. 12,000 is paid to partly secured creditors, Remaining balance of partly secured creditors of Rs. 8,000 (20,000 – 12,000) is included in unsecured creditors.

(14) The following is the balance sheet of the Unfortunate Ltd. as on 31-12-1985 :

Liabilities	Rs.	Assets	Rs.
Share Capital :		Buildings	2,00,000
4,000 6% preferential shares		Machinery	5,00,000
at Rs. 10 each	4,00,000	Patents	80,000
2,000 Equity shares of Rs. 100		Stock	1,10,000
each Rs. 75 per share paid up	1,50,000	Sundry Debtors	2,20,000
6,000 Equity shares of Rs. 100		Cash at Bank	60,000
each Rs. 60 per share paid up	3,60,000	Profit & Loss Account	2,40,000
10% Debentures (having floating			
charge on all the assets)	2,00,000		
Outstanding Interest on			
Debentures	10,000		
Sundry Creditors	2,90,000		
	14,10,000		14,10,000

On that date, the company went into liquidation. The dividend on preference shares was in arrears for two years which is payable on liquidation as per Articles of Association. Creditors include a loan of Rs. 1,00,000 on mortgage of buildings.

The liquidator realised the assets as follows :

Buildings	Rs. 24,000	Stock	Rs. 1,20,000
Machinery	Rs. 4,00,000	Debtors	Rs. 1,60,000
Patents	Rs. 60,000		

The expenses of liquidation amounted to Rs. 21,800. The liquidator is entitled to a commission of 3% on all the assets realised (except cash at bank) and a commission of 2% on the amount paid to unsecured creditors. Preferential creditors amounted to Rs. 30,000. All the payments were made on 31-3-1986.

Prepare the liquidator's final statement of account showing the distribution.

(Gulbarga, April 1984 & 1987)

Ans. : Total of liquidator's final statement of account Rs. 9,23,500.
Remuneration to liquidator Rs. 33,200 (Rs. 29,400 (*i.e.,* 3% on Rs. 9,80,000) Plus Rs. 3,800 *i.e.,* 1,93,800 × 2/102)
Account paid to unsecured creditors Rs. 1,90,000

Amount collected on calls Rs. 43,450 (*i.e.,* 7.25 per share on 6,000 equity shares)

Amount refunded to equity shareholders Rs. 15,500 (*i.e.,* Rs. 7.75 per share on 2,000 shares)

Note : Debenture interest is paid up to 31-3-1986 including outstanding interest.

(15) Balance Sheet of Fortunate Ltd. as on December 31, 1998 :

Liabilities	Rs.	Assets	Rs.
Share Capital :			
10,000, 9% Preference shares		Sundry assets	7,00,000
of Rs. 10 each	1,00,000	Building	1,80,000
20,000 Equity shares of		Profit and Loss A/c	1,00,000
Rs. 10 each fully paid	2,00,000	Preliminary expenses	20,000
10,000 Equity shares of			
Rs. 10 each Rs. 8 paid	80,000		
9% Debentures	3,00,000		
Bank Overdraft	1,20,000		
Trade Creditors	1,50,000		
Income Tax due	50,000		
	10,00,000		10,00,000

The debentures were secured by a floating charge on all the assets of the company. The debentureholders appointed a Receiver. A liquidator was also appointed, the company being voluntarily wound up. The Receiver took charge of sundry assets amounting to Rs. 5,00,000 and sold them for Rs. 4,00,000. The building and the remaining sundry assets realised Rs. 1,20,000 and Rs. 2,80,000 respectively. The cost of the Receiver amounted to Rs. 2,000 and his remuneration to Rs. 2,500. The expenses of liquidation were Rs. 3,000 and the remuneration of the liquidator was Rs. 2,500.

Prepare the accounts to be submitted by the Receiver and the Liquidator.

(Adapted from B. Com., Bombay & C.A. Inter)

Ans. : Receiver's Statement of Account Total Rs. 4,00,000

Receiver's Statement of Account Balance Rs. 45,500

Liquidator's Final Statement of Account Total Rs. 4,45,500

Amount paid to Equity shareholders :

Rs. 2 on 20,000 shares = 40,000

Re. 1 on 30,000 shares = 30,000

Rs. 70,000

Note : Preferential creditors *i.e.,* Income tax due and debentureholders are taken in receiver's statement of account.

(16) The liquidation of X Ltd. commenced on Ist July, 1998 and the assets were insufficient to pay the creditors. Unpaid amounts could not be realised from 'A' list contributories. Prepare a statement of liability of 'B' list contributories from the details given below :

Shareholders	No. of shares transferred	Date of transfer	Debts outstanding on the date of transfer
Ram	500	15th June, 1997	Rs. 10,000
Shyam	900	15th Sept., 1997	Rs. 12,000
Madan	600	15th Nov., 1997	Rs. 15,000
Sundar	300	15th March, 1978	Rs. 18,750

All the shares were of Rs. 25 each of which Rs. 15 were paid up.

(Adapted from B.Com. Madras & C.A. Inter)

Ans. : Amount to be realised from the contributors : Shyam Rs. 6,000; Madan Rs. 6,000 and Sundar Rs. 3,000.

Note : The liability against Sundar is Rs. 6,750. But his unpaid amount on shares is Rs. 3,000 only. He will not contribute anything more than Rs. 3,000. Hence, the loss of Rs. 3,750 will have to be suffered by the concerned creditors.

(17) You are asked by liquidator of a company to prepare a statement of account to be laid before a meeting of the shareholders from the following :

Balance Sheet of the company as on date of liquidation, *i.e.,* 1-1-1987 :

Liabilities	Rs.	Assets	Rs.
Share Capital :		Fixed Assets	4,00,000
4,000 Equity shares of		Book Debts	3,00,000
Rs. 100 each Rs. 80 called	3,20,000	Loss to date	1,00,000
1,000 Preference shares of			
Rs. 100 each Rs. 70 called	70,000		
Secured Loan from Banks			
on Building and Machinery	1,50,000		
Trade Creditors	2,60,000		
	8,00,000		8,00,000

The assets realised as follows :

1-4-1987: Fixed Assets Rs. 1,00,000, Book Debts Rs. 1,00,000, Expenses paid Rs. 4,000. 1-6-1987 : Fixed Assets (Final) Rs. 2,00,000, Book Debts Rs.1,00,000. 1-8-1987: Book Debts (Final) Rs. 50,000.

The liquidator is entitled to 5% on collections and 2% on the amount paid to equity shareholders.

Prepare the statements on the assumption that disbursements are made in accordance with law, as and when cash is available.

(Adapted from C. A. Final)

Ans. : Liquidator's Final Statement of Account Total : 1-4-87 Rs. 1,00,000; 1-6-87, Rs. 2,50,000 and 1-8-87 Rs. 50,000. Liquidator's remuneration : 1-4-87 Rs. 10,000; 1-6-87 Rs. 15,000 and 1-8-87 Rs. 3,250 (Rs. 2,500 *i.e.,* 5% on 50,000 plus Rs. 755 *i.e.,* 38,500 × 2/102).
Payments made to secured creditors : 1-4-87 Rs. 1,00,000 (*i.e.,* amount realised from the fixed assets) and 1-6-87 Rs. 50,000. Payments made to unsecured creditors : 1-4-87 Rs. 86,000 and 1-6-87 Rs. 1,74,000. Amount paid to pref. shareholders : 1-6-87 Rs. 61,000 and 1-8-87 Rs. 9,000. Amount paid to equity shareholders : 1-8-87 Rs. 37,745.

(18) The following is the Balance Sheet of Rashiko Ltd. on 31-12-1995 :

Liabilities	Rs.	Assets	Rs.
Share Capital :		Building	1,00,000
2,000 6% Pref. shares of		Machinery	2,50,000
Rs. 100 each	2,00,000	Patents	40,000
1,000 Equity shares of		Stock	65,000
Rs. 100 each Rs. 75 paid up	75,000	Debtors	1,00,000
3,000 Equity shares of Rs. 100		Bank	30,000
each Rs. 60 paid up	1,80,000	Profit & Loss Account	1,20,000
10% Debentures (having			
floating charge on assets)	1,00,000		
Interest on Debenture due	5,000		
Sundry Creditors	1,05,000		
Bills Payable	30,000		
Pref. Creditors for tax	10,000		
	7,05,000		7,05,000

On the above date the company went into voluntary liquidation. The dividend on preference shares was in arrears for two years. The sundry creditors include a loan of Rs. 50,000 on mortagage on building.

The liquidator realised the assets as follows :

Building Rs. 1,20,000, Machinery Rs. 2,00,000, Patents Rs. 30,000, Stock Rs. 60,000 and Debtors Rs. 80,000.

The legal expenses and cost of winding up amounted to Rs. 2,900 and Rs. 8,000 respectively. The liquidator is entitled to a commission of 3% on assets realised by him and 2% on the amount paid to unsecured creditors. All payments were made on 31-3-1996.

Prepare the Liquidator's Final Statement of Account. Also give working details.

(C.A. Inter)

Ans. : Total of Liquidator's Final Statement of Account Rs. 4,70,000. Liquidator's remuneration Rs. 16,600 (14,700 + 1,900) Payments made to Debentureholders Rs. 1,07,500 (1,00,000 + 5,000 + 2,500)

Amount paid to equity share holders :

(i) Excess of 15 per share on 1,000 equity shares	15,000
(ii) Balance equally on 4,000 equity shares	1,000
(*i.e.,* 0.25 paise per share)	16,000

(19) Bad Luck Limited went into liquidation. Its assets realised Rs. 1,75,000 excluding the amount realised by sale of securities held by the secured creditors. The following was the position :

Share capital : 500 shares of Rs. 100 each	
Secured creditors (securities realised Rs. 20,000)	17,500
Preferential creditors	3,000
Unsecured creditors	70,000
Debentures having a floating charge on the assets on the company	1,25,000
Liquidation expenses	6,250

Liquidator is to be paid a commission of 2% on the amount actually paid to unsecured creditors uncluding preferential creditors. Prepare Liquidator's Final Statement of Account.

(Bangalore April, 1995)

Total of liquidator's final statement of account Rs. 1,77,500; liquidator remuneration Rs. 907 (Rs. 46,250 × 2/102) and Amount distributed to unsecured creditors Rs. 42,343.

(20) Unfortunate Ltd. went into voluntary liquidation on 1-4-1994 on which date its position was as under :

Liabilities :	Rs.
Share Capital : 2,500 shares of Rs. 100 each Rs. 80 per share paid up	2,00,000
Secured Loan (Land, Building, Machinery)	50,000
Unsecured Loan	95,000
Preferential Creditors	5,000
	3,50,000
Assets :	
Land, Building, Machinery	40,000
Other Fixed Assets	1,30,000
Stock	52,500
Debtors	50,000
Loans	20,000
Cash	2,500
Profit & Loss Account	55,000
	3,50,000

Land, building and machinery were realised by secured creditors for Rs. 60,000. Other fixed assets realised Rs. 20,000, debtors Rs. 10,000, stock Rs. 5,000. Loans were completely bad, Liquidator is to be paid a commission of Rs. 500 (fixed) plus 1% of the amount paid to unsecured creditors, excluding preferential creditors. Liquidator's out of pocket expenses amounted to Rs. 500. Prepare Liquidator's Final Statement of Account.

(Bangalore, April 1996)

Ans. : Total of liquidators final statement of account Rs. 47,700; Surplus from secured creditors Rs. 10,000 and Liquidator's remuneration Rs. 911 (Rs. 500 + 411 *i.e.,* 41,500 × 1/110).

***Notes* :** (i) Amount paid to unsecured creditors Rs. 41,089.

(ii) Liquidator's out of pocket expenses are treated as liquidation expenses.

(21) The capital of Omega Co. Ltd. was :

(a) 1,000 Preference shares of Rs. 100 each fully paid.

(b) 4,000 Equity shares of Rs. 100 each fully paid.

(c) 3,000 Equity shares of Rs. 100 each Rs. 80 paid.

The creditors were Rs. 2,54,900 of which Rs. 10,900 were preferential and Rs. 54,000 fully secured. The assets realised Rs. 3,74,000 including those sold on behalf of fully secured creditors.

The cost of liquidation amounted to Rs. 12,000 and the liquidator's remuneration was 5% of the amount realised (excluding security of creditors) and 3% on the amount distributed to unsecured creditors. The liquidator made a call of Rs. 15 per share on the partly paid equity shares which was duly paid except by one member holding 200 shares.

Prepare Liquidator's Final Statement.

(Bangalore, November 1996)

Ans. : Total of liquidator's final statement of account Rs. 3,62,000; calls on shares Rs. 42,000 (2,800 shares × Rs. 150); liquidators remuneration Rs. 22,027 (16,000 + 6,027); Amount paid to equity shareholders Rs. 27,073 (Rs. 3.98 per share) and Amount paid to unsecured creditors Rs. 1,90,000 [2,54,900 – (54,000 + 10,900)].

Hint: 3% of liquidator's remuneration is calculated on Rs. 2,00,900 (1,90,000 + 10,900).

(22) The Un-Sound Ltd. went into Voluntary Liquidation on 31-3-1990 on which date the position was as follows :

	Rs.		Rs.
5,000 Equity shares of Rs. 100 each Rs. 80 paid	4,00,000	Land	80,000
		Other Fixed Assets	2,60,000
Land secured by Land	1,00,000	Stock	1,05,000
Unsecured Creditors (including Rs. 10,000 Preferential creditors)	2,00,000	Debtors	1,00,000
		Cash	5,000
		Loan	40,000
		P & L A/c	1,10,000
	7,00,000		7,00,000

Land was realised by secured creditors for Rs. 1,20,000. Other fixed assets realised Rs. 40,000, debtors Rs. 20,000 and stock Rs. 10,000. Loans were fully bad. Liquidator is entitled to a fixed remuneration of Rs. 1,000.

Prepare Liquidator's Final Statement of Account, assuming further that (1) Liquidator is entitled to an additional remuneration of 2% on the amount paid to unsecured creditors including preferential creditors. (2) Liquidator's out of pocket expenses amounted to Rs. 1,000. (3) The Liquidator made a call of Rs ?

(Bangalore, April 1997)

Ans. : Total of liquidator's final statement of account Rs. 95,000; Liquidator's remuneration Rs. 2,824 (1,000 + 1,824 *i.e.,* 93,000 × 2/102) and Amount paid to unsecured creditors Rs. 81,176.

***Notes* :** (i) The liquidators out of pocket expenses are treated as liquidation expenses.

(ii) Liquidator did not make any call.

(23) The Bad Luck Company went into voluntary liquidation on 31-6-1991. On that date, its Balance sheet was as follows :

Liabilities	Rs.	Assets		Rs.
15,000, 8% Preference shares of Re. 1 each	15,000	Machinery		25,000
30,000 Equity shares	30,000	Stock		18,000
	45,000	Debtors		14,500
(–) deficiency of P & L A/c	5,000	Cash		500
				58,000
	40,000	(–) 6% Debentures	10,000	
		Creditors	8,000	18,000
	40,000			40,000

The dividend on preference shares had been paid upto 30-6-1990. In this case, the preference shares had the right of getting their capital and arrears of dividend, before any amount is repaid to ordinary shareholders.

The liquidator sold the stock and machines for Rs. 36,500 and collected Rs. 14,500 from the debtors. In addition to the creditors mentioned above, he had to pay to the preferential creditors by way of taxes to the extent of Rs. 1,000. The liquidation expenses were Rs. 210. The debentureholders were repaid on 31-12-1991 along with interest upto this date.

2% on the amount realised by sale of stock and machines and collections from debtors, and 2% on the amount finally paid to the equity shareholders was to be the liquidator's remuneration.

Prepare the Liquidator's Final Account.

(Bangalore, November 1997)

Ans. : Liquidator's Final Statement of Account Total Rs. 51,500; Assets realised Rs. 51,500 (*i.e.,* 500 + 36,500 + 14,500); Paid to Debentureholders Rs. 10,300 (*i.e.,* 10,000+300 Interest); Paid to Pref. shareholders Rs. 16,200 (*i.e.,* 15,000 + 1,200 Dividend) and Liquidator's remuneration Rs. 1,310.

***Notes* :** (i) Liquidation remuneration is calculated as below :

2% on Rs. 51,000 (stock & machines and debtors)	=	Rs. 1,020
2% on Rs. 14,480 (Amount paid to equity shareholders)	=	Rs. 290
	Total	Rs. 1,310

(ii) Amount paid to Equity Shareholders is calculated as below :
Amount available after making the preferential payments is Rs. 14,770 (*i.e.,* cash collected Rs. 51,500 Minus Rs. 36,730. Preferential payments, *i.e.,* 210 + 1,020 + 1,000 + 10,300 + 8,000 + 16,200).
Out of this amount (*i.e.,* 14,770), a remuneration to the liquidator is also to be paid. The remuneration of liquidator is Rs. 290 (*i.e.,* Rs. 14,770 × 2/102). The balance amount of Rs. 14,480 (*i.e.,* 14,770 – 290) is paid to the equity shareholders. Payment per equity share Re. 1 = 0.483 paise (*i.e.,* 14,480/30,000).

(24) Bad Luck Ltd., went into voluntary liquidation on 31-12-1997. The following was the Balance sheet on that date.

Balance Sheet as at 31-12-1997

Liabilities	Rs.	Assets	Rs.
Share capital :		Land and Building	25,000
500, 6% Preference shares		Machinery	62,500
of Rs. 100 each	50,000	Furniture	10,000
250 Equity shares of		Stock	13,750
Rs. 100 each Rs. 75 paid	18,750	Sundry Debtors	27,500
750 Equity shares of		Cash at Bank	7,500
Rs. 100 each Rs. 60 paid	45,000	Profit and Loss Account	30,000
5% Debentures having a			
floating charge on all assets	25,000		
Interest Outstanding	1,250		
Creditors	36,250		
	1,76,250		1,76,250

The preference dividend was in arrears for two years. Creditors include a loan of Rs. 12,500 on the mortgage of land and building.

The assets were realised as follows :

	Rs.
Land and Building	30,000
Machinery	50,000
Furniture	7,500
Stock	15,000
Sundry Debtors	20,000

The expenses of liquidation amouted to Rs. 2,725. The liquidator is entitled to a remuneration of 3% on all assets realised except cash at Bank and a commission of 2% on amounts distributed among unsecured creditors.

Preferential creditors amounted to Rs. 3,750. The payment was made on 30th June, 1998. Prepare the liquidator's final statement of account.

(Karnataka, Oct. 1998)

Ans. : Liquidator's Final Statement of A/c Total Rs. 1,17,500; Liquidator's remuneration Rs. 4,150 [Rs. 3,675 (*i.e.,* 3% on Rs. 1,22,500) + Rs. 75 (*i.e.,* 2% on Rs. 3,750) + Rs. 400 (*i.e.,* 2% on Rs. 20,000)]; Amount paid to debentureholders Rs. 26,875 (25,000 + 1,250 + 625).

Hints :

(i) Amount paid to preference shareholders Rs. 56,000 (50,000 + 6,000)

(ii) Amount paid to unsecured creditors Rs. 20,000 [*i.e.,* Creditors Rs. 23,750 (*i.e.,* Rs. 36,250 Minus securities held Rs. 12,500) + 3,750 preferential creditors].

(iii) Amount paid to equity shareholders :

Paid to 250 equity shareholders at Rs. 15 each	Rs. 3,750
Paid to 1,000 equity shareholders at 25 paise	Rs. 250
	Rs. 4,000

******

7

HOLDING COMPANIES

Meaning

A holding company is one which holds more than half of the nominal value of the equity share capital of another company or which controls the composition of the Board of Directors of another company. The company which is so controlled by the holding company is termed as a "Subsidiary Company". For example, 'H' company holds 51% of the nominal value of the equity share capital of 'S' company, or if it is entitled to appoint 4 out of 7 directors of 'S' company, then 'H' company is called holding company of 'S' company and 'S' company is called a subsidiary company of 'H' company. According to Section 4(4) of the Companies Act, 1956, "A company shall be deemed to be the holding company of the another, but only if that other is its subsidiary." It means that there cannot be no holding company without there being one or more subsidiaries.

According to Section 4 (1) of the Companies Act, a company is subsidiary of other company if, the other company—

(a) controls the composition of its Board of Directors; or

(b) holds more than half in nominal value of its equity share capital; or

(c) if formed before 1st April, 1956 with both equity and preference shareholders having the same voting rights, the other company exercises or controls more than half of its total voting power.

Formation of holding company is the most popular form business combination to—

(i) eliminate the competition.

(ii) reduce cost through large scale operation.

(iii) ensure a smooth supply of raw materials.

(iv) get an assured market for the products.

(v) save the taxes etc.

Wholly Owned and Partly Owned Subsidiaries

When all the shares of a subsidiary company are held or owned by the holding company, the subsidiary company is called as wholly owned subsidiary company. In such a case, there will not be any outside shareholders and the entire profit of the subsidiary company belongs to the holding company. On the other hand, when a majority of shares *i.e.,* more than half the value of equity shares are held or owned by the holding company, the subsidiary company is called as 'partly-owned subsidiary company'.

Final Accounts

In England, it is compulsory for the holding company to present a consolidated Balance Sheet and consolidated Profit and Loss Account incorporating its own operations as well as the operations of subsidiary companies. But in India, the company law does not compel a holding company to prepare a consolidated Balance Sheet and Profit and Loss account. But, it just requires a holding company to attach to its Balance Sheet certain documents relating to its subsidiary. Under Section 212 of the Companies Act, the holding company has to attach the following documents to its Balance Sheet relating to its subsidiary—

(1) a copy of the Balances Sheet of the subsidiary,

(2) a copy of the Profit and Loss Account,

(3) a copy of the report of its Board of Directors,

(4) a copy of the Report of Auditors,

(5) (a) a statement of the holding company's interest in the subsidiary.

(b) the profits of the subsidiary so far as they concern the holding company.

Explanation of Certain Terms

1. Capital Profits and Revenue Profits. Any profit earned by the subsidiary company before the date of acquisition is treated as capital profit for the purpose of consolidated Balance Sheet. In other words, all the pre-acquisition profits/losses of the subsidiary company are capital profits/losses for the holding company. The profits which may be of revenue nature for the subsidiary company, may be capital profits so far as the holding company is concerned. While preparing the consolidated Balance Sheet, the capital profits or losses should be adjusted with the cost of control. The profit arising out of the appreciation of fixed asset on their revaluation even in the post-acquisition period is also a capital profit and the same is treated like profits pertaining to pre-acquisition period.

Any reduction in the value of fixed assets as on the date of acquisition, is treated as capital loss and deducted from the capital profits. But if any fall in the value of assets after the date of acquisition, it is termed as an ordinary revenue loss.

On the other hand, any profit earned by the subsidiary company after the acquisition date is termed as revenue profit. In other words, all post-acquisition profits/losses of subsidiary company are revenue profits/losses. While preparing the consolidated Balance Sheet, the revenue profits should be merged with the balance in the P & L A/c of holding company.

2. Pre-acquisition and Post-acquisition Profits. Profits made by the subsidiary company prior to the date of acquisition of shares by the holding company are called as pre-acquisition profits or capital profits. When the shares are purchased by the holding company, it will have a right over these profits also. Hence, such profits received would reduce the cost of shares acquired. The holding company's share of pre-acquisition profits is to be calculated and shown separately under the heading 'Capital Reserve' or adjusted against the 'Cost Control' if it is partly owned subsidiary and the remaining balance of pre-acquisition profit is to be added to the interest of the minority shareholders. If it is wholly owned subsidiary, the entire share of pre-acquisition profit is to be shown separately under the heading 'Capital Reserve' or adjusted against the 'Cost Control'. The position will be reverse in case of pre-acquisition loss.

The profits earned by the subsidiary company after the date of acquisition of shares by the holding company are called as 'Post-acquisition Profits' or 'Revenue Profits'. Such entire profits are the income to the holding company if it is wholly owned subsidiary. If it is partly owned subsidiary, only the portion belonging to the holding company is to be added to the profits of the holding company. The remaining balance of post-acquisition profits should be added to the interest of minority shareholders. The position will be reverse in case of post-acquisition loss.

3. Pre-acquisition and Post-acquisition Reserves. The reserves created by the subsidiary company prior to the date of purchase of shares by the holding company are called 'Pre-acquisition Reserves'. On the other hand, the reserves created by the subsidiary company after the date of purchase of shares by the holding company are called 'Post-acquisition Reserves'. The pre-acquisition and post-acquisition reserves are to be treated just like pre-acquisition and post-acquisition profits.

4. Majority and Minority Interest. Majority interest or holding company's interest is the share or claim or interest of the holding company in the net assets (*i.e.*, assets minus liabilities) of the subsidiary company. Net assets being nothing but aggregation of share capital, reserves, surplus, funds, etc. of the subsidiary company belonging to its shareholders. Majority interest or holding company's interest includes the following :

(i) Share in share capital of subsidiary company (*i.e.*, deducted from investment on assets side or deducted from the cost of acquisition of shares under goodwill).

(ii) Share in pre-acquisition reserve or capital reserve of the subsidiary company (added to capital reserve).

(iii) Share in post-acquisition of reserve or revenue reserve of subsidiary company (added to general reserve).

(iv) Share in pre-acquisition profit or capital profit of subsidiary company (added to capital reserve).

(v) Share in post-acquisition or revenue profit of subsidiary company (added to revenue profits).

(vi) Increase in the value of assets (before or after acquisition of subsidiary company (added to capital reserve).

(vii) Decrease in the value of assets of subsidiary company to (if it is pre-acquisition, it should be added to goodwill or deducted from capital reserve. If it is post-acquisition, it should be deducted from surplus *i.e.*, profit).

(viii) Share in pre-acquisition loss of subsidiary company (deducted from capital reserve or added to goodwill).

(ix) Share in post-acquisition loss of subsidiary company (deducted from surplus *i.e.*, profit).

Minority interest or outsider's interest is the share or claim or interest of minority shareholders or outside shareholders in the net assets of the subsidiary company. For example, if the holding company holds 75% of the equity share capital of the subsidiary company and the balance 25% belongs to outsiders, the share of the outsiders in the subsidiary company is called minority interest. In the consolidated Balance Sheet, all the assets and liabilities of the subsidiary company are consolidated with the assets and liabilities of the holding company and the minority interest in the subsidiary company will be shown as liability. Minority interest or outsider's interest includes the following :

(i) Share in share capital of the subsidiary company.

(ii) Share in pre- and post-acquisition reserves of the subsidiary company. (added to share capital of outsiders).

(iii) Share in pre and post-acquisition surplus of the subsidiary company (added to share capital of outsiders).

(iv) Share in increase in the value of the assets of the subsidiary company (added to share capital of outsiders).

(v) Share in pre- and post-acquisition losses of the subsidiary company (deducted from the share capital of outsiders).

(vi) Share in decrease in the value of assets of the subsidiary company (deducted from the share capital of outsiders).

The share of outsiders in the profit or losses will be calculated only with reference to equity shares held by the outsiders since the profits and reserves belong to only equity shareholders. If the preference shares are held by the outsiders, the face value of shares with the dividend due thereon will be included in the outsider's interest. If the subsidiary company is not earned profit and the preference share are cumulative, the dividend due should be shown by way of a note.

Chart Showing the Majority (Holding) and Minority (Outsiders) Interest in the Subsidiary Company

Sl. No.	Particulars	Total Interest	Majority Interest	Minority Interest
1.	Share capital	xxx	xxx	xxx
2.	Reserve : (a) pre-acquisition reserve	xxx	xxx	xxx
	(b) post-acquisition reserve	xxx	xxx	xxx
3.	Surplus : (a) pre-acquisition reserve	xxx	xxx	xxx
	(b) post-acquisition reserve	xxx	xxx	xxx
4.	Increase in value of assets (pre- or post-acquisition)	xxx	xxx	xxx
	"A"	xxx	xxx	xxx
	Deduct the following if any :			
1.	Decrease in the value of assets :			
	(a) pre-acquisition	xxx	xxx	xxx
	(b) post-acquisition	xxx	xxx	xxx
2.	Losses if any:			
	(a) pre-acquisition loss	xxx	xxx	xxx
	(b) post-acquisition loss	xxx	xxx	xxx
	"B"	xxx	xxx	xxx
	A – B	xxxx	xxx	xxx

5. Cost of Control or Goodwill and Capital Reserve. When the subsidiary company has accumulated profits or accumulated losses in its balance sheet at the time of acquisition of shares by the holding company, the holding company may acquire the shares of the subsidiary company at a premium or at a discount. If the holding company acquires the shares of the subsidiary company at a price above the face value, the excess price paid represents payment for cost control or goodwill. This amount of goodwill must further be increased by the holding company's share in the capital loss or be reduced by the capital profits. The goodwill already appearing in the books of holding and subsidiary is to be added to the amount of cost of control or goodwill to get the 'total goodwill'. The total cost of control/goodwill should be set off against the total capital reserve. The remaining balance of goodwill should be entered on the assets side of the balance sheet. The total amount of cost of control/goodwill is calculated as below :

		Rs.
Price paid for acquiring shares in subsidiary company *i.e.*, cost of shares purchased		xxxx
Less : Face value or nominal value of shares acquired or purchased		xxxx
		xxxx
Less : Holding company's share of capital profits		xxxx
		xxxx
Add : Holding company's share of capital losses	xxx	
Holding company's share of fictitious assets	xxx	
Holding and subsidiary companies' goodwill already appearing in the books	xxx	xxxx
Total cost of control or goodwill		xxxx

On the other hand, if the actual price by the holding company for the purchase of shares of subsidiary company is less than the paid up value or face value of shares in the subsidiary company, it is treated as 'Capital Reserve'. In other words, it is excess of shares acquired over the cost of shares *i.e.*, investments. This capital reserve will be increased by the pre-acquisition profits and reserves and reduced by the pre-acquisition loss. The total amount of capital reserve is calculated as below :

	Rs.
Face value/paid up value of shares in subsidiary company	xxxx
Less : Actual price paid for shares in subsidiary company	xxx
	xxx
Add : Holding company' share of capital profits and other capital reserves	xxx
	xxx
Less : Holding company's share of capital losses	xxx
	xxx
Add : Capital reserves already existing in the books of holding company	xxx
Total Capital Reserves	xxxx

The total capital reserve should be set off against the total goodwill. The remaining balance of capital reserve should be shown on the liabilities side of the balance sheet. In other words, if the goodwill is less than the capital reserve, it should be deducted from the capital reserves and the net capital reserves should be shown on the liabilities side of the balance sheet. On the other hand, if total capital reserve is less than the goodwill, it should be deducted from the goodwill and net goodwill should be shown on the assets of the balance sheet.

6. Inter Company or Mutual Indebtedness. While preparing the consolidated balance sheet, sums owed by holding company to its subsidiary and *vice versa.* Such amounts owed by one company to the other are called mutual owings, inter company debts, inter company transactions or inter company balances. Between holding company and its subsidiary companies several transactions on mutual interest may take place : goods may be supplied on credit, loans may be given and bills may be drawn and accepted. Such transactions represent mutual indebtedness which are to be eliminated while preparing the consolidated balance sheet. If such eliminations are not made, the assets and liabilities will be over stated in the consolidated balance sheet. Inter company eliminations should be made in the consolidated balance sheet as below :

(i) ***Inter company debtors and creditors.*** When one company sells goods to another company on credit, there will arise debts due from one company to another. If such dues are not settled on the date of consolidated balance sheet, they should be deducted both from the total debtors and total creditors in the consolidated balance sheet.

(ii) ***Inter company loans and advances.*** When the loans are advanced by one company to another, there will arise loans due from one company to another. If such loans and advances are not settled on the date of balance sheet, they should be deducted from the total loans and advances of both sides of the consolidated balance sheet.

(iii) ***Bills receivable and bills payable***. When one company accepts the bill drawn by another company, the amount of the bill outstanding, if any, on the date of consolidated balance sheet, should be deducted from the total bills receivable and total bills payable in the consolidated balance sheet. However, bills which have been discounted with a bank or which have been endorsed over to somebody else by the drawer company, will not constitute mutual debts. Hence, they will not be eliminated and will appear in the balance sheet as a liability.

7. Unrealised Profit. When the holding company sells goods to the subsidiary company or *vice versa*, the selling company will add some profit to the cost price of the goods. If such goods are sold out, the profit on such goods is said to be realized. But, if there is any unsold stock of such goods, the profit made on such unsold goods is said to be unrealized. This unrealized profit is not genuine profit. Therefore, this unrealized profit should be eliminated from the profits of the selling company. Similarly, if there is an unrealized profit, the unsold stock of the buying company is not valued correctly. Therefore, the stock of the buying company should be reduced to the extent of unrealized profit. The following journal entry should be passed to deduct the unrealized profit from the profit of the selling company and from the stock of buying company.

Profit and loss Account (Selling Company) Dr.

To Stock Reserve Account (Buying Company)

While eliminating the unrealized profit, earlier there was a practice of eliminating the amount of unrealized profit to the extent of interest of the holding company, since for the minority shareholders the profit is nothing but realized profit. But according to AS-21, it is now necessary to consider the whole amount of unrealised profit as stock reserve without adjusting the share of minority shareholders. Hence, the entire amount of unrealised profit (stock reserve) (and not just the holding company's share of unrealized profit included in stock) has to be eliminated from the P & L A/c on the liability side and also from the stock on the asset side of the consolidated Balance sheet. Thus, P & L A/c will now show only realised profit and stock will show as its true cost.

8. Revaluation of Assets and Liabilities. The holding company can decide to revalue the assets and liabilities of the subsidiary company on the date of the acquisition of shares. Any profit or loss on such revaluation of assets and liabilities is treated as a capital profit or loss. If the assets are undervalued and now the value of the assets is appreciated by the holding company, the difference between revised value and book value, should be adjusted on both sides of the consolidated balance sheet. The holding company's share of such difference (*i.e.*, capital profit) should be added to capital reserve or deducted from the cost of control (goodwill) and the remaining balance should be added to minority interest on the liability side. Similarly, such difference (*i.e.*, capital profit) should be added to the respective assets on the assets side. On the other hand, if the assets are overvalued and now the value of the assets is depreciated by the holding company, the difference between book value and revised value should be adjusted on both sides of the consolidated balance sheet. On the liabilities side, the holding company's share of such difference (*i.e.*, capital loss) should be deducted from the capital reserve or added to goodwill and the remaining balance should be deducted from the minority interest. On the assets side, such difference (*i.e.*, capital loss) should be deducted from the respective assets.

9. Share Premium. The share premium appearing in the books of holding company will appear in the consolidated balance sheet as share premium. But, the share premium appearing in the books of subsidiary company, will be divided between the holding company and subsidiary company. The holding company's share of share premium will be treated as capital reserve and added to capital reserve. The minority shareholders' share of share premium will be added to the minority interest.

10. Contingent Liabilities. Contingent liabilities are those liabilities whose occurrence is uncertain. They may happen or may not happen. They are two types : (i) External contingent liabilities and (ii) Internal contingent liabilities. External contingent liabilities arise between the company (*i.e.*, holding or subsidiary) and the outsiders. Examples are : Arrears of preference dividend, liability in respect of calls etc. On the other hand, internal contingent liabilities arise between the holding company and subsidiary company. Examples are : Guarantee given by holding company on behalf of subsidiary company or *vice versa,* liability in respect of bills of exchange drawn by holding company on the subsidiary or *vice versa* and discounted with bank etc. External contingent liabilities are shown at the foot of the consolidated balance sheet and internal contingent liabilities are to be eliminated from the footnote since they appear as actual liabilities in the consolidated balance sheet.

11. Dividend paid by the Subsidiary Company. When the dividend is paid by the subsidiary company to the holding company on its investment on shares, it should be dealt as below :

(a) ***When it is paid out of pre-acquisition profit.*** In the books of subsidiary company, it should not be taken into account at the time of the preparation of consolidated balance sheet, as the necessary adjustment would have been made already in the concerned accounts. But in the books of holding company, the dividend received should be credited to the cost of control or to the capital reserve. If the holding company has already credited the dividend received to the cost of control or to the capital reserve, no adjustment should be made in the books of holding company. On the other hand, if the holding company has already credited dividend received to the profit and loss account, the dividend should be debited to the profit and loss account and credited to the cost of control or to the capital reserve.

(b) ***When it is paid out of post-acquisition profit.*** No entry should be passed in the subsidiary books as above. But, in the books of holding company, the dividend received should be credited to the profit and loss account. If it is already credited to the profit and loss account, no entry should be passed in the books of holding company.

12. Abnormal Losses of Subsidiary Company. If the subsidiary company has suffered any abnormal losses (such as loss of stock by fire, theft, flood etc.) during the accounting period, it should be dealt as below :

(a) ***If it has taken place in the pre-acquisition period.*** It should be debited to the pre-acquisition profit or reserve of subsidiary company and the remaining portion of pre-acquisition profit or reserve should be allocated between the holding company and minority shareholders.

(b) ***If it has taken place in the post-acquisition period.*** It should be debited to the post-acquisition profit or reserve of subsidiary company and the remaining portion of post-acquisition profit or reserve should be allocated between the holding company and minority shareholders.

13. Cash or Goods In-transit. Cash or goods sent by one company to the another, but not received by the another company at the end of the accounting period, are called 'cash in-transit or goods in-transit'. These items should be shown on the assets side of the consolidated balance sheet.

Steps to be taken for the preparation of consolidated balance sheet

Following are the main steps to be taken while preparing the consolidated balance sheet :

First step : Calculation of total capital reserve and total goodwill.

Second step : Set off the total goodwill against total capital reserve or *vice versa.*

Third step : Calculation of minority interest and majority interest. The majority and minority interest should be entered in the appropriate places in the consolidated balance sheet.

Fourth step : All the assets and liabilities of the holding company should be entered directly in the consolidated balance sheet in the appropriate places.

Fifth step : All the assets and liabilities of the holding company should be entered in the consolidated balance sheet in the appropriate places.

Sixth step : Elimination of inter-company debts or transactions.

Seventh step : Elimination of unrealized profit included in stock.

Eighth step : Finally, completion of consolidated balance sheet.

Form of Consolidated Balance Sheet

Consolidated balance sheet means combining of separate balance sheets of holding company and its subsidiary company or companies into a single balance sheet.

There is no legal form prescribed for the consolidated balance sheet. However, it is preferable to prepare the consolidated balance sheet in the form prescribed by the Indian Companies Act. The following is the general proforma of consolidated balance sheet :

Consolidated Balance Sheet of Holding Company and its Subsidiary as on......................

Liabilities		Rs.	Assets		Rs.
Share Capital			**Goodwill**		
....shares of Rs.....each		xxxx	Cost of Shares acquired	xxx	
(Holding Co. share capital)			*Less*: Nominal Value of Shares	xxx	
Capital Reserve				xxx	
Share in Pre-acquisition			*Less* : Share of Capital Profits		
Reserve of Subsidiary	xxx		of Subsidiary	xxx	
Share in Pre-acquisition				xxx	
Profit of Subsidiary	xxx		*Add* : Share of Capital Losses		
Share in Capital Profits			of Subsidiary	xxx	
of Subsidiary	xxx		*Add* : Holding Co. Goodwill	xxx	
	xxx		Subsidiary Co. Goodwill	xxx	
Less : Share in Capital				xxx	
Losses of Subsidiary	xxx		*Less* : Capital Reserve		
	xxx		as per Contra	xxx	xxxx
Deduct as per Contra	xxx	–	**Buildings**		
General Reserve			Holding Co. Building	xxx	
Holding Co. Reserve	xxx		Subsidiary Co. Building	xxx	xxx
Share in Post-acquisition			**Machinery**		
Reserve of Subsidiary	xxx	xxx	Holding Co. Machinery	xxx	
Profit and Loss Account			Subsidiary Co. Machinery	xxx	xxx
Holding Co. Profit	xxx		**Furniture**		
Share in Post-acquisition			Holding Co. Furniture	xxx	
Profit of Subsidiary	xxx		Subsidiary Co. Furniture	xxx	xxx
	xxx		**Investments**		
Less : Holding Co. share			Holding Co. Investments	xxx	
in Unrealized Profit	xxx	xxx	Other Co. Investments	xxx	xxx
Debentures			(Except shares in subsidiary)		
Holding Co. Debentures	xxx		**Debtors**		
Subsidiary Co. Debentures	xxx		Holding Co. Debtors	xxx	
	xxx		Subsidiary Co. Debts	xxx	
Less : Inter Co. Debts	xxx	xxx		xxx	
Sundry Creditors			*Less* : Inter Co. Debts	xxx	xxx
Holding Co. Creditors	xxx		**Bills Receivable**		
Subsidiary Co. Creditors	xxx		Holding Co. B/R	xxx	
	xxx		Subsidiary Co. B/R	xxx	
Less : Inter-company Debts	xxx	xxx		xxx	
Bills Payable			*Less :* Inter-company Bills	xxx	xxx
Holding Co. B/P	xxx		**Stock**		
Subsidiary Co. B/P	xxx		Holding Co. Stock	xxx	
	xxx		Subsidiary Co. Stock	xxx	
Less: Inter-company Co. Bills	xxx	xxx		xxx	
					Contd.

Minority Interest		*Less* : Holding Co. Share in		
Subsidiary Company Share		Unrealized Profit	xxx	xxx
in Capital Reserve, Profits etc.	xxx	**Cash & Bank Balance**		
		Holding Co. Cash at Bank	xxx	
		Subsidiary Co. Cash at Bank	xxx	xxx
		Profit & Loss A/c		
		Holding Co. Loss (if any)		xxx
	xxxx			xxxx

Note : If the total amount of capital reserve is more than the total amount of goodwill, the total amount of goodwill should be deducted from total amount of capital reserve and the balance is shown in the outer column.

Illustration 1

From the following balance sheet of 'H' Co. Ltd. and its subsidiary 'S' Co. Ltd. prepare a consolidated balance sheet.

Balance Sheet as on 31st December, 2006

Liabilities	H. Co. Rs.	S. Co. Rs.	Assets	H. Co. Rs.	S. Co. Rs.
Share Capital			Sundry Assets	1,50,000	2,40,000
(Share of Rs.100 each)	3,00,000	2,00,000	Investments in		
Sundry Liabilities	50,000	40,000	shares of		
			'S' Co. Ltd. (2,000 shares)	2,00,000	
	3,50,000	2,40,000		3,50,000	2,40,000

Solution :

Consolidated Balance Sheet of H. Co. Ltd. and its Subsidiary 'S' Co. Ltd. As on 31-12-2006

Liabilities		Rs.	Assets		Rs.
Share Capital : H. Co. Ltd.		3,00,000	Sundry Assets :		
Sundry Liabilities :			H. Co. Ltd.	1,50,000	
H. Co. Ltd.	50,000		S. Co. Ltd.	2,40,000	3,90,000
S. Co. Ltd.	40,000	90,000			
		3,90,000			3,90,000

Note : Since all the shares are acquired by the holding company, there is no minority interest.

Illustration 2

From the following balance sheets, prepare a consolidated balance sheet.

Balance Sheet as on 31-12-2006

Liabilities	H. Co. Rs.	S. Co. Rs.	Assets	H. Co. Rs.	S. Co. Rs.
Share Capital			Shares in 'S' Co. Ltd.		
(Shares of Rs. 100 each)	2,00,000	1,00,000	(750 shares)	75,000	
Sundry Liabilities	20,000	10,000	Other Assets	1,45,000	1,10,000
	2,20,000	1,10,000		2,20,000	1,10,000

H. Co. Ltd. acquires shares in 'S' Co. Ltd. on 31st December, 2006.

Solution :

Consolidated Balance Sheet of H. Co. Ltd. and its Subsidiary of 'S' Co. Ltd. as on 31-12-2006

Liabilities		Rs.	Assets		Rs.
Share Capital: H. Co. Ltd.		2,00,000	Sundry Assets :		
Sundry Liabilities :			H. Co. Ltd.	1,45,000	
H. Co. Ltd.	20,000		S. Co. Ltd.	1,10,000	2,55,000
S. Co. Ltd.	10,000	30,000			
Minority Interest		25,000			
		2,55,000			2,55,000

Note : In this case, H. Co. Ltd. holds ¾ of share capital in S. Co. Ltd. while the rest ¼ is held by minority.

Illustration 3

A Co. Ltd. acquired all the shares in B. Co. Ltd. on 1st Jan., 1998 and the balance sheet of the two companies on 31st Dec., 2006 were as follows :

Liabilities	A. Co.	B. Co.	Assets	A. Co.	B. Co.
Share Capital	4,00,000	2,40,000	Fixed Assets	3,00,000	3,20,000
Reserve & Surplus :			Current Assets	2,20,000	2,40,000
Reserve on 1-1-98	1,60,000	1,20,000	Shares in 'S'		
Profit & Loss A/c	2,00,000	80,000	Co. Ltd. at Cost	4,00,000	
10% Debentures	1,00,000	90,000			
Creditors	60,000	30,000			
	9,20,000	5,60,000		9,20,000	5,60,000

The Profit and Loss Account of 'B' Co. Ltd. had credit balance of Rs. 24,000 on 1st Jan., 2006. Prepare the consolidated balance sheet as on 31-12-2006.

Solution :

Consolidated Balance Sheet of A Co. Ltd. and its Subsidiary B Co. Ltd. as on 31-12-2006.

Liabilities		Rs.	Assets		Rs.
Share Capital : A Co. Ltd.		4,00,000	**Goodwill** :		
Capital Reserve:			Cost of acquisition		
Prior Reserve of			of Shares	4,00,000	
B Co. Ltd.	1,20,000		*Less* : Nominal		
Prior Profit of			value of Shares		
B Co. Ltd.	24,000		in B Ltd.	2,40,000	
	1,44,000			1,60,000	
Deduct as per Contra	1,44,000	—	*Less* : Capital Reserve		
Reserve : A Co. Ltd.		1,60,000	as per Contra	1,44,000	16,000
Surplus : A Co. Ltd.	2,00,000		**Fixed Assets** :		
B Co. Ltd.	56,000	2,56,000	A Co. Ltd.	3,00,000	
10% Debentures :			B Co. Ltd.	3,20,000	6,20,000
A Co. Ltd.	1,00,000		**Current Assets** :		
B Co. Ltd.	90,000	1,90,000	A Co. Ltd.	2,20,000	
Creditors :			B Co. Ltd.	2,40,000	4,60,000
A Co. Ltd.	60,000				
B Co. Ltd.	30,000	90,000			
		10,96,000			10,96,000

Note : In this case all the shares are acquired by the A Co. Ltd. Hence, there is no minority interest.

Illustration 4

From the following balance sheets as at 31-12-2006 and particulars given below, prepare the consolidated balance sheet of XYZ Co. Ltd. and ABC Co. Ltd. as at 31-12-2006.

Liabilities	XYZ	ABC	Assets	XYZ	ABC
Share Capital	9,00,000	2,40,000	Goodwill	2,25,000	—
General Reserve :			Buildings	6,00,000	1,50,000
Balance as at			Sundry Assets	2,70,000	3,60,000
1-1-2006	1,80,000	75,000	Debtors	1,80,000	60,000
Creditors	2,00,000	1,00,000	Bills Receivable	60,000	30,000
Bills Payable	55,000	53,000	Share in Subsidiary :		
Profit and Loss A/c :			21000 shares at		
Balance as at			Rs. 20 each	4,20,000	
1-7-2006	1,35,000	30,000			
Net Profit for the					
Year 2006	2,85,000	1,02,000			
	17,55,000	6,00,000		17,55,000	6,00,000

(a) XYZ Co. Ltd. acquired shares in ABC Co. Ltd. on 1-7-2006.

(b) The debtors of XYZ Co. Ltd. included Rs. 18,000 due from the ABC Co. Ltd.

(c) The bills receivable of ABC Co. Ltd. included Rs. 12,000 due from the XYZ Co. Ltd.

Prepare the consolidated balances sheet as at 31-12-2006.

Solution :

Chart showing the Majority (Holding) and Minority (Outsiders) Interest in the Subsidiary Company

Sl. No.		Total Amount	Majority Interest	Minority Interest
1.	Share Capital (Ratio 7 : 1)	2,40,000	2,10,000	30,000
2.	General Reserve (75,000)			
	(a) Pre-acquisition Reserve	75,000	65,625	9,375
	(b) Post-acquisition Reserve	—	—	—
3.	Profit and Loss A/c (30,000 + 1,02,000)			
	(a) Pre-acquisition Profit (30,000 + 51,000)	81,000	70,875	10,125
	(b) Post-acquisition Profit (51,000)	51,000	44,625	6,375
		4,47,000	3,91,125	55,875

Consolidated Balance Sheet of XYZ Co. Ltd. and its Subsidiary ABC Co. Ltd. as on 31-12-2006

Liabilities		Rs.	Assets		Rs.
Share Capital : (XYZ Co. Ltd.)		9,00,000	**Goodwill :**		
Capital Reserve :			Cost of shares acquired	4,20,000	
7/8 of Pre-acquisition Reserve in ABC Co. Ltd.	65,625		*Less* : Nominal value of shares in ABC Co. Ltd. (7/8)	2,10,000	
7/8 of Pre-acquisition Profit in ABC Co. Ltd.	70,875			2,10,000	
	1,36,500		*Add* : Goodwill of XYZ Co. Ltd.	2,25,000	
Deduct as per Contra	1,36,500	–		4,35,000	
General Reserve :					
XYZ Co. Ltd.		1,80,000	*Less* : Deduct Capital Reserve as per contra	1,36,500	2,98,500
Profit & Loss A/c :			**Buildings** :		
XYZ Co. Ltd. :					
Balance as on 1-1-06	1,35,000		XYZ Co. Ltd.	6,00,000	
For the year 2006	2,85,000		ABC Co. Ltd.	1,50,000	7,50,000
7/8 of Post-acquisition Profit in ABC Co. Ltd.	44,625	4,64,625	**Sundry Assets** :		
			XYZ Co. Ltd.	2,70,000	
			ABC Co. Ltd.	3,60,000	6,30,000

Contd.

Creditors :			**Debtors :**		
XYZ Co. Ltd.	2,00,000		XYZ Co. Ltd.	1,80,000	
ABC Co. Ltd.	1,00,000		ABC Co. Ltd.	60,000	
	3,00,000			2,40,000	
Less : Due to			*Less* : Due from		
XYZ Co. Ltd.	18,000	2,82,000	ABC Co. Ltd.	18,000	2,22,000
Bills Payable :			**Bills Receivable :**		
XYZ Co. Ltd.	55,000		XYZ Co. Ltd.	60,000	
ABC Co. Ltd.	53,000		ABC Co. Ltd.	30,000	
	1,08,000			90,000	
Less : Due to			*Less* : Due from		
ABC Co. Ltd.	12,000	96,000	XYZ Co. Ltd.	12,000	78,000
Minority Interest (as per chart)		55,875			
		19,78,500			19,78,500

Note : Profits on or before 1-7-2006 are capital profits. Therefore, Rs. 30,000 and Rs. 51,000 (*i.e.*, ½ of the current year profits) are pre-acquisition profits or capital profits. The remaining half *i.e.*, 51,000 (*i.e.*, after 1-7-2006) is treated as post-acquisition profit or revenue profit.

Illustration 5

From the following information you are requested to prepare consolidated balance sheet of Monica Co.Ltd. and its subsidiary Lewinsky Co. Ltd. as on 31st December, 2006.

Balance Sheet as on 31-12-2006

Liabilities	Monica Co. Ltd.	Lewinsky Co. Ltd.	Assets	Monica Co.Ltd.	Lewinsky Co.Ltd.
Share Capital :			**Fixed Assets :**		
Eq. Shares of Rs. 100	8,00,000	4,00,000	Goodwill	2,00,000	50,000
Reserve & Surplus :			Plants	5,00,000	2,50,000
Capital Reserves	1,50,000	—	Buildings	2,00,000	1,00,000
General Reserves	1,40,000	1,00,000	**Investments :**		
Surplus	2,60,000	50,000	3,000 Shares in		
Secured Loans :	2,00,000		Lewinsky Ltd.	3,60,000	—
Unsecured Loans :	—	1,00,000	Other Securities	—	60,000
Current Liabilities &			**Loans & Advances:**		
Provisions :			Stock	1,20,000	90,000
Creditors	1,50,000	60,000	Debtors	1,50,000	1,00,000
Bills Payable	1,00,000	40,000	Bills Receivable	1,00,000	50,000
			Bank	1,70,000	50,000
	18,00,000	7,50,000		18,00,000	7,50,000

(a) Bills payable of Monica Co.Ltd. include Rs. 30,000 due to Lewinsky Co. Ltd.

(b) Sundry Creditors of Lewinsky Co. Ltd. include Rs. 50 due to Monica Co. Ltd.

(c) On the date of purchase of Rs. 3,000 shares of Lewinsky Co. Ltd., the Balance Sheet of Lewinsky Co. Ltd. showed a General Reserve of Rs. 40,000 and Surplus of Rs. 20,000.

(Karnataka, Oct. 1999)

Solution :

Statement Showing the Majority and Minority Interest in the Subsidiary Company (Ratio = 3 : 1)

Particulars	Total Rs.	Majority Rs.	Minority Rs.
(1) Share Capital	4,00,000	3,00,000	1,00,000
(2) General Reserve (Rs. 1,00,000) :			
(a) Pre-acquisition	40,000	30,000	10,000
(b) Post-acquisition	60,000	45,000	15,000
(3) Surplus (Rs. 50,000) :			
(a) Pre-acquisition	20,000	15,000	5,000
(b) Post-acquisition	30,000	12,500	7,500
	5,50,000	4,12,500	1,37,500

Consolidated Balance Sheet of Monica Co. Ltd. and its subsidiary Lewinsky Co. Ltd. as on 31- 12-1997

Liabilities		Rs.	Assets		Rs.
Share Capital (Monica)		8,00,000	**Fixed Assets :**		
Capital Reserve :			Goodwill :		
Capital Reserve (Monica)	1,50,000		Cost of acquisition		
Share of Monica in the			of shares	3,60,000	
Pre-acquisition			*Less:* Nominal value of		
Reserve of Lewinsky	30,000		shares acquired	3,00,000	
Share of Monica in the			Excess paid being		
Pre-acquisition			goodwill	60,000	
profit of Lewinsky	15,000		Goodwill (Monica)	2,00,000	
Profit of Lewinsky	1,95,000		Goodwill (Lewinsky)	50,000	
Deduct as per Contra	1,95,000	—		3,10,000	
General Reserve :			*Less* : Deducted as per		
General Reserve (Monica)	1,40,000		contra	1,95,000	1,15,000
Share of Monica in the			Plant : Monica	5,00,000	
Post-acquisition			Lewinsky	2,50,000	7,50,000
Reserve of Lewinsky	45,000	1,85,000	Building : Monica	2,00,000	
			Lewinsky	1,00,000	3,00,000

Contd.

Liabilities		Rs.	Assets		Rs.
Profit and Loss Account :			**Investments:**		
Surplus (Monica)	2,60,000		Other Securities : Monica		60,000
Share of Monica in the			**Loan and Advances :**		
Post-acquisition			Stock : Monica	1,20,000	
Profit of Lewinsky	22,500	2,82,500	Lewinsky	90,000	2,10,000
Secured Loan (Monica)		2,00,000	Debtors : Monica	1,50,000	
Unsecured Loan (Lewinsky)		1,00,000	Lewinsky	1,00,000	
Current Liabilities & Provisions				2,50,000	
Creditors : Monica	1,50,000		*Less :* Due from Monica	50	2,49,950
Lewinsky	60,000		**Bills Receivable :**		
	2,10,000		Monica	1,00,000	
Less : Due to Lewinsky	50	2,19,950	Lewinsky	50,000	
Bills Payable : Monica	1,00,000			1,50,000	
Lewinsky	40,000		*Less :* Due from		
	1,40,000		Lewinsky	30,000	1,20,000
Less : Due to Monica	30,000	1,10,000	Bank : Monica	1,70,000	
Minority Interest		1,37,500	Lewinsky	50,000	2,20,000
		20,24,950			20,24,950

Illustration 6

From the following balance sheets of 'A' Co. Ltd. and its subsidiary B Co. Ltd., prepare the consolidated balance sheet as on 30th Sept., 2006.

A Co. Ltd. acquired 75% of the share capital of B Co. Ltd., on 1st April, 2006. The balances to the General Reserve and Profit & Loss Account stood at Rs. 1,50,000 and Rs. 50,000 respectively on 1-10-2005. Out of Rs. 3,00,000 bills payable, bills amounting to Rs. 2,00,000 are payable to B Co. Ltd. and the latter has discounted bills worth Rs. 25,000.

Liabilities	A. Co.	B. Co.	Assets	A. Co.	B. Co.
Share Capital :			Goodwill	—	1,00,000
Authorised & issued			Buildings	10,00,000	3,80,000
5,00,000 shares of			Machinery	40,00,000	6,52,000
Rs. 10 each fully paid	50,00,000	—	Shares in B Co. Ltd.	8,50,000	—
1,00,000 shares of			Stock	15,00,000	3,48,000
Rs. 10 each fully paid	—	10,00,000	Debtors	6,00,000	1,20,000
General Reserve	5,00,000	2,00,000	Investments	—	2,00,000
Profit & Loss A/c	2,50,000	3,00,000	Bills Receivable	—	1,75,000
Creditors	4,50,000	1,50,000	Cash and Bank		
Bills Payable	3,00,000	—	balances	50,000	25,000
Debentures	15,00,000	—			
Bank Overdraft	—	3,50,000			
(unsecured)					
	80,00,000	20,00,000		80,00,000	20,00,000

Solution :

In this problem, profits on or before 1-4-2006 are capital profits or pre-acquisition profits. Therefore, out of Rs. 3,00,000, Rs. 50,000 and Rs. 1,25,000 (*i.e.*, ½ of the current year profits after deducting Rs. 50,000) are pre-acquisition profits. The remaining balances of profits (*i.e.*, after 1-4-2006) are to be treated as post-acquisition profits. The same treatment is applied in case of general reserves also.

Chart Showing the Majority and Minority Interest in the Subsidiary Company

Sl. No.	Particulars	Total Amount Rs.	Majority Interest Rs.	Minority Interest Rs.
1.	Share Capital (Ratio 3 : 1)	10,00,000	7,50,000	2,50,000
2.	General Reserve (2,00,000)			
	(a) Pre-acquisition Reserve (1,50,000 + 25,000 *i.e.,* half of 50,000 *i.e.*, 2,00,000 – 1,50,000)	1,75,000	1,31,250	43,750
	(b) Post-acquisition Reserve	25,000	18,750	6,250
3.	Profit and Loss Account (3,00,000)			
	(a) Pre-acquisition Profit (50,000 + 1,25,000 *i.e.*, half of 2,50,000 *i.e.*, 3,00,000 – 50,000)	1,75,000	1,31,250	43,750
	(b) Post-acquisition Profit	1,25,000	93,750	31,250
		15,00,000	11,25,000	3,75,000

Consolidated Balance Sheet of A Co. Ltd. and its Subsidiary B Co. Ltd. as at 30-9-2006

Liabilities		Rs.	Assets		Rs.
Share Capital : (A Co. Ltd.)			Goodwill :		
5,00,000 shares of Rs. 10 each		50,00,000	Cost of acquisition		
Capital Reserve :			of shares	8,50,000	
Pre-acquisition of Reserve			*Less* : Nominal		
of B Co. Ltd. (3/4)	1,31,250		value of shares (3/4)	7,50,000	
Pre-acquisition Profit				1,00,000	
of B Co. Ltd. (3/4)	1,31,250		*Add* : Goodwill		
	2,62,250		of B Co. Ltd.	1,00,000	
Deduct Goodwill				2,00,000	
as per Contra	2,00,000	62,500	Deduct as per		
General Reserve :			Contra	2,00,000	—
A Co. Ltd.	5,00,000		Buildings :		
B Co. Ltd. (3/4)			A Co. Ltd.	10,00,000	
Post-acquisition reserve	18,750	5,18,750	B Co. Ltd.	3,80,000	13,80,000

Contd.

	Rs.	Rs.		Rs.	Rs.
Profit & Loss Account :			**Machinery :**		
A Co. Ltd.	2,50,000		A Co. Ltd.	40,00,000	
B Co. Ltd. (3/4)	93,750	3,43,750	B Co. Ltd.	6,52,000	46,52,000
(Post-acquisition Profit)			**Investment :**		
Creditors :			B Co. Ltd.		2,00,000
A Co. Ltd.	4,50,000		**Stock :**		
B Co. Ltd.	1,50,000	6,00,000	A Co. Ltd.	15,00,000	
Bills Payable :			B Co. Ltd.	3,48,000	18,48,000
A Co. Ltd.	3,00,000		**Debtors :**		
Less : Due to B			A Co. Ltd.	6,00,000	
Co. Ltd. or B/P Set			B Co. Ltd.	1,20,000	7,20,000
off against B/R	1,75,000	1,25,000	**Bills Receivable :**		
Debentures :			B Co. Ltd.	1,75,000	
A Co. Ltd.		15,00,000	*Less :* Due from		
Bank Overdraft :			A Co. Ltd. or B/R Set		
B Co. Ltd.		3,50,000	of against B/P	1,75,000	—
Minority Interest		3,75,000	**Cash and Bank Balance :**		
(As per chart)			A Co. Ltd.	50,000	
			B Co. Ltd.	25,000	75,000
		88,75,000			88,75,000

Note : Bills to be eliminated only Rs. 1,75,000 (*i.e.,* 2,00,000 – 25,000 discounted).

Illustration 7

The following are the balance sheets of A Co. Ltd. and B Co. Ltd. as at 31-12-1998 :

Liabilities	A Ltd. Rs.	B Ltd. Rs.	Assets	A Ltd. Rs.	B Ltd. Rs.
Share Capital :			Goodwill	75,000	40,000
Equity Share of			Land & Building	4,50,000	1,20,000
Rs. 10 each	9,00,000	1,50,000	Plant & Machinery	3,00,000	90,000
10% Preference Share			Investments in		
of Rs. 100 each	1,00,000	—	12,000 shares		
Reserve & Surplus :			of B Ltd.	1,90,000	—
General Reserve	90,000	60,000	Stock	2,40,000	75,000
Profit and Loss A/c :			Debtors	1,50,000	80,000
On 1-1-1998	60,000	15,000	Bills Receivable	25,000	10,000
For the year 1998	1,50,000	60,000	Cash at Bank	95,000	10,000
Current Liabilities :					
Creditors	1,85,000	1,05,000			
Bills Payable	40,000	35,000			
	15,25,000	4,25,000		15,25,000	4,25,000

Additional Information

(a) A Ltd. acquired the shares in B Ltd. On 1-4-1998.

(b) General Reserve of B Ltd. was Rs. 10,000 in 1-1-1998.

(c) Bills Payable of B Ltd. included Rs. 20,000 accepted in favour of A Ltd. Out of which A Ltd. discounted the bills of Rs. 12,000.

(d) Creditors of B Ltd. included Rs. 60,000 for goods supplied by A Ltd. At cost + 25%. Half of the goods purchased included in stock of B Ltd.

(e) Plant and machinery of B Ltd. was undervalued by Rs. 20,000.

Prepare the consolidated balances sheet of A Ltd. and its subsidiary B Ltd. as on 31-12-1998.

(Adapted from Karnataka University)

Solution :

Chart Showing the Majority and Minority Interest in the Subsidiary Company

Sl. No.	Particulars	Total Amount Rs.	Majority Interest Rs.	Minority Interest Rs.
1.	Share Capital (Ratio 4 : 1)	1,50,000	1,20,000	30,000
2.	General Reserve (60,000) :			
	(a) Pre-acquisition Reserve (10,000 + 12,500 *i.e.*, $^3/_{12} \times 50,000$ *i.e.,* 60,000 –10,000)	22,500	18,000	4,500
	(b) Post-acquisition Reserve	37,500	30,000	7,500
3.	Profit and Loss Account (75,000) :			
	(a) Pre-acquisition Reserve (15,000 +15,000 *i.e.*, $^3/_{12} \times 60,000$)	30,000	24,000	6,000
	(b) Post-acquisition Reserve	45,000	36,000	9,000
4.	Increase in the value of Plant and Machinery :			
	Pre-acquisition (capital profit)	20,000	16,000	4,000
		3,05,000	2,44,000	61,000

Consolidated Balance Sheet of A Co. Ltd. and its Subsidiary of B Co. Ltd. as at 31-12-1998

Liabilities		Rs.	Assets		Rs.
Share Capital : (A Co. Ltd.)			**Goodwill :**		
Equity Shares of Rs. 10 each		9,00,000	A Co. Ltd.	75,000	
10% Pref. Shares of			B Co. Ltd.	40,000	
Rs. 100 each		1,00,000		1,15,000	
Capital Reserve :			Cost of acquisition		
Pre-acquisition Reserve			of Shares	1,90,000	
of B Co. Ltd. (4/5)	18,000			3,05,000	
Pre-acquisition Profit			*Less* : Nominal value		
of B Co. Ltd. (4/5)	24,000		of Shares	1,20,000	
Increase in the value of				1,85,000	
Plant & Machinery (4/5)	16,000		*Less* : Capital Reserve		
	58,000		as per Contra	58,000	1,27,000
Deduct as per Contra	58,000	—	**Land & Buildings :**		
General Reserve :			A Co. Ltd.	4,50,000	
A Co. Ltd.	90,000		B Co. Ltd.	1,20,000	5,70,000
B Co. Ltd. (4/5)	30,000	1,20,000	**Plant & Machinery :**		
(post-acquisition)			A Co. Ltd.	3,00,000	
Surplus or P & L A/c :			B Co. Ltd.	90,000	
A Co. Ltd.				3,90,000	
(60,000 + 1,50,000)	2,10,000		*Add* : Increase in value	20,000	4,10,000
B Co. Ltd. (4/5)			**Stock :**		
(post-acquisition)	36,000		A Co. Ltd.	2,40,000	
	2,46,000		B Co. Ltd.	75,000	
Less : Unrealised Profit	6,000	2,40,000		3,15,000	
Creditors :			*Less* : Unrealised Profit	6,000	3,09,000
A Co. Ltd.	1,85,000		**Debtors :**		
B Co. Ltd.	1,05,000		A Co. Ltd.	1,50,000	
	2,90,000		B Co. Ltd.	80,000	
Less : Due to A Co. Ltd.	60,000	2,30,000		2,30,000	
Bills Payable :			*Less* : Due from		
A Co. Ltd.	40,000		B Co. Ltd.	60,000	1,70,000
B Co. Ltd.	35,000		**Bills Receivable :**		
	75,000		A Co. Ltd.	25,000	
Less : Due to A Co. Ltd.			B Co. Ltd.	10,000	
or B/P set off against				35,000	
B/R (20,000 – 12,000)	8,000	67,000	*Less* : Due from B Co. Ltd.		
Minority Interest :			or B/R set off		
(As per chart)		61,000	against B/P	8,000	27,000
			Cash : A Co. Ltd.	95,000	
			B Co. Ltd.	10,000	1,05,000
		17,18,000			17,18,000

Note : (1) Inter-company bills of Rs. 8,000 discounted (*i.e.*, 20,000 – 12,000) only are to be eliminated.

(2) Calculation of unrealized profit :

Goods are supplied at cost + 25% profit *i.e.*, if cost is 100, the selling price of the goods will be 125 (*i.e.*, 100 + 125). So, for 120, profit is 20, then for Rs. 30,000 (half of the goods *i.e.*, ½ × 60,000), the profit will be Rs. 6,000 (*i.e.*, Rs. 30,000 × 25/125).

Illustration 8

From the following balance sheets and information given below, prepare the consolidated balance sheet of H. Co. Ltd. and its subsidiary S. Co. Ltd. as on 31-12-2006.

Liabilities	H. Co. Rs.	S. Co. Rs.	Assets	H. Co. Rs.	S. Co. Rs.
Share Capital :			Goodwill	1,00,000	60,000
Shares of Rs. 10			Land & Buildings	6,00,000	1,00,000
each Fully paid	12,00,000	2,00,000	Plant & Machinery	4,00,000	80,000
General Reserve	1,20,000	80,000	Investments :		
Profit & Loss A/c	2,80,000	—	16,000 shares in		
Bank Overdraft	—	1,00,000	S. Co. Ltd.	2,40,000	—
Creditors	2,50,000	1,50,000	Stock	3,20,000	80,000
Bills Payable	50,000	20,000	Debtors	2,00,000	1,00,000
			Bills Receivable	30,000	10,000
			Cash	10,000	20,000
			Profit & Loss A/c	—	1,00,000
	19,00,000	5,50,000		19,00,000	5,50,000

Additional Information :

(i) H. Co. Ltd. acquired the shares in S. Co. Ltd. on 1-7-2006.

(ii) General Reserve of S. Co. Ltd. on 1-1-2006 was Rs. 60,000.

(iii) Profit and Loss Account of S. Co. Ltd. showed a credit balance of Rs. 20,000 on 1-1-2006.

(iv) All the bills payable of S. Co. Ltd. were in favour of H. Co. Ltd. of which H. Co. Ltd. discounted the bills worth Rs. 12,000.

(v) Creditors of S. Co. Ltd. included Rs. 20,000 payable to H. Co. Ltd. for goods supplied.

(vi) Land and buildings of S. Co. Ltd. were found to be overvalued by Rs. 5,000.

(vii) Stock of S. Co. Ltd. included the goods of Rs. 10,000 supplied by H. Co. Ltd. at cost plus 25%.

Solution :

Chart Showing the Majority and Minority Interest in the Subsidiary Company

Sl. No.	Particulars	Total Amount Rs.	Majority Interest Rs.	Minority Interest Rs.
1.	Share Capital (Ratio 4 : 1)	2,00,000	1,60,000	40,000
2.	General reserve (80,000) :			
	(a) Pre-acquisition Reserve (60,000 + 10,000 *i.e.*, Half of 20,000 *i.e.*, 80,000 – 60,000)	70,000	56,000	14,000
	(b) Post-acquisition Reserve	10,000	8,000	2,000
3.	Profit and Loss Account :			
	Pre-acquisition Profit	20,000	16,000	4,000
	A	3,00,000	2,40,000	60,000
	Deduct the following :			
1.	Profit and Loss Account (1,00,000 + 20,000) :			
	(a) Pre-acquisition Loss (upto 1-7-98)	60,000	48,000	12,000
	(b) Post-acquisition Loss	60,000	48,000	12,000
2.	Decrease in the value of Land and Buildings : Pre-acquisition	5,000	4,000	1,000
	B	1,25,000	1,00,000	25,000
	A – B	1,75,000	1,40,000	35,000

Consolidated Balance Sheet of H. Co. Ltd. with its Subsidiary S. Co. Ltd. as on 31-12-2006

Liabilities		Rs.	Assets		Rs.
Share Capital :			**Goodwill :**		
(H Co. Ltd.) Share of			H. Co. Ltd.	1,00,000	
Rs. 10 each Fully paid		12,00,000	S. Co. Ltd.	60,000	
Capital Reserve :				1,60,000	
Pre-acquisition Reserve			Cost of acquisition		
of S. Co. Ltd. (4/5)	56,000		of Shares	2,40,000	
Pre-acquisition Profit				4,00,000	
of S. Co. Ltd. (4/5)	16,000		*Less* : Nominal value		
	72,000		of Shares	1,60,000	
Less : Pre-acquisition Loss				2,40,000	
of S. Co. Ltd. (4/5)	48,000		*Less* : Capital Reserve		
	24,000		as per Contra	20,000	2,20,000

Contd.

Less : Pre-acquisition			**Land & Buildings :**		
Decrease in the Value of			H. Co. Ltd.	6,00,000	
Land & Building (4/5)	4,000		S. Co. Ltd.	1,00,000	
	20,000			7,00,000	
Deduct as per Contra	20,000	—	*Less* : Decrease in		
General Reserve :			value	5,000	6,95,000
H. Co. Ltd.	1,20,000		**Plant & Machinery :**		
S. Co. Ltd. (4/5)	8,000	1,28,000	H. Co. Ltd.	4,00,000	
(Post–acquisition)			S. Co. Ltd.	80,000	4,80,000
Profit and Loss Account :			**Stock :**		
H. Co. Ltd.	2,80,000		H. Co. Ltd.	3,20,000	
Less : 4/5 Post-			S. Co. Ltd.	80,000	
acquisition Loss				4,00,000	
of S. Co. Ltd.	48,000		*Less* : Unrealised		
	2,32,000		Profit	2,000	3,98,000
Less : Unrealised			(10,000 × 25/125		
Profit	2,000	2,30,000	= 2,000)		
Bank Overdraft :			**Debtors :**		
S. Co. Ltd.		1,00,000	H. Co. Ltd.	2,00,000	
Creditors :			S. Co. Ltd.	1,00,000	
H. Co. Ltd.	2,50,000			3,00,000	
S. Co. Ltd.	1,50,000		Less : Due from		
	4,00,000		S. Co. Ltd.	20,000	2,80,000
Less : Due to			**Bills Receivable :**		
H. Co. Ltd.	20,000	3,80,000	H. Co. Ltd.	30,000	
Bills Payable :			S. Co. Ltd.	10,000	
H. Co. Ltd.	50,000			40,000	
S. Co. Ltd.	20,000		*Less* : Due from		
	70,000		S. Co. Ltd.	8,000	32,000
Less : Due to H. Co. Ltd.			**Cash :**		
(20,000 – 12,000)	8,000	62,000	H. Co. Ltd.	10,000	
Minority Interest		35,000	S. Co. Ltd.	20,000	30,000
(As per chart)					
		21,35,000			21,35,000

Illustration 9

The following balance sheets were presented to you :

Balance Sheets as on 31st December, 1998

Liabilities	H Co.	S Co.	Assets	H Co.	S Co.
Share Capital :			Fixed Assets	3,50,000	1,50,000
Shares of Rs. 100 each	5,00,000	2,00,000	Stock	90,000	40,000
General Reserve	1,00,000	—	Sundry Debtors	60,000	30,000
Profit & Loss A/c	80,000	—	Shares in S Ltd.		
6% Debentures	—	1,00,000	1,500 shares	1,20,000	—
Sundry Creditors	75,000	45,000	6% Debentures in		
Bills Payable	—	10,000	S. Ltd. acquired at par.	60,000	—
			Cash	75,000	35,000
			Profit & Loss A/c	—	1,00,000
	7,55,000	3,55,000		7,55,000	3,55,000

H Co. Ltd. acquired the shares on 1st May, 1998. The Profit and Loss Account of S Co. Ltd. showed a debit balance of Rs. 1,60,000 on 1-1-1998. All the bills payable of S Co. Ltd. were in favour of H Co. Ltd. All these bills have been discounted by the latter. Sundry creditors of S Co. Ltd. include Rs. 20,000 for goods supplied by H Co. Ltd. on which H Co. Ltd. made a profit of Rs. 2,000. Half of the goods are still on stock on 31-12-1998.

(Adapted from Managalore, Bangalore and Karnataka Universities)

Solution :

Calculation of Post-acquisition Profit

In this problem, the debit balance of P & L A/c has been reduced by Rs. 60,000 during the year 1998. This reduction represents profit of Rs. 60,000 earned during the year 1998. Out of Rs. 60,000, 1/3 of Rs. 60,000 should be considered as pre-acquisition profit, as the shares are acquired on 1st May, 1998 and the remaining balance is treated as post-acquisition profit. The calculation is given as below :

	Rs.
Total Loss as on 1-1-1998	1,60,000
Less : Balance of Loss as on 31-12-1998	1,00,000
Profit earned during the year (from 1-1-98 to 31-12-98)	60,000
Less : Profit up to 1-5-1998 (i.e., 60,000 × 4/12)	20,000
Post-acquisition profit (from 1-5-98 to 31-12-98)	40,000

Calculation of Pre-acquisition Loss

In this problem, it is clearly stated that the P & L A/c of S Co. Ltd. showed a debit balance of Rs. 1,60,000 as on 1-1-1998. This is considered as pre-acquisition loss. In this problem, there are both pre-acquisition profit and pre-acquisition loss. Therefore, it is better to set off pre-acquisition profit against pre-acquisition loss. There will be a net pre-acquisition loss of Rs. 1,40,000 (*i.e.*, 1,60,000 – 20,000). This calculation is shown as below :

	Rs.
Total Loss as on 1-1-1998	1,60,000
Less : Profit up to the date of acquisition (60,000 × 4/12)	20,000
Pre-acquisition upto 1-5-1998	1,40,000

Chart Showing the Majority and Minority Interest in the subsidiary company

Sl. No.	Particulars	Total Amount Rs.	Majority Interest Rs.	Minority Interest Rs.
1.	Share Capital (Ratio 3 : 1)	2,00,000	1,50,000	50,000
2.	Profit and Loss A/c :			
	Post-acquisition Profit (1,60,000 –120000 *i.e.*, 1,00,000 + 20,000)	40,000	30,000	10,000
		2,40,000	1,80,000	60,000
	Deduct the following :			
1.	Profit and Loss A/c :			
	Pre-acquisition Loss (1,60,000 – 20,000)	1,40,000	1,05,000	35,000
		1,00,000	75,000	25,000

Consolidated Balance Sheet of H Co. Ltd. and its Subsidiary S Co. Ltd. as on 31-12-1998

Liabilities		Rs.	Assets		Rs.
Share Capital : (H Co. Ltd.)			**Goodwill :**		
5,000 shares of Rs. 100 each		5,00,000	Cost of Control	1,20,000	
Capital Reserve :		—	*Add* : Pre-acquisition		
General Reserve :			Loss	1,05,000	
H Co. Ltd.		1,00,000		2,25,000	
Profit and Loss A/c :			*Less* : Nominal value		
H Co. Ltd.	80,000		of shares	1,50,000	75,000
Post-acquisition Profit			**Fixed Assets** :		
in S Co. Ltd. (3/4)	30,000		H Co. Ltd.	3,50,000	
	1,10,000		S Co. Ltd.	1,50,000	5,00,000
Less : Unrealised			**Investments** :		
Profit	1,000	1,09,000	In Debentures :		

(*Contd.*)

Debentures :			H Co. Ltd.	60,000	
S Co. Ltd.	1,00,000		*Less* : Due from		
Less : Due to H Co. Ltd.	60,000	40,000	S Co. Ltd.	60,000	—
Sundry Creditors :			**Stock :**		
H. Co. Ltd.	75,000		H Co. Ltd.	90,000	
S. Co. Ltd.	45,000		S Co. Ltd.	40,000	
	1,20,000			1,30,000	
Less : Due to			*Less* : Unrealised		
H Co. Ltd.	20,000	1,00,000	Profit	1,000	1,29,000
Bills Payable :			**Sundry Debtors :**		
S Co. Ltd.		10,000	H Co. Ltd.	60,000	
Minority Interest		25,000	S Co. Ltd.	30,000	
(As per Chart)				90,000	
			Less : Due from		
			S Co. Ltd.	20,000	70,000
			Cash : H Co. Ltd.	75,000	
			S Co. Ltd.	35,000	1,10,000
		8,84,000			8,84,000

Notes : (i) Inter company debentures are eliminated just like inter company debts.

(ii) Since half of the goods purchased from H Co. Ltd. by S Co. Ltd. are in stock only Rs. 1,000 is profit on such goods.

Illustration 10

Balance Sheet of H Ltd. and S. Ltd. as on 31st March, 1996.

Liabilities	H Ltd. Rs.	S Ltd. Rs.	Assets	H Ltd. Rs.	S Ltd. Rs.
Share of Rs. 10 each	3,00,000	2,00,000	Goodwill	20,000	30,000
10% Debentures	1,00,000	—	Fixed Assets	2,00,000	1,50,000
Creditors	63,000	20,000	Investments :		
Bills Payable	10,000	10,000	(i) 16,000 shares		
			of S Ltd.	1,20,000	—
			(ii) Govt. securities	10,000	5,000
			Debtors	60,000	25,000
			Stock	40,000	10,000
			Bills Receivable	3,000	—
			Profit & Loss A/c	20,000	10,000
	4,73,000	2,30,000		4,73,000	2,30,000

Notes : (a) Shares of S Ltd. were acquired on 31-12-1995.

(b) The Profit and Loss Account of S Ltd. on 1-4-1995 had a debit balance of Rs. 40,000.

(c) Bills Payable of S Ltd. were all in favour of H Ltd. of which bills of Rs. 8,000 were endorsed by H Ltd.

(d) Fixed assets of S Ltd. were undervalued by Rs. 25,000.

(e) Stock of H Ltd. includes goods valued Rs. 10,000 sold by S Ltd. at a profit of 20% of selling price.

Prepare consolidated balance sheet of H. Ltd. and S. Ltd. as on 31-3-1996. Give working notes.

(Karnataka, B.Com., April1997)

Solution :

In this problem, the debit balance of P & L A/c has been reduced by Rs. 30,000 during the year. This reduction represents profit earned during the year. Out of Rs. 30,000, ¾ (*i.e.*, for 9 months) of Rs. 30,000 should be considered as pre-acquisition profit (*i.e.*, 22,500), as the share are acquired on 31-12-1995 and the remaining balance (*i.e.*, Rs. 7,500) is treated as post-acquisition profit. Therefore, it is better to setoff pre-acquisition profit (Rs. 22,500) against the pre-acquisition loss [Rs. 40,000 as stated in the notes 'b']. There will be a net pre-acquisition loss of Rs. 17,500 (*i.e.*, 40,000 –22,500).

Chart Showing the Share of Majority and Minority Interest in the Subsidiary Company

Sl. No.	Particulars	Total Amount Rs.	Majority Interest Rs.	Minority Interest Rs.
1.	Share Capital (Ratio 4 : 1)	2,00,000	1,60,000	40,000
2.	Profit and Loss Account :			
	Post-acquisition Profit (40,000 – 32,500 *i.e.*, 10,000 + 22,500)	7,500	6,000	1,500
3.	Increase in the value of Fixed Assets : Pre-acquisition	25,000	20,000	5,000
		2,32,500	1,86,000	46,500
	Deducting the following :			
1.	**Profit and Loss A/c :**			
	Pre-acquisition Loss (40,000 – 22,500)	17,500	14,000	3,500
		2,15,000	1,72,000	43,000

Consolidated Balance Sheet of H Co. Ltd.
and its Subsidiary S Co. Ltd. as on 31-3-1996

Liabilities		Rs.	Assets		Rs.
Share Capital :			**Goodwill :**		
30,000 Shares of Rs. 10 each		3,00,000	H Co. Ltd.	20,000	
Capital Reserve :			S Co. Ltd.	30,000	
Face value of shares	1,60,000			50,000	
(1,600 × 100)			*Less* : Capital Reserve		
Less : Actual price paid for the			as per Contra	46,000	4,000
purchase of shares	1,20,000		**Fixed Assets :**		
	40,000		H Co. Ltd.	2,00,000	
Add : Capital Profits *i.e.*,			S Co. Ltd.	1,50,000	
increase in the value	20,000			3,50,000	
	60,000		*Add* : Increase in the		
Less : Capital Losses *i.e.*,			value	25,000	3,75,000
Pre-acquisition losses	14,000		**Investments in Govt.**		
	46,000		**Securities :**		
Deduct as per Contra	46,000	—	H Co. Ltd.	10,000	
10% Debentures :			S Co. Ltd.	5,000	15,000
H Co. Ltd.		1,00,000	**Debtors :** H Co. Ltd.	60,000	
Creditors :			S Co. Ltd.	25,000	85,000
H Co. Ltd.	63,000		**Stock :** H Co. Ltd.	40,000	
S Co. Ltd.	20,000	83,000	S Co. Ltd.	10,000	
Bills Payable :				50,000	
H Co. Ltd.	10,000		*Less :* Unrealised Profit		
S Co. Ltd.	10,000		(4/5 of 2,000)	2,000	48,000
	20,000		**Bills Receivable :**		
Less : Unendorsed Bills	2,000	18,000	H Co. Ltd.	3,000	
Minority Interest		43,000	*Less* : Unendorsed Bills	2,000	1,000
(As per chart)			**Profit and Loss A/c** :		
			H Co. Ltd.	20,000	
			Less : Post-acquisition		
			Profit	6,000	
				14,000	
			Add : Unrealised Profit	2,000	16,000
		5,44,000			5,44,000

Illustration 11

From the following balance sheets of A Co. Ltd. and its subsidiary, B Co. Ltd., prepare a consolidated balance sheet as at 31st Dec., 1998 to be presented to the shareholders of A Co. Ltd.

A Co. Ltd.
Balance Sheet as at 31st December, 1998

Liabilities	Rs.	Assets		Rs.
Authorised Capital :		Land & Buildings		25,000
20,000 shares of Rs. 20 each	2,00,000	Plant & Machinery		50,000
Issued Capital :		Fixtures		5,000
13,500 shares of Rs. 10		Investments in 'B' Ltd.		
each fully paid	1,35,000	at cost : 7,500 shares		90,000
6% Debentures (carrying		Stock in Trade		30,000
floating charge)	30,000	Sundry Debtors :		
Trade Creditors	15,000	'B' Ltd.	10,000	
General Reserve	30,000	Book Debts	20,000	30,000
Profit & Loss A/c	35,000	Cash at Bank		15,000
	2,45,000			2,45,000

B Co. Ltd.
Balance Sheet as at 31st December, 1998

Liabilities		Rs.	Assets	Rs.
Authorised Capital :			Land & Buildings	18,000
12,500 Shares of Rs. 10 each		1,25,000	Plant	13,000
Issued Capital :			Fixtures	500
10,000 Shares of Rs. 10 each			Stock in-Trade	45,500
fully paid		1,00,000	Sundry Debtors	50,000
Sundry Creditors :			Bills Receivable	5,000
A Co. Ltd.	9,500		Cash at Bank	27,500
Other Trade Creditors	25,000	34,500		
Profit and Loss A/c		25,000		
		1,59,500		1,59,500

The holding in the B. Ltd. was acquired on 1st January, 1998 at a premium of Rs. 2 per share on which date the balance to the credit of Profit & Loss A/c stood in the books of B. Ltd. at Rs. 10,000.

Transactions between the holding company and the subsidiary company include the purchase of goods by a subsidiary at cost plus 33 $^1/_3$%. The stock of B Co. Ltd. on 31st December, 1998 consisted of :

1. Goods purchased from A Co. Ltd. Rs. 15,008
2. Goods purchased from others Rs. 30,492.

Cash amounting to Rs. 500 was in transit from B Co. Ltd. to A Co. Ltd. at the close of business on 31st December, 1998.

(Adapted from Bangalore University)

Solution :

Chart Showing the Majority and Minority Interest in the Subsidiary Company

Sl. No.	Particulars	Total Amount Rs.	Majority Interest Rs.	Minority Interests Rs.
1.	Share Capital (Ratio 3 : 1)	1,00,000	75,000	25,000
2.	Profit and Loss Account :			
	(a) Pre-acquisition Profit	10,000	7,500	2,500
	(b) Post-acquisition Profit (25,000 –10,000)	15,000	11,250	3,750
		1,25,000	93,750	31,250

Consolidated Balance Sheet of A Co. Ltd. and its Subsidiary B Co. Ltd. as on 31-12-1998

Liabilities		Rs.	Assets		Rs.
Share Capital :			**Goodwill :**		
Authorised :			Cost of acquisition	90,000	
20,000 Shares of Rs. 10 each		2,00,000	*Less* : Nominal value		
Issued and subscribed :			of Shares	75,000	
13,500 Shares of Rs. 10 each		1,35,000		15,000	
Called up & Paid up :			*Less* : Capital Reserve		
13,500 shares of Rs. 10 each		1,35,000	as per Contra	7,500	7,500
Capital Reserve :			**Plant & Machinery :**		
Pre-acquisition Profit in			A Co. Ltd.	50,000	
B Co. Ltd. (3/4)	7,500		B Co. Ltd.	13,000	63,000
Deduct as per Contra	7,500	—	**Fixtures :**		
General Reserve :			A Co. Ltd.	5,000	
A Co. Ltd.		30,000	B Co. Ltd.	500	5,500
Profit & Loss A/c :			**Stock :** A Co Ltd.	30,000	
A Co. Ltd.	35,000		B Co. Ltd.	45,500	
B Co. Ltd. (3/4)	11,250			75,500	
(post-acquisition)			*Less* : Unrealised profit	3,752	71,748
	46,250		**Debtors** : A Co. Ltd.	20,000	
Less : Unrealised profit	3,752	42,498	(only outside debtors)		
6% Debentures : A Co. Ltd.		30,000	B Co. Ltd.	50,000	70,000
Trade Creditors :			**Bill Receivable :**		
A Co Ltd.	15,000		B Co. Ltd.		5,000
B Co. Ltd. (only			**Cash in Transit**		500
Outside creditors)	25,000	40,000	**Cash at Bank :**		
Minority Interest		31,250	A Co Ltd.	15,000	
(As per chart)			B Co. Ltd.	27,500	42,500
		3,08,748			3,08,748

Notes :

(i) Cash-in transit (500 *i.e.*, 10,000 – 9,500), is an asset. Hence, it should be shown on the assets side of the B/s.

(ii) The amount of unrealized profit included in stock is Rs. 3,752 (*i.e.*, 15,008 × $^1/_4$).

Illustration 12

A Ltd. purchased 40,000 shares of Re. 1 each in B Ltd. on 30th September, 1996. The summarized balance sheets of A Ltd. and B Ltd. on 31st December, 1996 were :

Liabilities	A Ltd. Rs.	B Ltd. Rs.	Assets	A Ltd. Rs.	B Ltd. Rs.
Share Capital :			Fixed Assets	90,000	93,000
Shares of Re. 1			Stock	15,000	20,000
each fully paid	1,00,000	50,000	Debtors	30,000	40,000
Reserves	40,000	30,000	Shares in B. Ltd.	65,000	—
Profit & Loss A/c	10,000	8,000	Bills Receivable	15,000	10,000
Creditors	60,000	60,000	Cash and Bank	5,000	3,000
Bills Payable	10,000	8,000			
Loan	—	10,000			
	2,20,000	1,66,000		2,20,000	1,66,000

On 1st January, 1996, the Profit and Loss Account of B Ltd. showed a debit balance of Rs. 10,000. B Ltd. made a transfer of the reserve on 31st December, 1996. Creditors of A Ltd. included Rs. 10,000 for goods purchased on credit from B Ltd. Stock of A Ltd. included unsold stock of Rs. 8,000 sold by B Ltd. at a profit of 25% on cost of goods sold. Bills Payable of B Ltd. included Rs. 6,000 accepted in favour of A Ltd. Bills receivable of A Ltd. included Rs. 5,000 received from B Ltd. There is a contingent liability of A Ltd. for the bills discounted Rs. 7,000 and for guaranteeing the loan granted to B Ltd. by Mehta Bros.

Your are required to draw the consolidated Balance Sheet.

(Adapted from Mangalore University)

Solution :

Calculation of Profit of B Ltd. during the year

	Rs.
Debit balance of P & L A/c as on 1-1-1996 set off against the current year's profits	10,000
Add : Credit balance of P & L A/c as on 31-12-1996	8,000
Add : Current year's profits transferred to reserves at the end of the current year	6,000
Profit earned during the year	24,000

Calculation of Pre-acquisition of Profit of B Ltd.

	Rs.
Profit from 1-1-1996 to 30-9-1996 (24,000 × 9/12)	18,000
Less : Debit balance of P & L A/c as on 1-1-1996	10,000
Net pre-acquisition Profits	8,000

Note : Pre-acquisition losses should be set off against pre-acquisition profits

Calculation Post-acquisition Profits of B Ltd.

	Rs.
Profits from 30-9-1996 to 31-12-1996 (24,000 × 3/12)	6,000
Less : Post-acquisition profits transferred to general reserve at the end of the year	6,000
Net post-acquisition profits	Nil

Calculation of Pre-acquisition & Post-acquisition Reserve of B Ltd.

Out of Reserve of Rs. 30,000 (as given in the B/s), Rs. 6,000 are transferred from the current year's profits at the end of the current year. Therefore, out of Rs. 30,000, Rs. 6,000 are treated as post-acquisition profits and Rs. 24,000 (30,000 – 6,000) are treated a pre-acquisition profits.

Charting Showing the Majority and Minority Interest in the Subsidiary Company

Sl. No.	Particulars	Total Amount Rs.	Majority Interest Rs.	Minority Interest Rs.
1.	Share Capital (Ration 4:1)	50,000	40,000	10,000
2.	Reserves :			
	(a) Pre-acquisition Reserve	24,000	19,200	4,800
	(b) Post-acquisition Reserve	6,000	4,800	1,200
3.	**Profit and Loss Account :**			
	(a) Pre-acquisition Profit	8,000	6,400	1,600
	(b) Post-acquisition Profit (6,000 – 6,000)	—	—	—
		88,000	70,400	17,600

Consolidated Balance Sheet of A Ltd. and its Subsidiary B Ltd. as on 30th September, 1996

Liabilities		Rs.	Assets		Rs.
Share Capital : (A Ltd.)			**Goodwill :**		
1,00,000 shares of Re. 1 each		1,00,000	Cost of acquisition	65,000	
Capital Reserve :			*Less* : Nominal value		
Pre-acquisition Reserve			of Shares	40,000	
of B Ltd. (4/5)	19,200			25,000	
Pre-acquisition Profit			Deduct as per Contra	25,000	—
of B Ltd. (4/5)	6,400		**Fixed Assets :**		
	25,600		A Ltd.	90,000	
Deduct Goodwill			B Ltd.	93,000	1,83,000
as per Contra	25,000	600	**Stock :**		
Reserve :			A Ltd.	15,000	
A Ltd.	40,000		B Ltd.	20,000	
B Ltd. (4/5)	4,800	44,800		35,000	
(post-acquisition)			*Less* : Unrealised Profit		
Profit and Loss A/c :			(8,000 × 25/125)	1,600	33,400
A Ltd.	10,000		**Debtors :**		
Less : Unrealised Profit	1,600	8,400	A Ltd.	30,000	
Creditors :			B Ltd.	40,000	
A Ltd.	60,000			70,000	
B Ltd.	60,000		*Less* : Debtor's set off	10,000	60,000
	1,20,000		**Bills Receivable :**		
Less : Creditors set off	10,000	1,10,000	A Ltd.	15,000	
Bills Payable :			B Ltd.	10,000	
A Ltd.	10,000			25,000	
B Ltd.	8,000		*Less :* B/R set off	5,000	20,000
	18,000		**Cash at Bank :**		
Less : B/P set off	5,000	13,000	A Ltd.	5,000	
Loan : B Ltd.		10,000	B Ltd.	3,000	8,000
Minority Interest		17,600			
(As per chart)					
		3,04,400			3,04,400

Note : **Contingent liabilities** : There are external contingent liabilities of A Ltd. for bills discounted for Rs. 7,000.

Hints : (i) Though B Ltd. has accepted the bills payable of Rs. 6,000 in favour of A Ltd., has only bills receivable of Rs. 5,000 in its hand. It means, the remaining bills of Rs. 1,000 might have been discounted by A Ltd. Hence, bills of only Rs. 5,000 will be mutual obligations.

(ii) There are two contingent liabilities in this problem. One is external contingent liability (*i.e.*, contingent liability of A Ltd. for bills discounted for Rs. 7,000). This should be shown at the foot of the consolidated balance sheet. Second is internal contingent liability (*i.e.*, contingent liability of "A" Ltd. for guaranteeing the loan granted to B Ltd. By Mehta Bros.). This should not be shown at the footnote of the consolidated balance sheet since it appears as actual liability in the consolidated balance sheet.

Illustration 13

Following are the Balance Sheets of H Ltd. and S Ltd. as at 31st December, 1998 :

Liabilities	H Ltd. Rs.	S Ltd. Rs.	Assets	H Ltd. Rs.	S Ltd. Rs.
Share Capital :			Goodwill	40,000	30,000
Shares of Rs. 100 each	5,00,000	2,00,000	Fixed Assets	3,60,000	2,20,000
General Reserve on			Stock	1,00,000	90,000
1st January, 1998	1,00,000	60,000	Debtors	20,000	75,000
Profit and Loss A/c	1,40,000	90,000	15,000 shares in		
Creditors	80,000	50,000	S Ltd. at cost	2,40,000	
Bills Payable	—	40,000	Bank	60,000	25,000
	8,20,000	4,40,000		8,20,000	4,40,000

The Profit and Loss account of S Ltd. showed a balance of Rs. 50,000 on 1st January, 1998. A dividend of 15% was paid in October, 1998 for the year 1997. This dividend was credited by H Ltd. to its Profit and Loss Account. H Ltd. acquired the shares on 1st July, 1998. The bills payable of S Ltd. were all issued in favour of H Ltd. which company got the bills discounted. Included in the creditors of S Ltd. is Rs. 20,000 for goods supplied by H Ltd. Included in the stock of S Ltd. are goods to the value of Rs. 8,000 which were supplied by H Ltd. at a profit of $33\frac{1}{3}$ on cost.

Prepare the consolidated balance sheet of H Ltd. and its subsidiary as at 31st December, 1998.

(Adapted from Mysore University)

Solution :

Calculation of Pre-acquisition Profit

Out of profit of Rs. 50,000 on 1-1-1998, the dividend of Rs. 30,000 (2,00,000 × 15/100) has been paid for the last year. Hence, the balance of profit of Rs. 20,000 (50,000 – 30,000) of the last year is treated as pre-acquisition profit. Again, as the shares of S Ltd. are purchased in the middle of the year, half of the current year profits *i.e.*, Rs. 35,000 (1/2 × 70,000 *i.e.*, 90,000 – 20,000) are to be treated as pre-acquisition profits.

Chart Showing the Majority and Minority Interest in the Subsidiary Company.

Sl. No.	Particulars	Total Amount Rs.	Majority Interest Rs.	Minority Interest Rs.
1.	Share Capital (Ratio 3:1)	2,00,000	1,50,000	50,000
2.	General Reserves :			
	(a) Pre-acquisition Reserve	60,000	45,000	15,000
3.	Profit and Loss Account :			
	(a) Pre-acquisition Profit (20,000 + 35,000)	55,000	41,250	13,750
	(b) Post-acquisition Profit (90,000 – 55,000 *i.e.*, 20,000 + 35,000)	35,000	26,250	8,750
		3,50,000	2,62,500	87,500

Consolidated Balance Sheet of H Ltd. and its Subsidiary S Ltd. as on 31-12-1998.

Liabilities		Rs.	Assets		Rs.
Share Capital :			**Goodwill :**		
5,000 shares of Rs. 100 each		5,00,000	H Ltd.	40,000	
Capital Reserve :			S Ltd.	30,000	
Pre-acquisition Reserve				70,000	
of S Ltd.(3/4)	45,000		Cost of acquisition		
Pre-acquisition Profit			of Shares	2,40,000	
of S Ltd. (3/4)	41,150			3,10,000	
Dividend received by			*Less* : Nominal Value		
H Ltd. from S Ltd. (3/4)	22,500		of shares	1,50,000	
	1,08,750			1,60,000	
Deduct as per Contra	1,08,750	—	*Less :* Capital Reserve		
General Reserve : H Ltd.		1,00,000	as per Contra	1,08,750	51,250
Profit and Loss A/c :			**Fixed Assets :**		
H Ltd.	1,40,000		H Ltd.	3,60,000	
Less : Dividend received			S Ltd.	2,20,000	5,80,000
out of pre-acquisition			**Stock** : H Ltd.	1,00,000	
profit to be credited			S Ltd.	90,000	
to capital reserve	22,500			1,90,000	
	1,17,500		*Less :* Unrealised		
S Ltd. (3/4)	26,250		Profit		
(Post-acquisition)	1,43,750		$\left(8,000 \times \frac{33\frac{1}{2}}{133\frac{1}{3}} = 2,000\right)$	2,000	1,88,000
Less : Unrealised profit	2,000	1,41,750			

Contd.

Creditors : H Ltd.	80,000		**Debtors** : H Ltd.	20,000	
S Ltd.	50,000		S Ltd.	75,000	
	1,30,000			95,000	
Less : Creditors set off against debtors	20,000	1,10,000	*Less* : Debtors set off against creditors	20,000	75,000
Bills Payable :			**Cash at Bank :**		
S Ltd.		40,000	H Ltd.	60,000	
Minority Interest (As per Chart)		87,500	S Ltd.	25,000	85,000
		9,79,250			9,79,250

Notes : (1) Bills discounted cannot constitute a mutual debt.

(2) Dividend received by H Ltd. from S Ltd. out of pre-acquisition profit should be treated as capital reserve. The holding company share of dividend of Rs. 22,500 received from the subsidiary company should be deducted from the profit of holding company and added to the capital reserve. The subsidiary company share should not be taken into account, as it has been already adjusted or taken in the concerned accounts at the time of preparation of consolidated balance sheet.

Illustration 14

From the following balance sheets of H Ltd. and its subsidiary S Ltd. as on 31-12-1993, prepare the consolidated balance sheet as on that date.

Liabilities	H. Ltd. Rs.	S. Ltd. Rs.	Assets	H. Ltd. Rs.	S. Ltd. Rs.
Share Capital :			Machinery	3,00,000	90,000
Shares of Rs. 100 each	5,00,000	1,00,000	Furniture	50,000	17,000
Reserves	2,00,000	75,000	Current Assets	4,40,000	1,43,000
Profit & Loss A/c	1,00,000	25,000	Shares in S Ltd.		
Creditors	1,50,000	50,000	800 shares at Rs. 200 each	1,60,000	—
	9,50,000	2,50,000		9,50,000	2,50,000

Adjustments :

(a) Reserves and Profit & Loss Account (credit balance) of S Ltd. stood at Rs. 25,000 and Rs. 15,000 respectively on the date of acquisition of its 80% shares held by H Ltd. on 1-1-1993.

(b) Machinery (book value Rs. 1,00,000) and Furniture (book value Rs. 20,000) of S Ltd. were revalued at Rs. 15,000 and Rs. 15,000 respectively. For the purpose of fixing the price of its shares, there was no purchase and sale of these assets since the date of acquisition on 1-1-1993.

(Gulbarga, April 1993)

Solution :

Chart Showing the Majority and Minority Interest in Subsidiary Company

Sl. No.	Particulars	Total Amount Rs.	Majority Interest Rs.	Minority Interest Rs.
1.	Share Capital (ratio 4 : 1)	1,00,000	80,000	20,000
2.	**General Reserves :**			
	(a) Pre-acquisition Reserve	25,000	20,000	5,000
	(b) Post-acquisition Reserve (75,000 – 25,000)	50,000	40,000	10,000
3.	**Profit & Loss Account :**			
	(a) Pre-acquisition Profit	15,000	12,000	3,000
	(b) Post-acquisition Profit (25,000 – 15,000)	10,000	8,000	2,000
4.	**Increase in value of Machinery :**			
	(a) Pre-acquisition Profit (capital profit : 1,50,000-1,00,000)	50,000	40,000	10,000
		2,50,000	2,00,000	50,000
	Less : Increase in depreciation on Machinery :			
	(a) Post-acquisition Loss (10% of Rs. 50,000 for 1993)	5,000	4,000	1,000
		2,45,000	1,96,000	49,000
	Less : Decrease in value of Furniture : Pre-acquisition Loss (capital loss : 20,000 – 15,000)	5,000	4,000	1,000
		2,40,000	1,92,000	48,000
	Add : Decrease in depreciation on Furniture : Post-acquisition Profit (15% of Rs. 5,000 for 1993)	750	600	150
		2,40,750	1,92,600	48,150

Consolidated Balance Sheet of H. Ltd. and its Subsidiary S Ltd. as on 31-12-1993

Liabilities		Rs.	Assets		Rs.
Share Capital :			**Goodwill :**		
50,000 Equity shares			Cost of acquisition		
of Rs. 10 each		5,00,000	of Shares	1,60,000	
Capital Reserve :			*Less* : Nominal		
Pre-acquisition Reserve			value of Shares	80,000	
of S Ltd. (4/5)	20,000			80,000	
Pre-acquisition Profit			*Less* : Capital		
of S Ltd. 4/5)	12,000		Reserve as		
Increase in value			per Contra	68,000	12,000
of Machinery	40,000		**Machinery :**		
	72,000		H Ltd.	3,00,000	
Less : Decrease in value			S Ltd.	1,35,000	4,35,000
of Furniture	4,000		(90,000 + 50,000 – 5,000)		
	68,000		**Furniture :**		
Deduct as per contra	68,000	–	H Ltd.	50,000	
General Reserve :			S Ltd.	12,750	62,750
H Ltd.	2,00,000		(17,000 – 5,000		
S Ltd. (4/5)	40,000	2,40,000	= 12,000 + 750)		
(post-acquisition)			**Current Assets :**		
Profit & Loss A/c :			H Ltd.	4,40,000	
H Ltd.	1,00,000		S Ltd.	1,43,000	5,83,000
Less : Net increase in depreciation					
(4,000 – 600) (4/5)	3,400				
	96,600				
S Ltd. (4/5)	8,000	1,04,600			
(post-acquisition)					
Creditors :					
H. Ltd.	1,50,000				
S. Ltd.	50,000	2,00,000			
Minority Interest		48,150			
(As per Chart)					
		10,92,750			10,92,750

Notes : (1) Depreciation on machinery is Rs. 10,000 (1,00,000 – 90,000). Hence, the rate of depreciation will be 10%. Similarly depreciation on furniture is Rs. 3,000 (20,000 – 17,000). Hence, the rate of depreciation will be 15%.

$$\frac{3,000 \times 100}{20,000}$$

(2) The value of machinery of S Ltd. is ascertained as below :

Value as given in the balance sheet		90,000
Add : Appreciation in the value as on 1-1-1993 not taken into account		50,000
		1,40,000
Less : Depreciation at 10% on the appreciated amount	$\left(\frac{50,000 \times 10}{100}\right)$	5,000
Value of machinery after adjustments		1,35,000

(3) The value of Furniture of S Ltd. is ascertained as below :

Value as given in the balance sheet		17,000
Less : Depreciation on furniture as on 1-1-1993 not taken into account (20,000 – 15,000)		5,000
		12,000
Add : Depreciation charged in excess	$\left(\frac{5,000 \times 15}{100}\right)$	750
Value of furniture after adjustments.		12,750

Illustration 15

You are given the balance sheets of two companies as on 31-12-1998.

Liabilities	Sky Ltd. Rs.	Stars Ltd. Rs.	Assets	Sky Ltd. Rs.	Stars Ltd. Rs.
Share Capital :			Fixed Assets	3,50,000	1,50,000
Shares of Rs. 100 each	5,00,000	2,00,000	Stock	90,000	40,000
General Reserve	1,00,000	—	Debtors	60,000	30,000
Profit & Loss A/c	80,000	—	6% Debentures in		
6% Debentures	—	1,00,000	Stars Ltd.	60,000	—
Creditors	75,000	45,000	Shares in Stars Ltd.	—	
Bills Payable	—	6,000	1,500 at Rs. 80 each	1.20,000	—
			Bills Receivable	10,000	—
			Bank	65,000	31,000
			Profit & Loss A/c	—	1,00,000
	7,55,000	3,51,000		7,55,000	3,51,000

Sky Ltd. acquired the shares on 1-5-1998. The Profit and Loss Account of Stars Ltd. showed a debit balance of Rs. 1,50,000 on 1-1-1998. During March, 1998, goods costing Rs. 6,000 were destroyed against which insurers paid only Rs. 2,000 to Stars Ltd. All the bills payable of Stars Ltd. are in favour of outsiders. Trade creditors of Stars Ltd. made a profit of Rs. 2,000. Half of the goods were still in stock on 31-12-1998. Prepare the consolidated balance sheet.

(Adapted from Bangalore University)

Solution :

Calculation of Pre-acquisition Profit, Pre-acquisition Loss and Post-acquisition Profit

The P & L A/c of Stars Ltd. as on 31-12-1998 showing the debit balance of Rs. 1,00,000 after charging the abnormal loss (*i.e.*, goods destroyed by fire) of Rs. 4,000. But the P & L A/c of Stars Ltd. as on 1-1-1998 showed a debit balance of Rs. 1,50,000. Therefore, Stars Ltd. has earned a profit of Rs. 54,000 [50,000 (*i.e.*, 1,50,000 – 1,00,000) + 4,000 abnormal loss]. Out of Rs. 54,000, 1/3rd of profits *i.e.*, 18,000 (54,000 × 1/3) should be considered as pre-acquisition profit, as the shares are acquired on 1st May, 1998. But, as the abnormal loss arose during the pre-acquisition period, it should be charged against the pre-acquisition profit. Therefore, the **net pre-acquisition profit will** be only Rs. 14,000 (*i.e.*, 18,000 – 4,000).

Similarly the debit balance of P & L A/c on 1-1-1998 is Rs. 1,50,000. This is considered as pre-acquisition loss. Then, there will be a **net pre-acquisition loss** of Rs. 1,36,000 (1,50,000 – 14,000).

Profit earned during the year is Rs. 54,000. Out of this profit, Rs. 18,000 is considered as pre-acquisition profit. The remaining balance of Rs. 36,000 (54,000 – 18,000) will be considered as **post-acquisition profit.**

Chart Showing the Majority and Minority Interest in the Subsidiary Company

Sl. No.	Particulars	Total Amount Rs.	Majority Interest Rs.	Minority Interest Rs.
1.	Share Capital (Ratio 3 : 1)	2,00,000	1,50,000	50,000
2.	Profit and Loss Account :			
	Post acquisition Profit	36,000	27,000	9,000
		2,36,000	1,77,000	59,000
1.	Deduct the following :			
	Profit and Loss Account :			
	Pre-acquisition Loss	1,36,000	1,02,000	34,000
		1,00,000	75,000	25,000

Consolidated Balance Sheet of Sky Ltd. and its subsidiary Stars Ltd. as on 31-12-1998

Liabilities		Rs.	Assets		Rs.
Share Capital :			**Goodwill :**		
5,000 Shares of Rs. 100 each		5,00,000	Cost of acquisition		
Capital Reserve		—	of Shares	1,20,000	
General Reserve :			*Add*: Pre-acquisition		
Sky Ltd.		1,00,000	Loss	1,02,000	
Profit & Loss A/c :				2,22,000	
Sky Ltd.	80,000		*Less* : Nominal value		
Stars Ltd. (3/4)	27,000		of Shares	1,50,000	72,000
(Post-acquisition)			**Fixed Assets :**		
	1,07,000		Sky Ltd.	3,50,000	
Less : Unrealised			Stars Ltd.	1,50,000	5,00,000
Profit	1,000	1,06,000	**Investments :**		
Debentures :			In Debentures :		
Stars Ltd.	1,00,000		Sky Ltd.	60,000	
Less : Due to Sky Ltd.	60,000	40,000	*Less* : Due from		
Sundry Creditors :			Stars Ltd.	60,000	—
Sky Ltd.	75,000		**Stock :**		
Stars Ltd.	45,000		Sky Ltd.	90,000	
	1,20,000		Stars Ltd.	40,000	
Less : Due to Sky Ltd.	20,000	1,00,000		1,30,000	
Bill Payable :			*Less* : Unrelised Profit	1,000	1,29,000
Stars Ltd.		6,000	**Sundry Debtors :**		
Minority Interest		25,000	Sky Ltd.	60,000	
(As per chart)			Stars Ltd.	30,000	
				90,000	
			Less : Due from		
			Stars Ltd.	20,000	70,000
			Bills Receivable :		
			Sky Ltd.		10,000
			Cash at Bank :		
			Sky Ltd.	65,000	
			Stars Ltd.	31,000	96,000
		8,77,000			8,77,000

Notes : (1) Inter company debentures are eliminated just like inter company debts.

(2) Since half of the goods purchased from Sky Ltd. by Stars Ltd. are in stock, only Rs. 1000 is profit on such goods.

(3) Abnormal loss is arrived as below :

	Rs.
Value of goods destroyed	6,000
Less : Amount recovered from insurers	2,000
Amount of abnormal loss.	4,000

EXAMINATION QUESTIONS

(A) Answer the following questions in two sentences each :

(Each carrying two marks)

(1) What is holding company?

(2) Define holding company. *(Karnataka, April 1997 & 1998)*

(3) What do you mean by subsidiary company?

(4) What do you understand by wholly owned subsidiary company?

(5) What is partly owned subsidiary company?

(6) What is capital profit? *(Karnataka, April 1996)*

(7) What are revenue profits?

(8) What do you mean by pre-acquisition profit?

(9) What is post-acquisition profit?

(10) What is meant by majority interest?

(11) What do you mean by minority interest?

(12) What is meant by cost of control in the holding company accounts? *(Karnataka, April 1997)*

(13) What do you mean by mutual indebtedness?

(14) What are inter company transactions? *(Mysore, Oct. 1989)*

(15) What the shares held by a holding company in its subsidiary company are not shown in the consolidated balance sheet? *(Karnataka, April 1996)*

(16) How do you deal with the revaluation of profit or loss?

(17) Give the meaning of pre-acquisition and post-acquisition reserve.

(18) Where do you show the contingent liabilities in the consolidated balance sheet?

(19) How do you deal with the abnormal loss of subsidiary company? *(Adapted from Bangalore University)*

(20) Where do you show the cash or goods in transit in the consolidated balance sheet? *(Mangalore, Oct. 1983)*

(21) What do you mean by unrealized profit?

(22) Why is a consolidated balance sheet of a holding company, with its subsidiary company prepared? Is it legally compulsory? *(Karnataka, April 1996)*

(23) What is consolidated balance sheet ? Is it compulsory to prepare it? *(Karnataka, Oct 1997)*

(24) Give the meaning of pre-acquisition and post-acquisition periods in the holding company.

(Karnataka, April 1998)

(25) How do you calculate minority interest?

(Karnataka, April 1998)

(26) What is wholly owned subsidiary

(Karnataka, April 1999)

(B) Answer the following questions :

(Each carrying 8 marks)

(1) Define holding company. When one company is treated as a subsidiary of another company?

(M.K. U., April 1983)

(2) How do you calculate the cost of control and capital reserve?

(3) Under what circumstances, a company becomes a subsidiary of another?

(4) What are inter-company owings? How are they treated in consolidation?

(5) Explain the steps involved in the preparation of consolidated balance sheet.

(6) State the documents which a holding company has to attach with its balance sheet in respect of its subsidiary as per Section 212 of the Company Act.

(I.C.W.A. Inter)

Simple Problems :

(7) A Co. Ltd. acquired all the shares of B. Co. Ltd. on 31-3-1998 on which date the balance sheet of two companies are as under :

Liabilities	A Ltd.	B Ltd.	Assets	A Ltd.	B Ltd.
Share Capital :			Sundry Assets	5,50,000	4,20,000
Shares of Rs. 100			100% Shares in		
each fully paid	6,00,000	3,00,000	B Ltd.	3,00,000	—
Reserves	80,000	—			
Profit and Loss A/c	70,000	—			
Sundry Creditors	1,00,000	1,20,000			
	8,50,000	4,20,000		8,50,000	4,20,000

Prepare a consolidated balance sheet as at 31st March, 1998.

Ans. : Consolidated B/S Total Rs. 9,70,000 (Liabilities 6,00,000 + 80,000 + 70,000 + 2,20,000; Assets : Rs. 9,70,000).

Hints : (i) Since all the shares are purchased by the holding company, there is no minority interest.

(ii) Since the shares are purchased at par, there is no capital reserve or goodwill.

(8) The summarized balance sheets of A Co. Ltd. and B Co. Ltd. as on 31st December, 1998 were as follows :

Liabilities	A Ltd. Rs.	B Ltd. Rs.	Assets	A Ltd. Rs.	B Ltd. Rs.
Share Capital :			Sundry Assets	6,00,000	8,00,000
Shares of Rs. 200			100% Shares in		
each fully paid	8,00,000	6,00,000	B Ltd.		
Reserves	2,00,000	—	(at cost)	6,50,000	—
Sundry Creditors	3,00,000	2,00,000	Profit & Loss A/c	50,000	—
	13,00,000	8,00,000		13,00,000	8,00,000

Prepare a consolidated Balance Sheet as at 31st December, 1998.

Ans. : Consolidated B/S Total Rs. 15,00,000 (Liabilities : 8,00,000 + 2,00,000 + 5,00,000; Assets : 14,00,000 + 50,000 + 50,000)

Note : Cost of Control or Goodwill Rs. 50,000 (6,50,000 – 6,00,000)

(9) You are given the following balance sheets of A Ltd. and B. Ltd. as on 31st December, 1998 :

Liabilities	A Ltd. Rs.	B Ltd. Rs.	Assets	A Ltd. Rs.	B Ltd. Rs.
Share Capital :			Sundry Assets	13,60,000	11,00,000
Shares of Rs. 50			100% Shares in		
Each fully paid	15,00,000	9,00,000	B Ltd. (at cost)	8,40,000	—
Reserves	3,00,000	—			
Sundry Creditors	4,00,000	2,00,000			
	22,00,000	11,00,000		22,00,000	11,00,000

Prepare consolidated balance sheet as at 31-12-1998 .

Ans. : Consolidated B/S Total Rs. 24,60,000 (Liabilities : 15,00,000 + 60,000 + 3,00,000 + 6,00,000) and Capital Reserve Rs. 60,000 (9,00,000 – 8,40,000).

(10) The following are the balance sheets of A Co. Ltd. and B Co. Ltd. as on 31st March, 1998 :

Liabilities	A Ltd. Rs.	B Ltd. Rs.	Assets	A Ltd. Rs.	B Ltd. Rs.
Share Capital :			Land & Building	2,00,000	2,00,000
Shares of Rs. 10			Plant & Machinery	1,00,000	80,000
each fully paid	7,00,000	4,50,000	Stock	1,50,000	1,20,000
General Reserve	40,000	—	Debtors	40,000	1,00,000
Debentures	1,00,000	—	75% Shares in B Ltd.	4,00,000	—
Bills Payable	60,000	50,000	Cash in hand	10,000	25,000
Creditors	75,000	25,000	Profit and Loss A/c	75,000	—
	9,75,000	5,25,000		9,75,000	5,25,000

Prepare a consolidated balance sheet as at 31-3-1998.

Ans. : Consolidated B/S Total Rs. 11,62,500; Minority Interest Rs 1,12,500 Goodwill Rs. 62,500 (*i.e.*, Cost of purchase Rs. 4,00,000 – Nominal value of shares purchased Rs. 3,37,500).

Note : Liabilities : 7,00,000 + 4,00,000 + 1,00,000 + 1,10,000 + 1,00,000 + 1,12,5000.

Assets : 62,500 + 4,00,000 + 1,80,000 + 2,70,000 + 1,40,000 + 35,000 + 75,000.

(11) Balance Sheet of S. Ltd. as on 31-12-1998 :

Liabilities		Rs.	Assets	Rs.
Share Capital :			Land & Buildings	5,00,000
50,000 Shares of Rs. 10 each		5,00,000	Machinery	3,00,000
General Reserve as on 1-1-1998		2,00,000	Current Assets	2,00,000
Profit and Loss A/c	1,50,000			
Add : Profit for 1998	50,000	2,00,000		
Creditors		1,00,000		
		10,00,000		10,00,000

H Ltd. acquired 40,000 shares of S Ltd. on 1st July, 1998, at Rs. 7,80,000. H Ltd. valued the machinery at Rs. 2,50,000 and current assets at Rs. 2,75,000. Calculate the minority interest.

(M.K. U., Oct. 1998)

Ans. : Minority interest Rs. 1,85,000 (Share Capital Rs. 1,00,000 + General Reserve Rs. 40,000 + Profit Rs. 40,000 + Increase in value of assets Rs. 15,000 – Decrease value of machinery Rs. 10,000).

Hint : Capital Profit Rs. 4,00,000 (2,00,000 + 1,50,000 + 25,000 + 75,000 – 50,000); Holding company share Rs. 3,20,000 (4/5) and Minority interest Rs. 80,000 (1/5).

(12) Balance Sheets as on 31st March, 1995 :

Liabilities	A Ltd. Rs.	B Ltd. Rs.	Assets	A Ltd. Rs.	B Ltd. Rs.
Share Capital :			Sundry Assets	5,17,600	3,04,000
Shares of Rs. 10			60% Shares in		
each fully paid	5,00,000	2,00,000	'B' Ltd. acquired		
Reserves	1,00,000	50,000	on 31-3-95 (cost)	1,62,400	—
Creditors	80,000	60,000	Preliminary Expenses	—	6,000
	6,80,000	3,10,000		6,80,000	3,10,000

Prepare a consolidated balance sheet as at 31-3-1995.

(Bombay, April 1995)

Ans. : Consolidated B/S Total Rs. 8,37,600 (Liabilities : 5,00,000 + 1,00,000 + 1,40,000 + 97,600; assets : 16,000 + 8,21,600); Goodwill or Cost of Control Rs. 16,000 and Minority Interest Rs. 97,600.

***Notes* :** (i) Accumulated losses or expenses of subsidiary company should be written off at the time of acquisition.

(ii) Calculation of cost of control or Goodwill

	Rs.
Cost of acquisition of shares	1,62,400
Less : Nominal value of shares	1,20,000
	42,400
Add : Preliminary Expenses (3/5)	3,600
	46,000
Less : Capital Reserve as per Contra (*i.e.*, 3/5 of prior reserve)	30,000
Goodwill or cost of control	16,000

(iii) Calculation of Minority Interest :

Share capital (2/5 of Rs. 2,00,000)	80,000
Add : Prior Reserve (2/5 of Rs. 50,000)	20,000
	1,00,000
Less : Preliminary Expenses (2/5 of Rs. 6,000)	2,400
Minority Interest	97,600

(C) Solve the following problems :

(Each carrying 15/16 marks)

(1) H. Ltd. acquired all the shares in S Ltd. on 1-1-1992 and the balance Sheets of the two companies as on 31-12-1992 were as follows :

Liabilities	A Ltd. Rs.	B Ltd. Rs.	Assets	A Ltd. Rs.	B Ltd. Rs.
Share Capital	50,000	30,000	Sundry Assets	65,000	70,000
Reserve on 1-1-1992	20,000	15,000	Investments :		
Profit & Loss Account	25,000	10,000	Shares in S. Ltd.		
Sundry Creditors	20,000	15,000	at cost	50,000	—
	1,15,000	70,000		1,15,000	70,000

The profit and loss account of S Ltd. had credit balance of Rs. 3,000 on 1-1-1992. Prepare the consolidated balance sheet as on 31-12-1992.

(Adapted from Karnataka University)

Ans. : Consolidated B/S Total Rs. 1,37,000; Goodwill Rs. 2,000; Capital Reserve Rs. 18,000 and P& L A/c Rs. 32,000.

***Note* :** Since all the shares are acquired by the holding company, there is no minority interest.

(2) The following are the summarized balance sheets of A Ltd. and its subsidiary B Ltd., as on 31-12-1996.

Liabilities	A Ltd. Rs.	B Ltd. Rs.	Assets	A Ltd. Rs.	B Ltd. Rs.
5,000 Ordinary shares of Rs. 100 each fully paid	5,00,000	—	Land and Buildings	1,00,000	40,000
			Plant and Machinery	1,00,000	50,000
			Stock in Trade	90,000	30,000
10,000 Ordinary shares of Rs. 100 each	—	1,00,000	Sundry Debtors	40,000	30,000
			Bills Receivable	5,000	—
			Bank	1,10,000	20,000
General reserve	10,000	40,000	Cash in Hand	5,000	5,000
Sundry creditors	20,000	30,000	Investments :		
Bills Payable	—	5,000	7,500 shares of B Ltd. at cost	80,000	—
	5,30,000	1,75,000		5,30,000	1,75,000

A Ltd. acquired shares in B Ltd. on 1-1-1996 when B Ltd. had 10,000 in general reserve. No dividend has been declared by B Ltd. in 1996.

All bills receivable of A Ltd. are drawn on B Ltd.

You are asked to prepare consolidated balance sheet of A Ltd. and its subsidiary B Ltd. as on 31-12-1996.

(Adapted from B.Com., Madras)

Ans. : Consolidated B/S Total Rs. 6,20,000.

Net Capital Reserve Rs. 2,500; Minority Interest Rs. 75,000; General Reserve Rs. 32,500 (10,000 + 22,500) and Ratio 3 : 1.

(3) From the Balance Sheets given below, prepare, a consolidated Balance Sheet of Moti Ltd. and its Subsidiary Choti Ltd.

Liabilities	Moti Ltd. Rs.	Choti Ltd. Rs.	Assets	Moti Ltd. Rs.	Choti Ltd. Rs.
Share Capital :			**Fixed Assets :**		
Shares of Rs. 10			Freehold Buildings	72,000	—
each	1,20,000	30,000	Lease hold Property	—	25,000
Reserves and Surplus	25,000	6,000	Machinery	30,000	10,000
Profit and Loss A/c	12,000	9,000	**Investments :**		
Secured Loan	—	—	2,000 Shares in		
Unsecured Loans	—	—	Choti Ltd.	25,000	—
Current Liabilities :			**Current Assets,**		
Creditors	15,000	5,000	**Loans & Advances:**		
			Stock at Cost	18,000	3,000
			Debtors	22,000	7,000
			Bank	5,000	5,000
	1,72,000	50,000		1,72,000	50,000

At the date of acquisition, by Moti Ltd., of 2,000 shares in Choti Ltd. the latter company had undistributed profits and reserves of Rs. 5,000, none of which has been distributed since acquisition.

(Adapted from My. U., B.Com.)

Ans. : Consolidated B/S Total Rs. 1,98,667; Goodwill Rs. 1,667; Minority Interest Rs. 15,000 & Ratio 2 : 1.

***Notes* :** (i) Capital Reserve of Rs. 3,333 is deducted as per contra.

(ii) The pre-acquisition reserve and profit of Rs. 5,000 should be allocated between pre-acquisition reserve and pre-acquisition profit in the ratio of total reserves and total profit of Choti Ltd. *i.e.*, 2 : 3 *i.e.*, 6,000 : 9,000. Then the pre-acquisition reserves will be Rs. 2,000 and pre-acquisition profit will be Rs. 3,000.

(4) H Ltd. acquired 80,000 shares of Rs. 10 each in S Ltd. on 1-1-1997. The summarised balance sheets of H Ltd. and S Ltd. on 30-6-1997 were :

Liabilities	H Ltd. Rs.	S Ltd. Rs.	Assets	H Ltd. Rs.	S Ltd. Rs.
Share Capital in			Machinery	6,00,000	4,50,000
Shares of Rs. 10 each	20,00,000	10,00,000	Furniture	20,000	40,000
Reserve	1,00,000	1,50,000	Shares in S Ltd.	8,80,000	
Profit and Loss A/c	50,000	45,000	9% Debentures		
9% Debentures	—	2,00,000	in S Ltd.	80,000	—
Creditors	4,00,000	2,00,000	Stock	5,20,000	6,50,000
Bills Payable	20,000	10,000	Debtors	1,80,000	2,70,000
			Bills Receivable	10,000	15,000
			Cash	2,80,000	1,80,000
	25,70,000	16,05,000		25,70,000	16,05,000

Bills Receivable of S Ltd. include bills for Rs. 8,000 accepted by H Ltd. and creditors of S Ltd. Include Rs. 20,000 due to H Ltd. An amount of Rs. 30,000 was transferred by S Ltd. from the current years profit to Reserves.

Prepare the consolidated Balance Sheet as on 30th June 1997.

(Mangalore University, B. Com.)

Ans. : Consolidated Balance Sheet Total Rs. 31,87,000; Net Capital Reserve Rs. 46,000 (*i.e.*, 1,26,000-80,000 Goodwill); Minority Interest Rs. 2,39,000 & Ratio 4 : 1.

Notes :(i) Out of reserves of Rs. 1,50,000, Rs. 30,000 were created at the end of the year. Hence, reserves of Rs. 30,000 are the post acquisition reserves and remaining reserves of Rs. 1,20,000 are the pre-acquisition reserve.

(ii) Current years profit of S. Ltd. is calculated as below :

P & L A/c credit balance (as shown in the B/S)	45,000
Add : Profits transferred to reserves at the end (as given in the problem)	30,000
Current year's profit	75,000

Out of Rs. 75,000, Rs. 37,500 (*i.e.*, for six months) is the pre-acquisition profit and Rs. 7,500 (*i.e.*, 37,500 – 30,000 transferred to reserves) is the post-acquisition profit.

(iii) Rs. 80,000 debentures of S Ltd. purchased by H Ltd. constitute inter company debts.

(5) From the following balance sheet and adjustments given below, prepare the Consolidated Balance Sheet as on 31-12-1984 :

Liabilities	Strong	Weak	Asset	Strong	Weak
Share Capital :			Plant & Machinery	8,00,000	1,20,000
Shares of Rs. 10 each	10,00,000	2,00,000	Investments :		
Reserve Fund on			15,000 shares in		
1-1-1984	10,00,000	60,000	Weak Ltd.	1,50,000	—
Profit & Loss A/c	4,00,000	1,20,000	Stock	6,10,000	2,40,000
Sundry Creditors	2,00,000	1,20,000	Sundry Debtors	1,30,000	1,70,000
Bills Payable	—	30,000	Bills Receivable	10,000	—
	1,70,000	5,30,000		17,00,000	5,30,000

Adjustments :

(1) The shares were acquired by Strong Ltd. in Weak Ltd. on 1-1-1984.

(2) The entire profit of Weak Ltd. has been earned after the shares were acquired by Strong Ltd.

(3) The bills payable of Weak Ltd. were all in favour of Strong Ltd.

(4) The stock of Strong Ltd. include Rs. 50,000 bought from Weak Ltd. which has been charged a profit of 25% on cost.

(Gulbarga, Oct. 1985)

Ans. : Consolidated B/S Total 20,60,000; Capital Reserve Rs. 45,000; Minority Interest Rs. 95,000; Profit & Loss A/c Rs. 4,82,500; Ratio 3 : 1 & Unrealised Profit Rs. 10,000.

Notes : (i) Pre-acquisition reserve is Rs. 60,000 and post-acquisition profit is Rs. 1,20,000.

(ii) Inter company bills of Rs. 10,000 should be eliminated. The remaining bills of Rs. 20,000 have been discounted.

(6) A Co., Ltd. acquired 80% of both the types of shares in B Co. Ltd. on 1-7-1991. The following are the balance sheets of the two companies as on 31-12-1991 :

Liabilities	A Co. Ltd.	B Co. Ltd.	Assets	A Co. Ltd.	B Co. Ltd.
Share Capital :			Goodwill	75,000	50,000
Equity shares of			Buildings	1,50,000	1,00,000
Rs. 10 each	4,50,000	2,00,000	Machinery	2,00,000	2,00,000
9% Preference shares			Investments :		
of Rs. 100 each	2,00,000	1,00,000	In shares of B Co. Ltd.		
General Reserve	80,000	60,000	Equity shares	2,00,000	—
Profit & Loss A/c	1,10,000	80,000	Preference shares	90,000	—
Creditors	65,000	45,000	Stock	80,000	70,000
Bills Payable	25,000	15,000	Debtors	40,000	30,000
			Bills Receivable	15,000	—
			Cash at Bank	60,000	50,000
	9,30,000	5,00,000		9,30,000	5,00,000

Additional Information :

(a) B Co. Ltd. had to its credit of general reserve and Profit & Loss Account Rs. 40,000 and Rs. 30, 000 respectively on 1-1-1991.

(b) Creditors of B Co. Ltd. included Rs. 25,000 for goods supplied by A Co. Ltd. at a profit of 20% on sales price. Goods worth Rs. 10,000 are still in stock of B Co. Ltd.

(c) Machinery of B Co. Ltd. was found overvalued by Rs. 20,000.

Prepare the consolidated balance sheet of A Co. Ltd. as on 31-12-1991.

(Karnataka, April 1992)

Ans. : Consolidated B/S Total Rs. 10,75,000; Goodwill Rs. 1,27,000; Pre-acquisition Reserve Rs. 50,000; Post-acquisition Reserve Rs. 10,000; Pre-acquisition Profit Rs. 55,000; Post-acquisition Profit Rs. 25,000; General Reserve Rs. 88,000; P & L A/c Rs. 1,28,400; Minority Interest Rs. 84,000; Unrealised Profit Rs. 2,000 and Ratio 4 : 1.

***Notes* :** (i) Investment in preference shares of B. Co. Ltd. is apportioned in the same manner as in case of equity shares.

(ii) Pre-acquisition-decrease in the value of machinery is Rs. 20,000 and Capital Reserve Rs. 68,000 (*i.e.*, 50,000 + 55,000 – 20,000 = 85,000 × 4/5 = 68,000 is deducted as per contra.

(7) The following are the summarised balance sheets of Alpha Ltd. and its subsidiary Beta Ltd. as at 31-12-1982 :

Liabilities	Alpha Rs.	Beta Rs.	Assets	Alpha Rs.	Beta Rs.
Share Capital :			Goodwill	60,000	20,000
Shares of Rs. 10 each	300,000	2,00,000	Land & Buildings	1,20,000	85,000
Reserve Fund	65,000	—	Machinery	65,000	42,000
Profit & Loss A/c :			Investments :		
Balance on 1-1-1982	10,000	—	Shares in Beta Ltd.	1,50,000	—
Profit for 1982	80,000	—	Govt. Securities	—	10,000
10% Debentures	1,00,000	—	Debtors	60,000	72,000
Creditors	10,000	35,000	Stock	85,000	40,000
Bills Payable	—	15,000	Bills Receivable	10,000	—
Public Deposits	—	1,30,000	Cash	15,000	11,000
			Profit & Loss A/c	—	1,00,000
	5,65,000	3,80,000		5,65,000	3,80,000

Additional Information :

(1) Alpha Ltd. purchased 12,000 shares of Beta Ltd. on 1-7-1982.

(2) The profit and loss account of Beta Ltd. showed debit balance of Rs. 1,50,000 on 1-1-1982.

(3) Creditors of Beta Ltd. included Rs. 10,000 for goods supplied by Alpha Ltd. on which Alpha Ltd. made a profit of Rs. 2,500. Half of the goods were still in stock of Beta Ltd.

(4) Bills Payable of Beta Ltd. are all drawn by Alpha Ltd. Prepare the consolidated balance sheet as on 31-12-1982.

(Gulbarga, Oct. 1983 & 1989)

Ans. : Consolidated B/S Total Rs. 7,78,750; Pre-acquisition Loss Rs. 1,25,000; Post-acquisition Profit Rs. 25,000; Goodwill Rs. 1,85,000; P & L A/c Rs. 1,04,250; Minority Interest Rs. 40,000; Unrealised Profit Rs. 1,250 and Ratio 3 : 2.

***Note* :** Inter company bills of Rs. 10,000 should be eliminated. The remaining bills of Rs. 5,000 have been discounted.

(8) Following are the balance sheets of H Ltd. and S Ltd. as at 31-12-1989 :

Liabilities	H Ltd. Rs.	S Ltd. Rs.	Assets	H Ltd. Rs.	S Ltd. Rs.
Share Capital :			Goodwill	30,000	20,000
Shares of Rs. 100 each	5,00,000	2,00,000	Fixed Assets	3,80,000	2,30,000
General Reserve			Stock	80,000	80,000
as at 1-1-1989	1,00,000	60,000	Debtors	30,000	90,000
Bills Payable	5,000	40,000	Bills Receivable	10,000	—
Creditors	75,000	50,000	Investments :		
Profit & Loss A/c	1,40,000	90,000	15,000 shares in		
			S Ltd. at cost	2,40,000	—
			Other Shares	10,000	10,000
			Cash at Bank	40,000	10,000
	8,20,000	4,40,000		8,20,000	4,40,000

The Profit and Loss Account of S Ltd. showed a credit balance of Rs. 50,000 on 1-1-1989. H Ltd. acquired the shares on 1-7-1989. The bills payable of S Ltd. were all issued in favour of H Ltd. included in the creditors of S Ltd. Rs. 30,000 for goods supplied by H Ltd. included in the stock of S Ltd. goods of the value of Rs. 10,000 which were supplied by H Ltd. at a profit of Rs. 25% on cost.

Prepare the consolidated balance sheet as at 31-12-1989.

(Mangalore, April 1985 modified)

Ans. : Consolidated B/S Total Rs. 9,70,500; Pre-acquisition Reserve Rs. 60,000; Pre-acquisition Profit Rs. 70,000; Post-acquisition Profit Rs. 20,000; P & L A/c Rs. 1,53,500; Unrealised Profit Rs. 2,000 and Ratio 3 : 1.

Notes : (i) Capital reserve Rs. 97,500 is deducted as per contra.
(ii) Inter company bills of Rs. 10,000 should be eliminated.

(9) The balance sheets of Moti Ltd. and its subsidiary Choti Ltd. as on 31-12-1983 were as follows :

Liabilities	Moti. Ltd. Rs.	Choti. Ltd. Rs.	Assets	Moti Ltd. Rs.	Choti Ltd . Rs.
Share Capital :			Buildings	60,000	20,000
Shares of Rs. 10 each	2,00,000	50,000	Machinery	2,00,000	25,000
General Reserve	30,000	20,000	Stock	50,000	35,000
Profit & Loss A/c :			Investments :		
Balance on 1-1-1983	30,000	10,000	3,000 Shares in		
Profit for the year	60,000	30,000	Choti Ltd. at cost	55,000	—
Creditors	40,000	30,000	Debtors	10,000	40,000
Bills Payable	25,000	5,000	Bills Receivable	—	10,000
			Cash & Bank Balances	10,000	15,000
	3,85000	1,45,000		3,85,000	1,45,000

Additional Information :

(1) Moti Ltd. acquired the shares in Choti Ltd. on 1-1-1983.

(2) Bills Receivable held by Choti Ltd. were all accepted by Moti Ltd.

(3) Included in the debtors of Choti Ltd. was Rs. 10,000 owing by Moti Ltd. in respect of goods supplied

(4) Included in the stock of Moti Ltd. were goods worth Rs. 5,000 supplied by Choti Ltd. at a profit of 20% on sales.

(5) Building of Choti Ltd. was undervalued by Rs. 10,000 and the directors decided to appreciate the value of building to bring upto its original value.

(6) The balance of General Reserve in Choti Ltd. on 1-1-1983 was Rs. 14,000.

Prepare the consolidated balance sheet.

(Gulbarga, April 1984)

Ans. : Consolidated B/S Total Rs. 4,64,000; Pre-acquisition Profit Rs. 20,000; Post-acquisition Profit Rs. 20,000; Pre-acquisition Reserve Rs. 16,000; Post-acquisition Reserve Rs. 4,000; Capital Reserve Rs. 2,600; General Reserve Rs. 32,400; P & L A/c Rs. 1,01,400; Minority Interest Rs. 48,000; Unrealised Profit Rs. 1,000 and Ratio 3 : 2.

Notes : (i) Goodwill of Rs. 25,000 is deducted as per contra.
(ii) Out of Rs. 10,000 increase in the value of building, Rs. 6,000 is added to Capital Reserve and Rs. 4,000 is added to Minority Interest.

(10) From the following balance sheets of H Ltd. and its subsidiary S Ltd., prepare the consolidated balance sheet as on 31-12-1986.

H Ltd. purchased 7,500 shares in S Ltd. on 1-7-1986. The balance to the credit of General Reserve and Profit & Loss Account of S Ltd. stood at Rs. 6,000 and Rs. 4,000 respectively on 1-1-1986. Out of Rs. 15,000 Bills payable of H Ltd., bills amounting to Rs. 10,000 were payable to S Ltd. and the latter had discounted bills worth Rs. 1,000.

Liabilities	H Ltd.	S Ltd.	Assets	H Ltd.	S Ltd.
Share Capital :			Goodwill	—	5,000
Shares of Rs. 5 each	2,50,000	50,000	Buildings	50,000	17,500
General Reserve	25,000	10,000	Machinery	1,50,000	30,000
Profit & Loss A/c	12,500	16,000	Shares in S Ltd.	42,500	—
Creditors	22,500	9,000	Stock	50,000	15,000
Bills Payable	15,000	—	Debtors	30,000	6,000
			Bills Receivable	—	9,000
			Cash	2,500	2,500
	3,25,000	85,000		3,25,000	85,000

(Karnataka, Oct. 1987)

Ans. : Consolidated B/S Total Rs. 3,53,500; Pre-acquisition Profit Rs. 10,000; Pre-acquisition Reserve Rs. 8,000; Post-acquisition Profit Rs. 6,000; Post-acquisition Reserve Rs. 2,000; Capital Reserve Rs. 3,500; General Reserve Rs. 26,500; P& L A/c Rs. 17,000; Minority Interest Rs. 19,000 and Ratio 3 : 1.

Note : Inter company bills of Rs. 9,000 (10,000 – 1,000) should be eliminated.

(11) The following were the Balance Sheets of H Ltd. and its subsidiary S Ltd. as on 31-12-1997.

Liabilities	H Ltd.	S Ltd.	Assets	H Ltd.	S Ltd.
Share Capital :			Buildings	90,000	—
Shares of Rs. 100 each	2,00,000	75,000	Machinery	2,00,000	—
General Reserve	45,000	15,000	Shares in Sagar Ltd. :		
Profit & Loss A/c :			450 shares at cost	97,500	—
Balance on 1-1-1997	60,000	30,000	Stock	60,000	1,27,500
Current year Profit	75,000	37,500	Debentures	15,000	45,000
Debentures	50,000	30,000	Bills Receivable	—	15,000
Creditors	25,000	15,000	Cash at Bank	15,000	15,000
Bills Payable	22,500	—			
	4,77,500	2,02,500		4,77,500	2,02,500

From the following information, prepare a Consolidated Balance Sheet as on 31-12-1999.

(a) Shares in S Ltd. were purchased by H Ltd. on 1-7-1999.

(b) As on 1-1-1999 balance of General Reserve of S Ltd. was Rs.10,000.

(c) Bills Receivable held by S Ltd. were all accepted by H Ltd.

(d) Debtors of S Ltd. included the amount of Rs. 9,000 for supply of goods to H Ltd.

(e) Stock of H Ltd. included goods from the above purchases from S Ltd. worth Rs. 6,000. The goods supplied by the S Ltd. to H Ltd. were at cost plus $33^1/_3$%.

(Mysore University, Oct. 1986 & Gulbarga, Oct. 1996 & 1997 Mod.)

Ans. : Consolidated B/S Rs. 5,72,750; Pre-acquisition Profit Rs. 48,750; Pre-acquisition Reserve Rs. 12,500; Post-acquisition Profit Rs. 18,750; Post-acquisition Reserve Rs. 2,500; Goodwill Rs. 15,750; General Reserve Rs. 46,500; P & L A/c Rs. 1,45,350; Unrealised Profit Rs. 1,500; Minority Interest Rs. 63,000 and Ratio 3 : 2.

***Notes* :** (i) Capital Reserve of Rs. 36,750 is deducted as per contra.

(ii) Inter company bill of Rs. 15,000 should be eliminated.

(12) The following were the balance sheet of A Ltd. and its subsidiary B. Ltd. as on 31-12-1984.

Liabilities	A Ltd. Rs.	B Ltd. Rs.	Assets	A Ltd. Rs.	B Ltd. Rs.
Share Capital :			Goodwill	25,000	—
Shares of Rs. 10 each	2,25,000	1,20,000	Buildings	60,000	70,000
General Reserve	45,000	24,000	Machinery	—	85,500
Profit & Loss A/c	70,000	35,000	Furniture	25,000	8,500
Creditors	60,000	80,000	Shares in B. Ltd. at cost	1,92,000	—
			Stock	40,000	25,000
			Debtors	33,000	55,000
			Cash at Bank	25,000	15,000
	4,00,000	2,59,000		4,00,000	2,59,000

From the following information prepare a Consolidated Balance sheet as on 31-12-1984.

(1) A Ltd. acquired 80% of shares in B Ltd. at Market price of Rs. 20 per share on 1-1-1984.

(2) The machinery of B Ltd. was overvalued to extent of Rs. 5,000.

(3) On 1-1-1984 the B Ltd. had Rs. 20,000 to the credit of General reserve and Rs. 20,000 to the credit of Profit & Loss A/c.

(4) The stock of A Ltd. included goods purchased from B Ltd. worth Rs. 6,000. The goods were supplied by B. Ltd. at cost plus 25%.

(Gulbarga, April 1991)

Ans. : Consolidated Balance sheets total Rs. 5,28,800; Pre-acquisition Profit 20,000; Pre-acquisition Reserve Rs. 20,000; Post-acquisition Profit Rs.15,000; Post-acquisition Reserve Rs. 4,000; Goodwill Rs. 93,000 General Reserve Rs. 48,200; P & L A/c Rs. 81,040; Unrealised Profit Rs. 1,200; Minority Interest Rs. 34,800 and Ratio 4 : 1.

***Notes* :** (i) Capital Reserve of Rs. 28,000 is deducted as per contra.

(ii) Out of Rs. 5,000 decrease in the value of machinery, Rs. 4,000 is deducted from Capital Reserve and Rs. 1,000 is deducted from Minority Interest.

(13) From the following balance sheet as at 31-12-1988 and the particulars given below, prepare consolidated balance sheet of Asha Ltd. and Nisha Ltd. as at 31-12-1988 :

Liabilities	Asha Ltd. Rs.	Nisha Ltd. Rs.	Assets	Asha Ltd. Rs.	Nisha Ltd. Rs.
Share Capital :			Goodwill	16,000	12,000
Shares of Rs. 100			Land & Buildings	50,000	40,000
each of fully paid	2,00,000	80,000	Machinery	80,000	44,000
General Reserve			Furniture	14,000	4,000
as on 1-1-1988	40,000	24,000	Investments :		
Profit & Loss A/c	56,000	36,000	600 Equity shares		
Bills Payable	—	16,000	in Nisha Ltd.	96,000	—
Creditors	32,000	20,000	Stock	40,000	36,000
			Debtors	8,000	30,000
			Cash at Bank	24,000	10,000
	3,28,000	1,76,000		3,28,000	1,76,000

(1) Asha Ltd. acquired the shares in Nisha Ltd. on 1-1-1988.

(2) All the bills payable of Nisha Ltd. were in favour of Asha Ltd. All these have been discounted by the latter.

(3) The Creditors of Nisha Ltd. included Rs. 8,000 payable to Asha Ltd. for goods supplied.

(4) The stock of Nisha Ltd. included the goods worth Rs. 3,200 supplied by Asha Ltd. at cost plus $33^1/_3$ %.

(5) The Profit & Loss account of Nisha Ltd. showed a credit balance of Rs. 8,000 on 1-1-1988.

(Karnataka, April 1989 & Gulbarga, Oct.1994)

Ans. : Consolidated B/S Total Rs. 4,00,700; Pre-acquisition Profit Rs. 22,000; Pre-acquisition Reserve Rs. 24,000; Post-acquisition Profit Rs. 14,000; Goodwill Rs. 29,500; P & L A/c Rs. 65,900; Unrealised Profit Rs. 800; Minority Interest Rs. 35,000 and Ratio 3 : 1.

***Notes* :** (i) Capital reserve of Rs. 34,500 is deducted as per contra.

(ii) Inter company bill of Rs. 16,000 have been discounted. Hence, they cannot be eliminated.

(14) The following are the balance sheet of H Ltd. and S Ltd. as on 31-3-1991.

Liabilities	H Ltd. Rs.	S Ltd. Rs.	Assets	H Ltd. Rs.	S Ltd. Rs.
Share Capital :			**Fixed Assets :**		
Shares of Rs. 10 each	3,60,000	2,00,000	Goodwill	20,000	10,000
Reserve & Surplus :			Sundry Assets	2,40,000	1,70,000
Profit & Loss A/c	—	5,000	**Investments :**		
Secured Loans :			12,000 Shares in		
Debentures	40,000	—	S Ltd. at cost	1,00,000	—
Current Liabilities :			Debentures in		
Creditors	80,000	50,000	H Ltd. at par	—	25,000
Bills Payable	10,000	5,000	**Current Assets etc. :**		
			Debtors	50,000	30,000
			Stock	60,000	20,000
			Bills Receivable	—	5,000
			Profit and Loss A/c	20,000	—
	4,90,000	2,60,000		4,90,000	2,60,000

Other Information :

(a) Shares in S Ltd. were acquired by H Ltd. on 1-10-1990.

(b) The Profit & Loss A/c of S Ltd. on 1-4-1990 showed a credit balance of Rs. 50,000.

(c) Sundry assets of S Ltd. were under valued by Rs. 10,000.

(d) Bills payable of S Ltd. were all favour of H Ltd.

(e) Stock of H Ltd. included goods worth Rs. 12,000 sold by S Ltd. at cost plus 20%. Prepare the Consolidated Balance Sheet as at 31-3-1991.

(Karnataka, Oct. 1992)

Ans. : Consolidated Balance Sheet Total Rs. 6,17,700; Pre-acquisition Profit Rs. 27,500; Post-acquisition Loss Rs. 22,500; Net Capital Reserve Rs. 12,500; P & L A/c (Loss) Rs. 34,700; Unrealised Profit Rs. 2,000; Minority Interest Rs. 86,000 & Ratio 3 : 2.

Notes : (i) Goodwill of Rs. 10,000 is deducted as per contra.
(ii) Out of Rs. 10,000 increase in value of Sundry assets, Rs. 6,000 is added to Capital Reserve and Rs. 4,000 is added to Minority Interest.
(iii) Inter company bill of Rs. 5,000 have been discounted. Hence they cannot be eliminated.
(iv) Inter company debentures of Rs. 25,000 should be eliminated.

(15) The following balance sheets of H Ltd. and its subsidiary S Ltd. as on 31-12-1976 are presented to you.

Liabilities	H Ltd. Rs.	S Ltd. Rs.	Assets	H Ltd. Rs.	S Ltd. Rs.
Share Capital :			Fixed Assets :	3,50,000	1,50,000
Shares of Rs. 100 each	5,00,000	2,00,000	Stock	90,000	40,000
General Reserve	1,00,000	—	Sundry Debtors	60,000	30,000
Profit & Loss A/c	80,000	—	Shares in S. Ltd.		
6% Debentures	—	1,00,000	15000 shares at cost	1,20,000	—
Sundry Creditors	75,000	45,000	6% Debentures in S Ltd. acquired at par	60,000	—
			Cash	75,000	25,000
			Profit & Loss A/c	—	1,00,000
	7,55,000	3,45,000		7,55,000	3,45,000

H Ltd. acquired the shares in S Ltd. on 1-5-1976. The profit and loss account showed a debit balance of Rs. 1,60,000 on 1-1-1976. Creditors of S Ltd. include Rs. 20,000 for goods supplied by H Ltd. on which H Ltd. made a profit of Rs. 2,000. Half of the goods were still in stock on 31-12-1976.

Prepare the consolidated balance sheet as on 31-12-1976.

(Mangalore, Oct. 1983)

Ans. : Consolidated B/S Total Rs. 8,74,000; Pre-acquisition Loss Rs. 1,40,000; Post-acquisition Profit Rs. 40,000; Goodwill Rs. 75,000; Unrealised Profit Rs. 1,000; P & L A/c Rs. 1,09,250; Minority Interest Rs. 25,000 and Ratio 3 : 1.

Notes : (i) Inter company debentures of Rs. 60,000 should be eliminated just like inter company debts.
(ii) Holding company's share of pre-acquisition loss (1,05,000) is added to goodwill.

(16) Major Ltd. acquired 80% of the shares of Minor Ltd. on 1-1-1989 at a total cost of Rs. 4,25,000. The balance sheets of the two companies as on 31-12-1989 are given below :

Liabilities	Major Ltd. Rs.	Minor Ltd. Rs.	Assets	Major Ltd. Rs.	Minor Ltd. Rs.
Share Capital :			Land & Buildings	4,65,000	1,85,000
Equity shares of			Machinery	1,50,000	1,09,000
Rs. 10 each	5,00,000	2,50,000	Stock	1,55,000	70,800
Preference shares			Investments :		
of Rs. 100 each	2,00,000		Shares in		
Reserve	3,50,000	15,000	Minor Ltd.	4,25,000	—
Profit & Loss A/c	3,00,000	1,50,000	Debtors	1,20,000	62,700
Sundry Creditors	70,000	65,000	Cash at Bank	1,05,000	52,500
	14,20,000	4,80,000		14,20,000	4,80,000

The following further information is relevant :

(a) The creditors in Major Ltd. include Rs 20,000 for goods purchased from Minor Ltd. on which the subsidiary company made a profit of Rs. 5,000.

(b) Half of the goods sold as above were still included in the stock of Major Ltd.

(c) The general reserve of Minor Ltd. represents the balance as on 1-1-1989. The Profit & Loss Account balance on 1-1-1989 was Rs. 50,000 out of which a dividend at 10% was paid for the year 1988.

(d) The machinery of Minor Ltd. is undervalued by Rs. 25,000. Prepare the consolidated balance sheet of Major Ltd. and its subsidiary as on 31-12-1988.

(Karnataka, Oct. 1990)

Ans. : Consolidated B/S Total Rs. 16,30,500; Pre-acquisition Profit Rs. 25,000 (50,000 – 25,000); Post-acquisition Profit Rs. 1,25,000 (1,50,000 – 25,000); Pre-acquisition Reserve Rs.15,000; Goodwill Rs. 1,53,000; P & L A/c Rs. 3,78,000; Unrealised Profit Rs. 2,500; Minority Interest Rs. 88,000 & Ratio 4 : 1.

***Notes* :** (i) Capital reserve of Rs. 72,000 is deducted as per contra.

(ii) Out of Rs. 50,000 pre-acquisition profit, Rs. 25,000 is paid for dividend. The remaining amount of Rs. 25,000 is treated as pre-acquisition profit. The holding company share of dividend of Rs. 20,000 is to be deducted from the profit of the holding company and added to the capital reserve. The minority shareholders have already withdrawn their share of dividend. Hence, their share should not be taken into account.

(17) The following are the balance sheets of H Ltd. and S Ltd. as at 31-3-1991.

Liabilities	H Ltd. Rs.	S Ltd. Rs.	Assets	H Ltd. Rs.	S Ltd. Rs.
Share Capital :			**Fixed Assets :**		
Shares of			Premises	1,50,000	1,28,000
Rs. 100 each	4,00,000	2,00,000	Equipments	1,07,000	1,00,000
Reserve & Surplus :			Furniture	20,000	10,000
General Reserve			**Investments :**		
(1-4-1990)	80,000	50,000	1,500 Shares in S Ltd.	1,80,000	—
Profit & Loss A/c	70,000	50,000	**Current Assets :**		
Current Liabilities :			Bills Receivable	5,000	—
Bills Payable	—	10,000	Stock	80,000	60,000
Creditors	30,000	20,000	Debtors	30,000	25,000
			Bank	8,000	7,000
	5,80,000	3,30,000		5,80,000	3,30,000

Additional Information :

(a) H Ltd. purchased the shares in S Ltd. on 1-4-1990 when the Profit & Loss A/c of S Ltd. showed a credit balance of Rs. 30,000.

(b) S Ltd. paid a dividend at 10% in October 1990 for the year 1989-90 and the dividend received by H Ltd. was credited to its P&L A/c.

(c) H Ltd. has received from S Ltd. bills amounting to Rs. 5,000 of which it holds on 31-3-1991 bills worth Rs. 3,000 only.

(d) The creditors of S Ltd. include Rs. 20,000 due to H Ltd. for supply of goods on which the latter company made profit at 20% on sales.

(e) The stock of S Ltd. includes half of the goods brought from H Ltd.

Prepare the Consolidated balance sheet.

(Karnataka, Oct. 1991)

Ans. : Consolidated Balance Sheet total Rs. 7,05,000; Pre-acquisition Profit Rs. 10,000; Post-acquisition Profit Rs. 40,000; Pre-acquisition Reserve Rs. 50,000; Capital Reserve Rs. 30,000; P & L A/c Rs. 83,500; Unrealised Profit Rs. 2,000; Minority Interest Rs. 75,000 and Ration 3 : 1.

Notes : (i) Inter company bills of Rs. 3,000 and debts of Rs. 20,000 should be eliminated.

(ii) The holding company share of dividend of Rs. 15,000 received from subsidiary company should be deducted from the profit of holding and added to capital reserve. The subsidiary company's share should not be considered, as it has been already taken in the concerned account at the time of preparation of Consolidated B/S.

(18) From the following balance sheets of Tata Ltd. and its subsidiary Byby Ltd., prepare the consolidated balance sheet as at 31-12-1984.

Balance Sheet of Tata Ltd. as at 31-12-1984

Liabilities	Rs.	Assets		Rs.
Authorised Capital :		Land & Buildings		50,000
20,000 Shares of Rs. 20 each	4,00,000	Plant & Machinery		1,00,000
Issued Capital		Fixtures		10,000
13,500 Shares of Rs. 20 each	2,70,000	Investments :		
6% debentures	60,000	75,000 shares in Byby Ltd.		
Sundry Creditors	30,000	at cost		1,80,000
General Reserve	60,000	Stock		60,000
Profit & Loss A/c	70,000	Sundry Debtors :		
		Byby Ltd.	20,000	
		Others	40,000	60,000
		Cash at Bank		30,000
	4,90,000			4,90,000

Balance Sheet of Byby Ltd. as at 31-12-1984

Liabilities		Rs.	Assets	Rs.
Authorised Capital :			Land & Building	36,000
12,500 shares of Rs. 20 each		2,50,000	Plant & Machinery	26,000
Issued Capital :			Fixtures	11,000
10,000 shares of Rs. 20 each		2,00,000	Stock	91,000
Sundry Creditors :			Sundry Debtors	1,00,000
Tata Ltd.	19,000		Cash at bank	55,000
Others	50,000	69,000		
Profit & Loss A/c		50,000		
		3,19,000		3,19,000

The holding in Byby Ltd. acquired on 1-1-1984 at premium of Rs. 4 per share on which date the balance of credit of Profit & Loss A/c stood in books of Byby Ltd. at Rs. 20,000.

The transactions between the two companies include the purchase of goods in Byby Ltd. at cost plus $33^1/_3$% from Tata Ltd. Stock of Byby Ltd. on 31-12-1984 consisted of :

(a) Goods purchased from Tata Ltd. Rs. 24,000.

(b) Goods purchased from others Rs. 67,000.

(Mysore, Oct. 1985 modified)

Ans. : Consolidated B/S Total Rs. 6,18,500; Pre-acquisition profit Rs. 20,000; Post-acquisition Profit Rs. 30,000; Goodwill Rs. 15,000; P & L A/c Rs. 88,000; Unrealised Profit Rs. 6,000; Minority Interest Rs. 62,500; Ratio 3 : 1.

Notes : (i) Capital reserve Rs. 15,000 is deducted as per contra.

(ii) Rs. 20,000 from debtors and Rs, 19,000 from the creditors should be eliminated. The difference being cash-in-transit is shown on the assets side of the B/S.

(19) From the Balance sheet and information given below, prepare the Consolidated Balance Sheet of Shiva. Ltd. and its subsidiary Parvati Ltd. as on 31-12-1986.

Liabilities	Shiva Ltd. Rs.	Parvati Ltd. Rs.	Assets	Shiva Ltd. Rs.	Parvati Ltd. Rs.
Share Capital :			Machinery	6,00,000	4,50,000
In shares of			Furniture	20,000	40,000
Rs. 10 each	20,00,000	10,00,000	Shares in Parvati Ltd.	8,80,000	—
Reserve Fund	1,00,000	1,50,000	10% Debentures		
Profit & Loss A/c	50,000	50,000	in Parvati Ltd.	80,000	
10% Debentures	—	2,00,000	Stock	5,20,000	6,50,000
Creditors	4,00,000	2,00,000	Debtors	1,80,000	2,70,000
Bills Payable	20,000	10,000	Bills Receivable	10,000	20,000
			Cash at Bank	2,80,000	1,80,000
	25,70,000	16,10,000		25,70,000	16,10,000

Adjustments :

(1) Shiva Ltd. acquired 80,000 shares of Rs. 10 each in Parvati Ltd. on 1-7-1986.

(2) Bills receivable of Parvati Ltd. include Rs. 8,000 accepted by Shiva Ltd.

(3) Creditors of Parvati Ltd. include Rs. 20,000 due to Shiva Ltd.

(4) An amount of Rs. 30,000 was transferred by Parvati Ltd. from the current year's profit to Reserve fund.

(5) The stock of Shiva Ltd. included goods worth Rs. 20,000 bought from Parvati Ltd. at profit of 25% on cost.

(Gulbarga, April 1987)

Ans. : Consolidated B/S Total Rs. 31,88,000; Pre-acquisition Profit Rs. 25,000; Post-acquisition Profit Rs. 25,000; Pre-acquisition reserve Rs. 1,35,000; Post-acquisition Reserve Rs. 15,000; Capital Reserve Rs. 48,000; General Reserve Rs. 1,12,000; P & L A/c Rs. 66,800; Unrealised Profit Rs. 4,000; Minority Interest Rs. 2,40,000; Ratio 4 : 1.

Notes : (i) It is assumed that the entire profit is earned by the subsidiary company during the current year.

(ii) Goodwill of Rs. 80,000 is deducted as per contra.

(20) The balance sheet of R Co. Ltd. as on 31-12-1990 are as given below :

Liabilities	R Co. Rs.	S Co. Rs.	Assets	R Co. Rs.	S Co. Rs.
Share Capital :			Buildings	80,000	30,000
Equity shares of			Machinery	70,000	75,000
Rs. 10 each	2,00,000	1,00,000	Investments :		
Reserve & Surplus :			8,000 shares in S Ltd.		
General Reserve	25,000	20,000	at cost	1,20,000	—
Profit & Loss A/c	40,000	30,000	Govt. Securities	—	10,000
Secured Loans :			Stock	60,000	30,000
6% Debentures	75,000	—	Sundry Debtors	40,000	15,000
Current Liabilities :			Bills Receivable	20,000	10,000
Sundry Creditors	50,000	20,000	Cash at Bank	20,000	10,000
Bills Payable	20,000	10,000			
	4,10,000	1,80,000		4,10,000	1,80,000

Other Information :

(a) R Co. Ltd. acquired 8,000 shares of Rs. 10 each at Rs. 15 per share in S Co. Ltd. on 1-4-1990.

(b) Rs. 10,000 and Rs. 15,000 were to the credit of general reserve and profit and loss account respectively on 1-1-1990 of S Co. Ltd.

(c) The creditors of S Co. Ltd. include Rs. 15,000 for purchase of goods from R Co. Ltd.

(d) The stock of S Co. Ltd. includes goods of Rs. 10,000 supplied by R Co. Ltd. at cost plus 25% profit.

(e) The Bills payable of S Co. Ltd. were all in favour of R Co. Ltd. and they were discounted.

(f) The buildings of S Co. Ltd. were overvalued to the extent of Rs. 5,000.

Prepare a Consolidated Balance Sheet as on 31-12-1990.

(Karnataka, April. 1993)

Ans. : Consolidated B/S Total Rs. 4,67,000; Pre-acquisition Profit Rs. 18,750; Post-acquisition Profit Rs. 11,250; Pre-acquisition Reserve Rs. 12,500; Post-acquisition Reserve Rs. 7,500; Goodwill Rs. 19,000; P & L A/c Rs. 47,400; Unrealised Profit Rs. 2,000; Minority Interest Rs. 29,000 Ratio 4 : 1.

Notes : (i) Capital reserve of Rs. 21,000 is deducted as per contra.

(ii) Since the bills are discounted cannot be eliminated.

(iii) Inter company debts of Rs. 15,000 should be eliminated.

(iv) Out of Rs. 5,000 decrease in value of buildings, Rs. 4,000 is deducted from the capital reserve and Rs. 1,000 is deducted from the minority interest.

(21) The following are the balance sheets of Maya Ltd. and Chaya Ltd. as on 31-12-1992 :

Liabilities	Maya Ltd. Rs.	Chaya Ltd. Rs.	Assets	Maya Ltd. Rs.	Chaya Ltd. Rs.
Share Capital :			Buildings	3,65,000	1,50,000
Equity Shares of			Machinery	2,00,000	1,30,000
Rs. 10 each	8,00,000	1,80,000	14,400 shares in		
General Reserve	80,000	60,000	Chaya Ltd. at cost	1,60,000	—
Profit & Loss A/c	80,000	—	Stock	1,35,000	30,000
Creditors	60,000	1,10,000	Debtors	80,000	20,000
Bills Payable	25,000	15,000	Bank	1,05,000	15,000
			Profit & Loss A/c	—	20,000
	10,45,000	3,65,000		10,45,000	3,65,000

Maya Ltd. acquired the shares in Chaya Ltd. on 1-7-1992. On 1-1-1992 Chayas Ltd. had Rs. 60,000 credit to its general reserve and Rs. 15,000 to its Profit & Loss A/c. Machinery of Chaya Ltd. were found overvalued to the extent of Rs. 20,000. Creditors Chaya Ltd. include Rs. 25,000 for goods supplied by Maya Ltd.

Prepare a consolidated balance sheet as on 31-12-1992.

(Karnataka, April 1995)

Ans. : Consolidated B/S Total Rs. 11,85,000; Pre-acquisition Loss Rs. 2,500; Post-acquisition Loss Rs. 17,500; Pre-acquisition Reserve Rs. 60,000; Capital Reserve Rs. 14,000; P & L A/c Rs. 66,000; Minority Interest Rs. 40,000 and ratio 4 : 1.

Notes : Inter company debts of Rs. 25,000 should be eliminated.

(22) The following were the balance sheets of Parent Ltd. and its subsidiary Child Ltd. as on 31-12-1983 :

Liabilities	Parent Ltd.	Child Ltd.	Assets	Parent Ltd.	Child Ltd.
Share Capital :			Buildings	1,00,000	28,000
Shares of Rs. 5 each			Machinery	80,000	12,000
Fully paid	2,00,000	50,000	Shares in Child Ltd.		
General Reserve	50,000		7,500 shares at cost	30,000	—
Profit & Loss Account	30,000	—	Stock	32,500	22,500
Creditors	20,000	15,000	Debtors	17,500	10,000
Bills Payable	—	35,000	Bills Receivable	25,000	—
			Cash at Bank	15,000	7,500
			Profit & Loss Account	—	20,000
	3,00,000	1,00,000		3,00,000	1,00,000

(1) The Parent Ltd. acquired the shares in Child Ltd. on 1-5-1983.

(2) The Profit & Loss Account of Child Ltd. showed as debit balance of Rs. 32,000 on 1-1-1983.

(3) Creditors of Child Ltd. included Rs. 5,000 for purchases from Parent Ltd.

Prepare the consolidated balance sheet as on 31-12-1983.

(Gulbarga, 1991)

Ans. : Consolidated B/S Total Rs. 3,58,500; Pre-acquisition Loss Rs. 28,000; Post-acquisition Profit Rs. 8,000; Goodwill Rs. 13,500; P & L A/c Rs. 36,000; Minority Interest Rs. 7,500 and Ratio 3 : 1.

***Note* :** Holding company's share in pre-acquisition loss of Rs. 21,000 is added to the goodwill.

(23) From the Balance Sheets as on 31-12-1997 and the information given below prepare the consolidated Balance Sheet of H Ltd. with its subsidiary S Ltd., as on 31-12-1997:

Liabilities	H Ltd. Rs.	S Ltd. Rs.	Assets	H Ltd. Rs.	S Ltd. Rs.
Share Capital :			Goodwill	50,000	1,00,000
Share of Rs 100 each	3,00,000	2,00,000	Buildings	1,00,000	75,000
Profit & Loss Account			Machinery	50,000	50,000
Balance on 1-1-97	35,000	30,000	Investments :		
Profit for the year	50,000	45,000	1500 Shares in		
General Reserve	30,000	20,000	S Ltd.	1,80,000	—
12% Debentures	1,00,000	87,500	Govt. Securities	25,000	30,000
Creditors	60,000	—	Stock	75,000	37,500
Bills Payable	15,000	—	Debtors	1,00,000	60,000
			Bills Receivable	—	10,000
			Cash at Bank	10,000	20,000
	5,90,000	3,82,500		5,90,000	3,82,500

(a) H Ltd. acquired the shares in S Ltd. on 1-5-1997.

(b) The general reserve of S. Ltd., on 1-1-1997 was Rs. 17,000.

(c) Bills receivable of S Ltd., were all accepted by H Ltd.

(d) The debtors of S Ltd., included the amount of Rs. 10,000 for supply of goods to H Ltd.

(e) The stock of H Ltd. included goods purchased from S Ltd. worth Rs. 5,000. The goods were supplied by S Ltd. at cost plus 25%.

(Karnataka, April 1998)

Ans. : Consolidated B/S Total Rs. 7,54,250, Pre-acquisition Reserve Rs.18,000 pre-acquisition profit Rs 30,000; Capital Reserve as per contra Rs. 47,250 goodwill Rs. 13,2750; P & L A/c Rs. 1,06,750; Unrealised profit Rs. 1,000; Minority Interest Rs. 73,750 and Ratio = 3 : 1

(24) The following are the Balance Sheets of R Ltd. and N Ltd. as at 31-12-1997.

Balance Sheet as at 31-12-1997

Liabilities	R Ltd. Rs.	N Ltd. Rs.	Assets	R Ltd. Rs.	N Ltd. Rs.
Share Capital :			Plant and Machinery	2,50,000	1,25,000
Equity shares of			Investment :		
Rs. 10 each	3,60,000	2,00,000	16,000 shares in		
Reserve Fund			N Ltd.	1,65,000	–
on 1-1-1997	25,000	15,000	Debtors	1,17,500	71,500
Profit and Loss A/c	70,000	12,500	Stock	45,000	83,500
Creditors	90,000	30,000	Bills Receivable	12,500	–
Bills Payable	45,000	22,500			
	5,90,000	2,80,000		5,90,000	2,80,000

R Ltd. acquired shares in N Ltd. on 1-5-1997. N Ltd. had a credit balance on profit and loss account of Rs. 5,000 on 1-1-1997. All bills receivable of R Ltd. were accepted by N Ltd. The plant and machinery of N Ltd. were undervalued to the extent of Rs. 5,000. Creditors of R Ltd. include Rs. 15,000 payable to N Ltd. The stock of N Ltd. included Rs. 6,000 supplied by R Ltd. at cost plus 20%.

Prepare the consolidated Balance Sheet on 31-12-1997.

(Karnataka, Oct. 1998)

Ans. : Consolidated B/S Total Rs. 6,81,500; Pre-acquisition Reserve Rs. 15,000; Pre-acquisition Profit Rs. 12,500; Post-acquisition Profit Rs. 5,000; Goodwill as per contra Rs. 5,000; Capital Reserve Rs. 17,000; Plant & Machinery Rs. 3,80,000; P & L A/c Rs. 73,200; B/R Rs. Nil; B/P Rs. 55,000; Unrealised Profit Rs. 1,000; Minority Interest Rs. 46,500 and ratio = 4 : 1

(25) From the following Balance Sheets as at 31-12-1998 and the particulars given below, prepare the consolidated Balance Sheet of Vinita Ltd. and its subsidiary Vanaja Ltd. as on 31-12-1998.

Additional Particulars :

(a) Vinita Ltd. acquired the shares in Vanaja Ltd. on 1-7-1998.

(b) All the Bills Payable of Vanaja Ltd. were in favour of Vinita Ltd.

(c) The creditors of Vanaja Ltd. included Rs. 16,000 payable to Vinita Ltd. for goods supplied.

(d) The stock of Vanaja Ltd. included the goods worth Rs. 6,400 supplied by Vinita Ltd. at cost plus $33^1/_3$%.

(e) The Profit & Loss Account of Vanaja Ltd. showed a credit balance of Rs. 16,000 on 1-1-1998.

Balance Sheets as on 31-12-1998

Liabilities	Vinita Ltd. Rs.	Vanaja Ltd. Rs.	Assets	Vinita Ltd. Rs.	Vanaja Ltd. Rs.
Share Capital :			Goodwill	32,000	24,000
Shares of Rs. 100 each	4,00,000	1,60,000	Other Fixed Assets	2,88,000	1,76,000
General Reserve	80,000	48,000	Investments :		
(1-1-1998)			(1,200 equity shares		
Profit and Loss A/c	1,12,000	72,000	in Vanaja Ltd.)	1,92,000	—
Bills Payable	—	32,000	Stock	80,000	72,000
Creditors	64,000	40,000	Debtors	16,000	60,000
			Bank	48,000	20,000
Total	6,56,000	3,52,000	Total	6,56,000	3,52,000

(Karnataka, April 1999)

Ans. : Consolidated B/S Total Rs. 8,01,400; Pre-acquisition Reserve Rs. 48,000; Pre-acquisition profit Rs. 44,000 (16,000 + 28,000); Post-acquisition Profit Rs. 28,000; Capital Reserve Rs. 69,000; Goodwill Rs. 59,000; P & L A/c Rs. 1,31,800; Stock Rs. 1,50,800; Unrealised Profit Rs. 1,600; Minority Interest Rs. 70,000 and Ratio 3 : 1.

******